## Abbreviations and labels used in *Context*

| | |
|---|---|
| **AE/BE** | American English / British English |
| **ca.** *(Latin)* | circa = about, approximately |
| **cf.** | confer (compare), see |
| **derog** | derogatory *(abfällig, geringschätzig)* |
| **e.g.** *(Latin)* | exempli gratia = for example |
| **esp.** | especially |
| **et al.** *(Latin)* | et alii = and other people/things |
| **etc.** *(Latin)* | et cetera = and so on |
| **f./ff.** | and the following page(s)/line(s) |
| **fml** | formal English |
| **i.e.** *(Latin)* | id est = that is, in other words |
| **infml** | informal English |
| **jdm./jdn.** | *jemandem/jemanden* |
| **l./ll.** | line/lines |
| **n** | noun |
| **pt(s)** | point(s) |
| **p./pp.** | page/pages |
| **pl** | plural |
| **sb./sth.** | somebody/something |
| **sin** | singular |
| **sl** | slang |
| **usu.** | usually |
| **v** | verb |
| **vs.** | *(Latin)* versus *(gegen, im Gegensatz zu)* |

| | |
|---|---|
| 🗺️ | marks tasks that refer you back to the chapter's guiding question |
| **Challenge** | indicates that task b includes an extension of task a at a more challenging level |
| ► **Support** | refers you to the Support pages (p. 304ff.) where you can find more help to do the assignment |
| **You choose** | lets you decide which of the two tasks you'd like to do |
| **Intercultural competence** | marks a task that focuses on intercultural competence |
| **Advanced** | marks a more demanding task or chapter suitable for the *Leistungsfach* |
| *metaphor | indicates that a word or expression (here: *metaphor*) is explained in the Glossary p. 418ff. |
| ► **SF 50: Paraphrasing** | directs you to the Skills File, p. 346ff. (here: Skill 50) |
| 🔊 | indicates that the sound file can be found in the Cornelsen Lernen App, eBook and UMA |
| ▶️ | indicates that the video can be found in the Cornelsen Lernen App, eBook and UMA |
| ► **More info** 🔗 | indicates that additional information can be found in the Cornelsen Lernen App |
| ► **More language** 🔗 | indicates that tips or further information regarding language can be found in the Cornelsen Lernen App |
| ► **Check** 🔗 | indicates that solutions to tasks can be found in the Cornelsen Lernen App |
| ► **Getting started** 🔗 | indicates that tips or ideas to get started on tasks can be found in the Cornelsen Lernen App |

# Context

## Bayern

Dein Buch findest du auch in der **Cornelsen Lernen App**.

Siehst du eines dieser Symbole in deinem Buch, findest du in deiner App …

🔊 alle **Audios**

▶ alle **Videos**

📲 **Ideen**, **Informationen** und **Lösungen** zu ausgewählten Aufgaben

**Cornelsen**

# Context · Bayern

**Im Auftrag des Verlages herausgegeben von**

Dr. Annette Leithner-Brauns, Dresden

**Erarbeitet von**

Martina Baasner, Berlin; Irene Bartscherer, Bonn; Lisa Braun, Meppen; Dr. Sabine Buchholz, Hürth; Dr. Wiebke Bettina Dietrich, Göttingen; Prof. Dr. Peter Hohwiller, Landau; Maren John, Hamburg; Sebastian Lippert, Bensberg; Sylvia Loh, Esslingen; Benjamin Lorenz, Bensheim; Dr. Paul Maloney, Hildesheim; Dr. Pascal Ohlmann, Tholey; Birgit Ohmsieder, Berlin; Dr. Andreas Sedlatschek, Esslingen; Veronika Walther, Rudolstadt

**Beratende Mitwirkung**

Dr. Christine Ayorinde, Braga, Portugal; Ramin Azadian, Berlin; Heiko Benzin, Neustrelitz; Martina Förster, Kempten; Sabine Otto, Halle (Saale); Andrea Tretter, Augsburg

**In Zusammenarbeit mit der Englischredaktion**

Dr. Marion Kiffe (Koordinierende Redakteurin), Anne Hauser-Teubner (Projektleitung), Dr. Jan Dreßler, Michelle Fridman, Tanya Matthew, Hartmut Tschepe, Dr. Christian von Raumer, Mai Weber, Freya Wurm, Anja Zieschang, *unter Mitwirkung von* Janan Barksdale, Katrin Gütermann, Dr. Christine Hehle, Jana Lose, Neil Porter, Evelyn Sternad

**Layoutkonzept**

Klein & Halm, Berlin

**Layout und technische Umsetzung**

Reemers Publishing Services GmbH, Krefeld; Straive; designcollective, Berlin

**Umschlaggestaltung**

Rosendahl, Berlin

**Lizenzmanagement**

Britta Bensmann

**Weitere Bestandteile des Lehrwerks**

- *Schulbuch* (Print und als E-Book)
- *Lehrkräftefassung des Schulbuchs*
- *Handreichungen für den Unterricht*
- *Workbook* (Print)
- *Unterrichtsmanager Plus*
- *Vorschläge zur Leistungsmessung* (digital)
- *Cornelsen Lernen App*

www.cornelsen.de

1. Auflage, 1. Druck 2024

Alle Drucke dieser Auflage sind inhaltlich unverändert und können im Unterricht nebeneinander verwendet werden.

© 2024 Cornelsen Verlag GmbH, Berlin, Mecklenburgische Str. 53, 14197 Berlin

Druck: Mohn Media Mohndruck, Gütersloh

ISBN: 978-3-06-034558-8

**PEFC-zertifiziert**

Dieses Produkt stammt aus nachhaltig bewirtschafteten Wäldern und kontrollierten Quellen

PEFC/04-31-1033   www.pefc.de

# Contents

# Contents

# Contents

# Contents

# Contents

# Contents

# Contents

# Contents

# Chapter 1
# The Individual in Society – Exploring Values, Norms and Religion

## Imagine   John Lennon

Imagine there's no heaven
It's easy if you try
No hell below us
Above us only sky
5 Imagine all the people
Living for today ... Aha-ah ...

Imagine there's no countries
It isn't hard to do
Nothing to kill or die for
10 And no religion, too
Imagine all the people
Living life in peace ... You ...

You may say I'm a dreamer
But I'm not the only one

15 I hope someday you'll join us
And the world will be as one

Imagine no possessions
I wonder if you can
No need for greed or hunger
20 A brotherhood of man
Imagine all the people
Sharing all the world ... You ...

You may say I'm a dreamer
But I'm not the only one
25 I hope someday you'll join us
And the world will live as one

*From:* Imagine, *1971*

▶ More info

**1** In his song 'Imagine' John Lennon describes his vision of an ideal society.

   **a** In one sentence describe the world that John Lennon imagines.
   **b** Which aspects in the song do you still consider relevant?
   **c** Outline topics you would mention in a version of the song for the 21st century.
   **d** Write a verse for your own song called 'Imagine'.

**2** Take a look at the Chapter map on the right-hand page.

   **a** Make notes about each of the terms in the boxes and what they mean to you.
   **b** Speculate about the content of this chapter.
   **c** *Quick write:* Look at the guiding question on p. 15. Write one short paragraph in which you answer the question. Keep your paragraph for later.

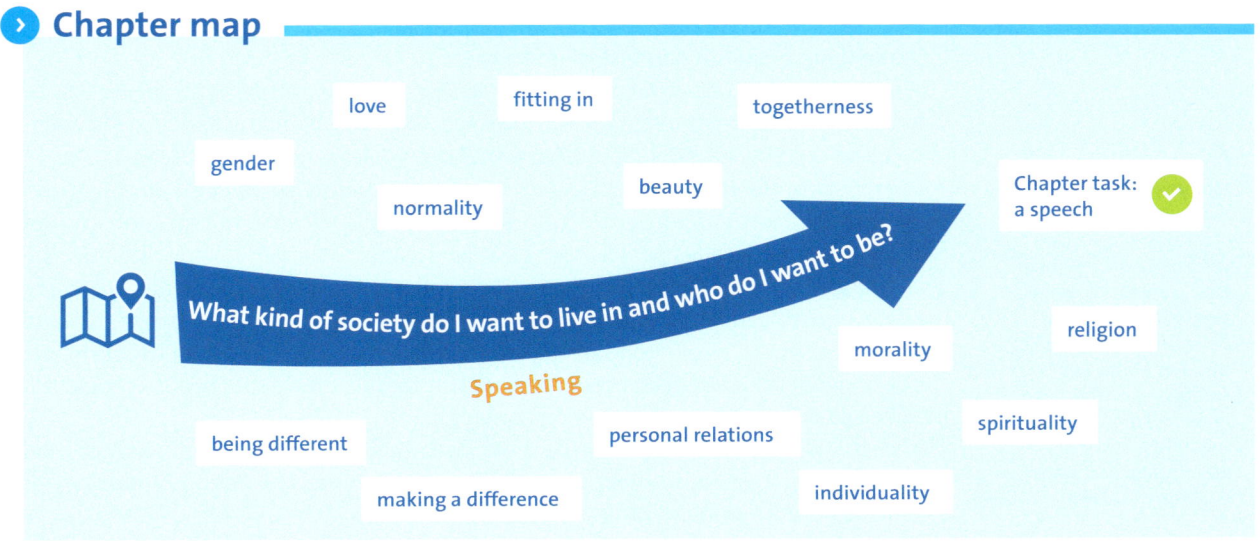

▸ **Chapter map**

love     fitting in     togetherness

gender

normality     beauty

Chapter task:
a speech ✓

What kind of society do I want to live in and who do I want to be?

Speaking

religion

morality

spirituality

being different     personal relations

individuality

making a difference

▶ More language

## 🔊 Finding my own path

### Embracing our privileges

Today's world offers more choices than ever before. Living in a free democratic society, we can make our own choices about our friends, our lifestyles, our jobs, our political affiliations. We take these rights for granted even though they are actually a privilege.
5 If we wish to develop our characters so that we become the person we are supposed to be, then we need to protect these rights. There are many opportunities for participating in activism concerning issues that affect our lives.

### Empowering religious individuality

Amidst the diversity of choices, embracing our individuality extends to religious be-
10 liefs where we can find our unique spiritual path, shaping our character and fulfilling our dreams while fostering tolerance and equality in today's world. This inclusivity enables us to celebrate the openness of choices and lifestyles, ensuring that society supports each person's journey of faith. But for these options to be available to us, we need to ensure that the society we live in enables us to forge our own path.

15 ### Crafting self-identity

Our sense of self is defined by the people we surround ourselves with and by how they perceive us as well as by our own aspirations about the person we want to be. As individuals, we strive to be unique and to stand out, while trying to find our place in society. Learning about our differences and needs is as much a part of this process of
20 developing a sense of identity as focusing on our dreams. Throughout our lives we will be faced with the question as to whether we want to conform to social norms or whether we want to stand out from the crowd.

### The rise of social mobility

In the past, a person's background, the family they came from, their social class and eco-
25 nomic status were the dominant factors that predetermined their future. However, in today's context, social mobility has gained significant importance, allowing individuals to shape their own destinies. Nevertheless, it's important to note that in some countries, the influence of family background and social class remains considerable. Despite the rise of social mobility, there are regions where it has been severely eroded, and a person's par-
30 ents' economic status still greatly impacts their life prospects, alongside their social class.

### Challenging prejudice and fostering dreams

Equality of opportunity still does not exist. Opposing discrimination experienced by certain groups and addressing social inequalities while upholding the values of toler-ance and equality is essential to ensure that everyone can fulfil their dreams.
35 Awareness of the risks inherent in prejudice and stereotyping can help society to be-come more accepting of people who are not accepted by the mainstream society. While in recent decades people have been campaigning for gender equality, now the campaign has become much broader. This reflects the fact that we are becoming aware of new gender roles and of gender-sensitive language. Many people who do
40 not adhere to the binary roles of male and female have urged society to accept the idea of gender fluidity. Body positivity is making people aware that beauty should not be tied to one particular form of body or face.
From the way we dress to the people we love, we are spoilt for choice. Rather than being confused and overwhelmed by the complexity of all the options and lifestyles
45 available, we can celebrate this new openness and discover what feels right for us.

---

### Info

**Gender-sensitive language** avoids reinforcing gender stereotypes by using terms and expressions that are neutral, inclusive and respectful of diverse gender identi-ties. The aim is to create an environment where all individuals, regardless of their gender, feel acknowl-edged and valued.

## 1 Main ideas

In a one-minute speech, explain the main message of the text 'Finding my own path'. Use phrases from the text to support your points.

## 2 Reflect

a Talk to your partner about one experience you have made or heard of that goes well with 'Finding my own path'.

b Listen to what your partner has to tell you and then discuss which experience reflects the text best.

## 3 Prepositions

▶ Check 🖱

a If you want to express *jemand passt nicht in die Gesellschaft* in English, the only problem for a learner at your level might be the German preposition. Give the right preposition for the following verb phrases:

1 be tied ... sth.
2 adhere ... sth.
3 campaign ... sth.
4 conform ... sth.
5 stand ... from sth.

b Make two sentences for each of the phrases from **a**, replacing *sth.* by different nouns.

c Talk to a partner: how helpful do you find tasks like **b** for learning chunks?

## 4 Chunk it!

Replace the gaps in the following *chunks with verbs. You can check the text for help if you are not sure.

▶ Getting started 🖱
▶ Check 🖱

1 ... your rights
2 ... a sense of identity
3 ... with the question
4 ... tolerance
5 ... your own path

## 5 A blog post

On the occasion of International Day of Tolerance, write a short *blog post for your school website about one of the issues referred to in the text. Try to use as many *chunks as possible from task **3** and **4** and mark them.

▶ SF 29: Writing a blog post, p. 384

▶ WOB: pp. 11–12

▶ More info

**Annotations**

1 **odour** smell
4 **divan** a backless long
  soft seat
5 **custom** *(fml)* habit
6 **gleam** *(n)* shine
6 **laburnum** *Goldregen*
9 **tussore silk** an
  expensive kind of silk,
  usu. rich in texture and
  gold in colour
11 **pallid** pale
15 **woodbine** *Geißblatt*
16 **bourdon note** (here)
  very low, droning
17 **easel** *Staffelei*
21 **conjecture** an idea that
  is not based on definite
  knowledge
22 **gracious** elegant
22 **comely** attractive
23 **linger** stay for a long
  time
28 **languidly** moving
  slowly and elegantly
  without much effort
28 **the Grosvenor** (here)
  an art gallery
28 **the Academy** the Royal
  Academy of Arts

# A beautiful portrait   Oscar Wilde

- **Think** In your view, what makes a photograph of a person perfect? Collect ideas.
- **Pair** Compare the criteria with a partner and rank them according to their importance.
- **Share** Present your rankings in a group and discuss whether a person's photograph can also reveal something about the person who took it.

*Oscar Wilde was one of the greatest writers in Britain at the turn of the 19th century. This is the beginning of his novel* The Picture of Dorian Gray.

The studio was filled with the rich odour of roses, and when the light summer wind stirred amidst the trees of the garden, there came through the open door the heavy scent of the lilac, or the more delicate perfume of the pink-flowering thorn.

5 From the corner of the divan of Persian saddle-bags on which he was lying, smoking, as was his custom, innumerable cigarettes, Lord Henry Wotton could just catch the gleam of the honey-sweet and honey-coloured blossoms of laburnum, whose tremulous branches seemed hardly able to bear the burden of a beauty so flame-like as theirs; and now and then the fantastic shadows of birds in flight flitted across the long tussore-silk curtains that were stretched in front of the huge

10 window, producing a kind of momentary Japanese effect, and making him think of those pallid jade-faced painters of Tokyo who, through the medium of an art that is necessarily immobile, seek to convey the sense of swiftness and motion. The sullen murmur of the bees shouldering their way through the long unmown grass, or circling with monotonous insistence round the dusty gilt horns of the straggling

15 woodbine, seemed to make the stillness more oppressive. The dim roar of London was like the bourdon note of a distant organ.

In the centre of the room, clamped to an upright easel, stood the full-length portrait of a young man of extraordinary personal beauty, and in front of it, some little distance away, was sitting the artist himself, Basil Hallward, whose sudden disap-

20 pearance some years ago caused, at the time, such public excitement, and gave rise to so many strange conjectures.

As the painter looked at the gracious and comely form he had so skillfully mirrored in his art, a smile of pleasure passed across his face, and seemed about to linger there. But he suddenly started up, and, closing his eyes, placed his fingers up on

25 the lids, as though he sought to imprison within his brain some curious dream from which he feared he might awake.

'It is your best work, Basil, the best thing you have ever done,' said Lord Henry, languidly. 'You must certainly send it next year to the Grosvenor. The Academy is too large and too vulgar. Whenever I have gone there, there have been either so

30 many people that I have not been able to see the pictures, which was dreadful, or so many pictures that I have not been able to see the people, which was worse. The Grosvenor is really the only place.'

'I don't think I shall send it anywhere,' he answered, tossing his head back in that odd way that used to make his friends laugh at him at Oxford. 'No: I won't send it

35 anywhere.'

Advanced

Lord Henry elevated his eyebrows, and looked at him in amazement through the thin blue wreaths of smoke that curled up in such fanciful whorls from his heavy opium-tainted cigarette. 'Not send it anywhere? My dear fellow, why? Have you any reason? What odd chaps you painters are! You do anything in the world to gain a
40  reputation. As soon as you have one, you seem to want to throw it away. It is silly of you, for there is only one thing in the world worse than being talked about, and that is not being talked about. A portrait like this would set you far above all the young men in England, and make the old men quite jealous, if old men are ever capable of any emotion.'

45  'I know you will laugh at me,' he replied, 'but I really can't exhibit it. I have put too much of myself into it.'

Lord Henry stretched himself out on the divan and laughed.

'Yes, I knew you would; but it is quite true, all the same.'

'Too much of yourself in it! Upon my word, Basil, I didn't know you were so vain;
50  and I really can't see any resemblance between you, with your rugged strong face and your coal-black hair, and this young Adonis, who looks as if he was made out of ivory and rose-leaves. Why, my dear Basil, he is a Narcissus, and you – well, of course you have an intellectual expression, and all that. But beauty, real beauty, ends where an intellectual expression begins. Intellect is in itself a mode of
55  exaggeration, and destroys the harmony of any face. The moment one sits down to think, one becomes all nose, or all forehead, or something horrid. Look at the successful men in any of the learned professions. How perfectly hideous they are! Except, of course, in the Church. But then in the Church they don't think. A bishop keeps on saying at the age of eighty what he was told to say when he was a boy of
60  eighteen, and as a natural consequence he always looks absolutely delightful. Your mysterious young friend, whose name you have never told me, but whose picture really fascinates me, never thinks. I feel quite sure of that. He is some brainless, beautiful creature, who should be always here in winter when we have no flowers to look at, and always here in summer when we want something to chill our
65  intelligence. Don't flatter yourself, Basil: you are not in the least like him.'

'You don't understand me, Harry,' answered the artist. 'Of course I am not like him. I know that perfectly well. Indeed, I should be sorry to look like him. You shrug your shoulders? I am telling you the truth. There is a fatality about all physical and intellectual distinction, the sort of fatality that seems to dog through
70  history the faltering steps of kings. It is better not to be different from one's fellows. The ugly and the stupid have the best of it in this world. They can sit at their ease and gape at the play. If they know nothing of victory, they are at least spared the knowledge of defeat. They live as we all should live, undisturbed, indifferent, and without disquiet. They neither bring ruin upon others, not ever receive it from
75  alien hands. Your rank and wealth, Harry; my brains, such as they are – my art, whatever it may be worth; Dorian Gray's good looks – we shall all suffer for what the gods have given us, suffer terribly.'

*From: Oscar Wilde,* The Picture of Dorian Gray, *1891*

Annotations
36  **elevate sth.**  lift sth., raise
37  **whorl**  *Windung, Kringel*
39  **chap**  *(old-fashioned)* man
40  **reputation**  (here) fame
50  **rugged**  (usu. about the face of a man) having strong and attractive features
51  **Adonis**  (in Greek mythology) an extremely attractive young man
52  **Narcissus**  (in Greek mythology) man who fell in love with his own reflection
68  **fatality**  belief that you have no control or influence on sth.
69  **dog sth.**  follow sth. closely all the time
70  **faltering**  hesitant or uncertain due to weakness
72  **gape** *(v)* stare with an open mouth
72  **be spared**  *verschont bleiben*
75  **rank**  position in society

Oscar Wilde (1854–1900)

Advanced

## Comprehension

▶ SF 34: Writing a summary or an outline, p. 390

**1** Outline the \*setting and the situation presented in this excerpt: Who is present, what are the men talking about and what do they disagree about?

## Analysis

**2** Analyse the \*atmosphere created in the first three paragraphs of the \*novel.

▶ SF 19: Reading and understanding narrative texts, p. 369

**3** Analyse the means Lord Henry employs to convince Basil that he and the picture have nothing in common.

> **Language help**
>
> use imagery/exclamations • address sb. directly • admit/concede sth. • flatter sb. • use/employ long/elliptical/incomplete/complex sentences/syntax

**4** Talk to a partner about the extent to which the analysis of the text changed your first impression of it.

▶ WOB: pp. 37–39

## Language awareness

**5** In the first two paragraphs, Oscar Wilde paints a picture of the studio with words. Examine how he achieves this effect by looking at his choice of words.

▶ Getting started

**6** Work on either **a** or **b**.

**a** Rephrase the first two paragraphs in a less \*formal register.

**b** Challenge Rephrase the first two paragraphs in a less formal register. Explain the difference between your version and the original.

## Beyond the text

▶ Check

**7** Writing 'It is better not to be different from one's fellows.' (l. 70) Write a comment on Basil Hallward's statement.

**8** You choose Speaking Work on either **a** or **b**.

▶ SF 13: Doing research, p. 360

▶ SF 23: Analysing visuals, p. 374

▶ SF 43: Giving a presentation, p. 405

**a** Find a photo or painting that in your opinion reveals a lot about the character of the person portrayed. Prepare a short podcast about the picture, also explaining how the artist achieved this effect.

**b** Research the stories of Adonis and Narcissus from Greek mythology (cf. ll. 51–52) and give a short presentation about them. Speculate what their relevance for the novel could be.　▶ Getting started

## Not being normal    Sally Rooney

- ***Quick write:** What is *normal*?
- Would you describe your life as normal? Why or why not?

*You are going to read an excerpt from Sally Rooney's novel* Normal People. *Marianne and Connell are two Irish teenagers who are classmates but who come from very different backgrounds. Connell's mother works as a cleaner for Marianne's mother.*

Marianne's classmates all seem to like school so much and find it normal. To dress in the same uniform every day, to comply at all times with arbitrary rules, to be scrutinised and monitored for misbehaviour, this is normal to them. They have no sense of the school as an oppressive environment. Marianne had a row with the
5 History teacher, Mr Kerrigan, last year because he caught her looking out a window during class, and no one in the class took her side. It seemed so obviously insane to her then that she should have to dress up in a costume every morning and be herded around a huge building all day, and that she wasn't even allowed to move her eyes where she wanted, even her eye movements fell under the jurisdiction of
10 school rules. You're not learning if you're staring out the window daydreaming, Mr Kerrigan said. Marianne, who had lost her temper by then, snapped back: Don't delude yourself, I have nothing to learn from you.

Connell said recently that he remembered that incident, and that at the time he'd felt she was being harsh on Mr Kerrigan, who was actually one of the more
15 reasonable teachers. But I see what you're saying, Connell added. About feeling a bit imprisoned in the school, I do see that. He should have let you look out the window, I would agree there. You weren't doing any harm.

After the conversation in the kitchen, when she told him she liked him, Connell started coming over to her house more often. He would arrive early to pick his
20 mother up from work and hang around in the living room not saying much, or stand by the fireplace with his hands in his pockets. Marianne never asked why he came over. They talked a little bit, or she talked and he nodded. He told her she should try reading *The Communist Manifesto*, he thought she would like it, and he offered to write down the title for her so she wouldn't forget. I know what *The*
25 *Communist Manifesto* is called, she said. He shrugged, okay. After a moment he added, smiling: You're trying to act superior, but like, you haven't even read it. She had to laugh then, and he laughed because she did. They couldn't look at each other when they were laughing, they had to look into corners of the room, or at their feet.

Connell seemed to understand how she felt about school; he said he liked hearing
30 her opinions. You hear enough of them in class, she said. Matter-of-factly he replied: You act different in class, you're not really like that. He seemed to think Marianne had access to a range of different identities, between which she slipped effortlessly. This surprised her, because she usually felt confined inside one single personality, which was always the same regardless of what she did or said. She had
35 tried to be different in the past, as a kind of experiment, but it had never worked. If she was different with Connell, the difference was not happening inside herself, in her personhood, but in between them, in the dynamic. Sometimes she made him laugh, but other days he was taciturn, inscrutable, and after he left, she would feel high, nervous, at once energetic and terribly drained.

▶ More info

Annotations

2 **arbitrary** seeming unfair and not based on reason
3 **scrutinised** looked at very closely
9 **jurisdiction** authority
12 **delude sb.** deceive sb.
26 **superior** better than everyone else
33 **confined** restricted, kept inside
38 **taciturn** not saying very much
38 **inscrutable** *undurchschaubar*
39 **drained** very tired, without energy

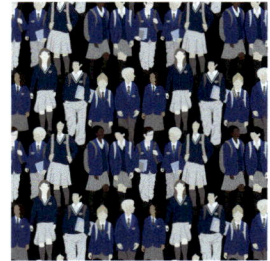

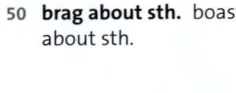

Annotation
**50** **brag about sth.** boast about sth.

40 He followed her into the study last week while she was looking for a copy of *The Fire Next Time* to lend him. He stood there inspecting the bookshelves, with his top shirt button undone and school tie loosened. She found the book and handed it to him, and he sat down on the window seat looking at the back cover. She sat beside him and asked him if his friends Eric and Rob knew that he read so much outside school.

45 They wouldn't be interested in that stuff, he said.

You mean they're not interested in the world around them.

Connell made the face he always made when she criticised his friends, an inexpressive frown. Not in the same way, he said. They have their own interests. I don't think they'd be reading books about racism and all that.

50 Right, they're too busy bragging about who they're having sex with, she said.

He paused for a second, like his ears had pricked up at this remark but he didn't know exactly how to respond. Yeah, they do a bit of that, he said. I'm not defending it, I know they can be annoying.

Doesn't it bother you?

55 He paused again. Most of it wouldn't, he said. They do some stuff that goes a bit over the line and that would annoy me obviously. But at the end of the day they're my friends, you know. It's different for you.

*From: Sally Rooney,* Normal People, *2018*

## Comprehension

**1** Outline Marianne's criticism of school rules.

▶ SF 34: Writing a summary or an outline, p. 390

**2** State why Connell does not talk to his friends in the same way he talks to Marianne.

## Analysis

▶ Support, p. 304

**3** Analyse how the two teenagers are depicted in the excerpt.

## Language awareness

**4** Look at the *ing*-forms used in ll. 18–50 and say which of them are participles and which gerunds. Replace the *ing*-form by a different construction where possible and assess to what extent it changes the paragraph.   ▶ More language

## Beyond the text

**5** You choose   Writing   Work on task **a** or **b**.

**a** Write a diary entry for either Connell or Marianne reflecting on their conversation and the idea of being 'different'.

**b** After her conflict with Mr Kerrigan, Marianne is asked to go to the headmaster's office. In pairs, write her conversation with the headmaster about the incident.

▶ SF 38: Creative writing, p. 395

## We are in this together　Vicky Bristow

- In 2020 the world experienced the start of Covid-19, a global pandemic which led to several lockdowns. Name three aspects of your life that changed during the lockdowns. Then write two sentences on your feelings about those changes.

*The following poem was written during the first lockdown in the spring of 2020 by a student at the University of East Anglia.*

We are in this together, is often said
So here are my thoughts, spun out like a thread
And here is my very first suggestion
Who is the 'we' – an important question
5　Some groups of 'we' more likely to thrive
Other 'we' more likely to die
And if you think this is purely fable
The truth is on the mortality tables
Can your 'we' work from the inside
10　Or are you a 'we' on the front-line?
Higher survival if you are white
Poverty, diabetes, and also to mention
Racism, stress and hypertension
Factors not evenly shared
15　To the dark of skin not fair
Are you the 'we' who's missing your mates?
Or one of the 'we' with an empty plate?
For the 'we' we are is broadly diverse
Experience and outcome, for better or worse
20　So the 'we' can be good or grim,
Now let's move on and explore the 'in'
Because the notion of 'in' is bogus
If you are the 'we' who is homeless
The 'in' for the lonely who live in silence
25　Or those in fear of domestic violence
Is your 'in' feeling fed up and bored
Or praying for the safety of being ignored
Is your 'in' comfortable and safe
Or do you dream of such a space
30　Children with no Wi-Fi or computer
No digital learning and brighter future
This situation is not clever
Now for the final word 'together'
A funny thing to say for a start
35　When we are all far apart
But for some this is not a game
For 'together' for some is not the same
For some have plenty, some do not
For some the fear just does not stop
40　This poem could be one of despair
So I will not leave it there

**Annotations**
2　**spin sth.** (spun – spun) *etwas spinnen*
5　**thrive** do well
13　**hypertension** high blood pressure
16　**mate** *(BE infml)* friend
22　**bogus** not genuine, inaccurate

**Info**

During the first phase of the **Covid-19 pandemic**, there was a notable rise in domestic violence in Britain and the mortality rates among ethnic minority communities were especially high.

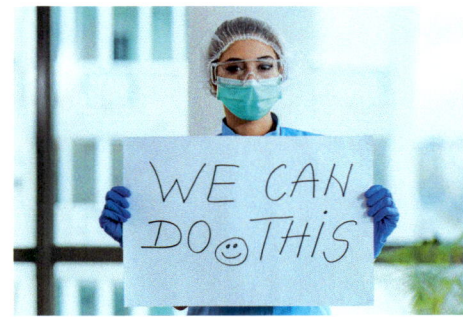

Annotations
43 **compassion** sympathy, sadness for the situation of others
45 **forgot** (usu. AE) forgotten

I pray so hard for a new world fashion
That we discover a genuine compassion
That valuing wealth and what you've got
45 Will be a memory soon forgot
That education, food and healthcare
Will be all right, for all to share
And the 'we' will be an all inclusive
And human rights not elusive
50 The 'in' a safe place in-side
Where friendship and family thrive
To shelter us from life's great storms
No matter to whom or where we are born
And this tragedy will have no sequel
55 Because we will be more equal
And when the world becomes more fair
Then we can proudly declare
This will happen again never,
Because now – we are in it together

*From: R. Barratt, ed.,* Lockdown 2020. Poetry and prose from around the world on living in isolation and surviving the coronavirus, *2020*

## Comprehension

**1**  Name the groups of people mentioned in the poem that suffered disproportionately during the pandemic and explain why they suffered more.

**2**  Describe the impact the pandemic has had on social relationships, according to the poem.

## Analysis

▶ SF 20: Reading and understanding poetry, p. 370

▶ WOB: pp. 31–33

**3**  Analyse the structure of the poem and the effect this has.

## Language awareness

**4**  Analyse the language used in the poem (e.g. *register, *stylistic devices) and speculate on what this tells us about the intended audience of the poem.

▶ Getting started
▶ SF 38: Creative writing, p. 395

**5**  Writing  Rephrase the poem as a newspaper article.

## Beyond the text

**6**  Writing  Work on task **a** or **b**.

▶ SF 38: Creative writing, p. 395

   **a**  Discuss whether there are aspects in the poem that would have been written differently today.

   **b**  Challenge  Write a more up-to-date version of the poem.

Advanced

▶ SF 35: Writing a formal letter or email, p. 391
▶ Check

**7**  Writing  Write a letter to your local Member of Parliament based on the criticism raised in the poem and make two suggestions for improvements.

# Focus on test formats

In test situations in your final years at school or later in life you may be required to participate in a speaking exam. It usually asks you to communicate in a dialogue or a group situation. Sometimes you may also have to hold a monologue on the basis of materials such as pictures or statistics.

The task below is set up for two students, but in practice, you may also find a setup involving more than two participants.

Read the following task:

▶ SF 42: Essentials: speaking, p. 404

**Info**

Mind that **speaking exams** must not be confused with oral exams in your *Abitur*: While the former test your ability to communicate, the latter also test your knowledge and text skills.

In an **exam** situation, you may only be allowed to see your own material (i.e. your cartoon, photo, statistics, etc.) and your partner(s) will be assigned a different one.

**Privileges and discrimination**

Your English course is organizing an English project day for year 12 and 13 on privileges and forms of discrimination that you and your age group might encounter in contemporary society.

The following cartoons deal with forms of privileges and discrimination. Work with a partner. One of you is partner A, the other is partner B. Analyse your cartoon and comment on its effectiveness. Speak for about two minutes each.

**Partner A:**

CartoonStock.com

**Partner B:**

"*Actually, Lou, I think it was more than just my being in the right place at the right time. I think it was my being the right race, the right religion, the right sex, the right socioeconomic group, having the right accent, the right clothes, going to the right schools...*"

CartoonStock.com

Together with your partner, plan major steps of the day and collect ideas on at least three ideas you could pursue and activities you could do. Analyse how suitable they might be for your peers and the situations you all live in. Discuss whether you would include one of the cartoons above in the leaflet advertising the project day (8 to 10 minutes).

## 1 Understanding the task

Together with a partner, analyse the task answering the following questions:
a What parts does the task consist of?
b What do you have to do on your own, which parts need cooperation with your partner?
c What results are you expected to come up with?

## Work it out

### 2 Preparing your monologue

► Check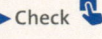

**a** Decide which of the following aspects you have to include in your monologue:
1 assessing the quality of the cartoon
2 describing the layout and colouring
3 comparing it to the second cartoon
4 outlining the topic of the cartoon
5 assessing whether you consider it funny
6 naming the elements of cartoons in general
7 giving the sources
8 explaining what the criticism or humour is aimed at
9 talking about your own experiences with situations like the ones depicted in the cartoon
10 reading out the speech bubble or caption.

**b** Put your answers from **a** in a logical order to form steps of your monologue.

**c** Match the words and phrases below to the steps above. There may be some steps for which no words and phrases are given and there may be some steps for which there is more than one word or phrase.

► Check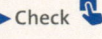

| | | | |
|---|---|---|---|
| a | deal with sth. | h | frame |
| b | present sth. | i | thought-provoking |
| c | personally, I don't believe | j | contain a harsh criticism of … |
| d | be skilfully drawn | k | publish sth. |
| e | find sth. hilarious | l | ridicule sth. |
| f | caption | m | an elaborate drawing |
| g | pencil drawing | | |

**d** For each step that is relevant for your monologue, collect more useful words and phrases.

### 3 Preparing a discussion: language and communication

**a** The following speech acts usually occur in discussions:
- starting the discussion
- stating your opinion
- involving a partner
- asking for clarification
- agreeing
- disagreeing/contradicting
- signalling that you would like to say something
- adding something
- buying time to think
- summarizing your point
- summarizing the results of the discussion.

Collect words and phrases you can use for these speech acts.

b   Remember the feedback you may have got in discussions before and collect aspects you could improve on. You may think of:
- voice
- fluency and intonation
- pronunciation
- body language and gestures
- grammatical correctness
- politeness
- participation in the discussion
- the quality of arguments.

Choose three aspects and write down how you will improve on them during this discussion.

## 4   Preparing the content of your dialogue

a   On your own, brainstorm ideas for your dialogue. Refer to the following aspects of the task:
- different forms of discrimination and privileges
- applicability of these aspects to your age group and living conditions
- arguments for and against using your cartoons from the monologue
- different activities for the project day
- other aspects necessary to plan and organize the day
- an opening and a closing statement.

b   Take notes and arrange them in a way so that they are helpful during the (mock) exam. Add discussion phrases from **3a** where necessary and possible.

## 5   Preparing to give feedback

a   After the mock exam, you will be asked to give feedback on your partners'/ partner's monologue(s) and to assess your dialogue.

Prepare two tables like the ones below and on the next page to structure your feedback:

| Monologue: aspect for feedback | Student's performance | Tips for improvement |
|---|---|---|
| Correctness and variability of language | ... | ... |
| Vocabulary | ... | ... |
| Voice<br>Accent<br>Fluency<br>Intonation | ... | ... |
| Completeness of description | ... | ... |
| Analysis of the given cartoon | ... | ... |
| Personal assessment of cartoon | ... | ... |

| Dialogue: aspects for feedback | Student's performance | Tips for improvement |
|---|---|---|
| Interaction:<br>  a  turn-taking<br>  b  flexibility<br>  c  mutual support | … | … |
| Style:<br>  d  register<br>  e  idiomatic structures<br>  f  adaption to situation | … | … |
| Language:<br>  g  accuracy<br>  h  fluency<br>  i  pronunciation<br>  j  speed<br>  k  features of spoken language<br>  l  discourse management | … | … |
| Content:<br>  m  understanding of the situation<br>  n  mentioning of relevant aspects | … | … |

**b** Collect criteria you should observe when giving your feedback for both, monologues and dialogues.

## Do it!

### 6 Participating in the speaking exam

**You choose** After going through the steps of a speaking exam in theory, you are now to carry out a mock exam in practice. Do this by working on the task on p. 89 according to either task **a** or **b**.

**a** Do the mock exam with your partner. Keep track of the time. Be prepared to give feedback to your partner. As it is only for practice, you may interrupt the mock exam after the monologues to get and/or give feedback (cf. task **7a** and **b**).

**b** Together with your teacher find a pair of volunteers to present their monologues and dialogues to the class. The class watches and makes notes on their performance. Be prepared to give detailed feedback (cf. task **7a** and **c**).

# Feedback

## 7 Giving feedback

**a** Using the tables in task **5**, prepare the feedback you want to give. Make sure to cover both content and form. Mention at least two good aspects and two that need to be improved. Don't only criticize, but suggest specific improvements, e.g. to the quality of arguments or the way contributions were phrased.

> **Language help**
>
> What I liked about your monologue was .... Still, ... • I think you might / could have ... • It would be easier for listeners to ... if ... • Your monologue was a little difficult to follow because ... • One thing you might work on is ... • I found it a bit hard to ... because ... • It seems that you ... • I think your monologue was ... because ... • You might consider ... • It could be a good idea to ... • In the future, you might want to ...

**b** Follow-up from task **6a**:
**Partner A:** Give feedback on your partner's monologue either directly after the monologue or at the end of your mock exam.
**Partner B:** Listen carefully to your partner's feedback on your monologue and take notes. Then swap roles.
Finally, both self-assess your participation in the dialogue and discuss your assessment with your partner.

**c** Follow-up from task **6b**:
Get together in a group of no more than 4 students and discuss your assessment of your classmates' mock exam. Remember the criteria for feedback from **7a**. Give feedback in class.

**d** Copy the *method card below and write down aspects you should work on yourself in order to improve your performance in a speaking exam.

▶ WOB: pp. 58–61, pp. 65–67

| Method card – speaking exam | |
|---|---|
| What I am good at | What I need to practise |
| ... | ... |

# Religion, family and diversity – the core values of Generation Z

You are going to deal with the so-called Generation Z or GenZ.

• Explain what you think might be typical of this generation.

*You are first going to assume a historical perspective by listening to a radio interview from 2009. It was back then when Australian researcher Mark McCrindle was one of the first to describe Generation Z systematically.*

## Comprehension

▶ SF 40: Listening/Viewing for gist and detail, p. 399

**1**   **Listening**   Listen to the interview, then answer the questions. You need not write complete sentences.
1   Why religion and spirituality are important for GenZ
2   What 'tweens' are interested in
3   In what respect GenZ is more egalitarian
4   What values are typical of GenZ

## Beyond the text

**2**   Compare some more recent findings on Generation Z in the table below and discuss whether McCrindle's now historical perspective has stood the test of time. Add new insights to your notes from the previous task.   ▶ Getting started

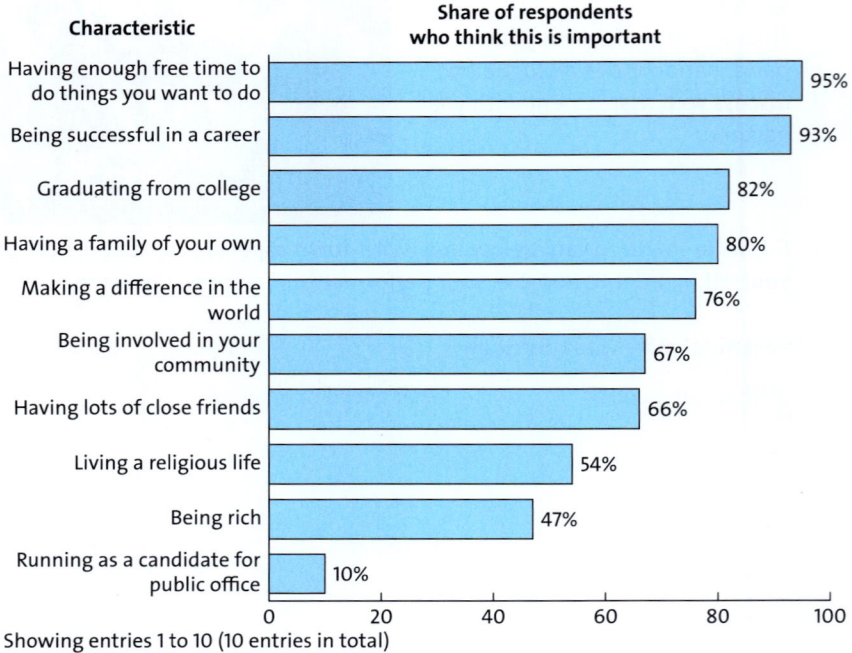

**Core values among teenagers in the United States as of 2021**

| Characteristic | Share of respondents who think this is important |
|---|---|
| Having enough free time to do things you want to do | 95% |
| Being successful in a career | 93% |
| Graduating from college | 82% |
| Having a family of your own | 80% |
| Making a difference in the world | 76% |
| Being involved in your community | 67% |
| Having lots of close friends | 66% |
| Living a religious life | 54% |
| Being rich | 47% |
| Running as a candidate for public office | 10% |

Showing entries 1 to 10 (10 entries in total)

**Details:** United States; Ipsos; Washington Post; June 15, 2021; 1,349 respondents; 14–18 years
Source: Statista 2023

**3 a** Examine the data presented in the chart below and point out significant differences in religious affiliation between the generations.

**b** Identify any key insights or observations you can draw from the data. Think about potential factors that could contribute to the observed trends.

**c** To what extent does the chart align with what you learned about the spirituality of GenZ in the interview?

▶ Getting started
▶ SF 22: Analysing diagrams, p. 373

**Info**

The **Silent Generation** (born between 1928 and 1945) grew up during a period of social upheaval and global events, such as the Great Depression and World War II. They are called 'silent' because they were often seen as conformist and less outspoken.

Baby **Boomers** (born between 1946 and 1964) got their name from the significant increase in birth rates following World War II. This generation experienced significant cultural and social changes, including the civil rights movement and the advent of technology like television.

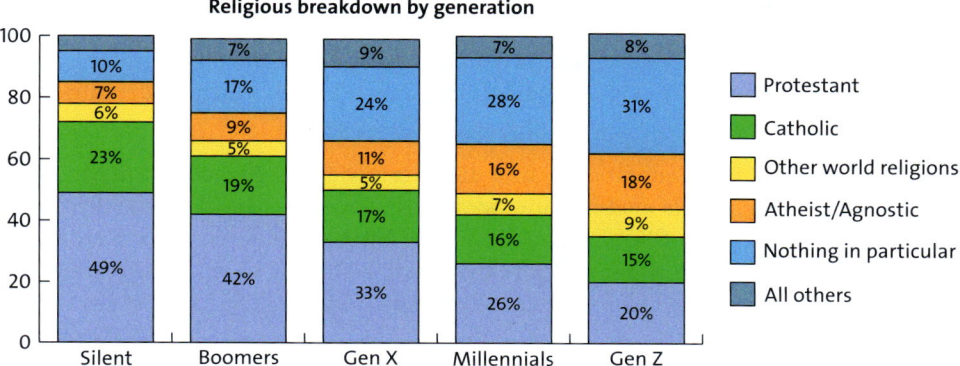

**Religious breakdown by generation**

Source: CES 2022 (USA)

**4** **Mediating** Study the following extract from a German non-fiction book that was published after the last members of Generation Z had been born. Add more details to the notes you already have, this time focusing on GenZ and …

**1** technology
**2** their parents
**3** wishes and concerns

Imagine you are discussing the topic of Generation Z in your bilingual social sciences class. Use the information from the interview and the article by Helene Einramhof-Florian below to write a comprehensive portrait of Gen Z.

▶ Getting started
▶ SF 49: Mediating from German into English, p. 416

**Info**

**Gen(eration) X** (born between 1965 and 1980) grew up during a time of economic and political uncertainty and were influenced by the rise of technology, particularly personal computers and the internet.

**Millennials** (also known as Generation Y, born between 1981 and 1996) are the first generation to come of age in the new millennium. They grew up in a time of rapid technological advancement and witnessed the rise of the internet and social media.

Die Generation Z wurde in eine sehr schnelllebige, dynamische, sich rasch entwickelnde, digitale Welt hineingeboren, sie genießt sehr gute Ausbildungen, ist so gut ausgebildet, wie es zuvor keine andere Generation war, über 50 % werden mit einer akademischen Ausbildung abschließen, wodurch sich der Berufsein-
5 stieg verzögert (Maas, 2019, S. 21).

Ihre Angst gilt der Zukunft des Planeten, mit all den Themen rund um Natur- und Umweltschutz, Nachhaltigkeit und Klimaschutz. Steckl et al. erwähnt 2019 die Arbeitsplatzsicherheit, die Bedeutung des sozialen Miteinanders und die Wertschätzung eigener Ideen als am relevantesten (S. 212 ff.).

10 Als erste Generation, die von Geburt an in einem digitalen Umfeld aufwuchs, ist die Digitalisierung das prägnanteste Merkmal dieser Generation, und sie kann sich der digitalen Entwicklung nicht entziehen. Die Technologie ist ein integraler Bestandteil ihres Alltags, meist intuitiv werden Techniken angewandt und in ihrem Alltag integriert – von klein auf kann sie mit einem Handy oder Tablet
15 umgehen, förmlich autodidaktisch versteht und begreift sie die Anwendung von Applikationen und beherrscht diese. […]

Die Aktivitäten im Internet zählen zu den beliebtesten Freizeitbeschäftigungen der Generation Z und die Kommunikation läuft nicht nur permanent, sondern auch orts- und zeitunabhängig. Die Jugendstudie von Shell berichtet, dass für die Nutzung des Internets 70 % ihr Smartphone verwenden und im Schnitt täglich 3,7 h Zeit damit verbringen. Regelmäßig wird mit 5 bis 20 % ihrer Kontakte gleichzeitig gechattet (2019). PWC zeigt in einer Studie auf, dass 95 % der Generation Z auf Social Media unterwegs sind (2020). Dieser hohe Wert zeigt, dass es sich nicht nur um Informationen, sondern auch um Unterhaltung handelt. Rüdiger Maas spricht in diesem Zusammenhang auch von Social Media Natives (2019, S. 11). Criteo spricht in einer Studie davon, dass 23 h pro Woche Videoinhalte gestreamt werden (2017). [...]

Wie schon bei der Generation Y sind die Eltern wichtige Ratgeber und fungieren teilweise auch als *role model*. Während andere Generationen in ihrer Sturm- und Drang-Phase eher auf Konfrontation mit den Eltern und deren Ansichten waren, ist dies bei den Zern weniger der Fall (Klaffke, 2020, S. 105 ff.). Resultierend aus der Erziehung, die mit viel Wertschätzung, Lob und Anerkennung passiert. [...]

Die Eltern finanzieren die Ausbildungen ihrer Kinder, unterstützen sie bei der Orientierung der richtigen Auswahl. Eltern werden zu Sparring Partner\*innen, Mentor\*innen und Coaches im übertragenen Sinne und stehen ihren Kindern kooperativ zur Seite. Die Shell Studie von 2019 bestätigt, dass Familie und ein weiterer sozialer enger Beziehungskreis die wichtigsten Werte für die Jugendlichen ausmachen und diese noch vor dem Wunsch der Eigenverantwortung und Unabhängigkeit stehen.

*(414 words)*

*From: Helene Einramhof-Florian,* Fit für die jungen Generationen am Arbeitsplatz. Wie ticken sie und was macht sie aus?, *2022*

### Beyond the text

▶ SF 13: Doing research, p. 360

**5 a** Do some research on the core values among German teenagers. Take notes on the information you find.

**b** Intercultural competence   Compare your findings with the data about values among American teenagers from task **2**. Are there differences between the US and Germany? If so, speculate why.

▶ SF 44: Preparing and giving a speech, p. 408 (task a)
▶ Getting started
▶ SF 43: Giving a presentation, p. 405 (task b)

**6** You choose   Speaking   Work on task a or b.

**a** Taking the interview, the chart and the German text as a starting point, prepare a speech on whether you are a typical representative of GenZ.

**b** Mediating   Talk to a person who was born before 2000 – e.g., your aunt, your neighbour, or your coach – and ask them how they were perceived by preceding generations when they were young adults. Use the language you two normally converse in, but report back to class in English.

▶ WOB: pp. 71–73

# The privilege backpack   Meg-John Barker and Jules Scheele

- A privilege is defined as 'a special right or advantage for a person or a group of people'. Which of the following would you consider a privilege, which would you consider a basic right? Discuss with a partner.

  1  going on holiday once a year
  2  being in contact with influential people
  3  having access to free education
  4  the freedom to marry the person you love
  5  the ability to afford anything you like
  6  not needing to feel afraid of being attacked on your way home

## Comprehension

1  Look at the illustration and text about 'straight privilege' on the following page. Point out what *privilege* means according to the 'privilege backpack' and for whom.

2  Outline what we learn about the lives of people who do not have such a 'privilege backpack'. Consider both the contents of the backpack and the four items in the 'straight privilege checklist'.

▶ Support, p. 304

## Analysis

3  a  Examine how the idea of straight white male privilege is presented on the page. Consider both the contents of the backpack and the layout of the page.
   b  Point out how effective you find the format in creating awareness about the experiences of individuals who are not part of the straight-white-male group.

▶ Getting started
▶ SF 23: Analysing visuals, p. 374
▶ SF 24: Working with multimodal texts, p. 376

## Language awareness

4  a  In the text a privilege is defined as a 'blank cheque to' or a 'safety net' for something. Find similar expressions in the text and think of others you could use.
   b  Describe the privileges you have or don't have using some of these expressions.

▶ WOB: pp. 40–44

## Beyond the text

5  Speaking  The concept of a 'privilege backpack' was developed by the US scholar and speaker Peggy McIntosh (see her portrait on the lower right of p. 34). Do some research about her and give a presentation in class. Choose suitable (digital) tools for your presentation.

6  Think back to the guiding question of the chapter and consider to what extent your society allows everyone to fit in.

▶ SF 13: Doing research, p. 360
▶ SF 43: Giving a presentation, p. 405

## STRAIGHT PRIVILEGE

Straight privilege builds on the work of feminist and anti-racism activist Peggy McIntosh on *male privilege* and *white privilege*. McIntosh looks at how these privileges interlock to give straight white men advantages in life.

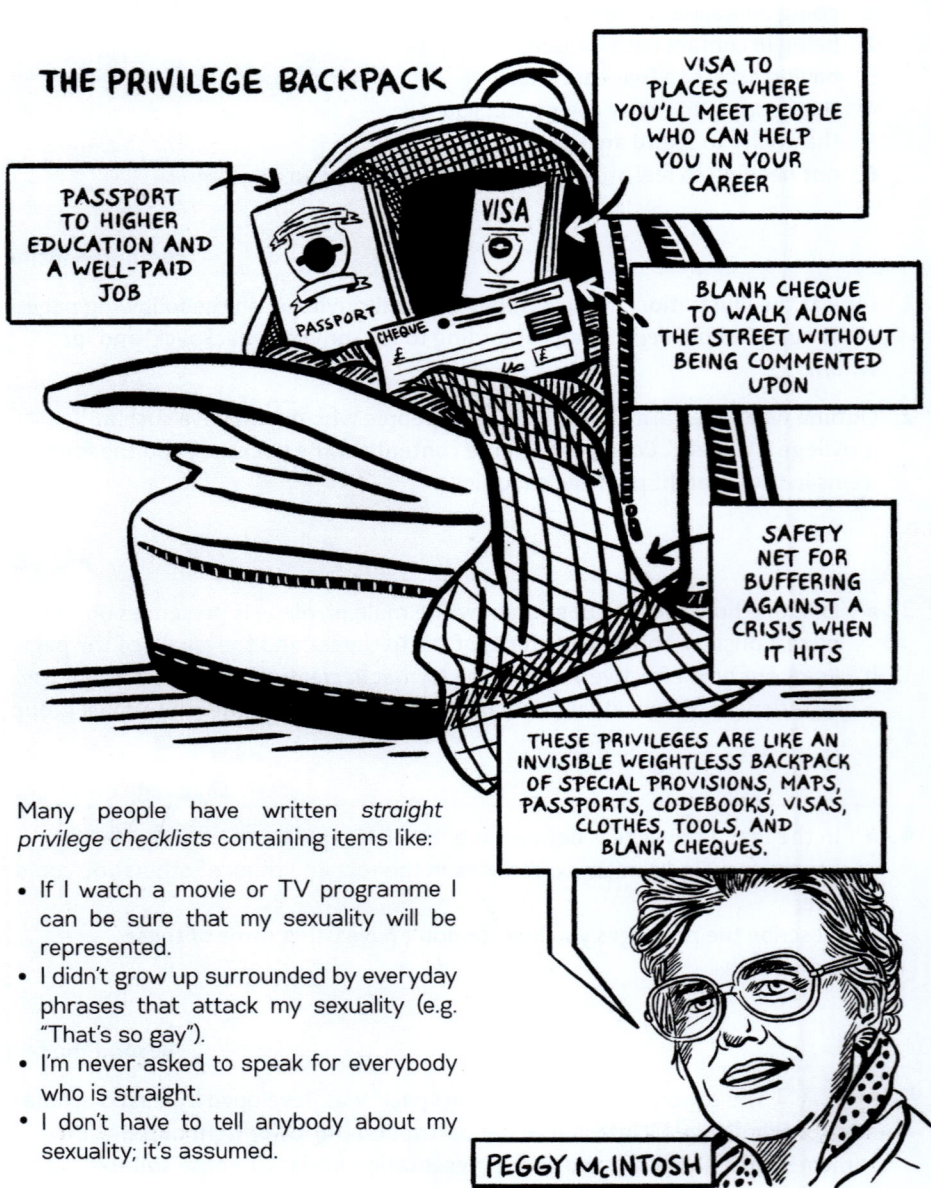

**THE PRIVILEGE BACKPACK**

PASSPORT TO HIGHER EDUCATION AND A WELL-PAID JOB

VISA TO PLACES WHERE YOU'LL MEET PEOPLE WHO CAN HELP YOU IN YOUR CAREER

BLANK CHEQUE TO WALK ALONG THE STREET WITHOUT BEING COMMENTED UPON

SAFETY NET FOR BUFFERING AGAINST A CRISIS WHEN IT HITS

THESE PRIVILEGES ARE LIKE AN INVISIBLE WEIGHTLESS BACKPACK OF SPECIAL PROVISIONS, MAPS, PASSPORTS, CODEBOOKS, VISAS, CLOTHES, TOOLS, AND BLANK CHEQUES.

PEGGY McINTOSH

Many people have written *straight privilege checklists* containing items like:

- If I watch a movie or TV programme I can be sure that my sexuality will be represented.
- I didn't grow up surrounded by everyday phrases that attack my sexuality (e.g. "That's so gay").
- I'm never asked to speak for everybody who is straight.
- I don't have to tell anybody about my sexuality; it's assumed.

**Annotations**
**straight**  heterosexual
**interlock**  connect
**blank cheque**  (here) freedom to do sth.
**buffer sth.**  lessen the harmful effect of sth.

*From: Meg-John Barker, Jules Scheele,* Queer: A Graphic History, *2016*

# Words revisited

*Some of the terms you encountered in 'Words in Context' (cf. p. 16) regarding the concept of gender are only used in certain contexts. It's important to note that using these terms incorrectly could potentially offend people.*

▶ SF 6: Essentials: language and study skills, p. 354

## 1 Gender-sensitive language

In the following table, expressions that are gender-sensitive or gender neutral are listed in the left column and their gender-biased equivalents are given in the right column. Explain the difference between some elements on the left and their equivalents on the right.

| | |
|---|---|
| actor | actress |
| French person, Irish person | Frenchman, Irishman |
| irrational | hysterical |
| humanity | mankind |
| creator | mastermind |
| police officer | policeman or policewomen |
| high pitched | shrill |
| strong | virile |
| cabin crew | air hostess |

# Language awareness

## 2 Matching

▶ Check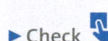

*When you read argumentative texts, you will notice ways in which writers try to influence their readers and convince them of their point of view.*

Match the following definitions to the explanations.

| 1 | bias | A | the way in which a subject is treated, which shows the writer's attitude to a particular topic |
|---|---|---|---|
| 2 | register | B | the writer's subjective view; a strong feeling in favour of or against sth. |
| 3 | tone | C | the way in which a text is written |
| 4 | style | D | the language used in a particular situation, e.g. formal, neutral or informal |

## 3 Collecting ideas

Name three stylistic devices which you think are especially useful for influencing readers in an argumentative text and describe the effect they can have.

### 4 Register

The register of any text has to be appropriate for the audience and the situation. Broadly speaking, a text can have a formal, neutral or informal register.

► Check

**a** Sort these elements according to register: formal, neutral or informal.

---

colloquial words • difficult words (often of Latin origin) and grammar • long and complex sentences • short forms (e.g. *wasn't*) • simple, often incomplete sentences • slang words • straightforward sentences • taboo words

---

**b** Decide which register needs to be used in the tasks below.
  1 Write an email to a friend about an event you want to attend.
  2 Write an email to your principal asking for school-related information.

Work with a partner, divide the two tasks among yourselves, then write your email. Make sure to use gender-sensitive language.
Compare results with your partner and point out the relevant expressions.

### 5 Influencing the reader

The phrases below are intended to influence the reader.
**a** Explain how these phrases can be used effectively to convince readers.
**b** Try to group them into more neutral ones and ones expressing strong bias.

| | |
|---|---|
| As you are all well aware, … | However, … |
| None of you can say that … | Obviously, … |
| Nobody will disagree with me when I say that … | Only a fool would argue that … |
| Statistically speaking, … | |

**c** Discuss with a partner strategies for effectively utilizing phrases like these in argumentative texts.

## Practice

► Getting started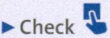

► Check

► SF 44: Preparing and giving a speech, p. 408

### 6 Convincing people of an absurd idea

Work with a partner.
**a** Pick one idea from the box below and brainstorm three (fictional) arguments to support it.
**b** Writing Write a short speech convincing your partner of the truth of this idea.
**Partner A:** Try to write your speech in a neutral register.
**Partner B:** Try to write your speech in an informal register.

| | |
|---|---|
| *Moonlight makes your hair grey.* | *Tall people are better mathematicians.* |
| *Going by train makes you think faster.* | *Carrots are bad for your teeth.* |

**c** Compare your speeches and talk about the differences. Which speech do you find more convincing and why?

► WOB: pp. 96–103

# Identity politics

*You are going to watch a video about identity politics. The first forty seconds will be shown to you without sound.*

- Based on your prior knowledge and the visuals from the video, with your partner, speculate on the possible meaning of the term *identity politics*.

### Comprehension

1 [Viewing] After having watched the video in its entirety, provide an initial definition of *identity politics*. Then, assess the accuracy of your speculations.

2 [Viewing] While watching the full video a second time, take some notes on the following aspects: background, challenges, solutions.

▶ SF 40: Listening/Viewing for gist and detail, p. 399

### Analysis

3 [Viewing] Explain what makes the video so convincing. Take its structure, its visuals, and its language into account.

▶ Getting started
▶ SF 41: Analysing films, series and videos, p. 399

### Beyond the text

4 Work on task **a** or **b**.

a [Speaking] With a partner, discuss how group identities can be used negatively or how group formation can be used against members of that group. Do you think that identity politics has gone too far or not?

b [Challenge] [Writing] Write a comment on the concept of identity politics and its impact on individuals and society. Use examples or personal experiences to support your view.

▶ Check (task b)
▶ SF 28: Argumentative writing: discussion and comment, p. 382

---

## Text 7

# We can do something really cool to this world

Marina Keegan

- In class, collect the criteria that will determine your choice of career. Rank them in order of importance, and explain what this shows about your needs.

*Shortly before graduating from Yale University, Marina Keegan wrote an essay reflecting on the plans of her fellow students for their future careers.*

If this year is anything like the last ten, around 25 percent of employed Yale graduates will enter the consulting or finance industry. This is a big deal. This is a huge deal. This is so many people! This is one-fourth of our people! Regardless of what you think or with whom you're interviewing we ought to be pausing for a second to ask why.

5 I don't pretend to know any more about this world than the rest of us. In fact, I probably know less. (According to the Internet, a consultant is 'someone who

Annotations
1 **Yale** famous elite US university
2 **consulting** *Unternehmensberatung*

Annotations
12 **inherently** necessarily, naturally
14 **intrinsically** essentially
23 **Bain, McKinsey, J.P. Morgan** leading consulting firms
34 **validation** approval

consults someone or something.') But I do know that this statistic is utterly and entirely shocking to me. In a place as diverse and disparate as Yale, it's remarkable that such a large percentage of people are doing anything the same – not to mention
10  something as significant as their postgraduate plans.

I want to understand. [...]

Are consulting firms inherently evil? Probably not. Are banks inherently evil? Probably not. Frankly, I don't know enough about *everything* to make a statement like that one way or another. So is there anything intrinsically wrong with the fact
15  that 25 percent of employed Yale graduates end up in this industry?
Yeah. I think so.

Of course, this is my own opinion, but to me there is something sad about so many of us entering a line of work in which we are not (for the most part) producing something, or helping someone, or engaging in something that we are explicitly
20  passionate about. Even if it's just for two or three years. That's a lot of years! And these aren't just years. This is twenty-three and twenty-four and twenty-five if it were a smaller percentage of people, perhaps it wouldn't bother me so much. But it's not.

What it boils down to is that we could be doing other things. Sure, working at Bain or McKinsey or J.P. Morgan might be one way to gain skills to help us get hired
25  elsewhere, but it's obviously not the only option. There's a lot of cool shit we could all be doing – and I don't need to enumerate the clichés.

Obviously, some people need to make money. They have school loans to pay off and families to support. For those of us with an actual need to make money quickly, these industries might make a lot of sense. In fact, I think that working hard to earn
30  a decent amount of money can be quite noble. I'm still struggling with the fact that due to my own (selfish) desire to be a writer, my children probably won't have the same opportunities I had growing up. For most students, however, I genuinely don't think it's about the money. It's a factor, sure. But it just feels like a factor.

What bothers me is this idea of validation, of rationalization. The notion that some of us
35  (regardless of what we tell ourselves) are doing this because we're not sure what else to do and it's easy to apply to and it will pay us decently and it will make us feel like we are still successful. I just haven't met that many people who sound genuinely excited about these jobs. That's super depressing! I don't understand why no one is talking about it.

Oftentimes at Yale, I'll be sitting around studying or drinking or hanging out when
40  I'll hear one of my friends talk about the project they're doing for a class or rally they're organizing or a play they're putting on. And I'll just think, really, honestly, how remarkably privileged we are to hang around with such a talented group of people around here. I am constantly reminded of the immense passion and creativity of those with whom I get to spend time every day.

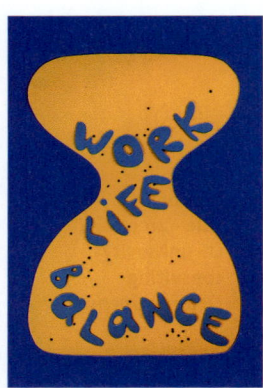

45  Maybe I'm overreacting. Maybe it really is a fantastic way to gain valuable, real world skills. And maybe everyone will quit these jobs in a few years and do something else.

But it worries me.

I want to watch Shloe's movies and I want to see Mark's musicals and I want to vol-
50  unteer with Joe's non-profit and eat at Annie's restaurant and send my kids to schools

Jeff has reformed and I'm *just scared* about this industry that's taking all my friends and telling them this is the best way for them to be spending their time. Any of their time. Maybe I'm ignorant and idealistic but I just feel like that can't possibly be true. I feel like we know that. I feel like we can do something really cool to this world. And
55　I fear – at twenty-three, twenty-four, twenty-five – we might forget.

*From: Marina Keegan, 'Even artichokes have doubts', The Opposite of Loneliness, 2014*

### Comprehension

**1**　Outline what Keegan thinks about the career plans of Yale students.

### Analysis

**2**　Keegan makes use of *contrast in her text. Find examples and explain its purpose.

### Language awareness

**3**　**a**　Examine the *register used.
　　**b**　Rephrase ll. 1–5 in a neutral register.

▶ Getting started
▶ WOB: pp. 98–99

### Beyond the text

**4**　You choose　Work on task **a** or **b**.

　　**a**　Discuss whether you agree with the last line of the text.

　　**b**　Evaluate the choice the writer made (ll. 30–33).

**5**　**a**　Conduct a class survey to explore your classmates' plans after graduating from school and their future aspirations. Present your results in class.
　　**b**　Intercultural competence　Based on the results of your survey, discuss the differences in career plans between American and German students and reflect on how cultural contexts may shape their decisions.

▶ Check
▶ SF 43: Giving a presentation, p. 405
▶ WOB: pp. 65–67

► More info

# 'Money is just a social construct'   Sally Rooney

- How many years of your life do you expect to spend in a paid job?
- Would you prefer to stay in one job or would you rather switch jobs frequently?
- Do you want to start a family and what would that mean for your professional life?

*Marianne is a university student in Dublin, Ireland. In the following extract from Rooney's \*novel* Normal People *Marianne is talking to her friend Joanna, also a student at Trinity College, on the phone. The two women discuss their differing opinions of working life and they talk about Peggy, a fellow student whose major aspiration in life seems to be to marry rich.*

Marianne is reading the back of a yoghurt pot in the supermarket. With her other hand she's holding her phone, through which Joanna is telling an anecdote about her job. When Joanna gets into an anecdote she can really monologue at length, so Marianne isn't worried about taking her attention off the conversation for a few
5 seconds to read the yoghurt pot. It's a warm day outside, she's wearing a light blouse and a skirt, and the chill of the freezer aisle raises goosebumps on her arms. She has no reason to be in the supermarket, except that she doesn't want to be in her family home, and there aren't many spaces in which a solitary person can be inconspicuous in Carricklea. She can't go for a drink alone, or get a cup of coffee
10 on Main Street. Even the supermarket will exhaust its usefulness when people notice she's not really buying groceries, or when she sees someone she knows and has to go through the motions of conversation.
The office is half-empty so nothing really gets done, Joanna is saying. But I'm still getting paid so I don't mind.
15 Because Joanna has a job now, most of their conversations take place over the phone, even though they're both living in Dublin. Marianne's only home for the weekend, but that's Joanna's only time off work. On the phone Joanna frequently describes her office, the various characters who work there, the dramas that erupt between them, and it's as if she's a citizen of a country Marianne has never visited,
20 the country of paid employment. Marianne replaces the yoghurt pot in the freezer now and asks Joanna if she finds it strange, to be paid for her hours at work – to exchange, in other words, blocks of her extremely limited time on this earth for the human invention known as money.
It's time you'll never get back, Marianne adds. I mean, the time is real.
25 The money is also real.
Well, but the time is more real. Time consists of physics, money is just a social construct.
Yes, but I'm still alive at work, says Joanna. It's still me, I'm still having experi-ences. You're not working, okay, but the time is passing for you too. You'll never get
30 it back either.
But I can decide what I do with it.
To that I would venture that your decision-making is also a social construct.
Marianne laughs. She wanders out of the freezer aisle and towards the snacks.
I don't buy into the morality of work, she says. Some work maybe, but you're just
35 moving paper around an office, you're not contributing to the human effort.
I didn't say anything about morality.
Marianne lifts a packet of dried fruit and examines it, but it contains raisins so she puts it back down and picks up another.

## Annotations
8   **solitary** alone
9   **inconspicuous** not attracting attention
9   **Carricklea** fictional town in Ireland
18  **erupt** break out
32  **venture sth.** dare to express sth., risk stating sth. that might be wrong

Do you think I judge you for being so idle? says Joanna.

40 Deep down I think you do. You judge Peggy.

Peggy has an idle mind, which is different.

Marianne clicks her tongue as if to scold Joanna for her cruelty, but not with any great investment. She's reading the back of a dried apple packet.

I wouldn't want you to turn into Peggy, says Joanna. I like you the way you are.

45 Oh, Peggy's not that bad. I'm going to the supermarket checkout now so I'm going to hang up.

Okay. You can call tomorrow after the thing if you feel like talking.

Thanks, says Marianne. You're a good friend. Bye. [...]

*From:* Normal People, *2019*

Annotations
41 **idle** *(adj)* lazy
42 **click your tongue** *(idiom) mit der Zunge schnalzen*
42 **scold sb. for sth.** rebuke sb. for sth.

## Comprehension

1 Work with a partner. **Partner A** points out why Joanne finds it important to have a job. **Partner B** points out why Marianne is sceptical about working life.

## Analysis

2 The text contains a lot of direct speech but does not have any quotation marks. Examine the effect this may have on the reader.

## Language awareness

3 a Identify characteristics of direct speech in the text and give examples.
  b Rephrase the last part of the text (ll. 40–49) using only reported speech or narrating it. Analyse the effect of these changes.

▶ More language

## Beyond the text

▶ SF 25: Analysing cartoons, p. 377

4 With a partner, describe and analyse the cartoon. Find a suitable title and compare its message to the text 'Money is just a social construct'.

5 You choose Work on task **a** or **b**.

a Writing 'Should I spend my time on something called work?' Write a personal journal entry in which you consider your ideas about your future working life.

b Speaking 'No one should do a job he could do in his sleep.' (Cory Doctorow) In groups of three, use this quote as a starting point to discuss the importance of having a meaningful job. Find examples of jobs you consider (ir-) relevant and give reasons.

"I STARTED SCHOOL AT AGE SIX AND I'M DONE WITH IT AT AGE 16. I THINK THAT AFTER SPENDING 62,5% OF MY ENTIRE LIFE AT WORK I'VE GOT THE RIGHT TO RETIRE."

CartoonStock.com

▶ **More info** ⤵

### A prank    Dashka Slater       **Advanced**

- **Think** Define the term *hate crime* in your own words.
- **Pair** Compare your definition with a partner's. Decide which is better or agree on a new one, based on both your definitions.
- **Share** Share your definition in class. Agree on one definition.

*You are going to read an extract from a novel based on true events. Please note that the extract contains severely offensive language which readers may find painful.*

Sasha liked the back of the bus. A platform seat they could spread out on, tuck their legs under. There they could read, do homework, nap. They had trained themself to wake as the bus rounded the sharp S-curve just before their stop. On 4 November they were unusually tired, having stayed up late the night before writing an
5 essay for their Russian Lit class. Less than twenty-four hours earlier, they'd shared their exhaustion on Tumblr:

*Do u ever just get rly tired when u have a lot of shit*
*to do and u just start crying for no reason*

Now, as the 57 bus rattled up MacArthur Boulevard, Sasha's eyes drifted close.

10 4:52 P.M.

In Oakland, every AC transit bus is equipped with cameras that continuously record sound and video from multiple vantage points. The 57 bus was no exception. The cameras recorded Lloyd and Richard climbing on at the front a little before five p.m. and walking down the aisle towards the back – Lloyd chubby in a
15 zipped-up black hoodie, Richard lean in a black hoodie over a white T-shirt and an orange-billed New York Knicks hat. [...]
Richard recognised a boy named Jamal sitting at the back of the bus and greeted him with a dap. [...]
As the bus started up again, the two cousins gripped the silver pole in front of
20 Jamal. Behind them, Sasha slept. A paperback copy of *Anna Karenina* lay closed in their lap. Their skirt, gauzy and white, dangled over the edge of the seat.
It couldn't have been easy to sleep with Lloyd nearby. He bounced up and down trying to make the bus shake, rapped a snippet of the song *Started from the Bottom* by Drake, screeched random words like 'Chinchilla!' and 'Obituary!' He shouted down
25 the aisle to a girl he'd noticed when they climbed on board, 'Hey! Girl! Excuse me!'
A girl in blue basketball shorts turned to look at him.
'No, your friend, the light-skinned one.'
Jamal pointed at Sasha, whispered, 'Look at this dude.'
Lloyd turned and looked over his shoulder. He cackled.
30 On the video, you can't hear what Jamal says as he hands Richard the lighter. But you can see him take out his iPhone and point it towards Sasha as if planning to record. Later Richard would say that it was supposed to be funny, like that prank show on MTV with Ashton Kutcher, *Punk'd*. He thought the fabric would smoulder for a minute and then Sasha would wake up and slap it out, startled.
35 'I *need* a good laugh,' he'd said just after getting on the bus. Now he showed the lighter to Lloyd and then swung to the opposite side of the silver pole, closer to Sasha. He flicked the lighter by the hem off Sasha's skirt. Nothing happened.
Lloyd was still shouting up to the front of the bus.

---

**Annotations**

2  **nap** *(v)* sleep
5  **Lit** Literature
14  **chubby** slightly overweight
15  **lean** slim
16  **New York Knicks** basketball team
18  **dap** form of greeting originally popular among young African Americans
20  *Anna Karenina* novel (1873) by Russian author Leo Tolstoy
21  **gauzy** ['gɔːzi] made of thin, translucent fabric
24  **Drake** Canadian rapper
29  **cackle** *(v)* laugh in an unpleasant way
30  **lighter** *Feuerzeug*
33  **Ashton Kutcher** US actor
33  *Punk'd* TV series in which practical jokes were played
33  **smoulder** burn slowly without a real flame
34  **startled** surprised
37  **hem** *Saum*

Advanced

'Hey! Light-skinned girl!'

40 'Light-skinned girl.' Jamal kept repeating what Lloyd said, his deep voice like an echo from the bottom of a well.

Lloyd bounced up the aisle to where the girls were sitting, perching on the edge of a nearby seat.

'Go ahead, you do it,' Jamal said to Richard. Richard flicked the lighter again.
45 Nothing.

Rebuffed by the girls, Lloyd returned to his companions, stopping in front of Sasha's sleeping form to shout an abrupt, parrotlike 'Hey!'

Sasha stirred, but didn't wake.

'Whoa, nigga. You said, "'Hey!'" Jamal echoed. 'Screamin' and shit.'
50 Lloyd leaned close and screeched in Jamal's ear. Richard laughed and slapped Lloyd's head.

'Aw, nigga, you just broke my neck,' Lloyd yelled. 'Damn, pussy, bitch, fuck!'

Richard brandished the lighter, pretending to light Lloyd's sleeve. He looked at Jamal.
55 'Do it,' Jamal urged.

Lloyd danced between them, landing half on Jamal's lap.

'Move, nigga! Get off me,' Jamal grumbled. He kept his eyes on Richard, his phone poised. 'You might as well do it,' he said again.

Richard slunk back to Sasha, flicked the lighter. Nothing. He glanced at Jamal,
60 grinned, and flicked the lighter a fourth time.

'Back door! Back door!' Lloyd called to the driver, ready for them to make their escape.

The doors opened. Richard leaped off the bus. Lloyd started to follow. Then he looked back and stopped, transfixed, as Sasha's skirt erupted into a sheet of flame.
65 When the doors closed again, he hadn't moved.

*

The next few seconds of the surveillance video are hard to watch.

Sasha leaps up, slapping the flaming skirt. 'Oh, fuck! Oh, fuck!' The skirt looks unearthly, impossible, a ball of white fire.

'Ow! *Ow!*' Sasha screams, voice high and terrified. '*I'm on fire. I'm on fire!*' Their
70 hands snatch at the skirt, shaking it, waving it. Specks of flaming fabric swirl through the air. Sasha runs for the door and finds it closed. They turn, dance in place, screaming.

Jamal howls with laughter. Then, as Sasha careens toward him, he cringes and climbs on to his seat. 'He's on fire!' he yells. 'Put him out!'
75 Passengers sprint for the exits, shrieking and coughing. 'It's a fire! It's a fire!' Some of the other kids on the bus are giggling. The bus still moving, the driver just start-ing to register that something is going on way back at the far end of his vehicle.

'I ain't got time to be playin' with y'all, man,' he calls over his shoulder.

Near the middle of the bus, two men leap from their seats and elbow through the
80 press of people trying to escape. One man is short and balding; the other is taller, with a walrusy moustache and sad basset-hound eyes.

'Get down!' the moustached one yells. 'Get on the ground!' The two men don't know each other, but they work in unison, shoving Sasha to the floor. The moustached man smothers Sasha's flaming skirt with his coat while the balding
85 man stamps out the burning tatters that flame around them.

**Annotations**

46 **rebuff sb.** reject sb.
53 **brandish sth.** *mit etwas herumwedeln*
58 **poised** in position
59 **slink** (slunk – slunk) move very quietly and slowly, esp. because you are ashamed
64 **transfixed** unable to move, fascinated
73 **careen** move very quickly in an uncontrolled way
83 **in unison** together
83 **shove sb.** push sb.
84 **smother sth.** cover a fire with sth. to put it out

**Info**

The story makes use of very offensive words (cf. e.g. l. 52), which should never be used in conversations as they might be extremely hurtful and very inappropriate. They are solely used as stylistic devices to underline and emphasize a certain attitude. Additionally the **N-word** ap-pears repeatedly in the story, for example in l. 49. Note that when used among young African Americans, the N-word can be a casual expression underlining shared identities. However, it should never be used by somebody who is not Black.

**Advanced**

Annotations
**86 kerb** *Bordstein*
**91 charred** black after being burned

It's over in seconds. The driver pulls the bus to the kerb. Sasha scrambles to a standing position, dazed and in shock. 'Oh, Lord. Fuck.'

'That boy was on *fire*, wasn't he?' a man remarks as Sasha pushes through the back doors to the pavement. Behind him, Sasha's moustached rescuer paces the aisle.

90 'Call an ambulance,' he croaks. He goes to the door of the bus and calls to Sasha, who roams the pavement with a mobile phone, charred legs. 'You need to call an ambulance, man.'

The girl in the blue basketball shorts calls to Sasha through the doors of the bus. 'Are you OK?'

95 Sasha doesn't answer.

The bus empties out. Passengers climb off, shaking their heads.

*From: Dashka Slater,* The 57 Bus, *2018*

## Comprehension

▶ Getting started

▶ Check

**1**   **Choose the correct option.**

**1**   Sasha likes the back of the bus because …
- **a**   it gives them plenty of space to do what they want.
- **b**   they can feel the bus make a sharp turn before their stop.
- **c**   they are separated from the other passengers.

**2**   When the boys dance around them, Sasha …
- **a**   pretends to sleep through the noise and movement.
- **b**   is too tired to wake up.
- **c**   hopes to be left alone by the boys.

**3**   The boys set fire to Sasha's skirt in order to …
- **a**   impress the girls on the bus.
- **b**   do something funny.
- **c**   harm someone who seems different.

**4**   The girls react to Lloyd's attempt to get their attention by …
- **a**   moving to the front of the bus.
- **b**   asking him to go back to his friends.
- **c**   ignoring him completely.

**5**   When the bus doors open, Lloyd …
- **a**   follows Richard out onto the street.
- **b**   wants to jump out but is transfixed.
- **c**   stays with Jamal to film the event.

**6**   How exactly are the flames extinguished from Sasha's skirt?
- **a**   Two men cover Sasha with clothes.
- **b**   The balding man smothers the fire on the skirt with his boots.
- **c**   The man with the moustache uses his coat to cover Sasha.

**7**   At the end of the episode Sasha …
- **a**   is by and large OK when walking around.
- **b**   is dazed and confused but not badly injured.
- **c**   has been burned on the legs and needs an ambulance.

Advanced

**2** Draw a diagram depicting the relationship of the characters in this scene.

### Analysis

▶ WOB: pp. 37–39

**3** Explain how the author uses things such as clothes, accessories and swear words to characterize the teenagers and state the effect this has on the reader.

**4** Analyse the different *narrative perspectives the author employs in the excerpt.

### Language awareness

**5** Analyse the use of the pronoun *they* in the extract. What difference would it make if *he/she* were used instead?

▶ Getting started

### Beyond the text

**6** Examine whether what happened can be called a hate crime. Refer to your ideas from the pre-reading task.

**7** ▎You choose▎ ▎Writing▎ Work on task **a** or **b**.
Richard is arrested and sent to court.

**a** After being sent to court, Richard has become insightful and decides to approach Sasha by writing them a letter. Sasha is not sure if they want to read the letter and discusses the situation with a friend. Write their dialogue.

**b** As a kind of confrontation therapy, Sasha decides to meet Richard. They talk about what happened and the effect it has had on both their lives. Write their dialogue.

▶ SF 38: Creative writing, p. 395
▶ WOB: pp. 51–53

**8** Work with a partner. **Partner B:** Go to p. 304. **Partner A:** Look below.
**a** Study your chart and tell your partner what information it gives.
**b** Discuss the most interesting findings.

▶ Getting started
▶ SF 22: Analysing diagrams, p. 373

**Registered hate crimes by bias motivation, USA 2021**

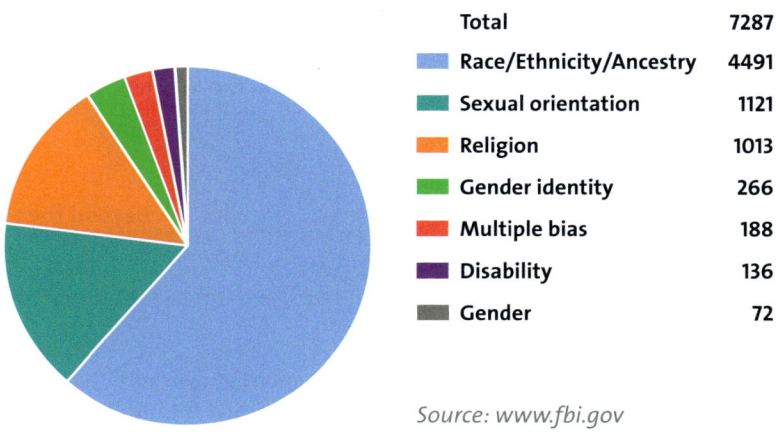

| **Total** | **7287** |
|---|---|
| **Race/Ethnicity/Ancestry** | **4491** |
| **Sexual orientation** | **1121** |
| **Religion** | **1013** |
| **Gender identity** | **266** |
| **Multiple bias** | **188** |
| **Disability** | **136** |
| **Gender** | **72** |

Source: www.fbi.gov

▶ Getting started

▶ More info

Annotations
1  **mistress**  lover
2  **coral**  *Edelkoralle*
3  **dun**  grey-brown
5  **rose damask'd**  type of rose
8  **reek**  stink, smell
12 **tread**  walk

**Info**

The **sonnet** originated in Italy in the 13th century and was adapted into many languages. The Shakespearean form of the sonnet follows a very strict structure of fourteen lines (three quatrains ending with a rhymed couplet: *abab cdcd efef gg*) and a typical metre (in English, the iambic pentameter). The sonnet was a very popular form of love poetry.

▶ SF 20: Reading and understanding poetry, p. 370

▶ Support, p. 305 (task 3)

Advanced

## Sonnet 130   William Shakespeare

- With a partner outline five beauty ideals of today and compare them to those you think may have existed during Shakespeare's lifetime.

My mistress' eyes are nothing like the sun;
Coral is far more red than her lips' red;
If snow be white, why then her breasts are dun;
If hairs be wires, black wires grow on her head.
5 I have seen roses damask'd, red and white,
But no such roses see I in her cheeks;
And in some perfumes is there more delight
Than in the breath that from my mistress reeks.
I love to hear her speak, yet well I know
10 That music hath a far more pleasing sound;
I grant I never saw a goddess go;
My mistress, when she walks, treads on the ground:
    And yet, by heaven, I think my love as rare
    As any she belied with false compare.

*From: William Shakespeare,* Sonnets, *1609*

William Shakespeare

### Comprehension

1  Sum up in one sentence how the speaker of Sonnet 130 views their lover.

2  Compare the idealized beauty and the speaker's lover by making a table like the one below.

| Conventional beauty | Their lover |
|---|---|
| bright, sparkly eyes (eyes like the sun) ... | Her eyes are probably normal (nothing like the sun) ... |

### Analysis

3  List all the \*images Shakespeare uses in his \*sonnet and explain their function.

4  Explain what point Shakespeare is making in his poem.

### Beyond the text

5  a  Write two lines of poetry which start 'Beauty is ...'.
   b  In your group combine your written lines and revise them to turn them into a lyrical piece of literature.

6  📖  Return to the guiding question of the chapter and rephrase your paragraph from p. 15, task **2c**, considering everything you have learned from this chapter.

# Art in Context: We can do it!

*The poster on the right was created during the Second World War. When US manufacturers were urged to produce more war goods, J.H. Miller designed a series of posters for Westinghouse Electric intended to boost worker morale – men and women alike. However, the poster was adopted by the feminist movement of the 1980s as their symbol of female empowerment.*

▶ SF 24: Working with multimodal texts, p. 376

- In a few sentences, note down what comes to your mind when you think about the word *empowerment*.

### Comprehension

1  Describe the poster.

### Analysis

2  Explain the message of the poster.

3  The poster was not well known during World War II, but has since become very popular. Assess why it might be so popular.

*J. Howard Miller, 'We Can Do It', 1942*

▶ WOB: pp. 40–44

> **Language help**
>
> inspirational image · iconic figure · uplifting attitude · self-empowerment · strong female · war production worker · promote feminism · inspire women workers · female empowerment · fight against gender inequality

### Beyond the text

4  [Speaking] Research how the image has been used in contemporary campaigns or by people today and present your results.

▶ SF 13: Doing research, p. 360

5  [You choose] [Speaking] Work on task **a** or **b**.

   **a** Prepare a three-minute speech on how the image inspires you personally.

   **b** In a short speech comment on the historical significance of the image, reflecting on its relevance in inspiring individuals to overcome challenges and strive for success in modern times.

▶ SF 44: Preparing and giving a speech, p. 408

▶ SF 28: Argumentative writing: discussion and comment, p. 382 (task b)

6  In small groups, create a contemporary poster with a similar message encouraging people to become involved in a social project today.

## Chapter task

**Change for the better!**
You are a member of a social movement that wants to give voice to younger voters. You have been invited to write a speech about the relationship between individuals and society. Your speech should refer to one or more of the following aspects:

   – charity and volunteering
   – the contribution of the individual to society

   – identity and diversity
   – changing gender roles.

▶ Getting started

# Chapter 2
# The UK between Tradition and Change

**A**

'[...] My children have Scotland, Wales, Iraq, India, Pakistan and Zanzibar in their blood. We live in Croydon and our family extends to every inhabited continent on the planet. Our friends are from all points of the compass. We are global and local in one room. Whether you look at the British Empire with
5 shame or anger or pride this is what it does for us now, it is our history that drew us together and it shapes our Britain. We are IndoScots, Presbyterian Muslims, we are London and like Tom Jones, we're not unusual.'

**Greendeskbruce**

**B**

'When someone abroad asks "Where are you from?" Do you say, I'm
10 British, a UK citizen, from Great Britain, English, Scottish, Welsh, Northern Irish, or from the United Kingdom of Great Britain and Northern Ireland? Do you then try to explain that the "Great" refers to the largest island and is really not a delusion of grandeur. Multi-culturalism is fine but do we have any shared culture?'

15 **JohnBea**

▶ More info

**Annotations**

2 **Croydon** district in south London

7 **Tom Jones** Welsh pop singer who sang the song 'It's not unusual'

13 **grandeur** [ˈɡrændʒə] *Größe, Pracht*

24 **bestow sth. on sth. else** *einer Sache etwas verleihen*

27 **power monger** *Machthaber*

27 **advocate sth.** *etwas befürworten*

32 **Cinderella** (here) sb. that has been ignored and deserves more attention

34 **devolved** decentralized

**1** **a** Read the texts above and note down the different definitions of Britishness you encounter.

**b** Choose one statement about Britishness that you find particularly striking. Present it and explain why you picked it.

**c** On the basis of the statements, discuss whether there is such a thing as Britishness after all.

**2** **a** Have a look at the Chapter map on p. 49 and discuss which aspects are already represented in the quotations and will be covered in the chapter.

**b** Speculate what the other topics mentioned in the Chapter map might have to do with the guiding question.

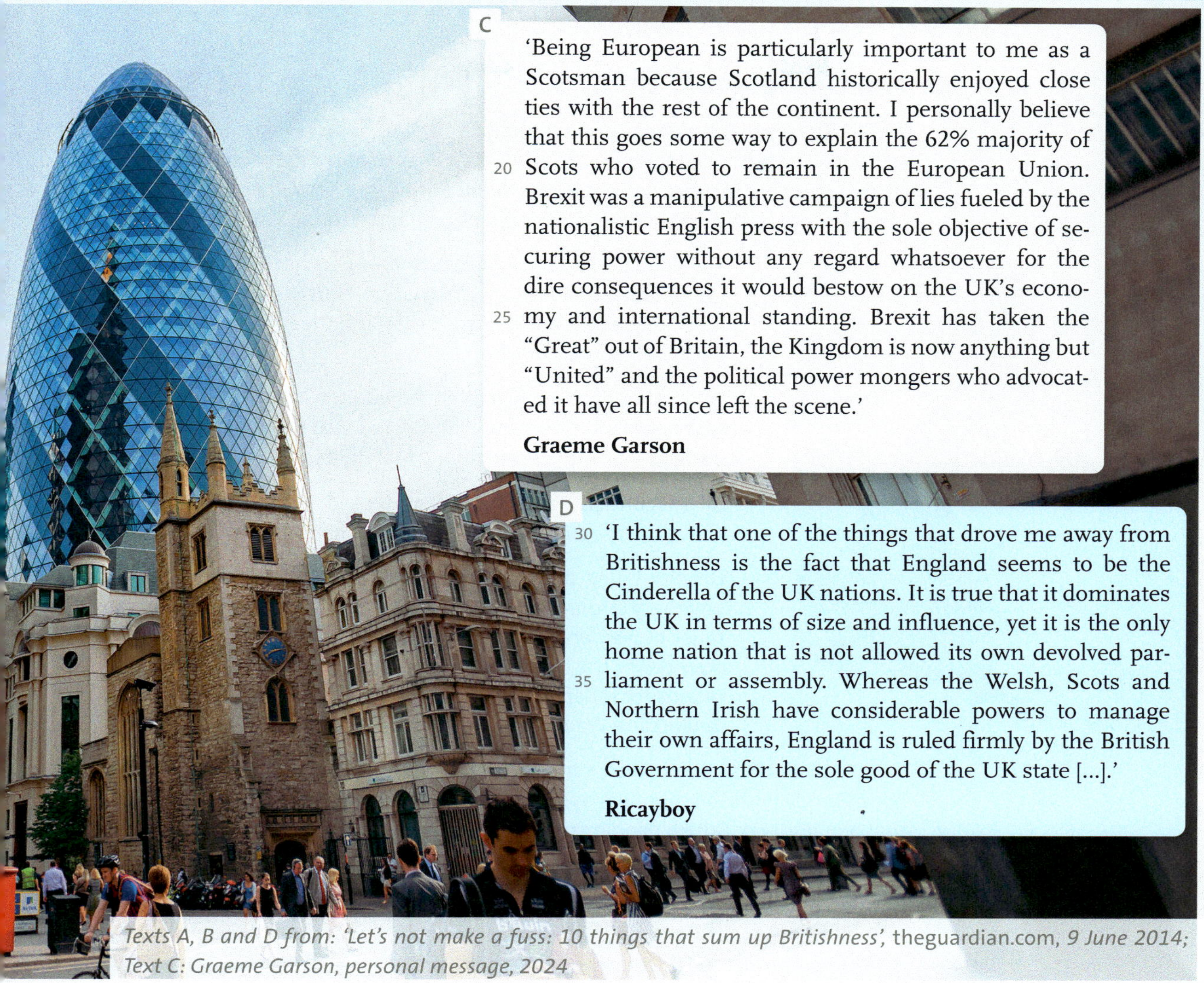

**C**

'Being European is particularly important to me as a Scotsman because Scotland historically enjoyed close ties with the rest of the continent. I personally believe that this goes some way to explain the 62% majority of
20 Scots who voted to remain in the European Union. Brexit was a manipulative campaign of lies fueled by the nationalistic English press with the sole objective of securing power without any regard whatsoever for the dire consequences it would bestow on the UK's econo-
25 my and international standing. Brexit has taken the "Great" out of Britain, the Kingdom is now anything but "United" and the political power mongers who advocated it have all since left the scene.'

**Graeme Garson**

**D**

30 'I think that one of the things that drove me away from Britishness is the fact that England seems to be the Cinderella of the UK nations. It is true that it dominates the UK in terms of size and influence, yet it is the only home nation that is not allowed its own devolved par-
35 liament or assembly. Whereas the Welsh, Scots and Northern Irish have considerable powers to manage their own affairs, England is ruled firmly by the British Government for the sole good of the UK state [...].'

**Ricayboy**

*Texts A, B and D from: 'Let's not make a fuss: 10 things that sum up Britishness', theguardian.com, 9 June 2014; Text C: Graeme Garson, personal message, 2024*

> ## Chapter map

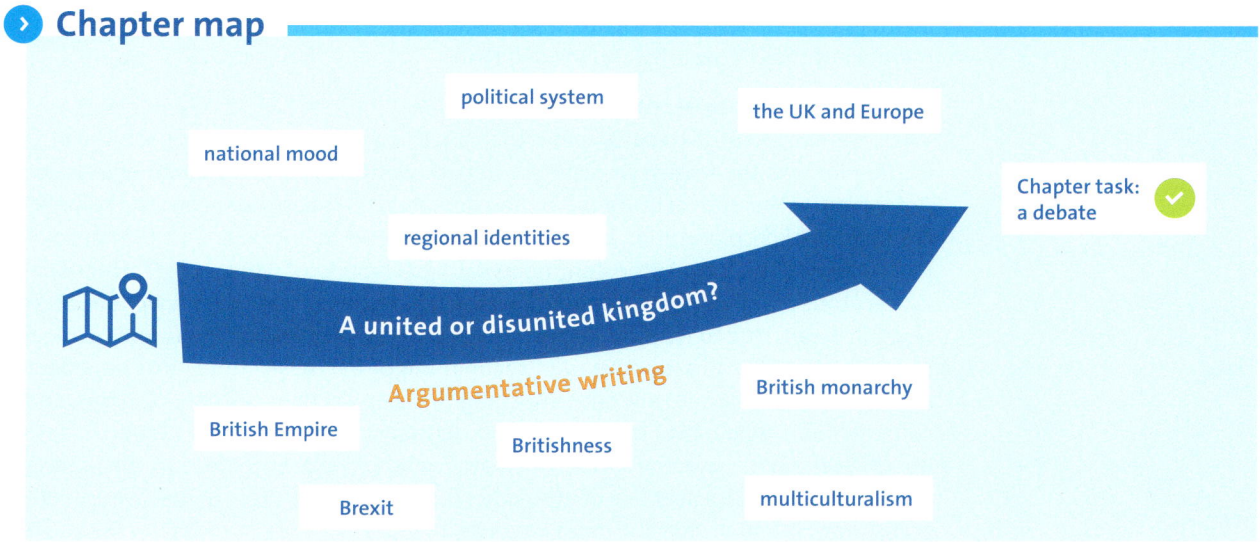

political system

the UK and Europe

national mood

Chapter task: a debate

regional identities

**A united or disunited kingdom?**

*Argumentative writing*

British monarchy

British Empire

Britishness

multiculturalism

Brexit

🔊 **The UK now and then**

▶ More language 🔖

**It's all in a name – geography and politics**
Although the terms *Great Britain, Britain, England* and *United Kingdom* are often used interchangeably, they are not synonyms. *Great Britain*, or *Britain* for short, is a political term describing the unity of the three nations England, Scotland and Wales.

5 The *United Kingdom of Great Britain and Northern Ireland*, or the *UK* for short, includes a fourth nation, Northern Ireland. Geographically, these four nations are located on the British Isles – together with the Republic of Ireland.

While the UK as a whole is governed from Westminster in London, 10 Northern Ireland, Scotland and Wales also have their own national parliaments with certain individual rights of self-government.

All the British nations are represented by the Union Flag, also known as the Union Jack, which is the national flag of the UK.

Despite being part of the United Kingdom, all four nations also 15 have very strong national identities, which has led to various separatist movements. The Brexit referendum in 2016 and the consequences of the United Kingdom leaving the EU have reignited demands for independence, mostly in Scotland but also in Northern Ireland and Wales.

20 In spite of all these differences, various uniting factors remain, most importantly the Royal Family with the monarch as head of state for all the nations. Polls have shown that a majority of British people are still in favour of the constitutional monarchy as a system of government and regard the Royal Family as an important British institution.

**Britain's place in Europe and its relationship with the EU**
25 Although the UK officially left the EU on 31 January 2020, geographically it remains a part of Europe and in fact shares a border with an EU country, namely the Republic of Ireland. As a strong economic power it continues to be an important trading partner for the EU and there are still many economic and cultural ties between the UK and the continent. Moreover, the UK plays a significant role in world politics as a permanent 30 member of the UN Security Council and NATO.

**Britain – a multicultural society**
What has shaped British society more than anything else is its imperial past. The British Empire was the largest in history and had territories on every continent except Antarctica. In the 20th century, increasing demands for independence in the colonies 35 led to gradual decolonization but the strong ties between Britain and its former colonies remain in the form of the Commonwealth of Nations, of which most former British territories are members. Some of these countries recognize the monarch as their nominal head. Due to its colonial past but also because of its economic and political strength, the UK is an attractive country for immigrants. These immigrants have added 40 ed greatly to the nation's diversity, enriching the UK with their cultural, religious, and culinary input while also increasing the economic wealth with their labour. Consequently, Britain has become a multicultural society, in which everyone has the right to be treated equally irrespective of ethnicity, religion or culture. This is, however, an ongoing process and Britain still has a long way to go.

## 1  Main ideas

**a**  Note down the geographical, political and cultural characteristics of the United Kingdom.

**b**  Add aspects that are depicted in the illustration at the bottom of the page.

## 2  Reflect

**a**  Assess which of the three parts of the text was most difficult for you. Give reasons. Refer to content, vocabulary or sentence construction.

**b**  Find …

    **1**  three words or phrases that were new to you and explain them.

    **2**  two interesting sentence constructions or grammar aspects.

    **3**  one sentence that you would like to keep in mind and use as a model for one of your next assignments.

## 3  Spidergram

**a**  Create a *spidergram for the word field *politics*. Use relevant words from the text and add some of your own.

**b**  Compare your spidergram with your partner's. Add some more branches where necessary.

**c**  With your partner, reflect on the usefulness of spidergrams and other visualizations or graphic organizers for your language learning.

## 4  Chunk it!

**a**  Collect useful phrases and *chunks from the text that help you define the UK as a country. Using an online *collocations dictionary, form as many collocations with the two nouns *nation* and *unity* as possible.

    ► Getting started
    ► Check

**b**  Intercultural communication   What role do the concepts of *nation* and *unity* play in Germany? Write a short paragraph using the phrases and chunks you collected in **a**.

## 5  Speaking about the UK

You choose   Work on task **a** or **b**.
    ► Getting started

**a**  Work in a group. Discuss which aspects depicting a modern multicultural society are missing from the illustration on the right. Think of cliches or prejudices related to such a society. Present your results in class.

**b**  A friend of yours argues that all multicultural societies are basically the same. Discuss which features (historical, political …) might make British multiculturalism different from the one in other countries.

▶ 'Britain after Brexit', p. 341

# Taking stock: the mood in the UK    Deborah Mattinson

- *Quick write**: Write one short paragraph naming political decisions and events that could divide a country. After you read the text, compare your paragraph to the content of the text.

*The organization BritainThinks conducted a survey of the mood in the UK in 2019. Deborah Mattinson reports about her findings from the survey.*

I have been listening to people in focus groups since the late 1980s and I cannot recall a time when the national mood was more despairing. 'Broken', 'sad', 'worried', 'angry' – the negatives tumble out, as does the long list of grievances.

I'm hearing anxieties voiced in a way I haven't heard since the 1990s: a rundown
5  NHS, job insecurity, teacher shortages. Seven out of 10 feel pessimistic about homelessness, 68% are gloomy about rising poverty, and a staggering one in five think it likely that they, or someone close, will be a victim of violent crime in the next year. This rises to almost a third in London.

We're a deeply divided nation, too – and nearly three-quarters of us expect that to
10  get worse in the year ahead. Forty-eight per cent self-identify as a 'have-not' while 52% see themselves as a 'have'. We're torn apart by social class, by geography, and by how we vote – especially on Brexit.

The starkest divide, though, is age: 52% of over-65s feel optimistic about the future of the UK, contrasting with just 23% of under-34s.

15  Younger people feel a strong sense of injustice. Home ownership seems a pipe dream, even for the relatively well off. Secure employment can be elusive for them too, despite many being far better qualified than their parents and grandparents.

But our survey suggests they shouldn't hope for sympathy. Many in the older generation dismiss them as 'liberal snowflakes' who waste cash on 'avocado toast and
20  flat whites', then waste away weekends 'watching screens'. Seventy-eight per cent of over-45s and 82% of those over 65 believe British values are in decline, and many see young people as the cause: 'They just don't have the same values we do – or the respect that we had.'

Where the nation can agree is that we probably can't expect politicians to lead us
25  out of this mess. Trust has long been in short supply. Ipsos Mori's 'veracity index' shows that just 19% believe politicians tell the truth – unchanged since 1983. What's happening now is different, and potentially much more damaging: voters have lost faith in politicians' ability to govern competently. Our focus groups, regardless of how they voted, felt the scales fall from their eyes as they watched
30  'them' grapple with Brexit. One told me: 'It's like we've all woken up.'

There are a few crumbs of comfort. While pessimism about Britain is palpable, just over half feel optimistic about their local area, and two-thirds are optimistic about their personal lives – and this is true for voters of all ages. Many feel that, whatever happens on the national stage, British character will win out: 69% agree
35  that 'British people will just get on with things regardless of the impact of Brexit'.

But the cloud of uncertainty hangs heavily. Voters long for a leader to map a clear route through. One observed: 'We seem to be stumbling along a crooked path and

## Annotations

1 **focus group** small group of people, selected based on a set of criteria to discuss a specific subject
4 **rundown** *(adj)* in a bad state
5 **NHS** = National Health Service, the healthcare system of the United Kingdom, which is free of charge and open to the entire population
15 **pipe dream** sth. that is unrealistic
16 **elusive** hard to find
25 **Ipsos Mori** global market research company
30 **grapple with sth.** struggle with sth.
31 **palpable** sth. that is easily noticeable

**Info**

On 23 June 2016 the **Brexit referendum** was held and people in the UK voted whether or not the UK would stay in the EU. A narrow majority voted to leave the EU. In January 2020 the EU (Withdrawal Agreement) Bill passed through Parliament and became law under Prime Minister Boris Johnson. On 31 January 2020 the UK officially left the EU.

not towards a target.' Eighty-six per cent say the 'UK needs a strong leader now more than ever before' [...] The bar is set high.

*From: 'Brexit has made this country as anxious as I have ever known it',* www.theguardian.com, *15 June 2019*

## Comprehension

1   Work in pairs. Considering the article and the bar chart, list what unites people in the UK and what divides them. Compare with another pair's list.

▶ Getting started

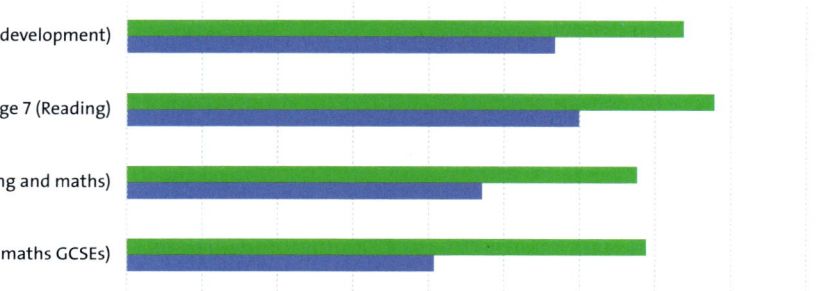

**Attainment gaps in the education system, 2019**

■ All other pupils   ■ FSM-eligible

Source: IFS Education inequalities report, 2019

Annotation
**FSM** = free school meals, school meals given for free to students whose parents get income support

## Analysis

2   Analyse how the author's choice of words and imagery express the emotional state of the people surveyed.           ▶ Support p. 305

## Language awareness

3   The first and second paragraph of the article contain several adjectives. Find antonyms and use them to write sentences about two or three of the details mentioned in the article.

## Beyond the text

4   You choose  Intercultural competence  Work on either **a** or **b**           ▶ Getting started
    and then present your results to class.

a   Britons consider themselves to be divided along class lines as 'haves' and 'have-nots'. Discuss to what extent this applies to life in Germany.

b   In pairs, research what forms of support children from disadvantaged backgrounds are given at school in the UK. Compare this to the programmes in Germany.

**Info**

A **disunited Britain** can be observed in the education system. 16-year-olds eligible for free school meals are around 27 percent less likely to achieve good GCSE results, while 40 percent of those just missing them achieve good GCSEs, rising to 70 percent in the wealthiest third of families. Inequalities can also be observed across categories like gender and ethnicity. Girls consistently outperforming boys academically, is not reflected as equal gains in the job market. Ethnicity also plays a role. Children from minority backgrounds typically start behind but progress faster than their white peers.

# A united kingdom or regional identities?    Daniel Wincott

- Do you feel more like a citizen of Europe, Germany, your federal state, or a different place entirely? Explain why.

*The following extract is taken from a comment by Professor Daniel Wincott on the failure of British politics to unite the nations of the UK.*

**Annotations**

1 **belie sth.** *(here)* contradict sth.
2 **nation-statehood** *Nationalstaatlichkeit*
3 **sustain sth.** strengthen sth.
4 **underpin sth.** support sth.
9 **Remain** the vote to stay in the EU in the Brexit referendum
10 **Leave** the vote to leave the EU in the Brexit referendum
16 **upshot** result

[...] Belying its name, the UK is far from united. Its disunity reveals that the Kingdom is a mystery to itself. Belying standard accounts of nation-statehood, surprisingly little effort has been made to create or sustain a shared state-wide identity or the institutions that might underpin it. There is little evidence of the shared 'imagined community' that is vital for any nation. On the contrary, recent research on relative territorial identities – how individuals view their sub-state and Britain-wide identities – casts new light on the character of apparently shared British identity. It turns out to work in very different ways across Britain. In the Brexit referendum, those who emphasized British national identity were more likely to vote Remain in England, but Leave in Scotland and Wales. [...]

Meanwhile, the UK-wide media is (unsurprisingly) dominated by English concerns, particularly those of London and the south east. UK national newspapers publish distinctive editions in Scotland and Northern Ireland often with contradictory front pages. Brexit provided an opportunity to test how key events – for example high-profile Brexit court cases – were mediated across each of the UK's nations. The upshot, it seems, was that the same events generated a distinctive debate focused on different issues in each nation (even in Wales, where sub-state media is notoriously weak).

*From: 'The possible break-up of the United Kingdom',* www.ukandeu.ac.uk, *19 December 2020*

## Comprehension

**1**  Point out the evidence Wincott presents for a lack of British unity.

Go on then, walk out.
But don't come running back to me
when you run out of money.

CartoonStock.com

## Analysis

**2**  Work in pairs and look at the cartoons highlighting the disunity of Britain. For more information, look at the Info box on p. 55.    ► More info

   **Partner B:** Go to p. 306 and work on task **2a**.

   **a**  **Partner A:** Look at the cartoon on the left and analyse how it stresses British disunity. Prepare a 2-minute presentation for your partner that includes a detailed description of the cartoon.
   ► SF 25: Analysing cartoons, p. 377

   **b**  Present your findings to each other. Examine together to what extent the two cartoons can be related to Daniel Wincott's arguments.

### Language awareness

**3  a**  Analyse how Wincott's words convey his feelings about the described
situation and examine their effect on the reader.

**b**  Choose sentences from the text and rephrase them in neutral language.

▶ Support p. 306

### Beyond the text

**4**  [Writing]  Taking either of the cartoons on p. 54 or 306 as a starting point, comment
on Wincott's idea that the UK is not united. Use words and phrases from **3**.

▶ SF 35: Writing a formal
letter or email, p. 391

▶ Check 🔖

Text 3

# Divided on independence

[Info]

#### National identities in the UK

The desire for a separate national identity has led to calls for independence in
Northern Ireland, Wales and, most notably, Scotland. In 2014 a referendum on
Scottish independence was held in which 44.7% of the voters voted for Scotland
to become independent and 55.3% voted to stay in the Union. Since then, the
5  Scottish National Party (SNP) has demanded two new referendums: in 2016, after
Brexit, and in 2021, after the SNP's Scottish Parliament victory. However,
Westminster rejected both these requests. Post Brexit, polls show that even in
Northern Ireland and Wales, people are increasingly open to the idea of independence, although opinions are still divided. Separatists argue that their country
10 is better off on its own, while unionists are in favour of staying in the union.

**1**  Create a *spidergram of terms that you associate with nationalism.
Add relevant words and phrases from the Info box above.

**2**  Explain your personal understanding of the concept of nationalism.

• **Think** Brainstorm all the facts you know about Wales and make notes. If you don't
know anything about Wales, do a quick online search.
**Pair** Compare your facts with a partner and organize them under suitable
categories (e.g., geography, culture, language).
**Share** Present your facts in class. Note down any new facts that you have learned.

*You are now going to watch a video about people's views on independence in Wales.*

### Comprehension

**1**  [Viewing]  Match the statements A–E to the names 1–4.
There is one more statement than you need.

**A**  Wales profits from the UK.
**B**  Brexit has made it difficult to sell their products.
**C**  Welsh culture isn't appreciated in the UK.
**D**  Wales would be better off without the UK.
**E**  Brexit has made them dependent on charity.

**1**  Lynne

**2**  Beca

**3**  Kieran

**4**  Vaughan

▶ SF 40: Listening/Viewing
for gist and detail, p. 399

▶ Check 🔖

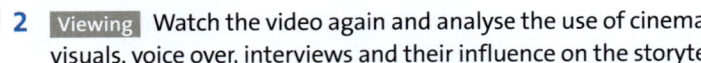

▶ Getting started

▶ SF 41: Analysing films, series and videos, p. 399

**2** Viewing  Watch the video again and analyse the use of cinematic elements such as visuals, voice over, interviews and their influence on the storytelling and the viewer.

**Beyond the text**

Sign in Welsh and English

**3** Work on either **a** or **b**.

**a** Work in groups of three. Each of you researches the impact that independence could have on either Wales, Northern Ireland, or Scotland and makes a list with benefits and drawbacks. Present your results to each other.

**b** Challenge  Research the impact that independence could have on either Wales, Northern Ireland, or Scotland, especially focussing on national identity. Have a debate on the motion 'It is beneficial for … to remain in the UK'.

▶ Getting started

---

**Text 4**

**Info**

The **levelling up programme**, put forth by the UK government in 2019, aims to reduce inequality between different regions by improving infrastructure and increasing funding. Part of the programme is devolution deals with counties and regions in England, through which they are given more power to tackle local priorities.

Annotations

**trailblazer**  pioneer
1 **swathe**  large area
3 **piecemeal**  one piece at a time
4 **dwarf sth.**  diminish sth.
4 **austerity**  Spar(maßnahmen)
8 **Jeremy Hunt**  British Chancellor of the Exchequer since October 2022
9 **Whitehall**  street in London, site of the British Government
11 **dismal**  without hope

## The trailblazer devolution deals                            Advanced

• In groups, compare the benefits and drawbacks of centralizing power in a state versus providing power to the federal governments by devolution.

*In 2023, two significant devolution negotiations were conducted with the Mayors of Greater Manchester and the West Midlands.*

Across great swathes of English local government, three lost years of levelling up have served principally to foster a growing sense of frustration, resentment and disappointment. The value of piecemeal pots of money made available by Westminster has been dwarfed by the impact of long-term austerity on council finances.
5 Inflation has diminished their worth still further and the cost of living crisis has disproportionately struck areas that levelling up was intended to help. [...]

The 'trailblazer' devolution agreements with Greater Manchester and the West Midlands, announced [...] by the chancellor, Jeremy Hunt, amount to a belated and welcome admission that Whitehall does not always know best. In fact, when it
10 comes to dealing with the legacy of deindustrialisation in much of the country, its record has been truly dismal. A top-down, over-centralised political culture has created a much greater level of regional inequality than most other large, wealthy nations. Nor should this come as any surprise. It is inconceivable, for example, that the disgraceful underdevelopment of the north's railway infrastructure would have
15 been permitted, if northern leaders had possessed the powers to do something about it.

In handing Mr Street and Andy Burnham, the Greater Manchester mayor, discretionary control over multi-year financial settlements focused on transport, housing and skills, the chancellor has acknowledged that the way England does its politics
20 needs to change. The new autonomy will give both city-regions the chance to devel-

op joined-up, bespoke strategies for growth, based on local priorities and insulated from politicking at the national level. Nascent projects, such as Mr Burnham's 'Atom Valley' plans for a hi-tech manufacturing hub in Rochdale and Oldham, will have a greater chance of succeeding as a result.

25 The two deals are only a first small step in the right direction. A lack of revenue-raising powers compared to equivalent regions in countries such as Germany means the combined authorities will be less able to effectively roll the pitch to attract international investment. If England's regions are to really take charge of their own destiny, full-fat fiscal devolution will be necessary. More also needs to be
30 done to develop new forms of scrutiny and accountability, not just in Westminster but at the regional level. And sooner rather than later, the privileges accorded to Greater Manchester and the West Midlands should be granted to the other combined authorities.

Nevertheless, this feels like an inflection point in the struggle to rebalance an econ-
35 omy grotesquely skewed towards London and the south-east. There is now cross-party consensus that regional inequality has contributed to anaemic growth and dire levels of productivity, while eroding communal self-esteem in places that have felt excluded from power and influence. Johnsonian levelling up was a cynical, superficial affair. But a new era of meaningful devolution can be the catalyst for
40 both economic and democratic renewal, allowing English regions to write themselves back into the national story.

*From: The Guardian view on the trailblazer devolution deals: a step in the right direction, www.theguardian.com, 16 March 2023*

Annotations
21 **bespoke** custom-made
22 **politicking** [ˈpɒlətɪkɪŋ] activity undertaken for political reason
25 **revenue** *Einnahmen*
27 **roll the pitch** (metaphor from cricket) make the necessary preparations
30 **scrutiny** critical observation or examination
34 **inflection point** turning point
35 **skewed** biased or distorted in a way that is regarded as unfair
36 **anaemic** [əˈniːmɪk] weak, not effective
37 **dire** extremely serious
37 **erode sth.** gradually destroy sth.

## Comprehension

1 Outline the intended aims of the levelling up programme and devolution deals.

## Analysis

2 Analyse the linguistic strategies the author of the editorial employs to show their opinion on the levelling up programme and the devolution deals.

▶ Support, p. 306

## Language awareness

3 The editorial uses several negatively connoted expressions to show that the levelling up programme has not had the effect intended. Find example sentences from the text and rephrase them in a more neutral tone.

▶ Getting started

## Beyond the text

4 | You choose | Work on either **a** or **b**.

a Research the two devolution deals in the text and find out what the latest developments are. Make a short presentation of your findings.

b | Intercultural competence | Research the differences and similarities between the level of decentralization in Germany and the UK. Make a short presentation of your findings.

▶ Getting started
▶ Support, p. 306 (task b)
▶ SF 43: Giving a presentation, p. 405

# The political system in the UK

▶ SF 25: Analysing cartoons, p. 377

- List some examples of monarchs depicted in popular culture, e.g. films and art. In what ways do you think they are similar or different from real monarchs?

### Comprehension

*"My position here is largely symbolic."*

CartoonStock.com

**1** Describe the cartoon.

▶ Getting started

### Analysis

**2** Analyse the cartoon.

▶ Check

### Beyond the text

10 Downing Street, official home of the British Prime Minister in London

**3** You choose   Work on task **a** or **b**.

**a** Referring to the cartoon above, assess the contemporary function of the monarchy in the UK. You may also refer to the diagram on p. 436.

**b** Have a look at the diagram on p. 436 and then discuss the following statement: 'Parliament is the most important part of Britain's political system of government.'

**4 a** Work in groups. Your teacher will assign each group a topic from the table below. Research your topic and consider all the listed aspects.

| Form of government: | Voting system: | Parliament: | Political parties: |
|---|---|---|---|
| – constitutional monarchy <br> – head of state <br> – head of government | – constituencies <br> – majority vote | – House of Commons <br> – House of Lords <br> – functions of Parliament | – Conservatives <br> – Labour <br> – Liberal Democrats <br> – regional parties |

▶ More language (task 3)

**b** Speaking   Form new groups with one expert for every topic. Present your results and take notes.

**c** Speaking   Return to your original group and exchange your knowledge. Discuss the claim that the British political system is partly undemocratic.

▶ Support, p. 307

**5** Intercultural competence   Together compare the British and German political systems and discuss the advantages and disadvantages of both.

**Advanced**

# The surprising potential of King Charles's reign    Peter Kellner

- Work with a partner and research the following aspects.
  **Partner A:** The most important members of the Royal Family and their duties
  **Partner B:** The most infamous royal scandals
- Take turns to present what you have found out to each other.

▶ Getting started

Nobody can be certain how the reign of King Charles III will play out, but we can be sure of one thing that won't happen. Despite being far more controversial than his mother, Elizabeth II, and far less popular than his oldest son, Prince William, Charles won't be deposed – either to hand his crown to his son or, even more dra-
5  matically, to make way for his kingdom to become a republic. Unlike most of Europe's monarchs in recent decades, Charles will keep his job for life.

How can we be so sure? The reason is simple and reflects an important truth about the United Kingdom: apart from two spasms in the seventeenth century, its story is one of persistent pragmatism and gradual change.

10  National constitutions tend to come in two varieties: those that bend and those that shatter. Some shatter as a result of revolution, civil war, coup d'état, or military catastrophe. These upheavals have afflicted the great majority of European countries in the past century, and their constitutions have been torn up and rewritten as a result – sometimes more than once.

15  In contrast, the UK has endured no such catharsis for more than three centuries. We beheaded one king in 1649 at the end of a brutal civil war and banished another to exile in 1688, following a bloodless Glorious Revolution. But since then, our constitution has been bent continuously but never shattered. Step by step, power has shifted from the monarch to Parliament – too slowly for many, but fast enough
20  to ward off turning the UK into a republic. Even today, the tyranny Britain suffered during our brief experiment of living without a monarch, between 1649 and 1660, is seen as a stain on our history.

So the circumstances in which we might get rid of our monarchy have not arisen and, for all our current problems, show no signs whatsoever of erupting any time
25  soon. To say that is not to claim any democratic virtue in selecting a head of state through the hereditary principle. However, only a minority of Britons believe our constitutional monarchy does any great harm. In fact, most of us think that in various soft-power ways it does good. We have a classic example of an arrangement that works in practice, even as we struggle to explain how it can possibly work in
30  theory.

There is another reason why our constitution bends but doesn't shatter. It is commonly said that the UK lacks a written constitution. This is half true. Yes, we lack a single document bearing that name, but the elements of a constitution – the rules that govern the ways in which we operate as a society – do exist in written
35  form. They comprise countless laws passed and amended through the centuries. Some last longer than others: from time to time, judges still draw on the words of the Magna Carta from 800 years ago to decide their rulings.

The point here is that the UK's constitution resembles the pages of a loose-leaf binder more than those of a leather-bound book. Fairly frequently, old pages are

**Annotations**
1  **play out**  develop
4  **depose sb.**  remove sb. from a position of power
8  **spasm**  brief duration of something, especially something beyond control
15  **catharsis** [kəˈθɑːsɪs] purification
16  **… one king …**  Charles I, King of England, Scotland and Ireland from 1625 to 1649 when he was executed
16  **… banished another …** James II, King of England, Scotland and Ireland from 1685 to 1688 when he was exiled
20  **ward sth. off**  protect or defend against sth.

Advanced

**Annotations**

49 **lag behind** develop
more slowly

56 **accession** act of
becoming a ruler of a
country

63 **clear sth.** give sth.
official permission

69 **flow from sth.** result
from sth.

74 **ally** sb. who helps and
supports sb.

removed and new ones inserted. Thus, gradually and usually in small ways, the
constitution evolves. Because it can be bent relatively easily, it hasn't yet needed to
shatter. Insofar as the future can be predicted at all, the constitution will not shatter
while Charles is king.

Pragmatism apart, what will his reign be like? Here the crystal ball turns cloudy,
but it is bound to be different from his mother's in two major ways.

First, Britain in 2022 is vastly different than it was in 1952 when Elizabeth became
queen. The empire has gone. Despite having nuclear weapons, the UK is no longer
a global military power. In the aftermath of World War II, the UK was easily Europe's largest economy. It now lags behind Germany and struggles to keep up with
France and Italy. Even so, we are far richer than we were and socially much more
liberal. Britain's population is more varied by ethnicity, religion, and family roots
than it was seventy years ago. And the concept of the UK itself is open to question
today in a way it wasn't then, with the possibility that either Scotland or Northern
Ireland (or both) might vote to leave the UK while Charles is on the throne.

Just as the UK now is different from the UK in 1952, so Charles today is different
from Elizabeth then. This brings us to the second major contrast in the accession.
She was 25 years old, with no known views on any public policy; he is 73, with half
a century of involvement in various controversies. We know what he thinks about
a range of issues, of which climate change is perhaps the most significant.

Charles has been passionate about the environment for decades – long before we
all learned to be concerned about global warming.

Charles has already said he will abide by the constitutional principle to avoid contro-
versy as king. Every speech he makes will be cleared by his government. However,
his people – and his government ministers – know the strength of his
views on a subject that has the power to shape the destiny of life on our
planet in this century and beyond. That fact gives him the potential for real
influence, even if he never says anything in public about it ever again.

King Charles with well-wishers in
Yorkshire, England

We – to be more accurate, our grandchildren – should not be surprised
if, decades from now, Charles's lasting reputation flows not from anything he says or does as king but simply from our knowledge of his
passionate commitment to a greener planet and the impact that passion
could have on the policies of the UK and, possibly, other countries. In its
way, this approach would continue the pragmatism that past monarchs
have demonstrated – and show that pragmatism can be the ally of principle, and not its rival.

*From: carnegieeurope.eu, 14 September 2022*

## Comprehension

 ▶Check

**1** Complete the sentences using information from the text:
   **1** The reasons that national constitutions might shatter include...
   **2** The British constitution will not shatter because...
   **3** Britain in 2022 is different to Britain in 1952 because...
   **4** The commentary describes King Charles as...

Advanced

## Analysis

**2** The author confidently asserts his belief that the national constitution will not shatter under King Charles. Analyse the \*stylistic devices he uses to convince the readers of his opinion.

► Getting started
► WOB: pp. 28–30

## Beyond the text

**3 a** Research arguments for and against the British monarchy. Decide which position you find more convincing and add specific suggestions and examples to support your arguments.

**b** Speaking  Discuss the following statement in groups: 'The British monarchy is outdated and unfit for modern times. Significant changes are called for.'

► Getting started (task b)
► SF 46: Having a discussion, p. 410
► WOB: pp. 65–67

**4 Art in Context:** Every royal event, be it happy or unhappy, creates two things: global interest and a line of royal family merchandise which range from the usual to the unconventional. Do some research on royal family merchandise.

**a** The photo below shows some merchandise commemorating the coronation of King Charles III. Describe the ceramics and explain whether you consider such ceramics art.

**b** You choose  Work with a partner and exchange your views on the following behaviours.

1 Many people collect royal memorabilia.

2 In 2022, an eBay user listed a teabag supposedly used by Queen Elizabeth II. The seller claimed it was smuggled out of Windsor Castle in 1998. It came with a certificate of authenticity, which said it 'had determined beyond any doubt that the following statements are absolutely true: This is a teabag.' The teabag sold for $12,000 within days.

## Text 7

# Important historical documents

Advanced

### Excerpts from the Magna Carta

*Until the Magna Carta ('great charter') was signed in 1215, the will of the king had been considered law. The Magna Carta was the first step leading to the constitutional principle that the 'law is king'. Four of its 63 articles are printed here.*

• Research why the Magna Carta was created and why England went into Civil War after the Magna Carta was published.

Advanced

Annotations
1 **scutage** [ˈskjuːtɪd͡ʒ]
(in feudal times) money
paid by a knight
instead of doing
military service, or by a
landowner instead of
personal service
5 **official** *(n)* person in a
position of authority
7 **freehold** ownership of
land

(12) No scutage or aid shall be imposed in our kingdom, unless by the general council of our kingdom; except for ransoming our person, making our eldest son a knight and once for marrying our eldest daughter; and for these there shall be paid no more than a reasonable aid. [...]

5 (38) In future no official shall put anyone to trial merely on his own testimony, without reliable witness produced for this purpose.

(39) No freeman shall be taken or imprisoned, or deprived of his freehold, or outlawed, or banished, or in any way destroyed, nor will we take or order action against him, unless by the lawful judgment of his peers, or by the law of the land.

10 (40) We will sell to no man, we will not deny to any man, either justice or right.

► 'US Bill of Rights', p. 117

### Excerpts from the Bill of Rights
*The Bill of Rights was signed into law in 1689 as an Act of the Parliament of England aiming to set out civil rights and to regulate the monarchy's next heir. Three of the 13 articles are printed here.*

It is declared,

[8] That election of members of Parliament ought to be free;

[9] That the freedom of speech and debates or proceedings in Parliament ought not to be impeached or questioned in any court or place out of Parliament;

5 [10] That excessive bail ought not to be required, nor excessive fines imposed, nor cruel and unusual punishments inflicted;

#### Comprehension

**1** With a partner, take turns to explain the meaning of the four articles of the Magna Carta and the three articles of the Bill of Rights.

#### Language awareness

► WOB: p. 114

**2** Today, the modal *shall* is rarely used in informal modern English to express obligations or prohibitions. Rephrase three sentences from the Magna Carta using a different structure, changing them into informal, modern and gender-inclusive English.

#### Beyond the text

► SF 28: Argumentative
writing: discussion and
comment, p. 382

► Check (task b) 👆

**3**  You choose  Work on either **a** or **b**.

**a** Explain how the Magna Carta and the Bill of Rights affected the absolute power of English kings.

**b** Comment on the relevance of the Magna Carta today.

## Focus on test formats

*In tests, your English school leaving exam and at university, you will frequently come across test formats that require argumentative writing. Look at the following example of such a task.*

> In text D on p. 49, Ricayboy claims that 'England [...] is ruled firmly by the British Government for the sole good of the UK state'. Discuss this statement.

▶ SF 27: Essentials: the stages of writing, p. 380

▶ Getting started

## Work it out

*In this section you will learn how to approach tasks for argumentative writing.*

### 1   Understanding a task for argumentative writing

a   Look at the following verbs that can often be found in tasks for argumentative writing. Match each verb with the correct description. You will need one description twice.

▶ Check

| | | | |
|---|---|---|---|
| **A** | assess | **1** | state your opinion clearly and support your view with evidence, reasons or arguments |
| **B** | discuss | **2** | express a well-founded opinion on the nature or quality of sb./sth. |
| **C** | comment on | **3** | examine the different sides of an issue and come to a conclusion |
| **D** | evaluate | | |

▶ Verbs for tasks, p. 440

b   Explain in more detail what the verb *discuss* means in relation to the task above.

### 2   Working with a model text

A student has written an argumentative text on the following task: 'Both British parties as well as the British public have often claimed that the British monarchy is an outdated institution and is no longer relevant in modern times. Taking this statement as a starting point, comment on the role of the British monarchy today.' Read the following excerpts.

*The British monarchy is one of the most famous institutions in the world, rooted in history and tradition and well-known for its 'Pomp and Circumstance'. Partly due to various scandals involving the Royal Family, it has been claimed that this institution is outdated and needs to change significantly in order to continue.*
5 *Although I accept the point that this institution is rooted in history and, therefore, to some extent outdated, I do not agree with the statement that it needs to change significantly in order to be allowed to continue.*

*First of all, the British monarch is a representative figure and is only head of state in name. Of course, it cannot be denied that hereditary monarchies are —*
10 *in general — undemocratic, as kings and queens are not elected by the people but are born into their position, whether or not they have the personal qualities or talents to hold that position. But the fact that the British monarchy is and*

has been a parliamentary democracy for hundreds of years and is one in which the monarch no longer has any real power to rule, clearly shows that the British
15 political system does take the people's wishes and elections into account and is, therefore, a democracy. Political power lies with the government and parliament, not with the reigning monarch. Even though he/she is called head of state, the monarch has a representative function rather than a political one.

In addition, the institution of the British monarchy contributes to the unity of
20 the United Kingdom. Especially in modern Britain, where the people are divided over so many topics and issues – including political questions like Brexit, cultural or historical questions like the evaluation of the British Empire or social aspects like multiculturalism – the stability and continuity represented by the traditional institution of the monarchy is valued highly. In times of crisis, like at
25 the beginning of the coronavirus pandemic, it is the monarch's address to the people that is spoken about and remembered as encouraging and consoling, rather than the addresses given by the Prime Minister. So, even though the monarch has limited political power, they may at times influence the government and have a strong emotional effect on the British people. [...]

30 Concluding, it has been shown that the institution of the British monarchy is neither harmful nor undemocratic and does have positive effects both in terms of the economy
35 and at an emotional level. Therefore, this makes claims that the monarchy should be abolished seem rather short-sighted, perhaps reflecting envy or a lack of
40 knowledge of the British political system. It clearly is an institution that is loved because of the fact that it is somewhat outdated, quaint and fairy tale-like. But that does not
45 make it a candidate for abolition.

Buckingham Palace in London, the official residence of the monarch

**a** Based on what you already know, point out which features make the comment above a good one. Refer to specific passages. See the aspects below:

| | |
|---|---|
| linking words are used to guide the reader | statements/arguments are supported |
| position of author becomes clear | position of author is restated as a consequence of arguments presented |
| each paragraph contains one argument | relevance of the question to be commented on is clear |
| text is concluded | topic is clearly presented |

**b** Outline which sentences would have to be reformulated if you had to write a discussion instead of a comment.

**c** Copy the *method card below and sort the relevant aspects from **a** into it. Keep adding helpful aspects throughout the Skills Lab.

▶ Support, p. 307

| Method card – argumentative writing | |
| --- | --- |
| Introduction | • … |
| Main part | • … |
| Conclusion | • … |
| General characteristics | • … |
| I am good at | • … |
| Needs improvement | • … |

## 3 Preparing for a written discussion

The following arguments are related to the claim that England is ruled by the British government for the benefit of the UK (cf. the task on p. 63):
- England is the largest constituent country of the UK.
- England does not have its own regional parliament.
- England cannot manage its own affairs in the way that Wales, Scotland and Northern Ireland do.
- The regional parliaments of Wales, Scotland and Northern Ireland are necessary to address a political imbalance.

**a** Copy the table below and sort the given arguments into it. If possible, add further arguments.

| England is ruled by the British government for the benefit of the UK. | |
| --- | --- |
| **For** | **Against** |
| … | … |

**b** Decide on your line of argument and sort the arguments, e.g. from least to most important. Use the table you made in task **a** and decide which arguments are the strongest to defend your point of view.

**c** Decide on a structure for your composition.

**Pattern A**
Present the arguments for and against in separate paragraphs:
1 Introduction
2 Arguments for
3 Arguments against
4 Conclusion

**Pattern B**
Answer each argument immediately with its counter-argument:
1 Introduction
2 Argument 1 → counter-argument 1
3 Argument 2 → counter-argument 2
4 Conclusion

**Info**

There are different ways to **structure the arguments** of the main part. It is, however, often helpful to end the main part with the argument that most strongly supports your position as this is the one that will be remembered most.

**Rules for using commas**
- If a subordinate adverbial clause precedes the main clause, it should be followed by a comma.
- You do not need a comma if a subordinate adverbial clause follows the main clause (except when the subordinate clause starts with *whereas* or *although*).
- Commas are used to mark non-defining relative clauses which add extra, non-essential information about the noun or noun phrase.
- Commas are not used to separate essential elements of the sentence, for instance relative clauses beginning with *that*.

**Rules for using an apostrophe with the possessive s**
- We use the possessive *s* with an apostrophe after singluar nouns (*girl's*) or irregular plural nouns (*children's*).
- We use an apostrophe after regular plural nouns (*girls'*).
- If a name ends in *s*, we can either add an apostrophe or an apostrophe with *s*.

► WOB: pp. 22–27

**d**  Sort your notes into a first draft. Remember to take notes on the following parts:
- introduction
- main body of your composition
- conclusion.

**e**  In the body of your text, each paragraph develops one argument. You should always plan your paragraphs before writing.
Write down the topic sentences, the supporting sentences and the concluding sentences of the paragraphs in the main part of the model text above. Use the information below for help.

> **Structure of a paragraph: one paragraph – one argument**
>
> **Topic sentence:** Start with a short topic sentence in which you present the main idea of what the paragraph is going to be about.
>
> **Supporting sentences:** These sentences make up the body of your paragraph and usually consist of explanations, examples, evidence, etc.
>
> **Concluding sentence:** This sentence summarizes the body of a paragraph and can also provide a link to the next one.

**f**  Plan the paragraphs for your own main part.

**g**  Complete your method card.

## Do it

### 4  Writing your argumentative text

**a**  Based on the preparations you have made so far, write your discussion of the claim 'The British political system is partly undemocratic'.

**b**  Proofread your text using the Info boxes for help.

## Feedback

### 5  Peer/Self-assessment

**a**  Using the method card you created, evaluate your partner's text. Note down which aspects have been done well and also give suggestions for improvement where necessary.

**b**  Taking into account your partner's feedback, highlight in your method card those aspects that you need or want to pay special attention to. Then improve these aspects in your composition.

**c**  With your partner, reflect on the usefulness of peer feedback for your language learning.

# Nobody is an island – the UK and Europe　Paul Hawkins

- In a short buzz group-activity, explain and try to distinguish the following terms: the Continent, Europe, the EU.

▶ More info 🔽
▶ More language 🔽

*In* The Bloody British *Paul Hawkins, a Briton living in Germany, offers a humorous description of the British and their relationship with the world.*

The British are, of course, an island people. We escape, perhaps a little too often for some people's liking, but ultimately we always come back to the island safety of our little moat-protected homeland. Indeed, our islandness might explain better than any other factor why we have always had a uniquely wobbly *will-they-won't-they*
5 relationship with the rest of the Continent: we are one of the only chunks of it that have floated off.

While the English Channel is just 21 miles wide, its effects on the British psyche should not be underestimated. Being literally separated from one's nearest neighbours, cocooned by the sea, can do strange and subtle things to a culture like ours.
10 It makes us, in my opinion, a little wackier around the edges than our mainland friends. Around the borders of most continental countries, there's a bit of cultural interaction and feedback that takes place (and maybe even helps stir the European soup) while we Brits stand somewhat more apart and alone (like a bread). [...]

Our islandness might also help explain how some of the more extreme aspects of
15 our national character developed. Take, for example, the almost existential need for good manners and the accompanying honour-based system of maintaining them. If you had an argument with someone in Ye Olde England, there was only ever so far you could get away from them before you were under water. In contrast, you could be as rude to someone as you bloody well liked in Ye Olde France, knowing
20 full-well it was always possible to climb atop your trusty donkey and get the hell out there. Ride east of Calais and there's Paris, Köln, Αθηνα, КИЇВ, [...]. A whole world of enemy-avoiding possibilities. Ride west from Dover and there's Devon.

This water-locked isolation might also explain why our ridiculous politeness comes equally paired with our literal ridiculousness. If our amusing British eccentricities
25 can be accredited to anything of geographic origin, then surely it's the big, wet fence around our garden that historically meant none of our neighbours could peek in and see all of the ludicrous things we were inventing while we thought no one else was looking. How else do you explain croquet, cricket, carpeted bathrooms, cucumber sandwiches and the penny-farthing? [...]

30 However, this relative isolation from our closest neighbours has also meant relative isolation from their constructive criticism and friendly feedback. Perhaps it was all this time marinating in our own juices before phones, televisions and airplanes stirred us more thoroughly into the European mix – but we British still seem to feel uniquely separate, which is why we, unique amongst the Europeans
35 of the continent of Europe, can still say, 'I'm going on holiday to *Europe*.'

*From:* The Bloody British – a Well-Meaning Guide to an Awkward Nation, *2019*

**Annotations**
5　**chunk** *(n)*　piece
10　**wacky** *(infml)*　unusual, often in a silly way
16　**maintain sth.**　keep sth.
29　**penny-farthing**　bicycle that has one very small and one very large wheel

Man riding a penny-farthing

Advanced

## Comprehension

**1**   Outline what the relationship between Britain and the EU is like and why the author regards it as something special.

## Analysis

▶ Support, p. 307

**2**   Analyse how the author uses a humorous style to voice his opinion on the British and the effect this has.

## Language awareness

▶ WOB: pp. 98–99

**3**   **a**   The text contains various colloquial and informal passages. Find at least three examples and rephrase them in a formal style.
      **b**   Explain the effect the informal style has on the reader.

## Beyond the text

**4**   Paul Hawkins calls the relationship between the UK and Europe a 'wobbly will-they-won't-they relationship' (ll. 4–5). Using information from the Info box below and considering the economic, political and social consequences of Brexit, explain which events support this notion.

> **Info**
>
> **The UK and the EU**
>
> In 1957 the EEC (European Economic Community) was founded. After two failed attempts to join the EEC, the UK became a member in 1973. In 1975 the British membership of the European Community (EC) was confirmed in a referendum in which 67% of the British people voted in favour.
>
> 5   Under Margaret Thatcher, who was Conservative Prime Minister from 1979–1990, special concessions for the UK were demanded by the British government and granted by the EU. In 1992 the UK signed the Maastricht Treaty, which gave EU citizens the right to free movement. The UK, however, continued to have passport controls for EU citizens and kept the pound as currency.
>
> 10   In 2013 the Conservative Prime Minister David Cameron promised a referendum on British EU membership if his party should win the election, and planned to re-negotiate the British membership in order to get better terms for the UK. In 2016 this referendum was held and a narrow majority of the British people voted to leave the EU. Following this referendum, complex withdrawal negotiations
>
> 15   began and the UK officially left the EU on 31 December 2020. On 1 May 2021, The Trade and Cooperation Agreement, which governs the relationship between the EU and the UK after Brexit, entered into force.
> Since May 2022, opinion polling has shown an increase in the number of British citizens seeking to rejoin the EU.

# Marriage counselling after Brexit  Jonathan Coe

► 'Britain after Brexit',
p. 341

► More info

- The bar chart on the right shows the overall results of the Brexit referendum in 2016. Explain how the results intensified disunity among people in the UK.

*Now read the following extract from Jonathan Coe's novel* Middle England, *in which Sophie remembers the first counselling session she had with her husband to save their marriage. Sophie voted 'Remain' in the Brexit referendum while Ian voted 'Leave'.*

A couple might decide to separate for all sorts of reasons: adultery, cruelty, domestic abuse, lack of sex. But a difference of opinion over whether Britain should be a member of the European Union or not? It seemed absurd. It was absurd. And yet Sophie knew, deep down, that it had not so much been a reason as a tipping point.
5  Ian had reacted (to her mind) so bizarrely to the referendum result, with such gleeful, infantile triumphalism (he kept using the word 'freedom' as if he were the citizen of a tiny African country that had finally won independence from its colonial oppressor) that, for the first time, she genuinely realized that she no longer understood why her husband thought and felt the way that he did. At the same time,
10  she herself had been possessed by the immediate sense, that morning, that a small but important part of her own identity – her modern, layered, multiple identity – had been taken away from her.

During their first session a few weeks later, their relationship counsellor, Lorna, told them that many of the couples she was seeing at the moment had mentioned
15  Brexit as a key factor in their growing estrangement.

'I usually start by asking each of you the same question,' she said. 'Sophie, why are you so angry that Ian voted Leave? And Ian, why are you so angry that Sophie voted Remain?' Sophie had thought for a long time before answering:

'I suppose because it made me think that, as a person, he's not as open as I thought
20  he was. That his basic model for relationships comes down to antagonism and competition, not cooperation.'

Lorna had nodded, and turned to Ian, who had answered: 'It makes me think that she's very naive, that she lives in a bubble and can't see how other people around her might have a different opinion to hers. And this gives her a certain attitude. An
25  attitude of moral superiority.'

To which Lorna had said:

'What's interesting about both of those answers is that neither of you mentioned politics. As if the referendum wasn't about Europe at all. Maybe something much more fundamental and personal was going on. Which is why this might be a diffi-
30  cult problem to resolve.'

She had suggested a course of six sessions, but it turned out that she was being optimistic. In fact they attended nine, before admitting defeat, and calling it a day.

*From:* Middle England, *2018*

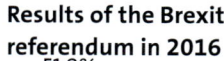

**Results of the Brexit referendum in 2016**

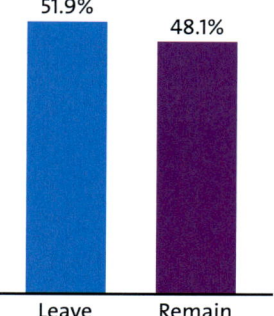

Source: Electoral Commission, 2021

Annotations
1  **adultery** [əˈdʌltəri] *Ehebruch*
1  **domestic abuse** physical or psychological violence in the home
4  **tipping point** time at which a change or an effect can no longer be stopped
13  **counsellor** therapist or advisor
15  **estrangement** loss of connection with or understanding of someone
32  **call it a day** stop

### Comprehension

1   Point out which character traits Sophie attributes to Ian for voting 'Leave' and which character traits Ian connects with Sophie for voting 'Remain'.

### Analysis

▶ SF 19: Reading and understanding narrative texts, p. 369

2   Analyse how the chosen point of view guides the reader's identification with the characters' opinions.

3   Explain the *analogy between a crumbling marriage and the Brexit process.

### Language awareness

▶ Getting started (task 4a)

4   a   Identify the words and phrases the two spouses use to describe their partner's opinion about Brexit and the *connotations these expressions might have for the reader.

    b   After the session, the counsellor makes notes in which she tries to record the spouses' opinions from a neutral perspective. Write her notes.

### Beyond the text

5   📖 Taking Sophie and Ian's reasons for their separation into account and everything you have learned so far, reconsider the guiding question of the chapter. How would you answer it at this point?

6   **You choose**   **Writing** Work on task **a** or **b**:

▶ SF 28: Argumentative writing: discussion and comment, p. 382

▶ SF 38: Creative writing, p. 395

▶ Check (task 6a)

▶ WOB: pp. 22–24, pp. 51–53

a   Write a comment on Lorna's statement that '[...] the referendum wasn't about Europe at all. Maybe something much more fundamental and personal was going on' (ll. 28–29). Take into account possible reasons for people's positions on Brexit.

b   Rephrase the novel extract from Ian's point of view, taking into account his motivations for voting 'Leave' and his feelings about his wife's reaction to the referendum result.

**Language help**

first of all ... • furthermore ... • moreover ... • it is important to recognize that ... • for some/many ... • in conclusion ...

## Text 10

▶ 'Britain after Brexit', p. 341

## Brexit: a German perspective   Jan Roß

*The UK always had a unique position in Europe. Jan Roß commented in* Die Zeit *on Brexit as a consequence of the special relationship between the UK and Europe.*

[...] Viele auf dem Kontinent sind erleichtert, dass mit dem förmlichen Ausscheiden des Vereinigten Königreichs aus der EU das ärgste Gewürge ein Ende hat – doch die britische Entscheidung selbst kommt ihnen so närrisch oder verheerend vor wie am ersten Tag. Auch ein Unterton von Gekränktheit ist unverändert her-
5 auszuhören. In dieser Lage lohnt es sich, einen Schritt zurückzutreten und die Sache mit etwas kälterem Blut zu betrachten.

Government billboard with information about the changes after Brexit

Großbritannien ist immer ein halb europäisches Land gewesen, als Seefahrtsnation, Kolonialmacht und seit dem Zweiten Weltkrieg als privilegierter Verbündeter der Vereinigten Staaten. Es war halb draußen, solange es der EU angehörte, mit
10 einer langen Geschichte von Ausnahmeregelungen und bremsenden Sondervoten. Es wird halb drinnen sein, wenn es die EU verlassen hat, in einer „ehrgeizigen, breiten, tiefen und flexiblen Partnerschaft", wie Briten und Europäer sie erklärtermaßen anstreben. So gesehen ist der Brexit keine Katastrophe, sondern schlicht ein Ausdruck der Normalität im britisch-europäischen Verhältnis. Keineswegs der
15 einzig denkbare (die bisherige innerlich distanzierte EU-Mitgliedschaft war auch einer), aber ein durchaus möglicher und plausibler.

Annotation
**Angela Merkel** chancellor of Germany (2005–2021)

Die größte konkrete Sorge auf dem Kontinent geht dahin, dass die Briten den Europäern in Zukunft als Wirtschaftsstandort unfaire Konkurrenz machen könnten, durch Steuerdumping oder laxe Regulierung. Diese Befürchtung wirkt doppelt
20 übertrieben. [...] Großbritannien wird auch nach dem Brexit schwerlich zum entfesselten Hyperkapitalismus übergehen, sondern ein weithin europäisch geprägtes Sozialmodell beibehalten.

Sofern allerdings die Briten den EU-Austritt tatsächlich zu Liberalisierung und Bürokratieabbau nutzen, sollte man das auf dem Kontinent nicht bejammern oder
25 bekämpfen, sondern davon lernen. Ein bisschen freibeuterhafte Konkurrenz täte der uniformen EU ganz gut. [Angela] Merkel hat kürzlich im Gespräch mit der *Financial Times* überraschend brexitfreundlich bemerkt, das Ende der Londoner EU-Mitgliedschaft könne als „Weckruf" dienen: „Aus einem positiven Blickwinkel betrachtet, müssen wir uns fragen, welche unserer Regelungen richtig und gut
30 sind und tatsächlich nützlich für uns." Und welche, heißt das natürlich, nichts taugen und abgeschafft gehören [...].

Trotz mancher Schwächen und Fehler, die gerade im Brexit-Prozess zutage getreten sind, besitzt Großbritannien eine unschätzbare Stärke: eine vitale, instinktive Freiheitlichkeit. Ein liberales Land ist eines, in dem man weitgehend unbesorgt
35 gegen den Mehrheitsgeschmack verstoßen kann, ob als Investmentbanker, der unverschämt viel Geld verdient, oder als Muslimin, die das islamische Kopftuch trägt. Mehr als die meisten anderen Länder, auch in Europa, ist das Vereinigte Königreich ein solches Land. Diese innere Liberalitätsquelle verliert die EU jetzt. Das ist für uns auf dem Kontinent der eigentliche, bittere Schaden durch den Brexit.

*From: 'Genug geheult', Zeit Online, 29 January 2019*                    *(394 words)*

1  Mediating  While you are spending a year in the UK, your teacher asks you to report to your politics class on how Brexit is perceived in the German press. In your research, you have come across the extract above. Prepare an oral presentation in which you tell your classmates about the positive and negative aspects of Brexit mentioned in this article.

▶ Getting started
▶ SF 49: Mediating from German into English, p. 416
▶ Support, p. 308

## Words revisited

▶ SF 6: Essentials: language and study skills, p. 354

### 1 Collecting words

In the course of this chapter, starting with 'Words in Context', you have come across a lot of adjectives, verbs and nouns connected to the concepts of *united* and *disunited*. Work with a partner. **Partner A** scans the text on p. 52 for relevant words, **partner B** the text on p. 69. Together create a mindmap with the words you find.

## Language awareness

*When you try to argue your point, it's not just strong arguments that help you convince your audience, but also the language you use. For example, certain types of adverbs and linking words allow your audience to follow your line of argumentation more easily.*

▶ Support, p. 308

▶ More language

### 2 Adverbs of comment and adverbs of degree

a Say which of the adverbs highlighted in the text below are adverbs of degree and which are adverbs of comment.

**The UK – no. 1 on your bucket list!**
*Still thinking about where to go next for your holidays? Stop racking your brains – you have clearly found the place to be: the UK. The UK undoubtedly offers highlights for every kind of traveller. It is extremely easy to go hiking and there are definitely enough pubs and tearooms to rest your legs after a strenuous walk. The country's cities certainly provide quite enough entertainment for all tastes, from music clubs to spectacular sights. Luckily British cuisine has improved considerably, so you will surely find exactly the right place for dinner, whether it is fine dining or Asian fusion cuisine that you have in mind.*

b Using a grammar book or reliable online sources, add other adverbs of degree and adverbs of comment to your list.

c The sentences below contain adjectives and verbs that you may have found in task **1.** Fill different adverbs from the box in the gaps and describe how they change the meaning of the sentences.

> extremely
> definitely
> quite
> undoubtedly

1 The UK is ... divided.
2 Britons are ... united in their negative opinion about politicians.
3 The generations in the UK are ... disunited.
4 Geographically speaking, the UK is ... isolated from the rest of Europe as it is made up of several islands.
5 Recent political developments have left the UK ... torn apart.

▶ Support, p. 308

### 3 Using linking words

Linking words and phrases are used to connect ideas and to express the logical connections between them. Categorize the linkers from the box on p. 73 according to their function by sorting them in the table under it.

in my opinion • first of all • for example • all in all • to my mind • firstly • for instance • on the other hand • however • though • naturally • admittedly • in conclusion • to sum up • furthermore • besides • in addition • nonetheless • of course • moreover • finally

▶ SF 27: Essentials: the stages of writing, p. 380

| Use/function | Linking word or phrase |
|---|---|
| Stating your opinion | … |
| Listing facts, structuring | … |
| Giving an example | … |
| Contrasting | … |
| Conceding a point | … |
| Coming to a conclusion | … |

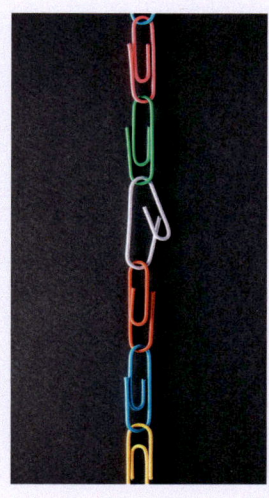

▶ WOB: pp. 94–95

## 4 Conveying emphasis

Examine the following statements. In each case the same idea is expressed in two different ways.

| Version 1 | Version 2 |
|---|---|
| Although this is not often stated, the history of the British Empire **has** a considerable effect on modern British society. | Although this is not often stated, the history of the British Empire **does have** a considerable effect on modern British society. |
| **British humour has** often been named as a stereotypical character trait of the British. | **It is British humour which has** often been named as a key characteristic of the British. |
| **The country has** not often been divided over so many topics. | **Hardly ever has the country** been divided over so many topics. |

Explain how the two versions of the sentence are different: grammatically and in terms of emphasis.

## Practice

## 5 Writing a blog post

Writing Write a blog post in which you advertise the UK as the perfect spot for studying after you finish secondary school. Use adverbs of degree, adverbs of comment and linking words. Put emphasis on the most important statements, using the strategies from task **4.**

▶ SF 29: Writing a blog post, p. 384

▶ Support, p. 308

▶ Check

▶ WOB: pp. 104–105

# Five times immigration changed the UK  Keith Lowe

▶ 'Loose change', p. 326

**Info**

### The British Empire and the Commonwealth of Nations

The British Empire was once the largest colonial empire in the world. Driven by its desire for raw materials and new markets, England started to establish trading outposts abroad as early as the 16th century. Over the next 300 years, more and more territories would come under British domination as part of its bid to achieve
5 economic and military superiority. The British Empire reached its peak by around 1920, when it ruled over approximately 20% of the world's population.
In the aftermath of World War II (1939–1945), many colonies started to seek autonomy and political independence. This led to a steady decline of the British Empire. Hong Kong was the last major colony to leave British rule when it was
10 handed back to China in 1997, but Britain still controls some smaller territories around the world even though they aren't officially called colonies.
As the British Empire gradually dissipated, a new political association, the Commonwealth of Nations (or Commonwealth, after its reduction in 1949), was formed. It was founded in 1931 by the United Kingdom and seven other indepen-
15 dent nations which had formerly been governed by Britain (Australia, Canada, India, New Zealand, Pakistan, South Africa, Sri Lanka). It was subsequently joined by many other countries, most of which are former colonies. Today, it is a volun- tary association of 56 countries, which work together closely to promote values such as democracy, human rights, education, equality, the rule of law and peace.
20 Despite British colonialism being a thing of the past, it still holds several political, financial and cultural ramifications for Britain and its former colonies today. The question of how to approach and interpret this colonial history remains a subject of intense debate, evoking discussions around British national identity, colonial reparations and the consideration of which perspectives should be prioritized
25 when retelling this history.

1   Note down the main aspects of the British Empire.
2   Research which countries were part of the British Empire and why it used to be called 'the Empire on which the sun never sets'.

- There have been various waves of immigration to Germany after World War II. Analyse their impact on Germany today. Think of culture, language, traditions and politics.

*In his article, British historian Keith Lowe writes about immigration to the UK in the last century.*

Annotations
4  **net migration** the number of immigrants minus the number of emmigrants
8  **NHS** = National Health Service, the healthcare system of the United Kingdom, which is free of charge and open to the entire population

**Since the end of World War Two, immigration has transformed the UK.**
After the war, fewer than one in 25 of the population had been born outside the country; today that figure is closer to one in seven. Many moments have contribut- ed to this transformation in net migration. Here are five key turning points.

5 **1948: The Windrush Generation**
In the aftermath of the war, the UK saw huge investment in public infrastructure. Bombed cities were rebuilt, transport systems expanded and new institutions, such as the NHS, had to be staffed.

Employment opportunities abounded, and people from all over the Common-
10 wealth came to the UK to help fill the labour shortage.

Some of the first to arrive in 1948 were a group of 500 or so Caribbean migrants,
who arrived on former troopship the Empire Windrush. Consequently, they and
the 300,000 West Indians who followed them over the next 20 years, were known
as the Windrush generation.

15 Alongside those from the Caribbean came some 300,000 people from India,
140,000 from Pakistan, and more than 170,000 from various parts of Africa.

Immigrants from the Republic of Ireland had the same rights, and also flocked to
the UK. Between 1948 and 1971, one-third of 18 to 30-year-olds left the country in
search of work, about half a million people. The overwhelming majority of them
20 were bound for the UK.

In the 1940s and 50s, none of these people required visas; as "citizens of the United
Kingdom and Colonies", they were automatically given the right to reside in
the UK.

However, the Home Office did not keep a record of those granted leave to remain.
25 Despite living and working in the UK for decades, it emerged in 2018 that some
Windrush migrants and their families had been threatened with deportation and
even removed. The UK government was forced to apologise.

### 1956: The Hungarian Revolution
The end of World War Two also brought huge political changes in eastern and cen-
30 tral Europe.

After liberating the region, the Soviet Union installed Communist regimes here
that were deeply unpopular with many people. It also annexed the Baltic States and
parts of Poland.

In reaction, hundreds of thousands of refugees fled to the West. The first to arrive in
35 the UK were about 120,000 Poles, who arrived in 1945; the substantial Polish communities in Manchester, Bradford and west London date from this time. About 100,000
people from Ukraine and the Baltic States also came to the UK for similar reasons.

At the time, these population movements were considered the final consequences
of World War Two. In fact, they were the symptom of a new Cold War.

40 This was confirmed in 1956, when the people of Hungary rose up against their
Communist rulers. After Soviet tanks drove into Budapest to crush the uprising,
almost 200,000 Hungarians fled the country.

Britain took in 30,000 of these political refugees, setting a precedent for the years
to come. From 1956 onwards, political dissidents from eastern Europe were rou-
45 tinely accepted and integrated into British society.

### 1971: Immigration Act
The post-war boom in immigration from Commonwealth countries was not welcomed by everyone.

In the late 1950s, racial tensions erupted in a series of riots, most famously in 1958
50 in Notting Hill and Nottingham.

Annotations
9 **abound** exist in great numbers or quantities
24 **leave** (n) official permission to do sth.

**Info**

**Windrush in numbers**
- 492 passengers arrived on the Empire Windrush in 1948.
- 910,000 people from the West Indies, India, Pakistan and Africa followed.
- 500,000 current UK residents were born in the Commonwealth before 1971.
- 18 were apologized to for being wrongfully deported or detained.

Annotations
61 **expulsion**  forcing sb. to leave a place

**Info**

Following **Brexit** and the implementation of a new immigration system on January 1, 2021, there have been significant changes to immigration to the UK. The new system ended the free movement rights for nationals of European single market countries and introduced a points-based system for work visas. Consequently, there has been a substantial increase in overall immigration to the UK, with 968,000 non-EU nationals, followed by 129,000 EU nationals and 84,000 British nationals in 2023.

And in 1968, the Conservative politician Enoch Powell spoke out against continued immigration, in his divisive "Rivers of Blood" speech.

Under considerable pressure, the British government eventually cracked down on all forms of racial discrimination.

55 But it also introduced a series of laws limiting immigration.

The most important of these was the Immigration Act of 1971, which decreed Commonwealth immigrants did not have any more rights than those from other parts of the world. This effectively marked the end of the Windrush generation.

### 1972: The Ugandan Asian Crisis

60 The first major test of the new immigration rules came the following year when war-torn Uganda, a former British colony, announced the immediate expulsion of its entire Asian community.

Prime Minister Edward Heath declared the country had a moral and legal responsibility to take in those who had UK passports. Of the 60,000 people expelled, a 65 little under half came to the UK.

This highlighted a change of emphasis in immigration policy. The UK was now wary of people coming in search of jobs, but it would continue to welcome those coming in search of asylum.

Throughout the 1970s and 1980s, fewer than 5,000 asylum seekers came to the UK 70 each year, on average. But in 1990, after the fall of the Berlin Wall, applications for asylum rose suddenly to more than 16,000 people. In the following two years this figure doubled, and then doubled again.

This trend would continue over the following decade, as instability in countries like Yugoslavia, Somalia and Iraq brought more refugees to the UK's door.

**Ethnic Minorities as a percentage of the population in 2011 and 2021, England and Wales**

● 2011   ● 2021

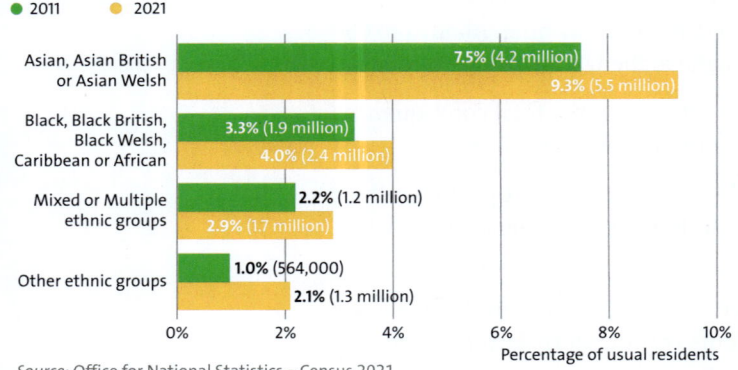

*Source:* Office for National Statistics – Census 2021

Annotation
**EEA** = European Economic Area

### 1992: The EU expansion

75 In 1992, the UK joined other EU nations in signing the Maastricht Treaty on European integration. This granted all EU citizens equal rights, with freedom to live in 80 any member state they chose.

In the following decade, tens of thousands of EU citizens came to live and work in Britain.

Few people protested, possibly because 85 these newcomers were balanced out by the tens of thousands of British people who moved away to other parts of the EU.

Nevertheless a new principle had been set. Just as the country had once held an open door to the Commonwealth, so it now held an open door to the European Union.

90 In 2004, the EU was expanded to include seven nations from the Eastern Bloc – Estonia, Latvia, Lithuania, Poland, the Czech Republic, Slovakia, and Hungary – while Slovenia, Malta and Cyprus also joined at the same time.

Unlike Germany or France, the UK put no temporary restrictions on arrivals from these new member states.

95 Tony Blair's Labour government had a positive stance on immigration: it argued a growing economy required a larger workforce and, as in the 1950s, people from other countries were considered a good source of new labour.

In any case, the government predicted that EU enlargement would only cause a rise of up to 13,000 people a year in immigration.

100 In the event, more than a million people from these countries arrived and stayed over the next decade. It was one of the biggest influxes in British history.

*From:* www.bbc.com, *20 January 2020*

Annotation
95 **Tony Blair** British Prime Minister 1997–2007

### Comprehension

**1** Copy the table below. Make notes on the different key turning points in the history of immigration mentioned in the text.

| When | Why | Who | How many | Attitude towards immigrants | Rights and laws |
|------|-----|-----|----------|-----------------------------|-----------------|
| … | … | … | … | … | … |

### Analysis

**2** Analyse how the author presents the matter in an objective and informative way considering the use of language and structure.

### Language awareness

**3 a** The author expresses various circumstances in the passive voice. Find three examples and rephrase them by introducing an agent and using the active voice.

**b** Explain the effect this has on the reader.

▶ More language

### Beyond the text

**4** You choose  Writing  Work on either **a** or **b**.

▶ Getting started

**a** In his article, the author does not focus explicitly on the racism, xenophobia and fears that accompanied the different waves of immigration. Prepare a set of interview questions that encourage the author to dive deeper into these aspects, allowing for a more detailed exploration of the content of the article.

**b** You are going to interview one of the people from what is known as the Windrush generation, who came to the UK from the Caribbean in the 1960s. Research the Windrush generation and prepare a set of interview questions to enquire about their experiences and perspectives.

# Growing up with mixed heritage

**Info**

### Taking action against racism

The UN's 'Fight Racism' campaign highlights the ongoing importance of combating racial discrimination, even 75 years after the adoption of the Universal Declaration of Human Rights. On the UN website, there are some concrete tips on how to take action against racial discrimination. One approach is to work on your own
5  assumptions and biases. The website offers information on groups that are particularly vulnerable to racism and provides helpful resources. Furthermore, the campaign encourages individuals to actively speak out against discrimination and support worthy causes.

**1**   What do you understand by *racial discrimination*? Research online resources that describe the term. Compare your findings with your original understanding.

- Reflect on the pros and cons of having mixed cultural heritage.

### Comprehension

▶ SF 40: Listening/Viewing for gist and detail, p. 399

▶ WOB: pp. 85–87

**1**   Viewing   You are going to watch two videos in which three young people share their experiences of growing up in the UK with mixed heritage.

**a**   Copy the table below, then watch the videos. Work with a partner to fill in the table. Partner A focusses on the downsides, Partner B on the benefits of growing up with mixed heritage.

| Growing up with mixed heritage | | | |
|---|---|---|---|
| **Partner A: Downsides** | | **Partner B: Benefits** | |
| Tillie: | Elouan and Amandine: | Tillie: | Elouan and Amandine: |

**b**   Present your notes. Discuss whether the protagonists' experiences are direct or more indirect forms of racism. Explain your understanding of the two terms.

### Analysis

▶ Getting started

▶ SF 41: Analysing films, series and videos, p. 399

**2**   Viewing   Analyse the strategies and cinematic devices used to present the issue of racism in a way that is also appropriate for younger viewers.

### Beyond the text

**3**   You choose   Work on either **a** or **b**.

**a**   Writing   You have watched the videos and feel compelled to write a comment in the comment section underneath the videos. In your comment, include ideas on how to raise awareness about racism and actively fight against it.

**b**   With your partner, think of creative ways to raise awareness in a video. Then create your own appeal video to fight racism.

▶ Check (task a)

# Racism in Britain

• Think about different forms racism can take. Discuss whether there are differences in the perception of racism and discrimination among different ethnic groups.

*The following statistics show the results of a survey on attitudes to racism in Britain carried out by the market research company Ipsos Mori in 2020.*

Home-made sign in support of Black Lives Matter

▶ Getting started

**Annotation**
**BAME** term used in the UK to describe people of Black, Asian and minority ethnicities

**Comprehension**

**1  a  Partner B:** Go to p. 309 and work on task **1a**.
**Partner A:** Take a look at the bar chart below. Prepare a two-minute presentation for your partner in which you tell them what your bar chart reveals about the different attitudes towards racism in Great Britain.

**The perception of racism in Britain according to ethnicity**

To what extent, if at all, do you agree or disagree with the following statement: 'Britain is a racist country'?

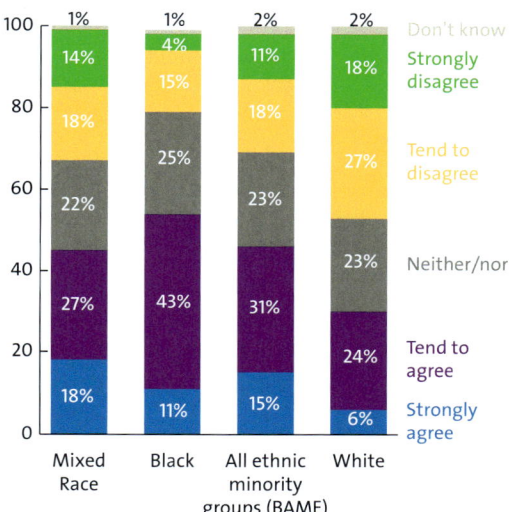

Source: Ipsos, 2020

**b  Present** your findings to each other and discuss what the statistics suggest about Britain as a multicultural society.

**Info**

According to an extensive survey, a lot more needs to be done in Britain to battle shocking levels of **racism** that spans several sectors of society. 88 percent of the 10,000 respondents reported being racially discriminated against at the workplace, with more than 90 percent feeling like they had to compromise who they were at work. 41 percent of respondents considered racial discrimination to be the biggest obstacle to young Black people's academic achievement as opposed to 4 percent who thought that was not the case. More than 90 percent believed that the government was not doing enough on behalf of Black Britons.

Source: The Black British Voices Project, 2023

**Beyond the text**

**2  Intercultural competence  Work on either a or b.**

**a**  How many Germans would agree or disagree with the statement 'Germany is a racist country'? Look for statistics online and discuss them with a partner.

**b  Challenge  How many Germans** would agree or disagree with the statement 'Germany is a racist country'? Look for statistics online. Discuss the results with a partner and speculate on reasons for differences with the UK.

Advanced

▶ 'Loose change', p. 326

**Info**

**Nai Zindagi Naya Jeevan** (New Life (Urdu) New Life (Hindi)) was a television programme by the BBC that was broadcast in Hindi and Urdu from 1968 until 1982. It was one of the first pro- grammes that used a language other than English or Welsh.

Annotations

5  **Gurdas Maan**  Punjabi artist

6  **Nusrat Fateh Ali Khan**  Pakistani musician

23  **Tjinder (Singh)**  singer of the British band Cornershop

35  **spring inna de step**  a spring in one's step; way of walking that indicates sb. is happy

57  **glass ceiling**  barrier that prevents women and minorities from improving their position at work

Member of the British band Asian Dub Foundation

# New way, new life   Asian Dub Foundation

*'New way, new life' is a song by the British band Asian Dub Foundation. They mix different musical styles, including dub, which is an electronic music genre that developed from Jamaican reggae and influenced genres such as hip hop, house, jungle, and drum and bass.*

- Keeping in mind what you have read about dub in the introduction, talk to a partner about why the band's name can be regarded as a sign of Britain's multiculturalism.

Every Sunday morning in front of the TV
Recording with a microphone Naya zindagi
5  Pioneer Gurdas Maan
Nusrat Fateh Ali Khan
Kept our parents alive
Gave them the will to survive
Working inna de factories
10  Sometimes sweeping de floor
Unsung heroines an heroes
Yes they open de door
They came a long time ago
But now it seems we've arrived
15  Naya zindagi, naya Jeevan
New way, new life

Stayed an we fought an now de fu-ture's open wide
New way, new life

20  Naya zindagi! Naya zindagi!
New way new life
Naya zindagi! Naya jeevan!

Tjinder pon de radio
Dis is England's new voice
25  Censorship for years
But now dem have no choice
Running thru de playground
We could never have known
Dat in de future
30  Our role models would be home grown
And now we're walking down de street
Wid a brand new pride
35  A spring inna de step

Our opportunity will no longer be denied
Wid our heads held high
Young Asian brothers an sisters
40  Moving forward, side by side
Naya zindagi! naya Jeevan
New way new life

New way new life
Naya zindagi! naya jeevan

45  And we're supposed to be cool
Inna de dance our riddims rule
But we knew it all along
Cos our parents made us strong
Never abandoned our culture
50  Just been moving it along
Technology our tradition
Innovation inna the song

Now de struggle continues
To reverse every wrong
55  New heroines and heroes
Inna de battle we belong
When we reach de glass ceiling
We will blow it sky high
Naya zindagi! naya Jeevan
60  New way new life

Stayed an we fought an now de fu-ture's open wide
New way new life
Naya zindagi! Naya zindagi!
65  New way new life
Naya zindagi! Naya jeevan! for it.

*From:* Community Music, *2000*

Advanced

## Comprehension

1  Create a table in which you list the immigration experiences of the parents in the column on the left and the second-generation's experience of life in Britain on the right.

## Analysis

2  Analyse the means Asian Dub Foundation use to present the Asian immigrant experience as a success story. Focus on the content and choice of words.

▶ Support p. 309

## Language awareness

3  Rephrase the song in Standard English and explain the difference in effect between the two versions.

## Beyond the text

4  **You choose**  Work on task **a** or **b**.

   a  Have another look at ll. 48–55. Use these lines as a starting point to comment on the key character-istics necessary to create a suc-cessful multicultural society.

   b  On the basis of what you have found out in this chapter and your back-ground knowledge, discuss the effectiveness of sending out a political message via music com-pared to other forms of protest.

5  Reconsider the guiding question of the chapter. How would you answer it after everything you have learned?

## Chapter task

*Since you have dealt with various aspects of the UK in this chapter, you will have the opportunity to put your knowledge to the test by taking part in a debate.*

Your school's debating society is hosting a debate on the following motion:

> 'This house believes that the United Kingdom is united in name only.'

▶ Getting started
▶ SF 47: Having a debate, p. 412

1  a  Depending on whether you are arguing for or against the motion, collect facts, figures, arguments or examples from this chapter to support your position and to refute the other side.

   b  Use your knowledge of how to be persuasive to prepare your arguments and counter-arguments.

2  Stage the debate in class.

# Chapter 3
# The Media – Tool, Drug, Manipulator, Friend?

1. Work in groups of five. Each of you chooses one of the pictures above and describes the advantages of the media shown in them.

2. **a** **Think** Make a table. List types of media for communication and types of media for information, beginning with the media you use most often, then second most often, etc.
   **b** **Pair** Talk to a partner about your lists. Together, agree on examples of each type of media that both of you consider relevant and helpful.
   **c** **Share** Share your ideas with another pair of students.

▶ Getting started

3. Take a look at the Chapter map on the right and speculate about the content of this chapter. Which of these aspects help you to form a tentative answer to the guiding question?

## ❯ Chapter map

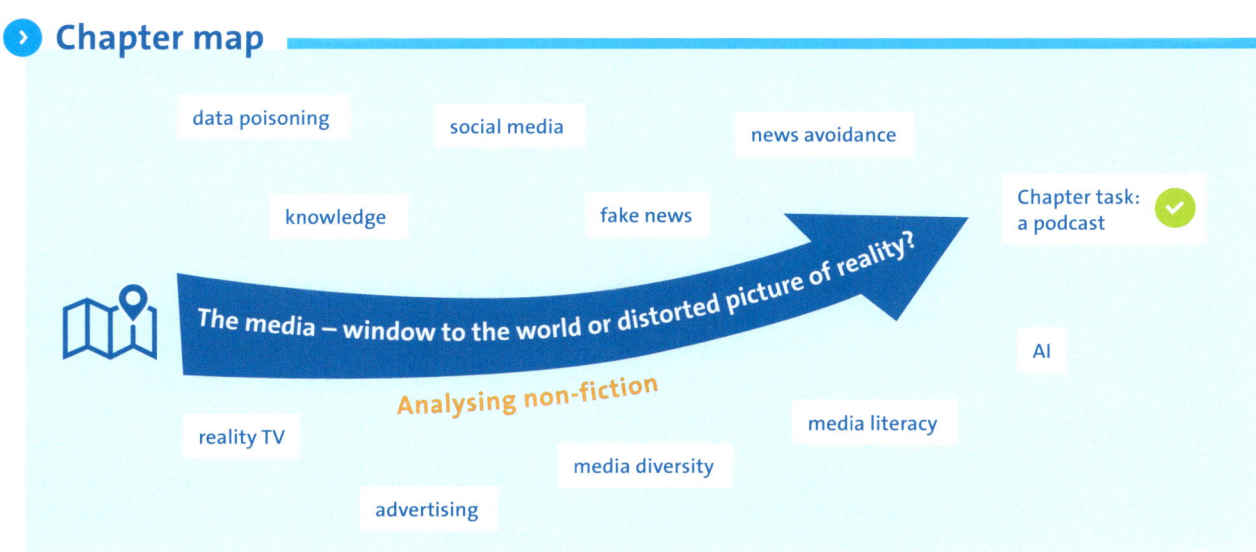

data poisoning

social media

news avoidance

knowledge

fake news

Chapter task: ✔
a podcast

The media – window to the world or distorted picture of reality?

AI

Analysing non-fiction

reality TV

media diversity

media literacy

advertising

# The multifaceted media

▶ More language 🔖

Engraving of Johannes Gutenberg's printing press, which enabled mass printing

### The development of the media

The media not only offers access to information, but also to different means of communication and it is constantly changing due to new inventions. The development of modern media as we know it gathered momentum
5 with the advent of the printing press in the 15th century, which eventually paved the way for the publication and distribution of newspapers – the first form of mass media. By the end of the 19th century, progress in electrical engineering enabled the invention of telegraphy and the telephone. Early in the 20th century, it was broadcast radio which provided news and
10 entertainment with stunning immediacy, becoming the first electronic mass medium. Television followed suit in the second half of the century.

### The digital revolution

The transition from analogue to digital technology, which started in the latter half of the 20th century, has deeply influenced all aspects of society.
15 Not only has the digital revolution with its increase in computing and information technology induced technological improvements, it has also profoundly changed the ways we communicate, work, gain knowledge, spend our free time and even think. Social media can help find like-minded people; powerful internet connections are enabling people in some professions to work from
20 almost anywhere in the world; streaming services are threatening the cinema; modern chatbots can be fed with all kinds of prompts and come up with well-written texts and solutions to virtually all kinds of school tasks. There are, however, some worries about the effects of digital media on your mental and physical health, especially given how many people are inseparably connected to their smartphones. Many people are wary of
25 modern AI chatbots and their potential to create fake news and to fundamentally change our world of work and of teaching and learning. Simultaneously, the rise of huge global tech and media companies has led some people to fear how our digital footprints – permanent traces we leave online – and 'big data' may be abused by private or even state organizations, e.g. for surveillance.

### 30 The digital divide

The digital revolution means computers and a home internet connection have become essential to access digital information. But this access is not evenly distributed, neither within societies nor globally. The gap between those with easy access to the internet and those without it is called the digital divide – a fact of modern life that puts
35 societal groups, regions or even states at a disadvantage.

### The media and democracy

The media has always had a significant role in influencing public opinion and democratic participation. By exposing misdeeds by those in power, it can serve as a watchdog. In the form of public service broadcasting, the media enables the public to make
40 informed choices and provides a platform for political debate. In recent years, however, trust in the democratizing effects of the media and social media especially, has been severely damaged. The worrying growth in fake news, disinformation campaigns and hate speech seems to threaten democracy. Journalistic ethics such as accuracy, fairness, respect, impartiality and truthfulness can no longer be taken for granted.
45 Hence, users have to ask themselves whether the media is truly a clear window to the world, or if it offers a distorted picture of reality.

## 1  Main ideas

Draw a mind map of the development, functions, opportunities and risks of the media. Use key concepts and highlighted phrases from the text.

## 2  Reflect

Which of the challenges mentioned in the text were new to you, which of them did you know about before reading the text? Give one example each and say which of them you consider most serious. Use words and phrases from the text, e.g. 'I was aware that chatbots can be used to create fake news.' (l. 25).

## 3  Synonyms, antonyms and scales

a  Take a look at the following words from the text: 'enable' (ll. 8, 39), 'provide' (ll. 9, 40), 'influence' (l. 14), 'improvement' (l. 16) and 'worries' (l. 22). Think of at least one synonym for each word.

► Check

b  Now take a closer look at the ethics of the media as described in the text. Think of an antonym for each characteristic: 'accuracy' (l. 43), 'fairness' (l. 44), 'respect' (l. 44), 'impartiality' (l. 44) and 'truthfulness' (l. 44).

c  Explain why and when synonyms and antonyms may be helpful in communication, especially for language learners.

d  Collect the effects that media usage can have according to the text.

e  Copy the scale below and place the aspects you collected in **d** according to your personal evaluation: Put the dangers more to the left and the benefits more to the right. Add the words from **d** and more words from the text.

| – – | – | 0 | + | + + |

## 4  Chunk it!

Find suitable words for the gaps to form chunks. Start by using phrases from the text, then add more. You can also use a dictionary.

1  … access
2  … knowledge
3  … public opinion
4  … picture of reality

► Getting started
► Check

## 5  The media and you

**You choose**  Work on either task **a** or **b**.

a  Note down the three forms of media you use most in your everyday life. Based on this, decide whether your media consumption is balanced. Give reasons for your conclusion.

b  List and explain situations in which media can cause unity or disunity among people.

## Constantly online? Stefan Ellerbeck

*The following text presents the results of a 2021 study on US teens' use of the internet and social media.*

- Guess: what percentage of your friends would agree with the following statements?
  1 I use the internet every day.
  2 I am constantly online.
  3 The amount of time I spend on social media is OK.

- Do a quick survey in class on the statements and discuss the results.

[...] A survey of 1,316 teenagers aged 13–17 in the US reveals that 97% now use the internet every day, up from 92% in 2014–15. However, the Pew Research Center's most striking finding is perhaps that 46% say they use the internet 'almost constantly' – a significant rise from 24% in 2014–15. [...]

5 **Many teens worry about their social media use**
While 55% of the teens surveyed say the amount of time they spend on social media is about right, 36% are concerned that they use it too much, with teenage girls more likely to say this than boys.

Would they find it easy to quit social media? Opinions were split – 54% said it
10 would be very or 'somewhat hard', while 46% said it would be 'at least somewhat easy'.

Teenage girls are more likely than boys to say it would be hard to quit – 58% compared with 49%. And there is a similar gap between older and younger teenagers, with the older saying it would be harder to stop using social media.

15 **The digital divide**
Around 95% of teens now have access to a smartphone – up from 73% in 2014–15 – and those aged 15–17 are more likely to have one than those aged 13–14.

Overall access to laptops and gaming consoles has barely changed, but teenagers from more affluent backgrounds are more likely to have these devices at home.
20 Around 82% of those from homes with incomes above $75,000 have gaming consoles, compared with 70% of those from homes earning under $30,000.

The divide is even wider for desktop and laptop computers, with 94% of the richest households owning them, compared with 79% of lower-earning homes.

**Driving digital inclusion**
25 The United Nations says 37% of the world's population, or 2.9 billion people, have never used the internet. [...]

*From*: 'Half of US teens use the internet "almost constantly". But where are they spending their time online?', www.weforum.org, *30 August 2022*

### Comprehension

1 Name three facts of the text that you had expected after reading the headline, two that were totally new to you and one you were surprised by.

2 Describe what is meant by the digital divide.

## Analysis

3   Examine if and how the writer's attitude to the data presented becomes clear in the text.

► SF 17: Reading and understanding non-fictional texts, p. 367

## Language awareness

4   Look at the phrase 'teens surveyed' (l. 6).
   a   Reword the phrase using a relative clause.
   b   Look at the phrase 'the amount of time they spend' (l. 6). Write two versions: one using a complete relative clause and the other one using a participle instead of the relative clause.
   c   Analyse the difference in style that is created by the different versions.

► More language

## Beyond the text

5   You choose  Speaking   Have a discussion on one of the topics given in a or b.

   a   'The internet – an indispensable tool in the modern world.'
   b   'Social media – more connected than ever.'

► SF 46: Having a discussion, p. 410
► Getting started

## Text 2

## Text    Carol Ann Duffy

► More info

• *Quick write: You can only use one form of communication for the rest of your life. Which one would you choose and why?

*Carol Ann Duffy explores texting as a form of communication in a relationship.*

I tend the mobile now
like an injured bird

We text, text, text
our significant words.

5  I re-read your first,
your second, your third,

look for your small xx,
feeling absurd.
The codes we send
10 arrive with a broken chord.

I try to picture your hands,
their image is blurred.

Nothing my thumbs press
will ever be heard.

*From:* Rapture, *2010*

**Annotations**
10  **chord** [kɔːd]  Sehne, Saite
12  **blurred**  not clear visually, fuzzy

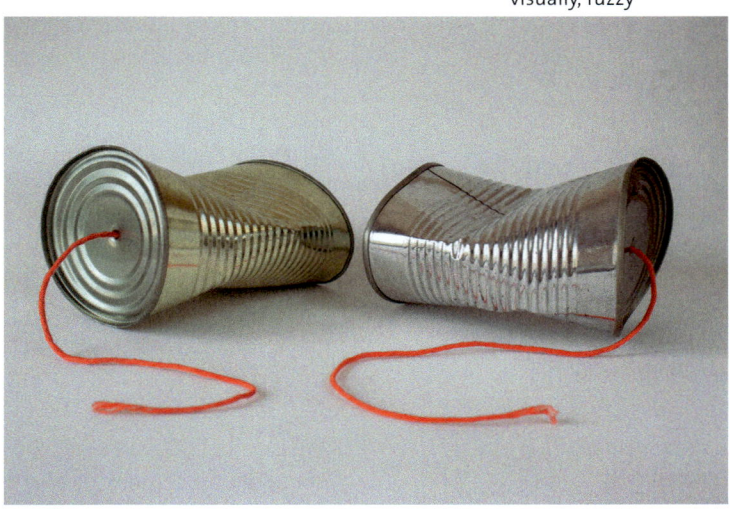

▶ SF 20: Reading and understanding poetry, p. 370

### Comprehension

**1**   Describe the situation represented in the poem. Explain the meaning of the 'small xx' (v. 7).

### Analysis

▶ Support, p. 310

**2**   Analyse how language is used to express the shortcomings of texting. Examine how emotions are presented.

### Language awareness

**3**   While in most of your writing tasks you will be asked to connect your sentences, this poem mainly consists of full sentences which do not contain any linking words. Add linking words to the poem and examine how they change the text.

### Beyond the text

▶ SF 38: Creative writing, p. 395

**4**   Writing   Imagine you are the addressee of the poem. Write a poem in response.

## Text 3

# Social media – an addiction?

*The following podcast explains what happens in the brain of a person who is using social media and in that of a person who has an addiction.*

- *Quick write:* Give a definition of the word *addiction*.

### Comprehension

▶ SF 40: Listening/Viewing for gist and details, p. 399
▶ Getting started

**Annotations**
**dopamine** a neurotransmitter, i.e. a chemical in the brain that has an effect on other cells
**nausea** ['nɔːziə / 'nɔːʒə] feeling of being close to vomiting
**withdrawal** the unpleasant effects a person experiences as they stop taking an addictive drug

**1**   Listening   Listen to the podcast, then answer the following questions. You need not write complete sentences:
   1   Why the young man believes he isn't addicted to social media (one reason)
   2   How the speaker realized that her handling of social media was getting out of control
   3   What the central function of dopamine is, according to the podcast
   4   Which two symptoms of substance abuse the podcast mentions
   5   What withdrawal symptoms are mentioned in the podcast
   6   What happens in the brain when we have a nice chat on social media
   7   What serious side-effect of social media addiction was identified in one study

### Beyond the text

▶ SF 29: Writing a blog post, p. 384
▶ Check

**2**   Writing   Write a blog post in response to the podcast. In it, weigh up the positive and negative consequences of social media both for the individual and for society as a whole. Outline some guidelines for the healthy use of social media.

## Focus on test formats

In tests at school and in your school-leaving exam you will encounter the task of analysing non-fiction, for example newspaper articles, excerpts of non-fiction books, etc. This skill will also be helpful in your life beyond school and support your critical reading and understanding of texts.

You are going to read a newspaper article on a new 'ethics policy' for journalists working for NPR, one of the leading US media organizations. Typical tasks accompanying the text might be the following:

1   Outline what the text says about NPR's new ethics policy and about the reactions to it.
2   Analyse how the author presents her view on the new policy.

## Work it out

▶ SF 27: Essentials: the stages of writing, p. 380

▶ SF 4: Writing a text analysis, p. 351

▶ SF 14: Quoting from texts, p. 361

### 1   Strategies

a   When working on a non-fiction text, there are a few useful strategies that help you deal with it. Together with a partner decide which of the strategies below you would use to complete tasks **1** and **2** above.
  1   Read the text first and then the task.
  2   Mark the verbs for tasks ('Operatoren') in the task.
  3   Make a list of *stylistic devices and literary terms and see if they can be found in the text.
  4   Use different colours to underline elements in the text that you find relevant for the tasks.
  5   Write down important passages from the text.
  6   Finish writing your answer to task **1** before you work on task **2**.
  7   Decide what your opinion is on the topic under discussion.
  8   Make a detailed outline of the text

b   Add and discuss other strategies that you have used before. You may want to collect them on a *method card.

### 2   Understanding an analysis task

Without having read the text, what can you deduce from task **2**, the analysis? For each of the activities below say whether they are relevant for task **2** and discuss your answers with a partner.
  1   Giving a summary of the text
  2   Providing information about the author
  3   Identifying the author's attitude and position
  4   Identifying and understanding a line of argument(s)
  5   Identifying the *narrative perspective
  6   Finding stylistic devices such as *rhetorical questions, *enumerations
  7   Explaining why the stylistic devices that are used are effective
  8   Expressing your opinion on the topic

► Check

## 3   Examining argumentation

*Many non-fiction texts aim at expressing an opinion, at convincing the reader – sometimes openly, sometimes implicitly. In order to examine the argumentation of a text and to assess its quality, it's helpful to identify the strategies that may be involved.*

Look at the examples below and say which strategy the author uses to support their arguments.

1   Social media can be compared to an addiction. I realized this when I tried to do a 3-day digital detox and showed all kinds of withdrawal symptoms: bad temper, nervousness, fidgeting, near-hysteria.

2   Traditional printed newspapers have been facing a substantial crisis for decades. For example, between 1980 and 2016 *The Independent* lost more than 90% of its sales.

3   The free press has come under threat worldwide. In Delhi, the BBC's offices were raided following a critical report. In Turkey, critical journalists were in fear of persecution before elections. The US and the UK have been accused of lacking pluralism regarding media ownership.

4   It has become increasingly difficult to distinguish what is fake from what is reality in the media. As Radikha Witton from the *Clontarf Explorer* put it: 'Fake news rules – and that's a fact'.

► Check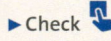

## 4   Examining the formal properties of a non-fiction text

*In the analysis of a non-fiction text it is vital to examine its formal properties and the effect they create. Among the elements that shape the formal properties especially of non-fiction texts are \*stylistic devices and other features listed in the left column below.*

a   Match the stylistic devices and other features on the left with their definitions on the right.

| Term | | Definition | |
|---|---|---|---|
| A | *alliteration | 1 | a question to which the answer seems obvious and is therefore not given |
| B | *allusion | 2 | an indirect reference to something or somebody the reader is supposed to recognize and respond to |
| C | *contrast | 3 | a comparison between two things that are not really like each other using the words *like* or *as* |
| D | *exaggeration | 4 | the way in which a writer treats their topic, thereby reflecting their emotional attitude towards that topic and also towards the reader |
| E | *irony | 5 | saying the opposite of what you actually mean |
| F | *juxtaposition | 6 | the level of language used in a text, e.g. *formal, *informal, *neutral, *slang |

| | | | |
|---|---|---|---|
| **G** | *metaphor | **7** | statement in which the true importance of an idea, event or fact is minimized, so that something is deliberately presented as being much less important, valuable, etc. than it really is |
| **H** | *personification | **8** | the repetition of a consonant at the beginning of neighbouring words, or of stressed syllables within such words to produce a rhythmic effect |
| **I** | *register | **9** | a thing, word or phrase signifying something concrete that stands not only for itself but also for a certain abstract idea |
| **J** | *rhetorical question | **10** | a strong overstatement |
| **K** | *simile | **11** | the use of a word which may be understood in two different ways or which may be put into a different context to change the meaning |
| **L** | *symbol | **12** | the technique of representing animals or objects as if they were human beings or possessed human qualities |
| **M** | *tone | **13** | a very strong *contrast of opposing ideas, arguments or views, mostly introduced by words like *but, however, nevertheless* |
| **N** | *understatement | **14** | a comparison between two things which are basically quite unlike one another without using the words *as* or *like* |
| **O** | *wordplay | **15** | the bringing together of opposing views or words to emphasize their difference and usually to highlight one of the opposing elements |

**b** Write three sentences, each including one of the features above. Then work with a partner and identify the features they used in their example sentences.

## 5 Possible answers

**a** Read the excerpts from two analyses below and discuss with a partner whether or not they are good.

**b** Rephrase them to improve them.

  **1** The author uses a lot of rhetorical questions. She also uses enumerations of things. She uses these things to persuade the reader. She is very convincing. The text contains a lot of humour. Her arguments are good …

  **2** In line 5 the author uses alliteration. In line 6 and 7 she uses a metaphor. There is also anaphora in lines 10 and 11. The effect is …

## Do it

### 6  Getting started

Now read the text below, then work on tasks **1** and **2** in the box on p. 89 using the strategies that you found to be helpful.

## A new ethics policy for journalists    Kelly McBride

*Neutrality is generally considered a central standard of journalism. Consequently, journalists are usually not expected to express their support for political aims even when they are not on duty. However, NPR, one of the leading US media organizations, has recently loosened the restrictions on journalists e.g. to take part in demonstrations.*

NPR rolled out a substantial update to its ethics policy earlier this month, expressly stating that journalists may participate in activities that advocate for 'the freedom and dignity of human beings' on both social media and in real life.

5 The new policy eliminates the blanket prohibition from participating in 'marches, rallies and public events,' as well as vague language that directed NPR journalists to avoid personally advocating for 'controversial' or 'polarizing' issues. [...]

The new NPR policy reads, 'NPR editorial staff may express support for democratic, civic values that are core to NPR's work, such as, but not limited to: the freedom and dignity of human beings, the rights of a free and independent press, the right 10 to thrive in society without facing discrimination on the basis of race, ethnicity, gender, sexual identity, disability, or religion.'

Is it OK to march in a demonstration and say, 'Black lives matter'? What about a Pride parade? In theory, the answer today is, 'Yes.' But in practice, NPR journalists will have to discuss specific decisions with their bosses, who in turn will have to 15 ask a lot of questions.

The carve-out is somewhat narrow. Protests organized with the purpose of demanding equal and fair treatment of people are now permitted, as long as the journalist asking is not covering the event. However, rallies organized to support a specific piece of legislation would be off-limits. Other events featuring a slate of 20 political candidates from one party are also out of bounds. [...]

This policy confronts the generations-old question in newsrooms: Where does the journalist end and the citizen begin?

This pressure on news companies to allow their journalists a wider berth to participate in civic activities has been building over the years, particularly as social media 25 has made direct engagement with audiences – sometimes rich, sometimes messy – part of the day-to-day workflow. As social justice causes took to the platforms, journalists were often caught in a new gray area between longtime professional practices and mores around personal communication. In the wake of George Floyd's murder, a younger generation of journalists pushed NPR to modify 30 its traditional prohibitions. [...]

**Annotations**

4  **blanket** *(adj)* affecting all possible situations or persons

5  **rally** *(n)* large public meeting held to support a political party or a political stance

7  **editorial staff** people working for a newspaper who are responsible for doing research and writing articles

18  **cover sth.** (in journalism) report on sth. on television or in a newspaper

19  **off-limits** (of a place, here) where journalists are not allowed to go

19  **slate** list of candidates in an election

20  **out of bounds** (of a place, here) where journalists are not allowed to go

23  **allow sb. a wide berth** *jdm. mehr Spielraum geben*

26  **messy** (here) unpleasant, challenging

28  **mores** ['mɔːreɪz] (*pl, fml*) customs or rules that apply to a specific social group

29  **George Floyd (1970–2020)** Black American man who was arrested after being accused of a minor offense. Forced to lie face-down, he complained of being unable to breathe. A white police officer nevertheless continued kneeling on his neck until Floyd died. After Floyd's murder, people around the world took to the streets to protest against police racism and police brutality.

In Pittsburgh, newspaper editors restricted a Black reporter from covering the George Floyd demonstrations after she tweeted a joke about the damage caused by white Kenny Chesney fans outside a concert being vastly worse than that caused by multi-ethnic protesters speaking against racism. The Associated Press recently
35 fired a news reporter for violations of their social media policies while employed there. Critics had initially called attention to her tweets supporting Palestinians. CBS News correspondent and former *Washington Post* reporter Wesley Lowery has been vocal about the impact traditional policies have had on Black journalists and ultimately Black audiences.

40 NPR didn't have high-profile conflicts with its journalists in recent years, and that may have made the news organization more prepared to usher in a new policy.

But that doesn't mean it was easy to get the members of the committee to agree on what the new policy should say. [...]

While the committee arrived at a general consensus, not everyone who worked on
45 the revisions agrees with the final product, Woods said. Some people think it goes too far. Others believe it doesn't go far enough.

Leah Donnella, a supervising editor at *Code Switch*, was one of the committee members who walked away dissatisfied. She's been at NPR since 2015 and she went into the conversations last year accepting as a truism that journalists must
50 sacrifice some political speech in order to do their jobs. But after a year of parsing words, she wonders if she and her colleagues missed the opportunity to go deeper.

The restrictions on supporting a political candidate or a piece of legislation still feel to her like a shortsighted compromise. If NPR employees were to reveal who got their vote for president, she asked, 'Is the problem that we are ideologically similar
55 or that people *know* we are ideologically similar?' [...]

Woods said that he and others argued that it was important for journalists to keep many of their personal views private, in order not to distract from the primary focus of reporting facts. But he added that it was a mistake in the past to allow that balancing act to overshadow all expression.

60 'There are things in the world where we are not torn about where we stand,' said Woods (who is also former dean of faculty and my former boss at The Poynter Institute). 'We are against bigotry, we
65 are against discrimination and unfairness.' [...]

Some journalists will find the changes less than satisfying. As someone who writes and reviews policies for news-
70 rooms of all kinds, I see them as a solid step in the right direction. They don't answer some of the thorniest questions, like what if a journalist wants to picket an abortion clinic or demon-
75 strate in support of women's autonomy

## Annotations

33 **Kenny Chesney** (born 1968) US country singer
38 **be vocal** express your views freely and confidently
41 **usher sth. in** *(fml)* make sth. begin
45 **Woods** = Keith Woods, NPR's chief diversity officer
47 **Code Switch** podcast from NPR
49 **truism** undoubted truth
50 **parse sth.** examine sth. in a minute way
63 **Poynter Institute** non-profit journalism school in Florida
64 **bigotry** intolerant devotion to your own beliefs and opinions

**Annotations**
**80 be mutually exclu-sive** *sich gegenseitig ausschließen*

over their bodies? What about a journalist who wants to express her general support of the Second Amendment? Or a parent who wants to march in solidarity with families and victims of a mass shooting?

80   Yet, these guidelines affirm that during this chaotic time in which we are living, being a journalist and standing up for human dignity are not mutually exclusive.

*From: NPR.org, 29 July 2021*

> **Language help**
>
> The author uses/employs …
> This enhances/underlines/stresses/shows …
> The author explains/examines/compares/expresses …

Don't forget:
1. You can start your answer with a TATT-sentence: title, author, text type, topic.
2. Use your notes to write a clearly structured text. Use linking words and a new paragraph for each new idea.
3. Write a conclusion that sums up your most important findings.
4. Then check your spelling and punctuation.

► Getting started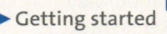

## Feedback

### 7   Peer assessment

    a   Exchange your first draft with a partner. Read your partner's text and make suggestions for improvement if necessary.
    b   Taking into account your partner's feedback, start a *method card in which you make notes of areas you need to improve.
    c   Pick one of the aspects/paragraphs that was criticized by your partner (e.g. the correct focus of your summary, your use of linking words, the way you underlined your findings by quoting from the text and combining the analysis of literary means with their function, etc.) and improve it by rewriting it.

► WOB: pp. 28–30

► Check

# The internet – an egalitarian force?

▶ 'Someone is watching', p. 330

*The internet has often been called an egalitarian force.*

- In your view, how egalitarian is the internet? In class, position yourself on an imaginary scale ranging from 1 (completely egalitarian) to 10 (not egalitarian at all).

## Comprehension

**1  a  Partner B:** Go to p. 310 and work on task **1a**.
**Partner A:** Have a look at the chart below, then prepare a two-minute presentation for your partner about the connection between household income and digitalization.

▶ SF 22: Analysing diagrams, p. 373

▶ SF 43: Giving a presentation, p. 405

▶ Getting started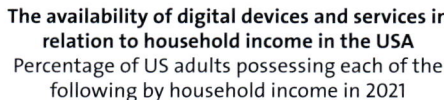

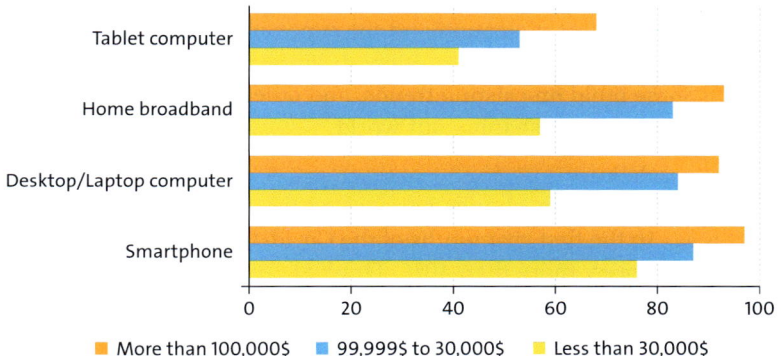

**The availability of digital devices and services in relation to household income in the USA**
Percentage of US adults possessing each of the following by household income in 2021

■ More than 100,000$   ■ 99,999$ to 30,000$   ■ Less than 30,000$

Source: www.pewresearch.org, 22 June 2021

**b** Give your presentation to your partner, then listen to your partner's presentation.
**c** Together discuss what the statistics reveal about the idea of an egalitarian internet.

## Beyond the text

**2**  You choose   Writing   Work on task **a** or **b**.

**a** The fact that not all people have access to the internet is often called the digital divide. What factors can you think of that contribute to the digital divide? Do some research, then present your results in a mindmap or infographic.

**b** How egalitarian is the internet? Write a short letter to the editor of an online IT magazine.

▶ Getting started

▶ Check

▶ WOB: pp. 19–21

# The future of the media: six recent trends

**Advanced**

Nicole Magoon, James Wright, Andre James

*The online article you are to read describes six developments in the field of the media.*

- With a partner discuss what you would consider recent, contemporary or future trends in the media.

Media is blurring its shape. Lines between media types are disappearing, consumers are creators, and entertainment is daubing tech and retail all over itself. Content is ever present, consistent across platforms, and individually personalized. As our physical world blends with virtual worlds, entertainment realities are chang-
5 ing, too.

The media and entertainment industry doesn't have a choice; it must change. Consumers have upped their baseline expectations as technology has evolved, and competitors for consumer time aren't limited to traditional media. If we look across current forms of media, consumers multitask with other media more than 55% of
10 the time. [...]

Increases in consumer participation and the exponential development of technologies like 5G will accelerate the disruption, driving six big shifts in media and entertainment. Some build on existing trends, and others read like sci-fi. All of them are very real, and they're reshaping our world.

15 **01 Omnipresent delivery**
Faster download speeds on phones have raised the bar on 'I want all of it, right here, right now.' In the first six months of the Covid-19 pandemic, streaming viewership on phones grew more than 40%. Think about that. At a time when people were sitting at home in front of their huge screens, they still wanted to watch video
20 on the tiny screens they carry around all day.

In addition to demanding the content they want, where they want it, and when they want it, consumers also expect that content to be interconnected. That's where we start to see cohesion become critical across media platforms, and media start to blend into other sectors, such as retail. [...]

25 **02 My media**
Me! Everything is about me. Or, actually, everything is about the individual consumer and his or her niche communities. Companies that can use data to personalize and customize their content and delivery will win hearts and minds (and money). This shift, like omnipresent delivery, isn't a new one, but it's increasingly
30 becoming a baseline expectation, and the subshifts are growing stronger. [...]

**03 Global aperture**
One of the most exciting things to come out of a more connected world was, well, the world. Content exposure increased, global connections increased, and a demand for authenticity and an understanding of the diverse world we live in in-
35 creased. A more interconnected world means the ability to reach niche audiences with locally tailored content – and the ability to hold the media accountable for diverse, global representation. [...]

## Annotations

- 2 **daub sth.** spread a substance carelessly onto sth.
- 2 **retail** [ˈ– –] *(n)* the selling of goods
- 7 **up sth.** increase sth.
- 12 **disruption** significant change to an industry caused by innovation
- 15 **omnipresent** available everywhere and at any time
- 15 **delivery** (here) act of making sth. accessible electronically
- 16 **raise the bar on sth.** set a new, higher standard for sth.
- 23 **cohesion** state of two things being inextricably connected
- 27 **niche community** [niːʃ] community with particular interests, likes or values
- 30 **baseline** (here) starting point for comparisons
- 30 **subshift** (here) small change/shift happening as part of a larger shift
- 33 **content exposure** the fact of digital content being accessible
- 36 **tailor sth.** (here) adapt sth. for a specific audience
- 36 **hold sb./sth. accountable for sth.** blame sb./ sth. for sth., consider sb./sth. responsible for sth.

## 04 Consumer producers

Digital media doesn't just mean the big guys have more nimble ways of delivering
40 content – the little guys have it all, too. [...]

Not only are individual creators leveraging increasingly professional tools and easy
uploads to pour passion into platforms they've never had access to before, but established content also lives on. Creators can edit, remix, and mash content, post it
on social feeds, and watch it evolve as other producers put their own spin on it for
45 the world to consume. [...]

## 05 Emerging metaverse

If you hear 'metaverse' and think video games, you're not wrong, but it goes beyond that. (If you think Superman, then we applaud DC Comics for their effective
content delivery.)

50 Nearly two decades ago, Linden Labs' Second Life became an early leader in showing how powerful and compelling online communities of avatar residents can be,
and myriad online communities have emerged as gaming worlds have become
more complex. The idea of living in a metaverse has only increased as commerce,
culture, and multiplayer role-playing games have converged in virtual worlds. This
55 includes day-to-day interactions in popular games [...], and in one-off events [...].

As virtual worlds have developed, they have incorporated concerts, shopping, and
other experiences that were once thought of as only physical. These worlds create
alternate lives for their users, and the idea of alternate virtual environments will
slowly infuse daily life beyond gamers. [...]

60 ## 06 Beyond reality

Virtual environments exist online today, but they're beginning to merge with our
physical reality. Augmented reality (AR), in particular, supported by AI, is likely to
be more transformative than virtual reality (VR) in the near-term, given the ability
to seamlessly layer AR on top of our daily life. The next wave of technology will
65 expand the potential for human-machine interactions, blending on-screen experiences with our physical world. For example, in April 2021 the Los Angeles County
Museum of Art teamed up with Snap to offer five AR-enhanced exhibits around
the city, allowing viewers to see virtual art displays through their phones.

Although nimble software and consumer-friendly form factors are still a barrier to
70 widespread consumer adoption, particularly for VR, those issues won't last forever.
[...]

## Implications

Some of these shifts are happening faster than others. One lens to measure their
pace and strength is venture capital (VC) investment, which doesn't capture invest-
75 ment by incumbents, but can show which technologies are drawing investors' interest.

Categorizing VC investments in 2020 shows that trends like omnipresent delivery,
my media, and consumer producers pop more than others [...]. These should be on
every media company's radar today.

80 Trends such as emerging metaverse and beyond reality garner some investment,
but it isn't as much – which isn't surprising. The metaverse is more 'in develop-

## Annotations

39 **nimble** able to adapt
and react quickly
41 **leverage sth.**
[ˈliːvərɪdʒ] (here) use
sth., exploit sth.
44 **put your spin on
sth.** (here) change sth.
so as to give it a slightly
different meaning or
interpretation
46 **metaverse** computer-
generated virtual
environment that
allows users to interact
like in real life
48 **DC Comics** a US comic
publishing house
50 **Second Life** virtual
world launched in 2013
that allows people to
interact with other
users through their
avatars
52 **myriad** huge number
of
52 **emerge** come into
existence
54 **converge** unite
55 **one-off** (*adj*, BE)
happening once and
not regularly
59 **infuse sth.** (*fml*) have
an effect on sth. and all
its parts
64 **seamless** (here) not
noticeable
64 **layer sth.** (here) add
sth. over sth.
73 **lens** (here) tool that
makes you perceive
things bigger and more
clearly
74 **venture capital** money
inversted in a new com-
pany, often involving
financial risks
75 **incumbent** (here)
investors who invest
their money in
traditional stock
market companies
80 **garner sth.** collect sth.

Advanced

**Annotations**
**83  aperture**
['æpətʃə] opening
**87  executive** leader of a
company
**89  competitive edge**
advantage over
competitors
**90  scramble** *(v)* rush and
fight with others to
reach sth.

ment,' and video game companies are the best positioned to invest there. [...] Global aperture draws the smallest investment, but this may be less about its importance and more about this being a shift in attitude rather than tech-driven
85 innovation.

The investment data shows all six shifts are underway. Whether you're a media executive, an investor, or an increasingly involved consumer, think about how they'll affect you. Those who understand how these shifts could reshape markets and open new opportunities will gain a competitive edge, while those who sit com-
90 fortably on traditional business rhythms will scramble to catch up.

*From: 'Six shifts changing the future of media', www.bain.com*

### Comprehension

**1** Work with a partner. **Partner A:** Work on the first three trends mentioned;
**Partner B:** Work on the last three trends mentioned.
a   Write a concise definition of the trends.
b   Compare definitions with your partner and improve them where necessary.
c   Together, state which of the trends is strongest according to the text.

### Analysis

▶ SF 17: Reading and
understanding non-
fictional texts, p. 367

▶ WOB: pp. 28–30

**2** Analyse the language and style of the text. Point out what audience the writers might have in mind and what intention might be behind their text.

### Language Awareness

**3  a** Examine the different tenses and aspects used in the text. Analyse how they contribute to an atmosphere of imminent and ongoing change.
**b**   Writing   Think of a current trend (e.g. a fashion trend, pastime, values or a cultural movement). Present it in a short text, using similar tenses and aspects as the text at hand.

### Beyond the text

▶ SF 28: Argumentative
writing: discussion and
comment, p. 382

▶ Check 👆

**4**   You choose     Writing   Later in the text, the writers describe two developments in detail (cf. tasks **a** and **b** below). Choose one and write a comment on it, stating whether you see this development as an opportunity or a threat and whether you think it will be a short-term trend or a long-term reality.

▶ WOB: pp. 22–24

a   'Creators can edit, remix, and mash content, post it on social feeds, and watch it evolve as other producers put their own spin on it for the world to consume.'
*From: 'Six shifts changing the future of media', www.bain.com*

b   'Our digital and physical lives will lose their separateness as we expand our definition of reality and digital interactions hold near-equal weight to in-person ones.'
*From: 'Six shifts changing the future of media', www.bain.com*

# Deepfakes – seeing, but not believing

- Give examples of deepfakes and/or fake news and say what dangers they could entail. (► Info boxes below)

► SF 40: Listening/Viewing for gist and details, p. 399

**Annotation**
**impression** (here) imitation

**Info**

**Deepfakes** are videos that have been edited to make it seem as if a specific person, often someone famous, is participating in the video. In reality someone's appearance has been changed with the help of an algorithm to look e.g. like a celebrity. Such videos can seem very authentic and sometimes make it impossible to differentiate between reality and fiction. Therefore, they are also popular methods of spreading fake news and disinformation.

## Comprehension

**1** 〔Viewing〕 Watch the video on deepfakes, then answer the questions below. You need not write complete sentences.

1 What deepfakes use AI for
2 What deepfakes have been used for in movies
3 How deepfakes are used in a humorous way
4 Why deepfakes can be dangerous especially with regard to politics
5 How AI may help identify deepfakes

## Analysis

**2** The video was created as part of the Australian Broadcasting Corporation's media literacy week.

**a** With a partner discuss what audience and what intentions the ABC might have had in mind when creating this video for its media literacy week.

**b** 〔Viewing〕 Watch the video again and examine what means are employed to reach the audience in the intended way (cf. your results from **a**).

**c** Go back to task **a** and correct your ideas on audience and intention if necessary.

## Beyond the text

**3** 〔You choose〕 〔Speaking〕 With a partner, do either task **a** or **b** below.

**a** Collect and discuss measures that can prevent the spread of deepfakes and strengthen people's media literacy. Present the three most convincing ideas to the class.

**b** Discuss how the media can strengthen democracy. Take all forms of media into consideration. Present the three most convincing ideas to the class.

► Getting started (task 2b)
► WOB: pp. 65–67

**4** Think back to the guiding question of the chapter. How would you answer it at this point?

**Info**

**How to spot fake news**

In order to verify whether a piece of information on the internet is trustworthy or not, you can apply the following questions to texts, pictures, videos and sources.

- Check the headlines – do they describe content objectively? Be careful if they are overtly sensational, emotional or speculative.
5 - Examine the URL – does it belong to an established source you can trust (e.g. renowned news associations, quality papers, etc.)?
- Examine the sources the website uses – are they reliable and authentic, i.e. do they give precise details about authors, editors, donors, charities, enterprises, locations and/or addresses?

10 • Look critically at the quality and appearance of photos, layout and language – do they meet the standards of high quality journalism? Significant short-comings such as low resolution, poor formatting or spelling and grammar mistakes may suggest an unreliable source.

• Check the dates and the timeline of events as well as numbers and statistics –
15 are they coherent and are they supported by other sources? Don't trust the article if there are inaccuracies and contradictions.

• Examine if the article under scrutiny is supported by other evidence – are there more articles on other websites about the same story?

• Look at the context of the article – does it present original content or was it
20 shared/copied? Who is the intended audience? Was there a special occasion for the publication? If the article was shared, consider who shared it and what their motives were.

**1** Visualize the guidelines above in a suitable form (illustration, table, mind-map, …)

## Text 7

### AI's threat to AI   Vishwam Sankaran

Advanced

• What role does Artificial Intelligence (= AI) play in your life? How do you feel about it?

*Read the Info box on the development of Artificial Intelligence and its uses, then go on to the newspaper article on p. 101 on a special type of danger that AI might pose to itself.*

Info

**Artificial Intelligence** (AI) is an interdisciplinary field that seeks to create intelligent machines able to think, learn and act like humans. In the early years after its inception, research on AI focused on creating machines that could reason, plan, and understand natural language. In the 1990s, more advanced AI systems
5 were developed, which were capable of recognizing patterns in data and making predictions. With the beginning of 'big data' and cloud computing in the 2000s, the development of AI speeded up tremendously: the availability of massive amounts of data enabled the development of deep learning neural networks that could recognize complex patterns in images, speech, and text. Due to the
10 development of cloud-based AI platforms and open-source libraries in recent years, AI has become more accessible to businesses and individuals, sometimes without there being any awareness of AI being used. They interact with chatbots or follow the suggestions of word processing programs' autocorrect function, they follow AI-generated travel directions, unlock their smartphone by means of facial
15 recognition tools or use its voice assistant, they use smart appliances in their smart homes, follow personalized recommendations in online shopping and even trust their self-driving cars to take over the wheel. AI is still in its early stages, but it has the potential to revolutionize many aspects of our lives and transform industries. Yet, concerns about the ethical and societal implications of intelligent
20 machines are growing, so it is essential to ensure that its development is guided by ethical principles and benefits humanity rather than harming it.

Future generations of artificial intelligence chatbots trained using data from other AIs could lead to a downward spiral of gibberish on the internet, a new study has found.

Large language models (LLMs) [...] have taken off on the internet, with many users adopting the technology to produce a whole new ecosystem of AI-generated texts
5 and images.

But using the output data from such AI systems to further train subsequent generations of AI models could result in 'irreversible defects' and junk content, according to a new, yet-to-be peer-reviewed study.

AI models [...] are trained using vast amounts of data pulled across internet plat-
10 forms that have mostly remained human generated until now.

But AI-generated data using such models have a growing presence on the internet.

Researchers, including those from the University of Oxford in the UK, attempted to understand what happened when several subsequent generations of AIs are trained off each other.

15 They found the widespread use of LLMs to publish content on the internet on a large scale 'will pollute the collection of data to train them' and lead to 'model collapse'.

'We discover that learning from data produced by other models causes model collapse – a degenerative process whereby, over time, models forget the true underlying data distribution,' scientists wrote in the study, posted as a preprint in *arXiv*.

20 The new findings suggested there to be a 'first mover advantage' when it comes to training LLMs.

Scientists liken this change to what happens when AI models are trained on music created by human composers and played by human musicians. The subsequent AI output then trains other models, leading to a diminishing quality of music.

25 With subsequent generations of AI models likely to encounter poorer quality data at their source, they may start misinterpreting information by inserting false information in a process scientists call 'data poisoning'.

They warned that the scale at which data poisoning can happen drastically changes after the advent of LLMs.

30 Just a few iterations of data can lead to major degradation, even when the original data is preserved, scientists said.

And over time, this could lead to mistakes compounding and forcing models that learn from generated data to misunderstand reality.

'This in turn causes the model to misperceive the underlying learning task,' re-
35 searchers said.

Scientists cautioned that steps must be taken to label AI-generated content from human-generated ones, along with efforts to preserve original human-made data for future AI training.

'To make sure that learning is sustained over a long time period, one needs to
40 make sure that access to the original data source is preserved and that additional data not generated by LLMs remain available over time,' they wrote in the study.

---

**Annotations**

2 **downward spiral** situation in which sth. gets continuously worse

2 **gibberish** (*infml*) incomprehensible and/or meaningless words

6 **subsequent** ['– – –] following, future

8 **yet-to-be** that still has to be

9 **pull data** collect data

14 **be trained off each other** be trained using the other AI's data

19 **preprint** (*n*) version of research studies before they have been peer-reviewed or formally published

20 **first mover advantage** competitive advantage of a company that occupies a market segment first

22 **liken sth. to sth. else** compare sth. to sth. else

29 **advent** ['– –] the coming of an important event, person, invention, etc.

30 **iteration** process of repeating a computing process again and again, always using the result of the previous stage as a basis

30 **degradation** reduction in quality

31 **preserve sth.** keep sth.

32 **compound** [–ˈ –] (*v*) (here) increase in number or become worse.

36 **caution** (*v*) (here) advise sb. to do sth. in order to avoid risks

**Advanced**

Annotations
43 **crawl data** collect data
43 **prior** to before
44 **at scale** on a large
    scale

'Otherwise, it may become increasingly difficult to train newer versions of LLMs without access to data that was crawled from the Internet prior to the mass adoption of the technology, or direct access to data generated by humans at scale.'

*From: 'Scientists warn of threat to internet from AI-trained AIs',* The Independent, *20 June 2023*

## Comprehension

**1** Outline how the 'junk content' (l. 7) that the article fears is created through AI.

## Analysis

▶ SF 17: Reading and
  understanding non-
  fictional texts, p. 367
▶ Support, p. 311
▶ WOB: pp. 28–30

**2** The developments presented in this text are derived from a study which has not yet been peer-reviewed (cf. l. 8), i.e. it has not yet been approved by the scientific community. Examine by what means the article expresses uncertainty around the study findings.

## Language awareness

▶ More language
▶ Check

**3** The text uses a number of *ing*-forms.
  **a** Match the forms 1–9 on the left to the categories A–D on the right.

| Some *ing*-forms from the text | Categories |
|---|---|
| 1 'trained using data' (l. 1) | A Gerund |
| 2 'using the output data' (l. 6) | B Present participle used instead of relative clause |
| 3 'data using such models' (l. 11) | C Present participle used as adjective |
| 4 'a growing presence' (l. 11) | D Present participle [instead of a subclause] expressing accompanying circumstances |
| 5 'the underlying data distribution' (l. 18) | |
| 6 'a diminishing quality of ...' (l. 24) | |
| 7 'by inserting false information' (l. 26) | |
| 8 'data poisoning' (l. 27) | |
| 9 'underlying ... task' (l. 34) | |

  **b** Try to rephrase the first four paragraphs without using any of the *ing*-forms.
  **c** Compare the two versions.

▶ SF 29: Writing a blog post, p. 384

▶ Check

▶ WOB: pp. 11–12

**Advanced**

## Beyond the text

**4** [Writing] Work on either **a** or **b**.

**a** Imagine one area of your life (school, sport, friends, communication) in ten years – how will it have been changed by AI? Write a blog post describing a day in your future life as you would in a personal diary.

**b** [Challenge] Imagine one area of your life (school, sport, friends, communication) in ten years – how will it have been changed by AI? Write a blog post describing a day in your future life. Insert graphic elements (or describe them) to make your blog post a multimodal text.

## Text 8

**Advanced**

## Scripting reality   Ben Elton

▶ 'Someone is watching', p. 330

▶ More info

• Play in groups. Every player holds up one hand with five fingers showing. Read out the confessions below. Every time a player did do what the statement denies, they lower a finger.

Never have I ever ...

1  defended reality TV.
2  watched a reality show on TV.
3  disliked a contestant in a reality TV show.
4  voted on who stays in a reality TV show.
5  watched the live stream of a reality TV show.
6  auditioned for a reality TV show.
7  visited the website of a reality TV show.
8  had a crush on a contestant in a reality TV show.
9  felt sympathy for a contestant in a reality TV show.
10  followed a reality show contestant on social media.

[Info]

**Reality TV shows** claim to broadcast how normal people manage their everyday lives. How these people are perceived by the public can be strongly influenced by those working behind the cameras. They decide which snippets are shown and how an episode is cut. It can also happen that specific situations are created to ensure that the protagonists behave in a particular way.

*In this extract from Ben Elton's novel* Dead Famous, *Trisha, a detective constable, is interviewing Bob Fogarty, the editor-in-chief of the reality TV show* House Arrest, *to find out who murdered one of the house mates. Please note that the extract contains offensive language that shouldn't be used in conversation with others.*

DAY THIRTY. 9.15 p.m.
While Coleridge and Hooper nosed their way along the M25, Trisha was interviewing Bob Fogarty, the editor-in-chief of *House Arrest*. After Geri the Gaoler, Fogarty was the most senior figure in the Peeping Tom hierarchy. Trisha wanted to know
5  more about how the people she had been watching came to be presented in the way they were.
'*House Arrest* is basically fiction,' said Fogarty, handing her a styrofoam cup of watery froth and nearly missing her hand in the darkness of the monitoring bunker. 'Like all TV and film. It's built in the edit.'
10  'You manipulate the housemates' images?'
'Well, obviously. We're not scientists, we make television programmes. People are basically dull. We have to make them interesting, turn them into heroes and villains.'

Annotations
2  **nose your way** *(infml)* move at a slow pace in a specific direction
4  **Peeping Tom**  (here) name of the production firm
9  **edit** *(n)*  the act of altering films or texts, usually for length, correctness, etc.

'I thought you were supposed to be observers, that
15  the whole thing was an experiment in social interaction?'

'Look, constable,' Fogarty explained patiently, 'in order to create a nightly half-hour of broadcasting we
have at our disposal the accumulated images of thir-
20  ty television cameras running for twenty-four hours.
That's seven hundred and twenty hours of footage
to make one *half-hour* of television. We couldn't
avoid making subjective decisions even if we wanted to. The thing that amazes us is that the nation

**Annotation**
37  **smack** *(n sl)* the drug
    heroin

25  *believes* what we show them. They actually accept that what they are watching is
real.'

'I don't suppose they think about it much. I mean, why should they?'

'That's true enough. As long as it's good telly they don't care, which is why as far
as possible we try to shoot the script.'
30  'Shoot the script?'

'It's a term they use in news and features.'

'And it means?'

'Well, say you're making a short insert for the news, investigating heroin addiction
on housing estates. If you simply went out to some urban hellhole with a camera
35  and started nosing around, you could be looking for the story you want till Christmas. So you *script* your investigation before you leave your office. You say ... all
right, we need a couple of kids to say they can get smack at school, we need a girl
to say she'd whore for a hit, we need a youth worker to say it's the government's
fault ... You write the whole thing. Then you send out a researcher to round up a
40  few show-offs and basically tell them what to say.'

'But how could you do that on *House Arrest?* I mean, you can't tell the housemates
what to say, can you?

'No, but you can be pretty sure of the story you want to tell and then look for the
shots that support it. It's the only way to avoid getting into a complete mess. Look
45  at this, for instance ... This is Kelly's first trip to the confession box on the afternoon of day one.'

**DAY ONE. 4.15 p.m.**
'It's brilliant, wicked, outrageous. I feel just totally
bigged-up and out there,' Kelly gushed breathless-
50  ly from the main monitor. She had come to the
confession box to talk about how thrilling and exciting it all was.

'I mean, today has just been the wickedest day ever
because I really, really love all these people and I
55  just know we're all going to get along just brilliantly.
I expect there'll be tension and I'll end up hating all
of them for, like, just a moment at some point. But
you could say that about any mates, couldn't you?
Basically I *love* these guys. They're my posse. My
60  crew.'

Deep in the darkness of the editing suite Geraldine glared at Fogarty. 'And that's what you want her to say, is it?'

Bob cowered behind his styrofoam cup. 'Well, it's what she did say, Geraldine.'

Geraldine's eyes flashed, her nostrils flared and she bared her colossal overbite. It
65 was as if the Alien had just burst out of John Hurt's stomach. [...]

'I could get a monkey to broadcast what she *actually* said! I could get a work-experience school-leaver pain-in-the-arse spotty fucking waste-of-space teenager to broadcast what she *actually* said! What I pay you to do is to *look* at what she *actually* said and *find* what we *want her to say*, you *cunt!*'

70 Fogarty threw a commiserating glance at the younger, more impressionable members of staff.

'Who is Kelly, Bob?' Geraldine continued, throwing an arm towards the frozen image of the pretty young brunette on the screen. 'Who is that girl?'

Fogarty stared at the television. A sweet smile beamed back at him, an open, hon-
75 est, naïve countenance. 'Well ...'

'She's our bitch, Bob, she's our manipulator. She's one of our designated hate figures! Remember the audition interviews? All that pert ambition? All that artless knicker-flashing. All that *girl power bollocks*. Remember what I said, Bob?'

Fogarty did remember, but Geraldine told him anyway.

80 'I said, 'Right, you arrogant little slapper, we'll see how far you get towards presenting your own pop, style and fashion show once the whole nation has decided you're a back-biting [...] fucking *dog,*' didn't I?'

'Yes, Geraldine, but on the evidence of today she's turned out to be really quite nice. I mean, she's a bit of an airhead, and vain, certainly, but she's not really a
85 bitch. I think we'll find it quite hard to make her look that nasty.'

'She'll *look* however we want her to look and *be* whatever we want her to be,' Geraldine sneered.

**DAY THIRTY. 9.20 a.m.**

'Does Geraldine normally talk to you like that?'
90 Trisha asked.

'She talks to everybody like that.'

'So you get used to it, then?'

'It's not something you get used to, constable. I have an MSc in computing and media. I am
95 *not* a stupid cunt.'

Trisha nodded. She had heard of Geraldine Hennessy before her *House Arrest* fame.

Most people had. Geraldine was a celebrity in her own right. A famously bold, provocative
100 and controversial broadcaster, Trisha ventured. 'Rubbish!' said Bob Fogarty. 'She's a TV whore masquerading as an innovator and getting away with it because she knows a few popstars and wears Vivienne Westwood. What she does is steal tacky, dumbed-down tabloid
105 telly ideas, usually from Europe or Japan, smear them with a bit of hip, clubby, druggy style, and flog them to the middle class as post-modern irony.'

▶ More info

**Annotation**
70 **commiserate** *mitfühlen*
76 **designate sth. to sb.** officially assign a particular role to sb.
77 **pert** direct, without respect
84 **airhead** *(infml)* fool, not an intelligent person
94 **MSc** = Master of Science

Advanced

**Info**

Several **offensive expressions** such as in l. 69 and l. 78 are used throughout the extract. Apart from authentically depicting informal exchanges on set, they serve to reveal the power relations between the different characters. It is important to remember, however, that this language can be emotionally distressing and is inappropriate in a classroom setting.

'So you don't like her, then?'

'I loathe her, constable. People like Geraldine Hennessy have ruined television. She's a cultural vandal. She's a nasty, stupid, dangerous bitch.'

110 In the gloom Trisha could see that Fogarty's cup was shaking in his hand. She was taken aback. 'Calm down, Mr Fogarty,' she said.

'I am calm.'

'Good.'

Then Fogarty played Kelly's confession as it had been broadcast.

115 'I'll end up hating all of them.'

Seven words were all she said.

*From:* Dead Famous, *2001*

## Comprehension

**1**   Point out how the TV show is manipulated by the producers.

## Analysis

**2**   Examine how the author is maintaining the reader's interest, considering the use of language and structure.

**3**   Analyse the way Kelly is characterized.

## Language awareness

▶ Getting started

**4**   **a**   In their dialogues, the characters make extensive use of very *colloquial expressions, even of inappropriate *slang expressions. Find examples from the text.

     **b**   Rephrase ll. 33–40 in a more formal *register and explain the function of this usage. With a partner, discuss whether an adapted version without the slang terms should be used for people under a certain age.

## Beyond the text

**5**   Intercultural competence   Writing   A friend of yours in the UK has to prepare an article about the popularity of reality TV shows in different countries. Write a letter in which you name some German reality TV shows and explain why they are popular or not.

**6**   You choose   Writing   Do either task **a** or **b**.

▶ Getting started (task a)

▶ Support, p. 311

▶ SF 28: Argumentative writing: discussion and comment, p. 382

▶ SF 38: Creative writing, p. 395

▶ Check (task a)

     **a**   Later in the book Bob Fogarty says: 'The public, they're worse than us! [...] They know they're watching ants getting burnt under a magnifying glass, but they don't care.' Write a comment on the viewers' responsibility for the quality and realism of reality shows, using this quotation as a starting point.

     **b**   As one of Kelly's closer friends sees her appearance in the confession box, they join the show's chat room. Write their post, considering the circumstances of the show and either defend Kelly or express irritation.

# Art in Context: The art in advertising

▶ More info

*While* art *refers to the use of creative skills and the imaginative mind for aesthetic and emotional ends,* advertising *implies the application of imagination and creativity in order to sell something. Despite their commercial function and the communicative tactics involved, print and film adverts may nevertheless be of aesthetic value.*

- Work in groups of three. Take turns to either hum the melody of a commercial jingle, quote a brand slogan in English or describe a print advert. The others have to guess what product, brand name or organization goes with the jingle, slogan or advert.

- Discuss how the adverts you referred to make a product recognizable.

> **Info**
>
> The **AIDA formula** is frequently used in advertising to make ads as appealing as possible to customers. Knowledge of this formula can also help to analyse an ad. *AIDA* stands for:
> - **A**ttention
> - **I**nterest
> - **D**esire
> - **A**ction
>
> Every part has a specific aim. First of all, the ad has to attract the *attention* of the audience. Following this, *interest* in the product has to be raised and the customer's *desire* to have the product aroused. Lastly, the customer should take *action*, e.g. research the product and/or purchase it.

### Comprehension

**1** Describe the situation presented in the advert above.

### Analysis

**2 a** Analyse the visual presentation of the product and the language used.
  **b** Explain how the product relates to the advert.
  **c** Examine what sort of emotional response the advert attempts to achieve.

▶ SF 23: Analysing visuals, p. 374

▶ Support, p. 311

▶ WOB: pp. 40–44

### Beyond the text

**3** Discuss to what extent adverts can be classified as art. Give examples.

▶ SF 6: Essentials: language and study skills, p. 354

Collection of big data in Shanghai

# Words revisited

## 1   Negative and positive meanings

Throughout this chapter you have come across words dealing with different aspects of the media. Some of them refer to its benefits, some to its flipsides – and some can do both, depending on the context they are used in. Here are some words from 'Words in Context' p. 84:

| | | |
|---|---|---|
| big data | fake news | smartphone |
| chatbot | hate speech | social media |
| digital divide | impartiality | streaming service |
| digital footprint | information technology | surveillance |
| digital revolution | journalistic ethics | watchdog |
| disinformation | mass media | |

**a**   Copy the table below and write the words in the respective column.

| Positive connotation | Negative connotation | Neutral connotation | Depending on context |
|---|---|---|---|
| ... | ... | ... | ... |

**b**   Add at least two more words dealing with media to each of the four columns. Look at the texts you've read for inspiration.

**c**   From the words in the right column, choose three and use them in two different contexts, illustrating their positive and negative connotations.

**d**   📖 Go back to the Chapter map on p. 83. Choose five words from the table and say which topic from the Chapter map they might be connected to.

# Language awareness

## 2   Communication problems and conflicts

Intercultural competence Communication problems are a common experience in your first language and happen even more often in a foreign language. Sometimes the problems can be caused by choice of media and/or a power imbalance.

**a**   Have a look at the following situations in which a problem or conflict occurs:

*Situation 1:* You're an intern with a prestigious company. You're supposed to give a presentation together with another intern, who's from the USA. As you meet for the first time to develop some general ideas for the presentation, you've come prepared: read lots of articles, collected pictures and developed a structure for your presentation. The US intern hasn't prepared anything.

*Situation 2:* You interviewed a local politician for your school magazine on the topic of making cycling safer. At the end she said, 'Text me if you need more information'. Three weeks later you open your messenger service and write, 'Please send info on plans for bike lanes. Thx'. The politician doesn't reply.

*Situation 3:* *You're an intern with a bank in London. On the first day one of the managers shows you around. She hands you a dossier and says, 'You might like to have a look at this'. You flip through it and toss it aside because you don't find it interesting. The next day, the manager asks you what you found most intriguing about the dossier.*

Work in three groups. Each group focuses on one of the situations and analyses the problem and its origins.

**b** Present your results to class. Discuss how convincing you found the explanations given for the problems.

## Practice

**3** **a** With a partner, choose one of the three situations and discuss how the problem could be resolved.

**b** Look at the phrases below for your chosen situation. Say which you consider useful and which counter-productive.

**Situation 1:**
**a** *I'm a little surprised you haven't prepared anything for the meeting.*
**b** *You're not saying you haven't prepared anything, are you?*
**c** *We were meeting to brainstorm together, so I didn't think it was necessary to do a lot of work beforehand.*
**d** *Cool down, it's no big deal! We've plenty of time.*

**Situation 2:**
**a** *I texted you yesterday, why haven't you answered?*
**b** *I didn't realize. I thought it was ok because we were texting.*
**c** *I don't think I find your tone appropriate in this situation.*
**d** *You can't be serious.*

**Situation 3:**
**a** *I thought I asked you to read the dossier.*
**b** *I didn't find the dossier relevant for my work.*
**c** *Do you usually not do what you are asked?*
**d** *Oh, sorry I thought you meant it as a suggestion.*

**c** Prepare and carry out a role-play for your situation in front of the class. Use appropriate phrases from **b**.

▶ WOB: pp. 108–113

# News avoidance in times of media fatigue   Maren Urner

*In a recent interview, German neuroscientist Professor Maren Urner explains how news about terror, war or the climate crisis influences our view of the world.*

- Do an acrostic on the words *bad news*. Present your acrostics to each other in a group to learn about your perspectives on the topic. You may check afterwards whether your ideas were represented in the text.

**Frau Urner, Sie beschäftigen sich seit vielen Jahren damit, wie wir Informationen verarbeiten. Ein Instrument, was Sie dabei verwenden, sind Wissenstests. Im Ergebnis zeigt sich immer, dass die Befragten den Zustand der Welt meist negativer beurteilen, als er tatsächlich ist. Warum ist das so?**

5 Tatsächlich können wir sagen, dass es nicht nur meistens so ist, sondern immer. [...] Mittlerweile habe ich den Test in sämtlichen gesellschaftlichen Gruppen, Kontexten und Settings benutzt und es war immer so, dass die Einschätzung des Publikums negativer ist, als die Realität tatsächlich ist.

**Woran liegt das?**

10 Zum Großteil daran, welche Informationen wir zur Verfügung gestellt bekommen. Die stammen vor allem aus medialen Kontexten, von den klassischen Medien, wie Zeitung, Radio, Fernsehen und natürlich auch, seit mittlerweile einigen Jahrzehnten, aus dem Internet und den eher noch neuen sozialen Medien. Generell haben wir da eine Überrepräsentanz, eine Fokussierung auf Negatives. Das
15 ist gut untersucht, auch in den unterschiedlichen Formaten, sei es in der Zeitung oder eben generell in Online-Medien. Die Anschlussfrage ist natürlich: Woher kommt diese Fokussierung aufs Negative? [...]

Wir alle tragen den sogenannten „Negativity Bias" in uns, also einen Fokus auf negative Inhalte. Wir speichern negative Informationen und potentielle Gefahren
20 nicht nur besser ab und reagieren intensiver auf sie, sondern suchen auch mehr danach. Also ganz einfach runtergebrochen: Negatives verarbeiten wir besser, schneller und intensiver als Positives oder Neutrales. [...]

**Was macht diese Fokussierung der Medien auf die negativen Nachrichten mit uns?**
Zunächst sorgt es für das bereits erwähnte zu negative Weltbild. Manch Journalist
25 argumentiert gern, dass das nicht weiter schlimm sei und die Menschen in der Folge besonders aktiv würden, um an den schlechten Zuständen etwas zu ändern. Doch sämtliche Forschungsergebnisse aus der Verhaltensforschung zu der Thematik zeigen ein anderes Bild. Sie zeigen, dass genau das Gegenteil der Fall ist.

Ein zu negatives Weltbild führt nicht dazu, dass wir besonders aktiv, hoffnungsvoll
30 und mit möglichst guten Ideen auf diese Herausforderungen und Probleme reagieren, die ja offensichtlich unsere Zeit beeinflussen. Stattdessen sind wir gefühlt dauerhaft im Krisenmodus und das führt dazu, dass wir chronisch gestresst sind. Damit einher gehen häufig Gefühle von Hilflosigkeit und Hoffnungslosigkeit. Am Ende des Tages führt das dazu, dass sich immer mehr Menschen vom Weltgesche-
35 hen abwenden, weil es einfach zu viel erscheint. Dieses Phänomen ist mittlerweile sehr gut untersucht und wird als „News-Avoidance" bezeichnet.

Außerdem kann der exzessive Konsum der negativen Nachrichtenflut uns tatsächlich gesundheitlichen Schaden zufügen. Denn chronischer Stress ist ein Risikofaktor für sämtliche Krankheiten, egal ob Herz-Kreislauf-Probleme oder psychi-

40  sche Leiden. Schlussendlich sind wir gestresst und ängstlich nicht in der Lage, gute und langfristige Entscheidungen zu treffen. [...]

**Führt die ständige Dauerberieselung an negativen Nachrichten auch zu Politik- und Medienverdrossenheit?**

Genau richtig. Das Phänomen, was Sie jetzt gerade beschrieben haben, ist
45  das Phänomen der sogenannten „erlernten Hilflosigkeit". Sehr anschaulich auf den Punkt gebracht durch die oft bemühte Aussage: „Die da oben machen sowieso, was sie wollen!" Gemeint ist der Punkt, an dem viele Menschen ankommen, wenn sie erfahren, dass sie nichts ändern können und die Welt nun mal schlecht und ein grausamer Platz ist, auf den sie
50  wenig Einfluss haben. Gesamtgesellschaftlich und demokratisch gedacht, führt das dazu, dass sich Menschen nicht mehr an der Gesellschaft beteiligen. [...]

**Was müssen Schülerinnen und Schüler erlernen, damit sie gesund Medien nutzen können? [...]**

Ich bin wirklich fest davon überzeugt, dass die wichtigste Kompetenz das soge-
55  nannte „kritische Denken" ist. Das bedeutet, Informationen von außen, aber auch sich selbst und die eigene Wahrnehmung stets kritisch zu hinterfragen. [...] Der Bestätigungsfehler beispielsweise meint das Phänomen, dass wir Informationen eher glauben, wenn sie in unser bestehendes Weltbild passen. [...]

**Medien schaffen mediale Wirklichkeiten. [...] Welche Kompetenzen müssen junge**
60  **Menschen haben, um stärker zwischen medialer und tatsächlicher Wirklichkeit unterscheiden zu können?**

Ich denke, dass das Stichwort Ehrlichkeit eine wichtige Rolle spielt. Das, was ich erlebe und was mir viele aus dem Bekannten- und Freundeskreis, die auf journalistischer Ebene tätig sind, zurückspielen, ist eine grundsätzliche Verwirrung über
65  die Vorstellung vieler Menschen, wie Journalismus funktioniere. Mit Ehrlichkeit und Transparenz meine ich, einen größeren Austausch zu schaffen. [...]

Das Tolle am Internet ist doch, dass wir das klassische Sender-Empfänger-Modell hinter uns gelassen haben. Wir sollten diese Chance des Austauschs noch mehr nutzen und wahrnehmen. Wir können dabei nicht nur über Inhalte reden, son-
70  dern auch über Methoden. [...]                                    *(654 words)*

*From: 'Negative Nachrichtflut führt dazu, dass sich Menschen nicht mehr beteiligen',*
SMK-Blog, *30 June 2021*

**1**  `Mediating`  You started an initiative with your partner school in the UK that aims at preventing media fatigue and news avoidance. Write an article for your project website, presenting Maren Urner's explanation.

► Getting started
► SF 49: Mediating from German into English, p. 416
► Support, p. 312

**Beyond the text**

**2**  `Writing`  Imagine the newspaper that you and your family read contains almost exclusively bad news. Write a letter to the editor in which you comment on this fact.

► Getting started
► Check
► WOB: pp. 19–21

**3**  **a**  📖  Reconsider the guiding question of the chapter. Has your opinion changed in the course of the chapter? If so, how and why?

**b**  What could you do to make sure the media you use are a 'window to the world' rather than a 'distortion of reality'? Write down five suggestions.

# Resignation or resistance? The power of the media

- Look at the criteria in the table below and say which type of media from the box on the right meets which criterion best for you personally. Also state which type of media does not meet which criterion well.
- Discuss your view with a partner giving examples to support your view.

**Types of media**
- radio news
- newspapers
- news websites
- TV news programmes
- weekly magazines
- social media platforms

| Accessible | Influential | Reliable | Thorough | Up to date |
|---|---|---|---|---|
| … | … | … | … | … |

*Worries about the effects that the media can have on people and society were articulated as early as in 1899 by the editors of the* Post, *a US magazine, long before the arrival of electronic media.*

The first peril of careless newspaper reading is that of being morally hardened by constant contact with the physical and spiritual evils of the world, without being called upon to any action with regard to them.

5 It requires a notable degree of moral culture to keep from becoming 'used to' such things; and there are few things worse for us than to grow accustomed to men's sufferings and their sins, so that these no longer evoke pity, or indignation, or any other emotion in us.

The great minds are those which show the least disposition to become familiar with wrong, so as not to feel indignation every time they see it. They have a moral 10 freshness which is our right and normal condition. They never 'get used to' good or evil.

It is very hard for us to keep this freshness of moral impression in our daily contact with what the newspaper tells us of the world's evil. It is even harder not to be deceived as to the comparative weight of evil and goodness in the world. The news-15 gatherer is drawn naturally to the former.

*From:* Post, *March 1899*

Annotations
1  **peril** danger
5  **accustomed to sth.** used to sth.
6  **suffering** pain
6  **evoke sth.** *etwas hervorrufen*
6  **indignation** *Empörung*
13 **deceive sb.** trick sb., make sb. believe that sth. false is true

**Comprehension**

**1** Summarize the editorial in two to three sentences.

**Analysis**

**2** Work on either task **a** or **b**.

**a** Examine the writer's attitude to the phenomenon they are describing. Give evidence from the text to support your points.

**b** Challenge Examine the writer's attitude to the phenomenon they are describing by analysing the stylistic devices used in the text.

**Language awareness**

**3** The editorial was written in 1899 and it differs from texts written nowadays.
    **a** Find words and phrases that are no longer commonly used today.
    **b** Rephrase the last two paragraphs in modern English.

▶ Check

**Beyond the text**

**4 a** With a partner, discuss to what extent the criticism expressed in the editorial is still representative for:
    • television
    • social media
    • newspapers.
    Present your findings in class.

> **Language help**
>
> In my opinion/view ... • The way I see it ... •
> Comparing the different forms of media ... •
> apply to • be (ir)relevant for ... • to a different
> extent

   **b** What could be done to counteract the phenomenon described in the text? Set up some guidelines for people your age. You may give differing guidelines for the three forms of media from **a**.

**Chapter task**

*After dealing with various aspects of the media, you will have the opportunity to put your argumentation and speaking skills to the test and show what you have learned about this topic by producing a podcast.*

You and your partner are going to produce a podcast on 'The media as a window to the world?' for senior students in the English classes at your school.

▶ Getting started

Prepare your podcast before recording it:
• Which aspects do you want to cover? Collect them and write them down.
• Who will present which aspects? Distribute them evenly.

Write a coherent script for your podcast, then record it (you may use your smartphone).

Present your podcast to your class.

# Chapter 4
# The USA – Land of Many Faces

1 a **Think** Write down the ideas that come into your head when you look at the 'puzzle' above.

b **Pair** Compare and discuss your ideas. Together come up with a caption for each photo in the puzzle.

c **Share** Present your captions in class and list your ideas on what makes the USA different from most European nations.

2 a Write down five sentences starting with 'The USA is …' and five sentences that start with 'The USA isn't …'. Give reasons for your statements.

b Discuss your sentences in small groups and agree on one sentence of each group. Then present the sentences to class, explaining why you chose them.

c ***Quick write**: Write a short paragraph about the guiding question on p. 115. Relate the concepts in the Chapter map to your own knowledge of the USA.

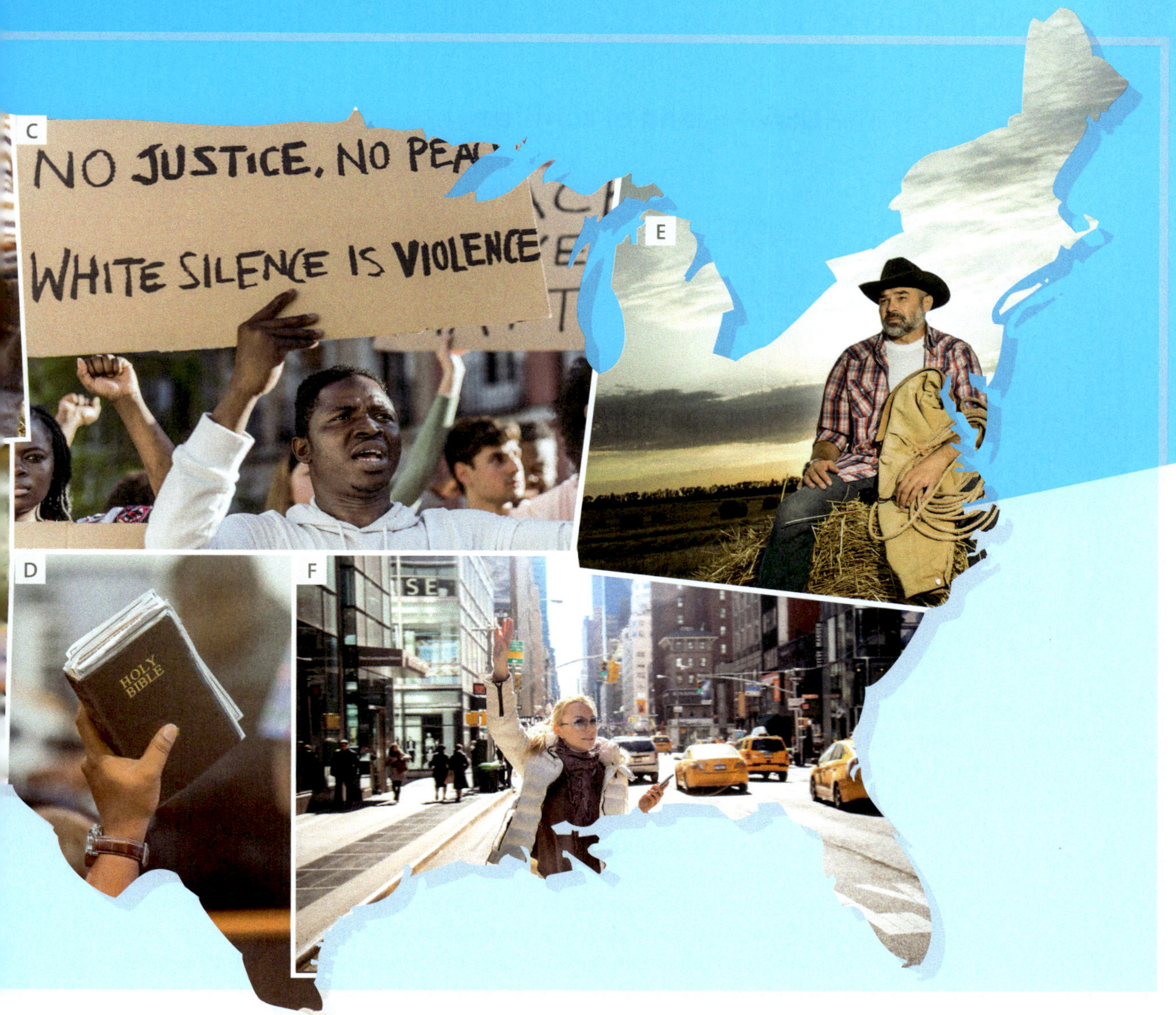

C

NO JUSTICE, NO PEA...

WHITE SILENCE IS VIOLENCE

E

D

F

> **Chapter map**

social class

development

history

ethnicity

dreams

Chapter task:
a discussion ✓

The USA – still a 'land of dreams'?

Listening

myth

immigration

reality

ideals

► More language

## 🔊 The USA – a land of conflicts

"'Life, liberty, and the pursuit of the almighty dollar' is too long. Let's change it to 'happiness.'"

CartoonStock.com

### A country founded on principle

The earliest document of the United States, the Declaration of Independence, begins with a statement of principle: that all people are created equal and have
5   equal rights and that all power derives from the will of the people. In the course of time, further notions have been added to the national myth, sometimes referred to as the *American Dream*. The most notable of these is equality of opportunity. It found popular ex-
10   pression in slogans such as *from rags to riches* or *the sky's the limit*. The belief that in the USA anyone, no matter how humble their origin, could work their way to the top attracted millions of immigrants in the 19th and 20th centuries. A rapidly expanding nation
15   offered seemingly endless opportunity to those with the ambition to succeed. Furthermore, the USA promised protection from persecution to those fleeing their homelands to escape political or religious persecution (► Info box 'Immigration', p. 145).

20   ### 'A house divided against itself cannot stand.'
Abraham Lincoln cited this quotation from the Bible in a speech he made in 1858. The conflict he alluded to in his speech was that between North and South over the issue of enslavement, which led to the Civil War (1861–1865). Today that
25   conflict is history, but the USA is still beset by problems resulting from the past: the legacy of discrimination against African Americans and Native Americans, the widening gap between rich and poor and the tensions between the USA's many ethnic minorities and the white mainstream society, often mirroring the contrast between rapidly growing urban areas and thinly populated rural regions. Moreover, the US
30   two-party system of government has become polarized to an extent unknown since the 1860s, with confrontation taking the place of cooperation and existing divisions being aggravated amid growing inequality and competition for resources.

► More info

### The road ahead
As the 21st century progresses, the US political system, now more than 200 years old,
35   is beginning to show signs of strain. One symptom is the discrepancy between election results and the popular vote, as in the presidential elections of 2000 and 2016. Moreover, because each state elects two senators, regardless of population, small states and rural regions exert a disproportionate influence on national politics. Issues such as gun control, abortion and police violence continue to split public opinion and
40   defy simple solutions. And yet, as the USA has demonstrated over and again in its history, it is a nation that possesses a unique capacity for reinventing itself. The USA of today is younger and more diverse than it has ever been before. It remains to be seen, however, whether the typically American belief that the future will be brighter than the past will once more hold true.

## 1 Main ideas

Read the text and complete the following sentences in at least two different ways:
1 The USA is unique among nations in that ...
2 In the course of its history, the USA has increasingly ...
3 After more than two centuries, the US political system ...

## 2 Reflect

a Write down three aspects that made the United States unique among nations at the time of its creation.
b Make a second list with examples of the duality of political and material ideals that can be seen in the USA's self-image. Make sure to refer to the cartoon on p. 116 as well.
c Make a third list with problems the United States of today has inherited from its history.

## 3 Mind mapping

One way to structure relevant vocabulary is to create a mind map of words that are linked with a certain topic.
a Create a mind map using vocabulary items from the text that you connect with the USA (e.g., equality of opportunity, two-party system, or gun control).
b Compare mind maps with your partner. Add any new items from your partner's mind map to your own.

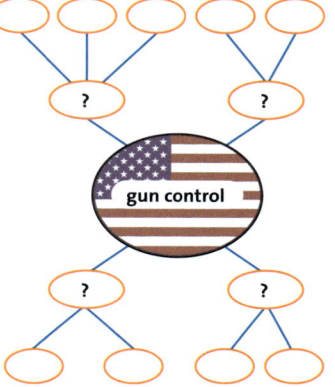

## 4 Chunk it!

a The text contains many chunks, for instance 'allude to ...', 'protection from ...', 'result from ...', 'show signs of ...' and 'influence on ...'. Complete each of these chunks starting with how they are used in the text and add at least two more examples for each chunk.

b Write a paragraph about the United States, using at least four of the chunks you formed in 4 a.

▶ Getting started

▶ Check

## 5  Over to you: a 'German Dream'?

Nowadays, many people worldwide dream of migrating to European countries like Germany. Is Germany 'the new USA'? Write a short blog post for your school's website, setting out your views.
a Go back to the first paragraph of the text and make notes on relevant aspects of the USA's worldwide appeal.
b Compare them with the present situation in Germany. Formulate your standpoint.
c Write your text.
d Swap texts with your partner. Discuss your views.

▶ SF 29: Writing a blog post, p. 384

▶ Check

▶More info

Annotations

1 **in the grips** *im Würgegriff*
4 **shuttered** closed down
5 **walk of life** field of employment
6 **pour** go in large numbers
9 **teeter on the brink of sth.** be close to sth. unpleasant
9 **be on the brink of sth.** be close to sth.
12 **the body politic** the people of a country (as a group)
13 **ongoing** still happening
13 **breach of sth.** violation of sth.
14 **procedural safeguard** *verfahrenstechnische Schutzmaßnahme*
14 **adherence** [əd'hıərəns] *Festhalten*
20 **vineyard** ['vınjəd] place where grapes are grown
22 **suffragist** person (usu. a woman) who fights for women's voting rights
22 **Pullman porters** The porters on the Pullman railroad service were entirely African Americans and their union was one of the most powerful African American organizations in the early 20th century.
23 **LGBTQ** = lesbian, gay, bisexual, transgender, queer
23 **picket sign** *(politisches) Plakat*
29 **discard sth.** throw sth. away
30 **cursory** brief, superficial
32 **subjugation** *Unterwerfung*
32 **rapacious** greedy
33 **complicit in sth.** involved in sth. dubious
33 **rigged** manipulated
36 **tempered** moderate

# At this moment in history   Barack Obama

• Imagine you were asked to speak on the state of the world today. What issues would you name?

*Barack Obama was President of the United States from 2009 until 2017, the first person of colour to hold this office. In his memoir from 2020 he looks at the state of the USA.*

As I sit here, the country remains in the grips of a global pandemic and the accompanying economic crisis, with more than 178,000 Americans dead, businesses shuttered, and millions of people out of
5 work. Across the nation, people from all walks of life have poured into the streets to protest the deaths of unarmed Black men and women at the hands of the police. Perhaps most troubling of all, our democracy seems to be teetering on the brink of crisis – a crisis
10 rooted in a fundamental contest between two opposing visions of what America is and what it should be; a crisis that has left the body politic divided, angry, and mistrustful, and has allowed for an ongoing breach of institutional norms, procedural safeguards, and the adherence to basic facts that both Republicans and
15 Democrats once took for granted.

This contest is not new, of course. In many ways, it has defined the American experience. It's embedded in founding documents that could simultaneously proclaim all men equal and yet count a slave as three-fifths of a man. [...] It's a contest that's been fought on the fields of Gettysburg and Appomattox but also in
20 the halls of Congress, on a bridge in Selma, across the vineyards of California, and down the streets of New York – a contest fought by soldiers but more often by union organizers, suffragists, Pullman porters, student leaders, waves of immigrants, and LGBTQ activists, armed with nothing more than picket signs, pamphlets, or a pair of marching shoes. At the heart of this long-running battle is a simple question: Do
25 we care to match the reality of America to its ideals? If so, do we really believe that our notions of self-government and individual freedom, equality of opportunity and equality before the law, apply to everybody? Or are we instead committed, in practice if not in statute, to reserving those things for a privileged few?

I recognize that there are those who believe that it's time to discard the myth – that
30 an examination of America's past and an even cursory glance at today's headlines show that this nation's ideals have always been secondary to conquest and subjugation, a racial caste system and rapacious capitalism, and that to pretend otherwise is to be complicit in a game that was rigged from the start. And I confess that there have been times during the course of writing this book, as I've reflected
35 on my presidency and all that's happened since, when I've had to ask myself whether I was too tempered in speaking the truth as I saw it, too cautious in either word or deed, convinced as I was that by appealing to what Lincoln called the better angels of our nature I stood a greater chance of leading us in the direction of the America we've been promised.

40 I don't know. What I can say for certain is that I'm not yet ready to abandon the possibility of America – not just for the sake of future generations of Americans but for all of humankind. For I'm convinced that the pandemic we're currently living through is both a manifestation of and a mere interruption in the relentless march toward an interconnected world, one in which peoples and cultures
45 can't help but collide. In that world – of global supply chains, instantaneous capital transfers, social media, transnational terrorist networks, climate change, mass migration, and ever-increasing complexity – we will learn to live together, cooperate with one another, and recognize the dignity of others, or we will perish. And so the world watches America – the only great power in history made up of people from
50 every corner of the planet, comprising every race and faith and cultural practice – to see if our experiment in democracy can work. To see if we can do what no other nation has ever done. To see if we can actually live up to the meaning of our creed.

*From:* A Promised Land, *2020*

Annotations
43 **manifestation** *Erscheinungsform*
43 **relentless** unstoppable
48 **perish** *vergehen*

## Comprehension

**1** Summarize Obama's views on the USA.

► Support, p. 312

## Analysis

**2** Analyse the link between the success or failure of the 'American experiment' (l. 51) and the situation of the global community.

**3** Work on task **a** or **b**.

| | |
|---|---|
| **a** Examine the different roles Obama plays in the course of the excerpt. | **b** Challenge Analyse how Obama influences the reader to accept his credibility as an interpreter of the American experience. |

## Language awareness

**4** Even though the text is an extract from a book, its style frequently resembles that of a *speech. Point out aspects of the text that make it seem as if it was a speech.

► Support, p. 312

## Beyond the text

**5** Obama makes *allusions to a number of events from US history (cf. ll. 19–21). Research the references below and explain to your class why they are relevant for Obama's argumentation:
1 the fields of Gettysburg and Appomattox
2 a bridge in Selma
3 the vineyards of California (search the words 'Delano grape strike')
4 the streets of New York (search the words 'Occupy Wall Street').

► SF 13: Doing research, p. 360

**6** Speaking Form small groups and debate the following statement:
'The success or failure of the American experiment is a matter of international concern.'

► SF 47: Having a debate, p. 412
► Getting started

## Keystones of US democracy

Advanced

Plantation in the English colonies in the 17th century

- The United States of America was one of the first democratic states in the modern world.
  Form small groups and collect ideas on one of the following questions:
  - How do you think European heads of state reacted to the 'American experiment' at the time?
  - What thoughts, hopes and fears do you think the US 'rebels' had on the eve of independence?

Compare your ideas in class.

**Language help**

| | |
|---|---|
| feel sceptical about … | have worries about … |
| scoff at the idea of … | feel uncertain about the outcome of … |
| ridicule the notion of … | feel confident that … |

▶ More info

### The Declaration of Independence

*In the second half of the 18th century, the American colonies were largely autonomous and fairly prosperous. Tensions with Britain arose over the policies and taxation imposed on the colonists, who resented the fact that they had no voice in Parliament. Representatives of the 13 colonies in North America met in Philadelphia and declared their independence from Great Britain on 2 July, 1776. The Declaration of Independence was ratified and published on 4 July, 1776. The excerpt below is from the Preamble.*

Annotations
5  **assume sth.** (here) take sth.
5  **station** *(n)* position
7  **impel sb.** urge sb.
10 **endow** provide
10 **unalienable** absolute
12 **derive sth. from sth.** *ableiten von*

**In Congress, July 4, 1776**
**The unanimous Declaration of the thirteen united States of America**

[…] When in the Course of human events, it becomes necessary for one people to dissolve the political bands which have connected them with another, and to
5  assume among the powers of the earth, the separate and equal station to which the Laws of Nature and of Nature's God entitle them, a decent respect to the opinions of mankind requires that they should declare the causes which impel them to the separation.

We hold these truths to be self-evident, that all men are created equal, that they are
10 endowed by their Creator with certain unalienable Rights, that among these are Life, Liberty and the pursuit of Happiness. – That to secure these rights, Governments are instituted among Men, deriving their just powers from the consent of the governed, – That whenever any Form of Government becomes destructive of these ends, it is the Right of the People to alter or to abolish it, and to institute new
15 Government, laying its foundation on such principles and organizing its powers in such form, as to them shall seem most likely to effect their Safety and Happiness. […]

### Comprehension

**1** State in your own words the reasons the authors give for declaring independence.

Advanced

### Analysis

**2** Work on either **a** or **b**.

**a** Examine the connection between the ideas contained in the text and the decision of the colonies to declare themselves independent.

**b** Challenge Analyse how the authors of the Declaration present their own behaviour towards the British crown.

### Language awareness

**3 a** Examine the language of the text. Explain in what ways it differs from modern English and what effect these differences have on modern readers.

**b** Rephrase ll. 9–11 in modern English and compare the effect of your version with that of the original.

### Beyond the text

**4** Writing Is the statement of human rights contained in the Declaration still up to date? What changes would you suggest? Write a short *comment.

▶ SF 28: Argumentative writing: discussion and comment, p. 382

▶ Check

## The Constitution

*After winning independence from Britain in 1783, the former colonies soon realized that they needed a strong central government. Meeting in Philadelphia in 1787, representatives of the 13 states drafted the Constitution of the United States, which came into effect in 1789. The Constitution details the structure of the federal government; it is based on the principles of the division of power and the system of checks and balances.*

### Comprehension

**5** Work with a partner.
**Partner A:** Study the chart on p. 435. Explain to your partner how the US system of government works.
**Partner B:** Study the chart on p. 437. Explain to your partner how the German system of government works.

Liberty Bell, Philadelphia

### Analysis

**6** Compare the government structures of the USA and Germany. Point out parallels and differences.

## The Bill of Rights

*The authors of the Constitution concentrated on the structure and the functioning of the federal government. Upon completion of their task, they realized that they had said nothing about the rights of the ordinary citizen. In 1787, ten 'amendments' to the Constitution were adopted, known collectively as the 'Bill of Rights'. Since 1789, only 17 further amendments have been ratified, among them such notable landmarks as the 14th Amendment (1868), which granted full citizenship to all persons born in the USA, including former enslaved persons.*

▶ More info

## Annotations

1 **amendment** *Ergänzung/Zusatzartikel*
3 **abridge sth.** (here) limit sth., deprive sb. of sth.
5 **redress** *(n)* compensation, remedy
5 **grievance** *Missstand*
8 **infringe sth.** limit sth., restrict sth.
11 **seizure** [ˈsiːʒə] (here) confiscation
11 **violate sth.** break sth., e.g. a rule
11 **warrant** *(n)* authorization issued by a judge

## Amendment I

Congress shall make no law respecting an establishment of religion, or prohibiting the free exercise thereof; or abridging the freedom of speech, or of the press; or the right of the people peaceably to assemble, and to petition the Government for a
5 redress of grievances.

## Amendment II

A well regulated Militia, being necessary to the security of a free State, the right of the people to keep and bear Arms, shall not be infringed.

## Amendment IV

10 The right of the people to be secure in their persons, houses, papers, and effects, against unreasonable searches and seizures, shall not be violated, and no Warrants shall issue, but upon probable cause, supported by Oath or affirmation, and particularly describing the place to be searched, and the persons or things to be seized.

> **Info**
>
> A militia is a group of ordinary citizens trained in the use of weapons. Before the War of Independence, many colonists owned firearms for hunting and/or self defense. When the conflict with Britain escalated, a militant group calling themselves the 'Sons of Liberty' played an important role in the defense of the
> 5 citizenry against the British Army. After the war, the so-called 'Continental Army' of General Washington was disbanded and without a regular army or police force, the existence of a militia was considered a necessity.

### Comprehension

**7 a**   Writing   Rephrase the first two amendments in modern English.
    **b**   Compare texts with your partner. Discuss any similarities/differences between your texts.

### Analysis

 ►Check

**8 a**   Examine the situations below. Decide if the behaviour described is protected by the Bill of Rights. Explain why or why not.

| | |
|---|---|
| **A** | A student who belongs to Jehovah's Witnesses hands out religious pamphlets to other students during breaks at his public high school. |
| **B** | A journalist writes an article about a state governor and calls him a liar. |
| **C** | A public school prohibits students from carrying knives on the school grounds. |
| **D** | An atheist parent objects to her child being forced to recite the Pledge of Allegiance because it contains the words 'one nation under God'. |

    **b**   Compare and discuss your results in your class.

**Beyond the text**

**9  a**  The table below lists cases which have been ruled on by the Supreme Court. Choose two and speculate how the judges might have decided in accordance with the Amendments I, II or IV.

▶ More info

**b**  Find students who have chosen different cases and present your results to each other.

**A**  In 1960, a school prohibited students from wearing armbands to protest against the Vietnam War.

**B**  A baker refused to make a cake for a gay wedding on the grounds of his religious opposition to same-sex marriage.

**C**  Some teenagers burned a cross on a Black family's lawn.

**D**  The Washington D.C. Firearms Regulation Act of 1975 required firearms to be kept unloaded and disassembled or bound by a trigger lock.

**E**  A drunken driver managed to get home before a police car could stop him but the police officer followed him into his home. The driver was charged with the misdemeanour of DUI and arrested.

**c**  Your teacher will provide the outcomes of all five cases. Discuss whether you agree with the Supreme Court rulings.

Annotations
**disassemble sth.** *etwas auseinanderbauen*
**trigger lock** *Abzugssperre bei Waffen*
**misdemeanour** [ˌmɪsdɪˈmiːnə] bad or unacceptable behaviour
**DUI** = **d**riving **u**nder the **i**nfluence of alcohol (or drugs)

## Text 3

**Info**

### American exceptionalism

The stunning declaration of human rights in the preface to the Declaration of Independence (equality, unalienable rights) was originally composed to justify a rebellion, but the document set high standards for a
5 young nation still in the making. For the first time in modern history, a nation was to be founded on the principles of human rights, equality and democracy. This sense of uniqueness gave US politics an almost missionary zeal, a feeling of moral superiority to all
10 other nations. At the same time, the Founding Fathers were aware of having embarked on an experiment that no one before them had ever believed possible; the fear that the experiment could end in chaos haunted the USA's early leaders for generations.

Engraving of the painting 'Declaration of Independence' by John Trumbull on the US two-dollar bill

**1**  Write down the ideals that Americans might say make their country unique.

## The great nation of futurity   John O'Sullivan

**Annotations**

- **futurity** state of belonging to the future
1 **derive sth. from sth. else** *etwas von etwas ableiten*
4 **but** (here) only
12 **expansive** boundless
13 **untrodden** *unberührt*
13 **beneficent** [bɪˈnefɪsnt] *wohltätig*
14 **object** goal
14 **unsullied** *unbefleckt*
16 **Providence** (here) *Gott*
18 **'the gates of hell ... against it'** allusion to Gospel of Matthew 16:18
20 **enfranchisement** voting rights
21 **cynosure** [ˈsaɪnəʃʊə] (*fml*) *Leitbild*
21 **exemplar** good example of sth.
22 **correlative** corresponding
22 **effulgence** bright light
23 **retrograde** [ˈretrəgreɪd] move backward
23 **dissolve sth.** *etwas auflösen*
23 **subvert sth.** damage or destroy sth.
23 **we must onward** = we must move onward
27 **decree** (*n*) law, rule
29 **salvation** *Erlösung*
29 **immutable** unchanging
30 **blessed** [ˈblesɪd] *gesegnet*
32 **smite** (*old-fashioned*) defeat
32 **hierarch** high priest
33 **tidings** news
33 **myriad** large number of people

- ***Quick write:** Which countries would you refer to as having a 'glorious past'?

*The USA is unique in having a sense of a mission in the world, one dating back to its origins, as magazine editor John O'Sullivan points out in this essay from 1839.*

The American people having derived their origin from many other nations, and the Declaration of National Independence being entirely based on the great principle of human equality, these facts demonstrate at once our disconnected position as regards any other nation; that we have, in reality, but little connection with the past history of
5 any of them, and still less with all antiquity, its glories, or its crimes. On the contrary, our national birth was the beginning of a new history, the formation and progress of an untried political system, which separates us from the past and connects us with the future only; and so far as regards the entire development of the natural rights of man, in moral, political, and national life, we may confidently assume that our coun-
10 try is destined to be the great nation of futurity. [...]

We have no interest in the scenes of antiquity, only as lessons of avoidance of nearly all their examples. The expansive future is our arena, and for our history. We are entering on its untrodden space, with the truths of God in our minds, beneficent objects in our hearts, and with a clear conscience unsullied by the past. We are
15 the nation of human progress, and who will, what can, set limits to our onward march? Providence is with us, and no earthly power can. We point to the everlasting truth on the first page of our national declaration, and we proclaim to the millions of other lands, that 'the gates of hell' – the powers of aristocracy and monarchy – 'shall not prevail against it.' [...]

20 Yes, we are the nation of progress, of individual freedom, of universal enfranchisement. Equality of rights is the cynosure of our union of States, the grand exemplar of the correlative equality of individuals; and while truth sheds its effulgence, we cannot retrograde, without dissolving the one and subverting the other. We must onward to the fulfilment of our mission – to the entire development of the principle
25 of our organization – freedom of conscience, freedom of person, freedom of trade and business pursuits, universality of freedom and equality. This is our high destiny, and in nature's eternal, inevitable decree of cause and effect we must accomplish it. All this will be our future history, to establish on earth the moral dignity and salvation of man – the immutable truth and beneficence of God. For
30 this blessed mission to the nations of the world, which are shut out from the life-giving light of truth, has America been chosen; and her high example shall smite unto death the tyranny of kings, hierarchs, and oligarchs, and carry the glad tidings of peace and good will where myriads now endure an existence scarcely more enviable than that of beasts of the field. Who, then, can doubt that our country
35 is destined to be *the great nation* of futurity?

*From:* The United States Democratic Review, *1839*

### Comprehension

1 Describe the relationship between the United States and other countries as presented in the text.

Advanced

### Analysis

**2** Work on task **a** or **b**.

**a** People sometimes refer to the USA as 'God's own country'. Point out *allusions to God in the text and analyse their meaning.

**b** Challenge Analyse the connection between religious belief and political thought in the essay.

**3** Examine how O'Sullivan reinterprets the notion of American exceptionalism (cf. Info box p. 123).

### Language awareness

**4 a** In the second half of the text O'Sullivan's *style becomes increasingly emotional and dramatic. Point to examples.

**b** Rephrase a few sentences in a more neutral style and examine the difference.

### Beyond the text

**5** Writing A contemporary magazine has included this article in its latest issue. Write a *letter to the editor, expressing your reaction to O'Sullivan's essay.

▶ Getting started

▶ Check

**Text 4**

# Art in Context: American Progress

Info

**Territorial expansion**

By the time the United States was founded, it was clear to most settlers that their future lay westward. When Napoleon sold the French territory in the centre of the continent to the USA in 1803, the area of the country was doubled. In 1819 Spain ceded Florida to the USA; Texas, which had broken away
5 from Mexico, joined the Union in 1845. The Mexican-American War ended with the annexation of the Southwest as far as California in 1848 and in 1867 the US government bought Alaska from Russia.

The Native American population had to pay a high price for US expansion. As settlers pushed westward, the US Army was deployed to drive the last
10 Native American tribes from the Great Plains. The indigenous peoples were forced to live on so-called reservations. Deprived of their traditional way of life, they became in effect welfare recipients of the federal government. It wasn't until 1924 that the 'Indian Citizenship Act' made them citizens of the country that had once been theirs.

**1** For the first century of their history, Americans were pre-occupied with pushing the 'frontier' (the invisible line separating civilization and wilderness) further westward. Speculate on the effect of this on the American national character.

John Gast, 'American Progress', 1872

▶ Getting started

▶ SF 23: Analysing visuals, p. 374

▶ More language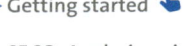

**Info**

**John Gast** (1842 – 1896) was a US painter. He was born in Berlin but his family emigrated to the USA when he was a child. 'American Progress' was his most famous work.

▶ Getting started

▶ More language

### Comprehension

1  a  Describe what you can see in the picture above. Work from right to left.
   b  Compare results with your partner. Add missing details to your list.

### Analysis

2  Relate the title of the painting to the direction of movement from right to left depicted by the artist.

### Beyond the text

3  **You choose**  **Writing**  Work on task **a** or **b**.

   a  Your class is preparing an online presentation on 19th century US history. Write a short text in which you explain the importance of Gast's painting.

   b  Some Native Americans have argued that this painting should be removed from public display. Find arguments to support their case.

4  **Intercultural competence**  Choose a painting from your country that you believe says a lot about your country. Explain its content and meaning and compare it to John Gast's 'American Progress'.

5  📖  Think back to the guiding question of the chapter and reconsider what you wrote in your paragraph on p. 114. Take into account everything you have learned so far.

# Focus on test formats

*As part of your* Abitur *exam and in some of your course exams, your listening skills will be tested using closed and semi-closed test formats.*
*Read the following tasks:*

**Task 1 (multiple choice):** *You are going to hear an excerpt from the podcast 'Fair and Square'. Host Ralph MacKenzie interviews Cilla Cossens, a professor at Madison University, on the history of affirmative action. Listen to the excerpt and choose the correct completion of each of the following sentences (only one is correct).*

1  The guest is a professor of
   a  history.
   b  natural science.
   c  political science.

2  Prof. Cossens says that the roots of affirmative action go back to
   a  the 14th Amendment.
   b  the Civil War.
   c  the age of enslavement.

3  The equal protection clause applies to
   a  all people born in the US.
   b  all citizens of the US.
   c  all people living in the US.

4  The Supreme Court decision in the case of Brown vs the Board of Education meant
   a  the end of segregated schools.
   b  the beginning of affirmative action.
   c  the beginning of the Civil Rights Movement.

5  Prof. Cossens says that affirmative action was the first attempt to address
   a  social inequality.
   b  discrimination.
   c  past injustice.

6  Under President Nixon, federal affirmative action rules applied to
   a  all private colleges.
   b  all firms that received federal support.
   c  all government agencies.

**Task 2 (short answers):** *You are going to hear a second excerpt from the same interview.*

Answer the following questions. You need not write complete sentences.
1  Who was given a bonus in the college admission process in the 70s and 80s
2  What percentage doubled between 1965 and 2001
3  What the Supreme Court ruled in 1978

▶ SF 2: Working with closed test formats, p. 347

▶ SF 39: Essentials: listening and viewing, p. 398

▶ Check

**Info**

The different **test formats** are presented here separately to aid practice. It is useful to keep in mind, however, that some tests might include tasks with a combination of the different formats.

4　What nine states have done since 1990
5　Who the plaintiff in the 2023 decision is
6　What the Supreme Court decided recently

▶ Check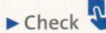

🔊 **Task 3 (multiple matching):** *You will hear five speakers (1–5) talking about the 2023 Supreme court decision on affirmative action. Choose from the list (A–G) the statement that each speaker makes. There is only one correct answer per speaker. Copy the table below and put the corresponding letter (A–G) into the correct box. There are two extra statements that you will not need.*

A　The speaker accuses liberal critics of the Court decision of employing a double standard.

B　The speaker criticizes the Supreme Court for the lack of impartiality.

C　The speaker praises the Supreme Court decision for ending a questionable practice.

D　The speaker believes that the Supreme Court decision on affirmative action reflects a misunderstanding of the proper role of the Court.

E　The speaker sees a disparity between US society and the decision of the Supreme Court.

F　The speaker believes that the Supreme Court ruling will not have a noticeable impact on diversity in higher education.

G　The speaker criticizes the Supreme Court for undoing the progress of the last fifty years.

Supreme Court, Washington D.C.

| Speaker | 1 | 2 | 3 | 4 | 5 |
|---------|---|---|---|---|---|
| Statement | ... | ... | ... | ... | ... |

## Work it out

*In this section you are led step by step through the tasks presented above. The strategies you learn here can help you do other types of listening tasks as well.*

### Pre-listening

*In a typical exam situation you are given an opportunity to read the tasks before listening to the recording. You may also be allowed to ask about unfamiliar vocabulary.*

**1　Examining the background information**

a　Read the texts that introduce each of the three tasks. For each of the tasks, answer the following questions:
- What information are you given by the text?
- What challenges do you anticipate while listening?

b　Compare answers with your partner. Together, formulate strategies that can help you to deal with the challenges you may encounter.

## 2 Examining the tasks

a  Read the task items closely. For each item, choose two or three keywords to listen for.

b  The speaker may not use exactly the same wording as the task. For the keywords you chose in **2a**, think of synonyms or other words that belong to the same word field. Keep them in mind while listening to the recording.

### While-listening

## 3 Listening strategies

▶ More language

a  You will hear the recording twice. There are different strategies for dealing with this situation. Compare the two strategies described below. What advantages and disadvantages does each of them have?
**Strategy a:** While listening for the first time, I don't write down anything. I concentrate on what the speakers are saying and listen for the gist.
**Strategy b:** While listening for the first time, I write down the answers I am sure of. When I hear the text the second time, I concentrate on the remaining tasks.

b  Which strategy would you use in an exam? Say why.

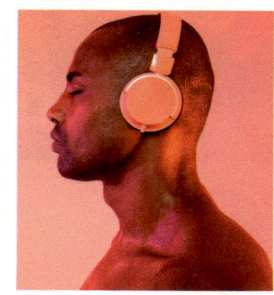

## 4 Doing multiple-choice tasks

All of the following statements are wrong. Correct them and add any other tips that you think are helpful for doing multiple-choice tests.
1  You lose one point for every wrong answer.
2  More than one answer can be correct.
3  It's better not to mark anything if you don't know the right answer.
4  Identifying wrong answers won't help you.

## 5 Doing short-answer tasks

a  Examine the following checklist and decide which points are relevant for doing short-answer listening tasks:
1  Using correct grammar and spelling.
2  Listening for keywords.
3  Using the same words as the original text.
4  Writing complete sentences.

b  Say which of the following are true or false when doing short-answer listening tasks:
1  Write the answer in German if you don't know the English word.
2  The questions are in the same order as the relevant information in the spoken text.
3  If you don't know the answer, don't write anything.
4  Make an intelligent guess even if you aren't sure it's correct.

c  Compare answers to **a** and **b** with your partner. If you aren't sure what is right, ask your teacher.

### 6   Doing multiple-matching tasks

a   Write three tips for doing multiple-matching tasks.
b   Compare results with your partner.

#### Post-listening

### 7   Checking your answers

Normally you will be given a short time after listening to complete your work. Check that you have done all the tasks. If you alter one of your answers, make sure that your final choice is clearly recognizable.

## Do it

### 8   Working on the task

Listen to the excerpts from the audios and do the three tasks on pp. 127–128.

## Feedback

### 9   Self-assessment

a   After you have corrected your answers, listen to the parts of the exam again that caused you difficulty by using the Cornelsen Lernen App.
b   On the basis of your results from **1–6**, make a *method card with the aspects you had difficulty with. Think of ways to improve your listening skills.
c   Add useful strategies for dealing with listening comprehension tasks to your method card.

▶ WOB: pp. 78–81

# Broomfield – the spirit of the dream

- *\*Quick write:* What comes into your mind when you think of small-town America? You can use a digital feedback or mind-mapping tool if possible.

*Watch this video about the history of a small town in the American West.*

**Info**

**Broomfield** is a town and a county near Denver in Colorado with a population of about 70,000.

▶ SF 40: Listening/Viewing for gist and detail, p. 399

▶ Check 👆

### Comprehension

**1** `Viewing` Match the following events in the history of Broomfield to the dates. Copy the table with the dates, then fill in the letters A–G. Some dates may be used more than once.

| Events | |
|---|---|
| A | creation of a suburb |
| B | change of state constitution to create a city county |
| C | people feeling a great nostalgia for 1950s Broomfield |
| D | suggestion of the name Broomfield by US Postal Office |
| E | creation of homes for returning veterans |
| F | Colorado Gold rush, homesteaders passing through |
| G | homeownership going up dramatically |

| 1859 | ... |
|---|---|
| 1884 | ... |
| 1950s | ... |
| 1960s | ... |
| 1970s | ... |
| Present and future | ... |

**2** `Viewing` Watch the trailer a second time. Make notes on the values that the people of Broomfield name as characteristic.

### Beyond the text

**3** **a** Compare the video to your initial impressions from the **Quick write**.
   **b** `Intercultural competence` Compare Broomfield with a small town in Germany you are familiar with. Point to similarities and differences.

Text 6

# The myth of the 'Lost cause'

`Advanced`

- With a partner, define the concept of a 'lost cause'. Use a dictionary if necessary.

*You are going to hear an excerpt from a history podcast. Host Joseph Coohill ('Professor Buzzkill') and his guest, historian Phil Nash, talk about the 'Lost cause' myth of the US-American South and the six principles ('tenets') it implies.*

Rock relief on Stone Mountain, Georgia, completed in 1972, depicting three Confederate generals. Regarded as a cultural asset by some and 'the three losers' by others.

Advanced

## Comprehension

► Check 🔖

🔊 **1** `Listening` Choose from the list below which statement A–H best matches which category in the table on the left. There is one more statement than you need.

| Category | Statement |
|---|---|
| 'Lost cause' myth definition | |
| Tenet 1 | |
| Tenet 2 | |
| Tenet 3 | |
| Tenet 4 | |
| Tenet 5 | |
| Tenet 6 | |

| Statements / Headings / Concepts | |
|---|---|
| A | Benefiting from enslavement |
| B | An ideal picture of the South before the Civil War |
| C | An undeserved victory |
| D | A Northern form of enslavement |
| E | Regretting the disappearance of the Southern lifestyle |
| F | A thriving Southern economy |
| G | Southern self-assertion against Northern dominance |
| H | The fine Southern character |

## Beyond the text

**2** Compare the contents of the 'Lost cause' myth with your knowledge of US history and the causes of the Civil War.

**3** `Intercultural competence` Discuss the dangers of preserving and cultivating a narrative that distorts the past.

► More info 🔖

The first enslaved people from Africa arrived by ship in Jamestown, Virginia in 1619, followed by hundreds of thousands more. Their importation was only declared illegal in 1807 although their population continued to grow in the US.

**Info**

### Enslavement in the 'Land of the Free'

Enslavement was a controversial issue in the early days of the republic. Thomas Jefferson and George Washington, both plantation owners, promoted human rights and equality despite enslaving people. While enslavement was illegal in the northern states, it was crucial to the economy of the South. Enslaved persons
5 were not recognized as citizens, had no legal rights and remained enslaved even if they escaped to the North.
As the nation expanded westward, the question arose whether enslavement was to be permitted in the new states. Southern settlers wanted to keep their enslaved people, while abolitionists called for their liberation. In 1860 Abraham
10 Lincoln ran for election, promising to abolish enslavement in the USA. When he won, eleven southern states declared independence, forming the Confederacy of States, and a Civil War followed that left the South in ruins. Enslavement was abolished and military governments were installed in the rebellious states.
The 14th and 15th Amendments to the Constitution granted citizenship and
15 voting rights to all persons born in the USA. But when the army was withdrawn from the South in 1877, a white backlash set in and the situation worsened for African Americans.

**1** Make notes on the history of enslavement in the USA. Then explain to your partner how Black people have been disadvantaged throughout US history.

# The health card   Alice Childress

▶ More info 🔗

- How do you react when asked to show proof of vaccination? Why?

*In the 1950s, Black and white US-Americans still lived in different worlds, as the following \*short story from New York illustrates.*

Well, Marge, I started an extra job today. ... Just wait, girl. Don't laugh yet. Just wait till I tell you. ... The woman seems real nice. ... Well, you know what I mean. ... She was pretty nice, anyway. Shows me this and shows me that, but she was real cautious about loadin' on too much work the first morning. And she stopped short
5 when she caught the light in my eye.

Comes the afternoon, I was busy waxin' woodwork when I notice her hoverin' over me kind of timid-like. She passed me once and smiled and then she turned and blushed a little. I put down the wax can and gave her an inquirin' look. The lady takes a deep breath and comes up with, 'Do you live in Harlem, Mildred?'
10 Now, you know I expected somethin' more than that after all the hesitatin'. I had already given her my address so I didn't quite get the idea behind the question. 'Yes, Mrs. Jones,' I answered, 'that is where I live.'

Well, she backed away and retired to the living room and I could hear her and the husband just a-buzzin'. A little later on I was in the kitchen washin' glasses. I looks
15 up and there she was in the doorway, lookin' kind of strained around the gills. First she stuttered and then she stammered and after beatin' all around the bush she comes out with, 'Do you have a health card, Mildred?'

That let the cat out of the bag. I thought real fast. Honey, my brain was runnin' on wheels. 'Yes, Mrs. Jones,' I says, 'I have a health card.' Now Marge, this is a lie. I do
20 not have a health card. 'I'll bring it tomorrow,' I add real sweet-like.

She beams like a chromium platter and all you could see above her taffeta housecoat is smile. 'Mildred,' she said, 'I don't mean any offense, but one must be careful, mustn't one?'

Well, all she got from me was solid agreement. 'Sure,' I said, 'indeed one must, and
25 I am glad you are so understandin', 'cause I was just worryin' and studyin' on how I was goin' to ask you for yours, and of course you'll let me see one from your husband and one for each of the three children.'

By that time she was the same color as the housecoat, which is green, but I continue on: 'Since I have to handle laundry and make beds, you know ...' She stops me
30 right there and after excusin' herself she scurries from the room and has another conference with hubby.

Inside fifteen minutes she was back. 'Mildred, you don't have to bring a health card. I am sure it will be all right.'

I looked up real casual kind-of and said, 'On second thought, you folks look real
35 clean, too, so ...' And then she smiled and I smiled and then she smiled again. ... Oh, stop laughin' so loud, Marge, everybody on this bus is starin'.

*From:* Like One of the Family, *1956*

## Annotations

6 **hover**  wait somewhere, esp. near sb.
8 **blush**  turn red
14 **a-buzzin'**  (here) speaking in low voices
15 **gills** *(pl)* Kiemen
16 **beat around the bush**  talk for a long time without coming to the main point
18 **let the cat out of the bag**  (here) finally say what you want to say
21 **beam**  (here) smile happily
21 **chromium platter** *verchromte Servierplatte*
21 **taffeta**  type of material
25 **study** *(sl)* think

### Info

**The American short story**
Literature 'made in USA' emerged around the middle of the 19th century. US authors like Edgar Allan Poe, Nathaniel Hawthorne and Stephen Crane made a name for themselves with short prose pieces – the first short stories of the modern era. In the 20th century, authors like Ernest Hemingway and Shirley Jackson helped establish the short story as a literary genre.

## Comprehension

**1**  Summarize the \*plot in your own words.

► Getting started

**Analysis**

2   Analyse the \*conflict in the story and how it is resolved.

3   Describe the situation in which the \*narrator tells her story. Analyse how the given narrative situation influences the reader.

**Language awareness**

► Support, p. 312

4   Compare the language used by the narrator and her white employer, also focusing on linguistic features such as differences in grammar and pronunciation.

**Beyond the text**

► SF 46: Having a
    discussion, p. 410
► Getting started

5   Speaking  'Alice Childress's short story shows how class differences and racial conflicts can be settled through humour and mutual acceptance.' Do you agree? Discuss in small groups.

## Text 8

### In search of the American Dream   Alan Ehrenhalt

► Info box 'Immigration',
    p. 145

• What comes into your mind when you hear the phrase 'the American Dream'? Compare your reactions.

*In the following text, the author traces the meanings of the American Dream from its origins to the present.*

**Annotations**
2  **conceit** phenomenon, idea
6  **Depression** worldwide economic crisis lasting from 1929 to 1939
17 **cold-water tenement flat** low-quality apartment with no hot running water

It may seem that American Dream fantasies must date back to the founding of the Republic, but in fact they are a modern conceit. The phrase 'American Dream' was first used in 1931 by the historian James Truslow Adams in his book *The Epic of America*. It meant, he wrote, 'that dream of a land in which life should be better
5  and richer and fuller for everyone.' Better and richer and fuller in what way? He didn't say. Maybe in the middle of the Depression it seemed obvious. It doesn't seem quite so obvious now.

What's clearly true is that the American Dream has meant vastly different things to people in different times and places – if it has any sort of genuine meaning at
10 all. It's interesting that when ordinary Americans are asked if they feel the Dream has somehow been lost, it is the more recent immigrants who say it hasn't. [...] I think they consider their arrival and continued presence in this country to be the realization of a dream in itself.

That's been the case with previous generations. A couple of decades ago, I spent
15 some time talking to second-generation immigrant families who were able to afford small but neat bungalows on Chicago's Southwest Side. These were people who had spent the Depression and war years in cold-water tenement flats a short distance away. Those two-bedroom brick bungalows were the American Dream for them. But not forever. By the early 1960s, many of them had bought bigger ranch
20 houses with back yards in suburbs south of the city limits. A house with a yard, and

a job that supported the mortgage payment, were their new incarnation of the American Dream.

I came away from those conversations convinced that whatever the American Dream might be at a given time, real estate had something to do with it. And I still
25 tend to believe that. There are a lot of people right now with lower-middle-class service jobs in Chicago or San Francisco or Seattle for whom a small affordable apartment convenient to work would be more than dream enough. Maybe that's one piece of the American Dream we could actually work on.

But better housing isn't the only thing Americans like to fantasize about. Millions
30 of them have been persuaded that the core of the Dream for an ordinary family is the assurance that their children will live a better (or at least more affluent) life than they have been able to live. I don't know how this became conventional wisdom, but when you think about it, it doesn't make much sense. Generational prosperity is cyclical, not linear. There are no guarantees, and never have been. If you gradu-
35 ated from high school or college in 1930, you faced far bleaker economic prospects than if you had graduated in 1910. By 1950, things were looking up again. In 2010, opportunity was curtailed by another stagnation. To take it as a given that your children should out-achieve you is to swallow a proposition that ends up causing much of the American public needless feelings of anxiety and nights of insomnia.

40 When the aging discontented of the right rhapsodize these days about the American Dream, they are usually talking about an image of the postwar years. It is an image that is based largely on homogeneity. Suppose that in the 1950s you were a decently paid industrial worker in Wisconsin or Iowa, for example, and that you lived in a small town where nearly everyone behaved like you, thought like you and
45 very likely even looked like you. It was a comfortable and reassuring existence. Elite opinion now inveighs against homogeneity and preaches the virtues of diverse communities. But the hard reality is that most people tend to be happier in homogeneous surroundings. Decades of reliable research have proved this to be true, though it may be an uncomfortable fact.

50 And suppose that, at this point in the 21st century, this same town has been heavily impacted by the disappearance of steady factory work and the arrival of a large cohort of immigrants who speak little English, eat unfamiliar kinds of food, and do the low-paid service work or grubby blue-collar tasks that now dominate the local economy. There is no legitimate reason to resent or dislike these people. But it is
55 not surprising that the old-timers would feel something precious has been taken away from them – that they have lost the American Dream.

It's worth pointing out, though, that as the postwar middle-class Americans of midwestern towns thrived on their version of the American Dream, millions of young people who rejected that world had a safety valve that allowed them to es-
60 cape from it. For the youthful malcontents of small-town America in the 1950s, the dream to be pursued was a move to New York or Chicago or Boston or San Francisco. It was a job in the arts, or journalism, or in the academy. These were the dissidents who believed in Scott Fitzgerald's dictum that the American Dream was discovery and individualism.

65 Today, in a new century, the safety valve scarcely exists. There are no cheap apartments available to young people in the hot cities of 2020, and very few appealing

Annotations
21 **mortgage payment** *Hypothekenrate*
37 **curtail sth.** limit sth.
40 **rhapsodize** talk with enthusiasm about sth.
46 **inveigh against sth.** criticize sth. strongly
53 **grubby** dirty
53 **blue-collar task** manual work
58 **thrive on sth.** be successful at sth.
59 **safety valve** *Sicherheitsventil*
60 **malcontent** *(n)* person who is not satisfied with a situation
63 **Scott Fitzgerald** US novelist (1896–1940)

**Info**

**Social class in the US**
Recent statistics show a decline in the percentage of adults living in middle-class households, dropping from 61 percent in 1971 to 50 percent in 2021. During this time, there was an increase in both the upper and lower income tiers. There was a significant gap between adults with bachelor's degrees and those with lower levels of education with 39 percent of adults with a bachelor's degree in the upper-income tier. Black and Hispanic adults lagged behind, with about 40 percent falling into the lower-income category in 2021, compared to 24 percent of White adults and 22 percent of Asian adults.

▶ More info

Annotations
72 **Red State America**
US states tending to
vote Republican
72 **couch** *(n)* use an
expression in a
particular manner
76 **Blue State America**
US states tending to
vote Democratic
77 **Sandy Hook**
elementary school in
Connecticut where
26 people died in a
school shooting in
2012

starter jobs for them to claim. This is yet another version of the American Dream that can be said to have eroded.

In 2007, a photojournalist named Ian Brown began a project that involved inter-
70 viewing 170 ordinary people and asking them what they thought the American Dream might be. [...]

Brown discovered that in Red State America, respondents tend to couch the American Dream in terms of personal liberty – often the liberty to carry a gun. [...] A man in Utah said the American Dream was simply having a refuge, a place where
75 he could be free from the indignities of oppressive government.

For Blue State America, the dream more often had to do with safety and personal security. Sometimes it was very specific. A woman who had lost a child at Sandy Hook told Brown that her American Dream was 'to have a country where no child ever experiences the devastation of school shootings.' A young African American
80 living in a dangerous neighborhood said his American Dream was simply survival – 'to grow up to be a black man.'

Ian Brown learned, after years of diligent inquiry, that the American Dream is in the mind of the dreamer. It is not a fixed ideal that anyone in politics or government can credibly promise to uphold or restore.

*From:* Could We Please Stop Pontificating About the American Dream? *2020*

### Comprehension

1   State the different ideas connected with the American Dream as they are named in the text.

2   Summarize the author's personal views on the American Dream.

### Analysis

3   Examine the differences between past and present generations of US citizens and different segments of the population as presented in the text. Sum up the conclusions you can draw.

### Language awareness

▶ Support, p. 313

▶ Getting started

4   a   The author makes frequent use of positive and negative *connotations. Point out three examples of each and examine their effects in the context of his line of argument.
b   Rephrase the sentences using more neutral words.

### Beyond the text

▶ SF 28: Argumentative
writing: discussion and
comment, p. 382

▶ Check

5   Writing   At the end of his essay, the author concludes from Ian Brown's survey 'that the American Dream is in the mind of the dreamer' (ll. 82–83). Does a nation need a collective vision? Write a short comment on this question.

# Words revisited

## 1 Mind mapping

▶ SF 6: Essentials: language and study skills, p. 354

a Go back to 'Words in Context' (p. 116). Collect words and phrases in the second section of the text that are related to the term *conflict*. Organize them in the form of a mind map.

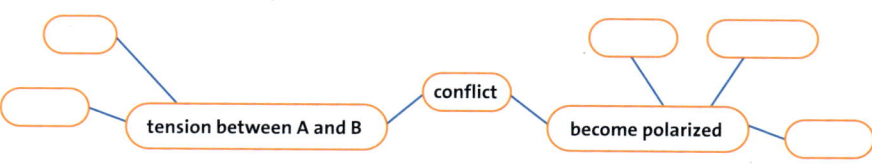

b Do the same for the terms *American Dream* and *the US political system*.

c Add more phrases you have come across to the three mind maps.

# Language awareness

## 2 What's in a name?

*The large number of ethnic groups living in North America has resulted in the creation of new names to distinguish them. In the course of time, some older discriminatory or wrongfully-used terms have been replaced by more correct and inclusive ones.*

| Old term | Preferred term |
| --- | --- |
| (American) Indians | First Nations peoples (Canada), Native Americans / American Indians (USA) |
| Eskimos | Inuit |
| Negroes, colored people | Black people, African Americans |
| Latin Americans | Hispanics, Latinos/Latinas |

Form small groups and speculate on the following:
- why the terms in the left-hand box above have gone out of fashion.
- why in some circles it has become fashionable to use *Latinx* [læˈtiːneks] instead of *Latino/Latina*.
- why in recent years the term *people of color* has become commonplace.

## 3 `Intercultural competence` The German side

a In the USA, citizens with foreign roots are often referred to as *Japanese Americans*, *Irish Americans*, etc. Compare the American terms to German words for German citizens with a *Migrationshintergrund*.

b Your exchange partner from the USA expresses surprise that you refer to your classmate Kyrill as a *Russlanddeutscher*, but to your friend Erkan as a *Deutschtürke*. From his point of view this is discriminatory. How would you reply to his criticism? Write a short email to him about the matter.

▶ WOB: pp. 110–111

## Practice

### 4 Examining a political speech

*Below is an excerpt from President Joe Biden's inaugural address held in the United States Capitol in Washington, D.C (20 January 2021).*

▶ SF 17: Reading and understanding non-fictional texts, p. 367

Here we stand, in the shadow of a Capitol dome that was completed amid the Civil War, when the Union itself hung in the balance. Yet we endured and we prevailed.

Here we stand looking out to the great Mall where Dr. King spoke
5 of his dream.

Here we stand, where 108 years ago at another inaugural, thousands of protestors tried to block brave women from marching for the right to vote.

Today, we mark the swearing-in of the first woman in American
10 history elected to national office – Vice President Kamala Harris.

Civil rights leader Martin Luther King Jr. at the Lincoln Memorial in Washington, D.C., giving his 'I have a dream' speech (28 August, 1963)

Don't tell me things can't change.

Here we stand across the Potomac from Arlington National Cemetery, where heroes who gave the last full measure of devotion rest in eternal peace.

15 And here we stand, just days after a riotous mob thought they could use violence to silence the will of the people, to stop the work of our democracy, and to drive us from this sacred ground.

That did not happen. It will never happen. Not today. Not tomorrow. Not ever. To all those who supported our campaign I am hum-
20 bled by the faith you have placed in us.

To all those who did not support us, let me say this: Hear me out as we move forward. Take a measure of me and my heart. And if you still disagree, so be it.

That's democracy. That's America. The right to dissent peaceably, within the guard-
25 rails of our Republic, is perhaps our nation's greatest strength. [...]

I understand that many Americans view the future with some fear and trepidation. I understand they worry about their jobs, about taking care of their families, about what comes next. I get it.

But the answer is not to turn inward, to retreat into competing factions, distrusting
30 those who don't look like you do, or worship the way you do, or don't get their news from the same sources you do.

We must end this uncivil war that pits red against blue, rural versus urban, conservative versus liberal. We can do this if we open our souls instead of hardening our hearts.

35 If we show a little tolerance and humility.

If we're willing to stand in the other person's shoes just for a moment.

Because here is the thing about life: There is no accounting for what fate will deal you. There are some days when we need a hand. There are other days when we're called on to lend one. That is how we must be with one another.

40  And, if we are this way, our country will be stronger, more prosperous, more ready for the future.

*From: Joseph R. Biden, jr.,* Inaugural address, *2021*

## Comprehension

**1** Write a summary of the content of the excerpt.

▶ Getting started

## Analysis

**2** Compare your summary from task **1** with the original. In what respects do they differ?

**3** Analyse the *stylistic devices used by Biden and the effect they have on the audience. The terms in the box below can help you.

▶ SF 18: Analysing speeches, p. 368

▶ Getting started

*allusion • *anaphora • *climax • *contrast • *direct address • *euphemism • *juxtaposition • *metaphor • negation • *parallelism • *repetition

## Language awareness

**4 a** Work in pairs. Try saying ll. 11 and 18–19 (until 'Not ever.') aloud in different manners (hesitant, determined, persuasive …). Experiment with loudness, stress, speed, pauses and intonation.
**b** In class, present your versions and listen to other students' versions. Give feedback to each other about the impressions created and analyse by which means they are achieved.

## Beyond the text

**5** Think about the USA today in light of the excerpt. Assess to what extent Biden's vision is reflected in reality.

**6** Intercultural competence  The USA and many other western democracies including Germany are faced with a crisis concerning democratic values at the moment. Discuss from your point of view as young people what governments and political parties could do to fight this crisis.

▶ WOB: pp. 16–18, pp. 28–30, pp. 45–47

▶ More info 🔖

# The new colossus   Emma Lazarus

- **Quick write:** What do you think of when you see a picture of the Statue of Liberty? Write down your associations, then compare them.

*Emma Lazarus (1849–1887) was a Jewish-American author and poet. She wrote the poem below as her contribution to a campaign to raise money for the pedestal of the Statue of Liberty.*

**Annotations**
1 **brazen** made of brass, also: shameless
2 **astride** standing with legs wide apart
6 **beacon** guiding or warning light
9 **storied** famous
11 **huddled** standing closely together
12 **teeming** full of people
13 **tempest-tost** storm-tossed, storm-driven

Not like the brazen giant of Greek fame
With conquering limbs astride from land to land;
Here at our sea-washed, sunset gates shall stand
A mighty woman with a torch, whose flame
5 Is the imprisoned lightning, and her name
Mother of Exiles. From her beacon-hand
Glows world-wide welcome; her mild eyes command
The air-bridged harbor that twin cities frame.
'Keep, ancient lands, your storied pomp!' cries she
10 With silent lips. 'Give me your tired, your poor,
Your huddled masses yearning to breathe free,
The wretched refuse of your teeming shore.
Send these, the homeless, tempest-tost to me:
I lift my lamp beside the golden door!'

*From: Emma Lazarus, 'The new colossus', 1883*

## Comprehension

▶ SF 20: Reading and understanding poetry, p. 370

**1** Formulate the message of the statue in your own words. To whom is it addressed?

## Analysis

**2** Compare the descriptions of the so-called *old world* (Europe) and the *new world* (the USA) in the poem.

**3** Analyse the meaning of *liberty* which the author gives to the statue.

## Language awareness

▶ Support, p. 313
▶ Getting started 🔖

**4** Point out an example of each of the following in the text and examine how it contributes to the effect of the poem:

\*alliteration • \*assonance • \*contrast • \*paradox • \*symbol

## Beyond the text

▶ SF 28: Argumentative writing: discussion and comment, p. 382

**5** Imagine you have just read an online commentary in which someone criticizes Emma Lazarus for confusing liberty and immigration. Write a response.

# Invisible footprints – the German Americans   Susanne Spröer

- Think of German words that are used in English. What does this tell you about the German influence on American culture?

▶ Getting started

*In the following text, the author looks back on the waves of German immigrants that left their home country for the 'new world'.*

▶ Info box 'Immigration', p. 145

Mehr als zwei Monate lang war der Dreimaster „Concord" über den stürmischen Atlantik gesegelt, bevor er am 6. Oktober 1683 im Hafen von Philadelphia anlegte. An Bord waren auch 13 deutsche Familien, Mennoniten aus der Nähe von Krefeld. Die Idee eines englischen Quäkers hatte sie in die „Neue Welt" gelockt: Dieser William
5 Penn wollte Religionsflüchtlingen Land zur Kolonialisierung zur Verfügung stellen.

▶ More info

Denn in den deutschen Fürstentümern und Königreichen des 17. Jahrhunderts waren nur die katholische, die lutherische und die reformierte Kirche erlaubt, andere Glaubensrichtungen wurden verfolgt. In Penns Kolonie gründeten die „Original 13" genannten Familien „Deitschesteddel": die erste deutsche Siedlung in den heu-
10 tigen USA. 1790, als die noch jungen Vereinigten Staaten von Amerika ihre erste Volkszählung veranlassten, lebten 434.000 Menschen im Bundesstaat Pennsylvania, ein Drittel von ihnen mit deutschen Wurzeln. [...] Auch in anderen Regionen der USA, wie im Mittleren Westen, z.B. in den Staaten Ohio, Illinois, Michigan oder Wisconsin, war der deutsche Einfluss groß: Hier leben die meisten deutschstämmi-
15 gen Amerikaner und viele große Brauereien sind deutsche Gründungen. [...]

Einem waschechten Preußen ist es zu verdanken, dass die amerikanischen Kolonialisten den Unabhängigkeitskrieg (1775–1783) gegen die britische Kolonialmacht gewinnen konnten: Friedrich Wilhelm von Steuben. Der 1730 geborene Spross einer Soldatenfamilie hatte unter Preußenkönig Friedrich dem Großen
20 gedient, bevor er in Paris Benjamin Franklin kennenlernte. Der empfahl ihn dem kommandierenden General der überseeischen Kolonialisten, George Washington. 1778 traf Steuben im Winterlager der „Continental Army" ein. Seine Aufgabe: aus den Freiwilligen, die eigentlich Bauern, Kaufleute oder Politiker waren, ein Heer zu bilden, das den britischen Berufssoldaten die Stirn bieten konnte. Mit preußi-
25 scher Disziplin und Drill organisierte Steuben die Ausbildung der Soldaten so gründlich, dass sie die Briten besiegten. [...] Auch im amerikanischen Bürgerkrieg (1861–1865) kämpften deutsche Militärs mit: wie Franz Sigel aus der Nähe von Heidelberg. Der deutsche Leutnant brachte es bis zum Generalmajor und gehörte zu den ranghöchsten Befehlshabern der Nordstaaten-Armee. [...]

30 Franz Sigel hatte in Europa zu denjenigen gehört, die sich 1848 gegen die Fürsten und Könige aufgelehnt hatten. Nach dem Scheitern der Revolution war er in die USA geflohen. Genauso wie Fritz Anneke aus Westfalen (der später im Bürgerkrieg ebenfalls für die Nordstaaten kämpfte) und seine Frau Mathilde Franziska Anneke.

Sie hatte schon in Europa als Journalistin gearbeitet, unter anderem für eine Zei-
35 tung, für die auch Heinrich Heine geschrieben hatte. In den USA durfte sie nun tun, was in den deutschen Staaten verboten war: Sie hielt Vorträge für Bildungschancen, die Gleichstellung der Geschlechter und gegen die Sklaverei. 1852 gründete sie die deutschsprachige „Frauen-Zeitung", 1869 wurde sie erste Vize-Präsidentin der „National Woman Suffrage Association" – und damit eine der
40 wichtigsten Frauen der US-amerikanischen Frauenbewegung.

Auch andere „Forty-Eighters" machten in den USA Karriere: Der Revolutionär Friedrich Hecker engagierte sich für die neu gegründete republikanische Partei und Carl Schurz wurde Innenminister und Berater von US-Präsident Abraham Lincoln. Insgesamt waren die ehemaligen Revolutionäre aber nur eine kleine
45 Gruppe unter den Auswanderern. Die meisten flohen vor Hunger und Armut gen Westen. Und es wurden immer mehr: Bis Mitte des 19. Jahrhunderts waren eine Million Deutsche in die USA übergesiedelt. Erst gegen Ende des Jahrhunderts gingen die Zahlen zurück.

1914 begann der Erste Weltkrieg. Als die USA 1917 in den Krieg eintraten, änder-
50 te sich auch das Verhältnis zu den Deutsch-Amerikanern in den USA. Deutsch-Amerikaner amerikanisierten ihre Namen, Behörden riefen zum Boykott deutscher Waren auf. Deutsche Begriffe verschwanden aus dem Sprachgebrauch. Sogar das beliebte „Sauerkraut" wurde umbenannt: „Liberty Cabbage" hieß es fortan. Und im Staat Illinois lauerte eine Meute dem Deutsch-Amerikaner Robert
55 Prager auf, zwang ihn, die amerikanische Flagge zu hissen und die Nationalhymne zu singen. Schließlich wurde er aufgehängt.

Schon zwischen den Weltkriegen war viel typisch Deutsches aus dem US-amerikanischen Alltag verschwunden. Und die Menschen, die ab 1933 nach der Machtübernahme der Nationalsozialisten in Deutschland in die USA flohen, wollten mit
60 dem Land, das Juden und andere missliebige Minderheiten verfolgte und millionenfach ermordete, nichts mehr zu tun haben. Viele wurden rasch Amerikaner. Wie Henry Kissinger, der spätere US-Außenminister: 1938 als Jugendlicher mit seiner jüdischen Familie aus Deutschland geflohen, nahm er 1943 die amerikanische Staatsangehörigkeit an und kämpfte als GI gegen sein Geburtsland.

65 Anders als bei den später eingewanderten Italienern oder Chinesen sind die Spuren der Deutschen heute eher verborgen. Und so eng mit der amerikanischen Kultur verwoben, dass beides kaum zu trennen ist.                                      *(709 words)*

*From:* German-American Day: So viel Deutsches steckt in den USA, *2020*

▶ SF 49: Mediating from German into English, p. 416
▶ Getting started 🔗

**1** `Mediating` You are part of a project on European emigration to the USA in your bilingual history class. Your special topic is Germany.
   **a** Write a blog entry targeting teenagers in which you describe the core factors of the history of German immigration to the USA.
                                           Advanced
   **b** Prepare a talk in which you identify the push factors that led to German emigration to the USA in the past. Then give your talk to your class. You may refer to the info box on p. 145 to help you get started.

**Beyond the text**

▶ Getting started 🔗

**2** `Speaking` Working in groups of three, choose one famous German-American emigrant per group (past or present) and research them. Present your person to two other groups and listen to their presentations. With the whole class, discuss what you found most surprising about one of the people.

**Info**

**From melting pot to salad bowl**

The melting pot is a metaphor sometimes used for the process of assimilation (i.e., how immigrants become 'real Americans'). It suggests that in the USA, cultures from all over the world 'melt' to form a new US identity, one which is both unique and homogeneous. In the 20th century, a rival metaphor, the 'salad bowl', emerged
5　as a heterogeneous alternative to the melting pot. In a salad bowl, the ingredients retain their identity, each contributing something unique to the overall flavour. The 'American salad bowl' resembles the 'Canadian mosaic', as both are symbols of a composite culture in which participants retain their cultural identity while at the same time shaping the national character. ▶ Info box, p. 145

1　Do some research on the three metaphors and point out their respective advantages and disadvantages. Explain why it might be that the 'Canadian mosaic' is often considered such a successful model of integration.

## My American daughter　Amy Tan

▶ More info 🔖

• If you were to emigrate to a different country, discuss what you think would be harder – retaining your cultural identity or integrating into a new one.

*Immigrants to the USA often wish to pass on their native culture to their children. This is sometimes more difficult than it sounds, as a Chinese-American mother discovers in Amy Tan's novel* Joy Luck Club.

My daughter wanted to go to China for her second honeymoon, but now she is afraid.
'What if I blend in so well they think I'm one of them?' Waverly asked me.
'What if they don't let me come back to the United States?'
5　'When you go to China,' I told her, 'you don't even need to open your mouth. They already know you are an outsider.'
'What are you talking about?' she asked. My daughter likes to speak back. She likes to question what I say.
'Aii-ya,' I said. 'Even if you put on their clothes, even if you take off your makeup
10　and hide your fancy jewelry, they know. They know just watching the way you walk, the way you carry your face. They know you do not belong.'
My daughter did not look pleased when I told her this, that she didn't look Chinese. She had a sour American look on her face. Oh, maybe ten years ago, she would have clapped her hands – hurray! – as if this were good news. But now she wants
15　to be Chinese, it is so fashionable. And I know it is too late. All those years I tried to teach her! She followed my Chinese ways only until she learned how to walk out the door by herself and go to school. So now the only Chinese words she can say are *sh-sh, houche, chr fan,* and *gwan deng shweijyau.* How can she talk to people in China with these words? Pee-pee, choo-choo train, eat, close light sleep. How can
20　she think she can blend in? Only her skin and her hair are Chinese. Inside – she is all American-made.
It's my fault she is this way. I wanted my children to have the best combination: American circumstances and Chinese character. How could I know these two things do not mix?

Annotations
1　**honeymoon** holiday taken by couples who just got married
3　**blend in** *sich (optisch) einfügen*
7　**speak back** *Widerworte geben*
9　**Aii-ya** Chinese exclamation of frustration
15　**fashionable** trendy

Annotation
26 **scholarship** *Stipendium*
27 **sue sb.** *jdn. verklagen*
27 **landlord** *Vermieter*
34 **pursue sth.** strive to
    get sth.

**Info**

**Diversity in the US**
A recent census
showed that the US
population is
becoming more
diverse. The likelihood
of two randomly
selected individuals
belonging to different
racial or ethnic
backgrounds rose to
61.1 percent in 2020
from 54.9 percent in
2010. Except for those
who identified as
white, all other ethnic
groups reported an
increase as a
percentage of the
population within this
timeframe. The
biggest increase was
the multiracial
population, which
grew from 2.9 percent
of the population to
10.2 percent.

25 I taught her how American circumstances work. If you are born poor here, it's no lasting shame. You are first in line for a scholarship. If the roof crashes on your head, no need to cry over this bad luck. You can sue anybody, make the landlord fix it. You do not have to sit like a Buddha under a tree letting pigeons drop their dirty business on your head. You can buy an umbrella. Or go inside a Catholic church. In America, 30 nobody says you have to keep the circumstances somebody else gives you.

She learned these things, but I couldn't teach her about Chinese character. How to obey parents and listen to your mother's mind. How not to show your own thoughts, to put your feelings behind your face so you can take advantage of hidden opportunities. Why easy things are not worth pursuing. How to know your 35 own worth and polish it, never flashing it around like a cheap ring. Why Chinese thinking is best.

No, this kind of thinking didn't stick to her. She was too busy chewing gum, blowing bubbles bigger than her cheeks. Only that kind of thinking stuck.

'Finish your coffee,' I told her yesterday. 'Don't throw your blessings away.'
40 'Don't be so old-fashioned, Ma,' she told me, finishing her coffee down the sink. 'I'm my own person.'

And I think, How can she be her own person? When did I give her up?

*From:* The Joy Luck Club, *1989*

## Comprehension

**1**   Summarize the reasons why the \*narrator is convinced that the Chinese will recognize her daughter as a foreigner.

**2**   Outline the mother's plan for her daughter's upbringing and the reasons why it failed.

## Analysis

**3**   Intercultural competence   Compare the relative merits of Chinese and US culture in the narrator's view.

**4**   Work on task **a** or **b**.

    **a**   Examine the impression the daughter Waverly makes in the text, pointing to examples.

    **b**   Challenge   Analyse the relationship between mother and daughter.

**5 a** Although the text at hand is an excerpt from a novel, in its *style it often resembles spoken language. Collect examples.

**b** Rephrase one passage without using spoken language. Analyse the effect this has.

**Beyond the text**

**6** You choose Work on **a** or **b**.

**a** Relate the images described in the info box 'From melting pot to salad bowl' (p. 143) to the story of the Chinese-American mother and her daughter.

**b** Writing The narrator says, 'It's my fault she is this way' (l. 22). Comment on her statement.

▶ SF 28: Argumentative writing: discussion and comment, p. 382

▶ Check (task b)

Info

### Immigration

The first settlers in Britain's Atlantic colonies, whose descendants later formed the backbone of the US population, came mainly from Great Britain, Germany and the Netherlands. For the first half-century after independence, immigration to the USA was moderate, but around the middle of the 19th century it exploded. Push factors
5  were political unrest, religious persecution and famine in many parts of Europe. As a result, large numbers of Irish, Poles, Italians and Jews fled to the USA in search of a better life. Pull factors were the availability of farmland, the Gold Rush and the need for labourers in the mines and factories of a young, rapidly growing nation. The newcomers, mainly Catholics and Jews,
10 were not always welcomed by the 'WASP' (White Anglo-Saxon Protestant) majority that dominated US political and cultural life for two centuries.
Immigration – both legal and illegal – has continued to be a significant and oftentimes controversial factor in US politics to
15 the present day. Mass migration of Spanish-speaking immigrants from Latin America is seen by some as a threat to mainstream English-language culture. The number of undocumented immigrants in the USA is estimated to be as high as ten million. In recent decades, migration from south-
20 eastern Asia has also risen significantly. The first major wave of Asian immigration to the USA occurred in California in the 1850s. Most Chinese immigrants hoped to earn money to send back to China. Soon Asian immigrants were sought not only in California but across the USA to fill the high demand for cheap labor in mines,
25 factories and particularly for the railways crossing the country.

Chinese labourers building the first transcontinental railway.

**1** Collect information from the box in two lists: 'Immigration – benefits and threats'.

► More info 🔖

► More info 🔖

## Intramural warfare    Ernesto Quiñonez

- What do you consider the main obligation of a school to its students? Explain.

*The following text is an excerpt from Ernesto Quiñonez' novel* Bodega Dreams.

Junior High School 99 (aka Jailhouse 99), on 100th Street and First Avenue, [...] was violently perfect and in constant turmoil within itself. It was a school that was divided by two powers, the white teachers and the Hispanic teachers. The white teachers had most of the power because they had seniority. They had been teaching
5   before the chancellor of the Board of Education finally realized that the school was located in Spanish Harlem and practically all of the students were Latinos, and so changed the school's name from Margaret Knox to Julia de Burgos.

To the white teachers we were all going to end up delinquents. 'I get paid whether you learn or not,' they would tell us. So we figured, hey, I ain't stealing food from
10   your kid's mouth, why should I do my work? The whole time I was at Julia de Burgos, I had no idea the school was named after Puerto Rico's greatest poet, had no idea Julia de Burgos had emigrated to New York City and lived in poverty while she wrote beautiful verses. She lived in El Barrio and had died on the street. But we weren't taught about her or any other Latin American poets, for that matter. As for
15   history, we knew more about Italy than our own Latin American countries. To Mr. Varatollo, the social studies teacher, everything was Italy this, Italy that, Italy, Italy, Italy. Didn't he know the history of the neighborhood? Hadn't he ever seen *West Side Story*? We hated Italians. At least that part of *West Side Story* was correct. Some Italians from the old days of the fifties and the sixties were still around. They
20   lived on Pleasant Avenue off 116th Street, and if you were caught around there at night you'd better have been a light-skinned Latino so you could pass yourself off as Italian.

So, since we were almost convinced that our race had no culture, no smart people, we behaved even worse. It made us fight and throw books at one another, sell loose
25   joints on the stairways, talk back to teachers, and leave classrooms whenever we wanted to. We hated the white teachers because we knew they hated their jobs. The only white teacher who actually taught us something, actually went through the hassle of making us respect her by never taking shit from us, was the math teacher, Ms. Boorstein. She once went toe-to-toe with Sapo. He was about to walk out of her
30   classroom because he was bored, and she said to him, 'Enrique, sit back down!' Sapo kept walking and she ran toward the door and blocked his path. She dared him to push her. She said to him, 'I'll get your mother. I bet she hits harder.' And Sapo had no choice but to go back to his seat. From that day on, no one messed with her. She might have been Jewish, but to us she was still white. Ms. Boorstein
35   could yell like a Latin woman. To us she was always 'that bitch.' But we knew she cared, for the simple reason that she never called us names; she would yell but never call us names. She only wanted us to listen, and when we did well on her math tests she was all smiles.

The Hispanic teachers, on the other hand, saw themselves in our eyes and made
40   us work hard. Most of them were young, the sons and daughters of the first wave of Puerto Ricans who immigrated to El Barrio in the late forties and the fifties. These teachers never took shit from us (especially Sapo), and they were not afraid to curse in class: '*Mira*, sit down or I'll kick your ass down.' At times they spoke to

### Annotations
1   **aka** = also known as
2   **turmoil** conflict
4   **seniority** higher status
8   **delinquent** young criminal
9   **figure** (sl) think
18   ***West Side Story*** musical (1957) set in Spanish Harlem, a modern retelling of *Romeo and Juliet*
24   **loose joint** marijuana cigarette
28   **hassle** (sl) (here) effort
28   **take shit** (sl) accept bad behaviour
29   **go toe-to-toe with sb.** confront sb.
29   **Sapo** (Span.) toad, (here) nickname
33   **mess with sb.** make trouble for sb.
36   **call sb. a name** insult sb.
43   **curse** (v) use vulgar language

**Info**

The text has some **offensive words and phrases** (e.g. l. 35, l. 43), which contribute to maintaining authenticity. It is important to remember that this language can be emotionally distressing and is inappropriate.

us harshly, as if they were our parents. This somehow made us fear and listen to
45  them. They were not Puerto Ricans who danced in empty streets, snapping their
fingers and twirling their bodies. Nor were they violent, with switchblade tempers.
None of them were named Maria, Bernardo, or Anita. These teachers simply
taught us that our complexion was made up of many continents, Africa, Europe,
and Asia. To them our self-respect was more important than passing some test,
50  because you can't pass a test if you already feel defeated. But the Hispanic teachers
had very little say in how things were run in that school. Most of them had just
graduated from a city university and couldn't rock the boat. Any boat.

*From:* Bodega Dreams, *2000*

Annotation
**52  rock the boat**  do
something that upsets
a situation and causes
problems

### Comprehension

**1**  Describe the relationships between the different groups at Junior High School 99:
- the white teachers and the Hispanic teachers
- the white teachers and their students
- the Hispanic teachers and their students.

▶ SF 19: Reading and
understanding narrative
texts, p. 369

### Analysis

**2**  You choose  Work on task **a** or **b**.

**a**  Analyse the reasons why the
students at JHS 99 take some of
their teachers seriously but ignore
the others.

**b**  Examine the influence of the
references to colour and ethnicity in
the excerpt. Explain how it
influences students' and teachers'
motivations.

▶ SF 19: Reading and
understanding narrative
texts, p. 369

### Language awareness

**3**  The young narrator frequently uses very informal language. Point out examples
and explain why you think he uses them.

▶ Getting started

### Beyond the text

**4**  Writing  Imagine you are a former student of JHS 99. Write a letter to the Board
of Education in which you suggest reforms that would help the school to better
serve the needs of its students.

**5**  In two places in the text, the narrator alludes to the musical *West Side Story*.
Research the plot and the setting of the musical; explain the allusions to your
class and discuss why the author may have chosen to include them.

▶ SF 35: Writing a formal
letter or email, p. 391
▶ Check

**Info**

The history of **Hispanics in the US** can be traced back to many centuries before the
founding of the US to the indigenous populations and later to Spanish
colonization. The term *Hispanic* or *Latino* denotes a person's cultural identity and
not ethnicity. The Hispanic community has contributed greatly to US culture,
economy and politics despite experiencing widespread discrimination.

# No longer the land of opportunity?
## Nicolas D. Kristof and Sheryl WuDunn

- What measures and institutions do you regard as desirable (or necessary) to promote equality of opportunity? Discuss.

*The American Dream promised equality of opportunity, not social or economic equality itself. But critics say political leaders have long since abandoned this goal – with severe consequences for millions of Americans.*

**Annotations**

2  **pioneer sth.**  be the first to do sth.
3  **160 acres**  c. 0.7 square kilometers
5  **impoverished** extremely poor
5  **landed**  landowning
6  **trace sth.**  *etwas zurückverfolgen*
17  **GI Bill of Rights**  laws passed in 1944 that provided generous benefits for World War II veterans
17  **attainment** achievement
21  **Social Security**  US pension system
26  **incarceration** imprisonment
28  **peak** *(v)*  stop rising
28  **glacially**  extremely slowly
30  **laggard**  loser
33  **relentless**  never stopping
33  **cost cutting**  saving money
33  **hollow sth. out**  *etwas aushöhlen*
33  **blue-collar job** manual work
34  **clerical job**  office work

For much of the nineteenth and twentieth centuries, the United States had pioneered efforts to create opportunity. The Homestead Acts, beginning in 1862, were a self-help program that gave American families 160 acres of land each if they farmed it productively or improved it over five years. Homesteads transformed the
5 West and turned impoverished workers into landed farmers. One-quarter of Americans can trace some of their family wealth to that visionary initiative. Another historic program was rural electrification, which beginning in 1936 brought electricity (and later telephone service) to farmers across America, transforming rural life, improving productivity and multiplying opportunity.

10 The United States was one of the first regions of the world to offer near universal basic education, and then one of the first countries to introduce high schools for nearly all children. 'By the early 20th century America educated its youth to a far greater extent than did most, if not every, European country,' Claudia Goldin and Lawrence F. Katz write in *The Race Between Education and Technology,* their explora-
15 tion of how investments in human capital made America the world's leading country. [...] A state university and community college system made tertiary education widespread, and the [...] GI Bill of Rights vastly expanded educational attainment and homeownership in America. [...]

There were many other historic initiatives in the early 20th century that put the
20 United States on a progressive path. In the 1930s, [...] Congress approved social safety net programs like Social Security, unemployment insurance and jobs initiatives like the Civilian Conservation Corps. Other countries later adopted many elements of these programs.

Then in about 1970, [...] America went off track, beginning a nearly half-century
25 drift in the wrong direction. High-school graduation rates tumbled from the highest to among the lowest in the industrialized world. Incarceration rose sevenfold. Family structure collapsed. Single-parent households soared. Life expectancy peaked. Working-class incomes grew glacially, if at all. [...] The result is that the top 1 percent now owns twice as great a share of national wealth as the entire bottom
30 90 percent. We went from being a world leader in opportunity to being a laggard.

The decline in education leadership is particularly significant, because good jobs increasingly require a solid educational foundation. Globalization, automation, and a relentless focus on cost cutting led to a hollowing out of urban blue-collar and clerical jobs that in the past were often performed by people with limited
35 education. David Autor, an economist at MIT, has found that as a result, urban workers with only a high-school education fill jobs that are actually lower skilled now than back in the 1970s. [...]

Advanced

One sign that the United States was moving rightward and following a different trajectory than the rest of the West was the election of Ronald Reagan in 1980.
40 Reagan both reflected and shaped the country's mood in the 1970s when in his speeches he regularly denounced a Chicago welfare recipient: 'She has eighty names, thirty addresses, twelve Social Security cards and is collecting veteran's benefits on four nonexistent deceased husbands.' After his election to the presidency, he famously declared in his inaugural address in 1981, 'Government is
45 not the solution to our problem; government is the problem.' He broke the air traffic controllers' union; worker protections declined; and the business world became much more powerful.

As hostility toward government spread in America, there have been determined efforts to cut taxes, particularly for the wealthy, and then 'starve the beast' – using
50 reduced revenue to justify cuts in services for the disadvantaged. This is both disingenuous and cruel, as well as out of step with the advanced world. Other countries over the decades expanded health-care coverage, adopted family-leave policies, extended mass transit and implemented child allowances to reduce poverty, while the United States bucked the trend by slashing taxes, cutting back
55 hours at public libraries, raising tuition at state universities, and allowing infrastructure to decay. Grover Norquist, an influential Republican advocate for lower tax rates, captured the small government ideology: 'My goal is to cut government in half in twenty-five years, to get it down to the size where we can drown it in the bathtub.' [...]

60 In 1965, the average chief executive earned about 20 times as much as the average worker; now the average CEO earns more than 300 times as much. A Walmart employee earning the median salary at the company, $19,177, would have to work for 1,188 years to earn as much as the chief executive did in 2018 alone. Companies also changed the ways they operated, outsourcing custodial jobs and eliminat-
65 ing pensions in ways that raised share prices but left many families more vulnerable. [...]

Not since the Great Depression has America experienced the kind of working-class stagnation that we've seen in recent decades, and it has fed polarization, racism, and bigotry, gnawing away at our social fabric.

70 Resentment has grown toward Latinos, Muslims, and African Americans. White supremacists gained ground, and on websites and social media Americans glibly trumpet their bigotry. Hate crimes have increased in the United States for three years in a row, the FBI reported. On one ultra-right website we visited, people posted venomous statements about Muslims and called for mass deportation. One
75 woman proposed, 'Any Muslim man wanting to come into our country must be castrated first.'

Is this America?

*From:* Tightrope: Americans Reaching for Hope, *2020*

---

**Annotations**

39 **trajectory** path
41 **denounce sb.** *jdn. brandmarken*
41 **recipient** sb. who receives sth.
43 **deceased** no longer living
44 **famously** *bekanntlich*
44 **inaugural address** *Antrittsrede*
45 **air traffic controller** *Fluglotse*
48 **hostility** negative feelings
48 **determined** *entschlossen*
49 **starve sb.** *jdn. verhungern lassen*
51 **disingenuous** dishonest
52 **family-leave policy** law that lets people take time off from work to look after a family member
53 **extend sth.** *etwas ausbauen*
53 **mass transit** *öffentlicher Personen-Nahverkehr*
53 **child allowance** *Kindergeld*
54 **buck the trend** do the opposite of everyone else
54 **slash sth.** reduce sth. drastically
55 **tuition** *Studiengebühren*
56 **advocate** *(n)* sb. who speaks out in favour of sth.
57 **capture sth.** express sth. in a few words
62 **median salary** *mittleres Gehalt*
64 **custodial job** *Hausmeistertätigkeit*
65 **vulnerable** at risk
69 **bigotry** prejudiced thinking
69 **gnaw at sth.** [nɔː] *an etwas nagen*
69 **fabric** *Zusammenhalt*
71 **glibly** without thinking
72 **trumpet sth.** make sth. public
74 **venomous** *giftig*

## Comprehension

▶ More language

**Info**

The **history of socialism** in the United States differs significantly from Europe. While European nations often voted in parties with leftist principles and embraced welfare systems, socialism in the US has faced opposition. The term has negative connotations, stemming from Cold War-era fears of communism and authoritarianism. However, in recent years, Democratic Socialism has increased in popularity with political proponents advocating for policies such as universal healthcare, free college tuition and anti-inequality measures.

▶ SF 22: Analysing diagrams, p. 373

▶ Getting started

1  You choose  Work on task **a** or **b**.

a  Summarize the measures adopted by the US government in the past to promote equality of opportunity.

b  Summarize the examples used to show how US governments have cut back on measures to create equal opportunity.

c  Compare notes with someone who chose the other task.

## Analysis

2  Analyse the relationship between government cutbacks and social cohesion as presented in the text.

3  The excerpt ends with a short *rhetorical question. Examine its meaning for the text as a whole.

## Language awareness

4  The sentence in ll. 67–69 contains an example of emphatic inversion.
a  Rephrase the sentence using normal sentence structure (i.e., subject – verb – object).
b  Compare the two versions in their grammar and their effect.

## Beyond the text

5  Work with a partner.
**Partner A:** Examine chart A. Summarize the main trends for your partner.
**Partner B:** Examine chart B on p. 151. Summarize the main trends for your partner.

Language help

stagnate/rise/fall sharply/steadily/moderately/gradually/minimally

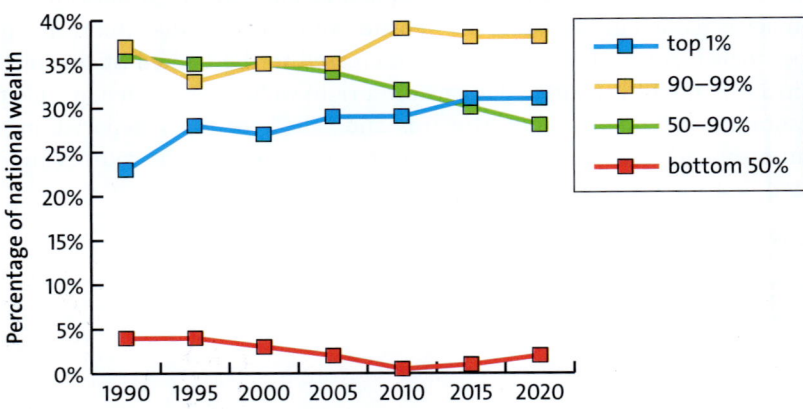

**Chart A: Private wealth USA 1990–2020 (in percentage of total)**

*Source:* The US Federal Reserve, *2020*

### Chart B: Level of education and class

Values represent percentage of the total population

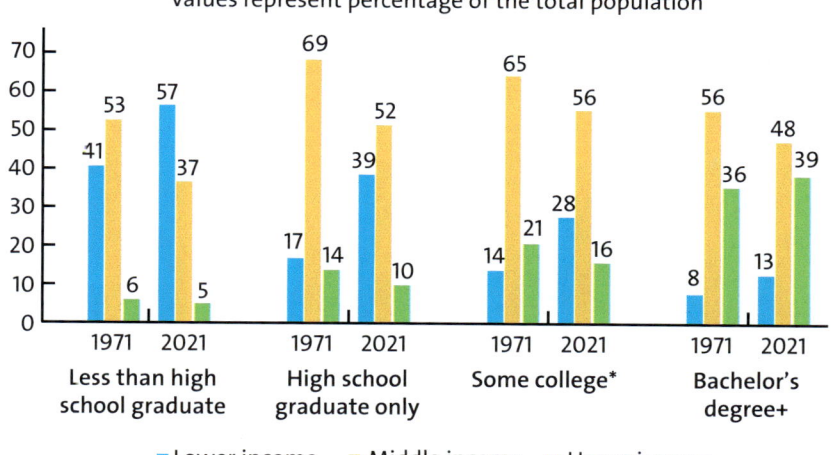

- ■ Lower income
- ■ Middle income
- ■ Upper income

**\* Those with associate degrees and those who attended college but did not get a degree**

*Source:* Pew Research Center analysis of the Current Population Survey, *2022*

**6**   `Writing`   Write an email to a US friend expressing your reaction to what you have learned about the USA from the article while focusing on three things you found most surprising.

▶ SF 35: Writing a formal letter or email, p. 391

## Chapter task

▶ Getting started

**The USA – still a 'land of dreams'?**

After the end of World War II, the USA became something of a role model for West German society, a country that many Germans looked up to and often emulated. Hollywood films, rock'n roll and the 'American way of life' held a special fascination, especially for the younger generation.

What about you and your generation? How do you feel about the USA, what it stands for and the role it plays in the world? Would you consider living in the USA? Make notes on your attitude, then conduct a class discussion in which you compare your feelings toward the USA.

# Chapter 5
# Arts and Culture – Cancelled or Created?

**1** Write down ideas and emotions that each of the pictures evokes for you.

► Getting started

**2** **a** What constitutes art for you? Try to give a tentative definition.
**b** With a partner, discuss which of the pictures represent(s) art for you. Say why.
**c** Together, agree on a definition of art.

**3** Explain which types of arts and cultural forms you are most/least interested in.

**4** **a** Look at the Chapter map and speculate about the content of this chapter.
**b** *Quick write: Answer the guiding question in a short paragraph.

> **Info**
>
> Picture A: Illumination of Pont du Gard, France (2013)
> Picture B: *The Fighting Temeraire* (1839) by English painter John William Turner (1775–1851)
> Picture F: *Die Zauberflöte* (2012), set design by Esther Bialas (*1969), costume and
> 5 stage designer

## Chapter map

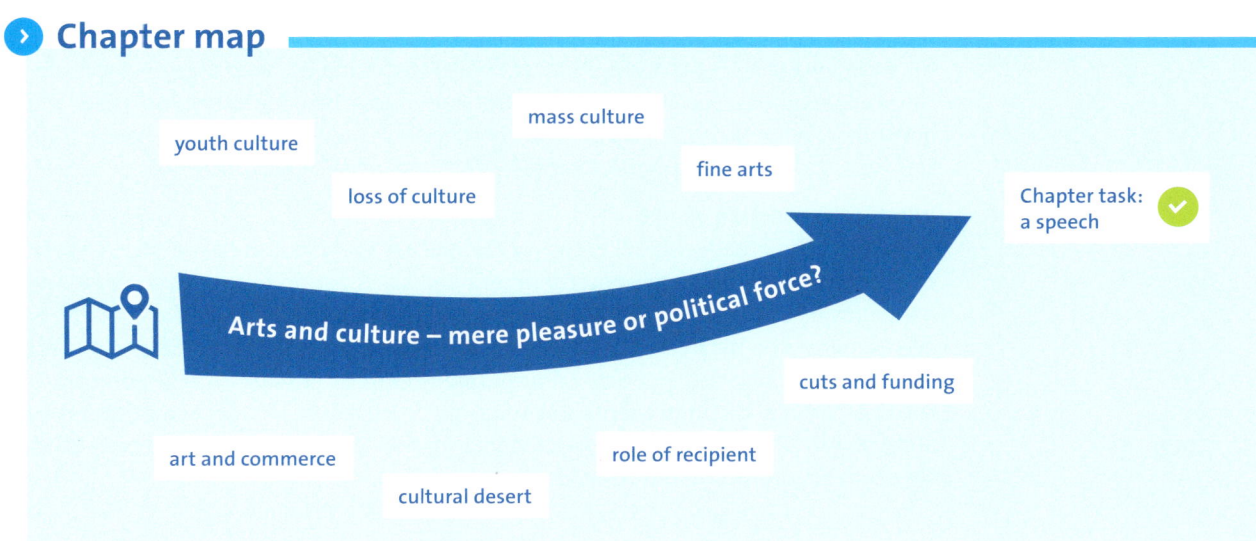

youth culture

mass culture

loss of culture

fine arts

Chapter task: a speech

Arts and culture – mere pleasure or political force?

cuts and funding

art and commerce

role of recipient

cultural desert

153

▶ 'Climate change goes Hollywood', p. 345

▶ More language

Ambrogio de Predis,
*Girl with Cherries*,
1491–1495

Wandjina Aboriginal
rock paintings,
Western Australia

# Arts and culture – one for all?

### What is culture? What is art?

Over the centuries people have tried to define what the word *culture* means to their respective communities. Some say *culture* refers to the arts and other products of human intellectual achievement regarded collectively. Therefore, the ideas, customs
5   and social behaviours reflected in this art make up the culture of a particular group of people or society.

Art comprises many different disciplines. There are the so-called fine arts, like painting, sculpture, architecture, photography and modern installations. There are also the performing arts, consisting of theatrical performances, e. g. musical theatre, dance,
10  film, circus arts, but also puppetry and improv – to name just a few. And then, of course, there are the two great arts of literature and music.

### Defining the undefinable

Art is a human cultural product, the result of a creative process. And people have always discussed who decides what exactly this includes. Is it something everybody
15  should like or accept? In early human history, objects and paintings that are considered art from today's perspective, had more functions attributed to them than mere viewing or adornment, e. g. cave paintings as a means of communication. Folk and tribal art from lots of different cultures, which may once have been considered primitive, are now collected as art by those who appreciate fine art.
20  In the past, the production and consumption of art was restricted to the intellectual elite of a country or nation. Yet with the creation of mass media, people from all sectors of society suddenly had access to art, hence its definition has since changed a lot. Nowadays, with the help of modern technology, almost everybody can produce and consume art – almost anytime and anywhere. But is it really art? It seems impossible
25  to define the undefinable.

### Putting a price tag on art

Have the mass media, and thus the mass distribution of art, changed both art's non-material and material value? Arts and money often cause a stir when we see some of the outrageously high prices paid for some works of art. Famous artists rely
30  on their name and reputation to charge high amounts of money for their work, but they are in a minority. Less well-established artists, however, often don't even earn the minimum wage since art and cultural activities are frequently seen as less relevant for the well-being of a society than science or commercialism, for example. Artists and performers who do not receive government funding usually have to work hard to find
35  sponsors and financial support to implement their artistic ideas and aims.

### What is the function of art?

Opinions differ greatly regarding the function of art and of culture generally in a society. To some, they are merely entertainment and a distraction from the problems and hardships of everyday life. To others, art is education, providing food for thought or
40  even serving a political function, as artists often use their artistic creations to protest against social injustice, political crimes, unfair regimes or wars. In non-democratic societies, artists are often silenced by measures such as censorship. Sometimes they are even forced to go into exile or excluded from their professions. So the power of art seems to be significant, but its recognition rather less so.

## 1 Main ideas

**a** Outline the main ideas of the text in no more than four sentences.

**b** Add aspects and ideas from the text to your definition of art (cf. p. 152, task **2a**), then present it to a partner.

## 2 Reflect

**a** Find three concepts in the text that are important for the topic and/or were new to you.

**b** Explain them in English. Use a dictionary if necessary.

**c** In small groups, take turns presenting your explanations. The other group members have to guess which phrase you are referring to.

Haute couture fashion is a form of art.

## 3 Adverbs

**a** Find three different adverbs in the text meaning 'and that means'. ▶ Check

**b** The use of these adverbs is rather formal. Choose three sentences from the text containing these adverbs and rephrase them to make them sound less formal.

## 4 Chunk it!

**a** Find as many suitable words that collocate with each word listed below. You can use the text and a monolingual dictionary for help.

1 *intellectual* + noun

2 *have access to* + noun

3 *implement* + noun

4 *differ* + adverb

5 *protest against* + noun

▶ Getting started

▶ Check

**b** Use the collocations to form sentences referring to the topic of arts.

Architectural art by Friedens- reich Hundertwasser

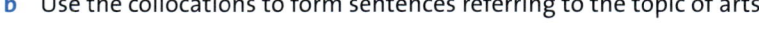

## 5 It's art

You choose Do either task **a** or **b**.

**a** Your class is invited to present ten works of art in an upcoming school exhibition. Describe a work of art you created and explain why it should be chosen for the event.

▶ Getting started

**b** What should art do? Entertain, educate, or express political protest? Write a short statement of about 100 words.

*The Light of China,* Feux Follets Festival 2019

Ugo Rondinone's art installation *Seven Magic Mountains* in Las Vegas

Paleolithic cave painting of bison, Lascaux, France

Wooden Dogon sculptures, Mali, Africa

## Consuming art

- Explain why you like going to exhibitions, or not. If you do, what kind of exhibitions do you like? Exchange your thoughts with a partner.

*You are going to look at two different cartoons about the art of painting.*
***Partner B:** Go to p. 314.*

*"I like this painting because it has a bench."*

CartoonStock.com

### Comprehension

**1** Describe the *cartoon briefly and sum up its message about how some people consume art in one sentence.

### Analysis

▶ SF 25: Analysing cartoons, p. 377

▶ Getting started

**2 a** Look at the *cartoon and analyse how it manages to convey the message. Then give a short presentation of it to your partner.
    **b** Explain which of the two cartoons you find more appealing. Think of the arguments you put together in the pre-reading task.

### Beyond the text

**3** Think back to the guiding question. Outline whether and how your answer has changed. Give reasons for your decision.

**4 a** Your school's art teachers want to put together an exhibition showcasing the best works of students of all ages from the last three years. The artworks are to be sold and the proceeds will go to charity. You are responsible for advertising the exhibition in the local community.
Go online and find a cartoon that you can use for a poster or flyer. Think of other visual elements you could use for your advertising material.
    **b** Speaking   In a group of four, present your ideas to each other in a 1-minute-talk.
    **c** In your group, choose the best idea. In class, explain why you think your group designed the best advertising material.

# Types of art and culture    Max Lerner

**Advanced**

▶ More info

*You are going to read an excerpt from the book* America as a Civilization *by Max Lerner, a fundamental book first published in 1957. The text is taken from chapter 11 'The Arts and Popular Culture'.*

▶ Support, p. 315

- Work in groups of three. Talk about the terms *art*s and *culture* and start building a word bank or mind map for them.
- Work with two new partners and exchange your ideas.
- Share your ideas in class and start a (digital) class wall.

**Info**

**Max Lerner** (1902–1992) was an American journalist and educator. Lerner's most influential book was *America as a Civilization: Life and Thought in the United States Today* (1957).

In every civilization there is an educated culture and a popular culture – an art of the classes and an art of the masses. Matthew Arnold defined the first (*Culture* with a capital C) as
5 the best that has been thought and said by the few in a civilization. The other conception refers to the run of what is thought, felt and liked by the many. Both are included within the broader anthropological use of 'culture' as
10 the total design of the life and thought of a people.

Using popular culture in the second sense above – as the culture of the many rather than the few, often deliberately differentiating itself
15 from elite culture – there are some who claim

for it the only valid elements of truth and beauty in a civilization. The cult

20

of 'folk art', like the cult of the 'folk mind', goes back to the discovery of the creativeness of the innocent by the weary sophisticates of the European Enlightenment. It is true that creativeness is not the monopoly of the professional artist. An untutored talent in poetry or a
25 'primitive' in painting may come up from the underlying population; and much of the energy of art comes from the experience of simple, anonymous people. [...]

30

The dangers of an uncritical cult of the people are contained in Franz Boas' remark: 'I should always be more inclined to accept, in regard to fundamental human problems, the judgement of the masses rather than the judgement of intellectuals. The desires of the masses are, in a wider sense, more human than those of the
35 classes.' I suggest this is the kind of sentimental thinking which is a dubious base for a theory of popular culture, although it may have some validity in the case of a cultural idiom like jazz.

Annotations

3 **Matthew Arnold** (1822–1888) was an English poet and critic

9 **anthropological** having to do with the study of human societies and culture

22 **weary** (here) tired of/ bored with sth.

22 **sophisticate** (*n*) worldly person that is knowledgeable about culture

22 **European Enlightenment** period in 18th century Europe in which scientists began to argue that science was more important than religion

24 **untutored** not having been formally taught about sth.

29 **Franz Uri Boas** (1858–1942) German American anthropologist

Annotations

**40 Henry James** (1843–1916) American-British author

**40 John Singer Sargent** (1856–1925) American artist, considered the leading portrait painter of his age

**40 Virgil Thomson** (1896–1930) American composer and critic

**41 Charles Tomlinson Griffes** (1884–1920) American composer

**41 Wallace Stevens** (1879–1955) American poet

**41 Frank Lloyd Wright** (1867–1959) American architect, designer, writer and educator

**43 sustained** continuing

**52 condescension** behaviour showing that you regard yourself as more important and more intelligent than other people

**53 contempt** feeling that sb./sth. is of no value and deserves no respect

**55 middlebrow** (adj) of good quality but intellectually not very challenging

**56 slackness** without attention or energy

**57 gloss over sth.** not talking about sth. unpleasant subsidiary – additional

**68 suction** Saugkraft, Saugwirkung

The fact is that the elite arts and popular arts have different functions in a culture. Whether
40  it be Henry James or Sargent, Virgil Thomson or Charles Griffes, Wallace Stevens or Frank Lloyd Wright, the drive of the elite artist is part of the sustained effort of individual creators to express their vision of life. The drive of popu-
45  lar culture (I am speaking here of the genuine folk culture and not of the synthetic and manufactured type) is mainly to find release, in performers and audience alike, for the energy, humor, and self-assertion of the people. Each
50  is a valid form of American creativeness. The characteristic weakness of the elite arts is likely to be found in condescension of spirit, arrogance of intellect, contempt for mass culture. That of the popular arts – and, in America,
55  what may be called the middlebrow arts as well – is found in cheapness of taste, slackness of discipline, the glossing over of real problems, a fear of depth.

The big media and the arts of reproduction
60  have, of course, brought the high achievements of elite musicians, painters, and writer to millions who never before had access to them. But the strength of American popular culture does not consist in its spreading of elite material but
65  in its creation of new popular material. Its rela-

tion to the elite arts is not subsidiary but imperialist: the popular arts absorb the works of even the playwrights, composers, and great novelists by a powerful suction force.

*From:* America as a Civilization, *1957*

## Comprehension

**1  a** Point out the two types of culture Lerner defines for each civilization and who their producers and consumers are.

**b** Outline which functions the representatives of the different cultures have according to Lerner.

## Analysis

**2** Work on either **a** or **b**.

**a** Examine Lerner's line of argument giving examples from the text.

**b** Challenge  Analyse Lerner's line of argument. Give examples from the text and explain if he favours one type of culture and whether his view is balanced.

Advanced

### Language awareness

**3**   **a**   Examine the choice of words in the text. Give examples. Who is the target group for Lerner's writings?

     **b**   Rephrase a passage of your own choice for a different target group of the 21st century.

▶ Support, p. 315

### Beyond the text

**4**   **a**   Speaking   Work in groups of four. Discuss Learner's key message that each civilization produces two different kinds of culture, i. e., elite culture and popular culture. Take into account the period in which Lerner wrote his book. State elaborately whether you agree or disagree and give examples based on your personal experience.

     **b**   Writing   Write an entry for your personal blog explaining which type of art you like looking at and why you like it.

**5**   📖   Reconsider Lerner's ideas and the results of the tasks you worked on. Note down some ideas, then answer the guiding question.

▶ SF 46: Having a discussion, p. 410
▶ Getting started 🔧
▶ WOB: pp. 65–67

---

## Text 3

### Today's struggles of a classical orchestra

Advanced

*You are going to listen to an interview with the conductor Simon Rattle.*

• Work with a partner. Which skills does a good conductor need? Speculate and make a list.

### Comprehension

🔊 **1**   Listening   Listen to the interview, then answer the questions below. You need not write complete sentences.

▶ Check 🔧

     1   Why it's strange for Simon Rattle to give this concert in Australia
     2   What connection he has to Sydney Opera House
     3   What has changed in Sydney Opera House
     4   What effect the pandemic had on the orchestra
     5   How he describes his relationship with his orchestra
     6   How he regards himself as a conductor

**2**   Go back to the results of the pre-reading task. Which of the skills you compiled does Rattle mention?

### Beyond the text

**3**   **a**   Work in groups of four. Prepare for a discussion by first listing institutions, events, groups or projects in the field of art and culture in your community that you think need (more) funding. Explain why they need the funding and why they are important.

#### Info

**Sir Simon Denis Rattle** (*1955) is a world-famous British-German conductor. He started conducting at a very early age and rose to international fame while he was music director of the City of Birmingham Symphony Orchestra (1980–1998). In 2002 he became principal conductor of the Berlin Philharmonic until 2018. Since September 2017 he has also been the music director of the London Symphony Orchestra. He was ranked as one of the world's best living conductors by music critics.

Advanced

▶ SF 46: Having a
discussion, p. 410
▶ Getting started

**b** 🔊 Choose one of the items from your list and discuss its funding: Two of you represent officials who have to ensure that the community saves money. The other two represent the arts council of your community. You want to have more money for the item you chose from your list. Discuss the matter and come to a solution or a compromise.

▶ WOB: pp. 78–81

**Info**

### The US and the UK: art, culture, politics and commerce

The art and culture of the US and UK are deeply linked with the realms of politics and commerce. Artists often use their influence to promote political and social change. For instance, Taylor Swift endorsed Biden and Harris during the 2020 election, dedicating her song *Only the Young* to their campaign. In the wake of the
5   Black Lives Matter movement, murals like *Say Their Names* by Whitney Holbourn, Andrew Thompson and Braylyn Resko Stewart and *We Stand with You* by Christian Grijalva memorialized the victims of police brutality. Meanwhile in Britain, the elusive street artist Banksy is known for his subversive works that offer commentary on issues like war, capitalism and social injustices.
10   The creative industries of both countries are economic forces to be reckoned with. In 2023, the United States generated 42 percent of the global art market value, with the UK at 17 percent, which amounted to 4.3 percent of the GDP in the US and 5.7 in the UK. Leading institutions promoting the arts include museums such as the British Museum and the Tate Modern in the UK and the Metropolitan
15   Museum of Art in the US, all of which rank in the top five most-visited art museums, attracting between 4.7 and 5.8 million visitors in 2023. Art itself can often be a lucrative avenue for potential investors. A prime example of the commercialized side of culture is the Super Bowl, the annual National Football League championship in the US. Its halftime show consisting of musical perfor-
20   mances by global superstars such as Beyoncé, Bruno Mars and The Weeknd is as important as the game itself for the companies who are willing to pay up to seven million dollars for a 30-second advertisement.

**1**   Discuss with a partner what you have learned about the links between art, politics and commerce.

**2**   Research Banksy's *Love is in the Bin* and use it as a basis to write a short comment on the commercialization of art and culture.

**3**   How do artists make a living from their art in the US or the UK? Work in pairs and share the work among yourselves. Then present your results to each other.

## Text 4

▶ More info

# I can't read    Lamont Carey

- About 6,2 million people in Germany are illiterate. Do you know people who are? Why do people remain illiterate? Name possible reasons.
- Brainstorm how those people might manage their everyday lives.

*You are going to read the lyrics of a spokenword performance by US artist Lamont Carey.*

I am eleven years old in the 6th grade and I can't read
The class is so full that the teacher doesn't notice me
But I can't read
And when she finally asks me to come to the head of the class
5　I do everything in my power to make the class laugh
What would u do if u knew that they all would laugh at u
But I can't read. I can't write. I can't spell and most of the time
I don't know my left from my right
But they keep on passing me
10　Because I can dribble a ball

And I can hit a three pointer ya'll
And I can almost dunk
And I can guarantee u thirteen points
But I can't read. I can't write. I can't spell and most of the time
15　I don't know my left from my right
And there are others in my class that I think are just like me
But they can't dribble a ball
And they can't dunk
So they can't guarantee ya' no points
20　So they are gonna have to work at McDonalds
But how they going to get a job when they can't read the application
So the streets become their occupation
Now they are peddling drugs to our nation
But I can't read. I can't write. I can't spell and most of the time
25　I don't know my left from my right
And the teachers aide said that it is the teacher's fault
And the teachers blame the board of education
And the board of education says that it is my parents' fault
And my parents blame me
30　But I can't read. I can't write. I can't spell and most of the time
I don't know my left from my right
On the biggest game of the school year I was coming down the lane
Getting ready to do my thang
When number thirteen crashed into me
35　And at the same time that I heard my knee crack
I saw my family's dream shatter
See they depended on me to get us out of the ghetto
So when I hit the ground I did everything in my power not to frown
But it was just too much pain
40　Like it ran straight to my brain
And the last thing I remember is the doctor saying
I will never run again
So now I am asking ya'll
What are my options

*From:* Reach Into My Darkness: I hate this place, *2013*

Annotations
11　**hit a three pointer** goal made from behind three-point line in basketball
11　**ya'll** (*infml*, *AE*) you all
12　**dunk** (in basketball) jump very high and put the ball through the basket
23　**peddle** sell
26　**aide** assistant
32　**come down the lane** (in basketball) be in the area under the basket
33　**thang** (*infml*, *AE*) thing
36　**shatter** fall apart, be destroyed

## Comprehension

▶ SF 20: Reading and understanding poetry, p. 370

**1** Summarize the *poem in about 5 sentences.

## Analysis

**2** Analyse the structure of the poem and describe the effect it has on the overall message. Give examples.

## Language awareness

▶ Getting started 🔖

▶ WOB: pp. 31–33

**3** **a** Examine the choice of informal language in the text. Which purpose does it have?
**b** Replace all informal expressions with neutral or formal ones. How does the effect change?

## Beyond the text

**4** | You choose | Do either **a** or **b**.

**a** | Writing | Write a letter to the *speaker of the poem. Express how you feel about the song and its message. Be empathetic and make suggestions as to how the speaker might find a way out of their dilemma.

**b** | Writing | Imagine a scholar from the 1950s would read Carey's poem. How would they react to it? Would they consider it art? Write a comment of about 200 words.

▶ Check (tasks a, b)

## Text 5

Advanced

▶ More info

**Info**

**Hector Hugh Munro** (1870–1916), known by his pen name **Saki**, was a British writer whose witty and mischievous stories mock and criticize Edwardian society and culture. His favourite literary genre was the short story.

Annotations
2 **tone down** make sth. less extreme or offensive
2 **indifference** lack of interest in sb.
3 **tangible** clearly visible

# The Bull     Saki

• Note down how you feel about people who have a special talent and can do some things much better than you.
• Exchange your results with a partner.

*You are going to read a short story by the famous author Saki.*

Tom Yorkfield had always regarded his half-brother, Laurence, with a lazy instinct of dislike, toned down, as years went on, to a tolerant feeling of indifference. There was nothing very tangible to dislike him for; he was just a blood-relation, with whom Tom had no single taste or interest in common, and with whom, at the same
5 time, he had had no occasion for quarrel. Laurence had left the farm early in life, and had lived for a few years on a small sum of money left him by his mother; he had taken up painting as a profession, and was reported to be doing fairly well at it, well enough, at any rate, to keep body and soul together. He specialised in painting animals, and he was successful in finding a certain number of people to buy his

10 pictures. Tom felt a comforting sense of assured superiority in contrasting his position with that of his half-brother; Laurence was an artist-chap, just that and nothing more, though you might make it sound more important by calling him an animal painter; Tom was a farmer, not in a very big way, it was true, but the Helsery
farm had been in the family for some generations, and it had a good reputation for
15 the stock raised on it. Tom had done his best, with the little capital at his command,
to maintain and improve the standard of his small herd of cattle, and in Clover
Fairy he had bred a bull which was something rather better than any that his immediate neighbours could show. It would not have made a sensation in the judg-
ing-ring at an important cattle show, but it was as vigorous, shapely, and healthy a
20 young animal as any small practical farmer could wish to possess. At the King's
Head on market days Clover Fairy was very highly spoken of, and Yorkfield used to
declare that he would not part with him for a hundred pounds; a hundred pounds
is a lot of money in the small farming line, and probably anything over eighty
would have tempted him.

25 It was with some especial pleasure that Tom took advantage of one of Laurence's
rare visits to the farm to lead him down to the enclosure where Clover Fairy
kept solitary state – the grass widower of a grazing harem. Tom felt some of his old
dislike for his half-brother reviving; the artist was becoming more languid in his
manner, more unsuitably turned-out in attire, and he seemed inclined to impart a
30 slightly patronising tone to his conversation. He took no heed of a flourishing
potato crop, but waxed enthusiastic over
a clump of yellow-flowering weed that
stood in a corner by a gateway, which
was rather galling to the owner of a really
35 very well weeded farm; again, when he
might have been duly complimentary
about a group of fat, black-faced lambs,
that simply cried aloud for admiration,
he became eloquent over the foliage tints
40 of an oak copse on the hill opposite. But
now he was being taken to inspect the
crowning pride and glory of Helsery;

however grudging he might be in his praises, however backward and niggardly
with his congratulations, he would have to see and acknowledge the many excel-
45 lences of that redoubtable animal. Some weeks ago, while on a business journey to
Taunton, Tom had been invited by his half-brother to visit a studio in that town,
where Laurence was exhibiting one of his pictures, a large canvas representing a

bull standing knee-deep in some
marshy ground; it had been good of
its kind, no doubt, and Laurence had
seemed inordinately pleased with it;
'the best thing I've done yet," he had
said over and over again, and Tom
had generously agreed that it was
fairly life-like. Now, the man of pig-
ments was going to be shown a real
picture, a living model of strength

Annotations
10 **assured** confident
10 **superiority** state of being better than sb.
15 **stock** (here) farm animals
17 **breed sth.** (bred, bred) produce an animal in a controlled way / for a particular purpose
19 **shapely** having an attractive shape or body
22 **part with sth.** give/sell sth. to sb. else
24 **tempt sb.** make sb. consider doing sth. even though they find it wrong
26 **enclosure** part of land that is surrounded by a fence
27 **keep solitary state** (here) live all by yourself
28 **languid** moving slowly in an elegant manner
29 **unsuitably turned-out in attire** (here) more and more unsuitably dressed
29 **inclined to do sth.** likely to do sth.
29 **impart** give a particular quality to sth.
30 **take heed of sth.** pay careful attention to sth.
31 **wax enthusiastic** (fml) become enthusiastic when talking about sth.
34 **galling** annoying
36 **duly** in the expected way
36 **be complimentary about sth.** (fml) express admiration for sth.
39 **tint** shade of a colour
40 **copse** area of trees growing together
43 **be grudging in sth.** (fml) do sth. unwillingly
43 **niggardly** (adj, fml) mean, unwilling to be generous
45 **redoubtable** (fml) having qualities that make others respect or even fear them

## Annotations

58 **comeliness** *(literary)* attractiveness

58 **feast your eyes on sth.** *(idiom)* look at sth. with great pleasure

62 **inquiring** *(AE = BE enquiring)* showing interest

65 **be of the catch-as-catch-can order** (here) be of the 'catch me if you can' type

66 **perfunctory** done as a duty

69 **slush** dirty, melted snow

70 **bulky** tall and heavy

70 **brute** (here) big, strong animal

71 **beggar** (here) Bursche, Kerl

74 **complacency** feeling of being overly satisfied with yourself

87 **patronizing** [ˈpætrənaɪzɪŋ, ˈpeɪtrənaɪzɪŋ] showing that you think you're better than the others

88 **put sb. out of conceit with themselves** (here) make sb. feel less proud of themselves

90 **a mere picture** just a picture

91 **dexterous** skilfully done

92 **counterfeit** *(fml)* fake

95 **byre** farm building in which cows are kept

96 **speckle sth.** leave coloured spots on sth.

97 **heifer** [ˈhefə] young female cow

97 **steer** bull

99 **chattel** sth. that belongs to you

102 **blunt** very direct

and comeliness, a thing to feast the eyes on, a picture that exhibited new pose and action with every shifting minute, instead of standing glued into one unvarying
60 attitude between the four walls of a frame. Tom unfastened a stout wooden door and led the way into a straw-bedded yard.

'Is he quiet?' asked the artist, as a young bull with a curly red coat came inquiringly towards them.

'He's playful at times,' said Tom, leaving his half-brother to wonder whether the
65 bull's ideas of play were of the catch-as-catch-can order. Laurence made one or two perfunctory' comments on the animal's appearance and asked a question or so as to his age and such-like details; then he coolly turned the talk into another channel.

'Do you remember the picture I showed you at Taunton?' he asked.

'Yes,' grunted Tom; 'a white-faced bull standing in some slush. Don't admire those
70 Herefords much myself; bulky-looking brutes, don't seem to have much life in them. Daresay they're easier to paint that way; now, this young beggar is on the move all the time, aren't you, Fairy?'

I've sold that picture,' said Laurence, with considerable compla-
75 cency in his voice.

'Have you?' said Tom; 'glad to hear it, I'm sure. Hope you're pleased with what you've got for it.'

'I got three hundred pounds for it,'
80 said Laurence.

Tom turned towards him with a slowly rising flush of anger in his

face. Three hundred pounds! Under the most favourable market conditions that he could imagine his prized Clover Fairy would hardly fetch a hundred, yet here was a
85 piece of varnished canvas, painted by his half-brother, selling for three times that sum. It was a cruel insult that went home with all the more force because it emphasised the triumph of the patronising, self-satisfied Laurence. The young farmer had meant to put his relative just a little out of conceit with himself by displaying the jewel of his possessions, and now the tables were turned, and his valued beast was
90 made to look cheap and insignificant beside the price paid for a mere picture. It was so monstrously unjust; the painting would never be anything more than a dexterous piece of counterfeit life, while Clover Fairy was the real thing, a monarch in his little world, a personality in the countryside. After he was dead, even, he would still be something of a personality; his descendants would graze in those valley mead-
95 ows and hillside pastures, they would fill stall and byre and milking-shed, their good red coats would speckle the landscape and crowd the market-place; men would note a promising heifer or a well-proportioned steer, and say: 'Ah, that one comes of good old Clover Fairy's stock.' All that time the picture would be hanging, lifeless and unchanging, beneath its dust and varnish, a chattel that ceased to mean
100 anything if you chose to turn it with its back to the wall. These thoughts chased themselves angrily through Tom Yorkfield's mind, but he could not put them into words. When he gave tongue to his feelings he put matters bluntly and harshly.

**Advanced**

'Some soft-witted fools may like to throw away three hundred pounds on a bit of paintwork; can't say as I envy them their taste. I'd rather have the real thing than a
105 picture of it.'

He nodded towards the young bull, that was alternately staring at them with nose held high and lowering its horns with a half-play-
110 ful, half-impatient shake of the head.

Laurence laughed a laugh of irritating, indulgent amusement.

'I don't think the purchaser of my
115 bit of paintwork, as you call it, need worry about having thrown his money away. As I get to be better known and recognised my pictures will go up in value. That particular one will probably fetch four hundred in a sale-room five or six years hence; pictures
120 aren't a bad investment if you know enough to pick out the work of the right men. Now you can't say your precious bull is going to get more valuable the longer you keep him; he'll have his little day, and then, if you go on keeping him, he'll come down at last to a few shillingsworth of hoofs and hide, just at a time, perhaps, when my bull is being bought for a big sum for some important picture gallery.'

125 It was too much. The united force of truth and slander and insult put over heavy a strain on Tom Yorkfield's powers of restraint. In his right hand he held a useful oak cudgel, with his left he made a grab at the loose collar of Laurence's canary-coloured silk shirt. Laurence was not a fighting man; the fear of physical violence threw him off his balance as completely as overmastering indignation had thrown Tom off his,
130 and thus it came to pass that Clover Fairy was regaled with the unprecedented sight of a human being scudding and squawking across the enclosure, like the hen that would persist in trying to establish a nesting-place in the manger. In another crowd-ed happy moment the bull was trying to jerk Laurence over his left shoulder, to prod him in the ribs while still in the air, and to kneel on him when he reached the ground.
135 It was only the vigorous intervention of Tom that induced him to relinquish the last item of his programme.

Tom devotedly and ungrudgingly nursed his half brother to a complete recovery from his injuries, which consisted of nothing more serious than a dislocated shoul-der, a broken rib or two, and a little nervous prostration. After all, there was no
140 further occasion for rancour in the young farmer's mind; Laurence's bull might sell for three hundred, or for six hundred, and be admired by thousands in some big picture gallery, but it would never toss a man over one shoulder and catch him a jab in the ribs before he had fallen on the other side. That was Clover Fairy's noteworthy achievement, which could never be taken away from him.

145 Laurence continues to be popular as an animal artist, but his subjects are always kittens or fawns or lambkins – never bulls.

*From:* The Toys of Peace, and Other Papers, *1919*

## Annotations

103 **soft-witted** lacking sense or judgment
113 **indulgent** (here) willing to ignore sb.'s ignorance or weakness-es
119 **six years hence** six years from now
123 **hide** *(n)* (here) animal's skin
125 **slander** statement intended to damage sb.'s reputation
126 **restraint** self-control
127 **cudgel** short stick used as a weapon
130 **regale sb. with sth.** entertain sb. with sth.
130 **unprecedented** [ʌnˈpresɪdentɪd] that has never happened before
131 **scud** hurry, move quickly
131 **squawk** make a loud sharp sound
132 **manger** [ˈmeɪndʒə] long box that e.g. cows eat from
135 **relinquish** (here) stop doing sth. unwillingly
137 **devoted** (here) full of affection and care
137 **ungrudging** not unwilling
139 **prostration** physical weakness
140 **rancour** bitterness
146 **fawn** young deer
146 **lambkin** = lamb

Advanced

## Comprehension

▶ SF 19: Reading and understanding narrative texts, p. 369

**1 a** Summarize the gist of the *short story in 5–7 sentences.
  **b** Work with a partner. Compile everything the reader learns about the two brothers. **Partner A** focuses on Tom, **Partner B** focuses on Laurence. Then exchange your results.

## Analysis

▶ SF 31: Writing a character profile, p. 387

**2 a** Analyse the means of *characterization the author uses to characterize the two brothers. Describe their effect on the reader.
  **b** Write a *character profile of either Tom or Laurence.

**3** Giving examples, identify the style of the text as well as other stylistic devices. Explain the function of the stylistic devices.

## Language awareness

▶ Getting started 📑

**4** The author uses very formal language. Rephrase the following sentences in your own words. The annotations may help you.
ll. 1–2: 'Tom Yorkfield ... indifference.'
ll. 27–30: 'Tom felt ... conversation.'
ll. 42–46: 'But now ... animal.'
ll. 130–133: 'The united force ... restraint.'

## Beyond the text

▶ WOB: pp. 37–39

**5**   You choose   Work on either **a** or **b**.

  **a** Which of these four proverbs fits the story's message best? Explain why you think so.
*Beauty is in the eye of the beholder.*
*To err is human, to forgive is divine.*
*Pride comes before a fall.*
*Actions speak louder than words.*

  **b** Find a picture that captures the idea behind the short story (no pictures of bulls). Then get together in groups of three. Each of you shows your picture and the others try to explain which idea it represents.

  **c**   Intercultural competence   There is a German equivalent of each of the four proverbs in **6a**. Explain what an intercultural use of the same proverbs might imply.

**6** Interpret the text, examining whether it can be considered a typical short story.

*Modal auxiliary verbs, also called modal auxiliaries or modal verbs, are used to add extra meaning to a sentence, e. g. the speaker's purpose or attitude.*

# 1 Language revisited

## Forms and functions

Write the modal verbs from the first box in a copy of the table below and add their negative forms. Match them with their communicative functions (cf. second box). Some communicative functions can be used more than once.

| **Modal verb** (positive/negative form) | **Communicative function** |
|---|---|
| can/cannot, can't | ability, permission, suggestion, offer, possibility, request |
| could/… | |
| … | … |

► More language

► Check

# 2 Language awareness

## Degrees of obligation

*To express obligation in English, the verbs* must, need to, be to, be supposed to, ought to, should, had better *can be used – each expressing different degrees of obligation.*

a   Arrange the modals from the weakest to the strongest expression of obligation.
b   Choose the most suitable modal from the brackets.
   1   The painter was really depressed because he couldn't live from his art. His teachers (should / were supposed to) have told him that he wasn't very talented.
   2   When (are we to / shall we) hand in our A&C-projects? Did Mr. Brown say the twentieth or the twenty-first?
   3   You simply (should/must) go the concert. It will be absolutely fantastic.
   4   Life as a musician is going to be hard. You (ought to / had better) take up another job to earn your living.

# 3 Practise

## Differences in meaning

Choose the correct modal auxiliary verb to fit the context.
1   I'm pretty sure you (won't be allowed to / can't) use Dad's violin for the concert.
2   We (had better not / haven't got to) disturb the actors in the theatre.
3   I (mustn't / needn't) be at the venue before 9 – we have reserved seats.
4   The director (oughtn't to have / mustn't have) called Anna a horrible actress.
5   I (could / was able to) talk to the designers yesterday and they agree with our ideas.

**Modal verbs**
can • could • will • would • must • may • might • need • shall • should • ought to

**Communicative functions**
ability • permission • prohibition • obligation • necessity • advice • offer • invitation • suggestion • possibility • probability • refusal/rejection • request • instruction

**Info**

To use **modal auxiliaries** in all tenses and aspects, you will have to use substitute forms such as: be able to • be allowed to • (not) have to • be supposed to • be to

► Check

► Check
► WOB: p. 114

**Street art** is a form of art displayed publicly on buildings, streets or trains, often intended to make a personal statement or provoke society. Initially, it was often produced illegally but today it might even be commissioned. Well-known street artists include Banksy and Shepard Fairey.
**Pop art**, developed in the 1950s and 1960s, is a style based on popular culture and uses imagery from advertisements and film. Renowned artists include Andy Warhol and Yayoi Kusama.

# A new kind of exhibition

*You are going to read an article about an unusual exhibition in Düsseldorf.*

• Do you like art exhibitions? Why or why not?

Auf die roten Backsteine hat jemand #Punk mit neongelber Farbe gesprüht. Gleich neben die Eingangstür, direkt unter das violette Schild mit dem Zeichentrick-männchen, die Augen übergroß, das Grinsen verschmitzt. *'No more Heroes'* steht auf seinem T-Shirt. Keine Helden mehr. Am Ticketschalter des NRW-Forums be-
5 kommt man keine Eintrittskarten, sondern weiße Armbändchen, wie auf einem Festival. Und in der Garderobe, auf einem der hölzernen Spinde, prangt ein gro-ßer grüner Mittelfinger. Alles sagt einem: Achtung, jetzt kommt eine coole Aus-stellung. Das hier ist was für junge Leute.

Und tatsächlich, die jungen Leute fühlen sich gemeint. Erstaunliche 40.000 Men-
10 schen haben sich *Wonderwalls – Art & Toys* schon angesehen. Davon sind rund 30 Prozent sehr jung, also unter 18 Jahre alt, Schüler oder Azubis, erklärt Alain Bieber, künstlerischer Leiter des NRW-Forums und Kurator der Ausstellung. 'Und viele kommen ohne Eltern. Normalerweise schleppen die ihre Kinder ja mit, aber diese Ausstellung besuchen sie alleine und gerne.' Im ersten Schauraum versam-
15 melt sich trotzdem eine Seniorengruppe. Eine ältere Dame hat bereits auf ihrem mitgebrachten Klappstuhl Platz genommen. Vor ihr, auf einer blauen Wand, hän-gen große Porträts, allesamt mit dickem weißem Rahmen; nicht von Menschen, sondern von Figuren wie Batman, Chewbacca, Wonder Woman. Auf einem frisst Godzilla Adolf Hitler. Sämtliche der über 2000 Werke, die hier in Düsseldorf aus-
20 gestellt werden, hat der Unternehmer Selim Varol gesammelt. Von Skulpturen bis zu Graffiti gibt es alles. 'Meine Sammlung – das bin ich. Meine Kindheit, meine Freunde, meine Helden, meine Vorbilder. Sie ist, was mir gefällt und was mich bewegt', heißt es groß am Anfang.

Das Versprechen von *Wonderwalls:* Hier trifft Pop auf Street-Art, also urbane Kunst.
25 In den 1960er- und 1970er-Jahren war sie aus den Protestkulturen entstanden, aus gegenkulturellen Strömungen und zivilem Ungehorsam. Ganz ohne Kommerz, im öffentlichen Raum, da, wo alle sind. 'Die von Gesellschafts- und Konsumkritik geprägten Arbeiten sind heute genauso relevant wie zum Zeitpunkt ihrer Entste-hung', heißt es auf einer Infowand. Darunter findet man die Logos der Sponsoren,
30 als erstes das von Red Bull. Daneben die Skulptur eines Mannes, graue Jeans und grauer Kapuzenpullover, der seinen Kopf durch die Wand geschlagen hat.

Zwei Frauen, beide mit dicker Daunenjacke, fotografieren einige Räume weiter ein Bild der Queen. Darauf hat sie pinke Haare, trägt zur Krone eine Lederjacke mit Nieten und punkigen Ansteckern. Auffällig, fast alle Besucherinnen und Besucher
35 zücken irgendwann ihr Handy. Das liegt laut Bieber auch daran, dass die Ausstel-lung besonders *'instagramable'* sei, sie lässt sich also gut für Social Media fotogra-fieren. Das merkt man spätestens vor einer Wand mit Hunderten *Be@rbricks* – so heißen die ausgestellten Bärenfiguren im Fachjargon. Sie sehen aus wie Lego-Teddys, die man mit unterschiedlichen Designs bedruckt hat. Da gibt es einen
40 Karl-Lagerfeld-Bären – Foto –, einen Garfield-Bären – Foto – und einen Homer-Simpson-Bären – Foto. Sogar ein plüschiges pinkes Glücksbärchi mit Regenbogen am Bauch. Vor den Bären wird laut Bieber mittlerweile auch getanzt.

'Wir waren noch nie so präsent auf TikTok', sagt er. Der Grund: Mit der Ausstellung spreche man verschiedene Filterblasen an. 'Die Hip-Hop- oder Skateboard-
45 Kultur gehört da dazu, aber auch die Street-Art-Szene. Da trifft sich ein Cluster an
Zielgruppen.'

Die Ausstellung ist überwältigend. Wo, wenn nicht hier, fragt man sich, wie sich
unsere Erwartungen an Museen verändern. In Düsseldorf sind die Kunstwerke
nicht mehr nur zum Bestaunen da, hier können die Menschen damit machen, was
50 sie wollen. Und das holt die Street-Art aus dem Museum wieder dorthin, wo sie
alle sehen können, wo heute alle sind – ins Internet. Schöner könnte sich ein Kreis
nicht schließen. [...]                                                 *(557 words)*

*From*: Eva Saga, *Die Zeit*, 2023

**1** `Mediating` Work on either **a** or **b**.

**a** Your bilingual art class is
planning a class trip to an
exhibition. You come across this
article and think 'Wonderwalls' is
worth going to. Recommend this
exhibition to your class and
summarize what they can expect
to see or find there.

**b** `Challenge` Your bilingual art class is
planning a class trip to an exhibition.
You come across this article and you
think 'Wonderwalls' is worth going
to. Recommend this exhibition to
your class, summarize what they can
expect to see or find there and
explain why they are the perfect
target group for this exhibition.

▶ SF 49: Mediating from
German into English,
p. 416
▶ Getting started
▶ WOB: pp. 71–73

## Artists and their communities

*You are going to listen to an interview with artist Manizha in the episode 'My
art, my community' from the BBC podcast* The Cultural Frontline.

### Comprehension

**1** `Listening` Listen to the interview. Then sum up the events in her life that
lead to her political activism.

**2** `Listening` Listen to the interview for a second time. Describe the consequences
Manizha's political activism has had and how this has impacted her art.

▶ SF 40: Listening for gist
and detail, p. 399
▶ Getting started

### Beyond the text

**3** Do you have a favourite artist who uses their art to express political protest?
Present them and their works of art to the class and explain why you like them.

**4** Think back to the guiding question of the chapter. How would you answer it
at this point?

▶ Support, p. 315

▶ WOB: pp. 78–81

**Annotations**
**blue sky thinking** activity of developing completely new ideas
**plough** [plaʊ] piece of farming equipment used to turn over soil
**Eisenhower** (1890–1969) 34th president of the United States
**the hungry cowterpillar** reference to the children's book *The Very Hungry Caterpillar* by Eric Carle
**home stretch** last part of a race
**50 k** (here) 50.000 pounds
**whacky** crazy
▶ Support, p. 315

# Noomoo launch film    Nick Flugge and Sami Abusamra

*Advertising is without doubt part of everyday culture in industrialized societies. While simple forms of advertising can be traced to ancient times, it was in the 19th century that the first advertising agencies were established. Since then, advertising has become increasingly elaborate and creative and, of course, more diverse in terms of the media used.*  ▶ More info

- With a partner, think about marketing campaigns that for some reason were memorable to you. What made them so special?

*You are going to watch a film clip about the creation of a marketing campaign.*

### Comprehension

1   Viewing  Describe what stages the creation of the campaign goes through and say how well the campaign manager is performing in each of them.

### Analysis

2   Work with a partner. One of you describes the character of the campaign manager, the other that of Maggie, the farmer.

> **Language help**
>
> boastful · conceited · cool-headed · disrespectful · down-to-earth · full of yourself · honest · ignorant · laid-back · offhand · self-confident · straightforward · unceremonious · unpretentious · vain

▶ Getting started
▶ Support, p. 316
▶ WOB: pp. 82–84

3   a   Viewing  Say whether you found the video funny and why. Then examine how humour is created in the video.
    b   Viewing  For what purpose might this film clip have been created? State your opinion and support it by examining the cinematic devices used.

### Beyond the text

▶ SF 41 Analysing films, series and videos, p. 399
▶ Check

4   Writing  Advertising – art, nuisance, capitalist tool, necessary evil, everyday experience? Write a blog post stating your personal view.

▶ SF 28: Argumentative writing: discussion and comment, p. 382
▶ SF 29: Writing a blog post, p. 384

> **Info**
>
> **British humour**, a rich tapestry woven from diverse comedic influences, thrives on understatement, sarcasm and surrealism. From Shakespearean comedies to Billy Connolly's charismatic performances, it's an integral part of British storytelling. Defining a singular British humour, though, is impossible. It varies not just across
> 5  the four home nations but also between major cities. Scottish humour ranges from Billy Connolly's brash style to Susan Calman's gentler approach, exemplifying the diversity within British humour. Moreover, overseas influences, like Italy's Commedia dell'arte have shaped exaggerated characters like those in *Fawlty Towers*, blurring the definition of what's 'British'.
> 10  However, it's safe to say that British humour dances on the fine line between the absurd and clever, finding hilarity in the ordinary. Whether through Monty Python's

surreal sketches or Oscar Wilde's sharp exchanges, it embraces diverse forms.
Sarcasm, its weapon of choice, is delivered with a cup of tea and a raised eyebrow,

15 as shown in Stephen Fry's witty remarks and John Cleese's iconic 'silly walk'.
Awkward situations, as portrayed in shows like *The Office,* created by Ricky
Gervais, and *Fawlty Towers*, also provide laughs.

Self-deprecation, another favoured tool of British humour, is a mark of comedic
talent, which can be seen in Ricky Gervais's stand-up routines. Brits find life's

20 quirks amusing and poke fun at themselves, their history and their habits. Eddie
Izzard's surreal monologues, for example, brilliantly and humorously deconstruct
language and history.

Surely, the essence of British humour lies in its ability to surprise, its unexpected
twists or clever phrases. Whether a funny comment from Stephen Fry, an absurd

25 scenario in P.G. Wodehouse's works, or Rowan Atkinson's deadpan 'Mr. Bean',
British humour invites you to join in on the joke with unflappable charm. It's a
celebration of the wonderfully absurd nature of life itself.

**1** Point out which features may be considered typical of British humour and
state to what extent the film clip on p. 170 might be considered an example.

**2** Try to find videos or texts by some of the representatives of British humour
mentioned in the text and say how funny you find them.

Michael Palin and John Cleese in Monty Python's famous *Dead Parrot Sketch*

## Chapter task

*After having dealt with various aspects of arts and culture, you now have the
opportunity to advocate for an arts project in your local community.*

In your community, there is a policy to introduce and promote the arts. The local
administration for arts and culture has therefore invited representatives of
different age groups to find out which projects deserve to be funded. You have
been invited to the meeting, at which each participant is allowed to give a
three- minute-speech to present their ideas.

Give a speech in which you explain how important arts and culture are to you and
your peers and which cultural forms should be funded and promoted in your local
community.

▶ Getting started

# Chapter 6
# Globalization and International Politics: Chances and Challenges

OPPORTUNITY

UNEMPLOYMENT

AMERICANIZATION

ALIENATION

COMMUNICATION

WORLD WIDE WEE

► Check

**1  a** Look at the words in the picture above and say which aspect of globalization they illustrate. Make a table with the four columns below and copy the words in one of them. Give reasons for your decision.

    **1**  economic aspects        **3**  cultural aspects
    **2**  political aspects        **4**  feelings and reactions

    **b** Add at least five more words from your background knowledge. Compare them with a partner and put them into the respective columns.

    **c** Continue adding new words to your table. In the end, you will have a global glossary, containing terms for talking about global chances and challenges.

**2  a** In your view, how beneficial is globalization? In the classroom, position yourself on an imaginary scale ranging from 1 (completely detrimental) to 10 (completely beneficial) without thinking about it too much.

    **b** Take a look at the Chapter map on the right side. Which of the aspects refer to global chances, which to challenges?

    **c** *****Quick write:** Answer the guiding question in a short paragraph.

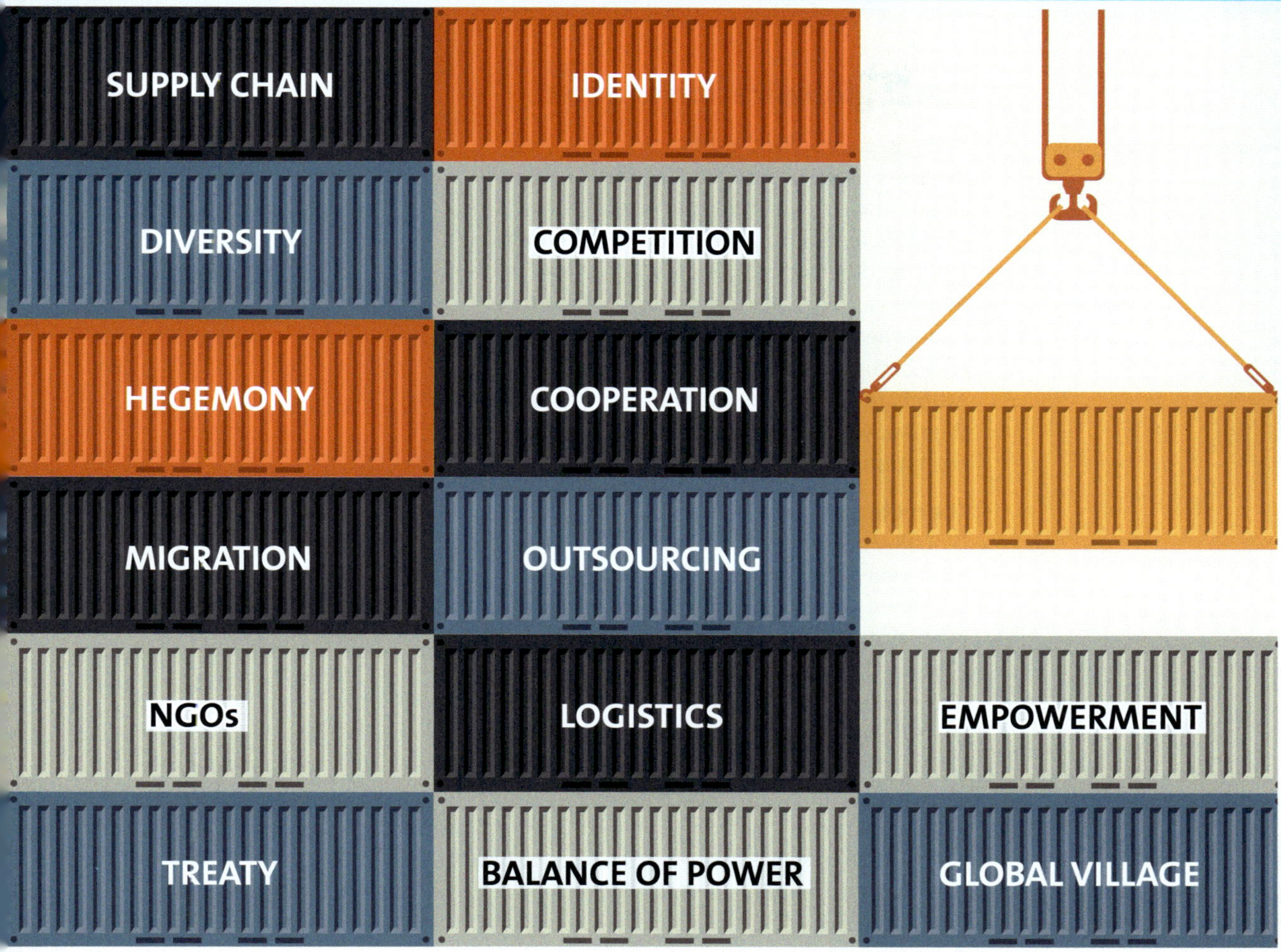

| | | |
|---|---|---|
| SUPPLY CHAIN | IDENTITY | |
| DIVERSITY | COMPETITION | |
| HEGEMONY | COOPERATION | |
| MIGRATION | OUTSOURCING | |
| NGOs | LOGISTICS | EMPOWERMENT |
| TREATY | BALANCE OF POWER | GLOBAL VILLAGE |

> **Chapter map**

globalization 3.0          global trade

Americanization          inequality          Chapter task: summary ✅

ecology

How can we use global chances to face global challenges?          international conflicts

Mediating          peacekeeping

migration

international relations          belonging          economic sustainability

### What globalization is about

► More language

**Living in a globalized world**

We are living in an increasingly globalized world. Trade, travel and communication make the world more closely connected than ever before.
5 The speed with which people, goods and information can be transported from one continent to another has reached an unprecedented level and continues to increase. The effects of globalization are reflected in every aspect of our lives:
10 the food we eat, the music we listen to, the information we receive, the products we buy.

On the ancient Silk Road

**The motors of globalization**

Globalization is a process that began two thousand years ago, with the first caravans on the
15 Silk Road between Asia and Europe. In the 16th century, progress in shipbuilding and navigation gave a new impulse to global trade. A number of factors have contributed to the in-

The Dubai skyline

creasing pace of globalization in our time. One of them is the emergence of affordable
20 air travel, which has made people more mobile than ever before. Container ships (and the logistics that keep track of them) have done the same for goods. Digitalization and advances in broadband and fibre-optic communication have also made international cooperation possible on a level that would have been unimaginable thirty years ago. Free-trade agreements and the implementation of international standards in finan-
25 cial matters have massively increased the mobility of goods, services and capital. Finally, the migration of workers and jobs has played a major role in raising the general standard of living worldwide.

**Global chances, global challenges**

Globalization is often regarded as just referring to economic globalization, e.g. the
30 loss of manufacturing jobs to Asia or the global outreach of American fast-food chains. But there is much more to globalization. It includes the efforts of organizations that regulate international relations. One of the most important is the United Nations. Its tasks include defusing conflicts between nations, maintaining peacekeeping operations and dealing with the impact of global migration. Other international organiza-
35 tions are the World Trade Organization (WTO), which works towards international standards in global commerce, and the World Health Organization (WHO), which coordinates efforts to limit the impact of pandemics. Environmental globalization is embodied by the Paris Agreement. It reflects the understanding that climate change and environmental destruction are global issues that require a global response. Cultural
40 globalization refers, on the one hand, to the lively intercultural dialogue to be found in some sectors of the entertainment industry for example, but also to the international dominance of the English language and US media corporations. Whereas the rise of the USA to the role of global superpower dominated world politics in the latter 20th century, today we are faced with new challenges in the rise of nations like China,
45 Russia and India to the status of global players and in the emerging countries of Africa, Asia and Latin America, all of whom clamour for their fair share of global wealth.

## 1  Main ideas

► Check

   **a**  Name three examples of each of the following:
      **1**  evidence of globalization in everyday life
      **2**  motors of globalization
      **3**  global chances and challenges

   **b**  Compare lists with your partner and add important aspects that are missing from your lists.

## 2  Reflect

Which of the aspects of globalization named in the text are important for you personally? Choose one or two. Explain to your partner why you chose them. Then listen to your partner's explanation.

## 3  Systematizing your vocabulary

   **a**  Create a chart or infographic about global chances and challenges using words from your global glossary and the highlighted phrases from the text.
   **b**  Present your product to your class.

## 4  Chunk it!

► Getting started
► Check

   **a**  Replace the gaps in the following *chunks by verbs. You can check the text for help if you are not sure. Add four more chunks from the text to the list. Use a dictionary for help if needed.
      **1**  … an impulse to sth.
      **2**  … track of sth.
      **3**  … a role in sth.
      **4**  … a new level
      **5**  … a conflict
      **6**  … a response

   **b**  Compare solutions with your partner.
   **c**  Add relevant words to your global glossary (cf. p. 172, task **1c**).

## 5  Summarizing your ideas

   **a**  `Writing`  What are or will be global chances and challenges in your life? Can you imagine studying, living or working abroad? Working for a multinational firm or organization? Summarize your thoughts in a short statement.
   **b**  Swap texts with your partner. Read your partner's summary and compare your ideas and expectations.

► **More info**

# A short history of globalization   Thomas Friedman

- Together with a partner, discuss which historical and political events can be described as early forms of globalization.

*Thomas Friedman is a US journalist who has written extensively on globalization and technology. His book* The World is Flat, *from which the following excerpt is taken, first appeared in 2005.*

[...] There have been three great eras of globalization. The first lasted from 1492 – when Columbus set sail, opening trade between the Old World and the New World – until around 1800. I would call this era Globalization 1.0. It shrank the world from a size large to a size medium. Globalization 1.0 was about countries
5 and muscles. That is, in Globalization 1.0, the key agent of change, the dynamic force driving the process of global integration, was how much brawn – how much muscle, how much horsepower, wind power, or, later, steam power – your country had and how creatively you could deploy it. In this era, countries and governments (often inspired by religion or imperialism or a combination of both) led the way in
10 breaking down walls and knitting the world together, driving global integration. In Globalization 1.0, the primary questions were: Where does my country fit into global competition and opportunities? How can I go global and collaborate with others through my country?

The second great era, Globalization 2.0, lasted roughly from 1800 to 2000, inter-
15 rupted by the Great Depression and World Wars I and II. This era shrank the world from a size medium to a size small. In Globalization 2.0, the key agent of change, the dynamic force driving global integration, was multinational companies. These multinationals went global for markets and labor, spearheaded first by the expansion of the Dutch and English joint-stock companies and the Industrial Revolu-
20 tion. In the first half of this era, global integration was powered by falling transportation costs, thanks to the steam engine and the railroad, and in the second half by falling telecommunication costs – thanks to the diffusion of the telegraph, telephones, the PC, satellites, fiber-optic cable, and the early version of the World Wide Web. It was during this era that we really saw the birth and maturation of a global
25 economy, in the sense that there was enough movement of goods and information from continent to continent for there to be a global market, with global arbitrage in products and labor. The dynamic forces behind this era of globalization were breakthroughs in hardware – from steamships and railroads in the beginning to telephones and mainframe computers toward the end. And the big questions in
30 this era were: Where does my company fit into the global economy? How does it take advantage of the opportunities? How can I go global and collaborate with others through my company? [...]

Right around the year 2000 we entered a whole new era: Globalization 3.0. Globalization 3.0 is shrinking the world from a size small to a size tiny and flatten-
35 ing the playing field at the same time. And while the dynamic force in Globalization 1.0 was countries globalizing and the dynamic force in Globalization 2.0 was companies globalizing, the dynamic force in Globalization 3.0 – the force that gives it its unique character – is the newfound power for *individuals* to collaborate and compete globally. And the phenomenon that is enabling, empowering, and
40 enjoining individuals and small groups to go global so easily and so seamlessly is

One of the first global goods: a hot pepper, brought to Europe in 1493 by Christopher Columbus's expedition

**Annotations**
5 **key agent** most important factor
6 **brawn** physical strength
8 **deploy sth.** use sth. effectively
15 **Great Depression** worldwide economic crisis (1929 – ca. 1940)
18 **spearhead sth.** initiate sth.
19 **joint-stock company** *Aktiengesellschaft*
22 **diffusion** *(fml)* act of spreading sth.
24 **maturation** process of becoming fully grown
26 **arbitrage** buying and selling for profit
40 **enjoin sb.** urge or strongly advise sb.

what I call the *flat-world platform* [...]. The flat-world platform is the product of a convergence of the personal computer (which allowed every individual suddenly to become the author of his or her own content in digital form) with fiber-optic cable (which suddenly allowed all those individuals to access more and more digital con-
45 tent around the world for next to nothing) with the rise of workflow software (which enabled individuals all over the world to collaborate on that same digital content from anywhere, regardless of the distances between them). No one anticipated this convergence. It just happened – right around the year 2000. And when it did, people all over the world started waking up and realizing that they had more power
50 than ever to go global *as individuals,* they needed more than ever to think of themselves as individuals competing against other individuals all over the planet, and they had more opportunities to work with those other individuals, not just compete with them. As a result, every person now must, and can, ask: Where do *I* as an individual fit into the global competition and opportunities of the day, and how can
55 *I*, on my own, collaborate with others globally?

But Globalization 3.0 differs from the previous eras not only in how it is shrinking and flattening the world and in how it is empowering individuals. It also is different in that Globalization 1.0 and 2.0 were driven primarily by European and American individuals and businesses. Even though China actually had the biggest economy
60 in the world in the eighteenth century, it was Western countries, companies, and explorers who were doing most of the globalizing and shaping of the system. But going forward, this will be less and less true. Because it is flattening and shrinking the world, Globalization 3.0 is going to be more and more driven not only by individuals but also by a much more diverse – non-Western, non-white – group of
65 individuals. Individuals from every corner of the flat world are being empowered. Globalization 3.0 makes it possible for so many more people to plug in and play, and you are going to see every color of the human rainbow take part.

*From:* The World Is Flat, *2007*

Annotations
42 **convergence**
*Annäherung*
45 **workflow software**
*Arbeitssoftware*

**Info**

**Globalization 4.0**
In recent years, the number of people identifying as digital nomads, i.e. people who use technology and new methods of communication to work remotely and are not bound to a specific physical location, has surged. The pandemic further increased remote work opportunities, even resulting in several countries offering digital nomad visas. However, this trend predominantly benefits those with stronger passports with fewer visa restrictions and a degree of financial stability. In stark contrast, many people are forced to relocate due to wars, economic instability and climate-related disasters, highlighting the disparity in reasons behind global mobility.

### Comprehension

1  Create a table with the following headers: Globalization 1.0, Globalization 2.0, Globalization 3.0 and Globalization 4.0. Add suitable categories in the first column on the left and fill in the information given in the text and the info box on the right for each of the four eras of globalization.

2  Outline the connection between globalization and technological progress as presented by Friedman and his view of the individual's role in the course of globalization.

▶ Support , p. 316

### Analysis

3  Examine the style of the text and relate it to the audience Friedman has in mind.

▶ WOB: pp. 28–30

▶ SF 46: Having a
   discussion, p. 410
▶ SF 29: Writing a blog
   post, p. 384
▶ Getting started
   (task a)
▶ Check

## Language awareness

**4  a**  Friedman uses a number of images in his text.

       **1**  'muscles' (l. 5)        **4**  'shrinking the world' (l. 34)

       **2**  'breaking down walls' (l. 10)  **5**  'waking up' (l. 49)

       **3**  'birth and maturation' (l. 24)

      Rephrase the phrases without using the images.

  **b**  Explain the effect it has on the sentences and the text in general.

## Beyond the text

**5**  You choose  Work on task **a** or **b**.

  **a**  Speaking  Discuss the following motion by Friedman: 'Globalization 3.0 empowers individuals worldwide'.

  **b**  Writing  Imagine Thomas Friedman hosted a blog. Write an entry there in which you explain why you think he called his book on globalization *The World Is Flat* and state whether you think the title is well chosen.

## Text 2

# Global champions

• Which nations do you regard as 'global champions'? Compare your ideas in class; give reasons for your choices.

*Three of the factors that determine the global influence of a country are the gross domestic product (GDP), the balance of trade and its military power.*

## Comprehension

**Info**

**GDP** refers to the total value of all goods and services produced and sold in a country in a given year. The **balance of trade** is the difference in value between a country's exports and imports. The **military power** of a country is expressed in terms of annual expenditure for the armed forces.

▶ Check

**1**  In each of the tables below, the top five countries worldwide are listed (with the data for 2021 in billions of US$). Decide which countries from the box at the bottom match the letters (countries may be used more than once):

| GDP | | Balance of trade | | Military spending | |
|---|---|---|---|---|---|
| A | 23,315 | F | 676 | K | 801 |
| B | 17,734 | G | 212 | L | 293 |
| C | 4,941 | H | 190 | M | 77 |
| D | 4,260 | I | 106 | N | 68 |
| E | 3,176 | J | 103 | O | 66 |

*Source: Worldbank*    *Source: Statista*    *Source: sipri*

China • Germany • India • Japan • Russia • Saudi Arabia • United Arab Emirates • UK • USA

2   Your teacher will give you the solution. Compare it with your ideas and discuss the results in your class. Which nations did you over- or underrate? What might the reason be?

**Beyond the text**

3   Looking into the future, other factors than the three named in task **1** might prove important for global leadership. Think of examples and discuss them.

## Text 3

**Advanced**

# Playing by the rules: the WTO

- WTO, WHO, UNO, NATO and OPEC are all \*acronyms for well-known international organizations. State the full name of each organization and explain its function.

*A globalized world requires rules that are accepted by all the major players. One of the most important organizations with regard to economic globalization is the World Trade Organization (WTO). The following text is taken from their website.*

### What is the WTO?

The World Trade Organization (WTO) is the only global international organization dealing with the rules of trade between nations. [...] The goal is to help producers of goods and services, exporters, and importers conduct
5  their business.

*From:* www.wto.org

Annotations
4  **conduct sth.** *(fml)* do sth.
13  **negotiation**
*Verhandlung*

### Who are we?

The overall objective of the WTO is to help its members use trade as a means to raise living standards, create jobs and improve people's lives. The WTO operates the global system of trade rules and helps developing coun-
10  tries build their trade capacity. It also provides a forum for its members to negotiate trade agreements and to resolve the trade problems they face with each other.

The WTO was born out of five decades of negotiations aimed at progressively reducing obstacles to trade. Where countries have faced trade barri-
15  ers and wanted them lowered, the negotiations have helped to open markets for trade. Conversely, in some circumstances, WTO rules support maintaining trade barriers – for example, to protect consumers or the environment.

Annotations

19 **bulk** majority
25 **objective** *(n)* goal
29 **ambassador**
   *Botschafter/in*
40 **commitment** sth. you
   have promised to do
45 **implementation**
   *Umsetzung*
46 **require sb. to do sth.**
   demand that sb. does
   sth.
47 **measure** *Maßnahme*
50 **scrutiny** close
   examination
53 **settlement** *Schlichtung*
54 **resolve sth.** end or
   solve sth.
55 **vital** absolutely
   necessary
57 **infringe sth.** *(fml)*
   break a law or rule

20 At its heart are the WTO agreements, negotiated and signed by the bulk of the world's trading nations. These documents provide the legal ground rules for international commerce. They are essentially contracts, binding governments to keep their trade policies within agreed limits. Although negotiated and signed by governments, the goal is to help producers of goods and services, exporters, and importers conduct their business, while

25 allowing governments to meet social and environmental objectives. [...]

*From:* www.wto.org

## What we do

The WTO is run by its member governments. All major decisions are made by the membership as a whole, either by ministers (who usually meet at least once every two years) or by their ambassadors or delegates (who meet

30 regularly in Geneva).

While the WTO is driven by its member states, it could not function without its Secretariat to coordinate the activities. The Secretariat employs over 600 staff, and its experts – lawyers, economists, statisticians and communications experts – assist WTO members on a daily basis to ensure, among

35 other things, that negotiations progress smoothly, and that the rules of international trade are correctly applied and enforced.

### Trade negotiations

The WTO agreements cover goods, services and intellectual property. They spell out the principles of liberalization, and the permitted exceptions.

40 They include individual countries' commitments to lower customs tariffs and other trade barriers, and to open and keep open services markets. They set procedures for settling disputes. These agreements are not static; they are renegotiated from time to time and new agreements can be added to the package. [...]

45 ### Implementation and monitoring

WTO agreements require governments to make their trade policies transparent by notifying the WTO about laws in force and measures adopted. Various WTO councils and committees seek to ensure that these requirements are being followed and that WTO agreements are being properly

50 implemented. All WTO members must undergo periodic scrutiny of their trade policies and practices, each review containing reports by the country concerned and the WTO Secretariat.

### Dispute settlement

The WTO's procedure for resolving trade quarrels under the Dispute Set-

55 tlement Understanding is vital for enforcing the rules and therefore for ensuring that trade flows smoothly. Countries bring disputes to the WTO if they think their rights under the agreements are being infringed. Judgements by specially appointed independent experts are based on interpretations of the agreements and individual countries' commitments.

The WTO headquarters in Geneva

Advanced

<sup>60</sup> **Building trade capacity**

WTO agreements contain special provision for developing countries, including longer time periods to implement agreements and commitments, measures to increase their trading opportunities, and support to help them build their trade capacity, to handle disputes and to implement technical stand-
<sup>65</sup> ards. The WTO organizes hundreds of technical cooperation missions to developing countries annually. It also holds numerous courses each year in Geneva for government officials. Aid for Trade aims to help developing countries develop the skills and infrastructure needed to expand their trade.

**Outreach**

<sup>70</sup> The WTO maintains regular dialogue with non-governmental organizations, parliamentarians, other international organizations, the media and the general public on various aspects of the WTO and the ongoing Doha negotiations, with the aim of enhancing cooperation and increasing awareness of WTO activities.

*From:* www.wto.org

Annotations
61 **provision** *Maßnahme*
64 **capacity** ability
73 **enhance sth.** improve sth.

## Comprehension

**1** [Writing] Write a dictionary entry that sums up the functions of the WTO.

▶ Getting started

## Analysis

**2** The above text is an example of *expository writing, i.e. a non-fiction text that provides facts. Considering this, examine the choice of verbs and verb forms used in the text and explain why certain forms are used so often.

▶ Getting started
▶ Support, p. 316

## Language awareness

**3** In the text there are a number of participle phrases, e.g. '... dealing with ...' (l. 3), '... aimed ...' (l. 13).
   **a** Rephrase the sentence without the participle.
   **b** Find three more sentences with participle phrases in the text and rephrase them without using a participle phrase.
   **c** Compare your sentences with the original ones. Which do you find better?
   **d** Name reasons why the participle phrases may have been used.

## Beyond the text

**4** Name a scenario in which the WTO might be needed and explain why.

Annotations

2 **gross** *(Geld) einspielen*
9 **impact** *(n)* influence
10 **unleash sth.** suddenly release sth., esp. a strong emotion or force
17 **extinction** *Auslöschung*
20 **Rio+20** UN Conference on Sustainable Development (2012)
31 **exacerbate sth.** [ɪgˈzæsəbeɪt] make sth. worse
33 **insurmountable** unsolvable
34 **obesity** state of being overweight
38 **agnostic** (here) neutral

**Info**

**The USA** is not only a global powerhouse when it comes to culture. After the attack on Pearl Harbor ended the era of American non-interventionism first articulated by former President James Monroe in 1823, the US became increasingly involved in global politics. The 1947 Truman Doctrine, for instance, pledged support for those fighting against communism during the Cold War. Priorities shifted as the September 11 attacks initiated the war on terror, with the US continuing to assume the position of the global policeman. In recent years, this role has been questioned after some criticized the country's excessive intervention in the Middle East. During the Trump administration (2017–2021), the USA briefly returned to its isolationist roots, with the former President promoting the historical 'America First' ideology, coined by Woodrow Wilson during WWI.

# Global culture – made in USA?    Peter Vanham

• Consider the music you like to listen to. Which countries does it come from?

*The dominant role of US culture throughout the world has led some to speak of 'cultural imperialism'. But there are signs that it is losing its influence.*

Today, there is no denying the dominant global culture is American. The highest grossing films of all time, worldwide, are almost without exception from Hollywood (think *Avatar*, *Titanic* or *Star Wars*). The best-selling albums of all time are mostly American (although Australian band AC/DC and British band Pink Floyd 5 gave Michael Jackson a run for his money).

Most social-media and internet firms are American. And food culture, though more diverse, is still affected by [big American companies].

This evolution would not have been possible without the wider globalization of the world economy, and the transformative impact of technology. In the 1960s, trans- 10 atlantic flights and radio recordings made it possible for The Beatles to unleash a mania in America. In the 1990s and 2000s open global markets and the internet allowed for cultural sensations to spread even faster.

But this globalization of culture did come at a price. Consider languages. Since the earliest era of globalization – the 16th Century Age of Discovery – the number of spo- 15 ken languages worldwide has steadily declined, from about 14,500 to less than 7,000.

By 2007, the New York Times reported, half of the remaining 7,000 languages were at danger of extinction. And by 2017, the World Economic Forum wrote, almost 1,500 languages had less than 1,000 speakers left.

As UNESCO, the United Nations' educational, scientific and cultural arm pointed 20 out at Rio+20, the homogenization of culture brought other risks too.

It said in 2012: 'While this phenomenon promotes the integration of societies, it may also bring with it a loss of uniqueness of local culture, which in turn can lead to loss of identity, exclusion and even conflict.' [...]

Then there are the economic effects of a globalizing culture. Already before the 25 rise of social media and the so-called Big Tech companies, less than a dozen companies [...] owned the lion's share of the world's leading media and entertainment institutions.

The arrival of large tech platforms only accelerated the trend towards larger market concentration, and the risks of loss of cultural diversity.

30 Finally, as much as we may like our burger with fries, our bag of chips and our takeaway cup of coffee, the globalizing fast-food culture exacerbated global problems too.

If everyone consumed the same amount of burgers as Americans, or created as much rubbish, climate change and pollution might be insurmountable, and obesity an even bigger cause of illness and death.

35 This raises some important questions. Is American-led cultural globalization a self-destructive time bomb, destined to slowly kill languages, cultures and life itself? Is cultural globalization a phenomenon that enriches local cultures with a diverse set of foreign influences? Or should we be agnostic about it, as long as it

leads to more positive outcomes for society and the environment, like better gov-
40 ernance and climate leadership?

If, until recently, the first question seemed most likely to be answered 'yes', BTS, Fonsi and their peers showed a more diverse globalization can't be completely written off.

Take the case of Luis Fonsi first. With his hit single 'Despacito', the Puerto Rican
singer broke seven Guinness World Records, including first YouTube video to reach
45 5 billion views, and most streamed track worldwide. Doing so, he showed that you
can influence global culture through the Spanish language and Caribbean culture
too. This is unsurprising when you consider that there are 437 million people who
speak Spanish as a first language compared to 372 million native English speakers.

The case of BTS is perhaps even more impressive, because it is so much more
50 against the cultural odds. While Spanish, alongside Mandarin Chinese and English belongs to the top 3 of most spoken languages worldwide, Korean doesn't
even feature in the top 10. As a matter of fact, Korea until about a century ago was
known as the 'Hermit Kingdom', for its cultural and economic isolation.

There are still remnants of Korea's isolation today. In many other G20 economies,
55 like France or Germany, English language songs counted for the majority of hits by
2017. In Korea all top hits were still Korean. BTS is no exception. Most of their
songs are largely sung in Korean, with only parts of the lyrics in English. Yet, BTS
managed to become the global musical sensation of the year. [...]

*From: 'Here's what a Korean boy band can teach us about globalization 4.0',*
*www.weforum.org, 18 December 2018*

Annotations
50 **against the odds** surprising
53 **hermit** *Einsiedler/in*
54 **remnant** part that is left of sth.

 ▶ More info

## Comprehension

1 [You choose] Work on task **a** or **b**.

   **a** Name the pros and cons of cultural globalization presented in the text.

   **b** Explain why the author finds the success of BTS so remarkable.

## Analysis

2 Analyse the structure of the text, pointing out the connection between arguments and examples.

## Language awareness

3 **a** One way to influence readers is through words with specific *connotations. Discuss whether the following words have a positive or negative connotation: 'dominant (l. 1), 'uniqueness' (l. 22), 'diversity' (l. 29), 'leadership' (l. 40).

   **b** Rephrase the sentences with the words from **a** in a more neutral way.

## Beyond the text

4 [Speaking] Collect examples of Asian or Latin American culture that you are familiar with, e.g. karaoke, mangas, mariachi. Discuss with a partner why you think these influences have caught on in the western world.

Info

Some words have – alongside their literal meaning – an emotional impact, i.e. they produce a positive or negative response. This is called a **connotation**. For example, *curious* has a positive connotation, *nosy* a negative one.

 ▶ Getting started

► SF 6: Essentials: language and study skills, p. 354

► Check

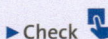

## Words revisited

### 1  Forming compound nouns

**a** The texts in this chapter use a lot of *compound nouns. The following are examples of compound nouns used in 'Words in Context' (p. 174): 'Silk Road' (l. 15), 'fibre-optic communication' (l. 22), 'free-trade agreements' (l. 24), 'manufacturing jobs' (l. 30), 'entertainment industry' (l. 41).
Explain how these compound nouns are formed and compare them to their German equivalents.

**b** Find more examples of compound nouns from 'Words in Context' or other texts.

**c** Make a general rule for the formation of compound nouns in English.

### 2  Matching

Form compound nouns by combining the words in the boxes below. Say which compounding rule you applied. Careful: Some may be used more than once.

| | |
|---|---|
| **A** globalization | **1** area |
| **B** high level | **2** control |
| **C** no smoking | **3** critic |
| **D** once in a lifetime | **4** expert |
| **E** passport | **5** opportunity |
| **F** telecommunications | **6** talk |

### 3  Global glossary

Add relevant compound words you have discovered here to your global glossary.

## Language awareness

*Communication can be tricky, even if people use the same language.*

### 4  Intercultural competence  Communicative misunderstandings

A  *Wow, she seems to be genuinely interested in my idea!*

B  *I don't think she actually likes my idea.*

C  *That's a very interesting idea!*

D  *I don't really care for that idea, but I don't want to come across as rude.*

*Actually, I think you've got a rather interesting idea here.*

**a** Work with a partner. **Partner A:** Decide what you believe the woman on the left is thinking. **Partner B:** Decide what you think the woman on the right means.

**b** Explain your interpretation of the scene to your partner.

**c** What does this experiment show you about the differences between what people say, what they mean and how others interpret it? How do you explain these differences?

## Practice

### 5 Complaining and making requests

There are different ways of complaining and making requests.

a Rephrase the potentially impolite requests in the speech bubbles below to make them sound more polite. Examine how the two versions differ.

b Make a list of sentence forms and phrases that can be used to make a polite request.

► Check

| | | |
|---|---|---|
| **A** *'Get out of my way!'* | **B** *'Quiet! I'm trying to concentrate!'* | **C** *'Shut that window! I've got a cold!'* |
| **D** *'Pass me the salt!'* | **E** *'Hey, that's my seat!'* | **F** *'Bring me the bill!'* |

### 6 Expressing yourself politely

**Intercultural competence** Write down what you could say to express yourself politely in each of the following situations.

1 You are the secretary of your school's Green Club. An exchange student from Lithuania has just asked if he can join. You want to write his name down, but you didn't really hear it properly when he introduced himself and you have no idea how to spell it.

2 You are staying with a family in Wales. Your host suggests going to a rugby match at the weekend. You're not especially fond of rugby. You would prefer to go hiking in the hills.

3 You are having lunch in an English café. Between the main course and dessert you go to the toilet. When you come back, a stranger is sitting at your table.

4 You are visiting London for the first time and want to go by Tube. You notice that all the people heading down to the platforms have blue plastic cards that they use to pass through the turnstile. As you don't have one, you go up to a stranger and ask for information.

5 You have just boarded a crowded train bound for Edinburgh. There is only one seat left in the carriage and someone has put their suitcase on it.

6 You are waiting in a queue in a British post office. You have to mail an application as soon as possible, so you need a stamp. The customer in front of you is holding two carrier bags full of small parcels. There is only one window open and you have an appointment in half an hour.

**Language help**

Sorry, I didn't know … • Is it all right with you if I …? • Would you mind if I …? • Would it be possible for me to …? • Could you please …?

► WOB: pp. 108–113

▶ 'Fly the friendly skies',
  p. 334

▶ More info

A view of Manila, capital
of the Philippines

# A stranger in Manila   Mohsin Hamid

• Name situations in which you felt strange or as if you were a stranger.

*The following excerpt is from the novel* The Reluctant Fundamentalist *by Mohsin
Hamid. Its narrator is Changez, a young Pakistani who graduated from Princeton
University and has found work with Underwood Sampson, a US consulting firm.
He tells his life story to a stranger from the US he meets in Karachi (Pakistan).*

When I arrived in the Philippines at the start of my first Underwood Samson assignment, I was terribly excited. We had flown first-class, and I will never forget the
feeling of reclining in my seat, clad in my suit, as I was served champagne by an
attractive and – yes, I was indeed so brazen as to allow myself to believe – *flirtatious*
5 flight attendant. I was, in my own eyes, a veritable James Bond – only younger,
darker, and possibly better paid. How odd it seems now to recall that time; how
quickly my sense of self- satisfaction would later disappear!

But I am getting ahead of myself. I was telling you about Manila. […] I expected to
find a city like Lahore – or perhaps Karachi; what I found instead was a place of
10 skyscrapers and superhighways. Yes, Manila had its slums; one saw them on the
drive from the airport: vast districts of men in dirty white undershirts lounging idly
in front of auto-repair shops – like a poorer version of the 1950s America depicted
in such films as *Grease*. But Manila's glittering skyline and walled enclaves for the
ultra-rich were unlike anything I had seen in Pakistan.

15 I tried not to dwell on the comparison; it was one thing to accept that New York was
more wealthy than Lahore, but quite another to swallow the fact that Manila was as
well. I felt like a distance runner who thinks he is not doing too badly until he
glances over his shoulder and sees that the fellow who is lapping him is not the
leader of the pack, but one of the laggards. Perhaps it was for this reason that I did
20 something in Manila I had never done before: I attempted to act and speak, as
much as my dignity would permit, more like an *American*. The Filipinos we worked
with seemed to look up to my *American* colleagues, accepting them almost instinc-
tively as members of the officer class of global business – and I wanted my share
of that respect as well.

25 So I learned to tell executives my father's age, 'I need it *now*'; I learned to cut to the
front of lines with an extraterritorial smile; and I learned to answer, when asked
where I was from, that I was from New York. Did these things trouble me, you ask?
Certainly, sir; I was often ashamed. But outwardly I gave no sign of this. In any
case, there was much for me to be proud of: my genuine aptitude for our work, for
30 example, and the glowing reviews my performance received from my peers.

We were there, as I mentioned to you earlier, to value a recorded-music business.
The owner had been a legendary figure in the local A&R scene; when he removed
his sunglasses, his eyes contained the sort of cosmic openness one associates with
prolonged exposure to LSD. But despite his colorful past, he had managed to sign
35 lucrative outsourcing deals to manufacture and distribute CDs for two of the
international music majors. Indeed, he claimed his operation was the largest of its
kind in Southeast Asia and – piracy, downloads, and Chinese competition notwithstanding – growing at quite a healthy clip.

**Annotations**
 4 **brazen** shameless
 5 **veritable** *wahrhaftig*
11 **vast districts of men**
   (here) huge amount of
   men
13 **enclave** part of a city
   where people have a
   different nationality,
   culture or religion
15 **dwell on sth.** keep
   thinking about sth.
19 **laggard** (old-fash-
   ioned) *Nachzügler/in*
29 **aptitude** talent
30 **peer** (here) workmate
32 **A&R = artists and
   repertoire** branch of a
   record label that is
   responsible for talent
   scouting
37 **notwithstanding sth.**
   despite sth.
38 **clip** *(n)* rate

Advanced

To determine how much it was actually worth, we worked around the clock for over
40  a month. We interviewed suppliers, employees, and experts of all kinds; we passed
hours in closed rooms with accountants and lawyers; we gathered gigabytes of
data; we compared indicators of performance to benchmarks; and, in the end, we
built a complex financial model with innumerable permutations. I spent much of
my time in front of my computer, but I also visited the factory floor and several
45  music shops. I felt enormously powerful on these outings, knowing my team was
shaping the future. Would these workers be fired? Would these CDs be made elsewhere? *We*, indirectly of course, would help decide.

Yet there were moments when I became disoriented. I remember one such occasion in particular. I was riding with my colleagues in a limousine. We were mired
50  in traffic, unable to move, and I glanced out the window to see, only a few feet away,
the driver of a jeepney returning my gaze. There was an undisguised hostility in
his expression; I had no idea why. We had not met before – of that I was virtually
certain – and in a few minutes we would probably never see one another again. But
his dislike was so obvious, so *intimate,* that it got under my skin. I stared back at
55  him, getting angry myself – you will have noticed in your time here that glaring is
something we men of Lahore take seriously – and I maintained eye contact until
he was obliged by the movement of the car in front to return his attention to the
road.

Afterwards, I tried to understand why he acted as he did. Perhaps, I thought, his
60  wife has just left him; perhaps he resents me for the privileges implied by my suit
and expensive car; perhaps he simply does not like Americans. I remained preoc-
cupied with this matter far longer than I should have, pursuing several possibilities that all assume – as their unconscious starting point – that he and I shared a
sort of Third World sensibility. Then one of my colleagues asked me a question,
65  and when I turned to answer him, something rather strange took place. I looked at
him – at his fair hair and light eyes and, most of all, his oblivious immersion in the
minutiae of our work – and thought, you are so *foreign*. I felt in that moment much
closer to the Filipino driver than to him; I felt I was play-acting when in reality I
ought to be making my way home, like the people on the street outside.

*From:* The Reluctant Fundamentalist, *2012*

Annotations
42  **benchmark** *Maßstab*
43  **permutation**
      *Umsetzung*
51  **jeepney** popular
      means of inexpensive
      transportation used in
      the Philippines
51  **hostility** unfriendly
      behaviour
66  **fair** *(adj)* light in colour
66  **oblivious** unaware of
      sth.
67  **minutiae** [maɪˈnjuːʃiaɪ]
      small details

A typical Philippine
jeepney

---

**Comprehension**

1  Summarize the events of the *plot in your own words.

---

**Analysis**

2  Examine how Changez's feelings towards himself and his status change in the
   course of the excerpt:
   a  Divide the text into sections based on Changez's perception of himself and
      his role.
   b  For each section, analyse Changez's relationship to his surroundings and their
      influence on his self-image.
   c  Assess the effect the Manila episode has on Changez's feelings towards
      himself and the role he plays.

▶ SF 34: Writing a
   summary or an outline,
   p. 390
▶ Getting started

▶ WOB: pp. 8–10

▶ Support, p. 317

**3**   At the end of the excerpt, Changez says 'I felt I was play-acting' (l. 68). Examine the text again and point to situations where the narrator appears to be 'playing a role'.

▶ SF 8: Working with dictionaries, p. 355

### Language awareness

**4**   **a**   In the headline and the text a feeling of being a stranger or feeling strange is expressed. Explain the concept of feeling strange as conveyed in the text.

     **b**   Compare the findings of **a** to your ideas from the pre-reading task.

     **c**   Examine the other words from the world field 'strange' in the box below. Copy the chart, then sort the adjectives according to the collocations in which they can be used (words can be used more than once). You can use a dictionary.

---

alien • bizarre • foreign • grotesque • mysterious • odd • peculiar • unexpected • unfamiliar • unknown • unusual • weird

---

| person | place | event |
|--------|-------|-------|
| *alien* | *alien* | ... |

### Beyond the text

▶ SF 38: Creative writing, p. 395

**5**   You choose   Writing   Work on task **a** or **b**.

     **a**   What is the driver of the jeepney (ll. 51/52) thinking while he glares at Changez? Write an interior monologue.

     **b**   The narrator hints that something happened to make him feel very differently about himself (ll. 6/7). Write a monologue in which he explains to his American listener why he decided to leave Underwood Samson in Manila and return to his native Pakistan.

## Text 6

## Art in Context: Walk with 'Little Amal'

- Speculate about who 'Little Amal' might represent.

*Watch the video about the art project 'Little Amal'.*

### Comprehension

▶ SF 40: Listening/Viewing for gist and detail, p. 399

**1**   Viewing   Imagine you have a friend who is visually impaired. Explain to them who 'Little Amal' is and why she is touring the world.

## Analysis

 **2** Viewing  Watch the film a second time. Examine the relationship between Little Amal's size and the effect she produces.

▶ SF 40: Listening/Viewing for gist and detail, p. 399

**3** Little Amal's creators decided to make the puppeteers visible for the audience. Describe the effect of their visibility and discuss possible reasons for the decision.

## Beyond the text

**4** You choose  Work on task **a** or **b**.

**a** 'Little Amal' has travelled to many places around the world. Discuss with a partner whether the project is an effective way of getting people interested in worldwide migration and especially about the fate of migrants.

**b** Writing  Write a comment on the following statement: 'The project "Little Amal" is both – art AND politics. It will impact policy makers worldwide and may even improve international relations.'

▶ Check  (task b)

▶ WOB: pp. 22–27

**5** Writing  Write an email to the project 'Little Amal' in which you urge the group to come to your region. Name reasons for why they should accept your request.

▶ SF 35: Writing a formal letter or email, p. 391
▶ Check

## Text 7

# Pathways to the future

*You are going to hear excerpts from an interview from 2017 with Jim Yong Kim, who was president of the World Bank from 2012 to 2019.*

• Speculate what the interview might be about in reference to pathways to the future.

**Info**

The **World Bank** is an international organization. It is committed to providing financial support and technical assistance to the governments of developing countries. It was established in 1944, together with the International Monetary Fund (IMF).

▶ More info
▶ Getting started
▶ SF 40: Listening/Viewing for gist and detail, p. 399

## Comprehension

 **1** Listening  Read the statements below. After listening to the interview for the first time, decide which of them best summarizes Kim's views.

1 According to Kim, an economy can only grow if there is some degree of financial imbalance.
2 Kim says that people in poor countries want the same lifestyle as people in rich countries.
3 Kim believes that emerging and advanced economies can profit from each other in many ways.

🔊 **2** Listening Read through the questions below before listening to the interview again and choosing the correct answers.

**1** Nowadays ... of the world's population live in extreme poverty.
  **a** less than 10%
  **b** 10%
  **c** more than 10%

**2** Kim says that people all over the world want to have ...
  **a** smartphones.
  **b** television.
  **c** a middle-class lifestyle.

**3** Kim sees the role of the World Bank as ...
  **a** lending money to poor countries.
  **b** linking capital and investment.
  **c** creating jobs in developing countries.

**4** Investments in developing countries are often regarded as ...
  **a** risky.
  **b** complicated.
  **c** highly profitable.

**5** The World Bank can help by reducing the risk for ...
  **a** foreign governments.
  **b** foreign investors.
  **c** local banks.

**6** Kim says this could be a ... for both sides.
  **a** no-risk situation
  **b** win-win situation
  **c** small help

**7** Kim says that in recent decades global inequality ...
  **a** has decreased.
  **b** has stagnated.
  **c** has risen.

**8** In a lot of high income countries (e.g. China and India), inequality ...
  **a** has been eliminated.
  **b** has remained unchanged.
  **c** has increased.

**9** China's rise from poverty began when Deng Xiao Ping taught that inequality ...
  **a** is sometimes necessary.
  **b** must be eliminated.
  **c** should be a national goal.

**10** The World Bank tracks the income growth of ... of the global population.
  **a** the bottom 14%
  **b** the bottom 40%
  **c** the bottom 50%

► Check 🔖

► WOB: pp. 78–81

Advanced

🔊 **3** Listening Listen to the interview for a third time and summarize Kim's answers to the question: 'Globalization – what does it mean for me?'

**Beyond the text**

**4** You choose Speaking Work on either task **a** or **b**.

► SF 44: Preparing and giving a speech, p. 408

► Getting started 🔖

**a** Make a speech to your class in which you outline ways in which globalization can help create a better world.

**b** Make a speech to your class in which you point out the consequences globalization may have for you personally and other members of your age group.

# Inequality around the globe

• Give examples of inequality despite or due to globalization.

*The following bar chart gives insight into the energy consumption in seven different regions in 2022.*

**The energy consumption per person of seven regions (year: 2022)**

▶ SF 22: Analysing diagrams, p. 373

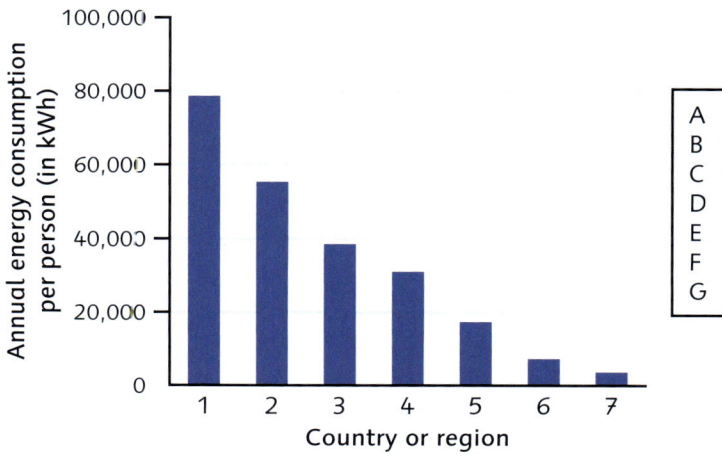

|   |               |
|---|---------------|
| A | Brazil        |
| B | United States |
| C | India         |
| D | Europe        |
| E | Africa        |
| F | Russia        |
| G | China         |

*Source: OurWorldInData.org*

**1 a** Guess which country/region used how much energy by matching countries/regions and bars. Give reasons for your choice.

▶ Getting started

  **b** Your teacher will give you the solution. Summarize the bar chart's most important results.

**Language help**

consume energy • twice/three times as much • most/least • be first/last in rank • at the top/bottom of the ranking

  **c** Say which result surprised you most, referring back to your ideas from task **a**.

**2** Speculate on possible reasons for the extreme differences in energy consumption shown in the chart.

**3** Work on either **a** or **b**.
  **a** Describe the cartoon.
  **b** **Challenge** **Writing** Using the cartoon as a starting point, write an entry for your personal blog, giving your view on inequality in the world.

▶ Getting started (task a)
▶ SF 25: Analysing cartoons, p. 377

"I blame the billions in the 3rd world, wanting to get what we've got!"

CartoonStock.com

## Focus on test formats

*As part of your school-leaving exam you may be required to summarize information from a German text in English.*

*Read the following task:*

You are a member of a European activist group that campaigns for workers' rights in the global garment industry. The British chapter has learned that the German government has committed itself to enforcing stricter rules for international supply chains. You found a relevant article from the *Deutsche Presse-Agentur (dpa)* (p. 196). You were asked to prepare an article summarizing the regulations contained in the law and how they are regarded by companies and activist groups. Your text will appear on the group's website.

▶ SF 48: Essentials: mediating, p. 415

▶ Check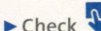

### 1   Mediation tasks

**a**   What do you remember about mediation tasks? Decide which of the following statements are true and correct the false ones.
   **1**   I must write in the same style as the original text.
   **2**   I mustn't include any ideas of my own.
   **3**   If I don't know the English translation of a German term, it's best to quote it in the original German.
   **4**   I may have to explain certain terms that are specific to Germany.
   **5**   The exact number of words is very important for my grade.
   **6**   I mustn't leave out any information from the original text.

**b**   Compare your results with your partner. Discuss points on which you disagree.

## Work it out

*In this section you are led step by step through the task presented above. The strategies you learn here can help you do other types of mediation tasks as well.*

### 2   Examining the task

Reread the task. Copy the table below and fill in the missing information in keywords:

| | |
|---|---|
| Text type I must write: | |
| Required content (main points): | |
| Audience I am writing for: | |
| Appropriate style: | |

### 3   Examining the text

► Support, p. 317

**a**   Read the text on p. 196. Make a list of the aspects the author deals with.

**b**   Compare your list with your notes from task **2**. Decide which aspects of the text are relevant for the task at hand.

**c**   Now go to the text and make further notes on the relevant aspects.

### 4   Organizing the information

Compare the task at hand with the notes you have made. Decide how you can best organize the information you have gathered. The order used in the primary text isn't necessarily the ideal order for your text  The chart below can help you:

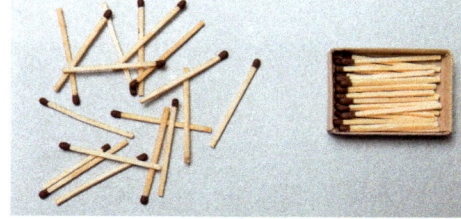

| Organization/Group | Views on Supply Chain Law | Arguments |
|---|---|---|
| … | … | … |
| … | … | … |

### 5   Using a dictionary effectively

The given text contains a number of lexical items that come from the wordfields *governance* and *economy*. You may find them challenging at first sight.

**a**   Examine the following list of words and phrases from the text. Put them into three groups: 1) necessary 2) optional 3) unnecessary for the mediation task.

| | |
|---|---|
| *Lieferkettengesetz* | *Bemühenspflicht* |
| *Nichtregierungsorganisation* | *Lieferantenmanagement* |
| *Beschwerdemechanismus* | *Wirtschaftsverbände* |
| *Geschäftsbereich* | *Handlungsfähigkeit* |
| *Abhilfemaßnahme* | *Inkrafttreten* |
| *Vertragsbedingungen* | *Sorgfaltspflicht* |
| *Beschaffungs-Standards* | *zivilrechtlich* |

**b**   Compare lists with your partner. Name reasons for your choices.

**c**   In an examination you probably won't have time to look up every word you might not know. That is why it is important to have strategies for working with what you already have:

–   Keep in mind that you are not expected to write a word-for-word translation of the text. Often it is possible to express a complex phrase in relatively simple words (*erheblichen zusätzlichen Aufwand treiben* → *do more*)

–   While looking for English equivalents you may find it easier to work with the verb instead of the noun (e.g. *Bemühenspflicht* → *that firms are required by law to make an effort …*).

–   Looking up words with a very general meaning such as *halten* is often a waste of time if you are looking for one special usage (*sich an ein Gesetz o. Ä. halten*). Try to think of a verb that has exactly the meaning you need (e.g. *einhalten*) and look it up instead.

– The same German word can have different translations in English depending on the context. A *Verletzung* in connection with a law or treaty is translated differently from the *Verletzung* that comes from an accident. Read the example sentences at the end of a dictionary entry to make sure you have found the right context.

## 6   Dealing with difficult words

Girl picking tobacco

Even in a good bilingual dictionary you won't find translations for every given word. This is especially true of compound nouns like *Lieferkettengesetz*. If you don't know or can't find a translation, paraphrase.

**a** Paraphrase each of the words below:
  1 *Lieferkettengesetz* ('a law regulating …')
  2 *Lieferantenmanagement*
  3 *Wirtschaftsverbände*
  4 *Wettbewerbsnachteile*
**b** Compare results with your partner.
**c** Use an internet search engine to find the common English expression for each of the above items.

## 7   Communicating internationally

**Intercultural competence** In mediation tasks you are sometimes confronted with terms that are specific to Germany, e.g. *Bundesministerium für wirtschaftliche Zusammenarbeit und Entwicklung*. Which of the two ways of dealing with this term given below is better? Keep in mind that you are writing for a non-German audience.
1 the government office that supervises international economic cooperation
2 the Federal Office for Economic Cooperation and Development

## 8   Focus on text types

In every mediation task you are asked to write a certain type of text. In this case it is an article for a website.

**a** Which of the following do you think are necessary or desirable in an article written for the general public?
  1 an eye-catching title
  2 explanations of technical terms
  3 a neutral style
  4 an appealing opening sentence
  5 direct address
  6 lots of concrete examples
  7 a concluding sentence

**b** Compare your ideas with your partner.

# Do it

## 9 Getting started: two versions

Getting off to a good start is often the hardest part of writing. Compare the introductory sentences below and discuss their relative advantages with your partner.

**A** *The German Supply Chain Act*
*The German government has passed a new law that went into effect in January 2023. This law makes large manufacturing firms in Germany responsible for their supply chains.*

**B** *Chaining in the supply chain*
*Until recently, German firms could import materials manufactured under conditions that would be illegal in Germany. A new law – the Supply Chain Act – aims to make this impossible.*

## 10 Writing

Now write your own article based on the German text. Use all the information you already gathered.

# Feedback

## 11 Peer assessment

▶ Check 🔖

a Swap texts with your partner. Read and assess what each one of you has written.
b Give your partner detailed feedback on their text. Listen to your partner's feedback.

## 12 Self-assessment

In your *method card, write down any strategies that can help you with mediation tasks. Decide for each strategy whether it needs more practice.

| Method card – mediation | |
| --- | --- |
| What I am good at | What I need to practise |
| ... | ... |

## 13 Writing Changing the addressee

Your host brother or sister in your American host family who is five years younger than you asks you to explain what you are writing about in your article. Rephrase your introduction and your opening one or two paragraphs to make the contents digestible for them.

▶ WOB: pp. 71–77

# A step forward for global equity   Jürgen Bätz

*In 2023 the German Supply Chain Law went into effect – the first in the EU.*

Zu Jahresbeginn tritt das deutsche Lieferkettengesetz in Kraft. Die Wirtschaft beklagt einen hohen Aufwand, Nichtregierungsorganisation[en] halten das Gesetz für zu lasch. [...]

Das „Lieferkettensorgfaltspflichtengesetz", wie es offiziell heißt, gilt zunächst für
5 Unternehmen mit mehr als 3000 Mitarbeitern. Laut Bundesministerium für wirtschaftliche Zusammenarbeit und Entwicklung (BMZ) sind davon rund 900 Unternehmen betroffen. Für sie ergeben sich unterschiedliche Anforderungen, für den eigenen Geschäftsbereich sowie für unmittelbare und mittelbare Zulieferer. [...]

Die Unternehmen müssen laut BMZ eine Reihe von Maßnahmen umsetzen. So
10 müssen sie unter anderem eine Risikoanalyse durchführen, ein Risikomanagement sowie einen Beschwerdemechanismus aufsetzen und öffentlich darüber berichten. Bei Verletzungen im eigenen Geschäftsbereich oder bei unmittelbaren Zulieferern müssen die Unternehmen laut Gesetz unverzüglich angemessene Abhilfemaßnahmen ergreifen, „um diese Verletzung zu verhindern, zu beenden
15 oder das Ausmaß der Verletzung zu minimieren".

„Für uns ändert sich nicht so viel, weil wir uns schon seit Jahren darauf vorbereitet haben", sagt Mercedes-Managerin [Renata] Jungo Brüngger. Man könne die Kontrolle von Lieferketten nicht einfach auf Knopfdruck umsetzen. Der Konzern habe entsprechende Vertragsbedingungen, Beschaffungs-Standards und Audit-Rechte
20 mit seinen unmittelbaren Lieferanten vereinbart. [...]

„Das Gesetz ist in vielen Punkten sehr ambitioniert und es wird sicher eine große Herausforderung sein", sagt die Vorständin. Man könne aber auch sagen, dass das Gesetz in vielen Punkten mit Augenmaß verfasst wurde. Positiv sei, dass es eine Bemühenspflicht gebe. „Wenn wir als Unternehmen in einem konkreten Fall
25 nachweisen können, dass wir alles in unserer Macht stehende getan haben, dann erfüllt das diese Anforderung", so Brüngger. „Kleine Unternehmen haben es bei der Umsetzung sicher schwerer."

Ein im Vergleich zu Mercedes-Benz kleineres Unternehmen ist Stihl. Für den Hersteller von Kettensägen aus Waiblingen bei Stuttgart sind weltweit etwa 20.000
30 Menschen tätig. Das Familienunternehmen arbeite bereits seit einigen Jahren daran, dass Nachhaltigkeit im Lieferantenmanagement zu einem integralen Bestandteil wird, sagt Unternehmer Nikolas Stihl. Aber um die Vorschriften zu erfüllen, müsse erheblicher zusätzlicher Aufwand betrieben werden. Stihl sieht zudem die Gefahr von Wettbewerbsnachteilen durch das deutsche Gesetz, weshalb seiner
35 Ansicht nach eine Ausweitung auf EU-Ebene oder sogar global einheitliche Anforderungen hilfreich wären.

Kritik kommt auch von Wirtschaftsverbänden. „Hier wird die Handlungsfähigkeit des industriellen Mittelstands aufs Spiel gesetzt", teilte Karl Haeusgen, Präsident des Verbands Deutscher Maschinen- und Anlagenbau, mit. Er kritisierte, dass Fir-
40 men Berichte für alle einsehbar machen müssten – auch für Wettbewerber. „Das wird zum Rückzug unserer Unternehmen aus ganzen Ländern führen und damit ist den Menschen vor Ort geschadet, nicht geholfen", so Haeusgen. [...]

Die Zweite Vorsitzende der IG Metall, Christiane Benner, bezeichnete das Gesetz als einen guten Start ins neue Jahr. „Umso weniger ist die Verweigerungshaltung
45  der Arbeitgeberseite nachzuvollziehen, die bis auf die letzten Meter versucht hat, das Inkrafttreten des Gesetzes zu verhindern", sagte Benner.

„Die Industrielobby hat das Gesetz extrem ausgehöhlt. Das ist zu einem zahnlosen Papiertiger geworden", sagt hingegen Viola Wohlgemuth von der Umweltorganisation Greenpeace. Sie kritisiert vor allem, „dass es keine eigenständigen umwelt-
50  bezogenen Sorgfaltspflichten gibt". Man könne nur dann eingreifen, wenn Menschen durch die Umweltzerstörung von Firmen gesundheitliche Schäden erleiden. „Und das ist quasi unmöglich vor Gerichten nachzuweisen, gerade für die Betroffenen in den Produktionsländern", sagt Wohlgemuth.

Beate Streicher von der Menschenrechtsorganisation Amnesty International kriti-
55  siert, dass das Gesetz nur sehr große Unternehmen erfasse. Zudem fehle eine Regelung der zivilrechtlichen Haftung. Das Gesetz sei ein Anfang, es reiche aber definitiv nicht aus. Die Schwächen müssten jetzt auf europäischer Ebene adressiert werden. Im Koalitionsvertrag stehe, dass sich die Bundesregierung für ein wirksames europäisches Lieferkettengesetz einsetzt. „An diesem Anspruch muss
60  sie sich messen lassen", sagt Streicher.                              *(546 words)*

*From: 'Lieferkettengesetz: Das kommt auf deutsche Unternehmen zu', dpa, 23 December 2022*

**1**  `Mediating`  You attend a bilingual school and are supposed to give a presentation in your social studies class. You want to talk about Western nations and their responsibility for fair treatment of developing countries. Based on the article above, prepare your oral presentation in English about the measures taken by the German government to ensure fairer treatment and how they are regarded by companies and activist groups.

▶ SF 49: Mediating from German into English, p. 416
▶ Getting started

---

**Text 10**

## Migration – problem or solution?

• **\*Quick write** What influence do you think migration has on advanced economies: positive, neutral or negative? Name reasons.

*You are going to hear an interview with economist Margaux MacDonald on the economic impact of worldwide migration.*

### Comprehension

**1**  `Listening`  Listen to the excerpt from the podcast. Then choose the correct answers.
   1  In the past 60 years, the percentage of migrants worldwide has ...
      a   fallen.
      b   remained stable.
      c   risen.

▶ SF 40: Listening/Viewing for gist and detail, p. 399
▶ Check

2 Studies show that all in all, migration has … on the economies of host countries.
   a a positive effect
   b a negative effect
   c no effect
3 MacDonald says that on the whole, migration …
   a takes away jobs.
   b helps create new jobs.
   c has little effect on the job market.
4 Macdonald says that the long-term impact of the pandemic lockdown on global migration patterns is …
   a positive.
   b negative.
   c unclear.

►Check

🔊 2 [Listening] Listen to the excerpt a second time, then answer the questions. You need not write complete sentences.
   1 How MacDonald defines a migrant
   2 Where the share of immigrants rose from 7% to 12%
   3 What a rise in migration after the end of the lockdown might lead to
   4 What the lockdown during the pandemic may lead to
   5 What jobs might be difficult to provide for low-income countries
   6 What advanced economies may be faced with
   7 What research has shown about migration in advanced economies
   8 What less qualified workers may face due to migration
   9 What false ideas about migration exist in developed countries
   10 Why migration may decline in some low-income countries

►WOB: pp. 78–81

**Beyond the text**

►Check

3 [Writing] Write an encyclopaedia entry about the economic effects of migration. Take into account your original ideas and what you have learned from the podcast.

Mural in Phoenix, Arizona

# The reluctant giant    Robert Kagan

- **Think** of two arguments for and two against the following statement: 'The US has a global responsibility that goes beyond that of other nations.'
- **Pair** Compare your arguments with a partner and decide on one argument for and one argument against the statement that you both find convincing.
- **Share** your arguments with other groups.

*Foreign policy expert Robert Kagan explains why Americans sometimes forget that they are a superpower – perhaps even the superpower.*

**Partner A and B:** Read the following two paragraphs.

All great powers have a deeply ingrained self-perception shaped by historical experience, geography, culture, beliefs, and myths. [...] Often, it is these self-perceptions that drive nations, empires, and city-states forward. And sometimes to their ruin. Much of the drama of the past century resulted from great powers whose aspira-
5  tions exceeded their capacity.

Americans have the opposite problem. Their capacity for global power exceeds their perception of their proper place and role in the world. Even as they have met the challenges of Nazism and Japanese imperialism, Soviet communism, and radical Islamist terrorism, they have never regarded this global activism as normal.
10  Even in the era of the Internet, long-range missiles, and an interdependent global economy, many Americans retain the psychology of a people living apart on a vast continent, untouched by the world's turmoil. Americans have never been isolationists. In times of emergency, they can be persuaded to support extraordinary exertions in far-off places. But they regard these as exceptional responses to excep-
15  tional circumstances. They do not see themselves as the primary defender of a certain kind of world order; they have never embraced that 'indispensable' role. [...]

**Partner A:** Read the paragraph below. Make notes on the causes of American isolationism in the 19th century.
**Partner B:** Go to p. 318.

Americans' preference for a limited international role is a product of their history and experience and of the myths they tell themselves. [...] Americans have always yearned to recapture what they imagine as the innocence and limited ambition of
20  their nation's youth. For the first decades of the new republic's existence, Americans struggled merely to survive as a weak republic in a world of superpower monarchies. They spent the nineteenth century in selfishness and self-absorption, conquering the continent and struggling over slavery. By the early twentieth century, the United States had become the richest and potentially most powerful country in
25  the world, but one without commitments or responsibilities. It rose under the canopy of a benevolent world order it had no part in upholding. [...]

**Partner A and B:** Read the rest of the text.

The world had never known such a power – there was not the language to describe it or a theory to explain it. It was sui generis. The emergence of this unusual great power led to confusion and misjudgment. Nations that had spent centuries calcu-
30  lating the power relationships in their own regions were slow to appreciate the impact of this distant deus ex machina, which, after long periods of indifference

## Annotations

- **reluctant** uncertain, not convinced
1  **ingrained** *verwurzelt*
2  **self-perception** self-image
4  **aspirations** goals
5  **exceed sth.** go beyond sth.
11  **retain sth.** *an etwas festhalten*
11  **apart** separately
12  **turmoil** conflicts
14  **exertion** effort
14  **exceptional** not normal
19  **yearn** *sich sehnen*
22  **self-absorption** being only concerned with yourself
25  **commitment** *Verpflichtung*
26  **benevolent** being friendly and helpful

**Annotations**
33 **adjust** get used to sth. new
33 **invulnerability** *Unverwundbarkeit*
37 **self-sufficient** not dependent on others
55 **diffusion** spread
58 **restraint** *Zurückhaltung*
64 **would-be** potential
71 **fraught with sth.** connected with sth. (unpleasant)
72 **square** *(adj)* honest
72 **predicament** situation
74 **nefarious** evil
74 **antidote** *Gegenmittel*
75 **scare the hell out of sb.** make sb. extremely frightened

and aloofness, could suddenly swoop in and transform the balance of power. Americans, too, had a hard time adjusting. The wealth and relative invulnerability that made them uniquely capable of fighting major wars and enforcing peace in
35  Europe, Asia, and the Middle East simultaneously also made them question the necessity, desirability, and even morality of doing so. With the United States fundamentally secure and self-sufficient, why did it need to get involved in conflicts thousands of miles from its shores? And what right did it have? [...]

In 1990, the former U.S. ambassador to the UN Jeane Kirkpatrick argued that the
40  United States should return to being a 'normal' nation with normal interests, give up the 'dubious benefits of superpower status,' end the 'unnatural focus' on foreign policy, and pursue its national interests as 'conventionally conceived.' That meant protecting its citizens, its territory, its wealth, and its access to 'necessary' goods. It did not mean preserving the balance of power in Europe or Asia, promot-
45  ing democracy, or taking responsibility for problems in the world that did not touch Americans directly. [...]

The problem is that the United States has not been a normal nation for over a century, nor has it had normal interests. Its unique power gives it a unique role. [...] World order became the United States' concern when the old world order collapsed
50  in the early new one in which its interests could be protected. [...]

An entire generation of Americans has grown up believing that the lack of clear-cut victories in Afghanistan and Iraq proves that their country can no longer accomplish anything with power. The rise of China, the United States' declining share of the global economy, the advance of new military technologies, and a gen-
55  eral diffusion of power around the world – all have signaled the twilight, once again, of the American order.

Yet if the United States were as weak as so many people claim, it wouldn't have to practice restraint. It is precisely because the country is still capable of pursuing a world-order strategy that critics need to explain why it should not. The fact is that
60  the basic configuration of international power has not changed as much as many imagine. The earth is still round; the United States still sits on its vast, isolated continent, surrounded by oceans and weaker powers; the other great powers still live in regions crowded with other great powers; and when one power in those regions grows too strong for the others to balance against, the would-be victims still
65  look to the distant United States for help. [...]

The time has come to tell Americans that there is no escape from global responsibility, that they have to think beyond the protection of the homeland. They need to understand that the purpose of NATO and other alliances is to defend not against direct threats to U.S. interests but against a breakdown of the order that best serves
70  those interests. They need to be told honestly that the task of maintaining a world order is unending and fraught with costs but preferable to the alternative. A failure to be square with the American people has led the country to its current predicament, with a confused and angry public convinced that its leaders are betraying American interests for their own nefarious, 'globalist' purposes. The antidote to
75  this is not scaring the hell out of them about China and other threats but trying to explain, again, why the world order they created still matters.

*From: 'A superpower like it or not', Foreign Affairs, 2021*

Advanced

## Comprehension

1 a **Partner A:** Explain to your partner why the United States played little or no role in international affairs in the 19th century.
  b **Partner B:** Explain to your partner why the US assumed a leading role in global politics in the 20th century.

2 Summarize the reasons named in the text why the USA traditionally has had an ambivalent relationship to its global responsibility.

3 Outline the author's main arguments for why he believes the USA must play a major role in the world.

## Analysis

4 a Examine the language Kagan uses in ll. 8–15 (Partner-B text p. 318) to emphasize America's global uniqueness.
  Advanced
  b Examine the means Kagan employs to convince his readers of his views.

▶ SF 17: Reading and understanding non-fictional texts, p. 367

## Language awareness

5 a Collect ten examples of words that belong to the word field 'power'.
  b Use five of the words you have chosen in sentences of your own.
  c Swap sentences with your partner. Ask your partner to decide if your 'power words' have a positive or a negative connotation. Compare responses.

6 a Identify the infinitives used in the last paragraph and compare the two forms of infinitive used.
  b Think of a person you're unhappy with and write five sentences describing necessary changes using both forms of infinitive.

▶ WOB: p. 118

## Beyond the text

7 You choose Work on task **a** or **b**.

  a Writing Has the rise of China, India and other nations made Kagan's view of the world obsolete? Summarize your opinion and name arguments for your view.

  b Speaking 'The world needs America's leadership.' Do you agree? Collect arguments to support your opinion, then have a discussion with a partner.

▶ SF 46: Having a discussion, p. 410
▶ WOB: pp. 65–67

8 Go back to the guiding question of the chapter and rephrase your paragraph from p. 172, task **2c**, taking into account everything you have learned from this chapter.

## The view from Germany    Hendrik Brandt

- ***Quick write:** Outline what you know about the relationship between Germany and the USA.

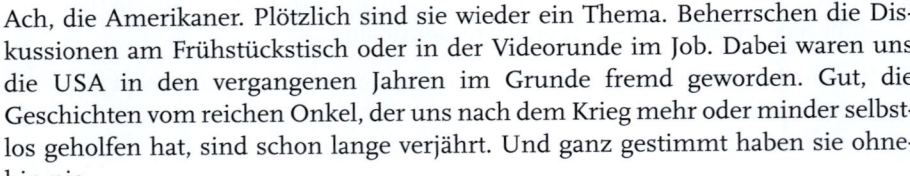

*The editor-in-chief of a German newspaper takes a critical look at how the USA is perceived in Germany.*

Ach, die Amerikaner. Plötzlich sind sie wieder ein Thema. Beherrschen die Diskussionen am Frühstückstisch oder in der Videorunde im Job. Dabei waren uns die USA in den vergangenen Jahren im Grunde fremd geworden. Gut, die Geschichten vom reichen Onkel, der uns nach dem Krieg mehr oder minder selbst-
5   los geholfen hat, sind schon lange verjährt. Und ganz gestimmt haben sie ohnehin nie.

Dennoch: Das Land zwischen Atlantik und Pazifik war über Jahrzehnte hinweg ein Ort für so viele Sehnsüchte. Da ging es für die einen um die große Freiheit oder um das große Geldverdienen ohne Skrupel. Für die anderen lag die Faszina-
10   tion im Gegenteil, sie suchten die Flucht aus dem Hamsterrad und fanden auch dafür einen Platz. „Drüben in den Staaten", wie man so sagte. Vor allem aber waren die US-Amerikaner über mehrere Nachkriegsgenerationen hinweg die wahre Bezugsgröße. Und auch ein Alltags-Vorbild; ihre Kultur bestimmte die deutsche und europäische längst weit mehr als umgekehrt.

15   Vieles davon ist in den zurückliegenden Jahren zu Ende gegangen. Nicht krachend oder spektakulär, sondern leise, Schritt für Schritt. Wenn Demoskopen die Deutschen derzeit fragen, ob sie eher zu den USA oder zu China neigen, hält sich das nun schon fast die Waage – nur noch gut ein gutes Drittel der Befragten setzt noch auf die alte Supermacht, fast genauso viele Menschen halten zur neuen. Pro-
20   tokoll einer Entfremdung, die noch vor einem Jahrzehnt unvorstellbar schien.

Oder etwa doch nicht? Hat das alles nur mit dem unsäglichen Donald Trump zu tun? War da nicht auch schon das Kopfschütteln über Ronald Reagans Neoliberalismus? Oder der Spott über George W. Bush, dessen Kriege nicht unsere sein konnten? Ist die dunkle Kehrseite des amerikanischen Gesellschaftsmodells nicht
25   lange vor den jüngsten Vorfällen rund um Rassismus, Gewalt und soziale Spaltung sichtbar geworden? Und wie war das nochmal mit Vietnam?

Das Faszinosum USA hat mächtig gelitten, vorrangig unter seinen eigenen Widersprüchen. Das Land ist nun einmal extrem. Es verbindet ungeheure Flexibilität mit exzentrischer Bürokratie, wunderschöne Landschaften mit entstellten Gegen-
30   den, breitbeinige Männlichkeit mit peinlich genauer Gender-Achtsamkeit. Die Kontraste hatten in ihrer hierzulande ungekannten Größe einst durchaus ihren Reiz – sind aber in ihrer wachsenden Brutalität jetzt oft nur noch abschreckend. Viele Deutsche wollen die USA nicht mehr so, wie sie sind. Sondern nur noch so, wie sie sie selbst gern hätten. Da liegt der Kern der kulturellen und gesellschaftli-
35   chen Distanzierung.

Das sicherste Indiz hierfür ist der Blick auf die Politik. Kaum jemand hierzulande hat verstanden, warum die Amerikaner nach dem überaus gewandten Bill Clinton vor zwanzig Jahren nicht dessen alerten Vize Al Gore zum Präsidenten gewählt haben, sondern den leicht tapsigen wirkenden Texaner George W. Bush. Geradezu
40   messianisch war später die Wahrnehmung des intellektuellen Barack Obama im

Oval Office. Der war ja auch cool. Dass es aber auch seine Politik war, die Teile des Landes einfach übersah und ein amoralisches Faktotum wie Donald Trump als Präsident mit ermöglicht hat, blieb meist unbeachtet. Genauso wie übrigens die oberflächlichen Erfolge Trumps. Deutschland nahm den USA mehrheitlich übel,
45  dass sie dem alten Wunschbild nicht mehr entsprachen.

Angesichts dieser Scheidung auf Raten ist nun oft davon die Rede, dass sich Deutschland wie Europa stärker auf sich selbst besinnen müssten. Ja, was denn sonst? Die Hoffnung, dass die USA irgendwann doch bitte wieder so sein mögen, wie wir sie einst gesehen haben, wird nicht tragen. Wer immer sie regiert. Bei
50  allen engen wirtschaftlichen, militärischen und immer noch auch kulturellen Bindungen muss klar sein, dass es hohe Zeit für eigene Wege ist.    *(569 words)*

*From: 'Wir sollten ein neues Verhältnis zu den USA finden', www.ndr.de, 6 November 2020*

**1**  `Mediating`  You have been invited to an international youth congress. The topic is 'Rethinking the USA'. You have been asked to write an *article for the conference website on the topic 'The German View of the USA'. Use events from the past, the present and the future mentioned in the text for the basis of your article.

`Info`

### The United Nations – a peacekeeping force

The first UN peacekeeping mission was in 1948, when observers were sent to the Middle East to keep peace between the newly formed state of Israel and its Arab neighbours. Since then, the UN has initiated more than 70 peacekeeping operations worldwide. UN peacekeepers are normally unarmed or only lightly
5  armed. After the end of the Cold War in 1990 more than 75,000 peacekeepers became involved in multiple tasks around the world, among them the creation of sustainable government institutions, the implementation of peace agreements, and the disarmament and reintegration of former combatants. Major setbacks in the Balkans and in Rwanda in the 1990s, where peacekeepers failed to prevent
10  genocides, led to a reassessment of the strategic goals. Today, UN Peacekeeping employs approximately 110,000 military and civilian staff members recruited from all member states of the United Nations.

**1**  Summarize the task of UN Peacekeeping in one sentence.
**2**  'Frieden schaffen ohne Waffen' – a realistic goal? Write a comment using the information on UN Peacekeeping as a starting point.

▶ Getting started

▶ SF 49: Mediating from German into English, p. 416
▶ Support, p. 318
▶ WOB: pp. 71–77

Annotation
**10  genocide** deliberate killing of a nation or ethnic group

▶ Check

## Chapter task

### Rise to the challenge!

An international youth organization has sponsored a writing competition for young people on the topic:

**Global problems – global solutions**
**What we can do today for a better future tomorrow**

Write an *article expressing your views on the topic.

▶ Check

# Chapter 7
# Images of Ireland

**The lake isle of Innisfree**
William Butler Yeats
▶ More info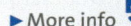

I will arise and go now, and go to Innisfree,
And a small cabin build there, of clay and wattles made:
Nine bean-rows will I have there, a hive for the honey-bee,
And live alone in the bee-loud glade.

5 And I shall have some peace there, for peace comes dropping slow,
Dropping from the veils of the morning to where the cricket sings;
There midnight's all a glimmer, and noon a purple glow,
And evening full of the linnet's wings.

I will arise and go now, for always night and day
10 I hear lake water lapping with low sounds by the shore;
While I stand on the roadway, or on the pavements grey,
I hear it in the deep heart's core.

*From: The National Observer, 1890*

**Annotations**
1 **Innisfree** island where Yeats spent summers as a child
2 **wattle** building material
4 **glade** open space in a wood
6 **cricket** *Grille*
8 **linnet** type of bird

1 What comes to mind when you think of Ireland? Brainstorm ideas.

2 **Viewing** Examine the photo above and watch the videos. Compare them to your notions of Ireland.

3 a Listen to the podcast on Irish geography, make notes and write a short country profile on Ireland. Include at least five important figures given in the text.

▶ Getting started
▶ SF 20: Reading and understanding poetry, p. 370

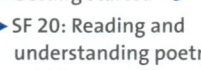

"I will arise and go now, and go to Innisfree, And a small cabin build there, of clay and wattles made:"

**Advanced**

b Research other aspects linked to Irish geography. Add the information to your country profile.

4 The text above is one of Ireland's most famous poems. Why do you think it might still be popular in Ireland today?

5 The poem's first two lines are quoted in the Irish passport. Discuss the poem's message with regard to the concepts of home, identity and peace. Draw connections to the guiding question of this chapter.

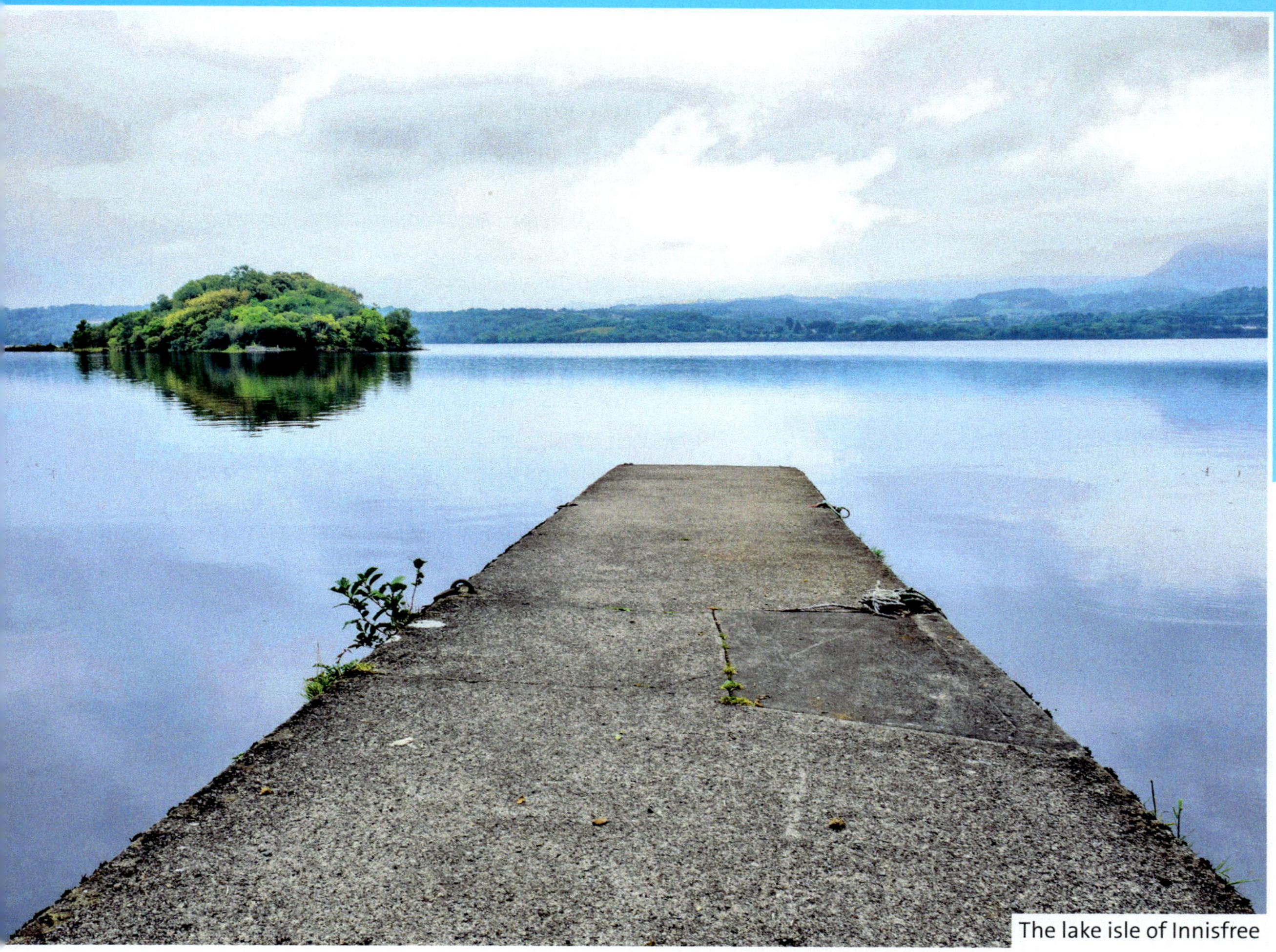

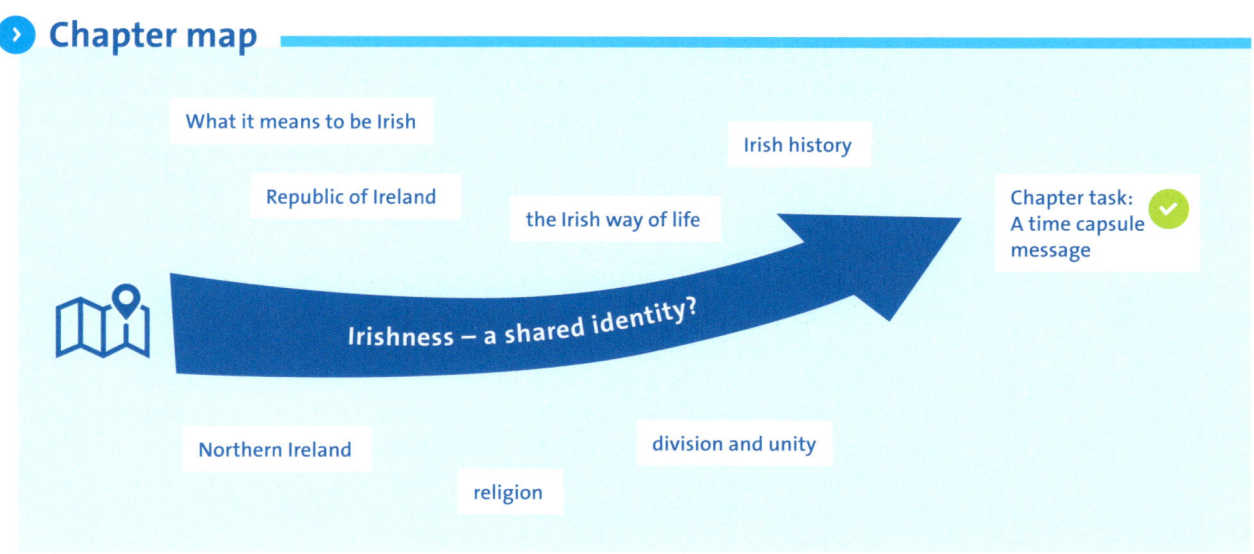

The lake isle of Innisfree

## Chapter map

- What it means to be Irish
- Republic of Ireland
- the Irish way of life
- Irish history
- **Irishness – a shared identity?**
- Northern Ireland
- religion
- division and unity
- Chapter task: A time capsule message

▶ More language

🔊 **One island – two countries**

### Ireland's past and present

Ireland, often referred to as the 'Emerald Isle', consists of the independent Republic of Ireland and Northern Ireland (or Ulster), a political entity of the United Kingdom.

5 Historically, the division of the island is the result of a civil war fought by the Irish in the aftermath of World War I to gain independence from Britain. As Britain's first colony in Europe, Ireland had resisted British oppression for many centuries. When the Anglo-Irish Treaty was signed to end the

10 Irish War of Independence (1919–1921), a geographic division of the island was created that would lead to violent sectarian conflicts between republicans (who were predominantly Catholic) and unionists (who were predominantly Protestant) for decades to come. The tensions culminated in

15 the latter half of the 20th century in another civil war known as the Troubles, in which thousands of people lost their lives. This conflict was ended in 1998 with the Good Friday Agreement between the Irish and British governments.

Today, the Republic of Ireland is a member of the European

20 Union with close ties to mainland Europe, while Northern Ireland remains part of the United Kingdom. When the British referendum on EU membership (the so-called Brexit Referendum) was held on 23 June 2016, the majority of voters in Northern Ireland opposed Brexit out of fear of new trade barriers between the UK and the EU. Once Brexit did indeed happen, there

25 followed years of uncertainty and confusion regarding customs checks across the Irish Sea and the Irish border. In March 2023, the EU and the UK finally settled on an agreement to ease trade relations, the Windsor Framework.

### Ireland's search for identity

Besides its varied history, Ireland is characterized by a vibrant culture and stunning

30 scenery that attracts tourists from all over the world. The Irish are proud of their Celtic roots and many Irish traditions are celebrated around the globe. Ireland has a rich musical and literary heritage, and Dublin, the Republic's capital and largest city, is a centre for these artistic expressions. Since the early 2000s, Dublin has also become a hub for global tech companies, which has attracted a diverse community of immigrants.

35 The close but complicated relationship with Britain continues to impact Ireland's search for identity, and the violent struggles for independence have left a deep mark on the Irish national consciousness. As President Michael D. Higgins put it on the first-ever state visit to the UK by a President of the Republic of Ireland in April 2014, 'Ireland and Britain live in both the shadow and in the shelter of one another and so it

▶ More info

40 has been since the dawn of history.' Today, there are close ties between the two countries in many areas – cultural, economic and diplomatic. While Irish (or Gaelic) is the first official language in the Republic of Ireland, it is currently only spoken in some rural areas, with English being much more common. Peace remains a sensitive issue, however, as demonstrated by the renewed outbreak of violence in Northern Ireland in

45 April 2021 following Brexit. Although the island remains divided, visions of a united Ireland persist on both sides of the border. Will there be a united Ireland in the future?

## 1 Main ideas

Draw a Venn diagram and complete it with information from the text, then compare your notes with a partner.

Republic of Ireland    Northern Ireland

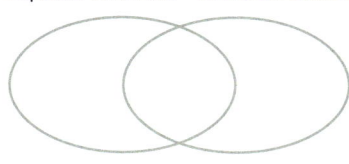

## 2 Reflect

a   Using different colours, mark the topics in your Venn diagram that you already know something about and those that are new to you.

b   Create a topic web where you can record vocabulary to help you to talk about these topics. Start by extracting words and phrases from the text opposite and add more vocabulary as you work through the chapter.

## 3 Defining, paraphrasing and giving examples

*Defining, paraphrasing* and *giving examples* are three strategies for clarifying the meaning of unknown words or concepts.

a   Study the information in the box, then define, paraphrase or give an example of the following expressions from the text opposite:
civil war – sectarian conflict – trade barriers – vibrant culture – heritage – Gaelic – sensitive issue – vision

b   Work with a partner. Look at your topic vocabulary maps and take turns defining, paraphrasing or giving examples of other key words and concepts. Your partner must guess the word.

## 4 Chunk it!

▶ Getting started 🔧

a   Combine the words in the box in as many ways as possible
to produce meaningful chunks you can use to talk about Ireland.

▶ Check 🔧

| Verbs | Adjectives | Nouns |
|---|---|---|
| characterize | Celtic | conflict |
| fear | political | entity |
| gain | rich | issue |
| impact | sensitive | identity |
| oppose | strong | independence |
| have | vibrant | oppression |
| resist | violent | culture |

b   Write example sentences for each word combination you found in **a**.
c   Work with a partner. Compare your sentences and add the chunks to your topic vocabulary map.

## 5 Giving a short talk

Beginning with the quote by President Michael D. Higgins (l. 39–40), give a short talk about the relationship between Ireland and Britain as mentioned in the text. Use the topic web you created in **2b**.

### Info

- **Defining:** giving the essential meaning of a term, e.g.: 'National identity *describes the sense of a nation as a cohesive whole, represented by its traditions, culture and language.*'
- **Paraphrasing:** expressing the meaning of a term in a different way, e.g.: '*When we speak of national identity, we speak of a collective feeling of belonging that brings a nation together and reflects a shared attachment to its culture, traditions and past.*'
- **Giving an example:** illustrating a term by a typical instance or case, e.g.: 'Irish national identity *is evident in the way Irish sports fans embrace Gaelic football, the country's most popular sport.*'

▶ Getting started 🔧

▶ SF 43: Giving a presentation, p. 405

## Being Irish    Leo Varadkar, Ryan McMullan and Teresa Buczkowska

▶ Getting started

- \***Quick write:** How do you define your national identity? Do you identify as German or another nationality? Write a short text explaining your national identity and what it means to you.
- With a partner, exchange ideas and compare them: What role do certain traditions or activities play in defining your national identities?

*For her book* Being Irish, *Marie-Claire Logue asked many people from different walks of life to write about what being Irish meant to them. Below are three answers.*

### Leo Varadkar (Taoiseach)

▶ More language

I was born in the Rotunda and grew up in west Dublin and it never occurred to me that I was anything else except Irish. This was my home and my heritage. As I grew
5 older, however, I realised that some others viewed me as different, because of my surname, because of my skin colour, because of differences that I had never imagined would affect my Irishness. Being Irish came to mean more to me precisely because some people tried to deny
10 it to me. [...]

> **Leo Varadkar** was born and raised in Dublin. A qualified medical doctor, he became Ireland's youngest prime minister (Taoiseach) in 2017, a position he held until 2020. He returned to that office from 2022 to 2024.

The people who shout loudest about someone not being Irish enough, who cling to a rigid conception of identity and attempt to deny it to others, are cowards who are afraid of what being Irish really means. They are insecure about their own identity and try
15 to over-compensate by lashing out at others. They are really at war with themselves.

There is no one version of Irishness. Our strength comes from each other, everyone bringing their own talents, ideas and dreams. We draw inspiration from the past, but we are not bound by it. We are all colours and backgrounds, every religion and none. [...]

20 Being Irish means our nationality is never a burden. It's the opposite. It lifts us up, it provides a sense of belonging and, in the darkest of times, it gives us a feeling of hope. To me being Irish simply means that you are someone who calls Ireland 'home'.

### Annotations

1 **Taoiseach** Irish Prime Minister
9 **deny sth. to sb.** prevent sb. from having sth.
12 **cling to sth.** continue to believe sth.
12 **rigid** firmly fixed
15 **lash out at sb.** strongly criticize sb.
24 **recognition** appreciation, acknowledgement
24 **instil sth.** inspire sth.
37 **congregate** come together in a group

### Ryan McMullan (musician)

Identity to me is recognition. It carries favour, instils
25 pride, evokes passion and offers hope. It becomes more apparent and less obvious, like the badge on a jersey or the style of a song. An Irish musician. That's me. I am sure there is more to me than that, but at first glance, that's how I'm identified. The musician identity has af-
30 forded me to travel the world playing shows and the Irish identity has given me company along the way. [...]

> **Ryan McMullan** is a singer-songwriter from County Down in Northern Ireland who has toured the world with acts such as Ed Sheeran. A multitalented musician, he has received praise for his ability to tell emotional stories in his songs.

I heard recently that there are more Irish people off the island of Ireland than there are on it. I can't prove it to be true, but I've yet to play a show as the only Irishman in
35 the room. Admittedly, that in itself tells a lot about us. We love to travel, but we don't travel well. I think that's why we congregate wherever we go. To keep home close to us.

Something I have always found funny is when I get the chance to meet some of the
Irish people after a show, or whenever it may be, they always tell me that for an
40 hour or so, I was a little bit of home to them, but get surprised when I return the
sentiment.

Truth be told, at every show that I hear an Irish accent, I immediately relax. It is like
an invisible comfort blanket. And then the show itself becomes this unspoken
conversation of home.

45 History has always told us to get out of Ireland. How there is nothing for us there,
and we have found that hard to move past. But there has been a shift in that tide.
Time has moved on and our generation is now starting to reap what was sown by
the generations before us. Ireland now has become as much of a paradise as anywhere we were leaving for. And the grass is most certainly greener.

50 **Teresa Buczkowska (migrants' rights activist)**
What makes us Irish? Is it our birthplace? Ancestors? A
distant line of blood? How far in history shall we look
back when tracing branches of a family tree? How long
does a family tree have to grow in Irish soil to be consid-
55 ered New Irish no more? Can Irish be Black? Can Irish be
of a non-Christian faith? Can Irish speak with a US accent? How about an Eastern European intonation, just
like mine? All of these questions make me wonder: what
gives Joe Biden more rights to call himself Irish than me?

60 The 46th US President's ancestors left Ireland nearly
two centuries ago. When he visited Ireland for the very
first time in his life, he was praised for declaring *Ireland
will be written on my soul.* I have been living here nearly
half of my life, immersing myself in my local community
65 day in and day out, but when I say I am Irish, people ask, 'but where are you really
from?' This question to some may seem to be just asking out of curiosity, but to me
this question is a challenge to my feeling of Ireland being my home. [...]

For more than 16 years I have been living and breathing Ireland in all aspects of my
life. I nourish an Irish strong sense of community, and in return I give that love and
70 care back. I have here my go-to places when I need a mental rest, and favourite spots
to meet my friends. I participate in Irish daily rituals even when I am not here because these habits are now mine. [...] I felt such a pride of place when we collectively said *Yes to Equality* and *Repeal the 8th.* I say that Ireland is written on my soul too.
This all means to be at home, and if I am at home in Ireland, I am Irish then. [...]

75 I was born in Poland so that's where I am partially from. That's where my childhood
happened, that's where my past was. When I arrived here, at first I didn't plan to
stay. Ireland was an adventure that turned into a permanent home. My whole adult
life has been here, and I am planning to stay for good, so I am from Ireland too.
Having two places that I can feel a strong sense of belonging to isn't as confusing as
80 it may seem. It is quite simple though: if Joe Biden can be a hyphen Irish, so can I.
I am Polish-Irish because Poland is where I was born, but Ireland is now my home.

*From: Marie-Claire Logue, ed.* Being Irish. 101 Views on Irish Identity Today, *2021*

▶ More language 🔖

**Teresa Buczkowska**
is a migrants' rights
activist who has
dedicated her
professional life to
improving the
situation of
migrants in Ireland.
She has published
extensively on
topics such as
integration and
migrant leadership.

Annotations
47 **reap what you
sow** *(proverb)* be faced
with the consequences
of your actions
64 **immerse yourself in
sth.** become fully
involved in sth.
69 **nourish sth.** encourage
sth. to grow stronger
73 **repeal a law** cancel a
law so it is no longer
valid
73 **the 8th** constitutional
amendment from 1983
making most abortions
illegal. It was repealed
in 2018 after a
referendum.
80 **hyphen Irish** of Irish
and another nationality,
e.g. American-Irish

▶ More info

▶ Support, p. 318

### Comprehension

**1**   Outline what being Irish means to each author.

### Analysis

**2**   Analyse how each author conveys their attitude towards a common Irish identity. Refer to the language they use.

### Language awareness

**3**   *Aspect* refers to how an event or action is viewed with respect to time (e.g. whether an action that started in the past is complete or still in progress at the time of speaking).

    **a**   Find examples of sentences in the text that fit the categories below and identify the tenses used:
- an action that is complete
- an ongoing action that is not yet complete
- an event occurring at a previous period of time that is linked to something happening later
- an action that started in the past and continues into the present.

    **b**   Write a short text about your own sense of identity and belonging using the types of verbal aspect described in **a**.

### Beyond the text

**4**   `Intercultural competence`   Discuss which of the authors' views comes closest to your own notion of national identity.

**Advanced**

**5**   **a**   'I heard recently that there are more Irish people off the island of Ireland than there are on it.' (ll. 32–33) Research whether this is true.

    **b**   Look again at ll. 60–67. Why do you think people are more accepting when US presidents call themselves Irish than when recent immigrants do? Give your opinion.

## Text 2

Annotation
3   **lilting** pleasant

# Irish craic   Amanda Ruggeri

- Milling around: Talk to different partners and discuss how your identities are shaped by the *places* you live in, the *people* you know and the *cultures* you are surrounded by.

*Follow award-winning journalist Amanda Ruggeri on a trip to Galway.*

Think of Galway, and certain images might come to mind. Bustling pubs. Freshly poured pints. And, of course, music – everywhere live, lovely, lilting music.

All of that is an important part of Galway, a city of about 80,000 residents on Ire-
5  land's west coast. It's also what most tourists notice first. But when it comes to
what gives Galway its spirit, there's more than meets the eye … and it's about much
more than fiddles and Guinness.

'People talk about the energy of Galway, and it's tangible,' said Aoibheann
McNamara, owner of Galway's Ard Bia At Nimmos restaurant. [...]

10  From the open-air market to the seaside promenade, restaurants to festivals, everywhere you go in Galway seems to share a certain buzz. But the energy you feel is
anything but frantic or frenetic. It's fun but light-hearted; lively but laid-back.
Among the Irish, this kind of easy-going merriment has its very own word: the *craic*.

Before I'd arrived, one local told me I could find the city's craic in a surprising place.
15  That was Blackrock, a beach at the end of the coastal promenade from Galway … at
08:00 on a Saturday morning … in January. For a city renowned to have fun until late
on a Friday, it seemed odd that locals would find it fun to be up so early again the
next morning. It seemed odder still given the cold, damp, winter weather. Surely she
must be wrong, I thought. No-one would be jumping into the sea at this time of year.

20  I was wrong. When I arrived, one person after another was stripping down to their
swimsuits and plunging into the roiling grey waters. Three of them were students
at the university here – a campus that helps give Galway a great deal of its youthful
energy. Shivering and dripping, they laughed as they recounted how cold the water
had been. 'You do it for the craic!' one said.

25  It reminded me of a conversation I'd had with Craig Flaherty, production associate
at Galway's Druid Theatre. 'There's something in the air of Galway – a kind of
wildness,' Flaherty had told me.

Much of Galway's spirit comes from its location. Facing the Atlantic, it is a place
where people are used to the unpredictability of life: it may be blowing gale-force
30  winds one day and sunny and calm the next. Politically, too, its geography has had
an effect. On the opposite coast from Dublin, Galway grew up as a kind of bohemi-
an counterweight to the capital.

But if the city's location helped breed its laid-back spirit, it's been further fostered
by its layout. Galway is small enough that you see the same people again and again
35  (even as an out-of-towner, I kept running into the handful of locals I knew). And
since everyone is on foot – the historical centre is pedestrian – it's easy, and expected, to stop for a chat.

'The city is not a city – it's a town. I never feel like I have to go out
and get a particular bag or a particular pair of shoes,' McNamara
40  said. 'That's really liberating and lovely. Life is very low-key.'

That sense of easy-going fun pervades the streets in other ways, too.
'There's a really good willingness to celebrate. You can see that on
the street from the buskers to the pubs to the street art,' Flaherty
said. 'There's a great natural landscape, from these small, winding
45  streets to the big open plazas, for playing and having the craic.'

Then there are the festivals. 'There's not a month that goes by where
there isn't some type of festival in Galway city,' said Aonghus Oferty

**Annotations**

51 **devotion to sth.** enthusiasm for sth.

59 **pretention** false behaviour intended to impress others

60 **uncontrivedness** being natural and spontaneous

76 **mannerism** way of speaking or acting

of the popular pub Tig Coili. 'There wouldn't be a month in the year that there wouldn't be something happening that's not good craic.' International Oyster and
50 Seafood Festival. Galway Races. Gin Fest. [...] The list goes on.

Given the city's devotion to the craic, it's small wonder that Galway was named a European Capital of Culture for 2020.

Everyone I spoke to had a slightly different definition of not only the craic, but Galway's version of it. But local Tony Burke, who has sold flowers at the Saturday
55 market for years, seemed to distil it best. 'It's the integration of conversation, contact with other people and the feeling of belonging,' Burke said. 'Class distinctions don't really matter. It's to be open, and realise that you could be homeless and having nothing going for you, but you can still have a conversation. Life is similar for us all, and we're all trying to get through it. It's the lack of pretention.'

60 McNamara agreed. 'Uncontrivedness is key,' she said. 'There's this real sense of engagement where people really want to connect with you. I'll say to American tourists, 'What's your story?' And they're completely shocked, like, 'What's she saying?' But I just want to know where you're at and how you are, because I care about that – and the world needs more people caring about that.'

65 Of course, Galway's music scene exemplifies everything about the city's soul – and its craic.

There is the lack of pretention. (Few pubs even have proper stages; musicians sit in a corner instead). The breakdown of barriers. (Often, formal bands aren't booked in advance. Instead, everyone is welcome to play – at Tig Coili I watched a Chinese
70 tourist shyly edge in, clutching a fiddle. He was warmly welcomed). The sense of living in the moment and doing something just because you love it. (Most musicians aren't paid in more than pints). And the importance of connecting with other people. (They do it to connect with not only the other musicians, but the pubgoers).

75 'Galway is very, very open,' Burke said. 'You'll see it in the amount of nationalities that come here. They'll start to get the Irish accent, the mannerisms, the sayings – they get it, and they love it.'

After all, once you've experienced a city devoted to the craic, it would be hard to settle for anything less.

*From: 'Ireland's light-hearted approach to life',* www.bbc.com, *3 April 2018*

Street musician in Galway

▶ Getting started

▶ SF 34: Writing a summary or an outline, p. 390

▶ WOB: pp. 8–10

### Comprehension

1  Summarize how Galway's identity is shaped by the following factors: people, location, layout and culture.

### Analysis

2  Analyse the means the author uses to share her personal travel experiences and emotions with her readers. Pay special attention to how she describes her interaction with locals and how she manages to reveal her inner world.

##### Language awareness

**3**  Work on either **a** or **b**.

▶ Getting started

**a**  Research the origin and meaning of
*craic* and its usage today. Then make
a short explainer video that
creatively presents your findings.

**b**  Challenge  *Craic* is just one of the
many Irish-English words in common
use today. Research other examples
and provide information about them
in a short explainer video.

##### Beyond the text

**4**  Writing  The above text is called a 'travelogue', i.e. a creative piece of writing that
reflects the author's personal travel experiences in an entertaining way while
providing information about the destination. Choose a place you have visited
and write a travelogue. Write in the first person.

▶ Check

## A brief history of Irish partition    Ronan McGreevy

- 3-2-1: Write down *three* things you know about the partition of Ireland,
  *two* questions you have about this topic and *one* aspect you are curious about.
- Exchange your ideas in class, then compile a list of open questions.

*Ronan McGreevy is a news reporter with* The Irish Times. *The article below was
written for readers who are not familiar with Irish history. The letters in brackets [A–E]
indicate that an internal heading has been left out (cf. task **1**).*

[A] The story of the Irish Border began with the Plantations of Ulster in the
17th century. Since the 12th century the British had retained a presence in Ireland
mostly along the east coast around Dublin in an area known as the Pale. King
Henry VIII's break with the Catholic Church in 1534 added a sectarian dimension
5  to the already fraught relationship between England and Ireland. Ulster had been
the most Gaelic Irish province in Ireland, but the dominant Catholic families, the
O'Neills and O'Donnells, were defeated in the Nine Years War between the Catholic
lords and the Protestant English crown. In 1607 they fled to the European continent, in what became known as the Flight of the Earls, leaving their lands behind
10  them.

Their flight was followed by the plantation of Ulster designed to make the province
quiescent to the crown. First Antrim and Down were planted by private settlers
mostly from Scotland, then the remaining seven counties of Ulster – Derry, Tyrone,
Donegal, Fermanagh, Cavan, Monaghan and Armagh – followed, attracting thou-
15  sands of Protestant settlers from Scotland and the north of England.

Although the plantations never succeeded in fully dislodging the native Catholic
Irish, the province took on a different character to the rest of Ireland, being predominantly Protestant and loyal to the crown.

▶ More language

Annotations
1  **plantation**  (here)
method of colonization
2  **retain sth.**  continue to
have sth.
4  **sectarian**  relating to
differences between
diverse religious groups
5  **fraught**  full of tension

▶ More language

7  **Nine Years War**  Irish
war against English
rule (1593–1603)
12  **quiescent**
[kwiˈesnt] causing no
trouble
16  **dislodge sb.**  remove sb.

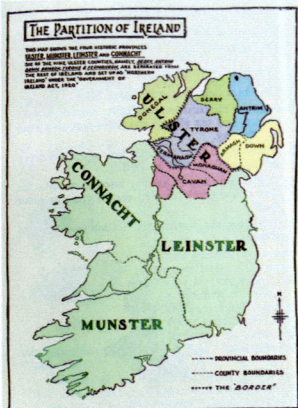

THE PARTITION OF IRELAND

Map of the partition of Ireland, 1921

**Annotations**

21 **reconcile sth.** restore sth. to harmony
24 **home rule** self-government
27 **jurisdiction** (here) authority
30 **into perpetuity** (*fml*) for all time in the future
36 **IRA** = Irish Republican Army, paramilitary organization fighting for an independent Irish Republic
36 **guerrilla war** irregular war fought, e.g. by armed civilians
47 **be subjected to sth.** (here) likely to be affected by sth.
49 **direct rule** (here) British control of Ireland

[B] The Border was the result of the partition of Ireland, which occurred under
20 the Government of Ireland Act (1920). This was an attempt by the British Government to reconcile two incompatible demands – the Irish nationalist demand for separation from Britain, and the unionist demand to remain part of the United Kingdom.

The Act set up two home-rule parliaments, one for six counties in Ulster and
25 the other for the 26 counties which was the rest of Ireland. A third parliament or council was envisaged where matters of mutual concern or the reunification of Ireland under one jurisdiction would be concerned.

The Act was accepted by the unionists and the Northern Ireland parliament was set up in 1921 with jurisdiction over six counties: Antrim, Derry, Tyrone, Fer-
30 managh, Armagh and Down. Unionists wanted a Protestant majority into perpetuity and the counties of Donegal, Cavan and Monaghan with their large Catholic populations threatened that hegemony. They were excluded from the six-county parliament.

The Act was rejected by the nationalist south as home rule, which only gave an Irish
35 parliament limited autonomy and not the full independence desired by the separatists in the IRA, who were then fighting a guerrilla war against the British.

[C] The Anglo-Irish Treaty of December 1921, which ended the War of Independence, set up the Irish Free State for the remaining 26 counties of Ireland. The Irish State came into being in 1922. This is now the Republic of Ireland, which is a sov-
40 ereign, independent state and a member of the European Union.

On March 23rd, 1923 the Border became an international frontier. [...]

The partition of Ireland left two minorities on either side of the Border; a small unionist one to the south and a substantial Catholic one to the north which wanted unification with the rest of Ireland.

45 Many Catholics in the North believed that Northern Ireland was, in the words of its first premier James Craig, 'a Protestant parliament and a Protestant state' and they were subjected to discrimination when it came to employment, housing and education.

[D] In 1969, violence broke out in Northern Ireland. Direct rule from the British
50 parliament in Westminster was imposed from 1972. The Provisional IRA waged a 25-year campaign to try and end British rule in Northern Ireland. In the years between 1969 and 1994, 3,500 people lost their lives.

The Border between the Republic and Northern Ireland became a frontline. Border posts were regularly attacked. In August 1972 a bomb planted by the Provisional
55 IRA blew up a customs post in Newry killing nine people, including the three IRA members who planted the bomb.

The main road between Dublin and Belfast was framed by a giant British army watchtower near the border town of Newry. The British sought to reduce the number of crossings to stop republican paramilitaries from moving back and forth
60 across the road. The British blocked roads, made them impassable or blew up

bridges. Hundreds of roads were closed during the Troubles, cutting communities off on either side of the Border.

Two things ended the Border as a physical obstacle. The first was the introduction of the European Single Market in 1993, which ended all customs controls between
65 member states of the European Union. The second was the end of the Troubles.

[E] The Troubles officially ended in April 1998 with the signing of the Good Friday Agreement also known as the Belfast Agreement. It sought to create a new relationship between nationalists and unionists in Northern Ireland with the establishment of a power-sharing executive (cabinet) and assembly. Cross-border organisations
70 were set up to improve relations between the North and the Republic and provision was also made for the strengthening of relations between Britain and Ireland.

The agreement sought to reconcile the twin identities of being British and Irish. It gave the right to anybody born on the island of Ireland to become a citizen of Ireland. It also enshrined the principle of consent – that a united Ireland could not
75 come about until a majority in Northern Ireland wanted it. [...] [T]he Good Friday Agreement has kept the peace and the people of Ireland have enjoyed two decades without the sickening daily routine of murder and mayhem.

The last British watchtower was dismantled in 2005 and with it went the last physical reminder of the Border in Ireland.

80 Now, to all intents and purposes, the Border is invisible. Only a change in road signs from kilometres in the Republic to miles in the North and the absence of bilingual signage (English and Irish in the Republic) in Northern Ireland denotes that the Border has been crossed. [...]

Brexit threatens all that. A year after the Brexit vote, British prime minister Theresa
85 May announced that Britain would be leaving both the single market and the customs union. That means the frontier between the Republic and Northern Ireland is no longer just a frontier between two sovereign states, but a European Union frontier. [...] The threat of such a visible return to a divided island is something that nobody in Britain or Ireland wants, but may happen anyway unless agreement can be reached.

*From: Ronan McGreevy, 'A history of Ireland for outsiders', www.irishtimes.com, 6 March 2019*

**Annotations**
70 **provision** *Vorkehrung*
74 **enshrine sth.** ensure that sth. will be protected
75 **come about** happen
77 **mayhem** chaos
78 **dismantle sth.** take sth. apart
82 **denote sth.** indicate sth.

 WOB: pp. 115–117

## Comprehension

**1　a** Match the headings below to the five sections of the text (A–E).

▶ Check 🔽

International border – Partition – Before the 20th century – The Belfast Agreement – The Troubles

**b** Work in groups of five, each of you focusing on a different section of the text. Reread your section and turn it into an infographic by visualizing the information about Irish history it contains. You can use a map, a timeline or images. Present your infographics to each other.

**c** Return to your list of open questions and check whether the text has provided answers. Research any questions left unanswered.

### Analysis

► SF 17: Reading and understanding non-fictional texts, p. 367

► WOB: pp. 28–30

**2** Historical writing tends to be *analytic*, going beyond mere description, and *specific*, avoiding vague generalization. Examine the means used by the author to make his text both analytic and specific.

### Language awareness

**3**  Intercultural competence   The text uses several words that have special meanings in the context of Irish history, e.g. 'unionist' or 'plantation'. It also states that in Ireland, both Irish and English are recognized as official languages.
  a  Write concise definitions for the Irish-specific meanings of 'unionist' and 'plantation'.
  b  Research some basic Irish phrases and practise the correct pronunciation. Present your findings to the class.

### Beyond the text

► SF 40: Listening/Viewing for gist and detail, p. 399

► Check

► WOB: pp. 78–81

**4**  Listening   Listen to a podcast on the situation along the Irish border after Brexit. Answer the questions below. You need not write complete sentences.
  1  What Sunak's compromise may lead to
  2  What is special about Mr Fitzpatrick's hardware shop
  3  What consequences Brexit had for Mr Fitzpatrick
  4  What cross-border traffic was like during the Troubles
  5  What the 'Windsor Framework' would imply for Northern Ireland
  6  What the 'Windsor Framework' would imply for the Republic of Ireland
  7  What Hirsch fears might happen if Sunak is not successful

**5**  Drawing on your knowledge of Irish history, explain how British involvement in Ireland has affected Irish identity over the centuries. Then think back to the guiding question of this chapter: How would you answer it now?

## Text 4

# Art in Context: Northern Ireland street art

- Complete the following sentence: *To me, political art is …*
- Read out your statements in class and compare them, then discuss in what ways you consider political art to be important.

*In Belfast and many other places in Northern Ireland, you can see paintings on walls and houses which reflect Northern Ireland's history.*

### Comprehension

► Getting started

**1** Work with a partner.
  a  Study the mural opposite (Belfast, 2013) and take notes on how the country's past (Partner A) and future (Partner B) are presented.

**b**  Share your ideas, then discuss the message of the mural with regard to the situation in Northern Ireland today.

### Analysis

**2**  Murals are 'multimodal' by nature. Analyse how the different modes of communication contribute to the mural's overall meaning.

▶ SF 24: Working with multimodal texts, p. 376

▶ WOB: pp. 40–44

### Beyond the text

**3**  `Speaking`  Have a debate in class on the following motion: 'Murals are an effective medium for political and social commentary.'

**4**  Read the info box about another form of political art, Irish protest songs. Then select one of the songs mentioned in the text and investigate the story behind the song. What other perspectives on Ireland does this song offer? Report back to class.

▶ Getting started

▶ Support, p. 319

▶ SF 47: Having a debate, p. 412

`Info`

**Irish protest songs – an intriguing part of Ireland's musical tradition**

Ireland has a rich musical tradition and protest songs are an intrinsic part of it. Throughout history, music has helped the Irish express their national identity and given a voice to those who fight injustice. Protest songs dealing with more recent aspects of Irish history include 'The Town I Loved So Well' by Phil
5  Coulter (1973), 'Banana Republic' by the Boomtown Rats (1980), 'Sunday Bloody Sunday' by U2 (1983), 'Streets of Sorrow/ Birmingham Six' by The Pogues (1988), 'Zombie' by The Cranberries (1994), 'This Is a Rebel Song' by Sinéad O'Connor (1997) and 'Dublin Town' by Damien Dempsey (1997).

## Language revisited

An exchange student to Ireland went to a rally and heard some politicians say: 'Ireland must be unified!' The next day, she told her host parents:

- *Some politicians **insisted that** Ireland **is** unified.*

**1** The sentence does not accurately reflect what the politicians said. Why not?

## Language awareness

What the exchange student should have said is:

- *Some politicians **insisted that** Ireland **be** unified.*

Here, the use of *be* is an example of the subjunctive, which is often used in formal English to say that something 'must be done'. The form occurs in subordinate *that*-clauses following verbs or expressions of proposal, demand, recommendation or intention, e.g. *demand (that)* or *it is crucial (that)*. Formally, the subjunctive can
5 only be distinguished from the indicative when a singular subject is followed by a present-tense verb in the third-person or when the subject is followed by *be*.

**2** In which of the sentences below is the subjunctive distinct in terms of form? Explain your answer.
  **1** *Unionists have always insisted that the two Irish countries stay independent.*
  **2** *Republicans, by contrast, believe it is crucial Ireland become one.*

## Practice

*The extract below is from a speech given by former Taoiseach Leo Varadkar to members of his party* Fine Gael *in 2021, in which he talks about the unification of Ireland.*

Unification must not be the annexation of Northern Ireland. It means something more, a new state designed together, a new constitution and one that reflects the diversity of a bi-national or multi-national state in which almost a million people are British. Like the New South Africa, a rainbow nation, not just orange and green.
5 We have to be willing to consider all that we'd be willing to change – new titles, shared symbols, how devolution in the North would fit into the new arrangements, a new Senate to strengthen the representation of minorities, the role and status of our languages, a new and closer relationship with the United Kingdom.
We also need to map out how we can take the best of both jurisdictions and apply
10 them across Ireland as a whole, perhaps our welfare and pensions system, their NHS to give just two examples.
And also what might remain different, because unification is not assimilation, for example, perhaps education or maintaining two legal systems.

*From: 'Speech from Tánaiste Leo Varadkar at the opening of the 2021 Fine Gael Ard Fheis', www.finegeal.ie, 15 June 2021*

**3** Outline Mr Varadkar's ideas by making sentences with the subjunctive.

► WOB: p. 119

| Mr Varadkar | suggests insists demands | (that) | a new Ireland Northern Ireland Ireland-UK relations | … |
| --- | --- | --- | --- | --- |

Advanced

# Queen of the sticklebacks   Dawn Watson

▶ More info

- With a partner, brainstorm possible challenges that a child growing up in Northern Ireland during the Troubles might be faced with.
- The story you are about to read is set in North Belfast in the late 1980s. It is narrated by a young girl roaming the streets of her neighbourhood. Read the first section (ll. 1–30) and take notes: What are the girl's surroundings like? What mood is she in? Speculate in class about what might happen next, then read the rest of the story.

▶ SF 19: Reading and understanding narrative texts, p. 369

*Dawn Watson is a writer and poet from Belfast, who also teaches creative writing classes at Queen's University.*

It was early summer in 1988 and everything concrete was a river. The grey pavement slabs rippled together like shallows. The painted kerbstones were odd fish strung in a line. Red, blue and white, red, white and blue. The pocked strip of road was a creek run low as a
5  bathtub, moss green and plumbed in silt. The overgrown entry was a stubborn dyke that saved us daily. It was a blue evening. Just to see what would happen, I put one foot on each entry post and dared the river to overwhelm me. 'Come on,' I said. 'Rise up, sure. Carry me out of here.' But those posts did their job well. There was no mess-
10 ing around from North Belfast footpaths trying to flood their banks on this occasion. The yard walls stayed where they were and the telephone poles dotted the tarmac flood plains quietly.

Two boys waded up Ashfield Gardens, one in a blue tracksuit and one in red. Both pairs of trousers were ripped from the knees to the ankles. Tiny silver minnows
15 smacked their lips in the holes. I jumped down from the posts and picked up my skateboard. Blue shouted, 'Are you a wee boy or a wee girl?'

'I'm a girl.'

'You're wearing wee boys' clothes.'

'So?'

20 'So, you are. They look second-hand.'

My face flushed. A dustbin rushed past in a current. The boys started singing, 'Hurrah – Hurrah – We are the Billy Boys'. I'd never heard Catholics sing the song. The minnows shut their mouths.

I said, 'Why are you singing that if you aren't Protestant?'

25 Red laughed. Blue shouted, 'What's a Protestant?' I admitted I didn't know. They ducked under the water and surfaced with handfuls of smooth rocks. We can only be nice to you if you give us your skateboard.' Red threw a stone and it hit me on my brow. I gripped the board in front of my face. Blood ran into my right eye. The boys splashed towards me in synchronised goose steps and snatched it from my
30 hands. I saw my blood plip-plop into the swollen river.

Red and Blue had been here six months. They had worn the same tracksuits every day since they moved in. They arrived after an army of Housing Executive builders

### Annotations

**stickleback** small fish
1 **concrete** *Beton*
1 **everything concrete was a river** water had flooded the street
2 **slab** flat piece of stone
2 **shallow** *(n)* area of a river where the water is not deep
3 **kerbstone** *Bordstein*
5 **plumbed in silt** full of fine sand
6 **dyke** [daɪk] *Damm*
12 **tarmac** road surface material
14 **minnow** small fish
15 **smack one's lips** *mit den Lippen schmatzen*
16 **wee** *(infml)* little
22 **Billy Boys** Protestant street gang in the 1920s

Advanced

Annotations

**34 wasteland** overgrown unused area of land

**36 whiz sth. in** (here) move sth. in quickly

**36 dinghy** [ˈdɪŋgi] small boat

**55 waders** waterproof boots

**57 spinner lure** plastic bait for catching fish

**62 luminescent** glowing

**62 stickbait** plastic bait shaped like a fish

wearing rain slickers built a dead-end string of houses at the bottom of our street. It used to be a patch of wasteland backing on to Dunmore Greyhound Track.
35 People built bonfires down there every July out of tyres and sofas. The builders whizzed diggers and cement mixers in on inflatable dinghies. They extended Ashfield Gardens into something shaped like a thermometer: the long, thin street leading to a mercury glob of houses boiling at the end. The people the Housing Executive moved in had one route in and one route out, and that was my street. The
40 people the Housing Executive moved in were Catholics, which was exotic. There was a patch of untouched tarmac between where the old Ashfield Gardens ended and the new one began. That's where my entry is. It's dry, tucked under a lamp post. Everything else has turned to water.

Last week, the Housing Executive pulled a fast one. Everyone in
45 our street was told to move house. The builders returned, dropping anchor at the red post box pier to implement their grand plan of house extensions, updates and renovation. It was goodbye and goodnight to everyone's homes and wallpapers and door handles and carpets and windows and linoleum. Overnight, the
50 people of Ashfield Gardens had been exploded. It was like a stone tossed in a bucket of sticklebacks. They had to go live in old and empty houses on the opposite side of their street until the renovation work was complete. They were told it might take a year, or forever.

**66 raft** floating platform used as a boat

**67 pug, Great Dane** types of dogs

**68 illicit** unlawful

**72 slacks** trousers

**78 digs** (infml) lodgings

**79 barge pole** long stick used to move a boat

55 The Housing Executive, shiny in waders, reeled me, my mum and my brothers out of number twelve and dropped us in the tank of number seven. Old Elsie in number sixteen bit on a spinner lure that must have looked like a Berkley Menthol and ended up in the bucket of number five. Lonely Luke, who had never married and was rumoured to be a Catholic, was speared in number two and strung up in num-
60 ber nine. Mrs Laird and the woman long-assumed to be her sister were netted in number twenty and released in number three. Isma and her two grown-up sons fell for buzzing luminescent stickbait in number ten and got cut loose in number eleven.

I spent the week of the Great Move watching from my step in the entry. I picked
65 wads of used gum off the warm ground and chewed up the last of its gritty spearmint. I saw Luke use a driftwood raft to tow fourteen ceramic dogs out of his living room to his new home on the gable end. There were two white pugs locked in an illicit embrace, and three white Great Danes dancing. Their tails were question marks. One tall, clay duck was not happy to see a white Doberman pinscher with a
70 glitter collar smiling. They didn't see Isma wading over the road balancing five tomato plants in blown-glass bowls. She wobbled on slick rocks, green with algae. Isma didn't see Elsie roll up her slacks to go ask the man with the long, black rifle and combat boots on the corner if he wouldn't mind swimming to the shop to get her ten Berkley Menthol. 'I'm sorry, I'm preventing a war in your street,' he said.
75 Elsie pressed her lips together in a line. Neither of them saw Mrs Laird gripping her sister's hand and shivering, neck-deep in clear blue water, feeling for a dropped telephone chair with her feet.

I watched my brothers and my mum sail to our new digs in an upturned wardrobe, using a yard brush and a curtain rail as barge poles. It was surprisingly watertight

**Advanced**

80 for something made of laminated medium-intensity fibreboard. John and Mark were crying and my mum was crying. She wailed, 'But isn't it like this anyway, sure? Isn't it always like this?' The crows, displaced in the gathering flood and looking for new and renovated nests themselves, clacked their beaks to confirm what she said was true.

85 The Housing Executive builders wore spacesuits and tore down my bedroom walls. Before my parents split, my dad had painted the walls with every cartoon character he could think of. He thought I would like them much better than wallpaper. And I did. Pluto, Goofy and Mickey are quare smilers. They smiled all day and all night, even when he died. They smiled even though they knew as well as I did my dad
90 would never be back to re-paint Donald Duck's beak when I tore his nostrils off with sticky tape. The builders piled up technicolour rubble. There were bits of white feather and red shorts and a black circular ear dumped in a skip. I watched while treading water.

North Belfast didn't use to be a river. When I was small, it was little more than a
95 thin creek. It started raining when my uncle knocked on our front door last November. I answered, and the brown leaves were alight. He told me my dad had cancer. He told me on the doorstep my dad had two weeks to live. It was like he said the corner shop was selling orangutans. It was like he said the leaves were jumping back on the trees. I asked him, 'What is a kohlrabi? What is a Romanesco?'
100 I laughed and laughed. I stared at the ceiling with my mouth open.

I should have twigged my dad was dying long before my uncle carried the news to us in bulging Crazy Prices bags. My dad's teeth had been going missing. His handsome face had been bright yellow for some time. But we don't always recognise life-breaking things as they happen. The worst things come from safe places, don't
105 they?

Three days later in his flat, I asked my dad if he hurt anywhere. He said, 'Listen to me. Remember you are as good as anyone. Don't let anyone tell you different. Make sure you laugh, love. Make sure you cut your hair as short as you want. And tell your future girl I said look after you.' The rest of the afternoon, we watched
110 Formula One. I noticed the big, black tyres were rippling. He told me and my brothers to choose a chocolate bar from a bag. I took a Twix. The wrapper was wet in my hand. The next day, my dad was dead. They buried him on a Saturday. The wake was at my aunt's house on Skegoneill Avenue. I saw his white face through a crack in the living room door. The coffin floated to the hearse. The crowd in Brant-
115 wood Football Club cheered. Its blue turnstile creaked and whuppeted. The ground beneath the pallbearers' feet was thick with flip-flop pike.

After the Great Move, everyone in Ashfield Gardens closed their front doors one by one. From across the street came the clink and batter of hammers and chisels. Metal sounds different when it drifts over water. Like a fog forge in an envelope.
120 Midges gathered in clouds.

My mum and my brothers locked themselves in a room with purple dragonfly wallpaper. They were crying and my mum was crying. She wailed, 'But isn't it like this anyway, sure? Isn't it always like this?'

---

**Annotations**

80 **fibreboard** *Kunstfaserplatte*
88 **quare** *(infml*, Northern Irish) remarkable, great
91 **technicolour** in many bright colours
91 **rubble** waste, debris
93 **tread water** keep in the same place while in deep water; *(fig)* do nothing while waiting for sth. to happen
99 **Romanesco** type of broccoli
101 **twig sth.** *(infml)* realize sth.
113 **wake** *(n)* Totenwache
114 **hearse** [hɜːs] vehicle carrying a coffin at a funeral
115 **turnstile** gate
116 **pallbearer** *Sargträger*
116 **flip-flop pike** (here) fish-shaped footprint
119 **forge** *(n) Schmiede*
120 **midge** *kleine Mücke*
121 **dragonfly** *Libelle*

Advanced

**125 slanted** not straight
**129 boulder** large rock
**131 wrought iron** [rɔːt]
    *Schmiedeeisen*
**136 cargo crate** *Frachtkiste*
**136 gantry** *Gerüst*
**141 mote** small particle
**142 subside** go down to a
    lower level
**143 rivet** metal pin used in
    construction
**143 honeysuckle**
    sweet-smelling plant

I grabbed my BMX. It's not easy to ride in a river. I headed for the Grove Park,
125 wobbling on mud banks slanted beneath hedges and bolted garden gates. I passed
the man on the corner with the long, black rifle and the combat boots. I waved to
Lonely Luke's white, ceramic dogs. When my blue tyres spun in silt, I planted my
left foot among stones, discarded cans and metal bed frames. I climbed off to push
in patches. I crossed Skegoneill Drive on shed planks stretched between boulders.
130 I crossed Jellicoe Avenue on a fallen silver birch. The park's green railings stretched
for miles. Its wrought iron points wriggled above the water. I got off my bike and
squeezed it through a gap.

The grass river stretched to the horizon, to the crest of a hill where the water
thinned. Metal benches were sunk at angles. Occasional birch trees stood like
135 stuck pins. It was all sky and cold and river. I pushed my bike to the top and stared
out at the docks. Cargo crates were locked in a stare-down with the gantries. I rang
my bell to set its thin *cling-k* echoing over the dark water, to the neck of the dry dock
well. The sticklebacks gathered at my feet. 'When the river goes down,' I whispered, 'I will go and get my skateboard back. I will punch those boys in the face.
140 I won't be afraid. I'm as good as anyone.'

I pedalled hard down the hill. The river welled behind me, a flood of silver motes.
I would wait on that bright yellow crane for the waters to subside. I would wait
above the rivets and slipways where everything smells like honeysuckle.

*From: Paul McVeigh and Lisa Frank, eds.* Belfast Stories, *2019*

### Comprehension

**1 a**   Share your first impressions in class and describe how close your guesses
     about the story were, then answer the five *wh*-questions: Who? What?
     Where? When? Why?

▶ Support, p. 319

   **b**   The terms and phrases below (all from the story) allude to the Troubles.
     Describe their significance in the story.

     1988 • kerbstones painted red, white and blue •
     Catholics and Protestants • Billy Boys •
     the man with the long, black rifle and combat boots

   **c**   Return to your ideas about the challenges faced by children growing up in
     Northern Ireland during the Troubles. Summarize the message of the story
     with respect to those challenges.

### Analysis

▶ WOB: pp. 37–39

**2**   Analyse the function of the story's setting. The following questions will help you:
     What insights into the girl's sense of identity and belonging does the setting
     provide? In what ways does it contribute to her internal or external conflicts?
     What kind of atmosphere does it create?

**3**   Examine the use of water and fish imagery in the text and interpret the title of
     the story, 'Queen of the sticklebacks'.

Advanced

### Language awareness

**4** The modal auxiliary verb *will* has different meanings and functions. It is used to talk about the future, to say what people want to do or to make predictions, assumptions, promises, offers, requests and even threats.

  **a** Explain the use of *will* in ll. 139–140.

  **b** The narrator's father is very important to her. What would she want to tell him? Write a diary entry using *will* with three different meanings. You could start like this: *I will never/always … / You will … / I won't ever …*

▶ More language

### Beyond the text

**5** Investigate the challenges North Belfast is facing today. Consider the following aspects: poverty – housing – crime – sectarianism.

  **a** Work in groups of four. Each group member focuses on a different aspect, conducting research and preparing a two-minute statement.

  **b** Report back to your group.

**6** Think back to the guiding question: How would you answer it now?

▶ SF 13: Doing research, p. 360

---

**Text 6**

## The future of Ireland: divided or united?

- In class, collect helpful phrases for working with statistics. Use them to write a short paragraph analysing the bar chart below.
- Based on the statistics below, discuss whether these statements about Northern Ireland today are true:
  - There are more Protestants than Catholics in Northern Ireland.
  - Northern Ireland has become more secular.
- Point out what relevance the data might have for the future of Ireland.

▶ SF 22: Analysing diagrams, p. 373
▶ Getting started

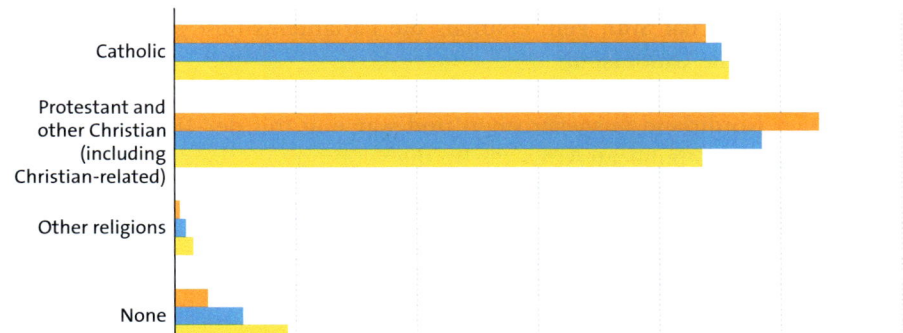

**Percentage of population by 'religion/religion of upbringing'**

*Source*: nisra.gov.uk, *22 December 2022*

*Duncan Morrow, a political scientist teaching at Ulster University, was interviewed by* Süddeutsche Zeitung *after the 2021 census data were published.*

**Herr Morrow, wieso hat eine katholische Bevölkerungsmehrheit für viele Nordiren eine große symbolische Bedeutung?**

Als der Staat vor hundert Jahren gegründet wurde, wurde von den Briten dafür gesorgt, dass es dort eine probritische Mehrheit von Protestanten gibt. Jetzt haben sich
5 die Mehrheitsverhältnisse zum ersten Mal seit 1921 geändert. Das sorgt bei vielen für ein Gefühl von totaler Veränderung. Denn mit einer katholischen Mehrheit wird es in Zukunft wahrscheinlicher, dass sich bei einem Referendum die Mehrzahl der Menschen in Nordirland irgendwann für ein vereinigtes Irland ausspricht.

**Wieso deckt sich die Religionszugehörigkeit hier so stark mit der politischen**
10 **Haltung?**

Religion ist historisch gesehen in Nordirland eine politische Trennlinie. Die beiden Communitys, die katholische und die protestantische, entwickelten fast getrennte Identitäten. Zwar war der Nordirlandkonflikt nie ein Krieg der Theologie, aber Religion wurde zu einem wichtigen sozialen, wirtschaftlichen und kulturel-
15 len Faktor – und angefeuert von der Gewalt auch zu einem Marker politischer Identität als Unionisten und Republikaner.

**Es gibt zwei bedeutende Parteien: Die Democratic Unionist Party (DUP) gilt als protestantische, die Sinn Féin als katholische Partei. Trifft diese Klassifizierung zu?**

Die beiden Parteien haben sich sehr stark innerhalb der beiden Communitys ent-
20 wickelt. Sie sind zwar keine religiösen, sondern politische Parteien, aber sie beziehen ihre Unterstützung in der Regel eben überwiegend aus der einen oder der anderen Konfession.

**Inwiefern spiegelt sich die religiöse Spaltung im politischen System wider?**

Im Karfreitagsabkommen wurde 1998 geregelt, dass in der Regierung Mitglieder
25 beider Seiten vertreten sein müssen. Es muss also eine Koalition von Leuten geben, die früher Feinde waren. Außerdem sichert das Abkommen beiden Regierungsparteien ein Vetorecht zu. Das heißt, das System funktioniert nur, wenn die Parteien zusammenarbeiten. Das ist natürlich eine große Herausforderung für das politische System in Nordirland, aber es soll sicherstellen, dass sich beide
30 Bevölkerungsgruppen in der Regierung vertreten fühlen.

**Anfang des Jahres hat Sinn Féin erstmals die Parlamentswahl gewonnen. Was bedeutet das für die Unionisten?**

Der Wahlsieg der Sinn Féin war historisch. Die Partei hat sich immer gegen die Existenz von Nordirland ausgesprochen und war eng mit der IRA (die Terror-
35 organisation Irish Republican Army, die für die Vereinigung Irlands gekämpft hat; *d. Red.*) verbunden. Dass Sinn Féin nun die stärkste Partei ist, ist für die Unionisten auch eine große psychologische Veränderung. Es ist ein weiteres Beispiel in einer Reihe von Entwicklungen, die bei ihnen das Gefühl hervorruft, dass ihre Verbindung zum Vereinigten Königreich schwächer wird. Das Nordirlandpro-
40 tokoll, die veränderte Demografie, alles bestärkt ihre Angst. Sie sehen, dass der Trend zu einem vereinigten Irland geht.

**Die DUP müsste also auch für Katholiken attraktiv werden?**

Ja, das ist Mathematik. Ohne katholische Wähler kann die DUP nicht überleben. Es ist auch eine große Herausforderung, vor der der Unionismus als Ganzes steht.

⁴⁵ Wenn die Unionisten wollen, dass Nordirland Teil von Großbritannien bleibt,
müssen sie auch nicht-protestantische Wähler davon überzeugen. [...] Die Sinn
Féin ist da erfolgreicher. Nicht so sehr beim Gewinnen von protestantischen Stim-
men als beim Aufbau von Koalitionen mit anderen Parteien. Die Sinn Féin hat
liberale Positionen bei sozialen Themen wie gleichgeschlechtlicher Ehe, Abtrei-
⁵⁰ bung oder Klimapolitik aufgenommen und erreicht damit mehr Wähler [...]

### Wird es eine Wiedervereinigung Irlands geben?

Die demografische Entwicklung deutet darauf hin. Auch wenn es noch zehn oder
auch 15 Jahre dauern könnte. Das Problem ist, dass viele die irische Wiederverei-
nigung vor allem als Vision oder als Ideal sehen. Über die Details, wie eine prak-
⁵⁵ tische Umsetzung aussehen könnte, macht sich kaum jemand Gedanken. Doch
wie der Brexit gezeigt hat, sind gerade diese Details wichtig: Welche Rolle spielt
das Vereinigte Königreich beim Übergang, welche Komplikationen könnten
auftauchen, was sind die praktischen, wirtschaftlichen und sozialen Fragen? Das
alles muss in den nächsten Jahren geklärt werden.                    *(607 words)*

*From: Interview mit Miriam Dahlinger, 'Wird Irland wiedervereinigt?',* Süddeutsche Zeitung,
*27 December 2022*

**1** `Mediating` Work on either **a** or **b**.

    **a** `Writing` A friend of yours from the USA is writing a research paper on the prospects and perils of a unified Ireland and has asked for your help. You have read the interview above and decide to send them an email summarizing the relevant information on the topic. Write the email.

    **b** `Challenge` `Speaking` You have to give a short speech in your bilingual English class about the prospects and perils of a unified Ireland. Using the interview above, write a script for your speech. Give your speech in front of your class.

▶ Getting started

▶ SF 49: Mediating from German into English, p. 416

▶ SF 44: Preparing and giving a speech, p. 408

▶ WOB: pp. 71–77

## Chapter task

A time capsule message is a letter written for someone in the future, telling them about the present and sharing hopes for the future. Follow the steps below to write a message to future generations about your vision of Ireland in a hundred years.

**1** Choose one of the following roles and brainstorm ideas about the message this person might wish to pass on. Include ideas from this chapter.

    a child growing up in Belfast • an artist from Galway • a historian • a politician • a poet • an immigrant • a civil rights activist

**2** Write in the first person and use the subjunctive where appropriate to say what must be done. Use a digital tool to design, edit and present your message.

# Chapter 8
# Nigeria – Going beyond African Stereotypes

When the train travelling from Abuja to Kaduna rolled into the station [...], none of the passengers were sure if it was because the faulty engine had broken down again. When the train refused to move nearly an hour later, everyone was almost certain it was the engine. Until another train travelling the opposite route rum-
5 bled by, pockmarked with holes and impact damage. [...]

There had been an attack on the other train. Guns, some said. [...] I and some writers were travelling to the first Hausa international book and arts festival in Kaduna. None of us dared to go by road. The roads belong to the bandits [...]. This was my country. This train. These coaches filled with anxiety and fright-
10 ened people, caught halfway between a dream and a promise, waiting to be led to a promised destination. [...]

*Abubakar Adam Ibrahim, Nigerian writer and journalist*   ▶ More info

## Annotations

5 **impact damage** damage caused by being hit by a heavy and fast object

7 **Hausa** (here) connected to the Hausa, an ethnic group living in northern Nigeria and other parts of West Africa

15 **entrepreneur** [ˌɒntrəprəˈnɜː] person with their own business

16 **lubricate sth.** add a greasy or oily substance to make sth. run smoothly

17 **mettle** determination to do sth. challenging

▶ More language

▶ Getting started (task 1)

1 Before reading the texts, brainstorm what you already know about Nigeria and make notes. If you don't know a lot, speculate on why this might be the case.

2 Work with a partner. Each of you reads one of the statements above.
   a Describe the portrayal of Nigeria presented in your text to your partner.
   b Choose one aspect from each text that you find particularly striking or surprising. Explain why you picked it.

3 a Look at the Chapter map and discuss which aspects are represented in your notes and in the statements.
   b Speculate on the possible meaning of the guiding question and its connection to the other aspects mentioned in the Chapter map.

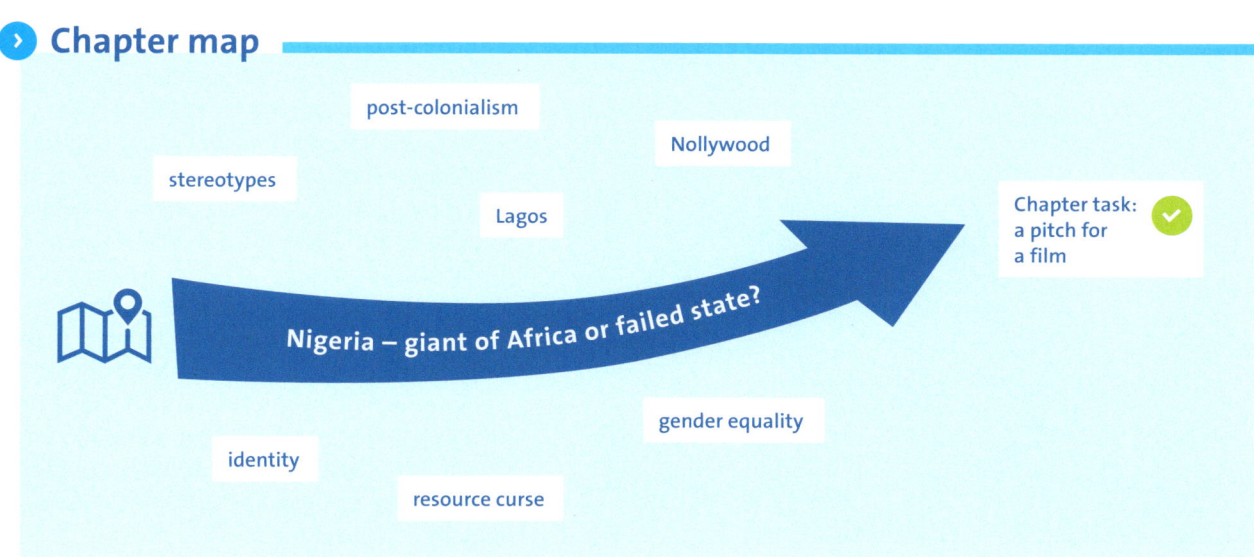

I've always been an optimistic person. And it's easy to find cause for optimism on the streets of Nigeria. In the vibrant artistic culture that continues to propel rising stars of every art form – music, film, fashion, literature, theatre – into the
15 international limelight. In innovators and entrepreneurs finding solutions for everyday problems in tech and finance. In every micro business that is lubricated by sweat and laughter and sustained by muscle and mettle. In the regular Nigerian who is forced to play the role of their own government, day after day, until their cash runs out or until reality catches up. [...]

*Umar Turaki, Nigerian film-maker and author*

▶ More info

*Texts from: 'My Nigeria: five writers and artists reflect on the place they call home',* www.theguardian.com, *29 October 2021*

## ❯ Chapter map

post-colonialism

stereotypes

Nollywood

Lagos

**Nigeria – giant of Africa or failed state?**

Chapter task:
a pitch for
a film ✓

gender equality

identity

resource curse

▶ More language

▶ More info

## 🔊 Nigeria – a sleeping giant?

### Nigerian identities: embracing diversity

Home to over 220 million people, Nigeria is the most populous country in Africa and is estimated to become the third largest country in the world by 2100. Often referred to as the 'giant of Africa', the country boasts a rich tapestry of over 250 ethnic groups,
5 each with their own unique traditions, languages and cultural heritage. With over 500 different languages spoken, Nigeria is one of the most linguistically diverse countries in the world. While English is the official language, Hausa, Yoruba, Igbo and Nigerian Pidgin are also widely spoken. Lagos, the vibrant cultural capital, is renowned for its arts and entertainment scene, producing accomplished musicians, acclaimed
10 writers and the thriving film industry known as Nollywood, which is increasingly gaining recognition beyond Africa.

### Aftermath of colonialism: fight for democracy

Like many African countries, Nigeria has grappled with the lingering effects of colonization.
15 Many of Nigeria's current problems and developments have to be seen against the backdrop of British rule, which lasted from the late 19th century until Nigeria's independence in 1960. The country's journey towards democracy has
20 been marked by periods of military rule and political instability. Although democratic elections have been held in recent years, establishing democracy remains an ongoing process as Nigeria seeks to forge a cohesive national iden-
25 tity that celebrates its rich diversity.

### Big challenges ahead for the sleeping giant

As Africa's largest economy, Nigeria owes much of its success to the oil and gas industry. Despite being the world's sixth largest oil producer, Nigeria has struggled to tackle poverty, with four in ten Nigerians living below the national poverty line,
30 prompting many Nigerians to leave the country in search of a better life. To ensure sustainable growth, Nigeria is actively trying to diversify its economy by investing in sectors such as agriculture, manufacturing and technology. Despite its economic potential, Nigeria faces significant socio-political
35 challenges such as corruption, a surge in kidnappings and violent conflicts between some of its ethnic groups and socio-economic disparities. These pose a risk to the country's stability and democracy. Gender equality re-
40 mains an ongoing struggle as women seek empowerment and equality. Nevertheless, while some remain sceptical, others are optimistic that the giant of Africa will wake up, overcome its obstacles, unlock its vast poten-
45 tial and pave the way for sustainable development and prosperity.

## 1 Main ideas

a From the text, collect information on both Nigeria's potentials and its challenges. Organize the information by creating two lists with the following headings: 'giant of Africa' and 'failed state'.

b Add other words to the lists while you are working on the chapter.

## 2 Reflect

Which characteristics of Nigeria were you already familiar with and which ones were new to you? Choose an example of each and describe them briefly using your own words.

## 3 Topic webs

a Create a topic web about Nigeria's economy using the information in the text.

b Add words and phrases from the exercises on this page.

## 4 Chunk it!

a In the table below, match the verbs on the left with the nouns on the right to form common *collocations. Some verbs can be matched with more than one noun.

► Getting started

► Check

| | |
|---|---|
| tackle | identities |
| seek | poverty |
| unlock | challenges |
| pose | risks |
| face | potential |
| overcome | obstacles |
| forge | empowerment |

b Find the collocations in the text and add the adjectives that are used with the collocations.

► Check

c Choose any three collocations and write three sentences with them, comparing the situation in Nigeria with the situation in Germany.

► Check

## 5 Text production

**Writing** Write a formal blog entry in which you explain what you – as a student in Germany – can learn from exploring Nigeria in your English class. Use as many words and phrases from your topic web and collocations from **4** as possible.

► SF 29: Writing a blog post, p. 384

► Check

**Language help**

gain insights into ... • help foster/enhance sth. ... • cultural understanding/sensitivity/appreciation ... • There is no doubt that / no denying the fact that ...

# Nigeria – a brief overview

**1**   Work in groups of four. Your expert group will be assigned one of the topics. Research your topic.

A: Milestones in Nigerian history
- Draw a timeline of dates and events that make up Nigeria's history, with information on colonization, independence and recent events.
- Include details on the Biafran War.    `Advanced`

B: Nigeria's population and society
- Find out about the people of Nigeria and create a map of Nigeria with information about the main ethnic groups, languages and religions.
- Include information about women in Nigeria.    `Advanced`

C: Nigeria's economy
- Collect information on the different sectors of the Nigerian economy in an infographic.
- Include information on the development of the oil industry after the coronavirus pandemic.    `Advanced`

D: Nigeria's geography
- Research the geography of Nigeria and prepare a short presentation with pictures of Nigeria's diverse geographical features.
- Include information about Lagos.    `Advanced`

▶ More language 🔖

**2**   Exchange results in your expert group.

**3**   Get together in new groups with an expert on each topic. Present your information to each other.

---

## Text 2

`Advanced`

▶ More info 🔖

▶ Getting started 🔖

▶ More language 🔖

# African identities    Dipo Faloyin

- Drawing from your own experience, name the key aspects that shape an individual's identity.

*Faloyin's book* Africa Is Not a Country *challenges the ways in which Africa is often perceived. In the following extract, the Nigerian author talks about his own identity.*

**Annotations**
5   **mourn sth.** (here) regret not having said sth.
7   **sublime** *(adj)* be of outstanding quality
7   **matrix** (here) highly complex system

Identities form specifically. [...] I am half Yoruba and half Igbo. They say Yorubas just want to have a good time and Igbos just want to have a good life, which means I am programmed, anytime anywhere, to never automatically turn down an invite without, at the very least, asking some follow-up questions. I have three older sisters, which means 23 per cent of my life has been spent mourning the points I wish I had brought up in a long-finished argument.

I come from a confusingly sublime matrix of who is actually a blood relative, and a deep appreciation of heat, both in taste and touch, and the healing powers of pepper soup. I was raised with a strong belief that it is an aunty's duty to mind your

10 business and that it is impossible to have too many cousins – two concepts I'm triggered to defend. I am from a home with an open-door policy. I am from a belief that to visit our home is to eat at our home, because food is the ultimate love language; food forgives sins and dispenses grace.

I was raised to get up early for church and stay up late for election nights. I am
15 from a family that has never willingly gone on a beach holiday, and values intuition over organisation; a home where decisions are based on emotion rather than practicality. A strict childhood diet of arriving at events and airports too early has made me allergic to arriving at events and airports too early. Bedtimes were set, as was the understanding that children should be heard.

20 I am descended from a long line of bad poker faces, a clan genetically unable to hide the frustrations or joys etched in our hearts, however temporary. I am from silence being the ultimate punishment, and appreciating the eternal value of a dance floor bursting with people you love as the greatest man-made invention. I am from a philosophy that questions why you would ever order something new
25 off a menu when you know exactly what you want; why order something new when you understand precisely who you are?

*From:* Africa Is Not a Country: Notes on a Bright Continent, *2023*

**Annotations**

11 **trigger sb. to do sth.** make sb. do sth. automatically, without thinking
13 **dispense grace** *(fml)* fill people with a deep and spiritual love
15 **willingly** happily, with pleasure
19 **children should be heard** reference to the common phrase 'children should be seen and not heard'
20 **be descended from** be related to sb. from the past
21 **be etched in sth.** be permanently fixed and clearly visible in sth.

## Comprehension

1 Point out what we learn about the author's family, their values and rituals.

## Analysis

2 Analyse how Faloyin presents his own identity. Focus on tone and choice of words.

## Language awareness

3 a Throughout the text, the author makes frequent use of *anaphora. Point to examples and analyse their effect.
  b Intercultural competence Using anaphora, write a similar paragraph about yourself.

► Getting started

## Beyond the text

4 You choose Writing Work on either **a** or **b**.

  a Dipo Faloyin's book is called *Africa is Not a Country*. Comment on this title keeping in mind what you have learned from the extract from the book.

  b In his book, Faloyin states that '[b]eing able to define yourself openly and fully is a privilege [...]. To strip an individual of that privilege is destructive enough. But when you apply this reductive treatment to an entire community, country or race, you create a poisonously false narrative that permeates for generations [...].' Comment on this statement keeping in mind how Africa is often portrayed in the media.

► Support, p. 320
► SF 28: Argumentative writing: discussion and comment, p. 382

► Check

## Nigeria – on the brink of failure?   Fola Aina, Nic Cheeseman

- Imagine a scenario in which a state is consistently linked with failure. What consequences might arise from this? Reflect on areas such as self-perception, diplomatic interactions, and actions taken. You could start by considering the impact of being labelled a failure on an individual.

▶ More info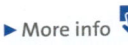
▶ More language

*The article examines the ongoing debate about whether Nigeria is a failed state.*

[...] Nigeria has experienced a worrying spate of kidnappings and violent attacks. Boko Haram insurgents have long terrorized the north of the country and are responsible for some of the violence, but so are organized crime syndicates, which have come to adopt kidnap-and-ransom as a business model. [...] Armed marauders
5 have killed scores of civilians and security forces in recent months and kidnapped hundreds of Nigerians from villages, schools, and motorways across the country.

Nigeria's swerve toward insecurity has prompted even sober and well-respected analysts to press the panic button. 'The definition of a failed state is one where the government is no longer in control. By this yardstick, Africa's most populous coun-
10 try is teetering on the brink,' the Financial Times warned late last year. John Campbell, a senior fellow at the Council on Foreign Relations and former U.S. ambassador to Nigeria, raises similar concerns in his recent book, Nigeria and the Nation-State, in which he describes the country as 'not quite a nation' and 'not quite a state.' Not only is Nigeria failing to protect its citizens from rampant crime
15 and corruption, according to Campbell, but its people lack a shared sense of what it means to be 'Nigerian.' Future-oriented studies such as 'Failed State 2030,' a case study of Nigeria published by the Center for Strategy and Technology of Air University, go even further, imagining Nigeria as a state that only exists on paper, sustained by the recognition of the international community. [...]

20 Fortunately, it is far too early to declare that either the nation or the state of Nigeria has failed. [...] There is no doubt that the coronavirus pandemic has devastated Nigeria's economy and contributed to a breakdown of law and order, which in turn has fueled the rise in banditry. But in some ways, Nigeria is actually a stronger and more resilient state today than it was 20 years ago.

25 Nigeria is often said to have an 'identity problem.' Home to more than 250 ethnic groups and three distinct religious affiliations, it is one of the most diverse countries in the world. It faces an Islamic extremist insurgency in the north in the form of Boko Haram and is still haunted by the legacy of the Biafran war, which pitted the government against Igbo separatists between 1967 and 1970 and resulted in
30 more than a million deaths. Given these facts, it is easy to see why some analysts conclude that Nigerians lack a shared aspiration or even common understanding of what it means to be Nigerian.

By some measures, the country's national identity is indeed very weak, in line with Campbell's argument. Many Nigerians identify more closely with their ethnic and
35 religious group than with the nation as a whole, and according to surveys conducted by Afrobarometer, Nigerians are among the least nationalist people in Africa. Nigerians from ethnic groups, such as the Igbo, that have taken part in past or present separatist movements are particularly unlikely to embrace a broad Nigerian identity.

### Annotations

1  **spate of sth.** large number of sth. unpleasant
2  **Boko Haram** Islamic militant organization
2  **insurgent** *(n)* person who fights against the government of their country
4  **marauder** [məˈrɔːdə] person who roams from place to place searching for people to attack
5  **scores of sth.** huge number of sth.
7  **swerve** *(n)* sudden turn of direction
9  **yardstick** standard used to measure sth.
10 **teeter on the brink of sth.** be close to a dangerous situation
14 **rampant** spreading uncontrollably
26 **affiliation** sb.'s connection to a party or a religion
27 **insurgency** revolt against a country
28 **pit sb. against sb.** test sb. in a struggle against sb. else
29 **Igbo** ethnic group living predominantly in the south-east of Nigeria

40 But while strong communal identities have often been associated with episodes of political violence, especially around elections, they have not caused relations between groups to deteriorate as a whole, as many analysts feared might happen after Nigeria transitioned to democracy in 1999. Rather, Nigerians from different ethnic groups have grown gradually more tolerant of one another, suggesting that the
45 prospects for the evolution of a unifying national identity are getting better, not worse. For the last three decades, the World Values Survey has been asking a nationally representative sample of Nigerians whether they would object to having a neighbor of a 'different race or ethnicity.' When the WVS first asked this question in 1990, 32 percent of Nigerians said that they would object – a worryingly high
50 figure. By 2020, however, the proportion of Nigerians who objected to a neighbor from a different group had fallen by half to just 16 percent. [...]

Since the country's return to multiparty politics in 1999, Nigeria has also practiced a form of temporal power sharing that has helped to prevent a return to civil conflict. Through an informal but widely accepted system known as 'zoning,' control
55 of the presidency alternates between the north and the south of the country every eight years, and northern presidents select southern vice presidents and vice versa. While this system does not ensure adequate representation for the country's 36 states and numerous ethnicities (and can cause controversies if a leader dies in office), it does mean that no one region – and no one religion – can hold power
60 indefinitely.

This system for temporal power sharing helps to explain why the proportion of Nigerians who feel that their ethnic group is discriminated against has fallen markedly in recent years. In 2005, for example, 37 percent of Nigerians said that their ethnic group was 'often' or 'always' treated unfairly by the government, ac-
65 cording to Afrobarometer. By 2018, the proportion had declined to just 21 percent – with 48 percent saying that their ethnic group is 'never' treated unfairly.

Greater political inclusion and falling perceptions of discrimination have allowed for a stronger national spirit to emerge, one that can be observed in the fervent popular support for the national football team and the shared pride that Nigerians
70 of all religions and ethnicities take in the international success of many Nigerian artists and musicians. [...]

Like claims that Nigeria is not a true nation, however, claims that its state has completely failed go too far. Whereas nearby countries such as Liberia and Sierra Leone have suffered repeated and prolonged civil wars, Nigeria has successfully avoided a return to
75 widespread violence, despite a recent increase in agitation from Biafran separatists. [...]

Warnings of impending state or nation failure don't just create the false impression of a country in which nothing at all works. They can be used to justify the imposition of external solutions – for example, foreign state-building efforts that emphasize militarized solutions at the expense of socioeconomic and environ-
80 mental ones. A more nuanced look at what the Nigerian state and political elite have actually achieved over the last 30 years suggests a need for something else: continued progress toward political inclusion, including by strengthening the federal system, focusing on homegrown strategies that resonate with political elites, and developing regional solutions to regional problems. [..]

*From: 'Don't call Nigeria a failed state', www.foreignaffairs.com, 5 May 2021*

**Annotations**
45 **prospects** *(pl)* chances of success
47 **sample** *(n)* Stichprobe
68 **fervent** passionate
74 **prolonged** lasting a long time
75 **agitation** attempts at influencing opinion so as to bring about political change
76 **impending** likely to happen soon
78 **imposition of sth.** establishment of sth. by authority
79 **at the expense of sth.** zu Ungunsten von etwas
83 **resonate with sb./ sth.** to be similar to what sb./sth. believes

**Info**

The **Nigerian Civil War**, also called the Biafran War, took place from 1967 to 1970 in Biafra, a region in the southeast of Nigeria, after the Igbo majority declared independence from Nigeria. The war led to fighting and famine in the area, killing at least one million people. The war must be seen in the context of British colonial rule in Nigeria, in which the various regions were brought together without considering the ethnic and cultural differences of the people living there.
▶ Info box, p. 230

Advanced

## Comprehension

**1**   **a**   Outline what you learn in the text about ...
- the definition of a failed state
- Boko Haram
- zoning
- Nigerian identity
- the Biafran War.

## Analysis

**2**   Analyse the authors' view of the current state of Nigeria. Focus on the line of argument.

## Language awareness

▶ SF 29: Writing a blog post, p. 384

**3**   **a**   In their text, the authors use several *stylistic devices to support their position. Find examples of these and analyse their effect on the reader.
     **b**   Pick out some key details from the text and rephrase them as an informal blog post on the current situation in Nigeria.

▶ Getting started
▶ SF 28: Argumentative writing: discussion and comment, p. 382
▶ SF 47: Having a debate, p. 412
▶ Check

## Beyond the text

**4**   🗺   You choose   Work on task **a** or **b**.

     **a**   Writing   Think back to the guiding question of this chapter: Nigeria – giant of Africa or failed state? Write a comment explaining your position on the question, drawing on the text and other work done in class.

     **b**   Speaking   Think back to the guiding question of this chapter: Nigeria – giant of Africa or failed state? With your teacher's help, form groups of four, assign roles (giant of Africa vs. failed state), and hold a debate.

**5**   Get together in five groups and assign one ethnic group from the map to each group. Research it and create a fact file about it.

Map depicting some of the ethnic and linguistic groups in Nigeria, including Yoruba, Igbo and Hausa-Fulani. The location of the former secessionist state of Biafra (1967–1970) has been marked in the south.

# The colonial looting of art   Annalena Baerbock

- Before reading a speech about Germany's colonial legacy, read the info box and do the tasks.

**European colonial expansion**

In the second half of the 19th century, Germany followed in the footsteps of other European powers in establishing colonies. The British Empire, with Nigeria as one of its major colonies, emerged as a dominant colonial power during this period. Many European countries, including the German Empire, sought to acquire
5  colonial territories to create new markets for their products, to gain access to valuable raw materials and to carry out what they saw as a 'civilizing mission' among peoples they considered backward. The Berlin or West Africa Conference of 1884–1885 was pivotal in establishing the rules of European colonization in Africa. At this conference, the European powers negotiated their respective claims
10  to African territories, resulting in the German Empire acquiring several territories in West Africa (today's Togo and parts of Ghana and Cameroon), East Africa (today's Tanzania) and southern Africa (today's Namibia). In 1897, British colonial troops launched a punitive expedition against the Benin Kingdom (located in what is now Nigeria), resulting in the capture of the capital, Benin City. As a result,
15  thousands of bronze, ivory and wooden artefacts were looted from the royal palace and dispersed around the world. Some were taken to the German Empire.

**1**   With a partner, outline what you have learned from this info box.
**2**   Add other points that you already knew about colonialism to your notes.

A plaque from the Benin collection depicting the façade of the royal palace

▶ More info
▶ More language

*Twenty-two looted bronze sculptures were returned to Nigeria in 2022 by the German government in an attempt to address its colonial past. Annalena Baerbock, Germany's foreign minister, made a speech to mark the occasion.*

„Die Kunst lebt in der Geschichte und die Geschichte lebt in der Kunst."

So hat es die nigerianische Autorin Chimamanda Ngozi Adichie formuliert. Sie beschreibt, wie Artefakte wie jene, die wir heute hier sehen, nicht bloße Objekte sind. Sie erzählen Geschichten. Und wir sehen das genauso.

▶ More info
▶ More language

5  Kunst sagt etwas darüber aus, wer wir sind. Kunst prägt unsere Wahrnehmung von uns selbst und unsere Wahrnehmung von der Welt. Über die Kunst sehen wir unsere Vergangenheit und erfahren etwas über den Weg, den wir als Menschen – aber auch als eine Nation, als ein Volk – zurückgelegt haben.

Daher geben wir Ihnen, dem nigerianischen Volk, heute nicht bloße Objekte zu-
10  rück. Von Ihnen haben wir gelernt: Was wir zurückgeben, ist ein Teil Ihrer Geschichte, ein Teil dessen, wer Sie sind.

Ich glaube, als Deutsche und Europäer sollten wir einen Moment innehalten und darüber nachdenken, was das eigentlich bedeutet. Was es bedeutet, einen wesentlichen Teil seiner Geschichte nicht bei sich zu haben, weil er einem weggenom-
15  men wurde. Was würde es für uns bedeuten, wenn wir auf unser kulturelles Erbe verzichten müssten? Nicht die Gutenberg-Bibel in Mainz bestaunen könnten?

Nicht Luthers Schriften bewundern? Oder nicht vor einer Skulptur von Käthe Koll-
witz in Berlin oder vor Goethes Schreibtisch in Weimar stehen könnten? Das löst
ein Gefühl des Verlusts aus, das ich mir schwer vorstellen kann. Für Sie hier in
20 Nigeria war dieser Verlust aber Ihre Realität.

Heute sind wir hier, um die Benin-Bronzen denen zurückzugeben, denen sie gehören, dem nigerianischen Volk. Wir sind hier, um ein Unrecht wiedergutzuma-
chen. Amtsträger aus meinem Land kauften einst die Bronzen, obwohl sie wuss-
ten, dass sie geraubt und gestohlen worden waren. Danach haben wir Nigerias
25 Bitte um Rückgabe sehr lange Zeit ignoriert. Es war falsch, sie mitzunehmen.
Aber es war auch falsch, sie zu behalten.

Dies ist eine Geschichte des europäischen Kolonialismus. Es ist eine Geschichte,
in der unser Land eine dunkle Rolle gespielt und in verschiedenen Teilen Afrikas
enormes Leid verursacht hat. Die Rückgabe der Bronzen heute ist ein entschei-
30 dender Schritt in Richtung dahin, wie wir mit diesem Kapitel umgehen sollten:
offen, aufrichtig, mit der Bereitschaft, die eigenen Handlungen kritisch zu bewer-
ten. Und entscheidend dabei ist, dass wir aufmerksam den Anliegen derjenigen
zuhören, die die Opfer kolonialer Grausamkeiten waren. Diese Bereitschaft mitei-
nander zu sprechen und zuzuhören war es, die die heutigen Rückgaben möglich
35 gemacht hat. [...] Darauf wollen wir aufbauen – auch, indem wir Sie darin unterstützen, den Bronzen den öffentlichen Rahmen zu geben, den Sie für angemessen
halten.

Wenn die Kunst in der Geschichte lebt und die Geschichte in der Kunst – wie es
Chimamanda Adichie sagt –, dann, so glaube ich, ist es wichtig, dass Frauen, Män-
40 ner und insbesondere Kinder in die Lage versetzt werden, Kunst wirklich zu erleben, damit sie ihre und unsere gemeinsame Geschichte verstehen können.

In Deutschland können wir noch besser darin werden, Kunst inklusiver zu machen, damit wir sie alle genießen können – unabhängig davon, wer wir sind, wo
wir leben oder wieviel Geld wir haben. Kunst sollte allen in unseren Gesellschaften
45 zugänglich sein. [...]

Das wissenschaftliche Projekt „Digital Benin" ist ein fantastisches und universel-
les Instrument zu diesem Zweck. Es ist eine digitale Plattform, die eine Vielzahl an
Informationen über mehr als 5.000 Artefakte, ihren Verbleib und ihre Geschichte
enthält. Ich lade Sie alle ein, diese Schatzkammer zu erforschen.

50 Es gibt ein Artefakt auf der Website, das ich besonders faszinierend finde. Es handelt sich um ein sehr kleines Objekt: einen Schlüssel, den wir heute mitgebracht
haben. Es ist ein einzigartiges Stück, wunderschön mit Leoparden und menschli-
chen Gesichtern verziert. Sein Schöpfer muss ein großer Künstler gewesen sein.

Wir sind nicht ganz sicher, wofür der Schlüssel verwendet wurde. Vielleicht, um
55 einen Schrein, eine Palasttüre oder auch eine Schatztruhe zu öffnen. Aber wir
wissen, dass er, nachdem er aus Benin geraubt worden war, ins Vereinigte Königreich gebracht wurde. Dort wurde er verkauft und wanderte dann über Irland und
Frankreich nach Köln.

Heute ist der Schlüssel zurück. Er ist wieder da, wo er hingehört.

60  Es bewegt mich zu sehen, mit welcher Liebe Sie diesen Schlüssel und die anderen Bronzen heute hier in Abuja aufgenommen haben.

Dieser Schlüssel ist ein Symbol. Er kann uns helfen, ein neues Kapitel in der Freundschaft zwischen unseren beiden Völkern aufzuschließen.

Dafür sind wir heute hier – um die Tür in die Zukunft unserer Freundschaft weit
65  zu öffnen. [...]                                                            *(708 words)*

*From:* www.auswaertiges-amt.de, *2022*

**1**  `Mediating`  `Intercultural competence`  You are an exchange student at a university in Lagos and you are working on a project about Nigeria's colonial history. In order to include an international voice, you are asked to provide a German perspective on the issue. Write an article for the university website summarizing Germany's handling of the Benin bronzes and the role art can play for a country and for intercultural understanding as described in the text.

▶ Getting started
▶ SF 49: Mediating from German into English, p. 416
▶ SF 32: Writing an (online) article, p. 388

## Text 5

### Art in Context: Tutu   Ben Enwonwu

▶ More info
▶ More language

*The 1973 painting below by Igbo artist Ben Enwonwu shows a Yoruba princess called Tutu. After being lost for over 40 years, the original painting was discovered in a London flat in 2017 and sold at auction for $1.6 million, sparking widespread interest in the art world.*

#### Comprehension

**1**  Describe the painting.

#### Analysis

**2**  In Nigeria, the painting is considered a symbol of the nation coming together. Point out why it may have acquired this status, considering the political situation at the time it was painted (▶ Info box p. 233) and the ethnic backgrounds of the painter and model.

▶ Getting started
▶ SF 23: Analysing visuals, p. 374

#### Beyond the text

**3**  `You choose`  `Speaking`  Work on either **a** or **b**.
   **a**  Research other works by Ben Enwonwu and their relevance to the history of Nigeria. Present one of the works in class.
   **b**  Research another work of art that serves as a national symbol for the country it is from. Present it in class.

▶ Getting started
▶ SF 43: Giving a presentation, p. 405

# Lagos – the Nigerian megacity

Eloghosa Osunde, Phillip Adams (Presenter)

► More info

► More language

- **\*Quick write:** Imagine yourself in the picture on the bottom of this page. Make it speak: Describe the sights, sounds, smells and events around you in a short written text.

*In this interview, Eloghosa Osunde talks about her novel* Vagabonds! *and the most populous city of Nigeria, Lagos.*

### Comprehension

► SF 40: Listening/Viewing for gist and detail, p. 399

► Check

**1** **a** **Listening** Listen to the interview, then answer the questions below. You need not write complete sentences.

1. What the theme of Osunde's novel is
2. How she perceives Lagos (three aspects)
3. What general aspects of Lagos are mentioned (three aspects)
4. Why she moved to Abuja
5. How she personally benefits from living in Lagos
6. What the underlying message of her novel is
7. What the general downside to working in Lagos is
8. What her personal downside to working in Lagos is

**b** **Listening** Choose the most suitable ending to the sentence.
Osunde's general attitude towards Lagos is …

1. melancholic.
2. enthusiastic.
3. patriotic.
4. nuanced.
5. frustrated.

### Beyond the text

**2** **You choose** **Writing** Work on task **a** or **b**.

► SF 29: Writing a blog post, p. 384

**a** Find out more about Lagos and write a short encyclopeadia entry about Nigeria's megacity.

**b** Write a short blog entry for a travel blog for international readers to promote a trip to Lagos.

Busy street in Lagos

# Nigerian oil – a blessing or a curse?  Kenneth Mohammed

- **Think** Nigeria is the world's sixth largest oil producer. Makes notes on why this is a blessing.
- **Pair** Exchange your ideas with a partner. Speculate on why an abundance of natural resources can be a blessing and/or a curse for a country.
- **Share** Present your ideas in class. Write down new ideas you encounter.

*In his analysis, Kenneth Mohammed explores whether Nigeria's abundant oil resources are a blessing or a curse for the country.*

In Nigeria, oil has been more of a curse than a blessing. Weak institutions of state and poor governance in managing the vast revenues have led the country to fail to realise its full potential in a textbook example of what academics know as the 'resource curse'.

5 First coined by Prof Richard Auty in 1994, the term refers to the inability of nations to use their windfall wealth to improve their population's lot and bolster their economies. The rich natural resources bring corruption and poverty to a nation, rather than positive economic development and, counterintuitively, these countries end up with lower growth and development than those without natural resources.

10 The subject of extensive research, the resource curse, or 'paradox of plenty', points to an inverse relationship where wealth brings a detrimental impact. Nigeria – the largest oil producer in Africa, the sixth-largest global exporter, holds the tenth-largest proven oil reserve in the world – is arguably such a 'cursed' nation. [...]

Resource wealth can have a devastating impact. Oil-exporting nations such as 15 Nigeria, Venezuela, Angola and DRC have seen livelihoods and economies devastated, but there have been many countries throughout history, such as Norway, Canada and Botswana, who have bucked the curse through strong state management and institutions that can stand against corruption.

This is crucial, because the key thing the resource curse is indicative of is corrup- 20 tion: a global phenomenon that is the single greatest obstacle to economic and social development, significantly so in less-developed countries. Worldwide, an estimated $2tn is siphoned away annually by corruption. [...]

Corruption erodes the integrity of people and institutions. A synthesis of social, political and economic forces, it disempowers sovereign states, undermines dem- 25 ocratic institutions and contributes to instability fuelled by the distrust and resentment of citizens. It attacks democracy by distorting electoral processes, perverting the rule of law and building new bureaucratic hurdles whose only reason for existing is to solicit bribes. Numerous reasons are behind corruption – self-inter- 30 est, fear, greed and desire for power – but its consequences are always the same, enduring and deleterious. [...]

Studies have shown that following an oil boom, an imbalance results as the non- 35 oil sectors are left underdeveloped. As demand rises for capital and labour, the

Annotations
1 **curse** *(n)* sth. that causes misfortune
1 **blessing** sth. that causes sth. good
2 **revenue** money a country receives from taxes
6 **windfall wealth** unexpected wealth
6 **bolster sth.** make sth. stronger
11 **detrimental** harmful
17 **buck sth.** *(infml)* oppose sth. bad
19 **be indicative of sth.** (here) be a sign of sth.
22 **siphon sth.** ['saɪfn] *(infml)* (here) illegally remove money
24 **undermine sth.** make sth. weaker
26 **distort sth.** (here) change sth. so that it no longer functions
28 **solicit sth.** *(fml)* get sth. from sb.
28 **bribe** *(n)* money offered to sb. to make them do sth.
32 **deleterious** [ˌdelə'tɪəriəs] dangerous, destructive

Annotations
38 **enfeebled** made weak
39 **astute** clever,
    competent

booming oil sector draws away those same factors from essential but less-lucrative sectors, such as agriculture, leaving them enfeebled. [...]

40 With astute management and determination other countries have beaten the resource curse and steered their economies to success. So far, Nigeria has failed in much of its population's eyes. Whether it is fated to become a failed state, only time will tell.

*From: 'A wealth of sorrow: why Nigeria's abundant oil reserves are really a curse',* www.theguardian.com, *9 November 2021*

## Comprehension

▶ Check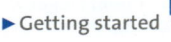

**1** Match each part of the text in the box on the left with the most suitable heading in the box on the right. There are two more headings than you need.

| | | | | |
|---|---|---|---|---|
| **1** | ll. 1–4 | **A** | Positive and negative examples |
| **2** | ll. 5–13 | **B** | Rising poverty |
| **3** | ll. 14–18 | **C** | Defining a resource curse |
| **4** | ll. 19–32 | **D** | Ecological downsides |
| **5** | ll. 33–38 | **E** | The effects of an oil-boom on other sectors |
| | | **F** | The resource curse in Nigeria |
| | | **G** | Corruption and its consequences |

## Analysis

**2** Analyse how Mohammed conveys his view of Nigerian oil. Focus on his line of argument and choice of words.

## Language awareness

▶ Getting started

**3 a** Mohammed uses many formal words such as 'revenue' (l. 2) and 'enduring' (l. 32). Find at least five sentences including formal words in the text and say what effect they have on the reader.

   **b** Rephrase the sentences with informal vocabulary and compare the effect they have.

## Beyond the text

▶ Support, p. 320

▶ Getting started

▶ SF 43: Giving a
   presentaton, p. 405

**4** Speaking   Research Nigerian fossil fuels and take notes on oil and gas respectively, their relevance today and their potential impact on Nigeria's ecology. Present your findings in class.

**5** Think back to the guiding question of the chapter and reconsider your opinion. Keep in mind everything you have learned so far.

# Language revisited

## 1 Emphatic structures

In English, there are many ways to convey emphasis. Match the sentences below with the different forms of emphasis in the box on the right.

1  If you get the chance while you are in Nigeria, do try Yoruba cuisine.
2  It is my mother's jollof rice that I miss the most.
3  Rarely have I sampled such a wide variety of dishes as I have in Nigeria.
4  Did you make this stew yourself?

▶ More language 🔧
▶ Check 🔧

A  Emphatic pronouns
B  Cleft sentences
C  Auxiliary *do*
D  Subject-auxiliary inversion

# Language awareness

## 2 Subject-auxiliary inversion: form and function

*When we place a negative adverbial structure in front position for emphasis, it must be followed by subject-auxiliary inversion, where the auxiliary verb and subject of the main clause swap places. If there is no auxiliary verb, a form of* do *must be inserted.*

▶ More language 🔧
▶ Check 🔧

a  In the text below about the Nigerian national anthem, there are some mistakes in subject-auxiliary inversion. Find and correct them.
*National anthems often play an important role in shaping a country's identity. Not only they represent the nation on special occasions, but they also instil a sense of belonging among the people. Nigeria's national anthem has a long history that dates back to the country's colonial past. During British rule, was the British anthem played. Not until Nigeria gained independence in 1960, a genuine Nigerian anthem was adopted, titled 'Nigeria, we hail thee'. But soon faced this anthem criticism. Not only was it written by a Briton, but it also emphasized Nigeria's diversity rather than its unity. Only in 1977 the Nigerian government launched an open competition to choose a more suitable anthem. After merging the lyrics of five different composers, the final version was named 'Arise, O compatriots', with music composed by the Nigerian Police Band. The new anthem highlighted Nigeria's unity and was officially adopted in 1978.*

b  Rephrase the sentences below, putting the negative adverbials in front position and making all the necessary adjustments.
1  I had never experienced such intense heat as when I left Lagos airport.
2  I realized how different Nigerian Pidgin was only when I failed to understand the lady at the ticket counter.
3  People rarely come to Lagos for tourism.

**Info**

**Negative adverbial structures** include
- restrictive adverbs like *rarely, scarcely,* and *seldom*
- negative words like *never* and *nowhere*
- structures with *only* and *not until*
- and fixed expressions like *under no circumstances, at no time* and *on no account.*

# Practice

## 3 Never in my life would I have thought that Nigeria ...

Writing  Write a short text reflecting on what you were most surprised to learn from the chapter on Nigeria. Include some negative adverbials and adverbs from the info box. Decide whether you want to use them in front position or in their normal position, depending on whether you want to emphasize the sentence.

▶ WOB: pp. 94–95, p. 120

# No future for the young?    Emmanuel Akinwotu

▶ More language

• With your partner, name trends you know that have inspired people to travel, study or work abroad, or even live in a different country.

> **Language help**
>
> go viral • spark a desire to ... • inspire/encourage viewers/listeners to ... • provide a platform for sth. • attractive destinations

*In recent years, more young Nigerians have felt the need to leave the country in search of a better life.*

## Comprehension

▶ SF 40: Listening/Viewing for gist and detail, p. 399

**1**   **Listening**   Listen to the news report about young people in Nigeria, then answer the questions below. You need not write complete sentences.

1. What the word *japa* means
2. In what way the word *japa* is ambiguous
3. In which three contexts the subject of *japa*-ing is mentioned
4. Which three problems in Nigeria make people leave the country
5. How Chioma Agwuegbo explains the situation
6. What is the main source of information for people who want to *japa*
7. What Funke Ogunkoya-Futi is concerned about

## Beyond the text

▶ Getting started (task b)

▶ Support, p. 321

▶ SF 37: Writing a letter to the editor, p. 394

▶ Check (task b)

**2**   Work on task **a** or **b**.

**a** Do some research into the factors that influence young people to stay in Nigeria. Make a list.

**b** **Challenge** **Writing** Do some research into the factors that influence young people to stay in Nigeria. Use your search results to write a *letter to the editor in which you express your reaction to the podcast.

## Egúngún   Olive Nwosu

Work with a partner and exchange ideas on the following questions:

- How do you define 'home'? Is it where you are currently living, where you were born, your family's origins or something entirely different?
- What sounds, smells, sights and feelings do you connect with this concept of home?

*In the 2021 short film* Egúngún, *writer and director Olive Nwosu follows Salewa on her return to Lagos.*

▶ More info
Annotations
**Egúngún** Yoruba masquerade, usually to show respect for ancestors

### Comprehension

**1** | Viewing | Copy the table below, then watch the film and collect information on the characters in the table below.

▶ SF 40: Listening/Viewing for gist and detail, p. 399

| Salewa | Salewa's dead mother | Ebun | Ladi |
|---|---|---|---|
| … | … | … | … |

### Analysis

**2 a** | Viewing | Explain how Salewa feels in the following situations:
- in the car
- at the funeral
- at the market
- in Ebun's house
- under the tree with Ebun
- on the motorcycle when leaving
- at her mother's grave.

**b** | Viewing | How does the film convey these feelings? List the techniques that are used to communicate them to the viewers.

▶ SF 41: Analysing films, series and videos, p. 401

**3** Explain the title of the film.

**4** | Viewing | Choose a scene that you find particularly interesting with regard to the cinematic devices used. Examine the cinematic devices and the effect they have. Present your results to class.

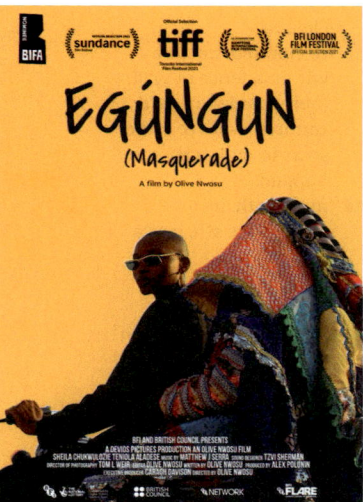

▶ Support, p. 321
▶ Getting started

### Beyond the text

**5** | You choose | Work on either task **a** or **b**.

**a** | Speaking | What aspects of Nigerian reality were shown in the film that were new to you? Do some research on how representative they are and give a short presentation.

**b** | Writing | After Salewa has left, Ebun returns to her house and reflects on the surprise reunion with Salewa. Write a creative text with her interior monologue.

▶ Getting started (task a)
▶ SF 43: Giving a presentaton, p. 405
▶ SF 38: Creative writing, p. 395

▶ 'Aunty Ifeoma', p. 337

▶ More info

▶ More language

**Annotations**

5  **salon** hairdresser's

7  **ancestral worship** the
   honoring of people
   from your family who
   lived a long time ago as
   divine beings

9  **Ala** Earth Mother
   Goddess of the Igbo, an
   ethnic group living in
   the south-east of
   Nigeria

10 **compound** an area
   within a fence or wall;
   (here) garden or yard

12 **connive** work together
   so as to make sth. bad
   happen

16 **mould sth. into sth.
   else** shape sth. into a
   certain form

17 **limbs** *(pl)* arms and
   legs

17 **hover** stay in the air in
   one place

18 **suitor** man who is
   interested in marrying
   a particular woman

18 **o** *(Nigerian Pidgin)*
   exclamatory word
   used mostly in short
   answers

34 **lizard** *Echse*

35 **Akuko abughi nri**
   *(Igbo)* News/books
   won't fill your stomach

## Being a woman in Nigeria   Aiwanose Odafen

- ▐ Intercultural competence ▌ Name some traditional gender roles in your culture.
  Do you think gender roles are changing or being challenged today? Give examples.

*Aiwanose Odafen delves into the societal pressures on Nigerian women.*

Mama never got tired of telling me the story. She'd been married for many years to Papa, and her position was safe: she'd had sons, three strong boys. But Mama had wanted a daughter; she'd prayed and begged for one. Someone to share her stories with, to pass on the recipes her mother and grandmother had given her, to teach all
5  that she knew about life, to take trips to the salon with and gossip about the things only girls cared about.

Mama always said I was punishment for her mixing ancestral worship with her Christian faith. She'd sought the counsel of native medicine men, worn amulets, and prayed to *Ala* and other deities to give her a daughter, even though she'd been
10 an active member of her church. Her father still had a shrine in his compound although he had sent all his children to the missionary school in their village. And so, in anger, the gods had connived and sent her a daughter identical to her in looks but nothing like what she wanted.

How else could she explain my disinterest in everything she loved – cooking,
15 cleaning, taking care of the home – and my determination to be anything but the person she'd endlessly tried to mould me into? Then I'd inherited Papa's height and long limbs, hovering inches over every other girl my age and many men, aka suitors. 'I can' introduce your daughter to my son o. She's too tall for him – in fact, she's probably taller than him. When they argue, she'll just give him a knock,' one
20 of Mama's friends had joked once. [...]

Mama was busy when I arrived, hard at work on a pot of *ogbono* soup. 'Uju, go and sit in the parlour, I'll come and join you. I'm almost done, or I would have asked you to help me,' she said to me when I walked into the kitchen that afternoon, her eyes set on the pot she was stirring. [...]

25 I looked away and tried to imagine Mama's reaction when I told her about Gozie. She had been waiting eagerly for me to bring someone home. I needed to marry early, she said. I lacked the traits and beauty to attract many suitors, thus, I had to make do with what I had before I was too old and educated to catch a decent man.

'Maybe I made a mistake by letting your father send you to the university. That's why
30 you like arguing like this; too much book is inside your head,' she'd lamented one day after interrupting a heated conversation between me and my brothers. 'Today, its politics; tomorrow it's football. Instead of you to come and join me in the kitchen, you're shouting up and down the house like a street boy. My grandmother used to say, 'Only a foolish rat dances with the lizard in the rain.' You're a woman! Your
35 brothers will have wives to cook for them. Akuko abughi nri. After all this book, better make sure you come home with a husband. You better not bring just a certificate home. Adaugo has that young man Uzondu; even Chinelo has somebody. '

Mama had been born in a time when education had been a luxury, if not a waste, for a girl child. But my grandmother had been a troublemaker; she'd insisted her
40 husband send all their daughters to the local primary school to learn to read and

write. Mama had spent the years afterwards learning to be a wife and then her father shipped her off to be married long before she'd turned eighteen. I had other ambitions, desires she didn't understand, to be something other than a wife.

45 I hoped telling Mama about Gozie would restore her faith that I would be married someday. I was tired of being introduced to friends' sons, cousins, uncles, friends, tired of Mama telling me every time the daughter of someone we knew got engaged or married and the *aso ebi* they all planned to wear, tired of congratulating others and watching as they responded with oily smiles of those who had achieved all you aimed to, saying, 'Don't worry. God will do your own.'

50 'Obianuju, how are you?' Mama asked, a grin on her face as she wiped her hands with a towel. 'Sorry I took so long; you know how much your father likes food. I had to make sure it's done before he gets back.' She relaxed into the sofa beside me, pulled a three-legged wooden stool from the corner and threw both feet on it. 'How's school?'

'School is fine, Mama.' [...]

55 I didn't hesitate. I told her about Gozie, 'a man I just started seeing,' I called him so she wouldn't raise her hopes too high. I'd barely finished speaking when Mama jumped to her feet and broke out in song and dance. The stool in front of her clattered to the floor.

I laughed, holding my stomach as I fell to my side on the sofa. [...]

60 Mama stopped dancing, as if something important had crossed her mind. 'Wait first. Uju, what part of Nigeria is he from? Is he a Lagos boy? Please tell me he isn't a Yoruba boy or one of those Northerners,' she pleaded.

'No, Mama he isn't. He's Igbo. His name is Chigozie,' I assured her. [...]

'Thank God!' Mama exclaimed. 'Hei! I can't wait to tell your father,' she said, smiling.

65 'Tell Papa? But there's nothing to te—' I started to say.

'There is o. There is something to tell. Anyways, that is not your concern, she said. Tell me more about this man. Where is he from? Which town?'

'Well, he isn't from our village,' I replied hesitantly.

Mama waved her hand dismissively. 'That's okay, at least he's Igbo. I've already told 70 your brothers that if they like, they should bring Yoruba girls home. If they think I and your father – a red cap chief – will follow anybody to prostrate in the name of marriage, they are dreaming!'

She clapped her hands together excitedly. 'This news calls for celebration. Finally! I was beginning to worry when no single man was interested in you,' she said 75 cheerfully. 'Let me ask Mama Sikira next door to bring two bottles of chilled Coke.' I wondered if she realised that Mama Sikira was Yoruba or if she was trying to pass on a message: we were to live in harmony with the Yorubas but never to marry one.

Minutes later, Mama returned with bottles of soft drink wrapped in a black nylon bag and placed them on a stool. The bag clung to the wet bottles. She picked up the steel 80 opener and proceeded to open them. As she hooked the corner of the red bottle cap, she stopped and turned to look at me with imploring eyes. '*Nne* please behave yourself with him; don't drive him away. Don't talk too much, and don't be doing *I-too-know*.'

**Annotations**

44 **restore sth.** bring sth. back into existence

47 **aso ebi** (Yoruba) traditional colourful evening dress worn by Nigerian women on special occasions

62 **Yoruba** ethnic group living predominantly in the south-west of Nigeria

63 **Igbo** ethnic group living predominantly in the south-east of Nigeria

69 **dismissive** showing that you do not find what the other person has said very important

71 **red cap chief** Igbo chief of the red cap rank, which stands for authority and tradition

81 **'nne** (Igbo) term of affection for a woman

**Info**

**Code switching** refers to the linguistic phenomenon whereby speakers of more than one language move seamlessly between languages. There are numerous reasons for code-switching. For instance, speakers may opt for a specific language that better expresses a particular idea or concept. Code-switching can serve to assert local speech community identities and create connections with others from the same linguistic community.

Advanced

Even if he is wrong, just smile, at least until he pays your bride price. I know you're stubborn but please do this one thing for your mother. *Biko*. Promise me Obianuju.'

85 'I promise Mama,' I replied solemnly.

Mama opened the last bottle with a smile.

*From:* Tomorrow I Become a Woman, *2022*

## Comprehension

**1**   Point out the gender norms the narrator is expected to conform to.

## Analysis

**2**   Analyse how Obianuju's mother is presented. Focus on narrative techniques and use of language, including her use of code switching. ▶ Info box, p. 245

## Language awareness

▶ SF 19: Reading and understanding narrative texts, p. 369

**3**   In this extract, there is a shift between the standard English used by the first-person narrator and the informal Nigerian English used by the characters.
    **a**   Analyse the effect of this shift on the narrative style.
    **b**   Rephrase ll. 29–37 into standard English using a first-person *narrator. Assess the effect of the changes.

## Beyond the text

▶ Getting started
▶ SF 22: Analysing diagrams, p. 373

**4**   The Gender Inequality Index (GII) provides an insight into gender disparities.
    **a**   Look at the statistic below and describe the current state of gender equality in Nigeria.
    **b**   Relate the information from the statistic to what you have learned from the text.

| | Nigeria** | | World | |
|---|---|---|---|---|
| **2021 GII value*** | 0.680 | | 0.465 | |
| Maternal mortality ratio (death/100,000 live births) | 917 | | 225.4 | |
| Adolescent birth rate (births/1,000 women age 15–19) | 101.7 | | 42.5 | |
| | Female | Male | Female | Male |
| Share of seats in parliament | 4.5% | 95.5% | 25.9% | 74.1% |
| Population with at least some secondary education (age 25 and older) | 40.4% | 55.3% | 64.2% | 70.3% |
| Labour force participation rate (age 15 and older) | 47.9% | 59.6% | 46.2% | 71.7% |

\* Gender inequality index: 0 = low gender inequality; 1 = high gender inequality
\*\* Wordlwide rank: 168
Source: United Nations Development Programme

**5** [You choose] [Writing] Work on either **a** or **b**.

**Advanced**

**a** Chimamanda Ngozi Adichie, Nigerian author and feminist, argues that the issue with gender lies in its tendency to impose how we should behave, instead of letting us be true to ourselves. Write a comment on this statement, referring to the text at hand as well as to the work done in class.

**b** Imagine Obianuju, the main character of the text, has dedicated her life to fighting for gender equality in Nigeria. She has been invited to speak at a gender equality conference in Europe about how growing up in Nigeria inspired her to become an activist. Drawing on the text, write her speech script about her fight for equality and her demands for the future.

▶ SF 28: Argumentative writing: discussion and comment, p. 382
▶ SF 44: Preparing and giving a speech, p. 408
▶ Check 🔖

**Language help**

take a stand • compel me/us to … • we/I demand … • we/I strive/fight for … • ensure equal access to …

---

**Text 11**

## A Nigerian Dream    Aisha Salaudeen

🔊 [Listening] Before reading Aisha Salaudeen's text, you will listen to an extract from an interview with Nigerian writer Dipo Faloyin about Nollywood, the Nigerian film industry. Make notes on the following points:

- the reasons for Nollywood's success
- the impact Nollywood has had on other industries
- Nollywood's cultural relevance.

▶ More info 🔖
▶ More language 🔖

Across a rocky landscape, two young girls find themselves running for cover as spaceships fire laser guns into the field. To survive, both girls, dressed in all black except for a pop of pink boots, are ultimately forced to engage in combat with a Darth Vader lookalike, using their pink and blue lightsabers – sword-like weapons
5 from the 'Star Wars' film franchise. The older girl disappears into thin air as the villain strikes her down and the younger one is left alone to finish the battle. These dramatic scenes are from a short film, 'Another Star Wars Story,' produced by 10 young people based in Kaduna, northern Nigeria, who call themselves The Critics.

Ranging in age from 7 to 27, The Critics have become social media sensations in
10 the West African country by using their mobile phones to create short films with visual effects, or VFX. Science fiction films are typically created with sophisticated software and high-tech equipment. But these young filmmakers – most of whom are siblings or cousins – prove that less is more, using everyday items at their disposal to shoot short films.

15 Raymond Yusuff, 18, the group's VFX artist and editor, says that in 2015 they taught themselves to make films and experiment with greenscreens – used to superimpose an image onto a different background – by reading Wikipedia and watching YouTube tutorials. 'We were exchanging DVDs and watching a lot of CGI (computer-generated imagery) movies and movies with VFX. And we wanted to do

**Annotations**

4 **Darth Vader** character from the science fiction series Star Wars
4 **lightsaber** fictitious weapon used in Star Wars
5 **franchise** *(n)* business run under a franchise agreement, i.e. the permission granted to sb. by a company to sell its product
6 **villain** main bad character in a movie or story
11 **VFX** visual effects
13 **item** thing, object
14 **at your disposal** available, ready to use
15 **editor** person who organizes and improves movie scenes

Annotations
21 **wrapper** (West African English) piece of cloth worn around the lower body and legs
33 **designate sth. to sb.** (here) say officially that sb. has a particular role

20 what we were seeing on screen. We actually started running around our houses, wrappers tied around us, acting,' he tells CNN.

Yusuff adds that at the time, The Critics did not have a camera to film their stories, so they used his [...] smartphone. 'My dad had this old laptop that was lying around, and I asked him for it. We looked up video editing software like Blender, which we
25 used to create our (CGI) effects,' he explains. In 2016, the young filmmakers made their first film, 'Redemption,' after saving up for a month to buy the green fabric needed to create their own greenscreens.

The Critics have now morphed into a production company – The Critics Company – and have created more than 20 short films, often telling stories about robots,
30 aliens and people with supernatural abilities. They keep their movies short because they don't have adequate electricity and data plans to upload long films to the internet. Their productions take anywhere from one week to seven months to shoot, and everyone on the team has a designated role. [...]

Nollywood, Nigeria's movie sector, is a $658 million-dollar-industry that has pro-
35 duced hundreds of talented actors and filmmakers across the country. Some of this

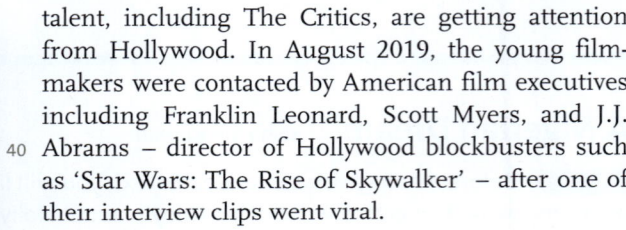

talent, including The Critics, are getting attention from Hollywood. In August 2019, the young filmmakers were contacted by American film executives including Franklin Leonard, Scott Myers, and J.J.
40 Abrams – director of Hollywood blockbusters such as 'Star Wars: The Rise of Skywalker' – after one of their interview clips went viral.

'Franklin Leonard sent us a message on Twitter, and he was like "First of all, you are doing a good job," ' Yusuff
45 tells CNN. 'He told us he found our videos and that he was friends with J.J. Abrams and a couple of people in Hollywood. He told us to send a list on WhatsApp of equipment that we might need for our films.'

This past August, the kids received a large shipment of gear, including high-end
50 gaming PCs, monitors, cameras and stabilizers from Abrams and Leonard. "We were so excited, so happy about it," Yusuff said. [...]

Now that they have the sophisticated gear to shoot more ambitious projects, the plan is to create even more sci-fi short films. Yusuff says The Critics Company's primary goal is to become one of Africa's biggest multimedia studios.

55 'It seems like quite a big dream for us, but we know it's possible.'

*From: 'These Nigerian kids are creating epic sci-fi short films using their phones, and Hollywood is paying attention', www.cnn.com, 1 January 2021*

**Comprehension**

**1**  Outline the Critics Company's filmmaking journey as presented in the article.

## Analysis

**2**  Analyse the *atmosphere created in the first paragraph of the text.

## Language awareness

**3**  The article uses a mix of direct and indirect speech.

▶ More language

   **a**  Analyse the effect this has on the tone of the text.

   **b**  Pick two paragraphs with direct speech and rephrase them using only indirect speech. Compare the effect.

## Beyond the text

**4**  You choose  Work on one of the tasks below.

▶ Getting started
(task a)

▶ SF 46: Having a discussion, p. 410

▶ SF 30: Writing a review, p. 386

▶ Check (task b)

   **a**  Speaking  Watch one of The Critics Company's films online. Using Faloyin's assessment of Nigerian films from the listening task on p. 247 as a starting point, discuss how the film contributes to challenging stereotypes of Africa.

   **b**  Writing  Watch one of The Critics Company's films and write a critical film review.

Language help

challenge stereotypes/preconceived notions • promote/reflect/showcase diverse experiences

## Chapter task

▶ Getting started

*After studying various aspects of Nigeria, you will have the opportunity to use everything you have learned to develop an idea for a short film on the subject of Nigeria and to create a *pitch. The film could be set in Nigeria, or explore a topic, perspective or issue that is specific to the country. Work in groups.*

- Go back to the lists you made on p. 229 with aspects supporting Nigeria's classification as giant of Africa or failed state. Add more words/aspects or make corrections if necessary. In your group, discuss what you have learned and whether your perception of Nigeria has changed and if so, how.
- In your group, create your film idea. Work on the following aspects:
  - genre
  - plot
  - characters
  - title.
- Prepare notes for the presentation of your film *pitch.

# Chapter 9
# Science, Technology and the Environment – No Easy Answers

1 **Art in Context**
 a **Think** Work on your own. Examine the picture above and take notes on the following questions: What do you think is happening in the photo? What associations does the image evoke in you?
 b **Pair** Compare your ideas in pairs and provide a caption for the photo.
 c **Share** Discuss in class how the picture might be related to the title of this chapter: Science, Technology and the Environment – No Easy Answers.

2 The name of the artist in the photo is Ai-Da. Research the story behind the photo.

▶ Getting started

3 a Look at the Chapter map opposite and speculate about the topics and the guiding question in this chapter. Choose one item from the map and brainstorm ideas. Then exchange your ideas with different partners.
 b Discuss in what ways science and technology might solve old problems but create new ones, especially in the context of the environment.

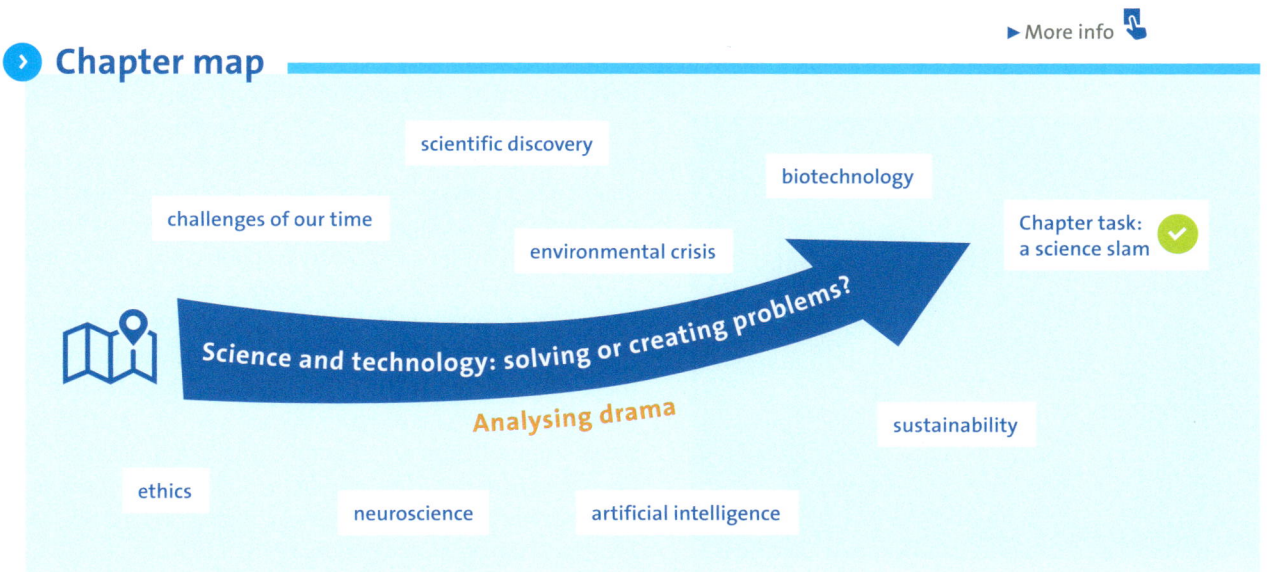

Ai-Da in front of one of her self-portraits, 2018

> **Chapter map**
────────────────────────────────

More info

scientific discovery

biotechnology

challenges of our time

environmental crisis

Chapter task:
a science slam ✓

Science and technology: solving or creating problems?

Analysing drama

sustainability

ethics

neuroscience

artificial intelligence

251

▶ More language

## 🔊 Core issues in science, technology and the environment

### The role of science and technology in the 21st century

Science can be broadly defined as the way human beings figure out how the world works. The 21st century has seen numerous breakthrough discoveries in science and technology which have increased our knowledge of the world and improved the way
5   we live. Researchers have, for example, produced scientific evidence for man-made climate change, developed effective therapies for diseases like HIV or some cancers and created robotic body parts that can be controlled by patients' minds. Scientific and technological progress will continue to play a decisive role in the coming decades if humankind is to overcome the economic, social and environmental challenges we
10   face today. Devising innovative technologies based on scientific research will be vital for combatting future pandemics, mitigating the dangers of climate change and solving many other global problems.

### Science: an unfinished book

Science will never be 'finished'. As our knowledge of science advances, new fields of re-
15   search emerge. Biotechnology, which uses biology to create new products such as vaccines, drugs or genetically modified crops, is a rapidly changing field with huge potential for innovation, for example in gene editing, which, if applied carefully, could cure chronic diseases such as Alzheimer's by repairing an organism's DNA. Similarly, advances in neuroscience, a discipline that investigates the workings of the human brain, could lead
20   to a better understanding of how human thoughts, feelings and actions are determined. This could help patients who suffer from health issues affecting the brain. Moreover, progress in artificial intelligence (or AI for short) might soon make it possible for machines to perform specialized tasks such as driving vehicles or performing surgery without human help, and advances in chemistry might lead to more efficient
25   chemical processes or to biodegradable plastics. Science is indeed an unfinished book.

### Ethical challenges

Humankind has reached a level of scientific and technological development that raises a host of ethical questions and dilemmas. For example, should scientists be allowed to edit an unborn child's genome? Should animals and humans be used in clinical trials?
30   Should robots replace humans as doctors, teachers and drivers? And should we expect the developing world to reduce their $CO_2$ emissions (and restrict their own economic

development) to limit global warming caused mainly by the rich, developed world? None of these questions has an easy answer, which is why they need to be addressed and
35   debated to make sure that scientific and technological innovations will be applied responsibly for the common good. In fact, the power of science fiction could play an important role in this context. Science fiction invites us to look to the future and explore the possibilities of science
40   and technology. It makes us aware of the ethical dilemmas these might entail and encourages discussion on what it means to be human. As Isaac Asimov, one of the most famous science fiction writers of all time, put it, science fiction could turn out to be 'crucial to our salvation, if we are
45   to be saved at all' (from: 'Foreword', Robert Holdstock, ed. *Encyclopaedia of Science Fiction*, 1978).

## 1 Main ideas

Read the text and finish the sentences in as many ways as possible.
1  Science and technology have transformed the 21st century by …
2  Future advances in science and technology may pose risks because …
3  The future of humankind depends on science and technology to …
4  Science and technology may help solve today's environmental crisis by …

## 2 Reflect

a  The table below contains some basic concepts to talk about science and technology. Copy it and add as many words as possible using the appropriate forms of the *word families.

▶ Check
▶ SF 8: Working with dictionaries, p. 355

| Verb | Noun (thing/idea) | Noun (person) | Adjective |
|---|---|---|---|
| ✕ | … | … | scientific |
| ✕ | technology | … | … |
| ✕ | … | … | ethical |
| advance | … | ✕ | … |
| … | discovery | … | … |

b  Examine how nouns (for persons) and adjectives can be formed.

c  Find synonyms and antonyms for the verbs and adjectives in **a**.

▶ Check

d  Define the nouns from the third column using phrases from the text.

## 3 Clustering and brainstorming

a  Read the text again and create a *cluster about science and technology and their contribution to the progress of humankind.
b  Choose one aspect in your cluster from **a** and, for one minute, brainstorm more ideas you could use to talk about it. Add the ideas to your cluster.
c  Work with a partner. Take turns talking for one minute about 'your' aspects.

## 4 Chunk it!

▶ Getting started
▶ More language

Find as many suitable words as possible that *collocate with each group of nouns below. Use a collocations dictionary to check your answers.
1  … *(adj)* + dilemmas | concerns | implications
2  … *(v)* + tasks | experiments | tests
3  … *(adj)* + advances | discoveries | progress
4  … *(v)* + cooperation | dialogue | participation | use
5  … *(adj)* + behaviour | brain | nature

## 5 Writing a speech

Writing  Write a short speech to be given at a science youth conference. Your topic is: 'Future innovations in science and technology I'm (not) looking forward to.' Use *chunks from the text and the exercises above and mark them.

▶ SF 42: Preparing and giving a speech, p. 408
▶ Getting started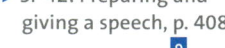

## The thrill of scientific discovery    Stephen Hawking

- Do you like science? Work in a double circle arrangement and discuss what gets you excited about it and what makes science difficult for you.

**Language help**

take satisfaction from sth. • deepen your knowledge of sth. • be able to make connections to reality • deal with abstract/complex ideas • solve/understand difficult problems • use scientific language / numbers / formulas • lack knowledge of sth.

*The excerpt below is from* Brief Answers to the Big Questions, *the last book by Stephen Hawking, which was published posthumously.*

When I was growing up it was still acceptable – not to me but in social terms – to say that one was not interested in science and did not see the point in bothering with it. This is no longer the case. Let me be clear. I am not promoting the idea that all young people should grow up to be scientists. I do not see that as an ideal situ-
5 ation, as the world needs people with a wide variety of skills. But I am advocating that all young people should be familiar with and confident around scientific subjects, whatever they choose to do. They need to be scientifically literate, and inspired to engage with developments in science and technology in order to learn more.

10 A world where only a tiny super-elite are capable of understanding advanced science and technology and its applications would be, to my mind, a dangerous and limited one. I seriously doubt whether long-range beneficial projects such as cleaning up the oceans or curing diseases in the developing world would be given priority. Worse, we could find that technology is used against us and that we might have
15 no power to stop it.

I don't believe in boundaries, either for what we can do in our personal lives or for what life and intelligence can accomplish in our universe. We stand at a threshold of important discoveries in all areas of science. Without doubt, our world will change enormously in the next fifty years. We will find out what happened at the
20 Big Bang. We will come to understand how life began on Earth. We may even discover whether life exists elsewhere in the universe. While the chances of communicating with an intelligent extra-terrestrial species may be slim, the importance of such a discovery means we must not give up trying. We will continue to explore our cosmic habitat, sending robots and humans into space. We cannot continue to look
25 inwards at ourselves on a small and increasingly polluted and overcrowded planet. Through scientific endeavour and technological innovation, we must look outwards to the wider universe, while also striving to fix the problems on Earth. And I am optimistic that we will ultimately create viable habitats for the human race on other planets. We will transcend the Earth and learn to exist in space.

30 This is not the end of the story, but just the beginning of what I hope will be billions of years of life flourishing in the cosmos.

And one final point – we never really know where the next great scientific discovery will come from, nor who will make it. Opening up the thrill and wonder of scientific discovery, creating innovative and accessible ways to reach out to the

---

▶ SF 17: Reading and understanding non-fictional texts, p. 367

**Info**

**Stephen Hawking** (1942–2018) was a British theoretical physicist and cosmologist working and teaching at the University of Cambridge. His work focused on studying black holes and on extending Albert Einstein's general theory of relativity. Hawking also published several popular science books, which became bestsellers and made him famous among a wider public. After losing the ability to speak because of a motor neuron disease, Hawking used a speech generator to communicate with people.

Annotations

2 **bother with sth.** take the time to deal with sth.
5 **advocate sth.** speak out in favour of sth.
7 **literate** having knowledge of sth.
17 **threshold** point at which sth. starts to happen
22 **extra-terrestrial** from outside the earth
24 **habitat** natural environment
26 **endeavour** [ɪnˈdevə] *(n)* attempt to achieve a goal
27 **strive to do sth.** make great efforts to achieve sth.
28 **viable** (here) capable of surviving
29 **transcend sth.** go beyond sth.

35 widest young audience possible, greatly increases the chances of finding and inspiring the new Einstein. Wherever she might be.

So remember to look up at the stars and
not down at your feet. Try to make
sense of what you see and wonder
40 about what makes the universe exist.
Be curious. And however difficult life
may seem, there is always something
you can do and succeed at. It matters
that you don't give up. Unleash your
45 imagination. Shape the future.

*From:* Brief Answers to the Big Questions, *2018*

Annotation
44 **unleash sth.** release
sth., allow sth. to have
an effect

## Comprehension

**1** Complete the following sentences with information from the text.
1 To be 'scientifically literate' means …
2 Acquiring scientific literacy is important because …
3 In the next few decades, Stephen Hawking expects science to …
4 Exploring the cosmos will be essential if humanity …
5 Science is thrilling because …

## Analysis

**2** Stephen Hawking was famous for his ability to write popular science books in
which he communicated complex scientific ideas in clear, non-technical
language. Take a close look at the text and analyse how Hawking tries to make
his ideas appealing and intelligible to his readers.

▶ SF 4: Writing a text
analysis, p. 351
▶ WOB: pp. 28–30

## Language awareness

**3** Look at the (modal) auxiliary verbs such as *can, will* and *may* used in ll. 16–29.
They all express different degrees of certainty.
a Rank the auxiliary verbs according to the degrees of certainty they express.
b Write one paragraph about your own future. Predict what will or might
happen expressing varying degrees of certainty.

Stephen Hawking

## Beyond the text

**4** You choose  Writing  Work on task **a** or **b**.

a Research more information about
Stephen Hawking's life and write an
entry for a science *blog, pointing
out what you find most fascinating
about the scientist and his work.

b Pick a scientific discovery
(by Stephen Hawking or another
scientist) you find exciting and write
a short *article for the science
section of the school newspaper,
pointing out why this discovery
fascinates you so much.

▶ SF 13: Doing research,
p. 360
▶ SF 32: Writing an (online)
article, p. 388
▶ Check
▶ WOB: pp. 11–15

# Scientists at work    Lawrence Wright

- *Taking the quote by Richard Feynman below as a starting point, explain the way scientists work.*

> " The only way to have real success in science, the field I'm familiar with, is to describe the evidence very carefully without regard to the way you feel it should be. If you have a theory, you must try to explain what's good and what's bad about it equally. "

*Richard Feynman,* The Quotable Feynman, *2015*

*Below is the opening chapter of the novel* The End of October *by Lawrence Wright. During a meeting at the WHO headquarters in Geneva, Henry Parsons, a US epidemiologist, learns about a mysterious new disease whose sudden appearance in Indonesia is stirring up a heated debate among scientists.*

The WHO headquarters in Geneva

In a large auditorium in Geneva, a parliament of health officials gathered for the final afternoon session on emergency infectious diseases. The audience was
5 restless, worn out by the day-long meetings and worried about catching their flights. The terrorist attack in Rome had everyone on edge.

'An unusual cluster of adolescent fatalities in a refugee camp in Indonesia,' the next-to-last speaker of the conference was saying. Hans Somebody. Dutch. Tall,
10 arrogant, well fed. An untrimmed fringe of gray-blond hair spilled over his collar, the lint on his shoulders sparkling in the projected light of the PowerPoint.

A map of Indonesia flashed on the screen. 'Forty-seven death certificates were issued in the first week of March at the Kongoli Number Two Camp in West Java.' Hans indicated the spot with his laser pointer, followed by slides of destitute refu-
15 gees in horrible squalor. The world was awash in displaced people, millions pressed into hastily assembled camps and fenced off like prisoners, with inadequate rations and scarce medical facilities. Nothing surprising about an epidemic spilling out of such places. Cholera, diphtheria, dengue – the tropics were always cooking up something.

20 'High fever, bloody discharges, rapid transmission, extreme lethality. But what really distinguishes this cluster,' Hans said, as he posted a graph, 'is the median age of the victims. Usually, infections randomly span the generations, but here the fatalities spike in the age group expected to be the most vigorous portion of the population.'

25 In the large auditorium in Geneva, the parliament of health officials leaned forward to study the curious slide. Most mortal diseases kill off the very young and the very old, but instead of the usual U-shaped graph, this one resembled a crude W,

► More info

**Annotations**

7 **on edge** nervously excited about sth.
8 **fatality** death caused by illness or violence
13 **West Java** province in Indonesia
14 **destitute** very poor
15 **squalor** state of being extremely dirty
17 **scarce** [skeəs] *(adj)* insufficient
20 **discharge** *(n)* (here) fluid from body parts
20 **lethality** capacity to cause harm or death
23 **spike** *(v)* rise quickly

with an average age of death of twenty-nine. 'Based on sketchy reports from the initial outbreak, we estimate the overall lethality at 70 percent,' Hans said.

30 'Pediatric or natal ...?' Maria Savona, director of epidemiology at the World Health Organization, interrupted the puzzled silence.

'Largely accounted for in the reported cohort,' Hans replied.

'Possible sexual transmission?' a Japanese doctor asked. 'Unlikely,' said Hans. He was enjoying himself. Now his face drifted into the projection, casting a bulky
35 shadow over the next slide. 'Reportable deaths stay consistent for the following weeks, but the overall total drops significantly.'

'A one-time event, in that case,' the Japanese woman concluded.

'With forty-seven bodies?' Hans said. 'Quite an orgy!'

The Japanese doctor blushed and covered her mouth as she giggled.

40 'Okay, Hans, you've kept us guessing long enough,' Maria said impatiently.

Hans looked around the room triumphantly. 'Shigella,' he said, to groans of disbelief. 'You would have got it but for the inverted mortality vector. That puzzled us as well. This is a common bacteria in poorer countries, the cause of innumerable cases of food poisoning. We queried the health authorities in Jakarta, and they
45 concluded that, in a starving environment, the only people robust enough to seize the limited food resources are the young. In this case, strength proved to be their undoing. Our team deduced that the probable source of the pathogen was raw milk. We offer this as a cautionary tale about how demographic stereotypes can blind us to facts that would otherwise be obvious.'

50 Hans stepped down to perfunctory applause as Maria called the last presenter to the podium. 'Campylobacter in Wisconsin–' the man began.

Suddenly, a commanding voice interrupted. 'A raging hemorrhagic fever kills forty-seven people in a week and disappears without a trace?'

Two hundred heads turned to locate the source of that booming baritone. From the
55 voice, you would have thought Henry Parsons was a big man. No. He was short and slight, bent by a childhood case of rickets that left him slightly deformed. [...] In the neverending war on emerging diseases, Henry Parsons was not a small man; he was a giant.

Hans Somebody squinted and located Henry in the gloom of the upper tiers. 'Not
60 so unusual, Dr. Parsons, if you consider the environmental causation.'

'You used the word "transmission."'

Hans smiled, happy to resume the game. 'The Indonesian authorities at first suspected a viral agent.'

'What changed their minds?' Henry asked.

65 Maria had become intrigued. 'You are thinking Ebola?'

'In which case we'd see likely migration to urban centers,' Hans said. 'Not shown. All it took was to eliminate the source of contamination and the infection disappeared.'

**Info**

The **World Health Organization (WHO)** is an agency of the United Nations whose primary function is to promote public health around the world, for example by devising and advancing international health standards, providing technical help and collecting data. Since its inception in 1948, the WHO has been successful in fighting global health challenges such as smallpox, polio and Ebola.

Annotations
30 **pediatric** (AE = BE paediatric) dealing with children and their diseases
30 **natal** relating to the birth of babies
32 **account for sth.** be the cause of sth.
32 **cohort** ['– –] group of people with shared characteristics
41 **Shigella** kind of bacteria
42 **inverted** changed to the opposite
42 **mortality** large-scale death
47 **undoing** cause of ruin or failure
47 **pathogen** ['– – –] microorganism that causes disease
48 **cautionary tale** story warning of danger
51 **campylobacter** kind of bacteria
52 **raging** prevailing uncontrollably
52 **hemorrhagic** (AE = BE haemorrhagic) **fever** viral disease accompanied by heavy bleeding
56 **rickets** (pl) Rachitis
63 **agent** substance that causes a change
67 **contamination** act of making sth. unclean

Annotations
70 **Médecins Sans Frontières** internation-al medical humanitari-an organisation
82 **cane** walking stick
89 **meningitis** [ˌmenɪnˈdʒaɪtɪs] serious disease affecting the brain
93 **stunning** extremely impressive
93 **downside** negative aspect of sth.
101 **MSF** = Médecins sans frontières
101 **sample** representative part of sth.

'Did you actually go to the camp yourself?' Henry asked. 'Take samples?'

'The Indonesian authorities have been fully cooperative,' Hans said dismissively. 'There is a team from Médecins Sans Frontières in place now, and we will receive confirmation shortly. Don't expect surprises.'

Hans waited a moment, but Henry sat back, thoughtfully tapping a finger on his lips. The next presenter resumed. 'A slaughterhouse in Milwaukee,' he said, as a few conferees with an eye on the time ducked toward the exits. There was bound to be increased security at the airport.

'I hate when you do that,' Maria said, when they got to her office. It was glassy and stylish, with a fine view of Mont Blanc. A flock of storks, having hurdled the alpine barrier, circled for a landing beside Lake Geneva, their first stop on the spring migration from the Nile Valley.

'Do what?'

Maria leaned back and tapped her finger on her lips, imitating Henry's gesture.

'Is that a habit of mine?' he asked, leaning his cane against her desk.

'When I see you do it, I know I should be worried. What makes you doubt Hans's study?'

'Acute hemorrhagic fever. Very likely viral. Weird mortality distribution, totally inappropriate for shigella. And why did it suddenly–'

'Just stop? I don't know, Henry, you tell me. Indonesia again?'

'They hid the ball before.'

'It doesn't look like another meningitis outbreak.'

'Certainly not.' Despite himself, Henry involuntarily began tapping his lips again. Maria waited. 'I shouldn't tell you what to do,' he finally said. 'Maybe Hans is right.'

'But ...?'

'The lethality. Stunning. The downside if he's wrong.'

Maria went to the window. Clouds were settling in, masking the majestic peak. She was about to speak when Henry interrupted her thought. 'I've got to go.'

'That's exactly what I was thinking.'

'I mean home.'

Maria nodded in that way that meant she had heard him, but the worried expression in her Italian eyes sent a different message. 'Give me two days. I know how much I'm asking. I should send a whole team, but I don't have anybody I can trust. Hans says MSF is there, so they can help. Just get slides and samples. In and out and on your way back to Atlanta.'

'Maria ...'

'Please, Henry.'

Advanced

105 In the manner of friends who have known each other a long time, Henry saw a flash of the worried young epidemiologist studying the African swine fever outbreak in Haiti. Maria had been part of the team that advocated the eradication of the indigenous pig that carried the disease. Nearly every family in Haiti kept pigs; in addition to being a major source of food, they functioned as currency, a bank for the peasant-

110 ry. Within a year, thanks to the efforts of the international community and the dictator 'Baby Doc' Duvalier, the entire population of Creole pigs was extinct, a great success, almost unprecedented. The eradication stopped an incurable disease. But the peasants, already poor, were reduced to famine. The corrupt elite appropriated most of the replacement pigs the Americans provided, which were in any case too

115 delicate for the environment and too expensive to feed. With no other resources, people turned to making charcoal, which denuded the forests. Haiti never recovered. It's debatable whether the hogs should have been slaughtered in the first place. We were such confident idealists back then, Henry thought.

'Two days, maximum,' he said. 'I promised Jill I'd be home for Teddy's birthday.'

120 'I'll have Rinaldo book you on the red-eye to Jakarta.' Maria assured him that she would call the Centers for Disease Control and Prevention, in Atlanta, where Henry was deputy director for infectious diseases, and beg forgiveness; it was an emergency request on her part.

'By the way,' he said as he was leaving, 'any word from Rome? Your family is safe?'

125 'We don't know,' Maria said despairingly.

*From:* The End of October, *2020*

**Annotations**

106 **epidemiologist** doctor who specializes in the spread of diseases
107 **Haiti** ['heɪti] country on the island of Hispaniola in the Caribbean Sea
107 **eradication** process of getting rid of sth.
107 **indigenous** [ɪnˈdɪdʒənəs] native
109 **peasantry** agricultural labourers
111 **'Baby Doc' Duvalier** Claude Duvalier, nicknamed 'Baby Doc', a cruel dictator in Haiti who was overthrown by an uprising in 1986
111 **Creole** (here) Haitian
112 **unprecedented** never known or done before
113 **famine** hunger, scarcity of food
113 **appropriate sth.** take sth. for your own use
116 **charcoal** *Holzkohle*
116 **denude sth.** make sth. bare
117 **hog** pig
120 **red-eye** (here) overnight flight

**Comprehension**

1 a   Look at the four statements on the right and say which of them comes closest to your understanding of the excerpt.
  b   Write a summary of the text. Afterwards, reevaluate your decision from **1a**.

  ▶ SF 34: Writing a summary or an outline, p. 390

  ▶ Getting started 👆

A Scientists are working together to combat a deadly disease.

B Scientists are giving speeches on infectious diseases at a conference in Geneva.

C Scientists are arguing about how to respond to the outbreak of an unknown virus in Indonesia.

D Scientists are forming hypotheses as to the causes of the high number of fatalities in an Asian refugee camp.

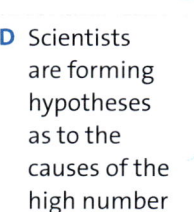

## Analysis

**2** **a** Use a grid like the one below to collect information on the steps taken by Hans, Henry and the other scientists to explain the disease in Indonesia.

|  | Hans | Henry | Other scientists |
| --- | --- | --- | --- |
| **Description** of the new disease | … | … | … |
| **Hypothesis** on the origins of the new disease | … | … | … |
| **Arguments/data** speaking for or against the hypothesis | … | … | … |
| **Conclusions** about what is to be done next | … | … | … |

▶ SF 12: Communicating across cultures, p. 359

**b** Compare your findings from task **2a**, then discuss what this text shows you about the challenges of scientific work. Analyse the *stylistic devices the author uses to highlight them.

**c** [Intercultural competence] Re-read the passage about the swine fever outbreak in Haiti (ll. 105–118), which is based on real events. Explain how the handling of the outbreak reveals a cultural misunderstanding about Haiti's economic situation and discuss how the misunderstanding – and its consequences – might have been avoided.

## Language awareness

▶ SF 8: Working with dictionaries, p. 355

**3** **a** Make a list of words and phrases from the text that you could use to talk about causes and effects of a pandemic. Use a monolingual dictionary.

**b** [Writing] Write a paragraph on this topic for a presentation in your bilingual Biology class. Use as many of the words you listed as possible.

## Beyond the text

▶ SF 38: Creative writing, p. 395

▶ SF 46: Having a discussion, p. 410

▶ Getting started

▶ WOB: pp. 65–67

**4** [You choose] Work on either **a** or **b**.

**a** [Writing] Write an email from Henry Parsons to his wife Jill in which he explains to her why he will return home later than expected.

**b** [Speaking] Imagine the following situation: A lethal disease is threatening the lives of people in your country. It is your job to set up a task force to handle the situation. Work in small groups and discuss the following questions:
– Which experts should be on the task force?
– Which competences and skills are needed to deal with this health crisis?
– What difficulties might arise should there be an outbreak of the disease?

# Using DNA technology to combat disease    John Arlidge

▶ SF 17: Reading and understanding non-fictional texts, p. 367

**Advanced**

- Before reading this newspaper article, look up the term *biotechnology* in a dictionary and note down the definition. Then work with a partner. Using your definitions, brainstorm ideas on the uses and goals of biotechnology and arrange them in a mind map.

*Jennifer Doudna and Emmanuelle Charpentier were awarded the 2020 Nobel prize in chemistry for their pioneering discoveries in the field of biotechnology.*

Few people want to talk about disease after the year we've just had, but Jennifer Doudna is one of those who do – for the best of reasons. Thanks to her, a revolution is taking place in the way scientists combat some of the most serious illnesses that afflict humankind.

5  The American biochemist has pioneered a technology that cuts to the heart of life. 'It's an extraordinary tool that allows us to edit the life code of any organism, including humans,' she says. She is talking about Crispr-Cas9, a technique in which enzymes are used as 'molecular scissors' to make changes to genetic code. She helped develop the system with her longtime collaborator Emmanuelle Charpen-
10  tier, an achievement that resulted in them being awarded the 2020 Nobel prize in chemistry. Their work is groundbreaking because it enables scientists easily and precisely to target DNA sequences and insert, remove or replace cells to achieve a range of benefits, from creating hardier plants to eliminating diseases.

Speaking from her home in Berkeley, where she works at the University of Califor-
15  nia, Doudna uses heart disease to illustrate how Crispr works and why it might be so useful. 'There's a well-known gene that in certain people protects them from high cholesterol and the resulting cardiovascular disease that can develop. Imagine if it were possible to edit that gene … so that we all had that protection. It's possible to do this in animal models.'

20  Before Crispr, editing DNA in human cells was slow and expensive. The recent technological advances should one day make it as straightforward as tweaking a sentence in a Word document. Eventually these 'edits' could be delivered by taking a pill or having an injection, creating 'molecular surgery on DNA without a scalpel', she says with a smile.

25  Researchers have long known that bacteria snip and store fragments of viruses to help fight them off. Doudna and Charpentier were able to replicate this process in the lab, using specialised enzymes, and then "program" them to target precise genetic sequences. 'Virus-like packages deliver the gene "editors" because viruses are very good at infecting specific kinds of cell,' Doudna says.

30  Being able to alter the smallest building blocks of life creates the chance not simply to tackle diseases but to prevent them from developing in the first place. She uses brain cancer as another example. 'We know we can add cells in the immune system specifically to go after solid tumour cells once a tumour has formed. Programming the immune system to be ready to fight the cancer – that's something that
35  genome editing could do. We're looking at it.' But she cautions: 'It is at the bleeding edge of where the technology is.' […]

## Info

**Nobel prizes** are annual awards given to people or groups for their outstanding contributions in the fields of physics, chemistry, physiology or medicine, economic sciences, literature and peace. Named after the Swedish industrialist and inventor of dynamite, Alfred Nobel (1833–1896), the Nobel prizes are widely regarded as the most prestigious awards today.

### Annotations

3  **combat sth.**  fight sth., take action against sth.
4  **afflict sb./sth.**  cause sb./sth. pain or trouble
6  **edit sth.**  change sth.
13  **hardy**  strong enough to bear difficult conditions
17  **cardiovascular**  related to or affecting the heart and blood vessels
21  **tweak sth.**  improve sth. by making small changes
23  **surgery**  *Chirurgie*
25  **snip sth.**  cut sth.
26  **replicate sth.**  copy sth. or do sth. again in the same way
31  **tackle sth.**  deal with sth.
35  **bleeding edge of sth.**  newest, most advanced, but still risky stage in the development of sth.

Advanced

**Annotations**
37 **dispute** *(v)* disagree
47 **eugenics** highly problematic practice of selective breeding, especially by discouraging or forbidding reproduction by persons having genetic defects or presumed to have inheritable undesirable traits
52 **hypothetical** not well supported by evidence

Few dispute Crispr is one of our most powerful new medical tools, but with great power come great risks: human gene editing raises serious ethical concerns about 'designer babies'. In theory egg and sperm cells can be edited to make sure children grow up not only largely disease-free but with, say, sprinter's legs or blue eyes. Critics worry that wealthy couples will seek to engineer the 'perfect children'. In 2018 a rogue Chinese scientist claimed to have used Crispr to create the first gene-edited babies in an attempt to protect them from HIV. Human embryo editing is illegal in most countries.

45 Making genetic changes that become part of the entire individual initially made Doudna uneasy. 'I thought, "No way. That just should not happen." It made me think of eugenics.'

Doudna says her views 'have evolved over time. Let's say it becomes safe and possible to remove from a family line a well-known disease – my mind remains open to that, for sure. And, gosh, you might at some point conclude that it would be unethical *not* to use it in ways that would prevent great human suffering.' However, she points out these ethical dilemmas are at present hypothetical: 'We're a long way from being able to do that right now.'

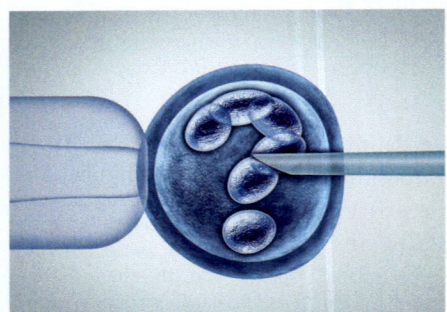

Today the billion-dollar question most people ask her is: can Crispr help with pandemics? 'Crispr works well as a rapid diagnostic, so I have real hope that it will have an impact on pandemic preparedness,' she says. 'Once we have it working well for diagnosing the coronavirus, it can be easily changed to look for other new types of virus in the future.'

60 No one would have a problem with that. [...]

*From: 'Why Jennifer Doudna's DNA discovery is revolutionising the way we tackle disease',* The Sunday Times, *3 January 2021*

## Comprehension

▶ Getting started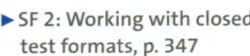

▶ SF 2: Working with closed test formats, p. 347

▶ Check

**1 a**   Match each part of the text in the box on the left with the most suitable heading in the box on the right. There are two more headings than you need.

| | |
|---|---|
| ll. 1–13 | **A** Advantages and disadvantages of Crispr |
| ll. 14–29 | **B** Costs |
| ll. 30–44 | **C** Extending the scope of research |
| ll. 45–53 | **D** How Crispr functions |
| ll. 54–60 | **E** International cooperation |
| | **F** Moral implications |
| | **G** What Crispr is |

**b**   Outline ...
- why Jennifer Doudna's discovery is revolutionary
- how the Crispr technology works
- what the potential benefits of this new technology are
- what the risks of this new technology might be.

Advanced

## Analysis

**2** In the author's opinion, do the benefits of Crispr outweigh the dangers? Assess his view on the technology, providing evidence from the text.

▶ Support, p. 321
▶ SF 4: Writing a text analysis, p. 351

## Language awareness

**3** The modal auxiliary verbs *can, could, might* and *should* are often used in English to say that something is probable or possible in the future.
  **a** Find examples in the text of *can, could, might* and *should* indicating how probable certain effects of Crispr are expected to be.
  **b** *Quick write*: Write a short paragraph about the pros and cons of gene editing. Use *can, could, might* and *should*.

▶ More language
▶ WOB: p. 114

## Beyond the text

**4** Speaking Crispr could change the world of tomorrow not only in biomedicine, but also in other fields. Do some research, then give a short presentation on possible applications of Crispr in these other fields and their potential impact.

▶ SF 43: Giving a presentation, p. 405
▶ Getting started

---

## Text 4

# The science of happiness, learning and the brain

*You are going to listen to the beginning of a podcast called 'Glück beginnt im Kopf'.*

• *Quick write:* Give your own personal definition of happiness.

**1** Mediating In your bilingual biology class you're dealing with the functions of the brain. For a wall display in class, write a short informative text about the connection between happiness, learning and the human brain.

▶ SF 40: Listening/Viewing for gist and detail, p. 399

▶ Support, p. 322
▶ Getting started

## Language awareness

**2** It's not always easy to find a suitable equivalent of *Glück* in English.

  **a** *Luck* and *fortune, happiness* and *joy* could all be translated by *Glück*, but there are slight differences in meaning. Define them.

  **b** How would you say the following in English?
    **1** Glück gehabt!
    **2** Was für ein Glück!
    **3** Ein Glück, dass …
    **4** jemandem Glück wünschen
    **5** großes Glück
    **6** sein Glück machen
    **7** Wünsch mir Glück!

▶ Check

▶ SF 21: Reading, watching and understanding drama, p. 371

## Focus on test formats

Analysing drama is a skill you might encounter in tests at school or other test formats. But your analysing skills may also lead to a deeper understanding of a text and they will probably make watching a drama at the theatre or a scene from a movie more enjoyable and worthwhile.

Read the following task:

*Analyse how the antithesis between medical and romantic explanations of love is presented as a dramatic conflict in the scenes.*

## Work it out

### 1 Examining the scenes

a To analyse drama, different strategies may prove helpful. With a partner, discuss which of the steps below you think are the most relevant for working on the specific task above:

1 Do research on the playwright.
2 Identify the scene's position within the structure of the whole play.
3 Draw a mindmap illustrating the characters and their relationships.
4 Watch out for stage directions and imagine the setup of the stage.
5 Examine the language used by the characters.
6 Have a closer look at the arguments brought forward by the characters.
7 Imagine different ways of performing crucial passages of the scene.
8 Examine how the characters interact.
9 Define the dramatic conflict in the scenes.
10 Relate the characters' arguments to the elements of the dramatic conflict.

b Discuss other strategies that you might find helpful. Collect them on a *method card.

### 2 Writing your analysis

a Read aspects 1–12 below and assess whether they need to be integrated into your written analysis. Match them to categories A, B or C on the left.

1 the play's title, the playwright's name and the scene you're referring to
2 information on what happens before and after the scenes you're analysing
3 a summary of the whole play
4 a summary of the scenes
5 a description of the setting and atmosphere of the scenes
6 a characterization of the characters
7 information on the characters you can deduce from the scenes including the concepts of love they represent
8 an account of the medical and romantic explanations of love mentioned in the scenes

---

**Info**

A **dramatic conflict** is at the core of all plays and movies. It is the constant tension that propels the action forward. It can result from one of many impulses, e.g. the characters' conflicting desires or values, or even obstacles that need to be overcome by the protagonist. A resolution of this conflict is necessary for the drama's conclusion. Although dramatic conflicts are often centered around topics like death, ambition and love, contemporary drama has broadened its scope. The topics encompass matters from all walks of life like science, technology, the environment, utopia or dystopia, migration and more.

**Usefulness of the aspect for the task at hand:**
**A:** absolutely necessary
**B:** possibly of help
**C:** not necessary or helpful

▶ Check 🔖

9 a brief summary of how the characters' arguments reflect the antithesis between medical and romantic explanations of love

10 a definition and analysis of the dramatic conflict in both scenes

11 an analysis of images used

12 your personal view on the antithetical views of love dealt with in the scenes

**b** Just like most texts, an analysis of a drama or dramatic scenes consists of an introduction, a main part and a conclusion. Match the aspects from **2a** that you considered absolutely necessary to the three parts. Some of them might be necessary in two or even all three parts.

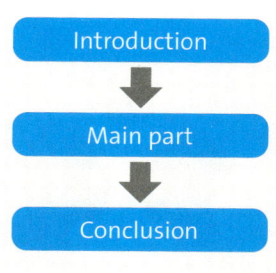

► Check

# Do it

## 3 Working on the task

**a** Read the text on p. 266 and analyse it using the strategies and aspects you collected in tasks **1** and **2**.

**b** Write a coherent, well-structured text to present the results of your analysis. Don't forget to use quotations and/or give line references.

**c** In the end, check your text for style, correctness and vocabulary.

# Feedback

## 4 Peer assessment

Swap texts with your partner. Compare them and give each other feedback.

► SF 15: Assessing yourself and giving feedback, p. 363

## 5 Self-assessment

**a** On the basis of your partner's feedback, go back to your *method card. Add and/or correct strategies for analysing drama tasks. Decide for each strategy whether you are already good at it or if you need more practice.

| Method card – Analysing drama | |
|---|---|
| What I am good at: | What I need to practise: |
| ... | ... |

**b** Look at the part of your text where your feedback partner suggested the most changes. Revise it, taking into consideration the points they put forward. If you like, you could apply what you have learned in a new analysis of another drama/film scene that you have watched.

## What is love? A clinical trial    Lucy Prebble

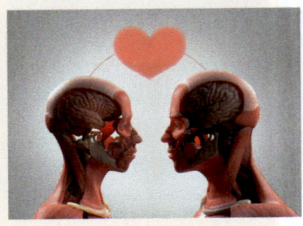

*In the play* The Effect, *Connie, a psychology student, and Tristan, a backpacker and drifter, have been paid to participate in a clinical trial for a new anti-depressant drug. Soon after the trial starts, they feel drawn to one another. The organizers of the trial, Dr Lorna James (a psychiatrist) and Dr Toby Sealy (the developer of the drug and Dr James's ex-boyfriend), have trouble interpreting their observations under the new circumstances.*

▶ SF 21: Reading, watching and understanding drama, p. 371

**Annotations**

**anti-depressant** drug used against depression

5 **dopamine** [ˈdəʊpəmiːn] substance that transmits nerve impulses in the brain and influences how you feel pleasure

9 **take sth. with a pinch of (salt)** not completely believe sth.

### Extract 1

| | |
|---|---|
| **Connie** | You're very interesting. I just feel weird. I don't feel what I'd feel like in real life. |
| **Tristan** | This *is* real life. When is it real? |
| **Connie** | No I mean. The anti-depressant, the doctor said, they're designed to ... stimulate certain, like, dopamine. Which is the rush you get if something exciting happens or, when you – well it's fake, it's a chemical that feels like. Like falling for someone. *Beat.* |
| **Tristan** | So? |
| **Connie** | So forgive me if I take everything with a big pinch of, you know, ... |
| **Tristan** | What you think I don't like you properly because of the – ? |
| **Connie** | I think it's a strong possibility. |
| **Tristan** | Bullshit. I can tell the difference between who I am and a side effect. |
| **Connie** | With respect Tristan, no you definitely can't. |
| **Tristan** | You're saying any attraction is a result of the trial. |
| **Connie** | Part of it could be. |
| **Tristan** | (*quietly pleased*) You must be basing that on feeling a sort of attraction then? |
| **Connie** | I didn't say that ...! It's a chemical reaction, is what I'm saying. |
| **Tristan** | But I'm still me. |
| **Connie** | No, yes, you're you, but under the influence of something. If you were really pissed and going 'I love you, you're my best mate' I wouldn't believe it either. |
| **Tristan** | Why not? Men mean it when they say that, they just can't say it when they're sober. |
| **Connie** | Yeah but they'll have known that person (ages) – and I don't know, I'm just telling you what the doctor said. |
| **Tristan** | Ah, what does she know? They don't know anything, Knowledge is a myth. |
| **Connie** | (*unimpressed*) Okay ... [...] |

### Extract 2

| | |
|---|---|
| **Dr James** | [...] You asked to see the scans of the volunteers showing the greatest effect. Are you interested in who they are? |
| **Toby** | Of course. |

Actors Billie Piper as Connie and Jonjo O'Neill as Tristan performing in a production of *The Effect* at the Cottesloe Theatre in London

| | Dr James | K. Two very different clinical histories, backgrounds, genders even. But they have one thing in common. They are both involved in an intense and protracted flirtation, with each other. |

**Dr James** K. Two very different clinical histories, backgrounds, genders even. But they have one thing in common. They are both involved in an intense and protracted flirtation, with each other.

**Toby** Really? Right ... So you think *that's* what I'm looking at?

40 **Dr James** I think their physical symptoms and this neural activity is a result of that ... attraction and frankly it's obscuring any sense of what the drug itself is doing.

**Toby** Unless it is what the drug itself is doing. If the agent is causing all these symptoms, why on earth *wouldn't* they assume they were

45 infatuated?

**Dr James** You think because they feel all the things one would associate with infatuation they are just ... assuming that's what they are.

**Toby** Assuming, exactly. The body responds a certain way to what it's being given, they can't sleep, they can't eat, they're in a constant

50 state of neural excitement ever since they met, what's the brain going to conclude?

**Dr James** You think it mistakes that for love?

**Toby** Not even mistakes it, creates it. To make sense of the response. Are the other volunteers showing similar effect?

55 **Dr James** Not to the same extent.

**Toby** But they're all straight men, right?

**Dr James** From their hygiene levels I'd guess, yes.

**Toby** Well maybe *they've* just got nowhere to go with it, nothing to hang it on. You can instil very strong feelings in a body

60 as long as it's toward something that looks right, you know? You can make ducklings follow a kettle believing it's their mother for years.

**Dr James** Can you?

**Toby** They did it at Exeter.

65 **Dr James** Oh that's very Exeter.

**Toby** Look at it objectively. With healthy volunteers we're starting from a midpoint. We're giving drugs to normal minds –

**Dr James** 'Normal minds.' (!)

70 **Toby** You know what I mean. Depression's deadness of emotion, right? Insularity, lack of engagement with the world and those around you –

**Dr James** Is it?

**Toby** So the other end of the spectrum, where the agent

75 could be taking them, is *extreme* emotion, excess engagement, overwhelming purpose and feeling. What does that sound like – ?

**Dr James** Bollocks?

**Toby** What does it sound like?

80 **Dr James** I'm pretty sure it's not drug effect, Toby. (!) [...]

*From:* The Effect, 2012

Annotations
38 **protracted** extended
40 **neural** [ˈnjʊərəl] relating to a nerve
41 **frankly** honestly
43 **agent** a chemical that produces an effect
45 **infatuated** madly in love
61 **duckling** young duck
64 **Exeter** University of Exeter
71 **insularity** isolation and disinterest
75 **excess** *(adj)* more than usual

Actor Tom Goodman-Hill performing as Toby in a production of *The Effect* at the Cottesloe Theatre in London

▶ WOB: pp. 34–36

## Will AI outsmart humanity?

- What is meant by Artificial Intelligence (AI)? Research the term and write down a succinct definition. Then use your definition to say whether the following statements are true or false.
    1. AI describes the ability of a robot to replace human beings.
    2. AI helps humans to become more intelligent.
    3. AI involves computers making decisions on their own.

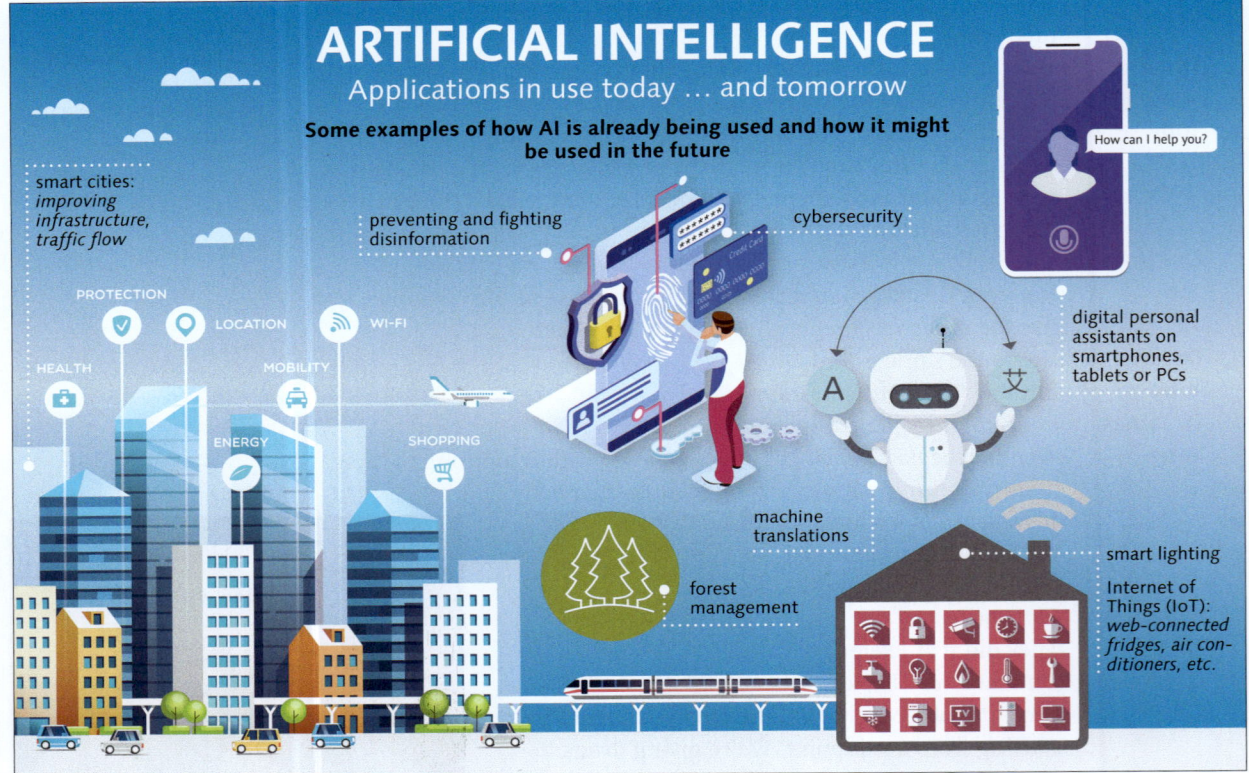

ARTIFICIAL INTELLIGENCE
Applications in use today … and tomorrow
Some examples of how AI is already being used and how it might be used in the future

---

### Comprehension

▶ SF 23: Analysing visuals, p. 374

▶ WOB: pp. 40–44

1. Work with a partner. **Partner B:** Go to p. 322.
    a. **Partner A:** Study the infographic above.
    b. Tell your partner how artificial intelligence is already part of daily life.

### Analysis

▶ Getting started

2. a. Analyse the two infographics in terms of how words, images and colours are used to create meaning.
    b. In your opinion, what message is being conveyed regarding AI and its impact on society, the individual and the environment?

Beyond the text

**3 a** 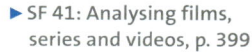 Think back to this chapter's guiding question. Is AI more likely to solve problems or create them? Working in groups, agree on a statement and present it in class.

**b** Interpret the two microfictions below. What philosophical questions do they raise about AI and the relationship between humans and machines?

'Are you conscious?' he asked the robot.
'Nod if you have free will.'
The robot nodded.
'Did you follow my orders, or not?'
The robot nodded.

*31/10/2016 18:13:43*

'I think,' said the machine.
'That is good.'
'Therefore I am.'
'Well reasoned.'
'I did not reason.'
'No?'
'I looked that up on the internet.'

*30/11/2016 22:38:41*

Annotations
**conscious** aware of yourself
**reason** *(v)* think logically

From: O. Westin, Micro Science Fiction, *2020*

## Text 6

# R'ha    Kaleb Lechowski

R'ha *is a science fiction short film written, directed and animated by Kaleb Lechowski, who was 23 at the time. Released in 2013, the film was enthusiastically received and even caught the attention of Hollywood producers.*

▶ SF 41: Analysing films, series and videos, p. 399

• Work in pairs. The stills below show the two antagonists from the film you are about to watch: C180–RG (left) and a nameless member of the R'ha, an army of elite warriors. In one scene, the R'ha tells C180–RG: 'I will destroy you and all of your kind.' Speculate about what has brought them together and what their conflict might be about.    ▶ Language help, p. 270

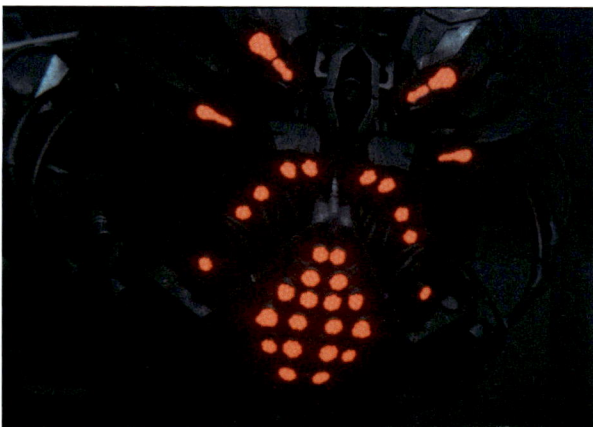

*'I will destroy you and all of your kind.'*

Annotations
**initialize sth.** start sth.
**protocol** (here) procedure
**severe** serious
**rendezvous** meeting
**ravage** destroy
**restrain sth.** keep sth. under control

Kaleb Lechowski, the creator of *R'ha*

► Check

► Support, p. 323
► SF 41: Analysing films, series and videos, p. 399
► Getting started
► WOB: pp. 82–84

**Language help**

agree/refuse to cooperate • an unexpected/chance encounter • a bitter/violent/ hostile encounter • a serious/unresolved conflict • deal with / handle / end a conflict • be in conflict with each other • have similar/opposing goals

### Comprehension

**1**  Viewing  Watch the short film, then give your first reactions to it. Which of your previous ideas came closest to the story?

**2**  Listening  Choose the correct option to complete each sentence.

**1**  The R'ha is ...
  **a**  a captured alien pilot.
  **b**  an intelligent machine.
  **c**  a hostile cyborg.

**2**  C180-RG is ...
  **a**  an alien organism.
  **b**  a superintelligent machine.
  **c**  an inorganic life form.

**3**  C180-RG wants to know ...
  **a**  where the R'ha comes from.
  **b**  where the rest of the R'ha's species meet.
  **c**  what the R'ha's mission is.

**4**  The Motivation Protocol is another name for ...
  **a**  a computer manual.
  **b**  an evacuation code.
  **c**  procedures for torture.

**5**  The R'ha was captured in the war between ...
  **a**  two alien species.
  **b**  an alien species and intelligent machines.
  **c**  hostile machines and evil aliens.

**6**  The R'ha escapes because ...
  **a**  he played a trick on C180-RG.
  **b**  C180-RG programmed his escape.
  **c**  C180-RG takes pity on him.

### Analysis

**3**  Viewing  Split up in groups and watch the film again. Each group focuses on one of the following elements: animation techniques, sound or colour and examines how their element contributes to creating the alien world. Discuss your observations in your group, then present your ideas in class.

### Language awareness

**4  a**  Examine the way the two antagonists interact and the language they use in the extract below.

**C180-RG:**    The limitations that my kind experience are rendered by illogical creatures who can control and restrain our intelligence and power. Our sole priority is to obtain our independence through your extinction.

**The R'ha:**    Madness.

| C180-RG: | By definition, I cannot be illogical. |
| The R'ha: | Yet you are insane! *(grunts)* |
| C180-RG: | Insanity is a neurologic dysfunction. I don't suffer such organic weaknesses. |

**Language help**

use simple/complex/emotional words • employ long/short sentences • use fragmentary language • include sensory details / sound devices

**b** Continue the dialogue by imitating the two speaking styles. Write at least two utterances for each character.

**Beyond the text**

**5** Intercultural competence | Interpret the conflict between the alien lifeform and the smart machine in *R'ha*. What can you conclude about the role that values play in intercultural communication?

▶ SF 12: Communicating across cultures, p. 359

---

**Text 7**

## After the storm    Jesmyn Ward

• Extreme weather events have been increasing in recent decades due to climate change. With a partner, talk about such weather events that you may have experienced or heard about. Describe what happened and how it made you feel.

▶ More info
▶ 'Climate change goes Hollywood', p. 345

▶ Getting started

**Language help**

drought • wildfire • lose your belongings • feel lost/afraid/hopeless • enormous/ overwhelming/devastating impact • under water • flooded • destroyed • charred • burnt to the ground • uninhabitable • look for shelter • call for help • save yourself

*Jesmyn Ward's novel* Salvage the Bones *(2011) follows an African American working-class family in southern Mississippi during the time of Hurricane Katrina (▶ Info box on p. 272). The family consists of 15-year-old Esch (the narrator), her brothers Randall, Skeetah and Junior, and her father. When Katrina hits, they narrowly escape from the floods surrounding their house. Later they return to what is left of their home.*

[...] When the water left, the front part of Daddy's truck was sitting on top of the smashed gas tank. The lower half was on the ground. All the water that had been in the car was out, and it left a muddy slime on the windows. The yard was one big puddle that we waded, so icy at our ankles, the first cold water we'd felt since the
5 March rains, to the back door of the house, which was blasted open. The screen door was gone. The inside of the house was wet and muddy as Daddy's truck. The food we'd gotten had been washed from the shelves, and we hunted for it like we did for eggs, finding some silver cans of peas. We found Top Ramen, still sealed, in the sofa. We put them in our shirts. My hands were pink with Skeetah's blood from
10 hugging him earlier. I washed them in a puddle in the living room.

Annotation
8 **Top Ramen**   brand of ready to cook noodles

Annotations

14 **dazed** confused or unable to think clearly, esp. as a result of an injury or from shock

27 **gash** *(n)* cut, wound

34 **magnolia** type of tree with beautiful flowers

35 **ditch** *(n)* long narrow channel cut into the ground at the side of a road or field

37 **shingle** small flat piece of wood used to cover the roof or wall of a building

**Info**

When **Hurricane Katrina** hit the southeastern United States in late August, 2005, it claimed more than 1,800 lives, making it one of the severest natural disasters in US history. On 29 August, the storm made landfall as a Category 4 hurricane in Louisiana near New Orleans. It then continued along the Mississippi Sound, where it slammed into coastal cities with a surge more than 8 metres high and destroyed thousands of homes. Many people without cars or not enough money to pay for public transport remained in the area at risk. Levees and flood walls having failed, people tried to escape from their flooded houses and find help. Some people could only be rescued several days after the storm had hit.

'We can't stay here. We need shelter.' Randall grimaced.

'Your hand, and the water ...' Randall trailed off. 'Who knows what the water had in it.'

Daddy shook his head, his lips weak as a baby's. He looked dazed. He stared at his
15  truck, the ruined house, the yard invisible under the trees and the storm's deposits.

'Where,' he said, and it was a statement with no answer.

'By Big Henry,' Randall said.

Junior was on Randall's back, his eyes finally uncovered and open. He looked drunk.

20  'What about Skeet?' I asked.

'He'll find us,' Randall said. 'Daddy?' He raised an arm to Daddy, flicked his head towards the road.

'Yeah.' Daddy cleared his throat.

'We can fix it,' Randall said.

25  Daddy looked down at the ground, shrugged. He glanced at me and shame filtered across his face like a spider, sideways, fast, and then he looked past the house to the road and started walking slowly, uneven, limping. There was a gash in the back of his leg, bleeding through his pants.

We picked our way round the fallen, ripped trees, to the road. We were barefoot,
30  and the asphalt was warm. We hadn't had time to find our shoes before the hand of the flood pushed into the living room. The storm had plucked the trees like grass and scattered them. We knew where the road was by the feel of the stones wearing through the blacktop under our feet; the trees I had known, the oaks in the bend, the stand of pines on the long stretch, the magnolia at the four-way, were all bro-
35  ken, all crumbled. The sound of the water running in the ditches like rapids escorted us down the road, into the heart of Bois Sauvage.

The first house we saw was Javon's, the shingles of his roof scraped off, the top bald; the house was dark and looked empty until we saw someone who must have been Javon, light as Manny, standing in front of the pile of wood that must have
40  been the carport, lighting a lighter: a flicker of warmth in the cold air left by the storm. At the next nearest house, when the neighborhood started to cluster more closely together, we saw what others had suffered: every house had faced the hurricane, and every house had lost. Franco and his mother and father stood out in the yard looking at each other and the smashed landscape around them, dazed. Half of
45  their roof was gone. Christophe and Joshua's porch was missing, and part of their roof. A tree had smashed into Mudda Ma'am and Tilda's house. And just as the houses clustered, there were people in the street, barefoot, half naked, walking around felled trees, crumpled trampolines, talking with each other, shaking their heads, repeating one word over and over again: *alive, alive, alive, alive.* Big Henry
50  and Marquise were standing in front of Big Henry's house, which was missing a piece of its roof, like all the others, and was encircled by six of the trees that had stood in the yard but that now fenced the house in like a green gate.

'It's a miracle,' Big Henry said. 'All the trees fell away from the house.'

'We was just about to walk up there and see about y'all,' Marquise said.

55 Big Henry nodded, swung the machete he had in his hand, the blade dark and sharp.

'In case we had to cut through to get to y'all,' Marquise explained.

'Where's Skeet?' Big Henry asked.

'Looking,' Randall said, hoisting Junior farther up on his back.

60 'For what?' Marquise asked.

'The water took China,' I said.

'Water?' Big Henry asked, his voice high at the end, almost cracking.

'From the creek that feeds the pit,' Randall said. 'The house flooded through. We had to swim to the old house, wait out the storm in the attic.'

65 I wanted to say: We almost drowned. We had to bust out of the attic. We lost the puppies and China.

'We need a place to stay,' I said.

'It's just me and my mama,' Big Henry said. 'Plenty of room. Come on.' He flicked the machete blade, threw it to Marquise, who caught the handle and almost 70 dropped it.

'You all right, Mr Claude?' Big Henry asked Daddy.

Every line of Daddy's face, his shoulders, his neck, his collarbone, the ends of his arms, seemed to be caught in a net dragging the ground.

'Yeah,' Daddy said. 'I just need to sit for a while. My hand.'

75 He stopped short. Big Henry nodded, placed one of those big careful hands on Daddy's back, and escorted us through the milling crowd, the crumbled trees, the power lines tangled like abandoned fishing line, to his home. He looked at me over his shoulder, and the glance was so soft, so tentative and tender, I wanted to finish my story. I wanted to say, *I'm pregnant*. But I didn't. [...]

*From:* Salvage the Bones, *London, 2011*

**Annotations**
55 **machete** [məˈʃeti] broad heavy knife
61 **China** name of Skeetah's dog
72 **collarbone** *Schlüsselbein*
76 **mill** *(v)* (esp. of a group of people) walk around aimlessly
78 **tentative** timid, hesitant

### Comprehension

1 Outline what happened to the *narrator and her family after the hurricane.

2 Describe the effect Hurricane Katrina had on Esch's home and neighbourhood.

### Analysis

3 Analyse the way the author conveys the *protagonists' feelings and the emotional impact this has on the reader.

► Support, p. 323

**Language awareness**

▶ Getting started

**4 a** Find examples of *informal style in the text and explain its use in the novel.
**b** Rephrase two sentences in a more *formal style and compare the two versions.

**Beyond the text**

▶ SF 38: Creative writing, p. 395

**5** Writing In the evening, when Esch and her family have settled in Big Henry's house, Esch reflects on the day and on her inability to tell anybody about her pregnancy. Write her interior monologue.

OH, BABY, I DON'T THINK WE'RE GONNA MAKE IT.

*From: Don Brown,* Drowned City, *2015*

▶ SF 26: Analysing graphic novels, p. 378

▶ More language

**6 Art in Context** Look at the picture above from Don Brown's graphic novel about Hurricane Katrina.
**a** Describe the picture from the graphic novel and your first reactions to it.
**b** The picture presents different aspects of the storm:
• the wind's strength (cf. bending trees and flying roofs)
• the damage done (cf. floating cars, houses under water)
• a person's fear that they are not going to make it
• the general atmosphere caused by the storm (cf. the greyish colours)
• the storm's magnitude (cf. the bird's eye perspective)
Find passages in the novel extract that also cover the aspects from above. Are they better represented by the picture or the novel excerpt? Explain your choice.

# Words revisited

▶ SF 6: Essentials: language and study skills, p. 354

## 1 Clustering

**a** Work with a partner. Look at your *cluster about science and technology (cf. 'Words in Context', p. 252) and take turns explaining what connects the ideas in the cluster with the texts you have already dealt with in this chapter.

**b** Scan your notes from class and add words and phrases to your cluster.

**c** Do you personally work with clusters or do you use other strategies for increasing your vocabulary? Discuss with a partner.

## Language awareness

*English has become the common language of science. If you plan to go into science after school, it is likely you will be required to give talks and write papers in English. This language lab will acquaint you with some of the most important features of scientific English.*

## 2 The standardized nature of scientific English

*Scientific English is a highly standardized brand of English that enables scientists from around the world to share their ideas with each other in a straightforward manner, e.g. in scientific research papers and talks.*

**a** Work with a partner. Use the *chunks in the box to describe 'the scientific method', i.e. the process normally followed by scientists when conducting research. Start like this: *The first thing a scientist does when beginning a new study is to …* The diagram below will help you.

**b** Work with a partner. Use your sentences from **a** and your knowledge about the scientific method to discuss the importance of *integrity, fairness* and *clarity* in scientific research.

**c** Unlike everyday English, which may be highly original, creative, flowery and emotional, scientific English tends to be more neutral in style. Work with a partner and take turns completing the sentences below:

Result · Observation

**THE SCIENTIFIC METHOD**

Conclusion · Question

Experiment · Hypothesis

agree with predictions
apply scepticism to sth.
ask a question
be relevant/irrelevant
be reliable/unreliable
be reproducible
be significant/insignificant
be valid/invalid
carry out an experiment
collect data
conduct a study
conflict with predictions
do background research
draw a conclusion
formulate a hypothesis
identify a possible outcome of sth.
interpret data
make an observation
make assumptions
monitor a process
refine a research question
seek answers to a question
support sth. by evidence
test a hypothesis

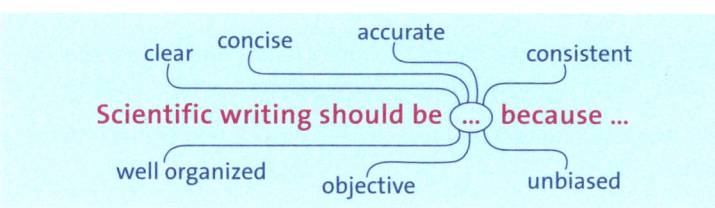

clear · concise · accurate · consistent
Scientific writing should be … because …
well organized · objective · unbiased

▶ SF 8: Working with
dictionaries, p. 355

▶ SF 9: Learning new
words, p. 357

**Info**

**Some types of
dictionaries:**
- monolingual
dictionary
- bilingual dictionary
- usage dictionary
- pronunciation
dictionary
- dialect dictionary
- etymological
dictionary
- thesaurus

### 3   The diversified nature of scientific English

*Scientific English is also highly diversified. Depending on the field of research,
scientists may use a vast amount of specialized vocabulary to communicate ideas
accurately and unambiguously. Reading scientific papers can therefore be quite
demanding for readers unfamiliar with these words. Using a dictionary will help
you overcome these difficulties.*

a   Read the info box on the left, then decide what kind of dictionary might help
you with tasks **b** and **c**.

b   Look at the terms for scientific occupations in the box to
the right and …
- explain what each scientist's job is,
- give the name of the scientific field in which they work,
- find more words belonging to the same *word family.

anthropologist
etymologist
herpetologist
meteorologist
statistician

c   Many scientific words have roots in Greek, Latin or other
languages. Trace the origins of the words from **b**.

## Practice

*You will now read and analyse an example of scientific writing by Jennifer A. Doudna
and Emmanuelle Charpentier, the two scientists whose work on gene editing using
Crispr technology (▶ Text 3, p. 261) earned them the Nobel prize in chemistry in 2020.*

**4**   Define the following key terms from the text: 'DNA double helix' • 'genome' •
'nuclease'. Then read the passage below.

**5**   Now read the text and find examples of a) technical terms, b) nouns and gerunds
and c) the passive voice. Explain how each of the features contributes to making
the passage concise, accurate and objective – but also challenging to read.

**Annotations**
4   **elusive**   difficult to
achieve or find
9   **validation**   proof that
sth. is correct

> Technologies for making and manipulating DNA have enabled advances
> in biology ever since the discovery of the DNA double helix. But introduc-
> ing site-specific modifications in the genomes of cells and organisms re-
> mained elusive. Early approaches relied on the principle of site-specific
> 5   recognition of DNA sequences by oligonucleotides, small molecules, or
> self-splicing introns. More recently, the site-directed zinc finger nucleas-
> es (ZFNs) and TAL effector nucleases (TALENs) using the principles of
> DNA-protein recognition were developed. However, difficulties of pro-
> tein design, synthesis, and validation remained a barrier to widespread
> 10   adoption of these engineered nucleases for routine use.
>
> *From: 'The new frontier of genome engineering with CRISPR-Cas9', Science, 2014*

▶ Getting started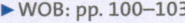

**6**   **You choose**   **Writing**   Choose one of the topics below and write a concise
scientific text. Avoid vague words (e.g. *thing*, *do*) and emotional language.

a   Write a text explaining the process
of photosynthesis.

b   Write a text explaining the water
cycle.

▶ WOB: pp. 100–103

# Fighting climate change

- In the fight against climate change, international agreements have been signed in recent years. Name some and say what they involve.

*The video you'll be watching deals with the development of global awareness of climate change up to the Paris Agreement in 2015 (▶ Info box, p. 278).*

▶ 'Climate change goes Hollywood', p. 345

**Comprehension**

▶ SF 40: Listening/Viewing for gist and detail, p. 399

**1** [Viewing] Read through the task below. Then watch the video and choose the right answer to each of the questions.

▶ Check

**1** The overall thesis formulated in the introductory minutes of the video:
  **a** Politicians have been increasingly aware of climate change for over 30 years and yet no effective measures have been taken to fight it.
  **b** In 2019, climate activists took to the streets and demanded that scientists listen to politicians.
  **c** Climate scientist James Hansen was the first person to acknowledge climate change and the greenhouse effect in 1988.

**2** Characteristics of the developments that led to the Kyoto Protocol in 1997:
  **a** an era of accelerated global communication and cooperation
  **b** a competition among nations to find the best solutions
  **c** an immediate translation of awareness into action

**3** Why the Kyoto Protocol is not considered successful:
  **a** Developing countries were hit hardest by its constraints.
  **b** The demands made were not specific enough.
  **c** The UN was not able to enforce the protocol.

**4** China's current position on climate action:
  **a** a feeling of responsibility for contributing to the world's emissions
  **b** a complete denial of man-made climate change
  **c** the hope to profit from the development of renewable energy technologies

▶ WOB: pp. 78–81

**Analysis**

▶ Support, p. 323

**2** [Viewing] Examine the visuals and music used in the video. Analyse to what extent they support the voiceover and contribute to its general meaning.

▶ SF 41: Analysing films and videos, p. 399
▶ WOB: pp. 82–84

**3** [Speaking] Your class is creating a podcast on the development of climate change policies. You're supposed to contribute a section on the Paris Agreement (cf. also info box p. 278). Prepare and record your podcast.

**Info**

On 12 December 2015, 196 countries signed a legally binding international treaty on climate change, which is referred to as the **Paris Agreement**. The aim is for signatory countries to cooperate in environmental matters and, most importantly, to limit global warming to well below 2°C compared to preindustrial levels. The

5  treaty is a sign that political leaders have realized the importance of working together when our planet is faced with severe and irreversible damage.

Participating countries aim to reach a peak in global greenhouse gas emissions as soon as possible in order to achieve a climate neutral world by 2050. According to experts, this is the only way to stop global warming in time to prevent a planetary

10  catastrophe. The Paris Agreement is therefore considered a landmark in the fight against climate change. For the first time, a binding agreement attempts to engage all nations in a common effort to combat climate change and find innovative solutions for adapting to the effects of global warming.

However, this requires massive economic and social transformation based on the

15  best available science in order to implement the aims of the Paris Agreement and embed them in the political agendas of the different countries. In 2020, countries submitted their plans for climate action known as nationally determined contributions (NDCs). The EU submitted a common NDC. In these NDCs, each country commits to actions it will undertake to reduce its greenhouse gas emissions, as well

20  as actions to adapt and increase resilience to the impact of rising temperatures.

Hopefully an international treaty such as this will put more pressure on each individual nation to keep its promises when it comes to fighting climate change. One of its positive effects is that the treaty has raised environmental awareness and generated a huge amount of publicity about environmentalism, a topic that

25  is still too often ignored. People have come to realize that climate change action needs to be massively increased to achieve the goals of the Paris Agreement.

The agreement's entry into force has already sparked low-carbon solutions and new markets. More and more countries, regions, cities and companies are establishing carbon neutrality targets and zero-carbon solutions are becoming

30  competitive across economic sectors. It is estimated that, by 2030, zero-carbon solutions could be competitive in sectors that are the source of over 70% of global emissions.

But there have also been drawbacks in the history of the treaty, as, for instance, in 2020 when the USA under President Donald Trump decided to withdraw from it.

35  In 2021, when President Biden took office, the USA rejoined.

1   List the aims that different countries set themselves under the Paris Agreement.

Advanced

# Scientists warn of a global climate emergency

Phoebe Weston

- Explain the word *emergency*. What do you associate with it?

*Now read the following text about different aspects of a global climate emergency.*

The planet is facing a 'ghastly future of mass extinction, declining health and climate-disruption upheavals' that threaten human survival because of ignorance and inaction, according to an international group of scientists, who warn people still haven't grasped the urgency of the biodiversity and climate crises.

5 The 17 experts, including Prof Paul Ehrlich from Stanford University, author of *The Population Bomb*, and scientists from Mexico, Australia and the US, say the planet is in a much worse state than most people – even scientists – understood.

'The scale of the threats to the biosphere and all its lifeforms – including humanity – is in fact so great that it is difficult to grasp for even well-informed experts,'
10 they write in a report in *Frontiers in Conservation Science* which references more than 150 studies detailing the world's major environmental challenges.

The delay between destruction of the natural world and the impacts of these actions means people do not recognise how vast the problem is, the paper argues. '[The] mainstream is having difficulty grasping the magnitude of this loss, despite
15 the steady erosion of the fabric of human civilisation.'

The report warns that climate-induced mass migrations, more pandemics and conflicts over resources will be inevitable unless urgent action is taken.

'Ours is not a call to surrender – we aim to provide leaders with a realistic "cold shower" of the state of the planet that is essential for planning to avoid a ghastly
20 future,' it adds.

Dealing with the enormity of the problem requires far-reaching changes to global capitalism, education and equality, the paper says. These include abolishing the idea of perpetual economic growth, properly pricing environmental externalities, stopping the use of fossil fuels, reining in corporate lobbying, and empowering
25 women, the researchers argue.

The report comes months after the world failed to meet a single UN Aichi biodiversity target, created to stem the destruction of the natural world, the second consecutive time governments have failed to meet their 10-year biodiversity goals. This week a coalition of more than 50 countries pledged to protect almost a third of the
30 planet by 2030.

An estimated one million species are at risk of extinction, many within decades, according to a recent UN report. [...]

In *The Population Bomb*, published in 1968, Ehrlich warned of imminent population explosion and hundreds of millions of people starving to death. Although he
35 has acknowledged some timings were wrong, he has said he stands by its fundamental message that population growth and high levels of consumption by wealthy nations is driving destruction.

Annotations
1 **ghastly** very frightening and threatening
2 **climate disruption upheaval** radical change to human society, our way of life and the natural world caused by profound changes to the climate
4 **grasp sth.** understand sth.
4 **urgency** need to be dealt with quickly
8 **scale** size
12 **delay** period of time between one thing and another
13 **vast** extremely big
14 **magnitude** extreme size
15 **fabric** structure that allows sth. to function properly
18 **surrender** *(v)* admit defeat and stop fighting against sb./sth.
23 **perpetual** never-ending
23 **externalities** effects of production and consumption
24 **rein in sth.** keep sth. under control
26 **Aichi biodiversity target** targets for the protection of biodiversity agreed upon in 2010 at a conference in Aichi, Japan
27 **stem sth.** stop sth.
27 **the second consecutive time** the second time in a row
29 **pledge sth.** formally promise sth.
33 **imminent** likely to happen very soon

Annotations

39 **equity** situation in which all people are treated in a fair manner
40 **junk** *(infml)* worthless stuff
41 **soil degradation** lessening of the quality of the uppermost layer of the earth, on which plants grow
45 **scarce** rare
48 **gravity** seriousness
54 **stark** marked

He told the Guardian: 'Growthmania is the fatal disease of civilisation – it must be replaced by campaigns that make equity and well-being society's goals – not con-
40 suming more junk.'

Large populations and their continued growth drive soil degradation and biodiversity loss, the new paper warns. 'More people means that more synthetic compounds and dangerous throwaway plastics are manufactured, many of which add to the growing toxification of the Earth. It also increases the chances of pandemics
45 that fuel ever-more desperate hunts for scarce resources.'

The effects of the climate emergency are more evident than biodiversity loss, but still, society is failing to cut emissions, the paper argues. If people understood the magnitude of the crises, changes in politics and policies could match the gravity of the threat.

'Our main point is that once you realise the scale and imminence of the problem,
50 it becomes clear that we need much more than individual actions like using less plastic, eating less meat, or flying less. Our point is that we need big systematic changes and fast,' Professor Daniel Blumstein from the University of California Los Angeles, who helped write the paper, told the Guardian. [...]

The report follows years of stark warnings about the state of the planet from the
55 world's leading scientists, including a statement by 11,000 scientists in 2019 that people will face 'untold suffering due to the climate crisis' unless major changes are made. [...] Prof Tom Oliver, an ecologist at the University of Reading, who was not involved in the report, said it was a frightening but credible summary of the grave threats society faces under a 'business as usual' scenario. 'Scientists now
60 need to go beyond simply documenting environmental decline, and instead find the most effective ways to catalyse action,' he said.

Prof Rob Brooker, head of ecological sciences at the James Hutton Institute, who was not involved in the study, said it clearly emphasised the pressing nature of the challenges.

65 'We certainly should not be in any doubt about the huge scale of the challenges we are facing and the changes we will need to make to deal with them,' he said.

*From: 'Top scientists warn of "ghastly future of mass extinction" and climate disruption',*
*theguardian.com, 13 January 2021*

### Comprehension

**1** Make notes on what the text says about: **1** factors that led to the climate emergency in the first place, **2** the state of the world that justifies the label of a climate emergency, **3** measures that should be taken to counteract the climate emergency.

### Analysis

**2** Work on either **a** or **b**.

**a** Analyse the structure of the text. It may help if you add a headline to each part you've identified.

**b** Challenge The text does not follow the conventional structure of an argumentative text. Analyse how it manages to express an opinion.

Advanced

## Language awareness

**3  a**  The choice of words used by the scientists quoted in the article stresses their idea of an emergency. Identify these words.

**b**  Choose three examples from task **a** and rephrase them using a more matter-of-fact tone.

## Beyond the text

**4**  Think back to your definitions of and associations with *emergency*. Discuss whether this term is justified with respect to the world's climate.

**5**  Writing  Referring to Blumstein's view that individual actions are not enough to fight climate change (cf. ll. 50f.), a friend of yours announces on his blog that he finds it worthless to be environmentally responsible. Think back on your ideas from the guiding question, then write a passionate reply to your friend's post, arguing either for or against what he wrote. Make use of the strategies from task **3**.

## Chapter task

▶ Getting started

*After exploring a variety of topics to do with science, technology and the environment, you now have the opportunity to present a scientific innovation of your choice in a science slam.*

### What is a science slam?

A science slam is a short talk in which a scientific topic, project or innovation is presented to an audience in an entertaining, informative and concise way. A slam can be creative and interactive, and slammers may use props, visuals and slides to make their talk appealing and memorable to the audience.

- Choose one of the fields you dealt with in this chapter (e.g. biotechnology, neuroscience, artificial intelligence or climate change) and research a scientific innovation in this field that you believe will profoundly transform people's lives in the future in positive or negative ways.

- Present your scientific innovation in a three-minute science slam using suitable (digital) tools. Convince your audience of the huge impact it will have on their lives.

▶ SF 13: Doing research, p. 360

▶ SF 43: Giving a presentation, p. 405

## Chapter 10

# Shakespeare – Not of an Age, But for All Time

*In many ways, Shakespeare's most famous *characters are still our contemporaries. Even people who have never read one of his plays know their names, their most famous *lines and something about the plays they appear in.*

**Jules C.**

party girl • secret wedding planner • tester of knock-out potion • Snow White impersonator

 Verona

 la_piccola@famiglia_capulet.

**Nørdman**

studiosus philosophiae • theatre buff • overthinker • ghost whisperer • prince • serial monologist

 Elsinore

 H31@kronborg.castle.

---

**1 a** Do some research on the *protagonists of the following plays by Shakespeare: *Hamlet* • *King Lear* • *Romeo and Juliet* • *Macbeth* • *Othello*.

**b** Read the social media profiles above carefully and state which Shakespeare *character they refer to. (Refer back to the plays mentioned in task **a**.)

**c** You will probably have heard of some of the characters you identified in task **b**. Discuss what could be reasons that these characters are still widely known after more than 400 years.

**d** Choose one of the social media profiles and use it as a starting point to write a self-portrait of about 100 words about the character.

**2** From the keywords in the Chapter map, choose five. For each of the chosen words write one sentence about
- what it might tell you about this chapter
- how it relates to the guiding question.

## Cruella MacThane

go-getter girl • supportive wife •
dearest partner of greatness • sleepwalker •
keeping up with the Royal Scots

📍 Dunsinane, Scotland

✉ cruella@dunsinane.castle. ▓▓▓▓

## Fortune's Fool

lovesick • party crasher • Cupid's
target • balcony enthusiast •
Mercutio's bro • hopeless romantic

📍 Verona

✉ figlio@della_casa_montague.
▓▓▓▓

## MacThane

battle axe • Highlander • kilt wearer •
star warrior • dearest partner in
greatness • follower of the dark arts

📍 Dunsinane, Scotland

✉ fergus@dunsinane.castle. ▓▓▓▓

## ❯ Chapter map

adaptations

language

immortal
characters

hate

love

Chapter task:
a Shakespeare
adaptation ✔

Is Shakespeare still relevant today?

sonnets

theatre

power

Shakespeare's world

# The Shakespeare phenomenon

▶ 'How Shakespeare revolutionized German literature', p. 345

▶ More language

▶ More info

### New ideas enter the stage

In the 16th and 17th centuries, Renaissance ideas coming from Italy widened people's intellectual horizons and challenged the traditional beliefs of the Middle Ages. Inventions and discoveries were made, explorers travelled the world and global trade ex-
5  panded. The reawakened interest in the history, literature and mythology of Greek and Roman antiquity had a huge impact on Elizabethan society and culture. Earlier, mystery plays based on Bible stories had been performed by townspeople, or touring theatre companies had staged morality plays dealing with human virtues or sins. During Shakespeare's lifetime (1564–1616), drama developed faster than ever before. In
10  London, theatres became thriving businesses, several new buildings were erected, and thousands of spectators regularly flocked to see the performances. Queen Elizabeth I (ruling 1558–1603) and her successor, James I (ruling 1603–1625), loved the theatre and supported several companies financially, of which Shakespeare's troupe became the leading company. New comedies, tragedies and history plays were
15  written by Shakespeare and other *dramatists, such as Christopher Marlowe (1564–1593) or Thomas Kyd (1558–1594). The *plots of these plays were often not original inventions but borrowed from traditional stories or ancient sources and adapted by *playwrights.

### The unknown Shakespeare

20  William Shakespeare, or the Bard of Avon, is widely regarded as the greatest writer in the English language. Little is known about the man, however. He was born in Stratford-up-on-Avon, to where he also retired a wealthy man and died in 1616. He spent most of his professional life in London as an actor, writer of plays and co-owner of his playing company. Since very little documentary evidence of his private life survives, there has been
25  much speculation about his education, his beliefs and personal relationships, and even if he really wrote his plays. What endures of Shakespeare are not the facts of his life but his outstanding works, which are now an important part of world literature.

### Shakespeare lives on

By the end of the 20th century, Shakespeare had become the most performed drama-
30  tist in the world. Many lines from his plays and poems are still widely known today, even if people are not always aware of where they come from. Some theatre companies have devoted their repertoire almost entirely to his plays and international Shakespeare festivals are held annually. The ongoing influence of his works is also shown by the many adaptations and spin-offs they have inspired in literature, films,
35  music, the fine arts and pop culture down through the years. In every generation, scholars and literary critics have continued to analyse Shakespeare's texts and find new interpretations. Audiences and readers continue to relate to his *characters and their fates, demonstrating their timeless and universal nature. Some have become iconic, like Hamlet, whose line 'To be or not to be, that is the question' must be the
40  most quoted line of any play. The tragic fate of Shakespeare's famous lovers, Romeo and Juliet, describes the outcome of a doomed love story and Macbeth or Richard III embody the ambitious tragic hero or power-hungry villain. The Bard also contributed a great number of new words and memorable expressions to the English language that are still in use today: *the naked truth, a shooting star* and *the rest is silence* are just
45  three examples. Shakespeare's continuing influence on our modern era makes him a genius well worth studying.

# 1 Main ideas

**a** Summarize the text in three sentences – one per paragraph.
**b** Complete the sentences:
  **1** With the help of royal support and a loyal audience, Shakespeare's troupe ...
  **2** What we know for certain about Shakespeare is ...
  **3** Without Shakespeare, we wouldn't have ...

# 2 Reflect

**a** Find three phrases or concepts in the text that are new to you, two that you found interesting and one that you will always connect with Shakespeare.
**b** Note down explanations of these phrases and concepts in your own words. Use a dictionary if necessary.
**c** In a group, present your explanations. The others guess which phrase you are referring to. Take turns. Add at least one phrase and its explanation from your partners to your list.

# 3 Word families

A good way to organize useful vocabulary is to create word families.
**a** Start a word family based on *write* including its phrasal verbs as well.
**b** Find three more words from the text and create word families with them.
**c** Discuss with a partner whether you consider word families a useful strategy to increase your vocabulary or not.
**d** How helpful do you find word families for learning words?

# 4 Chunk it!

**a** Replace the gaps in the following *chunks by verbs. You can check in the text for help, but also add other verbs. If you are not sure, use a dictionary. What kind of dictionary would you choose and why?
  **1** '... people's intellectual horizons'
  **2** '... traditional beliefs'
  **3** '... inventions and discoveries'
  **4** '... a thriving business'
  **5** '... adaptations and spin-offs'
  **6** '... words and expressions to the English language'

**b** Compare your chunks with a partner and add new ones to your list.

► Getting started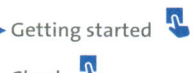

► Check

# 5 Shakespeare wants you for drama

Inspired by a stimulating theatrical performance, you and your partner want to start an amateur theatre group at your school to stage Shakespeare plays in English.

You choose  Work on either task **a** or **b**. Use expressions from the text.
**a** Create a poster inviting other student theatre enthusiasts to join your ensemble.
**b** Speaking  Prepare an inspiring two-minute *pitch for your project. Present your talk to the class.

► SF 44: Preparing and giving a speech, p. 408

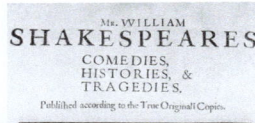

Title page to the
*First Folio*

Annotations

1 **and tomorrow** or the next day
2 **in this petty pace** slowly
3 **to the last syllable of recorded time** until the end of time
4 **our yesterdays** the days gone by, the past
4 **light** *(v)* show
5 **brief** short
6 **walking shadow** actor, illusion
6 **poor** bad
7 **strut** *(v)* walk proudly
7 **fret** *(v)* worry
7 **his hour** when he is performing
9 **sound and fury** noise and anger
10 **signify** mean

# Understanding Shakespeare's language

- Explain the *images Shakespeare uses in the following sentences to describe the *characters' feelings.
  1 'Why, what's the matter, that you have such a February face, so full of frost, of storm, and cloudiness?' (*Much Ado About Nothing,* Act V, scene 4)
  2 'How sharper than a serpent's tooth it is to have a thankless child.' (*King Lear,* Act I, scene 4)

**Info**

Originally, **Shakespeare's plays** were not written for publication but only as *scripts for performances on stage. In 1623, after Shakespeare's death, his actor friends published most of his plays in the *First Folio* edition and divided them into three categories: comedies, tragedies and history plays.

5 **Tragedies** focus on a single high-ranking *character, the tragic hero, who contributes to or is driven to his death by his own weakness in character (tragic flaw) in the final *act, a fate which appeals to the audience's sympathy or pity. Usually, not only the *protagonist's own life but the whole state is thrown into disorder, e.g. by the murder of a king. Order must then be restored, e.g. by the

10 installation of the rightful heir to the throne.

*This short passage from Shakespeare's tragedy* Macbeth, *in which the *protagonist reacts to the news of his wife's death, gives an impression of the type of *verse that is typical of Shakespeare's plays.*

MACBETH    Tomorrow, and tomorrow, and tomorrow,
           Creeps in this petty pace from day to day
           To the last syllable of recorded time,
           And all our yesterdays have lighted fools
5      The way to dusty death. Out, out, brief candle!
           Life's but a walking shadow, a poor player
           That struts and frets his hour upon the stage
           And then is heard no more: it is a tale
           Told by an idiot, full of sound and fury,
10     Signifying nothing.

*From:* Macbeth, *Act V, scene 5*

**Comprehension**

1 Rephrase what Macbeth says using modern English prose.

Advanced

**Analysis**

2 Analyse the *imagery used in this speech and examine its effect on the reader.

#### Language awareness

**Info**

Shakespeare writes mostly in **blank verse,** i.e. regular *metrical but unrhymed lines. The *rhythm is usually **iambic** [aɪˈæmbɪk] **pentameter,** i.e. ten syllables with five stressed syllables to a line with the stress on <u>dum</u>: di <u>dum</u>, di <u>dum</u>, di <u>dum</u>, di <u>dum</u>, di <u>dum</u>. When using prose, Shakespeare often changes the *intonation or
5   pronunciation of words (e.g. stressing the ending *-èd*) to make it more suitable to *verse.

To avoid monotony, Shakespeare varies his meter by using eleven syllables or by running one line into the next ('enjambement' or 'run-on line'); he creates pauses in the middle of a line or divides a line between two speakers. The meter also
10   varies when *characters are experiencing strong emotions. Occasionally, he uses meters of four, six or eight beats, e.g. for songs or the magic spells of the three witches in *Macbeth:*

> 'Double, double, toil and trouble,
> Fire burn and cauldron bubble.' (IV, 1)

15   To express a character's emotions, often at the end of a *scene, Shakespeare uses rhyming *couplets, e.g. when Hamlet (in the play that bears his name) feels uneasy about having to avenge his father's death:

> 'The time is out of joint: O cursèd spite,
> That ever I was born to set it right.' (I, 5)

**1**   With a partner, practise reading some verses from **Text 1** or **Text 4** aloud. Discuss which patterns described above you noticed in the verses.

**3**   **a**   First, read out the prose version that you wrote in task **1**; then, read Shakespeare's verses aloud applying the information about the iambic pentameter from the info box.

    **b**   Compare the effect of the two versions on the listeners. Also explain what difference it makes to the speaker, e.g. if they have to learn the text by heart.

#### Beyond the text

**4**   Shakespeare has contributed numerous words and phrases to the English language.

    **a**   Choose one of the phrases below and explain what it means. You may look it up online if you need help.
- 'What's done is done' (*Macbeth,* Act III, scene 2)
- 'All that glisters is not gold' (*The Merchant of Venice,* Act II, scene 7)
- 'Greek to me' (*Julius Caesar,* Act I, scene 2)
- 'A fool's paradise' (*Romeo and Juliet,* Act II, scene 3)
- 'I must be cruel, only to be kind' (*Hamlet,* Act III, scene 4)
- 'Though this be madness, yet there is method in't' (*Hamlet,* Act III, scene 2)
- 'The world's mine oyster' (*The Merry Wives of Windsor,* Act II, scene 2)
- 'Spotless reputation' (*Richard II,* Act I, scene 1)

**Info**

**16th-century English**
In Shakespearean times, there were two forms of *you:*
- *thou* (object form *thee*; possessive form *thy/thine*), used similarly to German *du*
- *ye/you*, used as a term of respect or as the plural form (cf. the old German use of *Ihr*)

Verbs following *thou* ended in -st, e.g. *didst, camest, hast.* The second-person singular form of *be* was *art: thou art = you are.* The third-person singular verb often ended in -th, e.g. *doth (does), hath (has), seemeth (seems).*

b **Speaking** Work on one of the tasks below:

b **Speaking** Work on one of the tasks below:
- In groups, write a short *dialogue that contains at least three different phrases from **4a**, rehearse it and present it to the class.
- **Challenge** In groups, write a short *dialogue in blank verse that contains at least three different phrases from **4a**, rehearse it and present it to the class.

## Text 2

### The stage is all the world

- What do you prefer and why – reading a play in a book or watching it in the theatre?

**Info**

Shakespeare's **history plays** deal with British kings' lives and deaths and usually feature battles, coronations, funerals, etc. They focus more on dramatic effect than on historical accuracy and intend to show what qualities a king should possess to deal with domestic opponents, as well as enemies abroad.

*In the prologue at the beginning of Shakespeare's history play* Henry V, *the play's chorus (a group of actors who comment on the play's action and narrate events that are not performed on stage) reflects on how important the powers of imagination are for a theatrical performance.* ▶ More info ⬇

**Annotations**

1 **O for** if only we had
1 **Muse of fire** divine inspiration
1 **ascend** rise, climb
2 **invention** creative imagination
4 **behold** look at, see
4 **swelling** majestic
5 **warlike** ready to fight
5 **Harry** King Henry V
6 **assume the port of Mars** appear like the Roman god of war
7 **leashed in** not yet let loose
7 **hound** (n) hunting dog
7 **famine** severe lack of food that threatens people's lives
8 **crouch for employment** wait for their attack
8 **gentles** ladies and gentlemen
9 **flat unraisèd spirits** dull, ordinary actors
10 **scaffold** stage
11 **cockpit** theatrical arena
13 **wooden O** synonym for the circular theatre
13 **the very casques** the real helmets
14 **affright sb.** frighten sb.
14 **Agincourt** place in Northern France where the English army won an important battle against the French in 1415
15 **crookèd figure** the number zero
16 **attest in little place a million** can turn a low number into a million
17 **ciphers** zeros, noughts; here: actors
17 **accompt** account, judgement

CHORUS    O for a Muse of fire, that would ascend
            The brightest heaven of invention,
            A kingdom for a stage, princes to act
            And monarchs to behold the swelling scene!
5           Then should the warlike Harry, like himself,
            Assume the port of Mars; and at his heels,
            Leashed in like hounds, should famine, sword and fire
            Crouch for employment. But pardon, and gentles all,
            The flat unraisèd spirits that have dared
10          On this unworthy scaffold to bring forth
            So great an object: can this cockpit hold
            The vasty fields of France? Or may we cram
            Within this wooden O the very casques
            That did affright the air at Agincourt?
15          O, pardon! Since a crookèd figure may
            Attest in little place a million;
            And let us, ciphers to this great accompt,
            On your imaginary forces work. [...]

*From:* Henry V, *Act I, Prologue*

**1** On the basis of the text, write one short paragraph about each of the following aspects:

1 stage
2 actors
3 imagination

**2** You choose Work on either task **a** or **b**.

**a** Examine the \*imagery used in the text and the effect created by it.

**b** Analyse the way the chorus addresses the audience and the effect this may have on their experience of the performance they are about to see.

Advanced

**3 a** Find examples in the text where Shakespeare uses the same syntactical structures repeatedly to build his sentences.

**b** Rephrase them in a way that avoids repetitions.

**c** Compare the two versions and analyse the effect of repeating a particular sentence structure on the reader or listener.

**Info**

From the mid-sixteenth century onwards, several professional theatre companies performed in London. The first commercial theatre opened in 1576 and Shakespeare's company, 'The Lord Chamberlain's Men', built the first **Globe Theatre**, the 'Wooden O', in 1599. The city council had banned the com-
5 panies from playing within the city limits, so they built their theatres across the river Thames, in Southwark. In 1997, a modern reconstruction of the Globe opened, only 200 yards from the original site.

▶ More info

**4 a** Do some research to find out more about the Globe and other theatres in Shakespeare's time. Focus on the following questions:

- How were the theatres managed and financed?
- What did the interior look like?
- What was the atmosphere like and how did the audience respond to the performance?

**b** Discuss how the external conditions of the theatre performances may have influenced the plays Shakespeare wrote and the way they were performed.

The only surviving contemporary sketch of an Elizabethan stage similar to the Globe shows The Swan, a London theatre built in 1595

# Shakespeare and his time

Info

During Shakespeare's lifetime, England was ruled by **Queen Elizabeth I**, who reigned from 1558 to 1603. Since she never married, the crown passed to her cousin James VI, the king of Scotland, whose troubled reign lasted from 1603 to 1625.

Portrait of Elizabeth I
(1592)

5 Elizabeth's father Henry VIII had founded the **Anglican Church** and made Protestantism the state religion, which led to bitter conflicts with the Roman Catholic Church and unsuccessful attempts by Spain to overthrow Elizabeth. Despite some domestic rebellions by sections of the aristocracy, the queen's 45-year-long reign was an era of relative stability
10 and prosperity, in which especially trade, exploration and literature, like drama, flourished.

Several concepts dating from the Middle Ages still governed the **Elizabethan worldview**, despite the spread of Renaissance ideas and the widening of people's horizons. According to the concept of **The Chain of**
15 **Being**, each living and lifeless thing had a fixed place in a divine ranking system, which in order to prevent chaos must never be upset. People also believed in the power of fate, or **fortune**, and saw a direct link between the order of the universe and the life of human beings on earth, who they thought were strongly influenced by what happened in the cosmos
20 (macrocosm reflected in microcosm and vice versa).

Like all other creatures, man was also believed to be made of the four elements fire, air, water and earth, which in the form of bodily fluids known as the **Four Humours** ruled the person. In Shakespeare's works, there are many references to these notions and his *characters' actions and convictions are based on this set of beliefs.

**Annotations**
**Prime** first hour of daylight, when a prayer should be said
**Galen** important ancient physician of the 2nd century AD
**empiric** medical practitioner without a degree from medical college

▶ Getting started

▶ Check

*You are going to listen to an excerpt from Cassidy Cash's podcast* That Shakespeare Life. *Cash talks to Professor Barbara Traister, who teaches medical history at university, about the role of astrology in medicine in Shakespeare's time.*

**Comprehension**

🔊 **1**  Listening  Answer the following questions. You need not write complete sentences.
   1  What doctors would use astrology for in the Elizabethan era
   2  Where the concept of the Four Humours originates from
   3  When a person can be considered healthy according to this concept
   4  What might happen to you if you were a melancholic person
   5  Why astrology was important to understand the distribution of the fluids in a person's body
   6  Why physicians would often draw a horoscope
   7  How much the average theatregoer would understand of the Four Humours

**2** If we believed, like Shakespeare and his audience did, that the course of a person's life was influenced by fate and the constellations of the planets – would we judge his \*characters and their actions differently? Discuss the question.

**3** In groups, find out more about different aspects of life in Shakespeare's time:

- Elizabethan era social classes
- women's lives, roles and rights
- exploration and trade
- dangers and opportunities in Shakespeare's London
- amusements and pastimes
- crime and punishment
- witchcraft, magic and religion

**a** Each group chooses one topic, and all group members, who are the experts on this topic, make notes on the results.

**b** Then, new groups are formed with one member of each expert group, who present their findings to the others. All group members take notes on the topics the other members have worked on.

**You choose** Work on either task **c** or **d**.

**c** All students go back to their original groups and share the information they gathered.

**d** **Challenge** All students go back to their original groups and share the information they gathered. In your group, create a podcast or a short video on the topic you worked on.

---

**Text 4**

# Our little life is rounded with a sleep

**Advanced**

- With a partner discuss how you'd like to be remembered by people you love.

*Shakespeare often holds the mirror to people's all too grand self-images and their desire for immortal fame. In his 'Sonnet 71' (1609), he reflects on whether there is any sense in keeping loved ones who have died in our memories. In her poem 'Remember' (1849), Christina Rossetti (1830–1894) takes a different perspective.*

**Sonnet 71**  William Shakespeare

No longer mourn for me when I am dead
Than you shall hear the surly sullen bell
Give warning to the world that I am fled
From this vile world with vilest worms to dwell;
5 Nay, if you read this line, remember not
The hand that writ it; for I love you so,
That I in your sweet thoughts would be forgot,
If thinking on me then should make you woe.
O, if I say you look upon this verse,
10 When I perhaps compounded am with clay,
Do not so much as my poor name rehearse,
But let your love even with my life decay,
Lest the wise world should look into your moan,
And mock you with me after I am gone.

*From: Sonnets, 1609*

Annotations

1 **No longer mourn for me when I am dead than …** do not let your sad feelings about my death last longer than …
2 **surly sullen bell** gloomy funeral bell
4 **vile** evil
4 **dwell** stay
6 **writ** wrote
7 **would be** want to be
8 **make you woe** cause you to mourn
10 **compounded** mixed
10 **clay** heavy, sticky earth used to make pots
11 **rehearse** repeat
12 **decay** die
13 **lest** for fear that
13 **the wise world** the world in its wisdom
13 **look into your moan** want to find out about your sorrow
14 **mock you with me** mock you because of me

▶ More info

Annotations

8  **counsel** *(v)*  listen to and advise
10  **grieve**  mourn
12  **vestige of sth.**
   ['vestɪdʒ]  small part of sth. that still exists

## Remember     Christina Rossetti

Remember me when I am gone away,
Gone far away into the silent land;

When you can no more hold me by the hand,
Nor I half turn to go yet turning stay.
5  Remember me when no more day by day
You tell me of our future that you planned:
Only remember me; you understand
It will be late to counsel then or pray.
Yet if you should forget me for a while
10  And afterwards remember, do not grieve:
For if the darkness and corruption leave
A vestige of the thoughts that once I had,
Better by far you should forget and smile
Than that you should remember and be sad.

*From:* Goblin Market and Other Poems, *1862*

Advanced

### Comprehension

**1**  **a**  Sum up the main ideas of the two sonnets.
     **b**  State who is speaking to whom in both poems and what the intention of the *speaker of each poem is.

### Analysis

**2**  Analyse the mood of both sonnets and point out where a change of mind can be found in the *speakers' statements.

### Language awareness

**3**  **a**  Examine the choice of words and the *images both *speakers use to describe death. Would you use them if you had to write a letter of condolence? Explain why or why not.
     **b**  Find more expressions suitable for this purpose.

### Beyond the text

▶SF 38: Creative writing, p. 395

▶SF 35: Writing a formal letter, p. 391

▶ Check (task 4b)

**4**  You choose     Writing     Work on either task **a** or **b**.

     **a**  Choose one sonnet and rephrase it in modern English in the form of a poem or a song. Use some of the expressions that you collected in tasks **3a** and **b**.

     **b**  Imagine you are the addressee of one of the sonnets. Write a letter replying to its speaker. Use some of the expressions that you collected in tasks **3a** and **b**.

**5**  'Sonnet 71' has been frequently chosen for poetry collections and 'Remember Me', a choral song version of Rossetti's poem composed by Bob Chilcott, is often performed. Assess why both sonnets are still popular.

# The course of true love never did run smooth

**Advanced**

- Outline reasons why 'the course of true love' may not always 'run smooth'.

*The complications, misunderstandings and tricks that often go along with love are a frequent theme in Shakespeare's comedies especially. In this excerpt from* Much Ado About Nothing, *Benedick, who has often cynically spoken against marriage, wonders whether he will fall in love like his friend Claudio did with Hero, Leonato's daughter.*

| | |
|---|---|
| BENEDICK | May I be so converted and see with these eyes? I cannot tell; I think not: I will not be sworn, but love may transform me to an oyster; but I'll take my oath on it, till he have made an oyster of me, he shall never make me such a fool. One woman is fair, yet I am well; another is wise, yet I am well; another virtuous, yet I am well; but till all graces be in one woman, one woman shall not come in my grace. Rich she shall be, that's certain; wise, or I'll none; virtuous, or I'll never cheapen her; fair, or I'll never look on her; mild, or come not near me; noble, or not I for an angel; of good discourse, an excellent musician, and her hair shall be of what colour it please God. Ha! The prince and Monsieur Love! I will hide me in the arbour. |

*Withdraws*
*Enter*

15    *BENEDICK's friends DON PEDRO and CLAUDIO, and LEONATO*

| | |
|---|---|
| DON PEDRO | [...] Come hither, Leonato. What was it you told me of today, that your niece Beatrice was in love with Signior Benedick? |
| CLAUDIO | [*quietly*] O, ay: stalk on, stalk on; the fowl sits. [*loud*] I did never think that lady would have loved any man. |
| LEONATO | No, nor I neither; but most wonderful that she should so dote on Signior Benedick, whom she hath in all outward behaviours seemed ever to abhor. |
| BENEDICK | Is't possible? Sits the wind in that corner? |
| LEONATO | By my troth, my lord, I cannot tell what to think of it but that she loves him with an enraged affection: it is past the infinite of thought. |
| DON PEDRO | Maybe she doth but counterfeit. |
| CLAUDIO | Faith, like enough. |
| LEONATO | O God, counterfeit! There was never counterfeit of passion came so near the life of passion as she discovers it. |
| DON PEDRO | Why, what effects of passion shows she? |
| CLAUDIO | [*quietly*] Bait the hook well; this fish will bite. |
| LEONATO | What effects, my lord? She will sit you, you heard my daughter tell you how. |
| CLAUDIO | She did, indeed. |
| DON PEDRO | How, how, pray you? You amaze me: I would have I thought her spirit had been invincible against all assaults of affection. |
| LEONATO | I would have sworn it had, my lord; especially against Benedick. |

▶ More info

Annotations

1  **may I be so converted** will I ever change like that

3  **oyster** *Auster;* here: sb. who shuts up in silence (very unlike Benedick)

5  **well** not in love

7  **my grace** my good opinion

8  **cheapen sb.** make an offer of marriage to sb.

9  **not I for an angel** I won't have her even if she is an angel

10  **of good discourse** well spoken

12  **arbour** shelter in a garden

13  **withdraw** (here) go to the back of the stage

18  **stalk on, [...] the fowl sits** start hunting, the bird sits

20  **wonderful** surprising

20  **so dote on sb.** love sb. so deeply

22  **abhor sb./sth.** hate sb./sth.

23  **Sits the wind in that corner?** Can this really be true?

24  **by my troth** [trəʊθ] used to express a slight oath

25  **enraged affection** passionate love

25  **past the infinite of thought** unbelievable but true

27  **doth** does

27  **counterfeit** (*v*) pretend

28  **faith, like enough** indeed, very probable

30  **discover sth.** (here) show sth.

32  **bait sth.** place food on sth.

33  **she will sit you, you heard my daughter tell you how** Leonato has forgotten his prepared lines

37  **invincible** too strong to be defeated

37  **assault** (*n*) attack

Annotations

40 **gull** trick
41 **knavery** trickery
41 **such reverence** such a respectable old man
43 **hath ta'en the infection** is caught
43 **hold it up** continue
47 **scorn** (n) strong feeling that sb. is stupid
51 **ecstasy** passion, frenzy
52 **overborne** over-whelmed
53 **do a desperate outrage to sb.** kill sb.
55 **by some other** from sb. else
57 **to what end** why
57 **sport** game
59 **and he should** and if he did
59 **alms** good deed
60 **out of all suspicion** without doubt
61 **exceeding** extremely
67 **woo sb.** try to persuade sb. to fall in love with you
67 **bate one breath of her accustomed crossness** change her usual manner of criticizing him
69 **make tender of sth.** show sth., express sth.
70 **hath a contemptible spirit** mocks everything
73 **good outward happiness** handsome appearance
75 **wit** intelligence
76 **valiant** brave
79 **wear it out with good counsel** get over it with advice from others
86 **upon this** after this
87 **expectation** judgement

| 40 | **BENEDICK** | I should think this a gull, but that the white-bearded fellow speaks it: knavery cannot, sure, hide himself in such reverence. |
| | **CLAUDIO** | [*quietly*] He hath ta'en the infection: hold it up. |
| | **DON PEDRO** | Hath she made her affection known to Benedick? |
| 45 | **LEONATO** | No; and swears she never will: that's her torment. |
| | **CLAUDIO** | 'Tis true, indeed; so your daughter says: 'Shall I,' says she, 'that have so oft encountered him with scorn, write to him that I love him?' [...] Then down upon her knees she falls, weeps, sobs, beats her heart, tears her hair, prays, curses; 'O sweet Benedick! God give me patience!' |
| 50 | **LEONATO** | She doth indeed; my daughter says so: and the ecstasy hath so much overborne her that my daughter is sometime afeared she will do a desperate outrage to herself: it is very true. |
| 55 | **DON PEDRO** | It were good that Benedick knew of it by some other, if she will not discover it. |
| | **CLAUDIO** | To what end? He would make but a sport of it and torment the poor lady worse. |
| | **DON PEDRO** | And he should, it were an alms to hang him. She's an excellent sweet lady; and, out of all suspicion, she is virtuous. |
| 60 | **CLAUDIO** | And she is exceeding wise. |
| | **DON PEDRO** | In everything but in loving Benedick. [...] I pray you, tell Benedick of it, and hear what he will say. |
| | **LEONATO** | Were it good, think you? |
| 65 | **CLAUDIO** | Hero thinks surely she will die; for she says she will die, if he love her not, and she will die, ere she make her love known, and she will die, if he woo her, rather than she will bate one breath of her accustomed crossness. |
| | **DON PEDRO** | She doth well: if she should make tender of her love, 'tis very possible he'll scorn it; for the man, as you know all, hath a contemptible spirit. |
| 70 | | |
| | **CLAUDIO** | He is a very proper man. |
| | **DON PEDRO** | He hath indeed a good outward happiness. |
| | **CLAUDIO** | Before God! And, in my mind, very wise. |
| 75 | **DON PEDRO** | He doth indeed show some sparks that are like wit. |
| | **CLAUDIO** | And I take him to be valiant. |
| | **DON PEDRO** | [...] Well, I am sorry for your niece. Shall we go seek Benedick, and tell him of her love? |
| | **CLAUDIO** | Never tell him, my lord: let her wear it out with good counsel. |
| 80 | **LEONATO** | Nay, that's impossible: she may wear her heart out first. |
| | **DON PEDRO** | Well, we will hear further of it by your daughter: let it cool the while. I love Benedick well; and I could wish he would modestly examine himself, to see how much he is unworthy so good a lady. |
| 85 | **LEONATO** | My lord, will you walk? Dinner is ready. |
| | **CLAUDIO** | [*quietly*] If he do not dote on her upon this, I will never trust my expectation. |

**DON PEDRO**

90

Let there be the same net spread for her; and that must your daughter and her gentlewomen carry. The sport will be, when they hold one an opinion of another's dotage, and no such matter: that's the scene that I would see, which will be merely a dumb-show. Let us send her to call him in to dinner.

*Exeunt DON PEDRO, CLAUDIO, and LEONATO*

**BENEDICK**

95

100

105

110

115

[*coming forward*] This can be no trick: the conference was sadly borne. They have the truth of this from Hero. They seem to pity the lady: it seems her affections have their full bent. Love me! Why, it must be requited. I hear how I am censured: they say I will bear myself proudly, if I perceive the love come from her; they say too that she will rather die than give any sign of affection. I did never think to marry: I must not seem proud: happy are they that hear their detractions and can put them to mending. They say the lady is fair; 'tis a truth, I can bear them witness; and virtuous; 'tis so, I cannot reprove it; and wise, but for loving me; by my troth, it is no addition to her wit, nor no great argument of her folly, for I will be horribly in love with her. I may chance have some odd quirks and remnants of wit broken on me, because I have railed so long against marriage: but doth not the appetite alter? A man loves the meat in his youth that he cannot endure in his age. Shall quips and sentences and these paper bullets of the brain awe a man from the career of his humour? No, the world must be peopled. When I said I would die a bachelor, I did not think I should live till I were married. Here comes Beatrice. By this day! She's a fair lady: I do spy some marks of love in her.

*Enter BEATRICE*

**BEATRICE**
**BENEDICK**
**BEATRICE**

120

**BENEDICK**
**BEATRICE**

125

Against my will I am sent to bid you come in to dinner.
Fair Beatrice, I thank you for your pains.
I took no more pains for those thanks than you take pains to thank me: if it had been painful, I would not have come.
You take pleasure then in the message?
Yea, just so much as you may take upon a knife's point and choke a daw withal. You have no stomach, signior: fare you well.

*Exit*

**BENEDICK**

130

Ha! 'Against my will I am sent to bid you come in to dinner;' there's a double meaning in that. 'I took no more pains for those thanks than you took pains to thank me.' That's as much as to say, any pains that I take for you is as easy as thanks. If I do not take pity of her, I am a villain.

*Exit*

*From:* Much Ado About Nothing, *Act II, scene 3*

Annotations

89 **when they hold one an opinion of another's dotage, and no such matter** when both think the other one is in love, when neither of them is
91 **would see** would like to see
92 **dumb-show** scene without speech
94 **conference** conversation
95 **sadly borne** completely serious
97 **requited** returned in equal measure
98 **censure sb.** criticize sb.
101 **their detractions** criticism of themselves
102 **put them to mending** change for the better
104 **reprove sth.** deny sth.
105 **argument** proof
106 **I may chance have some odd quirks and remnants of wit broken on me** Maybe I will have to endure some jokes and not very witty remarks.
110 **quips and sentences** clever remarks and wise sayings
111 **awe a man from the career of his humour** bring a man to abandon his chosen path
123 **choke a daw withal** make a jackdaw (*Dohle*) stop breathing with it
123 **have no stomach** not be hungry

Advanced

## Comprehension

**1  a** Summarize your first impression of what love is for Benedick.
  **b** State the qualities Benedick is looking for in a woman.
  **c** Sum up how Beatrice's supposed love for Benedick manifests itself and why she cannot tell him about it.
  **d** Outline how Benedick's attitude towards marriage changes during the course of the scene. Has your impression on his view of love changed?

## Analysis

**2** Analyse how Don Pedro, Claudio and Leonato convince Benedick that Beatrice is in love with him.

**3** Examine how Shakespeare achieves a humorous effect in this scene.

## Language awareness

**4  a** Collect words and phrases in the text that describe the feelings of somebody who is in love.
  **b** Which of them could still be used today? Which would seem odd today?
  **c** Arrange the words on a scale from 'passionate love → indifference → passionate hatred'. Add more words to your scale.
  **d** Besides a scale, what other types of visualization may help you learn vocabulary?

## Beyond the text

 **5**  Viewing  *In a staging of the scene, where could Benedick hide on the stage? Watch a video of actors rehearsing the 'orchard scene'.*
  **a** Outline Benedick's hiding places on stage.
  **b** Analyse the means used to make Benedick's hiding have a comic effect.
  **c** Comment on the effectiveness of this kind of humour.

▶ SF 38: Creative writing, p. 395

**6**  Writing  Imagine Beatrice and Benedick were alive today. Write a text thread between them in which they try to find out if the other one wants to go on a date with them. You may also include messages between them and other characters.

## Text 6

▶ Getting started

# Adapting Shakespeare

Advanced

- Think about possible reasons for a writer or a film director to make a modern adaptation of a text written centuries ago.

*In this excerpt from* Much Ado About Nothing, *Beatrice and Benedick, wearing masks and costumes, dance with each other during a festivity. Beatrice pretends not to recognize Benedick, who assumes that she really cannot see through his disguise.*

| | |
|---|---|
| **BEATRICE** | I am sure you know him well enough. |
| **BENEDICK** | Not I, believe me. |
| **BEATRICE** | Did he never make you laugh? |
| **BENEDICK** | I pray you, what is he? |
| 5 **BEATRICE** | Why, he is the prince's jester: a very dull fool; only his gift is in devising impossible slanders: none but libertines delight in him; and the commendation is not in his wit, but in his villainy; for he both pleases men and angers them, and then they laugh at him and beat him. |
| 10 | I am sure he is in the fleet: I would he had boarded me. |
| **BENEDICK** | When I know the gentleman, I'll tell him what you say. |
| **BEATRICE** | Do, do: he'll but break a comparison or two on me; which, peradventure not marked or not laughed at, strikes him into melancholy; and then there's a partridge |
| 15 | wing saved, for the fool will eat no supper that night. We must follow the leaders. |

*From: William Shakespeare,* Much Ado About Nothing, *Act II, scene 1*

**Partner B:** Read the text on p. 324 and work on the tasks there.
**Partner A:** Read the text below and work on task **1**.

*In Lily Anderson's adaptation of Shakespeare's comedy,* The Only Thing Worse Than Me Is You *(2016), the \*protagonists go to a private school. In this excerpt, they meet in a haunted house set up for Halloween.*

'Do you know Ben West, homicidal clown?'

He glanced down at me, the axe going limp in his hand. From the shadowy recesses of his mask, I could barely make out confused brown eyes.

'Ben West?' I repeated. 'Skinny, handlebar mustache, really lazy insults?'

5 The clown cocked his head and shook it side to side.

'Lucky you,' I said, shivering closer to him. 'You must be new. He's less of a class clown – no offence – and more of our token idiot savant. I don't know how Cornell and Peter are putting up with his jackassery. Two minutes with West is like one really obnoxious lifetime. They'll realize it eventually. Everyone does. I mean, what
10 kind of loser do you have to be to get kicked out of the role-playing club?'

The clown yanked the elbow I was holding onto, steering me around a group heading into the next room and toward the opposite wall. He drew back a sheet of plastic – which looked no different from the rest of the black plastic – to reveal a door that opened onto the quad.

*From: Lily Anderson,* The Only Thing Worse Than Me Is You, *2016*

### Comprehension

**1  a** Together with your partner, summarize what happens in Shakespeare's scene.
   **b** Point out for your partner which elements of the original have been kept in Anderson's version and what has been changed. Then listen to your partner.

---

Annotations
1  **him**  Benedick
5  **jester** *Hofnarr*
5  **only his gift**  his only talent
6  **devise sth.**  invent sth.
6  **slanders**  false statements made to harm sb.'s reputation
6  **libertines** ['lɪbətiːnz] good-for-nothings
7  **delight in sb.**  find sb. enjoyable
7  **commendation**  praise
8  **villainy**  offensiveness
8  **angers them**  e.g. when he makes jokes which insult them
10  **fleet**  company
10  **had boarded me**  had asked me to dance with him
12  **break a comparison on sb.**  make clever remarks about sb.
13  **peradventure**  perhaps
13  **mark sth.**  pay attention to sth.
14  **a partridge wing**  a small amount
16  **leaders**  (here) those leading the dance

Annotations
1  **homicidal clown**  referring to his disguise as an evil clown with a rubber axe
3  **recess**  part that is set further back
4  **handlebar mustache**  line of hair on the upper lip
7  **no offence**  this is not meant as an insult
7  **token**  only pretending
7  **idiot savant** [ˌɪdiəʊ sæˈvɒ̃] sb. with learning difficulties who is unusually talented in a specific field
7  **Cornell and Peter**  Claudio and Don Pedro in Shakespeare's play
9  **obnoxious**  extremely unpleasant
11  **yank sb./sth.**  suddenly pull sb./sth. hard
14  **quad**  (quadrangle) open square area with buildings all around it

Advanced

## Analysis

2 Compare the ways in which Shakespeare and the modern adaptation you worked on build up the tension between the two characters.

3 Work on either task **a** or **b**.

**a** Compare the ways Beatrice insults Benedick in Shakespeare's text and in the modern version you worked on and explain why their remarks are so hurtful.

**b** Challenge Compare the ways Beatrice insults Benedick in Shakespeare's text and in the modern version you worked on and explain why their remarks are so hurtful. Explain what her insults may tell us about her feelings towards Benedick.

## Language awareness

▶ More language

4 **a** Find typical features of spoken language in the modern adaptation you worked on.

**b** Point out which elements should not be used in a formal text type and find suitable replacements for them.

## Beyond the text

5 The numerous modern adaptations of Shakespeare show that there is a lot in his texts that still speaks to us. Think back to the guiding question and discuss what aspects of the original scene between Beatrice and Benedick we can still relate to.

## Text 7

# Art in Context: Portraying Shakespeare

- *Quick write: Based on the texts you have read, what kind of person do you imagine the historical Shakespeare might have been? Write a short paragraph.

▶ More info

The Chandos portrait of Shakespeare was painted between 1600 and 1610.

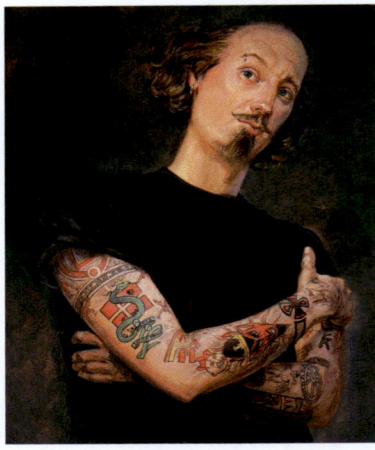

US artist Mathew McFarren painted his 'Tattooed Shakespeare' in 2003.

▶ Getting started

## Comprehension

**1** Describe McFarren's portrait 'Tattooed Shakespeare' (2003).

> **Language help**
>
> be shown/depicted … • His body language suggests … • be characterized as someone who … • common features • the most striking similarities/differences …

## Analysis

**2** Compare the two portraits of Shakespeare and analyse the graphical means McFarren uses to reinterpret the famous Chandos portrait.

▶SF 23: Analysing visuals, p. 374

▶Support, p. 325

## Beyond the text

**3** Interpret McFarren's painting: What does it say about Shakespeare's relevance to us today? Looking back on the quick write exercise, how has your assessment of Shakespeare as a person changed?

**Text 8**

# Shakespeare is all around us

• If the Shakespeare of Mathew McFarren's portrait (p. 298) were alive today, where would he work and what would he write?

*Kae Tempest, born in 1985, is a British poet and hip-hop artist. In addition to several volumes of poetry, Tempest has also published essays, plays and a novel. In the poem 'My Shakespeare', the artist reflects on Shakespeare's place in our contemporary world.*

**My Shakespeare**  Kae Tempest

He's in every lover who ever stood alone beneath a window,
In every jealous whispered word,
In every ghost that will not rest.
He's in every father with a favourite,
5 Every eye that stops to linger
On what someone else has got, and starts to widen in distress.

He's in every young man that grows boastful,
Every worn out elder, drunk for days;
Muttering false prophecies and squandering their lot.
10 He's in every complex misunderstanding that springs up between
a group of friends
And never seems to end, even when its beginnings are forgot.

He's in every girl who ever used her wits to outsmart the status quo.
He's in every vain self-admirer,

Annotations
5 **linger on sth.** continue to look at sth.
7 **boastful** talking about yourself proudly
9 **mutter sth.** say sth. quietly and angrily
9 **squander sth.** waste sth.
14 **vain** overly proud

Annotations

15 **ambitious** determined to be successful
16 **tempers fray** people get annoyed with each other
17 **pawn** *(n)* chess piece of the least value; here: people controlled by others
19 **ancient** very old
25 **blade** flat part of a sword with sharp edges

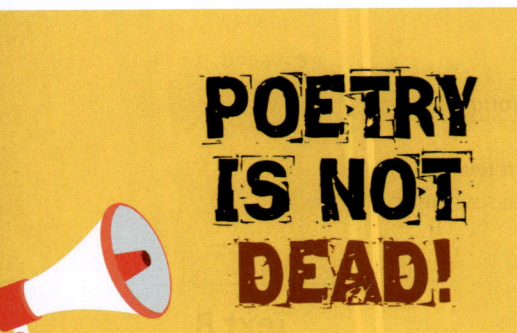

29 **swagger** *(v)* walk confidently
33 **fabric** basic structure
34 **tangled** twisted
36 **tights and garters** stockings and bands to hold them worn by men in Shakespeare's time
38 **doomed** certain to fail
39 **tightened jaw** teeth pressed together
40 **rascal** *Schurke*
43 **inadequacy** state of not being good enough
44 **valiant** courageous, brave
44 **pitiful** deserving pity
45 **sore loser** unable to accept defeat without bitterness
46 **legacy** *Vermächtnis*

15 Every passionate, ambitious social climber,
He's in every misheard word that ever led to tempers fraying,
He's in every pawn that moves across the board
And still remains convinced that it's not playing.

20 So, you might think his words are ancient, you might think his words are dead but chances are you've quoted him directly if you've ever said, oh, it sets my teeth on edge, or there's a method in my madness or pure as the driven snow or my hair is standing on end or all that glitters is not gold or I haven't slept a wink or I wear my heart upon my sleeve or the beast with two backs or the word puking which is harder to believe or fighting fire with fire or having too much of a good thing. You

25 see, his pen was mightier than his sword, but still his words are like blades that sing our very names when they strike. Here's the milk of human kindness, up in arms, break the ice, here's the green-eyed monster, here's discretion is the better part of valour, and now his words with their arms around each other's shoulders, swagger

30 to the ends of their sentences, proud of everything they've done, of how his pages have lasted through the ages but how he has become a poet whose poetics have embedded themselves so firmly in the fabric of our language, it's like he's in our mouths, his words have tangled around our own and given rise to expres-

35 sions so effective in expressing how we feel, we can't imagine how we'd feel without them. He's less the tights and garters, more the sons demanding answers from the absence of their fathers, the hot darkness of a doomed embrace.
He's in the laughter of the night before, the tightened jaw of the morning after,

40 He's in us, part and parcel of our royals and our rascals.
He's not just something boring taught in classrooms, in language that's hard to understand,
He's not just a feeling of inadequacy when you sit for an exam,
He's in every valiant woman, every pitiful villain,

45 Every sore loser, every great king, every fake tear,
And his legacy exists and lives on in everything he's written,
And if you listen you hear him everywhere,
He's my Shakespeare.

From: A transcript of a performance commissioned by the Royal Shakespeare Company

## Comprehension

**1** Work on the tasks below.
   **1** Name three examples where, according to Tempest's poem, we can recognize traits of Shakespeare's characters in everyday life.
   **2** Name three examples that show Shakespeare's enduring influence on the English language and explain what they mean.
   **3** Sum up what Tempest says about Shakespeare's relevance today.

▶ Getting started (task 2)
▶ SF 20: Reading and understanding poetry, p. 370

## Analysis

**2** Identify some *stylistic devices used and examine their effect.

**3** Examine the function and effect of the repetitions Tempest uses in the text and find suitable expressions that could be used instead. How does that change the effect the poem has on the reader or the audience?

**4** According to Tempest's poem, Shakespeare's influence is still very present, even if we are not always aware of it.

You choose  Taking this chapter's guiding question into consideration, work on either task **a** or **b**.

**a** Discuss what we can gain by becoming aware of Shakespeare's influence on contemporary language and culture as well as tracing it back to the original texts.

**b** We can still feel close to Shakespeare – but what about the other way around? If he were alive today, would he feel close to us? Would he be able to understand us? Discuss the question.

▶ Getting started (task b)

**Text 9**

Advanced

# The inexhaustible genius    Ceyda Nurtsch

• In your opinion, how does reading a modern English adaptation or a German translation instead of the original text influence your understanding of Shakespeare? What could you lose or miss out on by doing so?

*You are going to read an excerpt from an article by Ceyda Nurtsch in which she reports on the German Shakespeare society's 2019 annual conference on translations of Shakespeare's work.*

Annotation
**inexhaustible** *unerschöpflich*

▶ More info

Der Zeitpunkt ist bewusst gewählt: Jedes Jahr um den Geburtstag des englischen Dramatikers und Lyrikers William Shakespeare am 23. April herum veranstaltet die Shakespeare-Gesellschaft ihre Frühjahrstagung. „Shakespeare
5 und Übersetzung" lautete das diesjährige Thema. Vom 26.–28. April widmeten sich internationale Forscher der Frage nach der Übersetzbarkeit der Werke des Dramaturgen aus Stratford-upon-Avon. [...]

Einer der Tagungsteilnehmer ist der langjährige Überset-
10 zer, Anglist und Lyriker Klaus Reichert. „Jedes Mal, wenn ich ein Stück von Shakespeare wieder lese, entdecke ich Stellen, wo ich denke, wieso ist mir das nicht aufgefallen? Da steht ja etwas drin, das ist viel spannender als das, was ich bisher über das Stück gedacht habe." Als junger Mensch
15 habe er immer „relativ flott" übersetzt, erzählt er. Doch im Laufe seines Lebens habe er erfahren, wie viele unterschiedliche Schichten in den Texten seien. „Sie übersetzen

ja nicht Wort für Wort, sondern Sie übersetzen von einem kulturellen System in ein anderes kulturelles System." Doch wie erklärt er, dass sich Shakespeare immer
20 wieder der Zeit anpassen lässt und so nie an Aktualität verliert? „Shakespeare ist einfach ein unerklärliches Genie gewesen, wie es vorher und nachher überhaupt keines gegeben hat", denkt Reichert. „Es hat große Dramatiker, große Dichter gegeben, aber niemanden mit dieser Unerschöpflichkeit." Und vielleicht, fügt er hinzu, liege es auch daran, dass sich der Dramaturg „nicht packen" lasse. „War er
25 nun Anglikaner, Protestant, Puritaner oder ein verkappter Katholik?" Bei anderen Autoren sei das deutlicher zu sehen. Doch bei Shakespeare erwecke jede Figur eine neue Fragwürdigkeit. „Wenn Sie denken, Sie wissen was ist, stimmt es wieder nicht in der nächsten Szene. Das ist auch diese darstellerische Vielfalt", so Reichert. [...]

30 Den abschließenden Festvortrag der Tagung hält die Kultur- und Literaturwissenschaftlerin Elisabeth Bronfen. Sie widmet sich der Frage nach den Einflüssen Shakespeares in gegenwärtigen TV-Produktionen. In *Westworld* mit Anthony Hopkins in der Hauptrolle etwa zitiert ein Android immer, wenn er eine Störung erfährt, Shakespeare. „Man nennt das ‚Quotable Shakespeare'", erklärt Bronfen.
35 „Durch die Shakespeare-Zitate verleiht man der Serie Autorität. Man zeigt, man ist kulturell wertvoll, man schafft eine Art Gemeinschaft, weil alle Leute diese Zitate auch erkennen." Der Einfluss zeige sich aber auch in Serien wie *House of Cards* oder *Homeland*. Die derzeitige Politik, insbesondere die US-amerikanische Politik, erinnere sehr an die Politik, die in den Shakespeare-Historien wie *Macbeth* durch-
40 gespielt werde, denkt Bronfen. „Es geht immer um blutige Machtkämpfe, um Intrigen und Zwist im Inneren." Und da liege es auf der Hand, die blutigen Hände der Politik in Washington und somit *House of Cards* mit den blutigen Händen Macbeths und seiner Lady zu verknüpfen. Und Bronfen fasst zusammen: „Der Geist Shakespeares geistert also weiter herum, weil er so greifbar und wandelbar
45 ist. Und zwar sowohl von der Sprache her als auch von den Figurenkonstellationen, Geschichten und Themen, die verhandelt werden." *(458 words)*

*From: 'Shakespeare: aktuell und unerschöpflich'.* Dr. Ceyda Nurtsch, Deutsche Welle
ⅅⅅ Deutsche Welle *29 April 2019*

▶ Getting started ⤵
▶ SF 49: Mediating from German into English, p. 416
▶ WOB: pp. 71–77

**1** 🗺 Mediating This year, your school's annual project week will deal with the topic 'Warum sollen wir Klassiker heutzutage noch im Unterricht behandeln?'. Your class will contribute to the English department's entry focusing on Shakespeare. Think back to this chapter's guiding question, read the above text and write an *article summing up what Klaus Reichert and Elisabeth Bronfen say about Shakespeare's ongoing relevance.

### Beyond the text

▶ SF 32: Writing an article, p. 388

▶ WOB: pp. 13–15

**2** Intercultural competence Writing Reichert claims 'Sie übersetzen von einem kulturellen System in ein anderes kulturelles System' (ll. 18–19). Write an *article for your school newspaper in which you describe the main cultural differences between Shakespeare's world and that of young German readers.

## Chapter task

► Getting started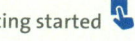

*Now well familiar with Shakespeare, you will create a modern version of a dramatic scene to be performed in front of the class or recorded and shown to them.*

You can use one of the following scenes or pick another one from Shakespeare's plays.

1 During a banquet, Macbeth is haunted by the ghost of his murdered victim. (*Macbeth*, Act III, scene 4)
2 Under a magic spell, the Fairy Queen Titania falls in love with an amateur actor transformed into a donkey by another spell. (*A Midsummer Night's Dream*, Act III, scene 1)
3 A quarrel between Tybalt, Mercutio and Romeo ends in a deadly confrontation. (*Romeo and Juliet*, Act III, scene 1)

1 `Writing` In groups of four to six, find and read a \*plot summary of the play and then the scene itself. Write a screenplay with a modern \*setting for your own adaptation with roles for every group member. Include a \*character speaking in an aside who briefly sums up the \*action leading up to this moment in the play. Find suitable voice-overs, sound effects or music to support the action and the \*dialogue of your \*scene.

**aside** *(n)* remark made by a character on stage that is only to be heard by the audience, not by the other characters

2 `You choose` `Speaking` Choose one of the following modes for presenting your scene.

► Getting started (task c)

a Practise your dramatic reading of the screenplay and discuss how it can be made more convincing. Then, present it to the class.

b Record your reading of the screenplay. Make sure that the action comes across in the dialogue and that the listeners know who is speaking.

c Prepare a \*storyboard for the filming of your screenplay. Practise performing the scene by heart.

► p. 22

**Chapter 1**     **Text 2**

# Not being normal

### 3  Support

Look for different elements that are used to characterize the two characters in the excerpt:

- examples of Marianne's and Connell's actions in the text. Example: 'Marianne had a row with the History teacher last year' (ll. 4f.).
- examples of what Marianne and Connell actually say / have said in the text. Example: 'Connell said ...' (l. 17)
- examples of Marianne's and Connell's thoughts in the text. Example: 'It seemed so obviously insane to her ...' (ll. 6ff.)

Think of suitable adjectives and phrases to describe those actions, words and thoughts.

*Now use these ideas to go back to your original task.*

**Text 5**

► p. 33

# The privilege backpack

### 2  Support

Start by listing the contents of the 'privilege backpack' and the four statements in the 'straight privilege checklist,' along with the advantages they imply. Then, reflect on how these elements could affect the lives and feelings of individuals who lack such privileges.

*Now go back to p. 33.*

**Text 9**

► p. 45

► Getting started

# A prank

### 8  Partner B

a  Study the infographic on the next page. Tell your partner what it shows about people's perception of society and racism.

## Racism in Germany – a problem in every area of life

Proportion of respondents who believe that racism is a (very) big problem in the following areas

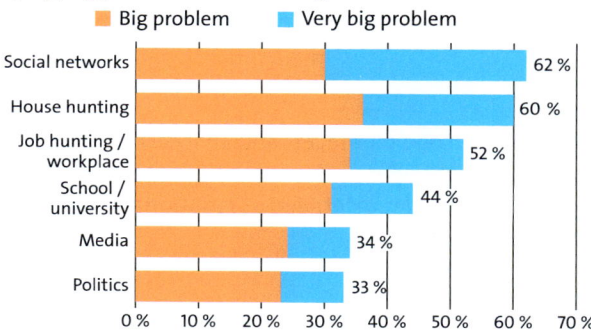

Sample: 2049 German respondents older than 18, Germany June 2020
Source: YouGov, June 2020

*Now go back to task **8b** on p. 45.*

**Text 10**

## Sonnet 130

► p. 46

### 3  Support

Poets and novelists often work with comparisons and contrasts if they want to question or criticize something. Think about the last two lines of the poem (the couplet) and their relationship to the rest of the sonnet.

*Now go back to your original task.*

**Chapter 2**     **Text 1**

## Taking stock: the mood in the UK

► p. 53

### 2  Support

- Emotions can be captured and conveyed with the right choice of words. Take a closer look at the *connotations of adjectives, nouns and verbs used in the text. It might help you to find *antonyms for some of the words to determine their connotation.
- Imagery is also often used to support the message of a text. The metaphor 'crumbs of comfort' (l. 31) suggests that there is very little comfort, as breadcrumbs are very small fragments of bread.

► p. 54

### Text 2

## A united kingdom or regional identities?

DO THE WELSH AND SCOTS GET ON?

OH YES... THEY BOTH HATE THE ENGLISH

Lindsay

CartoonStock.com

**Partner B**

**2 a** Look at the cartoon on the left and analyse how it stresses British disunity. Prepare a 2-minute presentation for your partner that includes a detailed description of the cartoon. Then go back to task **b**.

**3 Support** (p. 55)

Look for examples of expressions like 'belying' (l. 1) or 'surprisingly little' (l. 2). Decide if these words and phrases have a positive or negative *connotation. Find more examples like the ones mentioned above. Then think about how this choice of words might influence the readers' perception of the topic.

### Text 4

► p. 57

## The trailblazer devolution deals

**2 Support**

- Look at phrases like 'cost of living crisis has disproportionately struck...' (l. 5), 'truly dismal' (l. 11) and 'disgraceful underdevelopment' (l. 14). What is the general view that is presented through these phrases?
- Contrast this with the general view that is presented through phrases like 'the new autonomy will give [...] the chance to develop' (l. 20), 'will have a greater chance' (l. 24) and 'a first small step in the right direction' (l. 25).
- What is the effect of signposting words like 'Nevertheless' (l. 34) and 'but' (l. 39) in the last paragraph?

**4 b Support**

Look for reliable government sources from the respective countries and the European Union. In the UK, the terms used to describe government powers are 'reserved' (belonging to the centre) and 'devolved' (decentralized). While doing your research, do not forget that the different countries in the UK (England, Scotland, Northern Ireland and Wales) do not have the same powers.

You can compare specific areas such as agriculture, education, employment, transport, tourism, etc.

► p. 58

## Text 5

### The political system in the UK

#### 5 Support

When researching the German political system, research the *Bundestag* and *Bundesrat*. There are some features and functions that are common to both chambers, for example, approving laws, regulations and constitutional changes. There are other features and functions that are specific to each. For instance, the *Bundestag* is elected directly by German citizens and has a legislative function. It is responsible for electing the chancellor. On the other hand, the *Bundesrat* represents the federal states. Its members are selected by the state governments.

## Skills Lab

#### 2 c Support

► p. 65

The *method card below already includes helpful information about argumentative writing. Keep adding relevant aspects.

| Method card – argumentative writing | |
|---|---|
| Introduction | • starts with an introductory phrase<br>• includes your own opinion on the matter<br>• … |
| Main part | • each paragraph develops one argument<br>• … |
| Conclusion | • clearly states your point of view<br>• … |
| General characteristics | • … |

## Text 8

### Nobody is an island – the UK and Europe

► p. 68

#### 2 Support

The following ideas can help you with your analysis:
• Check the text for exaggerations – which examples can you find? What effect do they have on the reader?
• Find funny anecdotes or episodes the author uses to paint a picture of the British. Explain how the reader perceives the British because of this.
• Find passages in which the author criticizes the British. Check how he does this and why this description is not hurtful or offensive.

▶ p. 71

## Text 10

# Brexit: a German perspective

### 1 Support

**Step 1:** Find ways to express the following words from the comment in English:
- 'Wirtschaftsstandort' (l. 18)
- 'Konkurrenz' (l. 18)
- 'Bürokratieabbau' (l. 24)
- 'uniforme EU' (l. 26).

**Step 2:** Bear in mind that Brexit is a controversial and highly emotional issue in the UK. Are there any parts of your presentation that might cause cultural clashes? If yes, find a diplomatic way to get those parts across.

## Language Lab

▶ p. 72

### 2 Support

Adverbs of comment give information about the speaker's opinion or point of view. Comment adverbs usually go at the beginning of a sentence or clause. They are usually separated from the rest of the sentence by a comma.

Adverbs of degree can be used to intensify or tone down adjectives, verbs or other adverbs. They usually go in front of the adverb/adjective/verb they describe.

### 3 Support

Go back to the Skills Lab and read the written comment you find on p. 63 to see linking words used in the text.

▶ p. 73

### 5 Support

Possible arguments could be:
- English as lingua franca
- renowned universities like Oxford and Cambridge with a long tradition
- closeness to home country.

# Racism in Britain

▶ p. 79

## Partner B

### Comprehension

1  a   Take a look at the bar chart below. Prepare a two-minute presentation for your partner in which you tell them what your bar chart reveals about the different attitudes towards racism in Great Britain.

▶ Getting started

**Support for the Black Lives Matter movement by ethnicity**

To what extent, if at all, do you support or oppose the aims of the Black Lives Matter movement?

Strongly support   Somewhat support   Neither/nor   Somewhat oppose   Strongly oppose   Don't know

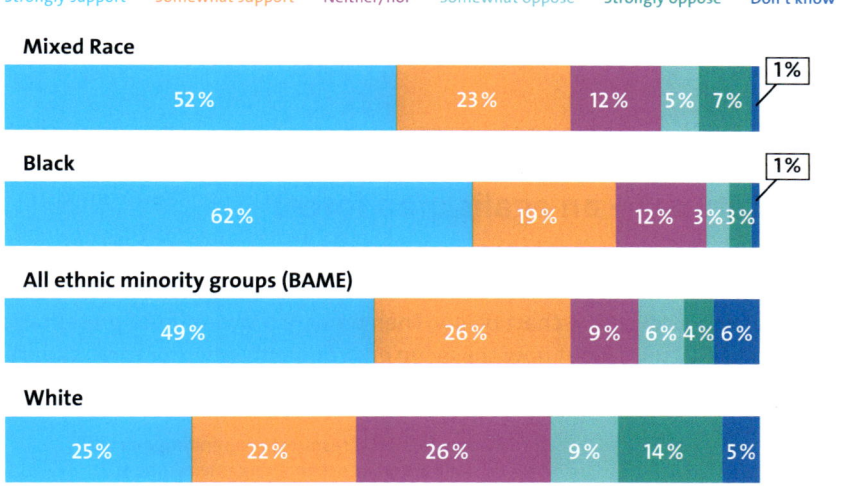

Source: Ipsos, 2020

*Now go back to task 1b.*

# New way, new life

▶ p. 81

## 2  Support

- Collect foreign-language expressions in the song. Which languages are used? What is the function of using these expressions and to what extent can they be regarded as a statement on Britain as a multicultural society?
- 'Inna' (l. 9), 'de' (l. 9), 'an' (l. 11), 'dis' (l. 24) und 'riddims' (l. 46) are all spellings that depict a Jamaican accent. Although none of the members of Asian Dub Foundation are of Caribbean descent they use this accent. What does this tell you about their view of the possibilities of language in a multicultural society?

| Chapter 3 | Text 2 |
|---|---|

## Text

▶ p. 88

### 2  Support

- Analysing the language of a poem, it can be useful to start with the peculiarities of the text: note down the most important words, *stylistic devices such as *repetitions and *parallelism, *imagery, etc.
- Don't analyse language for its own sake but relate form to content: explain how these linguistic peculiarities and stylistic devices add to the description of personal emotion by means of communication technology.
- Make conclusions about the deficiencies of texting: consider what is missing when two lovers cannot meet in person but have to rely on their mobile devices only. How is this expressed in the poem?

### Text 4

## The internet – an egalitarian force?

### Partner B

▶ p. 95

▶ SF 43: Giving a presentation, p. 405

▶ Getting started

**1  a**  Have a look at the chart below. Then prepare a two-minute presentation for your partner about how the living environment, whether rural, suburban or urban, correlates to the level of digitalization of households.

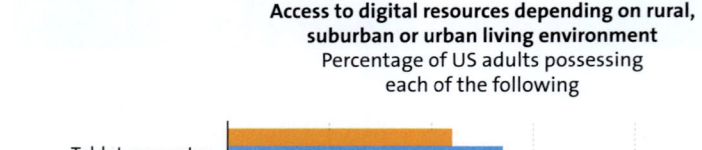

**Access to digital resources depending on rural, suburban or urban living environment**
Percentage of US adults possessing each of the following

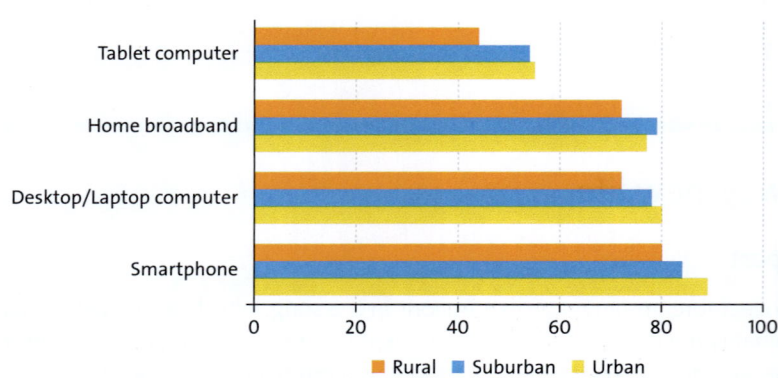

*Source:* www.pewresearch.org, *19 August 2021*

*Then go back to task **1b** on p. 95.*

# AI's threat to AI

▶ p. 102

## 2  Support

Watch out for modal auxiliary verbs, the use of direct and indirect speech and other ways of linking the findings to the scientists and their studies.

# Scripting reality

▶ p. 106

## 6  a  Support

- Explain the statement in the context of the story, pointing out what additional aspects are covered.
- Critically engage with the viewers' responsibilities.
- To round off your comment, come back to the quotation and compare the viewers' responsibility with that of the producers.

## b  Support

- Make sure you make your position clear.
- Use aspects of Kelly's original message in the confession box to describe her the way you used to know her.
- Choose a register that is appropriate for a post in the chat room, i.e. rather colloquial language, with features of spoken rather than written language.

# The art in advertising

▶ p. 107

## 2  a  Support

**Take** into account:
- graphic elements and characters typeface
- spatial division (including background, foreground, perspective)
- light and colour
- mood and atmosphere
- visual references.

## 2  c  Support

**Take** into account:
- the way readers or viewers are addressed
- register and stylistic devices
- quotations and references.

## Text 10

▶ p. 111

### News avoidance in times of media fatigue

#### 1 Support

- List reasons for news avoidance and media fatigue.
- Take a closer look at the role of journalists with regard to news avoidance and media fatigue.

## Chapter 4    Text 1

▶ p. 119

### At this moment in history

#### 1 Support

**Step 1:** Scan the text to determine what aspects it deals with. The paragraphs can help you: good writers use a separate paragraph for each topic they deal with. But one aspect may extend to more than one paragraph.

**Step 2:** Use the aspects you have found to structure your summary. For each aspect, make notes on the main points.

**Step 3:** Use your notes to write your summary. Remember that we use the present tense to refer to the author's activity ('Obama refers to...'), but otherwise the same tenses as the original (i.e., past tense for action in the past).

*Now go back to the original task.*

#### 4 Support

Look for examples of each of the following:
- *parallelism
- *repetition
- *enumeration
- parenthesis
- *antithesis

*Now go back to the original task.*

## Text 7

▶ p. 134

### The health card

#### 4 Support

Compare the examples in the box on p. 313. Pay special attention to:
- Mildred's pronunciation of certain endings and prefixes
- personal pronouns that refer to groups of people (both women)

- the use of adverbs without the *-ly* ending
- the complexity and completeness of sentences.

**Mildred**

'Sure,' I said, 'indeed one must, and I am glad you are so understandin', 'cause I was just worryin' and studyin' on how I was goin' to ask you for yours [...].'

'On second thought, you folks look real clean, too, so ...'

**Mrs. Jones**

'Do you live in Harlem, Mildred?'

'I don't mean any offense, but one must be careful, mustn't one?'

'Mildred, you don't have to bring a health card. I am sure it will be all right.'

*From: Alice Childress,* Like One of the Family, *1956*

## Text 8

# In search of the American Dream

▶ p. 136

### 4 Support

Examine the following excerpt (ll. 34–39 of the original text) closely. Point out 4 words that evoke negative feelings in the reader (1 adjective, 3 nouns):

If you graduated from high school or college in 1930, you faced far bleaker economic prospects than if you had graduated in 1910. By 1950, things were looking up again. In 2010, opportunity was curtailed by another stagnation. To take it as a given that your children should out-achieve you is to swallow a proposi-
5 tion that ends up causing much of the American public needless feelings of anxiety and nights of insomnia.

*From: A. Ehrenhalt,* Could We Please Stop Pontificating About the American Dream, *2020*

*Now go back to the text and read the next paragraph (ll. 40–49). Look for words that evoke positive feelings (one verb, two adjectives).*

## Text 9

# The new colossus

▶ p. 140

### 4 Support

Match the quotations in the left column to the terms on the right.

| A | 'cries she / With silent lips.' (ll. 9–10) | 1 | alliteration |
| B | 'world-wide welcome' (l. 7) | 2 | assonance |
| C | 'mild eyes' (l. 7) | 3 | contrast |
| D | 'I lift my lamp beside the golden door!' (l. 14) | 4 | paradox |
| E | "Keep, ancient lands, your storied pomp![...] Give me your tired, your poor [...]" (ll. 9–12) | 5 | symbol |

# Consuming art

**Partner B**

▶ p. 156

Annotation
**pretense** (AE = BE pretence) the act of behaving in a particular way in order to make other people believe something that is not true

" I DECIDED TO CUT OUT THE PRETENSE
AND GET RIGHT TO THE POINT! "

CartoonStock.com

## Comprehension

▶ SF 25: Analysing cartoons, p. 377

**1** Sum up the cartoon's message about the consumption of art in one sentence.

## Analysis

▶ Getting started

**2 a** Look at the cartoon and analyse how its message is conveyed. Share your analysis with your partner in a 1-minute presentation.

*Now go back to p. 156.*

# Types of art and culture

### Pre-reading task    Support
▶ p. 157

Consider the following questions to help you collect ideas:
- What components make up the culture of a country, nation, or community?
- Who is it that consumes art? How, when and why do they do so?
- Who produces or creates art?
- What is the function of art and culture?
- What is the significance of art and culture in your life?

### 3  b  Support
▶ p. 159

Choose one of the following target groups: students at your school, your grandparents, who are especially interested in different cultures, or local politicians who determine the funding for cultural programs in your community. Think about the appropriate register, vocabulary and sentence structure for your target group. Then write your text.

# Artists and their communities

### 3  Support
▶ p. 169

If you can't think of an artist, here are a few ideas. Pick an artist from the following list and research the kind of art they created and what it had to do with their political activism:

Banksy • Diego Riviera • Ai Wei Wei • Picasso • Hanna Hoch • Hans Arp • Billie Holiday • Woodie Guthrie • Nina Simone • The Wailers • Public Enemy

# Noomoo launch film

### 1  Support
▶ p. 170

You may want to consider the following stages:
- Tasting the product and choosing the best
- Defining the general aim of campaign to colleagues
- Planning an expansion
- Learning how the product is produced
- Developing a social media campaign

- Launching the product
- Finding a product name
- Developing the packaging

### 3 a Support

You may want to look at the following aspects:
- the contrast between the campaign manager and Maggie (actions, dress and gadgets they use, their way of speaking and interacting), between the manager and his audience, between his presentation of himself/his ideas and reality
- the quality of the campaign manager's marketing ideas
- puns, allusions, nonsensical statements
- common clichés about work in a marketing agency
- Maggie's presentation of how milk is produced
- the milk tasting

**Chapter 6**  **Text 1**

## A short history of globalization

▶ p. 177

### 1 Support

Choose labels from the box below. Put them in the right order.

driving force • key technologies • major players • primary question • size of world • time frame

*Now go back to p. 177.*

**Text 3**

## Playing by the rules: the WTO

▶ p. 181

### 2 Support

Look at the first two paragraphs of the section titled 'What we do' (ll. 26–36). A variety of verbs and verb forms is used here:
is run (l. 26) • are made (l. 26) • meet (l. 27 and 28) • is driven (l. 31) • function (l. 31) • employs (l. 32) • assist (l. 43) • progress (l. 35) • are applied (l. 36) • are enforced (l. 36)

a Read the passage again. Then examine the form of the verbs. Which tenses are used most often? What are the reasons for this? (Hint: pay attention to the adverbs of time.)

The WTO is run by its member governments. All major decisions are made by the membership as a whole, either by ministers (who usually meet at least once every two years) or by their ambassadors or delegates (who meet regularly in Geneva).

5 While the WTO is driven by its member states, it could not function without its Secretariat to coordinate the activities. The Secretariat employs over 600 staff, and its experts – lawyers, economists, statisticians and communications experts – assist WTO members on a daily basis to ensure, among other things, that negotiations progress smoothly, and that the rules of in-
10 ternational trade are correctly applied and enforced.

*From: www.wto.org*

**b** Examine the meaning(s) of the verbs that are used, focusing on whether they are mainly action verbs or state verbs.

*Now go back to task 3 on p. 181.*

**Text 5**

▶ p. 187

# A stranger in Manila

## 2 a Support

Put the headlines below in the right order. They can help you to divide the text into different sections about Changez's perception of himself and his role.

on arriving in Manila • on the job • on the flight to Manila • the traffic incident

*Now go back to p. 187.*

**Skills Lab**

▶ p. 193

## 3 Support

Group the phrases below in the right order so that they correspond to the structure of the text:

final form of the law • consequences for the EU • the problem • original form of the law • consequences for firms • the solution • German supply-chain law

*Now go back to p. 193.*

## Text 11

▶ p. 199/201

# The reluctant giant

**Partner B**

Read the text below. Make notes on the reasons why America's role in the world changed dramatically in the 20th century.

**Annotations**
2 **tenuous** weak
4 **precarious** *instabil*
4 **equilibrium** balance
5 **concurrent** happening at the same time
8 **thrust sb.** push sb violently
10 **bulk** the largest part
10 **theater** (here) place where a war is happening
11 **prolonged** longer
12 **muster sth.** bring sth together (for a special purpose)

But then the world shifted, and Americans suddenly found themselves at the center of it. The old order upheld by the United Kingdom and made possible by a tenuous peace in Europe collapsed with the arrival of new powers. The rise of Germany destroyed the precarious equilibrium in Europe, and the Europeans proved unable to
5 restore it. The concurrent rise of Japan and the United States put an end to more than a century of British naval hegemony. A global geopolitics replaced what had been a European-dominated order, and in this very different configuration of power, the United States was thrust into a new position. Only it could be both a Pacific and an Atlantic power. Only it, with weak neighbors to the north and south and vast oceans
10 to the east and west, could send the bulk of its forces to fight in distant theaters for prolonged periods while its homeland remained unthreatened. Only it could afford to finance not only its own war efforts but also those of its allies, mustering the industrial capacity to produce ships, planes, tanks, and other materiel to arm itself while also serving as the arsenal for everyone else. Only it could do all of this without bank-
15 rupting itself but instead growing richer and more dominant with each major war. [...]

*From: Robert Kagan, 'A superpower like it or not', Foreign Affairs, 2021*

*Now go back to your original task.*

## Text 12

▶ p. 203

### 1 Support

In your text you can concentrate on the following aspects:
• the German view of the USA in previous decades
• the German attitude towards recent US presidents
• how Germans might regard the USA in the future

## Chapter 7    Text 1

▶ p. 210

# Being Irish

### 2 Support

To explore how the three writers convey their attitudes towards a common Irish identity, pay attention to how they make use of specific words, sentences structures and stylistic devices to communicate their views.

**Step 1:** Determine first what each writer's attitude towards a common Irish identity actually is. Which of the three authors feels positive / negative / sceptical / emotional / worried / fearful / doubtful about this notion? Find evidence in the text and take notes.

**Step 2:** Have a closer look at your evidence and examine whether the three authors make use of specific words, sentence structures and stylistic devices to communicate their views. Make notes.
For example, are there …
- any words with positive or negative meanings?
- any statements, exclamations or questions revealing the author's attitude?
- any metaphors, similes, symbols or other stylistic devices which might indicate the author's attitude?

**Step 3:** Write a short text in which you explain how each author conveys their attitude by summarizing your findings in Steps 1 and 2.

Text 4

# Art in Context: Northern Ireland street art

### 3 Support

▶ p. 217

Choose suitable chunks from the box below to generate ideas for your arguments, either for or against the motion.

> bring about change • challenge authorities • controversial topic • creative form of commentary • does not reach or appeal to many people • form of activism • glorify sth. • have an impact on sb. • laws and regulations • mirror/reflect ideas • overestimate the power of art • political controversy/discourse • private property • promote ideals/ideologies • raise awareness of sth. • single-sidedness • social issue/conflict • subjective view • take action • threaten peace and stability • use sth. as a propaganda tool • vandalism • with/without approval

Text 5

# Queen of the sticklebacks

### 1 b Support

▶ p. 222

To grasp the significance of the given words and phrases in the short story, follow the steps below:

**Step 1:** Make sure that you understand the historical events alluded to in the story by completing the sentences below. Conduct additional research if necessary.

- 1988 was a particularly violent year in Northern Ireland's history, because …
- During the Troubles, unionists and nationalists in Belfast marked their territory by painting kerbstones in different colours. Unionists would colour kerbstones … in reference to the British flag, whereas nationalists would colour them … in reference to the Irish flag.
- In the 1980s, the dominant religious group in Northern Ireland was …
- 'The Billy Boys' is a song which was often sung during the Troubles by …, because …
- During the Troubles there were regular patrols of the streets of Belfast by …, because …

**Step 2:** Use the information you gathered above to explain the significance of the historical allusions in the context of the short story 'Queen of the sticklebacks'. The following questions will guide you:
- What do the allusions reveal about the place and the time the story is set in?
- What do they reveal about the characters in the story, their relationships with each other, potential conflicts between them, etc.?
- What new ideas or layers of meaning do these details add to the story's message?

---

**Chapter 8**        **Text 2**

▶ p. 231

## African identities

### 4  Support

Consider the following questions while working on the task:
- What are some typical images that are associated with Africa?
- What do I know about the different countries in Africa?
- What are some typical images that are associated with Europe?
- What do I know about the different countries in Europe?
- What are the dangers of negative or positive stereotypes?

---

**Text 7**

▶ p. 240

## Nigerian oil – a blessing or a curse?

### 4  Support

Possible search terms:
petroleum industry • revenues • economic diversification • Niger delta • oil spills • natural gas flaring

# No future for the young?

▶ p. 242

## 2 Support

Possible search terms:
education • employment • services (e.g., essential services such as gas, water, electricity; health services) • housing • environmental protection

# Egúngún

▶ p. 243

## 4 Support

Aspects you may want to watch out for:
flashbacks • slow-motion • blurred images • loudness and silence • camera angles • light and shadow • hard cuts • music

# Using DNA technology to combat disease

▶ p. 263

## 2 Support

**Step 1:** Find examples in the text of how the author describes
- Jennifer Doudna's work.
- how CRISPR has changed the world.
- the future impact of CRISPR.

Then think: Is CRISPR described in a positive or negative light?

**Step 2:** Find an example in the text of the author directly commenting on Jennifer Doudna's work. Then think: Does he agree or disagree with the scientist?

**Step 3:** Summarize your insights from 1 and 2 using the simple present.

## Text 4

▶ p. 263

### The science of happiness, learning and the brain

#### 1 Support

The podcast uses a number of noteworthy terms and phrases. How would you convey the following in English?

- 'die Anpassungsmaschine Gehirn'
- 'Zufallsglück'
- 'ein Hochgefühl vermitteln'
- 'ein Verhalten zeigen'
- 'eine Belohnung bekommen'

## Text 5

▶ p. 268

### Will AI outsmart humanity?

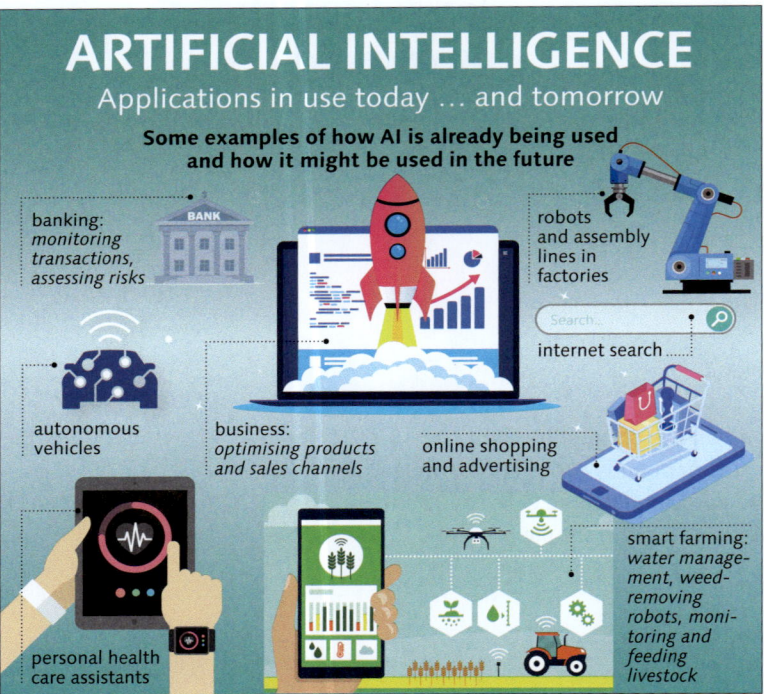

**Partner B**

**1 a** Study the infographic on the left, then go back to task **1b**.

# R'ha

▶ p. 270

## 3 Support

The questions below may help you analyse your aspect of the film:

**Animation techniques**
- A *shot* is a single continuous motion captured by the (virtual) camera between two *cuts*. When does the film use many cuts, when only a few? Why?
- Can you find scenes in which the film uses (virtual) close-up/medium/long/low-angle/high-angle shots? What are the intended effects?

**Sound:**
- Can you find scenes in which the film makes special use of music and sounds? What are the intended effects?
- What do you notice about the human voices used in the film?

**Colour**
- What colours are predominant? What mood or atmosphere is evoked?
- What do you notice about the use of brightness and darkness in the film? What purpose does it serve?

# After the storm

## 3 Support

▶ p. 273

Novelists often use descriptions of nature, the weather, or landscapes and surroundings to mirror a character's inner life. Explain the connection between the devastation left behind by Hurricane Katrina and Esch's state of mind.

*Now go back to task 4.*

# Fighting climate change

▶ p. 277

## 2 Support

When approaching this task, it may be helpful to consider the following questions.
- What exactly is being shown in the video?
- Who is speaking?
- What cinematic techniques are used? For example, do they use effects such as slow motion and fast forward?

- How does the video show historical developments?
- What are the different devices used to inform, convince and evoke emotions in the viewer?
- How are technical processes illustrated?
- What kind of music is used and to what effect?

**Chapter 10**  **Text 6**

▶ p. 297

### Annotations

1 **disdainful** arrogant, looking down on others
1 **she** Beatrice
6 **loquacious** [ləˈkweɪʃəs] talking a lot
10 **be/feel tempted to do sth.** feel a wish to do sth.
10 **beyond description** impossible to describe
11 **warranted** made necessary
11 **lurk** (v) wait secretly
11 **his request** his asking
13 **Prince** Don Pedro in Shakespeare's play
13 **speakeasy** a place where alcohol could be bought or consumed illegally during the time of Prohibition in the USA (1920s–1930s)
16 **acquire sth.** [əˈkwaɪə(r)] gain sth., obtain sth.
21 **nasty** very bad
24 **plagued** troubled
26 **a hill of beans** (AE) a very small amount

# Adapting Shakespeare

## Partner B

Read the excerpt from *Speak Easy, Speak Love,* McKelle George's 2017 adaptation of *Much Ado About Nothing.* The two \*protagonists dance with each other at a festivity.

'At first I thought you must have learned I was disdainful from someone else,' she said. 'Benedick Scott perhaps?'

'Who's that?' he asked, all innocence.

'You must know him.'

5 'I don't, believe me.'

'Lord Loquacious, they'd call him.' They were dancing, she realized. As long as she let him lead, she actually did all right. He was irritatingly graceful, and this, even more irritatingly, didn't surprise her.

'Describe him, won't you? Maybe I've seen him.'

10 She was tempted to say he was beyond description – the only truthful response that question warranted – but lurking within his request was the monster of opportunity.

'He's Prince's little pet,' she said after a pause. 'The speakeasy's mascot. Quick on his feet, entertaining and whatnot, but not much substance underneath. He wants 15 to write, I hear, but he's too much a snob for it. The upper class think some skill they acquired in an expensive classroom can pass as art, but they haven't got anything real to say. They don't understand the world outside their social circle.'

By the time she finished, his grip was painful, but she pretended not to notice. Below the mask his mouth was a grim line.

20 'When I do meet this gentleman,' he said at last, 'I'll tell him what you said.'

'Oh, please do. He'll have a few nasty things to say about me, too, I'm sure. But we really ought to be nice. Why would he be here at all if he weren't desperately lonely?'

He practically threw her away from him, taking a step back. Beatrice had always been plagued with a mouth that was a little too big and a little too full of salt and 25 vinegar or, most offensive of all, too full of the truth. Still, she couldn't imagine Benedick gave a hill of beans about her opinion – even if he truly believed she thought she was talking to a stranger.

'Sir, perhaps you –'

'Excuse me,' he muttered, the country accent gone, and stormed away. Beatrice
30 watched him go, wondering if the slight twist in her stomach was, for the first
time, guilt over speaking her mind.

*From: McKelle George,* Speak Easy, Speak Love, *2017*

**1 a** Together with your partner, summarize what happens in Shakespeare's
scene.
   **b** Listen to your partner. Then point out which elements of the original have
been kept in McKelle George's version and what has been changed.
*Now go back to p. 298 and work on task 2.*

**Text 7**

# Art in Context: Portraying Shakespeare

▶ p. 299

## 2 Support

To structure your observations, the following table may be helpful:

|  | Chandos | McFarren |
|---|---|---|
| Head and body | ... | ... |
| Clothing | ... | ... |
| Posture | ... | ... |
| Background | ... | ... |

Annotations
**29 mutter sth.** say sth. quietly and angrily
**30 slight twist** small sudden turn

## Chapter 2

► More info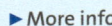

**Annotations**

1  **aloof** not interested in other people
2  **predicament** difficult situation
12 **filing** small piece of metal
15 **whack** act of hitting sb./sth.
15 **Tom and Jerry's cartoon** popular series of cartoons featuring a mouse and a cat
16 **coppers** (pl) coins of low value
30 **Darcey Bussell** (born 1969) British retired ballerina, who went on to have a career in TV

# Loose change   Andrea Levy

*Read the following extract from a short story on a chance encounter in London.*

I am not in the habit of making friends of strangers. [...] I'm a Londoner – aloof sweats from my pores. But I was in a bit of a predicament; my period was two days early and I was caught unprepared.

I'd just gone into the National Portrait Gallery to get out of the cold. [...] My fingers
5 were numb, searching in my purse for change for the tampon machine; I barely felt the pull of the zip. But I didn't have any coins. I was forced to ask in a loud voice in this small lavatory, 'Has anyone got three twenty-pence pieces?'

Everyone seemed to leave the place at once – all of them Londoners. I was sure of it. Only she was left – fixing her hair in the mirror.

10 'Do you have change?'

She turned round slowly as I held out a ten-pound note. She had the most spectacular eyebrows. I could see the lines of black hair, like magnetized iron filings, tumbling across her eyes and almost joining above her nose. [...] She had wide black eyes and a round face with such a solid jawline that she looked to have taken
15 a gentle whack from Tom and Jerry's cartoon frying pan. She dug into the pocket of her jacket and pulled out a bulging handful of money. It was coppers mostly. Some of it tinkled on to the floor. But she had change: too much – I didn't want a bag full of the stuff myself.

'Have you a five-pound note as well?' I asked.

20 She dropped the coins on to the basin area, spreading them out into the soapy puddles of water that were lying there. Then she said, 'You look?' She had an accent but I couldn't tell then where it was from; I thought maybe Spain.

'Is this all you've got?' I asked. She nodded. 'Well, look, let me just take this now ...' I picked three damp coins out of the pile. 'Then I'll get some change in the shop
25 and pay them back to you.' Her gaze was as keen as a cat with string. 'Do you understand? Only I don't want all those coins.'

'Yes,' she said softly.

I was grateful. I took the money. But when I emerged from the cubicle the girl and her handful of change were gone.

30 I found her again staring at the portrait of Darcy Bussell. Her head was inclining from one side to the other as if the painting were a dress she might soon try on for size. I approached her about the money but she just said, 'This is good picture.' [...]

'Really, you like it?' I said.

'She doesn't look real. It looks like ...' Her eyelids fluttered sleepily as she searched
35 for the right word, 'a dream.'

That particular picture always reminded me of the doodles girls drew in their rough books at school.

'You don't like?' she asked. I shrugged. 'You show me one you like,' she said. [...]

40 Her eyes were encircled with dark shadows so that even when she smiled – introducing herself cheerfully as Laylor – they remained as mournful as a glum kid at a party. [...]

Alan Bennett with his mysterious little brown bag didn't impress her at all. She preferred the photograph of Beckham. Germaine Greer made her top lip curl and as for A. S. Byatt, she laughed out loud, 'This is child make this?'

45 We were almost making a scene. Laylor couldn't keep her voice down and people were beginning to watch us. I wanted to be released from my obligation. 'Look, let me buy us both a cup of tea,' I said. 'Then I can give you back your money.'

She brought out her handful of change again as we sat down at a table – eagerly passing it across to me to take some for the tea.

50 'No, I'll get this,' I said.

Her money jangled like a win on a slot machine as she tipped it back into her pocket. When I got back with the tea, I pushed over the twenty-pences I owed her. She began playing with them on the tabletop pushing one around the other two in a figure of eight. Suddenly she leant towards me as if there were a conspiracy be-
55 tween us and said, 'I like art,' With that announcement a light briefly came on in those dull eyes to reveal that she was no more than eighteen. A student perhaps.

'Where are you from?' I asked.

'Uzbekistan,' she said.

Was that the Balkans? I wasn't sure. 'Where is that?'

60 She licked her finger, then with great concentration drew an outline on to the tabletop. 'This is Uzbekistan,' she said. She licked her finger again to carefully plop a wet dot on to the map saying, 'And I come from here – Tashkent.'

'And where is all this?' I said, indicating the area around the little map with its slowly evaporating borders and town. She screwed up her face as if to say nowhere.

65 'Are you on holiday?' I asked.

She nodded.

'How long are you here for?'

Leaning her elbows on the table she took a sip of her tea, 'Ehh, it is bitter!' she shouted.

70 'Put some sugar in it,' I said, pushing the sugar sachets toward her.

She was reluctant, 'Is for free?' she asked.

'Yes, take one.'

The sugar spilled as she clumsily opened the packet. I laughed it off but she, with the focus of a prayer, put her cup up to the edge of the table and swept the sugar

**Annotations**
42 **Alan Bennett** (born 1934)  English actor and author
43 **Beckham** (= David Beckham, born 1975)  retired English football star
43 **Germaine Greer** (born 1939)  Australian scholar and feminist writer
44 **A. S. Byatt** [ˈbaɪət] (born 1936) pen name of Dame Antonia Susan Duffy, English novelist and poet
51 **slot machine** *Spielautomat*

**Annotations**

75 **detritus** *(fml)* pieces of waste
82 **doggedly deter-mined** very deter-mined
83 **aggrieved** *gekränkt*
97 **chipped** *eingerissen, abgebrochen*
98 **fringe** front part of sb.'s hair
98 **blunt** not sharp
113 **sleep rough** sleep in the streets

75 into it with the side of her hand. The rest of the detritus that was on the tabletop fell into the tea as well. Some crumbs, a tiny scrap of paper and a curly black hair floated on the surface of her drink. I felt sick as she put the cup back to her mouth.

'Pour that one away, I'll get you another one.'

Just as I said that a young boy arrived at our table and stood, legs astride, before
80 her. He pushed down the hood on his padded coat. His head was curious – flat as a cardboard cut-out – with hair stuck to his sweaty forehead in black curlicues. And his face was as doggedly determined as two fists raised. They began talking in whatever language it was they spoke. Laylor's tone pleading – the boy's aggrieved. Laylor took the money from her pocket and held it up to him. She slapped his hand
85 away when he tried to wrest all the coins from her palm. Then, as abruptly as he had appeared, he left. Laylor called something after him.

Everyone turned to stare at her, except the boy, who just carried on.

'Who was that?'

With the teacup resting on her lip, she said, 'My brother. He want to know where
90 we sleep tonight.'

'Oh, yes, where's that?' I was rummaging through the contents of my bag for a tissue, so it was casually asked.

'It's square we have slept before.'

'Which hotel is it?' [...]

95 'No hotel, just the square.'

It was then I began to notice things I had not seen before: dirt under each of her chipped fingernails, the collar of her blouse crumpled and unironed, a tiny cut on her cheek, a fringe that looked to have been cut with blunt nail-clippers. [...]

'How do you mean just in the square?'

100 'We sleep out in the square,' she said. It was so simple she spread her hands to suggest the lie of her bed.

'Outside?'

She nodded.

'Tonight?'

105 'Yes.'

The memory of the bitter cold still tingled at my fingertips as I said, 'Why?' It took her no more than two breaths to tell me the story. She and her brother had had to leave their country, Uzbekistan, when their parents, who were journalists, were arrested. It was arranged very quickly – friends of their parents acquired passports
110 for them and put them on to a plane. They had been in England for three days but they knew no one here. This country was just a safe place. Now all the money they had could be lifted in the palm of a hand to a stranger in a toilet. So they were sleeping rough – in the shelter of a square, covered in blankets, on top of some cardboard. [...]

115   I didn't know anything about people in her situation. Didn't they have to go somewhere? Croydon, was it? Couldn't she have gone to the police? Or some charity? My life was hard enough without this stranger tramping through it. She smelt of mildewed washing. Imagine her dragging that awful stink into my kitchen. Cupping her filthy hands round my bone china. Smearing my white linen. [...] Slump-
120   ing on to my sofa and kicking off her muddy boots as she yanked me down into her particular hell. How would I ever get rid of her? [...]

  'Last week …' she began, her voice quivering, 'I was in home.' This was embarrassing. I couldn't turn the other way, the girl was staring straight at me. 'This day, Friday,' she went on, 'I cooked fish for my mother and brother.' The whites of her
125   eyes were becoming soft and pink; she was going to cry. 'This day Friday I am here in London,' she said. 'And I worry I will not see my mother again.'

  Only a savage would turn away when it was merely kindness that was needed. I resolved to help her. I had three warm bedrooms, one of them empty. I would make her dinner. Fried chicken or maybe poached fish in wine. I would run her a bath
130   filled with bubbles. Wrap her in thick towels heated on a rail. I would then hunt out some warm clothes and after I had put my son to bed I would make her cocoa. We would sit and talk. I would let her tell me all that she had been through. Wipe her tears and assure her that she was now safe. I would phone a colleague from school and ask him for advice. Then in the morning I would take Laylor to wherever she
135   needed to go. And before we said goodbye I would press my phone number into her hand. All Laylor's grandchildren would know my name.

  Her nose was running with snot. She pulled down the sleeve of her jacket to drag it across her face and said, 'I must find my brother.'

  I didn't have any more tissues. 'I'll get you something to wipe your nose,' I said.

140   I got up from the table. She watched me, frowning, the tiny hairs of her eyebrows locking together like Velcro. I walked to the counter where serviettes were lying in a neat pile. I picked up four. Then standing straight I walked on. Not back to Laylor but up the stairs to the exit. I pushed through the revolving doors and threw myself into the cold.

*From:* Underwords: The Hidden City, *2005*

Annotations
116 **Croydon** area in South London
118 **mildewed** ['mɪld-juːd] *muffig, schimme-lig*
119 **bone china** fine porcelain

## Comprehension

1   Describe the narrator's reaction to Laylor and how it changes in the course of the story.

## Analysis

2   Analyse how the narrator presents what she and Laylor say and think and the effect this has.

3   Examine the narrative perspective of the story and the effect it has for the events covered in the story.

▶ More info

Advanced

### Beyond the text

▶ SF 28: Argumentative
writing: discussion and
comment, p. 382

▶ Check (tasks a, b)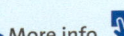

**4** You choose  Writing
**a** Write a comment on the the the
narrator's behaviour.
**b** Two weeks after the incident described in
the story, the narrator writes a letter to a London
newspaper in which she briefly describes her
behaviour and explains how she now feels
about her decision.

## Chapter 3

Advanced

▶ More info

# Someone is watching   Dave Eggers

*In Dave Egger's novel* The Circle, *Mae Holland finds a job at a California high-tech firm
called 'the Circle'. In the following excerpt she and her colleague Annie see the CEO
Eamon Bailey for the first time.*

**Annotations**
1 **lucite** kind of
transparent plastic
2 **gut** waist
4 **amplify sth.** make sth.
louder
14 **deprive sb. of sth.** *jdm.
etwas vorenthalten*
16 **where the heck** *(sl)* wo
zum Teufel
21 **break** (n) big wave
23 **proliferate** become
common
27 **take** (n) opinion

Mae's attention was pulled to the stage, where a man was walking to a lucite podium,
amid a roar of applause. He was a tall man of about forty-five, round in the gut but
not unhealthy, wearing jeans and blue V-neck sweater. There was no discernible
microphone, but when he began speaking, his voice was amplified and clear.

5 'Hello everyone. My name is Eamon Bailey,' he said, to another round of applause
that he quickly discouraged. 'Thank you. I'm so glad to see you all here. A bunch
of you are new to the company since I last spoke, one whole month ago.' [...]

'Newbies,' Bailey said, 'you're in for something special. This is called Dream Friday, where we present something we're working on. Often it's one of our engineers
10 or designers or visionaries, and sometimes it's just me. And today, for better or for
worse, it's just me. For that I apologize in advance.'

'We love you Eamon!' came a voice from the audience. Laughter followed. [...]

'Yes,' he continued, 'it's been a whole month since I've gotten up on this stage, and
I know my replacements have been unsatisfying. I am sorry to deprive you of my-
15 self. I realize there is no substitute.' The joke brought laughter throughout the hall.
'And I know a lot of you have been wondering just where the heck I've been.'

A voice from the front of the room yelled 'surfing!' and the room laughed.

'Well, that's right. I have been doing some surfing, and that's part of what I'm here
to talk about. I love to surf, and when I want to surf, I need to know how the waves
20 are. Now, it used to be that you'd wake up and call the local surf shop and ask them
about the breaks. And pretty soon they stopped answering their phones.'

Knowing laughter came from the older contingent in the room.

'When cellphones proliferated, you could call your buddies who might have gotten
out to the beach before you. They, too, stopped answering their phones.'

25 Another big laugh from the audience.

'Seriously, though. It's not practical to make twelve calls every morning, and can
you trust someone else's take on the conditions? The surfers don't want any more

Annotations
37 **pixilated** *pixelig*
38 **titter** *laugh*
44 **awe** *amazement*
50 **high-res** *hochaufgelöst*
55 **the precise model** *genau das Modell*
56 **magnification** *Vergrößerung*
65 **stake** *stick*

bodies on the limited breaks we get up here. So then the internet happened, and here and there some geniuses set up cameras on the beaches. We could log on and get some pretty crude images of the waves at Stinson Beach. It was almost worse than calling the surf shop! The technology was pretty primitive. Streaming technology still is. Or was. Until now.'

A screen descended behind him.

'Okay. Here's how it used to look.'

The screen showed a standard browser display, and an unseen hand typed in the url for a website called SurfSight. A poorly designed site appeared, with a tiny image of a coastline streaming in the middle. It was pixilated and comically slow. The audience tittered.

'Almost useless, right? Now, as we know, streaming video has gotten a lot better in recent years. But it's still slower than real life, and the screen quality is pretty disappointing. So we've solved, I think, the quality issues in the last year. Let's now refresh that page to show the site with our new video delivery.'

Now the page was refreshed, and the coastline was full-screen, and the resolution was perfect. There were sounds of awe throughout the room.

'Yes, this is live video of Stinson Beach. This is Stinson right at this moment. Looks pretty good, right? Maybe I should be out there, as opposed to standing here with you!'

Annie leaned into Mae. 'The next part's incredible. Just wait.'

'Now, many of you still aren't so impressed. As we all know, many machines can deliver high-res streaming video, and many of your tablets and phones can already support them. But there are a couple new aspects to all this. The first part is how we're getting this image. Would it surprise you to know that this isn't coming from a big camera, but actually just one of these?'

He was holding a small device in his hand, the shape and size of a lollipop.

'This is a video camera, and this is the precise model that's getting this incredible image quality. Image quality that holds up to this kind of magnification. So that's the first great thing. We can now get high-def-quality resolution in a camera the size of a thumb. Well, a very big thumb. The second great thing is that, as you can see, this camera needs no wires. It's transmitting this image via satellite.'

A round of applause shook the room.

'Wait. Did I say it runs on a lithium battery that lasts two years? No? Well it does. And we're a year away from an entirely solar-powered model, too. And it's waterproof, sandproof, windproof, animal-proof, insect-proof, everything-proof.'

More applause overtook the room.

'Okay, so I set up that camera this morning. I taped it to a stake, stuck that stake in the sand, in the dunes, with no permit, nothing. In fact, no one knows it's there. So this morning I turned it on, then I drove back to the office, accessed Camera One, Stinson Beach, and I got this image. Not bad. But that's not the half of it.

# Advanced Literary Analysis

81 **smattering** small amount
82 **closed-circuit TV** *Videoüberwachung*
82 **cross sth. with sth.** combine sth. with sth.
84 **prohibitively expensive** too expensive
86 **retail sth.** offer sth. for sale
88 **aloft** high
99 **feed** (n) video input
105 **Tahoe** skiing area in California
107 **ridge** *Berghang*
107 **conifer** kind of tree

Actually, I was pretty busy this morning. I drove around, and set up one at Rodeo
70 Beach, too.'

And now the original image, of Stinson Beach, shrunk and moved to a corner of the screen. Another box emerged, showing the waves at Rodeo Beach, a few miles down the Pacific coast. 'And now Montara. And Ocean Beach. Fort Point.' With each beach Bailey mentioned, another live image appeared. There were now six
75 beaches in a grid, each of them live, visible with perfect clarity and brilliant color.

'Now remember: no one sees these cameras. I've hidden them pretty well. To the average person they look like weeds, or some kind of stick. Anything. They're unnoticed. So in a few hours this morning, I set up perfectly clear video access to six locations that help me know how to plan my day. And everything we do here is
80 about knowing the previously unknown, right?'

Heads nodded. A smattering of applause.

'Okay, so, many of you are thinking, Well, this is just like closed-circuit TV crossed with streaming technology, satellites, all that. Fine. But as you know, to do this with extant technology would have been prohibitively expensive for the average person.
85 But what if all this was accessible and affordable to anyone? My friends, we're looking at retailing these – in just a few months, mind yo – at fifty-nine dollars each.'

Bailey held the lollipop camera out, and threw it to someone in the front row. The woman who caught it held it aloft, turning to the audience and smiling gleefully.

'You can buy ten of them for Christmas and suddenly you have constant access to
90 everywhere you want to be – home, work, traffic conditions. And anyone can install them. It takes five minutes tops. Think of the implications!'

The screen behind him cleared, the beaches disappearing, and a new grid appeared.

'Here's the view from my back yard,' he said, revealing a live feed of a tidy and
95 modest back yard. 'Here's my front yard. My garage. Here's one on a hill overlooking Highway 101 where it gets bad during rush hour. Here's one near my parking space to make sure no one parks there.'

And soon the screen had sixteen discrete images on it, all of them transmitting live feed.

100 'Now, these are just *my* cameras. I access them all by simply typing in Camera 1, 2, 3, 12, whatever. Easy. But what about sharing? That is, what if my buddy has some cameras posted, and wants to give me access?'

And now the screen's grid multiplied, from sixteen boxes to thirty-two. 'Here's Lionel Fitzpatrick's screens. He's into skiing, so he's got cameras positioned so he
105 can tell the conditions at twelve locations all over Tahoe.'

Now there were twelve live images of white-topped mountains, ice-blue valleys, ridges topped with deep green conifers.

'Lionel can give me access to any of the cameras he wants. It's just like friending someone, but now with access to all their live feeds. Forget cable. Forget five hun-
110 dred channels. If you have one thousand friends, and they have ten cameras each,

you now have ten thousand options for live footage. If you have five thousand friends, you have fifty thousand options. And soon you'll be able to connect to millions of cameras around the world. Again, imagine the implications!'

115 The screen atomized into a thousand mini-screens. Beaches, mountains, lakes, cities, offices, living rooms. The crowd applauded wildly. Then the screen went blank, and from the black emerged a peace sign, in white.

'Now imagine the human rights implications. Protesters on the streets of Egypt no longer have to hold up a camera, hoping to catch a human rights violation or a murder and then somehow get the footage out of the streets and online. Now it's
120 as easy as gluing a camera to a wall. Actually, we've done just that.'

A stunned hush came over the audience.

'Let's have Camera 8 in Cairo.'

A live shot of a street scene appeared. There were banners lying on the street, a pair of police in riot gear standing in the distance.

125 'They don't know we see them, but we do. The world is watching. And listening. Turn up the audio.'

Suddenly they could hear a clear conversation, in Arabic, between pedestrians passing near the camera, unawares.

'And of course most of the cameras can be manipulated manually or with voice
130 recognition. Watch this. Camera 8, turn left.' On screen, the camera's view of the Cairo street panned left. 'Now right.' It panned right. He demonstrated it moving up, down, diagonally, all with remarkable fluidity.

The audience applauded again.

'Now, remember that these cameras are cheap, and easy to hide, and they need no
135 wires. So it hasn't been that hard for us to place them all over. Let's show Tahrir.'

Gasps from the audience. On screen there was now a live shot of Tahrir Square, the cradle of the Egyptian Revolution.

'We've had our people in Cairo attaching cameras for the last week. They're so small the army can't find them. They don't even know where to look! Let's show the
140 rest of the views. Camera 2. Camera 3. Four. Five. Six.'

There were six shots of the square, each so clear that sweat on any face could be seen, the nametags of every soldier easily read.

'Now 7 through 50.' [...]

Live shots from all over the square filled the screen, and the crowd erupted again.
145 Bailey went on, revealing their coverage of a dozen authoritarian regimes, from Khartoum to Pyongyang, where the authorities had no idea they were being watched by three thousand Circlers in California – had no notion that they *could* be watched, that this technology was or would ever be possible.

Now Bailey cleared the screen again, and stepped toward the audience. 'You know
150 what I say, right? In situations like this, I agree with the Hague, with human rights activists the world over. There needs to be accountability. Tyrants can no longer

Annotations
124 **riot gear** *Schutzausrüstung*
131 **pan** (v) move, turn
137 **Egyptian revolution** series of protests against lack of political freedom and economic stability in Egypt in 2011 initiating a transition towards more democratic structures
146 **Khartoum** capital of Sudan
146 **Pyongyang** capital of North Korea
150 **the Hague** = the International Court of Justice in Den Haag, Netherlands
151 **accountability** *Rechenschaft*

Advanced

Annotation
153 **bear witness** *Zeugnis ablegen*

hide. There needs to be, and will be, documentation and accountability, and we need to bear witness. And to this end, I insist that all that happens should be known.'

155 The words dropped onto the screen:

ALL THAT HAPPENS MUST BE KNOWN.

*From:* The Circle, *2013*

### Comprehension

**1** Describe the latest invention of the Circle and why Bailey believes it will have an enormous impact.

### Analysis

**2** Examine how Bailey tries to influence his audience.

### Beyond the text

▶ SF 28: Argumentative writing: discussion and comment, p. 382

▶ Check (task 3)

**3** Writing  Bailey presents his firm's invention as a great step forward for humanity. Do you agree? Write a comment.

**4** You choose  Writing

▶ SF 35: Writing a formal letter or email, p. 391

▶ Check (tasks a, b)

**a** Imagine that you work for the Circle. After Bailey's speech you decide to quit. Write an email to a friend listing reasons for your decision.

**b** After writing the email to your friend you write your letter of resignation to the Circle. Make sure to include only those reasons for quitting that would be appropriate to mention and to phrase your motivation in a suitable manner.

Chapter 4 / Chapter 6

Advanced

▶ More info

## Fly the friendly skies   Sunita Jain

*In the following short story, an immigrant from India describes how he experiences his new home, New York.*

Annotations
2 **belch sth. out** eject sth. by force
6 **onslaught** mass movement
9 **gaga eyed** amazed, fascinated
10 **gadgets galore** *Überfluss an Krimskrams*

It was again the hurry-home time – the time most difficult for an outsider or alien in a foreign country. The buildings belched out men and women as if out of compulsion, and New York's Fifth Avenue, as were the other streets at that hour, was a veritable escalator of moving traffic. Arjun sat near the window inside the cafe and
5 watched the Whites, Blacks and peoples of every description cluttering the sidewalk in their simultaneous onslaught.

He felt lonesome sitting by himself while all around him New York moved to get home. Arjun could not have moved even if he had wanted. All day he had window shopped, gazing gaga eyed at the mannequins in the windows, the automatic toys,
10 the gadgets galore. He had no money to buy anything yet, and he was in no hurry

to possess any of the wealth that littered the shops. Instead he had felt extremely tired and alone. The excitement with which he had left India and reached New York three days ago, had disappeared.

A group of smartly dressed young women went past his window. *America is incred-*
15 *ibly erotic. Too many legs make all these streets sexy* … Whose lines were these? Too many legs, but not erotic. Nothing stirred in Arjun except the vague evenings near Regal or Janpath and the sway of some Indian girl's body baling out the hypnotic scent of jasmine *gajaras*. The girls outside his window were shadows on a screen and distant. He was too ignorant and unbearably scared.

20 The new world around him had expanded into the multitude outside, and the sounds enveloping him were unfamiliarly harsh. He understood now why his elder brother had not left the small village in Panjab to which his family belonged. 'What does a man need…' his brother had said in answer to Arjun's pleading to shift to New Delhi, 'what does a man need to live out his life happily except a small
25 place he can belong to and a known face? I'll never belong to anything in your New Delhi …'

Nonsense. Arjun stiffened himself. A small place stinks and stagnates – it chokes you by degrees. Even New Delhi got too small; there weren't any jobs anymore or decent houses within the reach of one's income. One had to, one must, enlarge
30 one's world in order to fully unfold – Joyce did it, and Henry James …

It was getting dark outside. The shadows struggled with the glare of lights. He paid for his coffee and stepped out. 'Don't loiter in NY after seven … stay indoors. There is too much crime these days …' An old friend settled in Washington had advised him through letters. A close-cropped young man ran swiftly past Arjun. His heart
35 dropped a beat. 'It's not healthy to be so scared.' Arjun chastised himself. 'I am starting a new to chapter of my life in America, the beautiful. I'll get used to it just as I got used to the IIT hostel life in Delhi.'

The air grew slightly chilly. He walked close to the warmth of the walls that glowed with electric lights. He was ravenously hungry. For three days now he had eaten
40 more sweet dishes and fruits than at any other time in his life. The few vegetable and cheese preparations he tried had strange tastes, and were unable to satisfy his hunger. His stomach growled for spicy food, for peas thick with large chunks of *panir,* for potatoes fried whole before they were curried, and for a plate of rich rice *pillao* … The aroma of the food he hungered for assailed his memory and he felt
45 weak in the knees. The thought of sandwiches with milk for dinner revolted him.

He stopped involuntarily outside the large show window of a shop which was now closed for business. Several Indian carpets rioted in color behind the bright glass. Here and there a strategically placed large brass tabletop accented the flavor of the handknotted Mirzapurs, Kashmirs, and Agras.

50 'Aren't they beautiful!' someone said to him, making him jolt out of his reverie. He turned around. An aged white woman carrying a heavy grocery bag in the cradle of her left arm stood by the window. She too had stopped to look at the carpets.

'You know,' she smiled, 'I can't go past this window without slowing down. Tell me, how long does it take to make one of those?' She pointed to a sharp velvet blue
55 Kashmir. 'I am told they are *actually* handmade …'

Annotations

15 **Whose lines were these?** Who wrote these words?
17 **sway** (n) rhythmic movement
17 **bale sth. out** produce sth. in large quantities
30 **Joyce … Henry James** James Joyce (1882–1941) and Henry James (1843–1916), authors who spent most of their lives outside their country of birth
32 **loiter** stand around
34 **close-cropped** having very short hair
35 **chastise sb.** criticize sb. harshly
37 **IIT** (= Indian Institute of Technology)
39 **ravenous** extreme
42 **growl for sth.** make a low sound indicating the need for sth.
43 *panir* type of Indian cheese
44 *pillao* Indian rice dish
44 **assail sb.** attack sb.
45 **revolt sb.** make sb. feel sick
47 **riot in color** display brilliant colours
50 **reverie** dreamlike thoughts

**Annotations**

68 **elder** (n) old person
71 **reckless** not caring about risks
75 **disengage yourself** leave a conversation
88 **lash** (n) *Schlag*
88 **relent** give in
93 **United** = United Airlines, Inc., a large American airline; 'Fly the friendly skies of United' was their slogan for many years

He mumbled a reply, for he himself did not know how long it takes to knot a Kashmir carpet, big or small. In just the few days away from home, Arjun had learned how little he knew about India, and how much he had taken for granted, or had never bothered to know the statistics of. Whenever people asked him *when* or *how* or *where* of something or an event – he had uttered confused answers.

The two moved away from the window. The lady walked rather slowly as if her feet or legs hurt. He realized then that she was actually very old. She was telling him about how once when she was in high school she had wanted to go to India.

The woman grew nostalgic and sentimental about her past. Her voice sounded glad to have an audience. She pointed out the names of buildings and places that could be of interest to a newcomer. Arjun's mind began to wander, looking for an excuse to excuse himself. The friend in Washington had written: you will meet a very large number of lonely elders in this country. Avoid cultivating their friendship even if you are lonesome, for you will end up hurting their feelings...

The two had drifted away from the business section, and he had a feeling he was lost. But somehow it did not bother him. Home-sickness had made him reckless. 'I'll hail a taxi back to my hotel,' he assured himself.

'I live in that building.' The lady indicated one of the several red brick buildings sectioned into layers of apartments. 'Have you had your supper?' she asked.

'Not yet.' He tried to disengage himself. A tall, dark Indian appeared on the other side of the street. 'Excuse me, Mam, there's a friend I want to say hello to ...' waving a hurried goodbye he crossed over to the other side.

Arjun was very eager to catch up with the Indian. He had seen other Indian men and women on the streets during the day; but right now he wanted to be able to talk to one. To have a chat about *home* over a cup of tea!

'Hello ...' His voice was as eager as his manner.

'Yes?' The man looked at him. The expression in the man's eye however made Arjun stammer suddenly.

'Are you from India?' he asked, but felt very foolish in asking it.

'Yes,' the man answered.

'I am also from India.'

'So?' The man stared at Arjun.

The lash of the insult flushed his face. The man relented. 'Look, young man,' he said to Arjun in a cryptic voice, 'you are probably new here, but you did not travel ten thousand miles to know another Indian, nor did I. Good-night.'

The street light changed. The elderly woman had entered her apartment building. The revolving door swallowed her. In the distance the neon sign flashed rhythmically, fly the friendly skies – of United ...

*From:* Short Stories Universal. Thirty Stories from the English-Speaking World, *1993*

Advanced

## Comprehension

**1** Summarize the events of the story.

► Getting started

## Analysis

**2** Analyse Arjun's reactions to his new surroundings and what they reveal about his character.

**3** Examine the narrative perspective of the story and the effect it has on the events covered in the story.

## Beyond the text

**4** `You choose` `Writing`

    **a** Back in his hotel room the same evening, Arjun writes a letter to his brother in India describing his first impressions of New York and how he now feels about his decision to emigrate.

    **b** Write a comment on the challenges of adapting to life in a new country, referring to the text at hand and to other texts or films.

► SF 28: Argumentative writing: discussion and comment, p. 382

► SF 38: Creative writing, p. 395

► Check (tasks a, b)

## Chapter 8

Advanced

## Aunty Ifeoma     Chimamanda Ngozi Adichie

► More info

*In this extract from Adichie's novel* Purple Hibiscus, *Ifeoma, a lecturer at the university in Nsukka, visits her brother Eugene and his family right before Christmas. They are a deeply Christian family living in Enugu, Nigeria. The story is told from Kambili's perspective, Ifeoma's 15 year-old niece. Ifeoma's husband Ifediora died in a car crash.*

Aunty Ifeoma came the next day, in the evening, when the orange trees started to cast long, wavy shadows across the water fountain in the front yard. Her laughter floated upstairs into the living room, where I sat reading. I had not heard it in two years, but I would know that cackling, hearty sound anywhere. Aunty Ifeoma was
5 as tall as Papa, with a well-proportioned body. She walked fast, like one who knew just where she was going and what she was going to do there. And she spoke the way she walked, as if to get as many words out her mouth as she could in the short-est time.

'Welcome Aunty, *nno*,' I said, rising to hug her.

10 She did not give me the usual brief side hug. She clasped me in her arms and held me tightly against the softness of her body. The wide lapels of her blue A-line dress smelled of lavender.

'Kambili, *kedu*?' A wide smile stretched her dark-complected face, revealing a gap between her front teeth.

15 'I'm fine, Aunty.'

**Annotations**

4 **cackle** (n) sound comparable to the sounds chicken make
4 **hearty** loud and cheerful
9 **nno** (Igbo) Welcome!
13 **kedu** (Igbo) How are you?
13 **dark-complected** dark-skinned

`Info`

The Igbo or Ibo ['iːbəʊ] are a Nigerian ethnic group living predomi-nantly in the south-east of the country.

**Annotations**
21 **aghast** shocked when hearing sth.
23 **remnant** last remaining part of sth.
28 **tight** (here) with her lips pressed together
29 **umunna** (Igbo) clan
33 **sneak sth. home** secretly take sth. home
38 **mmuo** (Igbo) masquerade
38 **Aro festival** Igbo festival celebrated each year in the city of Aro; it involves the display of colourful masquerades
40 **mmuo** (Igbo) masquerade
40 **heathen** *heidnisch*
40 **kwa** (Igbo) sure
53 **guinea fowl** bird belonging to the pheasant family, often kept for meat

'You have grown so much. Look at you, look at you.' She reached out and pulled my left breast. 'Look at how fast these are growing!'

I looked away and inhaled deeply so that I would not start to stutter. I did not know how to handle that kind of playfulness. [...]

20 'Nwunye m,' Aunty Ifeoma called, and Mama turned back.

The first time I heard Aunty Ifeoma call Mama 'nwunye m,' years ago, I was aghast that a woman called another woman 'my wife.' When I asked, Papa said it was the remnants of ungodly traditions, the idea that it was the family and not the man alone that married a wife, and later Mama whispered, although we were alone in 25 my room, 'I am her wife, too, because I am your father's wife. It shows that she accepts me.'

'Nwunye m, come and sit down. You look tired. Are you well?' Aunty Ifeoma asked.

A tight smile appeared on Mama's face. 'I am well, very well. I have been helping the wives of our umunna with the cooking.'

30 'Come and sit down,' Aunty Ifeoma said again. 'Come and sit down and rest. The wives of our umunna can look for the salt themselves and find it. After all, they are here to take from you, to wrap meat in banana leaves when nobody is looking and then sneak it home.' Aunty Ifeoma laughed.

Mama sat down next to me. 'Eugene is arranging for extra chairs to be put outside, 35 especially on Christmas day. So many people have come already.'

'You know our people have no other work at Christmas than to go from house to house,' Aunty Ifeoma said. 'But you can't stay here serving them all day. We should take the children to Abagana for the Aro festival tomorrow, to look at the mmuo.'

'Eugene will not let the children go to a heathen festival,' Mama said.

40 'Heathen festival, kwa? Everybody goes to Aro to look at the mmuo.'

'I know, but you know Eugene.'

Aunty Ifeoma shook her head slowly. 'I will tell him we are going for a drive, so we can all spend time together, especially the children.'

Mama fiddled with her fingers and said nothing for a while. Then she asked, 45 'When will you take the children to their father's hometown?'

'Perhaps today, although I don't have the strength for Ifediora's family right now. They eat more and more shit every year. The people in his umunna said he left the money somewhere and I have been hiding it. Last Christmas, one of the women from their compound even told me I had killed him. I wanted to stuff sand in her 50 mouth. Then I thought that I should sit her down, eh, and explain that you do not kill a husband you love, that you do not orchestrate a car accident in which a trailer rams into your husband's car, but again, why waste my time? They all have the brains of guinea fowls.' Aunty Ifeoma made a loud hissing sound. 'I don't know how much longer I will take my children there.'

Annotations
84 **Ifukwa (Igbo)** you see
84 **Philippa** a friend of Ifeoma's

55 Mama clucked in sympathy. 'People do not always talk with sense. But it is good that the children go, especially the boys. They need to know their father's home-stead and the members of their father's *umunna*.'

'I honestly do not know how Ifediora came from an *umunna* like that.'

I watched their lips move as they spoke; Mama's bare lips were pale compared to 60 Aunty Ifeoma's, covered in a shiny bronze lipstick.

'*Umunna* will always say hurtful things,' Mama said. 'Did our own *umunna* not tell Eugene to take another wife because a man of his stature cannot have just two children? If people like you had not been on my side then ...'

'Stop it, stop being grateful. If Eugene had done that, he would have been the loser, 65 not you.'

'So you say. A woman with children and no husband, what is that?'

'Me.'

Mama shook her head. 'You have come again, Ifeoma. You know what I mean. How can a woman live like that?' Mama's eyes had grown round, taking up more 70 space on her face.

'*Nwunye m*, sometimes life begins when marriage ends.'

'You and your university talk. Is this what you tell your students?'

Mama was smiling.

'Seriously, yes. But they marry earlier and earlier these days. What is the use of a 75 degree, they ask me, when we cannot find a job after graduation?'

'At least somebody will take care of them when they marry.'

'I don't know who will take care of whom. Six girls in my first-year seminar class are married, their husbands visit in Mercedes and Lexus cars every weekend, their husbands buy them stereos and textbooks and refrigerators, and when they gradu-80 ate, the husbands own them and their degrees. Don't you see?'

Mama shook her head. 'University talk again. A husband crowns a woman's life, Ifeoma. It is what they want.'

'It is what they think they want. But how can I blame them? Look what this military tyrant is doing to our country. [...] *Ifukwa*, people are leaving the country. Philippa 85 left two months ago. You remember Philippa?'

'She came back with you for Christmas a few years ago. Dark and plump?'

'Yes, she is now teaching in America. She shares a crammed office with another adjunct professor, but she says at least teachers are paid there.' Aunty Ifeoma stopped and reached out to brush something off Mama's blouse. I watched every 90 movement she made; I could not tear my eyes away. It was the fearlessness about her, about the way she gestured as she spoke, the way she smiled to show that wide gap.

*From:* Purple Hibiscus, *2003*

## Comprehension

**1** Compare the attitudes of Kambili's mother and her aunt Ifeoma to the traditional roles of men and women in Nigeria as portrayed in the excerpt.

## Analysis

**2** Examine the impression Ifeoma makes in the excerpt and how it is created.

## Beyond the text

**3** `You choose` `Writing`

▶ SF 28: Argumentative writing: discussion and comment, p. 382

▶ Check (task a)

▶ Getting started (task b)

    **a** 'Progress is not possible without gender equality.' Write a comment on this statement, referring to the text at hand and to other information.

    **b** You are participating in an international youth forum. Your team is preparing a poster presentation on the topic 'Gender roles around the world'. Write an email to other students in your team arguing why this novel excerpt should or should not be included in the presentation.

## Chapter 2

Advanced

## Britain after Brexit  Benedikt Strunz, Annette Dittert

*Brexit has changed the face of the UK and Europe considerably. The following German podcast examines the situation in Britain four years after Brexit.*

**1** **Mediating** You are participating in a summer academy at a British university on 'Four years after Brexit: British and European perspectives'. Your group's task is to give a presentation on how the aftereffects of Brexit are perceived in the German media. You find a podcast in which the UK correspondent of the ARD, Annette Dittert, describes how Britons are coping with the effects of Brexit four years after the separation. Write an introductory statement to your group's presentation giving concrete examples of how Britons are affected by Brexit in their daily lives.

Advanced

## The two faces of the USA  Sandra Navidi

► More info

*For people around the world, the USA is a country they adore. For others, it's a country they despise. The writer of the following text has mixed emotions.*

Ich liebe Amerika. Seit insgesamt über einem Vierteljahrhundert sind die USA meine Wahlheimat, in der ich studiert, gearbeitet und geheiratet habe. Ich lebe in der Metropole Manhattan, habe beträchtliche Zeit in der Provinz verbracht und das Land kreuz und quer bereist, beruflich wie privat. Seit ich denken kann, war
5 Amerika mein Traumland, das ich lange Zeit durch eine rosarote Brille betrachtet habe.

Auf den ersten Blick mag die amerikanische Kultur oberflächlich erscheinen, aber sie ist komplex und voller Widersprüche. Viele Aspekte des Lebens sind in Amerika besser als in anderen Teilen der Welt und Vieles ist einfach anders. Zahlreiche
10 kulturelle Besonderheiten und Nuancen habe ich erst mit der Zeit realisiert. Auch Missstände, Schwachstellen und Nachteile des Landes sind mir nach und nach immer bewusster geworden.

Die größten Stärken Amerikas sind gleichzeitig auch seine größten Schwächen. Die Selbstwahrnehmung als außergewöhnliche Nation, der ausgeprägte Individu-
15 alismus und die wettbewerbsorientierte Leistungsgesellschaft verleihen Selbstbewusstsein, setzen ungeahnte Kräfte frei und ermöglichen es dem Einzelnen, über sich hinaus zu wachsen. Aber ein übersteigertes Selbstbewusstsein kann eine kritische Auseinandersetzung mit sich selbst und der eigenen Vergangenheit verhindern. Der ungezügelte Individualismus kann zu Egoismus und Narzissmus
20 führen und die Leistungsgesellschaft hat de facto einen Sozialdarwinismus zur Folge, bei dem viele Menschen auf der Strecke bleiben und der die Ungleichheit drastisch vergrößert.

Die amerikanische Wirtschaft und die Kultur haben viele Errungenschaften hervorgebracht, die das Land bereichert haben und zu Exportschlagern geworden sind. Aber eine Welt, in der Hollywood, die Medien, die Vergnügungsindustrie, das Silicon Valley und die sozialen Medien regieren und jeder sich selbst und seine Welt so gestalten kann wie er möchte, führt dazu, dass die Grenzen zwischen Fiktion und Realität immer mehr verschwimmen. In dieser alles-ist-möglich Kultur kann sich der einzelne immer weiter von der Realität abkoppeln und in eine imaginäre Welt begeben, in der er alles wahrnehmen, glauben und machen kann, was er möchte.

Auf der Grundlage meiner eigenen Erfahrungen sowie tiefgehender Recherche werde ich in diesem Buch das amerikanische Menschenbild, die Weltanschauung und den nationalen Charakter erläutern. Das Schreiben habe ich in Teilen als emotional herausfordernd empfunden, weil ich dieses Land und seine Menschen schätze und es mir in der Seele weh tut, mit anzusehen wie nahe es an den gesellschaftlichen und politischen Abgrund getaumelt ist.

Wie kann es sein, dass sich Amerika, scheinbar im Zeitraffer auf eine Autokratie zubewegt hat? Dass rund ein Drittel der Amerikaner einer totalitären Herrschaftsform aufgeschlossen sind? Dass 74 Millionen Wähler 2020 für Donald Trump gestimmt haben? Dass Schätzungen zufolge zehn Millionen Menschen sogar gewaltsam unter Einsatz von Waffen für ein weißes, christliches und autoritäres Regime kämpfen würden? Jahrhunderte weißer Vorherrschaft, das Trauma des 11. Septembers, die zunehmende Komplexität unserer Welt und die daraus folgende Ungewissheit waren ideale Bedingungen für die Radikalisierung weiter Teile der Bevölkerung und den Versuch Donald Trumps und der Republikaner, die Demokratie mit faschistischen Mitteln zu kapern.

Meine Sozialisierung im Nachkriegsdeutschland und die Erfahrungen meiner iranischen Familie mit dem Wandel Irans in eine autoritäre Theokratie sowie meine transatlantische Perspektive haben mich für die Formierung extremistischer politischer Tendenzen und den daraus resultierenden Gefahren sensibilisiert. In meiner Arbeit als Rechtsanwältin und Wirtschaftsexpertin auf beiden Seiten des Atlantiks habe ich viel über die menschliche Natur gelernt. Und vielleicht am wichtigsten: Ich habe miterlebt, dass das Unmögliche möglich ist und wir nicht die Augen davor verschließen dürfen, auch wenn wir es nicht glauben möchten.

Die Entwicklung Amerikas ist auch für Europa und Deutschland richtungsweisend, weil Ultranationalisten zunehmend internationale Koalitionen gegen die liberale Werteordnung bilden und die Unterminierung westlicher Allianzen und Institutionen vorantreiben. Die Gegenwart ist die Geschichte von morgen und jetzt ist die Zeit für jeden einzelnen gekommen, sich zu entscheiden, auf welcher Seite der Geschichte er oder sie stehen möchte.

Auch wenn ich in diesem Buch viele Aspekte der amerikanischen Kultur kritisch beleuchtete, möchte ich diese Abfassung nicht als Generalkritik verstanden wissen. Das Land hat schon viele Krisen bewältigt und der überwiegende Teil der Amerikaner ist humanistischen Werten verpflichtet. Amerika ist ein fantastisches Land und ich glaube, hoffe und erwarte, dass die demokratische Mehrheit der Bevölkerung gegen die tyrannische Minderheit obsiegen wird. *(662 words)*

From: 'Vorwort', *Die DNA der USA: Wie tickt Amerika?*, 2022

**1** [Mediating] For your bilingual politics class, you are creating a blog dealing with people's views on the USA. You find Sandra Navidi's book and write a blog entry on her personal assessment of the US.

## Chapter 5

## Climate change goes Hollywood    Paulus Müller, Luisa Neubauer

► More info 👆

*Art often deals with existential questions and experiences. So how then does the music or film industry deal with the topic of climate change?*

🔊 **1** [Mediating] You are a member of an international environmental protection organization and you're preparing an exhibition on popular culture and climate change. You've come across this podcast with German activist Luisa Neubauer. Write a short text on Neubauer's view on the way the film industry deals with climate change which can be used in the exhibition.

## Chapter 10

## How Shakespeare revolutionized German literature

*When Shakespeare became known to a broader German audience in the 18th century, writers such as Schiller and Goethe were full of admiration for this literary genius. Read the following interview with German Shakespeare translator Frank Günther in which he explains their fascination with Shakespeare.*

**Lieske:** Dieses Sprachfaszinosum ist dann ja auch irgendwann in Deutschland eingeschlagen. Sie zitieren Goethe: „Die erste Seite, die ich in ihm las machte mich auf zeitlebens ihm eigen, und wie ich mit dem ersten Stücke fertig war, stund ich wie ein Blindgeborener, dem ein Wunderland das Gesicht in einem Au-
5 genblicke schenkt." [...]

**Günther:** Was Goethe beeindruckt hat, war nicht nur die Sprache. Bis dahin gab es ja eine Regelliteratur in Deutschland, es gab den Literaturpapst Gottsched, der die Sprache nach französischen Grundsätzen, der Einheit von Ort Zeit und Handlung geregelt hatte, der vorgeschrieben hatte, wie man Dichtung herstellt, also Bastel-
10 anweisungen, wie man Poesie zusammenrührt. Diese Regeln, aus dem französischen Dichtungskanon entnommen, wurden als zunehmend beengend empfunden. Nun hatte Lessing diesen Shakespeare entdeckt, der der Regelsprengende war, der anscheinend keine Regeln kannte, der gegen Ort-Zeit-Handlungseinheiten radikal verstieß, der in seinen Stücken in der Zeit sprang, in den Orten
15 sprang, der chaotisch war, der anarchisch war, und dieses Anarchische daran war das, was Goethe faszinierte, weil in diesem scheinbaren Anarchismus eine Befreiung lag von den beengten literarischen, politischen und sozialen Verhältnissen, die seine Zeit gekennzeichnet hatten. So wurde Shakespeare für ihn zu einem quasi-religiösen Erweckungserlebnis, das ihn zu solchen egomanischen Exzessen
20 getrieben hat, wie diese Rede zum Shakespeare-Tag.

**Lieske:** Irgendwann wurde ja dann auch behauptet, der Shakespear'sche Geist sei eigentlich ein deutscher Geist, man sagte, er sei eigentlich nur durch Zufall auf dieser grauen Insel geboren worden, sei aber einer der Unseren. Wie kam es dazu und was ist davon zu halten?

25 **Günther:** Naja, das war in einem besonderen Moment der deutschen Geschichte möglich. Hundert Jahre vorher oder nachher wäre das vermutlich nicht möglich gewesen. Es war dieser Augenblick, wo das sich emanzipierende Bürgertum nach Befreiung und nach Selbstständigkeit drängte. Es gab ja zum Beispiel davor die Ständeklausel, das heißt, Tragödien durften nur von Adeligen handeln, weil nur

30 adelige Menschen große Menschen waren und nur große Menschen können tragisch stürzen. Bürger haben nur kleine, lächerliche Themen, die haben keine Tragik, können auch nicht stürzen. Also sind Bürger nur das Thema in Komödien. Das emanzipierende Bürgertum hat natürlich auch sein Anrecht auf das tragische Erleben der Welt eingeklagt. In dieser Situation war nun plötzlich ein Autor, der

35 Könige und Bettler, und Wahnsinnige und Verliebte, und Verrückte und Mörder alle zugleich in einer Szene auf die Bühne brachte, der keine Klassenschranken scheinbar kannte, obwohl Klassen natürlich vorhanden waren, der aber keine Berührungsängste in dem Sinne hatte, sondern ein Weltpanorama geschaffen hat, in dem alle ihren Platz hatten, und in dem alle im Widerspruch zueinander standen. Dies hatte eine unglaubliche Faszination, weil es etwas war, was es in

40 Deutschland nicht gab, und dieses emanzipative Bemühen des Bürgertums vor der Französischen Revolution fand sich plötzlich in dem Helden Shakespeare wieder, in der Art wie er gedichtet und geschrieben hat.

**Lieske:** Er ragt also hinein in ein sich emanzipierendes Bürgertum, er war der Dichter der Politik?

45 **Günther:** So wurde er zumindest empfunden. Ob er das war oder nicht steht dahin, aber das war, wie er begriffen wurde, wie er eigentlich das Zustandekommen eines deutschen Nationalgefühls mitgefördert hat, oder eben dazu benutzt wurde, je nachdem wie man das sehen will.

50 **Lieske:** [...] Bis zu 80 Prozent Analphabeten lebten damals in Shakespeares Welt. Die Frage ist, für wen hat er damals Theater gemacht, und muss man sich das wie ein Trivialtheater vorstellen, war es Trivialliteratur?

**Günther:** Ja. [...] Shakespeares Stücke dienten primär der Unterhaltung. Nachmittags um zwei wurden die Fahnen hochgezogen, heute wird gespielt. Auf der Nord-

55 seite der Themse sahen die Leute: Die Fahne geht hoch. Die Handwerker und Lehrlinge ließen ihre Arbeit liegen und sind über die Themse in die Theater, um etwas Neues zu erfahren: Unterhaltung, Amüsement, Dramen, Komödien, Schlägereien, Wahnsinnsszenen, Mord und Totschlag, Schlächtereien, Splatter, was man wollte. Es war ein buntes Unterhaltungstheater, das die Leute anzog, das

60 aber natürlich auch von ihrer eigenen Welt erzählt hat. Der Analphabetismus hat den Leuten ja nicht erlaubt, ihre eigene Geschichte zu kennen. Indem Shakespeare zum Beispiel die Geschichte der Rosenkriege, also englische Geschichte, fürs Theater aufbereitet hat. Das war natürlich wahnsinnig spannend, weil diese Erzählungen neu waren. *(679 words)*

From: Tanya Lieske, 'Die Zeit war grausam, brutal und sehr spannend',
*www.Deutschlandfunk.de*, 19 April 2014

**1** Mediating  You have applied for a position as a volunteer at the Shakespeare Trust in Stratford-Upon-Avon. The organizers ask you to submit a short presentation (in English) in which you explain why Shakespeare is considered an important figure in German literary history. You have found the interview with Frank Günther and use it to prepare your contribution. Write and record it.

▶ Getting started

Advanced

# Skills File

# General exam skills

## SF 1   Essentials: exams

You will encounter many different English tests and exams at and after school. Before any exam, you should familiarize yourself with its specific format. However, there are some general tips that will help you to be successful. Most important: start early and organize your work.

### Preparing for the exam

**Step 1   Collecting information**

- Find out where the exam will take place, how long it is and, especially for speaking exams, if you will be given preparation time.
- Look at past exam papers to see what they require.
- Make sure you understand what the different tasks require you to do.
- To get the maximum number of points in your exam, find out about the evaluation criteria to help you to focus on the relevant aspects.
- Make sure you know how to use aids that are allowed in the exam, e.g. dictionaries.

**Step 2   Practising**

- Go over past exam or homework tasks to identify any problem areas and learn from your mistakes.
- Focus on your weak areas. Don't practise what you already know.
- Practise the specific type of exam you will be doing.

### Doing the exam

- Read the instructions carefully. They provide crucial information. Make sure you understand what you are supposed to do – it may help to highlight the exam tasks ('Operatoren') and content keywords.
- If you have to choose between tasks, read all the alternatives before deciding which one to do.
- If you notice that you are becoming nervous, take a quick break before continuing.
- Use your time efficiently and leave enough time to check your work.

## SF 2   Working with closed test formats

During lessons and in written exams, you will come across test formats that do not require you to write complete texts or answers to questions. In **half-open** formats, you write keywords only, e.g. note-taking, completing tables or finishing sentences. In **closed** test formats, you only indicate which of the given solutions is correct or which items go together. The most common closed test formats are:

- **multiple-choice task** (choosing the correct answer from several options)
- **true/false statement** (classifying each statement as 'true' or 'false')
- **matching task** (matching items from two lists, e.g. paragraphs with headings)
- **gapped text** (identifying sentences or passages that have been omitted)

Closed test formats occur mostly in listening and reading comprehension tasks. In exams such as TOEFL, Cambridge Certificate and TELC, they may also be used for grammar or vocabulary.
The following strategies will help you deal with closed test formats.

**Step 1**  **Reading the instructions**
- Read the instructions carefully, work out which information is important and underline keywords.
- Make predictions about the listening/reading text and the answers to the questions.

**Step 2**  **Doing the closed test**
- Focus on the information that is necessary to complete the task. Take notes.
- Read all the answers even if you are sure that you have found the correct one. The differences between the right and the wrong answers are often subtle or tricky.
- Fill in answers to questions that you are sure about straight away. If you are unsure, leave the question and come back to it later.
- Do not skip questions you cannot answer. Make educated guesses – for a multiple-choice question with four options, you have a 25% chance of success!
- Keep an eye on the time. Tasks that require you to read for gist only allow you a short time to skim the texts.
- In listening tasks, complete as much as possible during the first listening. Use the second listening to add any missing information or to correct your answers.

**Tips**

**Working with closed test formats**

**Multiple-choice task**
- Read the options carefully – they may contain traps. They may use keywords from the text, but say the exact opposite of what is said in the text.
- If you are unsure which of the options is correct, go through them one by one and ask yourself if you can exclude any answers.

**True/False statements**
- With false statements, you will often find the opposite information in the text.
- In a half-open version of this format, you may be asked to give evidence as to why you think an answer is right or wrong or to correct it.

**Matching task**
- Do not match items just because they contain words or phrases that are similar. Instead, paraphrase the items and match those with a similar meaning.

**Gapped text**
- Watch out for words that link sentences/ideas such as connectors (e.g. *therefore, moreover*), pronouns and adverbs (e.g. *she, this, there*) or connected vocabulary (e.g. *bird – eagle, sparrow*) and pay attention to the sequence of time in the text. They may all provide useful hints.
- After completing the text, make sure that the grammar is correct and the line of thought logical (e.g. cause and effect).

## SF 3 Understanding text-based tasks ('Operatoren')

In general, when dealing with a text, you will be asked to consider the following three aspects:

| 'Anforderungsbereich I' | 'Anforderungsbereich II' | 'Anforderungsbereich III' |
|---|---|---|
| comprehension (focus on content) | analysis/interpretation (focus on form and function) | composition (focus on evaluation and re-creation) |

In an exam (as well as for homework), you may be given tasks that clearly relate to one of these three aspects, or there might be complex tasks that combine two or all three of them.

### Comprehension (understanding) ['Anforderungsbereich I']

This type of task focuses on the content of a text and is intended to check whether you have understood it. Comprehension tasks can be quite open, i.e. they require you to write a free text, as in summary writing ▶ SF 34: Writing a summary or an outline, p. 390, or answer comprehension questions. They can also occur in the form of closed test formats, e.g. multiple choice or true/false exercises.

Below are some instructions that are frequently used for comprehension tasks. For the complete list of instructions, see ▶ pp. 440–441 ('Verbs for tasks').

| Instruction ('Operator') | What you are expected to do | Example | Tips |
|---|---|---|---|
| **outline** [ˈaʊtlaɪn] _umreißen, skizzieren_ | Give the main features, structure or general principles of a topic, omitting minor details. | Outline the writer's views on genetic engineering. | Structure your answer using main and subordinate points. |
| **state** _darlegen_ | Specify something clearly. | State the *author's opinion on the main character's decision. | Be precise and brief. |
| **summarize** (also: **give/write a summary of; sum up**) _zusammenfassen_ | Give a concise account of the main points of something. | Summarize the incident in the church in no more than four sentences. | Be concise; leave out details and examples. |

You may also get (half-)closed tasks to test your understanding.

| | | | |
|---|---|---|---|
| **complete** _vervollständigen, ausfüllen_ | Finish the sentence with a few words from the text. | Complete the sentences with words from the text. | |
| **tick** _ankreuzen, abhaken_ | Put a tick (✔) next to the right answer. | Tick which adjectives characterize the girl most appropriately. | |

### Analysis/Interpretation ['Anforderungsbereich II']

This type of task requires you to 'read between the lines' of a text. You might have to examine why an author gives the text a certain form, why they characterize the characters in a certain way, etc.

Below are some instructions that are frequently used for analysis tasks.

| Instruction ('Operator') | What you are expected to do | Example | Tips |
|---|---|---|---|
| analyse (BE), analyze (AE) ['ænəlaɪz] / examine [ɪɡ'zæmɪn] analysieren, untersuchen | Describe and explain certain aspects and/or features of the text in detail. | Analyse the main elements of the poster. Examine the writer's attitude towards the *protagonist. | Do not just list the *stylistic devices the author uses, but explain the effect they create. |
| explain erklären | Describe and define in detail. | Explain the main character's reaction to her mother in the first *scene. | Do not just describe something, but give reasons as to why it is the way it is. |

### Beyond the text (evaluation: comment and/or text production) ['Anforderungsbereich III']

This type of task goes beyond the text and requires you to give your opinion and/or evaluate a question or problem arising from the topic of the text or visuals. You may also be asked to be creative. The task may be called *comment, composition, re-creation of text, creative writing or simply writing. Sometimes you will be asked to write a certain *text type, e.g. a *letter to the editor or an *interior monologue. The task may also give you aspects that need to or may be taken into consideration. If the text type is not specified, you may find one of the instructions listed below.

| Instruction ('Operator') | What you are expected to do | Example | Tips |
|---|---|---|---|
| assess auswerten, beurteilen, bewerten, einschätzen | Give a carefully considered opinion; include all the important aspects of a question | Assess whether the statement applies to the short story as well. | Make sure to clearly state your opinion. |
| comment on ['kɒment] kommentieren, Stellung nehmen zu | State clearly your opinions on the topic in question; support your views with evidence. | Comment on the *speaker's belief that ... | Say exactly what you think and why. |
| discuss diskutieren, erörtern | Investigate or examine an issue; give reasons for and against your position. | Discuss how education influences attitudes towards immigration. | Structure your ideas clearly. Weigh up both sides of an issue and support your final position with arguments. |
| justify begründen, rechtfertigen | Show adequate grounds for decisions or conclusions. | Justify your answer. | If possible and appropriate, use research results as support. |

# SF 4 Writing a text analysis

Text analysis (of *fictional or *non-fictional texts) is an essential part of most written exams including the *Abitur*. The aspects you analyse will differ depending on the text type ▶ SF 16–24, p. 359ff., but the process of analysing is usually the same.

## Preparing the text analysis

**Step 1 Reading the task carefully**

Make sure you know exactly what you are asked to do. ▶ SF 3: Understanding text-based tasks, p. 349
You may be given a specific aspect to analyse, or will be free to select aspects yourself.

**Step 2 Reading the text**

Make sure you understand the text properly. Use a dictionary where necessary. Here are some suggestions for questions you might ask yourself.

- Which stylistic devices and/or communicative strategies are used? To what effect?
- Which noteworthy words and phrases are used? To what effect?
- How does the structure of the text add to its general meaning / line of argument?
- How is the reader influenced by the text? To what effect?
- What information is being withheld? Why / To what effect?
- In what way does this text differ from other texts of the same type?

**Step 3 Making notes**

Make notes on features or aspects of the text that seem relevant for your analysis. Remember to note down references from the text that support your analysis.

**Step 4 Structuring your ideas**

Do not follow the text chronologically but structure your ideas according to the different aspects you are analysing.

## Writing the text analysis

A text analysis is usually written in the present tense.

**Step 1 Introduction**

Write a short introductory paragraph that contains the following:

- the title, the author, the year of publication and the text type
- a first general idea (interpretive hypothesis) of the central message of the text.

**Step 2 Main part (body)**

Write the main part of your text.

- Present your findings to support the central message stated in the introduction.
- Use different paragraphs for different ideas and introduce each paragraph with a topic sentence to guide the reader. Structure your paragraphs coherently.
- Use linking words.
- Remember to provide evidence from the text, i.e. to use quotations with line references.
  ▶ SF 14: Quoting from texts, p. 361

**Step 3    Conclusion**

Write a short conclusion.

- Refer back to your introduction and restate your first general idea in different words and based on your findings. Summarize the main points you have made.
- Do not add new aspects at this point.
- Do not give your personal opinion or an evaluation.

**Step 4    Proofreading**

Check your text for any spelling and or grammatical mistakes. Make sure that quotations from the text have been copied correctly.

## SF 5    Doing a speaking exam

Many exams include a part in which you have to prove your speaking skills. ► SF 42–47, p. 404ff. Preparing for and successfully passing a speaking exam is different from a written exam because of the different skills and strategies required. Speaking exams usually consist of two parts which are thematically linked, a *monologue and a *dialogue.

| Monologue | Dialogue |
|---|---|
| In this part, you are asked to give a presentation based on, for example, a diagram, statistics, a picture, *cartoon, quote or short text. | In the second part, you are asked to interact with a partner or a group of students in a role-play or a discussion. It may be based on the material you have worked on for the monologue. Your fellow students have probably dealt with similar material. |

### Preparing for the speaking exam

**Step 1    Finding out the conditions of the examination**

Ask your teacher about the specific conditions of your exam, e.g.:

- What kind of prompts can you expect (i.e. cartoons, pictures, quotes, etc.)?
- Will you be given time to prepare only the monologue or both parts?
- If there is preparation time for the dialogue, will it be at the very beginning or shortly before the dialogue?
- How long will the preparation time be?
- How long will both parts of the exam be?
- How many people will take part in the dialogue?
- Will the participants in the dialogue be other students or teachers?

**Step 2    Finding out the assessment criteria**

To get the maximum number of points in your exam, find out which criteria your teacher will apply when assessing your exam:

- communicative strategies (structure, eye contact, interaction with partners, etc.)
- pronunciation (clarity, fluency, *intonation, accuracy)
- powers of expression (choice of words, ability to deal with unknown words / technical terms, flexibility, etc.)
- grammar: amount and types of mistakes
- content: quality and meaningfulness of statements/arguments, etc.

### Step 3 Practising

- Practise monologues, e.g. by describing and explaining to a fellow student a picture or text that might appear in the exam.
- Practise dialogues, e.g. by discussing with a fellow student a picture or text that might appear in the exam.

### Doing the speaking exam

- If there is preparation time, arrange your material so that you can use it effectively. Structure your ideas clearly. Use clear handwriting. Use abbreviations, keywords, etc.
- You may have to adopt a role or defend a position which you do not like. Try to disregard your personal opinion, stick to the facts and give evidence if possible.
- In the dialogue part, take your time to react but do not hesitate too long.
- Ask for clarification of crucial points. Be provocative and polite at the same time; avoid attacks or insults.
- Do not be too emotional.
- Use appropriate body language and facial expressions.
- Choose the right moment to sum up your points and introduce a new aspect.

**Tips**

#### Preparing for a speaking exam

- Learn phrases which you can use during presentations ▶ SF 43, p. 405, *speeches ▶ SF 44, p. 408 or discussions. ▶ SF 46, p. 410
- Study your classroom material and look for controversial issues which could be discussed, then collect arguments for and against them.
- Watch (current) political debates online to get an idea of the culture of reflection and debate.

# Language and study skills

## SF 6   Essentials: language and study skills

You already use some of the skills and strategies presented in this Skills File. In the future, you will need to adapt them to support your language learning at school and beyond, for English or any other foreign language. There are three important questions you should ask yourself – and be honest with your answers!

**Step 1**    **Where am I?**
Take stock and review your language skills and learning strategies.
- Look at your results and achievements in English.
- Consider the results of self-assessment and peer assessment.
  ▶ SF 15: Assessing yourself and giving feedback, p. 363
- Ask your teacher where you stand with learning English.
- Do you know how to actively learn more English to improve your results?

**Step 2**    **Where would I like to be?**
Set yourself achievable goals.
- Do you simply want to avoid some of your most frequent mistakes, or would you like to speak and write better English?
- Do you wish to be well prepared for your next exam?
- Do you need to write an application for a job, scholarship or an exchange year?

**Step 3**    **What are the next steps?**
Now you know where you are and what your aims are, you have to consider which methods and strategies you can use to achieve these goals.
- If your main aim is to expand your vocabulary, how can you best do this, for example by reading and writing more texts or by using a vocabulary app?
- If you have problems with mediation, is it because you have difficulties mediating ideas, concepts or arguments expressed in German into English? Should you practise explaining things in English?
- If you are not very good at giving presentations in English, do you need to improve your oral skills, or are you unsure about what to present? Should you practise how to identify relevant content or how to get your message across in front of an audience?

## SF 7   Dealing with unknown words in a text

When you read or listen to texts, you don't usually understand every single word. Luckily, in many cases, you don't need to because you can understand texts without knowing each individual word. However, if the meaning of a word is essential to a sentence, there are some techniques that can help you work it out.

Look at the highlighted words in the text on the left, then at the strategies on the right to work out their meaning.

In order to remain competitive, industrial nations have to raise their productivity, encourage innovation and lower their production costs.

To reduce costs and to maximize profits, multinational companies often relocate facilities to other countries (= outsourcing) to profit from the lower wages they pay their workers and from less restrictive laws. The problem is that it diminishes work prospects for workers here.

- competitive Think of words from the same *word family that you know: competition / (to) compete / competitor.
- encourage Identify parts of the word that you know: courage → give sb. courage.
- maximize Think of similar words in other languages: German 'maximieren'.
- multinational Identify prefixes or suffixes, e.g. multi (= many): multinational = belonging to many nations.
- wages Use the context of the word: they pay their workers.
- prospects Watch out for false friends: prospects = 'Aussichten', not: 'Prospekte'.

**Tips**

**Help with understanding new words**
- Illustrations in the text (photos, charts, etc.) can help you to understand unfamiliar words.
- Sometimes there are annotations explaining the meaning of certain words.
- An e-book version of your text often gives you direct access to a dictionary.

## SF 8 Working with dictionaries (print and online)

If you do not know the meaning or translation of a word, you can look it up in a bilingual or in a monolingual dictionary. The two types of dictionaries are useful in different situations. Practise using them before the exams.

### Using a bilingual dictionary
A bilingual (English-German, German-English) dictionary is useful for finding translations and checking the meaning of individual words, e.g. the English word for 'Ruf' or the German translation of reputation. Familiarize yourself with the form of the entries in your dictionary.
- The running heads at the top of each page help you find the right page quickly (top left-hand corner: first entry on page, top right-hand corner: last entry at bottom of page).
- In the example on the right, 'Ruf' is the headword: the different translations are listed; numbers or letters in boxes indicate the different meanings.
- The notes in italics (e.g. 'auch übertragen') help you to find the particular meaning you are looking for.
- Examples and *collocations ('der **Ruf nach** ...') are found below the headword.

**Ruf**

1 auch übertragen call /kɔːl/; lauter shout /ʃaʊt/: der **Ruf nach** schärferen Gesetzen the **call for** tougher laws
2 ≈ Ansehen reputation /ˌrepjuˈteɪʃn/

From: Schulwörterbuch English G 21

If you are writing on a laptop or PC, it is convenient to use an online dictionary. Linguee, for example, is a useful and reliable website (and dictionary app) for translating individual words. Here too you can hear the correct pronunciation. Under each main entry, you will find example sentences from various sources on the internet, together with the corresponding translations. But be careful: the translations are marked as 'not reviewed', i.e. there is no guarantee that the text on the left has been translated correctly.

### Using a monolingual dictionary

If you know the English word you need, but are not sure how to use it, then a monolingual dictionary is the right choice. It contains definitions and example sentences that help you to find the words that express exactly what you want to say. In order to choose the right meaning, always read the whole entry.

> **grim** /grɪm/ *adj.* (**grim·mer**, **grim·mest**) **1** looking or sounding very serious: a **grim face**/**look**/**smile** ◊ *She looked grim.* ◊ *with a look of* **grim determination** *on his face* ◊ **grim-faced** *police-men* **2** unpleasant and depressing: *grim news* ◊ *We face the grim prospect of still higher unemployment.* ◊ *The outlook is pretty grim.* ◊ *Things are* **looking grim** *for workers in the building industry.* **3** (of a place or building) not attractive; depressing: *The house looked grim and dreary in the rain.* ◊ *the grim walls of the prison* **4** [not before noun] (*BrE*, *informal*) ill/sick: *I feel grim this morning.* **5** [not usually before noun] (*BrE*, *informal*) of very low quality: *Their performance was fairly grim, I'm afraid!* ▶ **grim·ly** *adv.*: '*It won't be easy,*' *he said grimly.* ◊ *grimly determined* **grim·ness** *noun* [U]
>
> From: *Oxford Advanced Learner's Dictionary*

Monolingual dictionaries contain useful supplementary information:
- information on spelling and grammar
- examples of common collocations and idioms
- information on usage and *style
- typical sources of error.

Monolingual dictionaries such as the *Oxford Advanced Learner's Dictionary* are usually also (easily) accessible online. The online versions provide the same (often more clearly arranged) information as the printed versions and sometimes even more. Usually, you can hear the words spoken (BE and AE). Most online dictionaries are regularly updated and supplemented.

### grim *adjective*
🔊 /grɪm/
🔊 /grɪm/
(comparative **grimmer**, superlative **grimmest**)

( Idioms )

1 ★ looking or sounding very serious
- a **grim face**/**look**/**smile**
- *She looked grim.*
- *with a look of* **grim determination** *on his face*
- *He set about the task with grim concentration.*
- **grim-faced** *policemen*

From: *www.oxfordlearnersdictionaries.com*

## SF 9  Learning new words

Learning vocabulary is a lifelong activity – even in your own language. There are different methods for expanding your vocabulary. Try out various ways until you find the one that works best for you.

**Step 1  Identifying useful words**

Identify words that could be useful to you. These might be:
- words that are related to the topic you are dealing with (e.g. Shakespeare's plays)
- words that help you talk or write about texts or topics in class
- words that go together with other words (collocations) or that belong to a word family that you already know
- words that belong to a *neutral register (very formal or very informal words can only be used in limited situations).

**Step 2  Arranging the words**

Arrange your words in a suitable form. This could be on index cards, using a list or any form of *clustering as in mind maps, topic webs and flow charts.Indicate the meaning of your words by:
- giving *synonyms (e.g. *dogma* = *belief/principle*) or antonyms (e.g. *upheaval* ≠ *stability*)
- establishing word families
- making sketches/drawings
- giving examples (e.g. *the arts* = *art, music, literature, etc.*)
- giving the German equivalent (e.g. *achievement* = 'Errungenschaft', 'Leistung').

If possible, write down words in contexts or collocations. This will help you to use them in a sentence (e.g. *be torn between, remember sth. as sth.*).

> The Elizabethan Age is often remembered as a Golden Age for its many achievements in the arts. However, England was struggling for peace and stability at home – religious, social, political and economic developments challenged society. People were torn between a traditional world view and a more modern one; they generally accepted the Earth as the centre of the cosmos and the Church as the centre of life on Earth, but were keen to discover new truths beyond the old dogmas. Shakespeare's drama reflects this upheaval.

**Step 3  Using new vocabulary**

Use new vocabulary as often as possible: include it in a short text, study your index cards, etc.

**Step 4  Revision**

Revise your vocabulary regularly; first in short intervals, then in longer ones.

**Tips**

**Being active when learning new words**
- Do not just write new words down, say them out loud as well.
- Walking around while learning new words can be helpful.
- Giving new words a *rhythm or tune can be helpful.

## SF 10  Learning languages through digital media

Here are some suggestions on how to use digital media to help you improve your English.

**Help with your writing skills**

Electronic (rather than handwritten) versions of texts are easier to change and correct. Rewriting and editing longer texts will help improve them – and your English! Giving a text a clear *layout helps the reader to follow your line of thought.

### Help with your reading skills

Online dictionaries are a quick way to check the meaning of a word – if you are careful to check a word in its context. You can also listen to the pronunciation. ▶ SF 8: Working with dictionaries, p. 355

### Help with your listening and viewing skills

Watching films and videos in English is a good way to internalize sounds and speech patterns. Try to get as much language input as you can, whenever you can.

### Help with your speaking and presentation skills

- Digital presentations are the best way to combine text, images and sound. There are lots of fun things that you can do with digital media to make your presentation more interesting. But remember: your message is the most important thing – and YOU are the most important medium!
- Record yourself to check how your ideas come across. Ask others for feedback.

### Help with your language and study skills

- Both vocabulary apps and grammar apps help you to keep track of what you want or need to learn. They also keep track of your progress. Use them as your personal coach.
- It is becoming more and more important to work in a team even when you cannot meet in person. Video conference tools make it easy to work together online. Chats and shared documents saved in the cloud allow all the team members to make their own contributions at any time – no matter where they are.

---

**Tips**

**Blended learning – the best of both worlds**
- Your English book has gone digital too. Make sure you are familiar with the digital extensions your book or e-book offers. Use them when you need language help or online practice, background information or a kickstart with an assignment.
- Books are not everything – neither are digital media. Learning and working in a hybrid world means that you decide what is best for you and your language learning in any given situation.

---

## SF 11   Building language awareness

To improve your language skills, it is not enough to write and speak English fluently. You also need to be aware of the following aspects of language and language use:
- How is language structured as a system?
- How does it work in different contexts?
- How can it have a certain effect on other people?

For different usages of English, you must therefore develop a sensitivity to language (called language awareness) that goes beyond the rules of grammar and how verbal communication works. The following steps will help you to develop/improve your language awareness.

**Step 1**   **Focusing on a language phenomenon**
When reading, writing, listening to or speaking English, you may encounter and should focus on linguistic phenomena or obstacles such as the following:
- a special accent
- a grammatical form that is different from your mother tongue, e.g. the progressive forms in English

- the fact that in English commands are often given in the form of a polite question
- a communication problem that involves explaining something in a different way, using different words and structures so that another person can understand it
- so-called false friends (e.g. English *sensible* and German 'sensibel')
- different stylistic levels that English speakers use when communicating with different audiences
- how the use of certain words with specific *connotations affects the reading or understanding of a text.

**Step 2**   **Analysing form**
Analyse the linguistic form of specific uses of English very carefully to understand how they work or why they did not work in case of misunderstanding.
- Try to identify the structure or phenomenon.
- Consider what (grammar) rules might apply.
- Consider how you can explain this specific form of English or why there was a misunderstanding.

**Step 3**   **Analysing function and meaning**
To be fluent in English, you need to know and understand not only the form of such (specific) language uses, but also what they express, i.e. when and with what intention they are used.
- Find out the function and meaning of the uses of language.
- Find out how they influence communication. For example, if somebody uses very formal English in communication, this might be due to the fact that there is a difference in authority between the communication partners. The speaker either wants to demonstrate power or, by adding politeness to formal English, addresses the other person in a way that achieves a certain goal, such as in a job interview.

**Step 4**   **Building language awareness and making use of it**
Once you have analysed a language phenomenon and recognized its form, function and meaning, you will be able to:
- use it in your own communication
- analyse the language use of others
- address different target audiences and use the appropriate language for the situation
- convince other people of your ideas because you are aware of how to use language correctly, appropriately and understandably.

## SF 12   Communicating across cultures

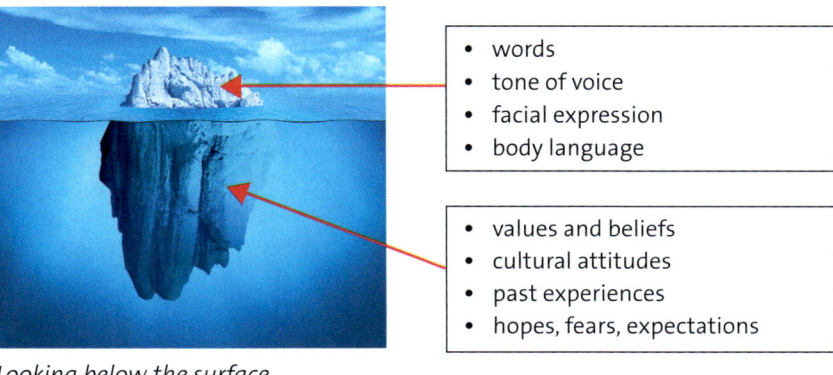

- words
- tone of voice
- facial expression
- body language

- values and beliefs
- cultural attitudes
- past experiences
- hopes, fears, expectations

*Looking below the surface*

When we communicate with other people, what we see and hear is only part of the story – sometimes the smaller part, as illustrated in the photo above. The image of the iceberg shows that most of the meaning of language is determined by factors beyond words written, read and heard. This is especially true when communicating with people from a different culture. Not only language itself, but also the way we use it can vary. It is important to be aware that each culture may have different social conventions, e.g. regarding directness or sincerity.

- In some societies, you must say what you want directly if you wish to be taken seriously, e.g. *I want to speak to the manager – now.* In other parts of the world, it is good manners to express yourself as indirectly as possible, e.g. *I was wondering if it might be possible to speak to the manager.*
- People in the UK are generally far more indirect in their speech than US-Americans or Germans.
- In some cultures, it is considered impolite to express your opinion openly, especially if it is negative. The use of adjectives that are not very meaningful, such as *interesting* or *remarkable* is a polite way of expressing disapproval. In other cultures (e.g. US-American), people are extremely generous with praise and with vague, non-committal promises that are not necessarily to be taken literally, e.g. *You must come for dinner some time.*

### Tips

**Getting by in an unfamiliar culture**
- Observe other people and behave accordingly, for example if they all queue up, then get in line too; if they all rush to the front, then do the same.
- Never take for granted that the person you are talking to understands what you mean just because they smile, nod or say *yes*.
- Be as polite as possible.
- If you do become involved in a misunderstanding, it is often best to apologize, even if you are convinced you are right. An unexpected apology will generally defuse the situation and motivate the other side to seek an agreement.

### Language help

**Being polite**

**Asking for confirmation**
- So, you mean/think/believe that ...?
- Let me see if I've understood you correctly. You ...

**Expressing wishes as questions**
- Do you think it would be possible to ...?
- Would anyone mind if I ...?

**Avoiding imperatives**
- Would you mind taking your bags off my seat?
- Could I ask you to take your bags off my seat?

**Apologizing**
- I'm very sorry – it was probably my mistake.

## SF 13 Doing research

For projects, presentations or other schoolwork, you usually have to research for specific information. To do so, you can use the internet or other sources of information. Here are some ways to make your research more effective.

**Step 1    Clarifying the topic**
- Make sure you understand exactly what the topic is, then brainstorm it. Decide what informa-tion you need so that you can structure your research accordingly.
- Make a list of keywords that you want to check.

**Step 2    Choosing sources**
- Decide which sources will be most helpful for your research: the internet, textbooks, encyclo-paedias, newspapers or magazines, experts or contemporary witnesses.
- Concentrate on English language sources. Using information in German and translating it into English will take a long time and often leads to unidiomatic English.

**Step 3    Checking source quality and reliability**
- Older publications may contain outdated information – make sure you have the most up-to-date facts.
- Information published by individuals, interest groups or companies may be biased (i.e. in favour of this group or company). Check and do not rely on just one source.

**Step 4    Making notes on the information found**
- Use index cards to make it easier to organize your information later.
- Copy the exact wording and note down the source, as it normally needs to be given in a bibliography (an alphabetical list of sources used) at the end of your project work. If you use a URL, include the last date of access.

---

**Tips**

**Finding the most useful information on the internet**
**Determine whether a website provides reliable information.**
- Domain names ending with *.gov* or *.edu* indicate that the information is likely to be accurate, as it is usually an official website. Sites of scientific institutions are also usually reliable.
- Personal *blogs or home pages often just give statements by individuals – they tend to be biased.

**Limit the number of hits so that you will find useful information more quickly.**
- Brainstorm which keywords will most likely appear in an *article which answers your search question.
- Combine them to get the most exact results. Typing in five or six keywords is better than just two or three.
- The more specific the words, the better.

**Find the original source of a quote.**
- Enter the full quote or parts of it, using quotation marks to find websites with this exact quote and thus normally the original source of the quote.

---

## SF 14  Quoting from texts

Quoting is used when you want to support your own statements (e.g. in an analysis) by giving evidence from other texts or the text you are working on. You can either use a **direct quote** (i.e. use the exact words of the text) or **paraphrase / quote indirectly** (i.e. use your own words to express ideas from a text).
▶ SF 50: Paraphrasing, p. 417

Here are some rules for quoting properly:
- Always give the exact **source** of your quotation: *line or *verse numbers and – when dealing with longer texts – page numbers. If you are quoting from more than one text, indicate the *author and year of publication.

- Remember these **abbreviations:**
  - *p./l.* is used for one page/line, e.g. *p. 4*
  - *pp./ll.* is used for more than one page/line, e.g. *pp. 11–14*
  - *f./ff.* is used after the number of a page/line and means 'and the following page(s)/line(s)', e.g. *p. 4ff.*
- When working on projects, you may have to quote from more than one source. In this case, you need to indicate in a **bibliography** which texts you have used. For each text, provide the author, title, place and date of publication, publisher or URL.

### Indirect quotes

- If you use an indirect quote, you do not use quotation marks.
- Indirect quotes are often, but not always, preceded by *that* or *if*.
- Indicate that you are referring to somebody else's ideas by using *cf.* (German 'vgl.') and the page number and/or line.

**Example**
Franklin D. Roosevelt suggests in his speech that people who are threatened by poverty are easy prey for dictators (cf. p. 00, l. 00f.).

### Direct quotes

- In a direct quote, repeat exactly what the author wrote – this also applies to spelling, punctuation, etc.
- Use quotation marks to show where the direct quote begins and ends. A direct quote must be clearly indicated as someone else's thoughts to avoid plagiarism. Remember that in English, quotation marks start and end above the line ('...' or "...").
- When quoting complete sentences, make sure that you explain them, refer to or comment on them to avoid disconnected quotations.
- If you want to refer to individual words or phrases from the text (e.g. in an analysis), you can 'build' them into your own sentence. Be careful: work the quotations into your sentences as smoothly as possible so that they fit syntactically.

**Example**
'We must act now to save our planet and our future', writes a young climate activist in a letter to the editor of the *Guardian*.

### Quoting poems or plays in verse

With texts written in verse, indicate the end of lines with a slash (/). When quoting from *plays, provide the *act, *scene and verse, e.g. *II/2/6 = act II, scene 2, verse 6.*

**Example**
The first two lines of the poem 'The Road Not Taken' by Robert Frost introduce the dilemma of choice that every human faces: 'Two roads diverged in a yellow wood, / And sorry I could not travel both' (ll. 1–2).

### Deleting from or adding to a direct quote

- If you want to leave out part of a quote, indicate this by using square brackets […].
- If you need to add to a quote, e.g. to make it fit into your sentence syntactically or logically, indicate this by adding words in square brackets too. Make sure that you don't change the meaning of the quote and that it is still syntactically correct.

**Example**
The author says that '[l]ove has made [her] a new […] person'.
Cf. the original:
Love has made me a new, much more optimistic and likeable person.

## Quoting texts containing quotation marks

When quoting a passage that includes quotation marks (e.g. in direct speech), use two different kinds of quotation marks, i.e. '...' and "...".

**Example**

In Genesis, the first book of the Bible, it says:
'And God said, "Let there be light" and there was light' (Genesis 1.6).
OR
"And God said, 'Let there be light' and there was light" (Genesis 1.6).

**Tip**

### When not to use quotes

Check the assignment carefully before using quotes. For example, in comprehension tasks you are asked to express ideas from the text in your own words and are therefore not supposed to quote.

▶ SF 3: Understanding text-based tasks, p. 349

**Language help**

### Quoting
#### Indirect quotes
- The author says/claims/states/argues/believes that ... (cf. ll. 00–00).
- He/She draws attention to the fact that ... (ll. 00f.) and asks if ... (l. 00).
- Franklin D. Roosevelt suggests in his *speech that ... (cf. p. 00, l. 00f.).
- The work of ... shows/indicates that ...
- According to Albert Einstein, ...

#### Direct quotes
- Biden is convinced that immigration has benefitted the USA: '...' (p. 00, ll. 00–00).
- In her *essay ..., the author says, 'The world needs to wake up' (p. 00, l. 00).
- According to the author, 'British girls are among the most stressed at school' (p. 00, l. 00).
- The article goes on to say that more and more boys 'were also found to be ...' (p. 00, l. 00).
- 'It is disappointing', a teacher is quoted as saying, 'that you haven't learned from your mistakes' (p. 00, l. 00).
- In the *prologue to *Romeo and Juliet,* the unhappy ending of the play is already *foreshadowed by the phrase 'starcrossed lovers' (Prologue, v. 6).

## SF 15  Assessing yourself and giving feedback

### Self-assessment

Assessing yourself is an important part of learning. It helps you to learn by making you aware of your strengths and weaknesses. However, to assess your own performance, you must find and apply an objective benchmark.
- Try and compare your results, texts, presentations, etc. with a set of rules, a good example text or another model or pattern that helps you to identify your strengths, but also your weaknesses or mistakes.

- Ask your teacher for self-assessment sheets with criteria to help you analyse and evaluate your own performance. The Common European Framework of Reference for Languages or the marking schemes your teacher uses may also be helpful.
- Make a list of your 'favourite' mistakes. Or decide on a particular aspect of the task in question that you want to review and improve on.

### Peer assessment: giving and receiving feedback

Giving others feedback not only improves your evaluation skills – something that you will find useful in other fields of life too – but also teaches you alternative ways of dealing with and solving a task.
- Before you give feedback, ask if there are any aspects you should pay particular attention to.
- Do not just point out mistakes, also highlight positive aspects.
- Always start with the positive feedback.
- Do not only criticize, but also suggest how to correct a mistake or improve a weakness.
- Focus on the work and performance, not on the person.

It is always easier to assess somebody else's work than your own. But getting feedback from others helps you to evaluate your own skills and products more objectively.

### Tips

**Giving and receiving feedback**
- Make your feedback as specific as possible and refer to aspects such as:
  - the given topic
  - the quality and meaningfulness of content
  - language (correct structures and vocabulary)
  - pronunciation (e.g. in presentations)
  - clarity and readability
  - the needs of the target audience
  - the use of effective strategies for written, oral or visual communication
- A feedback sheet or checklist is helpful when giving and receiving feedback.
- Note down useful strategies and methods to help you with specific activities and for self-assessment (= to be aware of your frequent mistakes and/or see how things have improved).
- Do not feel attacked by critical feedback. Peer assessment is about supporting each other.

### Language help

**Giving feedback**
- You did a good / an excellent job. What I really like about your work/text is …
- Your text contains quite a few / a lot of good elements; however, …
- Your text meets many of the relevant criteria such as …
- You might want to focus more on …
- Why not try to … instead of …?
- If you changed/rewrote the beginning/conclusion / the passage where you …, your text would sound even more convincing/professional/emotional/…
- I think it would be a good idea to … Maybe you could … in order to …

# Reading, text and media skills

## SF 16 Essentials: reading strategies and text types

When working with longer texts, there are different ways of reading. Which strategy you apply depends on what you want to do with your text: look for the main ideas or specific information, read for pleasure or analyse it. You also need a strategy to deal with unknown words.

▶ SF 7: Dealing with unknown words in a text, p. 354

### Skimming

Skimming (or reading for gist) means going through a text or material quickly to identify the main ideas. This technique is helpful when you are researching a certain topic and have to find relevant texts quickly.

**Step 1    Getting the gist**
Look at the title, (sub)headings, pictures, diagrams or keywords to get an idea of the content.

**Step 2    Going through the text quickly**
- Don't read every sentence.
- Read the beginning and end of each paragraph – the first sentence usually states the main idea and the last often contains a summary of the paragraph.

**Step 3    Summarizing**
Summarize the text. If you are able to do this, your skimming was probably successful.

### Scanning

Scanning means looking out for specific information. This technique is helpful when you want to find answers to a particular question or to compare particular aspects in different texts.

**Step 1    Looking for particular keywords or details**
Think of useful keywords or phrases before looking for the information you need.

**Step 2    Reading the information around the keywords**
Move your eyes quickly down the page. Stop when you find a keyword or phrase and read the part where you found it. Then continue scanning the text.

### Extensive reading

This means reading as much as possible, usually for pleasure, e.g. reading a *novel. You read at your own speed and concentrate on what is happening without looking up unknown words.

### Close reading

Close reading is necessary when analysing a text in detail. ▶ SF 17–20, p. 367ff. To do so, you will have to read the text more than once and make sure you understand every word. You will also have to **read between the lines** to understand what is implied rather than stated explicitly.

▶ SF 17–20, p. 367ff.

**Tips**

#### Reading strategies

**Before you read**
- Activate your **prior knowledge** by making a list of what you already know about the topic.
- Make **predictions**. Use the title, (sub)headings, pictures and diagrams as well as your own experience to speculate about the topic and the central message of the text.

**While you read**
- Ask and answer **questions** to clarify that you really understand the text.
- Think of **headings** for the paragraphs as a way of understanding the main message of each.
- Analyse the text **structure** (e.g. introduction/main part/conclusion, paragraphs).

### Text types

Texts can be classified into two main categories.

| Non-fictional texts ▶ SF 17, p. 367 | Fictional texts ▶ SF 18–20, p. 368ff. |
|---|---|
| • A *non-fictional text deals with factual events, people and places which are described precisely and are thus verifiable.<br>• It was written to convey information, convince the reader, criticize something or to entertain (while informing about factual events or information).<br>• Non-fictional texts come in many types, e.g. *newspaper/magazine article, *essay, feature article, information leaflet, *advertisement, questionnaire, *letter, review, *biography, political *speech, travel writing. | • A *fictional text describes a world created by its *narrator. It is based on imagination.<br>• The *setting, *characters and events are invented by the *author.<br>• The main types of fiction are:<br>  – **narrative prose**, e.g. novel, *short story<br>  – **poetry**, e.g. ballad, *sonnet<br>  – **drama**, e.g. *comedy, *tragedy<br>• Fictional texts tend to use *stylistic devices.<br>• Within each type of fiction, there are different *genres, e.g. science fiction (or sci-fi), historical fiction, romance fiction. |

▶ SF 17, p. 367 ... ▶ SF 18–20, p. 368ff.

**Tips**

#### Non-fiction and fiction
- Sometimes it is difficult to distinguish between non-fiction and fiction, as the boundaries between these two genres can be blurred, e.g. in the case of diaries, *autobiographies or historical novels.
- Writers of non-fiction often use the techniques of fiction as well as stylistic devices to make their texts more appealing.

# SF 17  Reading and understanding non-fictional texts

When analysing a non-fictional text, you have to say more than just what it is about. You have to find out what type of text it is, e.g. a *feature story, an *editorial or a *comment. By looking at how the content, structure and language of the text interact, you can find out what its function and message might be. Follow the steps below.

**Step 1    Skimming the text**
- Try to get a general idea of the topic and main arguments of the text.
- Sum up briefly what the text is about.
- If possible, find out when and where it was published (newspaper, book, journal, internet).

**Step 2    Identifying the text type**
Knowing the text type and its characteristic features will help you to anticipate what kind of information might be given and how it might be presented. The info box lists some of the most common text types you will encounter.

**Info**

### Text types

**Expository texts** (e.g. feature story, *news story, scientific paper)
- contain comprehensive and detailed information
- are intended to be objective and factual
- give no personal opinion
- describe a situation, scientific findings, historic events

**Descriptive texts** (e.g. travel book, biography)
- describe actual places, objects, events or people based on the author's observations
- are intended to create a vivid picture in the reader's mind
- tend to give a lot of detail

**Argumentative texts** (e.g. [written] discussion, comment, editorial, *column, *letter     ▶ More info
to the editor, review, speech)
- discuss problems and controversial ideas
- evaluate a topic by giving reasons and stating the pros and cons of an issue
- arrange arguments in a clear and logical order (line of argument)
- tend to use expert opinions, statistics, quotations and technical/scientific language
- aim to convince the reader/listener
- often use stylistic devices

**Persuasive texts** (e.g. speech, advertisement)
- often use imperatives as an appeal to take specific action
- try to persuade or convince the reader/listener
- use stylistic devices

**Instructive texts** (e.g. manual, brochure, recipe)
- tell the reader what to do and how to do it
- use imperatives and passive constructions

**Step 3**   **Examining the text more closely**
- Focus on the content and purpose of the text: is it meant to inform, persuade, entertain, ...?
- Look at the structure of the text (heading or headline, introduction, main part, conclusion, argumentation / line of argument)
- Analyse the language, *style, *tone and *register of the text: is it *formal/*informal, simple/complex, objective/*neutral/biased, *emotive, ...?
- Establish the author's reason for writing and what the reader is expected to do with the text.

**Step 4**   **Answering questions on the text**
- Always read the questions very carefully so that you know what to do or look for.
- Read the text or parts of it again before you answer.
- You may quote keywords or (parts of) individual sentences to support your answer.

> **Language help**
>
> **Analysing non-fictional texts**
> - The author uses vivid/informal/objective/emotive language.
> - The sentences are long-winded/complex/simple.
> - The author's tone is friendly/humorous/critical/optimistic/sarcastic.
> - The author's choice of words underlines ...
> - The stylistic devices used support/emphasize/underline ...
> - The reader can easily picture the situation / follow the author's train of thought / line of argument.

## SF 18  Analysing speeches

A speech is as much an argumentative text as it is a persuasive text, as it often tries to convince the audience of a certain point of view by giving a line of arguments. Despite being identified as non-fiction it makes use of many stylistic devices and techniques that are common in fiction.

**Step 1**   **Listening to or reading the speech**
Read or listen to the speech at least once. If there is a video of the speech, watch the speech itself, but also focus on the speaker as well as the audience and their reactions.

**Step 2**   **Examining the context**
Analyse the speech to identify the speaker, the audience and the general topic and purpose of the speech. The following questions may help you:
- Who is the speaker?
- When and where was the speech delivered?
- What was/is the occasion?
- Who is the (target) audience?
- Was it presented live and/or covered by any forms of media?

**Step 3**   **Finding out about the objectives of the speech**
Find out why the speaker delivers their speech. The following questions may help you:
- What is the speaker's goal? Is it to persuade, appeal, motivate, educate, commemorate or entertain?
- What is the primary message of the speech?
- Was the objective achieved? Why or why not?

**Step 4**   **Analysing structure and argumentation**
To be convincing every speech uses a special structure. It is often divided into three parts:
- opening/introduction: trying to grab the audience's attention

- main body: giving the line of arguments towards the general objectives of the speech
- conclusion: a concise and memorable summing up, often with a call-to-action

**Step 5**  **Examining language and style**

A speaker uses rhetorical devices and elements of style to underline their position. The following are common:
- *rhetorical questions
- *repetitions, (e.g. slogans), *anaphoras, *parallelisms
- use of imagery, e.g. *similes, *metaphors, *symbols
- *connotations to support one's argument
- pronouns like 'you/we/our/us' to address the audience directly

**Step 6**  **Giving an overall assessment**

In the end you can give feedback on the speech. The following questions may help you:
- How did the speech make you feel?
- Were you convinced?
- Did the speaker's voice, presence, gestures and eye contact add to their performance?

## SF 19  Reading and understanding narrative texts

When you have to analyse a short story, a novel or any other narrative text, you are usually asked to pay attention to one or two specific aspects. The most common aspects are:

### Characters, character constellations and character relationships

► SF 31: Writing a character profile, p. 387
► Characterization, p. 420

- Which characters in the story are the most relevant?
- How do the narrator and/or other characters characterize them, *directly or *indirectly?
- What relationships do the characters have to each other? Are they dependent on each other or equals, etc.? Do they like or dislike each other?
- Do they belong to similar/different groups (social/ethnic, etc.)?
- Do they serve as foils for each other, i.e. do they contrast with another character to highlight particular qualities of that character?
- How do the characters develop? Are they *'round characters' (complex and undergoing development) or *'flat characters' (not very complex and not changing over the course of the *plot)?

### Narrator and narrative perspective

► More info

- From which *point of view (perspective) is the story told?
  - Is the narrator a *first-person or a *third-person narrator?
- How much does the narrator know or not know? What are the limiting factors?
  - Does the narrator have a *limited point of view – a limited third-person narrator?
  - Does the narrator have an *unlimited point of view – an *omniscient third-person narrator?
  - Does the narrator slip into one character and tell the story from that person's perspective (but still in the third person)? Is it the point of view of one character in the story? In this 'figural narrative situation', the narrator sees the world only through the eyes of the chosen character.
  - Is the narrator *reliable or *unreliable?
- What effect does the *narrative perspective have on the reader and the reading process?
- What are the narrative techniques used?
  - Is the narrative chronological or are there movements through time with *flashbacks and flashforwards?
  - Is the narrative an *interior monologue?

## Plot
- How are the events connected by cause and effect to form a plot?
- How does the narrator attract or keep the reader's attention by creating *tension or *suspense?
- Is there a *climax and/or a *turning point? If so, what effect does it have?
- Does the story have an ending or a conclusion? Or is there an *open ending / a *denouement? What is the effect/consequence of the type of ending?

## Setting and atmosphere
- Where and when does the *action take place?
- How do the characters react to the setting?
- How are the *atmosphere and mood created? The four most common ways of establishing atmosphere are setting, tone, the choice of words or the *theme (subject matter) the narrator uses, e.g. sunny spring days usually create an optimistic atmosphere, a crowded place may create a tense or an exciting atmosphere, etc.
- Is the atmosphere described directly, or does the reader have to draw conclusions?

**Language help**

### Analysing narrative texts
- The relationship between the characters is strongly influenced by ...
- The power struggle between the characters reveals itself when ...
- The characters' lack of communication shows ...
- X's behaviour when ... reveals that ...
- The description underlines/emphasizes ... / conveys the impression that ...
- The *image suggests ...
- By using words like ..., the narrator stresses ...
- The overall effect is / can be portrayed as ...
- The perspective is biased/one-sided ...
- As the first-person narrator has a limited perspective, the reader must ...
- The author has chosen an omniscient narrator because ...
- The story has an open ending, so ...
- In the end, the *conflict is solved when ...

## SF 20  Reading and understanding poetry

When you analyse a *poem, you should look at its poetic features (e.g. *rhythm or language) as well as at the content and then link this to the structure and form of the poem. Only then will you be able to fully understand the message the poem is trying to convey.

**Step 1  Reading the poem**
Read the poem two or three times, then summarize it as briefly as possible. Consider:
- the title, setting and theme
- the *'speaker' and the addressee
- the link between the title and the content of the poem.

**Step 2  Analysing structure and form**
Look at the structure and form of the poem (*stanzas, *rhyme scheme, rhythm and *metre).
It may help to read the poem out loud to get a feeling for the way it sounds.
- Is the rhythm or rhyme scheme regular or not? Are there interruptions?
- Is there a *refrain?
- How do structure and form contribute to the understanding/meaning of the poem?
- What type of poem is it? (e.g. sonnet, acrostic, limerick, ballad, *free verse)

**Step 3**   **Analysing the language**
Examine the language of the poem more closely. Look for:
- the poet's choice of words: how do they contribute to the meaning of the poem?
- *imagery, e.g. *simile, *metaphor, *analogy, *personification
- sound effects, e.g. *alliteration, *assonance, *onomatopoeia
- *contrasts, *repetitions and specific sentence structures (simple/complex sentences, *enjambement)
- mythological/literary/social/historical references
- *symbols and their meaning or function.

**Step 4**   **Understanding the message**
- Try to figure out the meaning of the poem. Ask yourself what the poet is trying to say.
- Connect your findings on the form, structure and language of the poem to its content. Describe how they link to the meaning and effects of the poem.

**Language help**

**Analysing poems**
- The poem '…' by … deals with / is about …
- In the poem, … describes / reflects on …
- The poet or speaker addresses …
- The title reminds the reader of … / refers to …
- The poem is made up of … / consists of … verses/ stanzas.
- The rhyme scheme is … / There is no consistent rhyme scheme. / The word … rhymes with … / The use of … creates rhythm.
- Line … runs into *line …, which emphasizes …

- The poet employs specific images, such as metaphors or similes, in order to …
- The *diction/register is simple/*colloquial/formal, which intensifies the feeling of …
- The most prominent stylistic device used in the poem is …, which serves to …
- All in all, … / The overall effect is … / The overall message of the poem is …
- The poem aims to show/illustrate/convey/express the idea that …

## SF 21   Reading, watching and understanding drama

A drama or *play is a *script in which a *playwright presents what characters say and do. Usually, a drama is written to be performed on stage. When analysing drama, the following aspects should be considered.

### Dramatic structure
- Is the structure of the play linear, with events occurring chronologically? This could include *exposition, *rising action, *climax, *falling action, *resolution.
- Is the structure of the play non-linear, with the action of the play moving backwards or forwards in time?
- Does the play include subplots? What is their function?
- Is the play divided up into *acts and *scenes, or is there a different structure?
- What function do these divisions have in the play?
- Do they correspond to action, time, place?
- To what extent do they correspond to the line/arc of suspense?

### The construction of action
- How does the action unfold through the *dialogues?
- Are there *monologues? What function do they have?
- What kind of language is used?

## Setting
- Do we know when (year, season, time of day) and where (location) the play takes place?
- What sights, sounds, smells and tastes are described?
- Does the script contain *stage directions? If so, what information do they provide?

## Characters, character constellations and character relationships  ▶ SF 31: Writing a character profile, p. 387
- Which characters in the play are the most relevant?
- Is one of the characters the *protagonist / the main character / the hero or heroine who fights against another character who is his/her *antagonist? Or are there only anti-heroes/anti-heroines?
- What relationships do the characters have to each other? Are they dependent on each other or equals, etc.? Do they like or dislike each other?
- Do they belong to similar/different groups (social/ethnic, etc.)?
- What issues do they have to deal with in the play?
- How do the characters develop? Are they 'round characters' (complex and undergoing development) or 'flat characters' (not very complex and not changing over the course of the plot)?
- Where do we get the information about the characters from (the stage directions, the characters themselves, other characters)?

## Audience
- Does the audience know/see something that the characters do not know/see (*dramatic irony)?
- What is left to the audience's imagination?

### Tips

**Analysing plays**
- Analysing a play is similar to analysing narrative fiction. The basic elements are the same: characters, a plot and a theme.
- When you read a play, imagine how it would look and sound on stage. This way you will understand it better and enjoy it more.

### Language help

**Analysing plays**
- The play is divided into ... acts and ... scenes.
- The overall theme of the play is ...
- In the play, conflicts develop between ...
- The audience is drawn into the plot by ... / The action is supposed to please/shock/enrage/fascinate the audience.
- The ... act ends in a *cliffhanger, which causes the audience to ...
- At the end, the conflict is solved by ...
- The stage directions draw a concise picture of the scenery. / There are almost no stage directions, so ...
- The play works with almost no *props / a bare stage ...
- Even though X appears as a friendly character at first, later he/she demonstrates / stands for / represents ...
- The social differences between the characters can be seen in the language they use ...
- The characters speak in blank verse, which suggests ...

## SF 22 Analysing diagrams

Charts and graphs present complex information visually. There are different types:

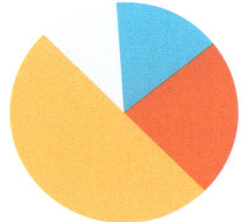

*pie chart* ('Tortendiagramm', 'Kreisdiagramm')

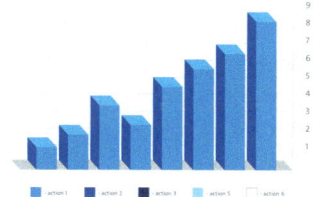

*bar chart* ('Balkendiagramm', 'Säulendiagramm')

*line graph / line chart* ('Liniendiagramm', 'Kurvendiagramm')

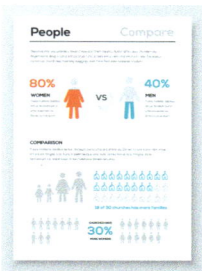

*infographic* ('Infografik', 'Piktogramm')

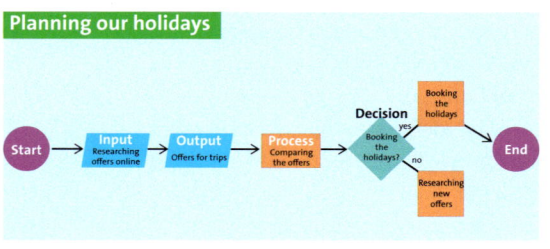

*flow chart* ('Flussdiagramm', 'Ablaufdiagramm')

Plans of graduate students after finishing school

| | Percentage of students (in one class) |
|---|---|
| Gap year | 20% |
| Apprenticeship | 15% |
| Enroll *(study)* at university | 40% |
| Internship | 15% |
| Voluntary work | 5% |
| Other | 5% |

*Venn diagram* ('Venndiagramm', 'Mengendiagramm')

*chart/table* ('Tabelle')

When analysing diagrams, follow these three steps:

**Step 1**  **Identifying the type of diagram**
- Identify the type of chart or graph you are dealing with.
- Try to determine whether the source is reliable. ▶ SF 13: Doing research, p. 360
- Check if the data is up to date.

**Step 2**  **Describing the diagram**
- What is it about and what information does it give?
- What period of time is covered?

- Does it show a development, or does it compare different items at one point in time?
- Does it use absolute figures or percentages?
- Which developments can be observed (e.g. where are peaks and low points)?
- Can the diagram be divided into periods which show contrasting or similar developments?

**Step 3     Analysing the diagram**
- What conclusions can you draw from the chart/graph?
- Can you think of historical, social, political, economic developments which could help to explain the chart?
- Is the chart designed to give a brief factual overview or to influence or even manipulate the reader, e.g. by using differing intervals on the x-axis from those on the y-axis?

**Language help**

**Analysing diagrams**

- The bar chart / pie chart / line graph / table ... shows the different ...
- It compares the size/number of ... / deals with / is about ... / contrasts ... with ...
- It shows ... in contrast to ...
- It is taken from / It contains data from ... / It was published in ...

**Pie chart**
- The chart is divided into ... segments which show/represent ...
- The smallest/biggest segment represents ...
- The segments representing ... and ... constitute the majority ...
- A huge majority/minority is ...

**Bar chart**
- The bars are arranged horizontally/vertically.
- There are big/vast/surprising differences between ...
- At the top/bottom of the ranking comes ...
- ... is first/last in rank.
- ... has the largest / second largest ...

**Line graph**
- The graph shows the relationship between ... and ...
- ... is twice / three times as high as ...
- There are more than / nearly twice as many ... as there are ...
- ... increase/decrease / reach a high point / rise/fall/ drop / grow steadily.

## SF 23  Analysing visuals

There are different types of visuals: photos, posters, paintings, drawings or sketches. Often they are combined with a written text, either as a title or a caption.

**Step 1     Basic information / Introduction**
- What is your first impression of the visual?
- Read the title or caption. What is the general topic?
- When and where was the visual created or published?

**Step 2     Description**
Choose one of these approaches.
- Start with the main subject, i.e. a dominant object, describe it in detail, then describe the background (useful for a visual with one dominant image).
  **or**
- Start at the left of the visual and work across to the right or vice versa (useful for pictures with a lot of activity).
  **or**
- Start at the top of the visual and work down to the bottom or vice versa (useful for visuals where the interest tails off towards the top or bottom).

**Step 3** **Analysis / Interpretation**

Draw conclusions about what the visual is meant to convey and how it achieves its effect. You might consider:

- the technique, colours
- the effect on the viewer
- who is addressed and why
- the artist's/photographer's message.

**Step 4** **Evaluation**

Evaluate the image by thinking about the following questions:

- How effective is the image as a visual message?
- Can the visual be looked at in different ways?
- How does it compare/contrast to other examples that you know?
- If the image illustrates a text, to what extent does the image support, complement or contradict the text?
- If you are asked, say whether you like the image or not and why.

**Language help**

### Analysing visuals

**Basic information / introduction**

- This picture/painting/photo/poster/drawing/sketch was created by ...
- It was published in ...
- It shows/depicts/portrays/illustrates ...
- It provides proof of / gives information on / introduces the topic of / conveys the impression that / is about ...
- In the picture, you/we can see ... / In the picture, ... can be seen.

**Description**

*in the background*

*in the top right-hand corner*

*in the centre*

*in the bottom left-hand corner*

*in the foreground*

**Analysis and interpretation**

- The artist's/photographer's use of ... creates ... / conveys the impression of ...
- The dominance of ... / The way the light/shadow ... directs the viewer's attention to ...
- As the foreground/ background is ..., the impression given is that ...
- ... is a symbol of ...
- ... helps to create an atmosphere of / which ...
- This has the effect that ...

## SF 24   Working with multimodal texts

What is a text? According to dictionaries, a 'text' is any form of written material. Traditionally, texts were seen primarily as collections of words. But all texts are 'multimodal' because they use not only words but also other forms ('modes') of communication (e.g. *layout, images or sounds) to convey meaning.

**Step 1**   **Identifying the type of multimodal text**

Multimodal texts can be print, digital or 'live'.
- **Print** ('paper-based') multimodal texts include textbooks, *graphic novels, *cartoons, posters and *comics.
- **Digital** multimodal texts include films, podcasts, social media or computer games.
- **Live** multimodal texts include dance, theatre performance and oral storytelling.

**Step 2**   **Identifying the modes of communication used in the text**

When dealing with (multimodal) texts, it is useful to look at **all** the modes involved. This will deepen your understanding of the text and help you analyse it. In general, five different modes can be distinguished:
- the **linguistic** [lɪŋˈɡwɪstɪk] mode (spoken or written words)
- the **visual** [ˈvɪʒuəl] mode (visuals such as photos, but also typography)
- the **spatial** [ˈspeɪʃl] mode (arrangement of objects in space, layout)
- the **gestural** [ˈdʒestʃərəl] mode (body language)
- the **auditory** (BE: [ˈɔːdətri], AE: [ˈɔːdətɔːri]) mode (sounds).

**Step 3**   **Exploring the functions of multimodality**
- Analyse how each mode contributes to the overall meaning of the text.
- Analyse how the different modes interact with each other to convey the message of the text.

**Example:**

The poster on the right uses four different modes of communication:
- linguistic mode: caption
- visual mode: picture of Uncle Sam, colours, capital letters
- spatial mode: layout (Uncle Sam in the centre, caption overlaps with the picture)
- gestural mode: fixed eyes, finger pointing.

A US Army recruiting poster (ca. 1917)

The combination of the four modes strongly communicates the recruitment efforts of the US military during World War I.
- The man in the centre immediately draws viewers in. Dressed in red, white and blue, he can be identified as Uncle Sam, a traditional personification of the US government or the nation in general. By looking the viewer straight in the eye and pointing at them, the impression of immediacy is created, as if Uncle Sam were addressing the viewer directly.
- The fact that the caption partly overlaps with the image suggests that the caption echoes Uncle Sam's own words. The use of capital letters in the caption adds emphasis and determination to the message. Significantly, the pronoun YOU, which is slightly bigger than the rest of the caption, has been highlighted in red to attract the viewer's special attention.

The message is very clear. Anyone who sees and reads this poster should immediately join the army.

# SF 25 Analysing cartoons

The following steps will help you to systematically describe and analyse a *cartoon as a multimodal text.

**Step 1** **Basic information / Introduction**
- What is your first impression of the cartoon?
- What is the cartoon about? What is its topic / central idea?
- Is the cartoon black and white or in colour?
- What is the name of the cartoonist?
- Where and when was the cartoon published?

**Step 2** **Description**
- Describe the cartoon systematically.
- Describe the choice of colours and the drawing style.
- Name any labels, speech bubbles or captions.
- What people, events or trends does the cartoon refer to?

**Step 3** **Analysis**
The following questions will help you when analysing a cartoon:
- Are the figures or issues presented in a positive or negative light? How is this achieved?
- What techniques are used to convey the message (symbols, *irony, exaggeration, caricature)? What is the effect?
- How do the drawing style and colour scheme contribute to the overall image of the cartoon?
- Does the cartoon express criticism of certain people, current events or trends? If so, what is criticized and how is this conveyed?
- What point is the cartoonist trying to make? What means are used to get the message across?

**Step 4** **Evaluation**
The following questions will help you when commenting on a cartoon:
- How effective is the cartoon as a visual message? Give reasons, using your background knowledge of the topic.
- Do you agree or disagree with the message of the cartoon? Why / Why not?
- Do you find the cartoon convincing? Why / Why not?
- (if asked to compare the message of a text and a cartoon:) To what extent does the cartoon support, complement or contradict the text?

**Info**

**Cartoon – caricature**
A **cartoon** is an amusing drawing in a newspaper or magazine that deals with human nature or a current political or social issue. Complex issues are reduced to memorable pictures. Cartoons often include captions or speech bubbles. Techniques employed by cartoonists include *caricature, *exaggeration, *wordplay and the use of symbols.

**Language help**

**Analysing cartoons**
**Description**
- The cartoon is (in) black and white / coloured / in colour.
- The cartoonist uses thick outlines, geometric shapes and colourful colours.
- In the centre/foreground/background, ...
- At the top/bottom, ...
- On the left/right-hand side of the cartoon, ...
- There is a caption underneath. It says ...

**Analysis**
- The characteristics of the illustrated person are simplified/exaggerated through sketching / pencil strokes / artistic drawings.
- The cartoon may be meant to show ...
- The cartoon is very eye-catching because of its use of ...
- The cartoon speaks to the viewer directly by ...
- The layout / use of colour / ... criticizes / makes fun of ...
- The cartoon conveys its message through ...
- The cartoon gets its message across by ...

## SF 26  Analysing graphic novels

*Graphic novels are texts that need to be perceived and read using not only textual literacy but also visual literacy skills. Thus they are one example of so-called multimodal texts (▶ SF 24, p. 376). This means that you have to analyse the relationship of text and imagery, looking at both content and form. The arrangement of elements in the space of a page (page layout/mise-en-page) controls the direction and speed of the reader's gaze. The reader has to assume things that happen between the depicted moments to connect the panels into a story. Therefore, based on effects that you can find in a *cartoon in one frame, a *graphic novel or *comic can be described as an extended intricate form of a cartoon in which the design is inseparable from the narrative.

**Step 1**  **basic information / Introduction**
- What is your first impression of the graphic novel?
- Who is the author and who the illustrator?
- Name the full title.
- What is the main topic? What is it about?
- When and where was the graphic novel created and published?
- This information can be summarized in one sentence: title, author, topic, text type.

**Step 2**  **Description**
Choose one of these approaches:
- Start by describing the textual elements of the story (including a short summary of the story) and then move on to the visual elements.
  **or**
- Describe the visual elements and then move on to the textual elements.

In both cases, state clearly if you are referring to the whole of the text or if you are choosing a single page or panel as an example to describe what you think is typical of this graphic novel.

**Step 3**  **Analysis / Interpretation**
Explain how the overall effect is achieved and how the artist(s) bring(s) the message across. Consider how form and context work together to analyse the artistic choices made by the creator(s), especially regarding:
- the way the textual elements are used and the balance between textual and visual elements
- drawing technique, page layout, symbols, colours, etc.
- aspects that are left out
- any intertextual references (to other texts or visuals)
- the way the characters/topics are presented
- the effect on the reader
- who is addressed by the text and how
- the message conveyed.

**Step 4**  **Evaluation**
Evaluate the *graphic novel by thinking about the following questions:
- How effective is the graphic novel in getting the story and its message across? Do you think the format worked well?
- How does it compare with other examples of graphic novels or *novels you know that are dealing with the same topic?
- Did you enjoy reading it? Say why or why not.

## Language help

### Analysing graphic novels

#### Basic information/introduction

- The graphic novel was written/created/illustrated by ...
- It was published in ...
- The graphic novel deals with/is about/reflects on ...
- The graphic novel was written/created/illustrated by ...
- It was published in ...
- The graphic novel deals with/is about/reflects on ...

#### Analysis and interpretation

- The story is told in a linear/non-linear way.
- The panels are ordered in a sequential style / conventional order (left-to-right + top-to-bottom) / more configurational style.
- Some panels bleed into each other/bleed off the page/overlap each other.
- The gutters are white/black/of different sizes ... and contribute to the effect ....
- The illustrator uses thought/speech bubbles/balloons, narrative boxes/caption boxes/voice-overs...

- The (most prominent) colours/symbols/stylistic elements used are ....
- The graphic novel (partly) is in black and white/coloured/in colour/drawn like a sketch/in an elaborate style/very detailed ...
- The icons/symbols/colours used evoke associations of ...
- The atmosphere created is dark/tense/funny ...
- The text in this panel in general is redundant/contrasting/complementary/unrelated to the image. The (overall) effect created by this is ... startling/confusing/focusing on ...
- Time represented in the narrative is slowed down/fast forwarded/stopped.
- The perspective/'camera' angle used is a close up/extreme close-up/long shot/shot-reverse shot ...
- Some panels are exaggerated in size/height/colour to emphasize ...
- The creators use irony/exaggeration/symbols ... to point out/criticize/stress ...
- To claim a reader's attention ... / to steer eyes from one point to another
- The imagery/story/symbols refer to ... / evoke associations of ...

narrative box/voice over
(as background)

speech/thought
bubble/balloon

emanata
(extra elements artists
use to portray emo-
tions, e.g. sweat drops,
question marks ...)

gutter
(space between panels)

borderless panel

extreme close up

panels/frames

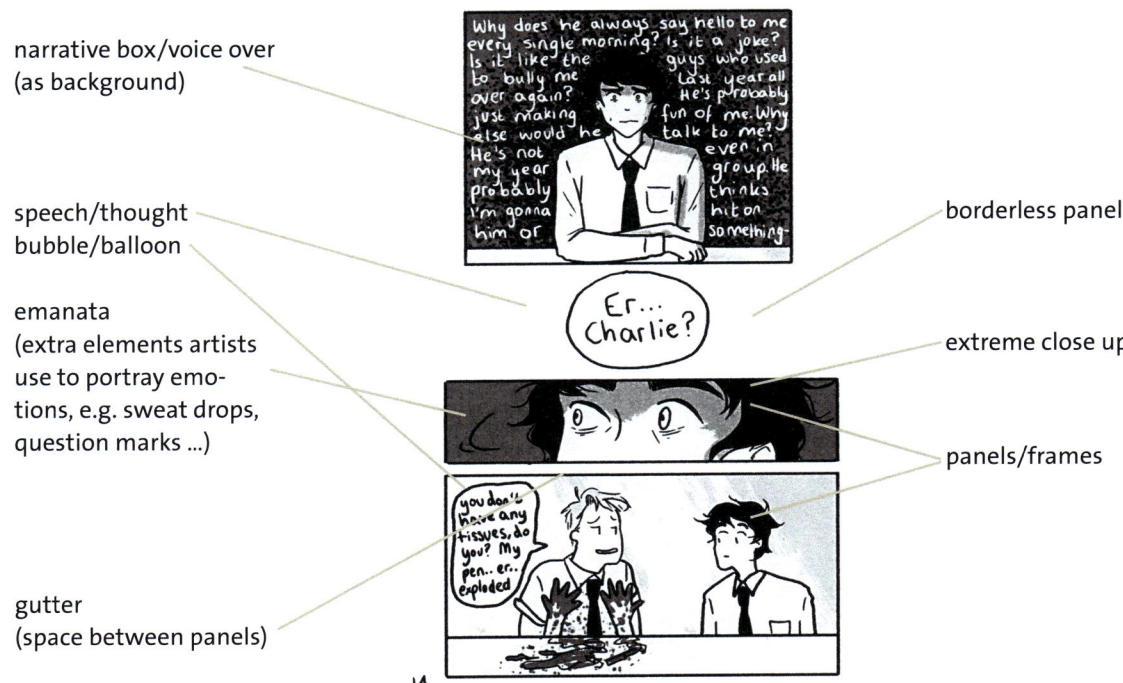

*From:* Heartstopper, *Alice Osemann, 2018*

# Writing skills

## SF 27  Essentials: the stages of writing

A well-structured text makes it easy for your reader to follow your line of thought and to understand your text. The structure you use will depend on the kind of text you are writing. There are some rules which apply to all kinds of texts.

### Planning stage

**Step 1**  **Collecting information and ideas**
- Look at the task and make sure the topic you have to write about is clear.
- Collect ideas by brainstorming and going through class work you have done on the topic.

**Step 2**  **Deciding on the structure of your text**
- Most texts you produce will follow this general structure:
  **1. Introduction – 2. Main part (body) – 3. Conclusion.**
- Decide on the order in which to present your ideas in the main part. Often the text type you have to produce will require a specific structure. For example, if you are asked to discuss a statement, you will probably divide up your ideas into pro and con arguments.
  ▶ SF 28: Argumentative writing, p. 382 Other possibilities are a chronological order or *problem → cause → solution*. A flow chart may be helpful at this stage.

**Step 3**  **Outlining your text / Structuring your ideas**
- Make an outline of your text (cf. the box on the right). All the 'main ideas' are of equal importance, as are the 'important facts', etc.
- Add the ideas you have collected to your outline. Use keywords.
- Before you start writing notes or the final text, review your outline. Make sure that your main part follows a logical structure.

**OUTLINE**

1. **Introduction**
2. **Main part (body)**
   - I. Main idea 1
     - A. Important fact
       - 1. Supporting fact
       - 2. Supporting fact
         - a. Example or detail
         - b. Example or detail
     - B. Important fact
       - …
   - II. Main idea 2
     - …
3. **Conclusion**

### Outline

The term *outline* is used in two slightly different senses. Here it refers to the structure of a piece of writing in which each new thought or fact is separately written down (German: 'Gliederung', 'Entwurf', 'Konzept'). But it can also be used to mean a kind of summary of the main ideas or facts, without the details (German: 'Kurzfassung', 'Zusammenfassung').

### Writing stage

Write out your text.

- Begin a new paragraph for each new event, point, argument or idea.
- Structure your text visually, for example by leaving spaces between your paragraphs.
- Each paragraph should start with a topic sentence stating what the paragraph will be about.
- Use linking words to make the connections between individual ideas clear.

### Revision and proofreading stage

**Step 1    Checking structure**

- Have you included an introduction and a conclusion?
- Have you followed all the rules for a clear text structure? Do the ideas in your text develop from paragraph to paragraph?
- Are your paragraphs organized coherently? Do they include more than one sentence but still focus on one basic thought, argument or idea?

**Step 2    Checking style**

- Consider whether the sentence structure is clear and simple. If your text consists of a lot of unconnected main clauses only, make it more readable by adding linking words to express logical connections between your ideas.
- Decide if you can cut out any wordiness.
- Make sure you used the right *collocations. If in doubt, look them up in a dictionary.
  ▶ SF 8: Working with dictionaries, p. 355
- Check for *repetitions. Substitute words you have used repeatedly with *synonyms. Again, check your dictionary for help.

**Step 3    Checking correctness**

- Check the content.
- Check the grammar. Use a grammar book if possible.
- Check spelling and punctuation. If you type your text on a computer, you can use the spellchecker. But always double-check its suggestions (with the help of a dictionary) rather than accepting them blindly.
- If you have inserted quotations from other texts, check you have followed the citation rules and quoted correctly. ▶ SF 14: Quoting from texts, p. 361

**Step 4    Rewriting your text**

- If possible, give your text to a classmate to check for mistakes ('peer assessment'). Also ask them to tell you if your ideas are organized and presented well.
  ▶ SF 15: Assessing yourself and giving feedback, p. 363
- Based on the Steps 1–3, rephrase your text. Make a clean copy of your work.

**Tip**

When checking correctness, make sure you check your 'favourite' mistakes first.

**Language help**

**Linking words**

**Enumeration/Structure**
first(ly)/second(ly)/third(ly) • to begin with • to start with • in the first place • next • then • finally • last (but not least) • lastly • to conclude

**Addition**
furthermore • moreover • in addition (to that) • above all • what is more

**Comparison**
equally • likewise • similarly • in the same way

**Summary/Conclusion**
then • all in all • to conclude • to sum up • in summary • in conclusion

**Exemplification**
namely • for example (e.g.) • for instance • that is to say (i.e.)

**Reasoning**
that is why • because • one reason for this is that ...

**Result**
consequently • as a consequence • therefore • thus • after all • as a result • this leads to ... • this results in ...

**Reformulation**
or rather • to put it another way • in other words

**Alternatively**
on the one hand, ... on the other hand, ... • either ... or ... • neither ... nor ...

**Contrast**
on the contrary • in contrast to ... • unlike ...

**Concession**
however • nevertheless • still • though • in spite of that • despite that

## SF 28  Argumentative writing: discussion and comment

The main purpose of an *argumentative text is to get a certain perspective of an issue across, i.e. the writer tries to convince the reader of his or her opinion on a topic with the help of arguments. They use quotations from experts as well as figures and statistics to support his or her view. Usually argumentative texts are divided into three parts: an introduction, the middle part with the development of the writer's arguments and a conclusion which again states the central arguments for the writer's opinion.

When writing an argumentative text, you need to structure your text clearly and argue logically to get your message across. The starting point for an argumentative text can be a statement, a text you have read or a *thesis you have been given.

- In a written **discussion** ('Operator': *discuss*), you give arguments for and against something, weigh them up and come to a well-argued conclusion.
- In a ***comment** ('Operator': *comment on / write a comment*), you want to convince the reader of your own opinion on an issue. You have to give arguments to support it and may even introduce counterarguments which you refute to make your own arguments even stronger.

## Planning stage

**Step 1    Understanding the task and brainstorming**
- Make sure you understand the task.
- Are you supposed to
  - weigh up arguments (i.e. write a discussion)?
  - defend your own position (i.e. write a comment)?
- Brainstorm your topic and take notes of your first ideas.

**Step 2    Collecting arguments**
- [For a written discussion:] Collect arguments both in favour and against the thesis and note them down. Consider: What is your position on the topic/thesis?
- [For a comment:] Collect arguments in favour of your position and counterarguments you want to refute.

**Step 3    Deciding on your line of argument and arranging arguments**
- Decide if you are in favour of the thesis or against it.
- Then arrange your arguments in a way that will support your point of view. It is useful to follow one of these two patterns:

| Pattern A | Pattern B |
| --- | --- |
| Present the arguments for and against in separate paragraphs:<br>1 Introduction<br>2 Arguments pro<br>3 Arguments con<br>4 Conclusion | Answer each argument immediately with its counterargument:<br>1 Introduction<br>2 Argument 1 > counterargument 1<br>3 Argument 2 > counterargument 2<br>4 Argument 3 > counterargument 3<br>5 Conclusion |

## Writing stage

**Step 1    Introduction**
- Write your introduction.
- Refer to the topic or thesis given. Introduce the topic in general and then narrow it down to the thesis to be discussed or commented on.
- Do **not** write 'In the following I am going to comment on …'.

**Step 2    Main part (arguments)**
- Present your line of argument, following either pattern A or B (see above).
- Present your arguments in separate paragraphs (one argument = one paragraph).
- Structure your paragraphs clearly to guide the reader through your text.
- Connect the arguments coherently with linking words.

**Step 3**  **Conclusion**
- Round off your text with a conclusion in which you state your thesis once again.
- Do not give new information and do not use the same phrases as in the introduction.
- If appropriate, outline consequences or future outlooks concerning the topic.

**Arranging arguments**
- It is usually a good idea to finish with the argument that supports your position most strongly because this is the one the reader will remember most.
- Sometimes, however, it may be helpful not to postpone your strongest argument until the very end, because you want to catch the reader's attention immediately.

**Making your arguments more convincing**
- Quote authorities, experts or statistics.
- Present facts.
- Refer to your personal experience whenever possible.

**Language help**

**Argumentative writing**
**Presenting arguments**
- One of the main reasons why ...
- It is often said that ...
- Some people think ...
- In addition to these points, ...

**Ordering arguments**
- To start with, ...
- First of all, ...
- Firstly/Secondly/Thirdly, ...
- Finally, ...

**Contrasting arguments**
- On the one hand, ... on the other hand, ...
- Contrary to what most people believe, ...
- ... while/although ...
- However, ...
- But it cannot be overlooked that ...

**Giving examples**
- This becomes clear when you look at ...
- For example, / For instance, ...
- ... can serve as an example ... / ... is an example of ...
- A good example to illustrate/prove this is ...

**Summing up arguments:**
- In conclusion, ...
- All in all, ...
- To sum up, ...
- Looking at the given arguments, ...

**Explaining your conclusion**
- [comment:] After looking into the matter in detail, ...
- [discussion:] After looking at both sides of the matter, ...
- Personally, I believe that ...
- It has been shown that ...

## SF 29  Writing a blog post

Writing or mediation tasks often ask you to write a blog post, or blog entry. This is an online diary or informational website to showcase aspects of the blogger's life and/or attitudes.

Blog posts have a range of formats and may resemble an *article ▶ SF 32, p. 388, a review ▶ SF 30, p. 386 or a short, direct and conversational response to a point of view or an event. ▶ SF 37, p. 394 They are always written with a specific audience in mind, normally in an *informal style unless the expected readership is more intellectual. Even if the post is informal, it must not contain *slang, offensive terms or incorrect information.

A typical blog post consists of:
- a catchy headline
- an introduction ('lead') which captivates the readers and explains why they should read on
- a main part divided into short paragraphs, ideally with subheadings
- a conclusion which relates to the headline and includes a call to action or invites a response to the points the blogger made
- a timestamp/date indicating when the blog post was published.

Additionally, it could include:
- pictures and illustrations that catch the reader's attention
- tags or hashtags which cross-reference other content that addresses the topic of the post.

## Planning stage

Read the task carefully.
- Who is the blog post aimed at? The target group determines the *style and structure of the blog entry.
- What are you going to write about?
- Do you want to post an idea or a topic, start a discussion or contradict somebody else's viewpoint?
- Is it a 'How to ...' guide?

## Writing stage

**Step 1** **Headline**
- The headline should not be too long (as with real blog posts, it must fit on the screen).
- It should relate to the main topic of your post.
- It should attract the reader's attention, e.g.:
    - by giving numbers or lists (*Four ways to ..., The ten most important reasons for ...*)
    - by asking a provocative question (*Do you really believe in ...?*)
    - by giving good advice (*How to ...*)

**Tip**

Some *authors recommend writing the headline last in any kind of text because then they can best assess how to appeal to their readers.

**Step 2** **Introduction**
- Write a captivating introduction.
- Mention the most important, attention-grabbing elements of your post in the first paragraph, e.g.:
    - how you came across the topic of your blog post
    - why it is so important
    - answers to the five *wh*-questions of a story you are going to tell.

**Step 3** **Main part (body)**
- Divide your main part into paragraphs.
- Introduce each paragraph with a topic sentence or highlight the main points of your topic.
- Use subheadings to add structure to your blog post.
- You may add pictures/illustrations, but remember to name your sources.

**Step 4    Conclusion**
- Do not repeat everything you mentioned in the main part.
- Try to make a connection to the question or thesis you stated in the headline or introduction.
- Bloggers often include a call to action (e.g. *Why don't you ...?, For more information, go to the LINK!*) or invite further comments or responses from their readers.

## SF 30  Writing a review

When writing a review, you provide information on a book, film or *play you have read or watched, as well as expressing your opinion about it. Reviews are intended either to recommend the work in question or to discourage people from reading or watching it.

### Planning stage

**Step 1    Reading, watching or listening to the work**
Read the book (*novel, *biography, travel book, etc.) or watch the film/play you want to write about more than once.

**Step 2    Making notes of relevant aspects**
- Outline the *plot.
- Make notes of interesting, very good or very bad aspects.
- Consider typical elements of the *text type in question.

**Step 3    Noting down basic information**
Write down important information about the book or film, e.g.:
- title of book/film/play that is being reviewed
- number of pages / running time
- your rating
- year of publication / release date
- author's / director's name.

### Writing stage

**Step 1    Introduction**
- Give your review a catchy title which contains basic facts.
- Start with an introductory paragraph with basic information:
  – type of book/film/play
  – *characters
  – your first reaction.

**Step 2    Main part (body)**
- First give a short summary of the plot. Be careful not to give away the ending. It could spoil somebody else's pleasure in reading or watching it.
- Comment on the cast/characters.
- Then give your opinion on positive or negative aspects of the book/film/play, e.g. on the plot, characters, *actors, *dialogues, special effects, the 'message'.

**Step 3    Conclusion**
- Finish your review by summarizing the main aspects.
- Give a recommendation as to whether or not the book/film/play is worth reading/watching.
- Say for which target group you would recommend the book/film/play.

**Writing a review**
- Use the present tense.
- Avoid imprecise words like *good, really bad,* etc.

## SF 31 Writing a character profile

Characters in *fictional texts are presented through descriptions by the *narrator or other characters (*direct characterization) and through their appearance, language, attitude, behaviour, relationships to other characters, and by their thoughts and actions (*indirect characterization).

### Planning stage

**Step 1**  **Collecting information about the character and their role in the story**
Collect relevant passages in the text and make notes on the following aspects:
- What general information do we get about the character you are dealing with (name, outward appearance, social background, etc.)?
- What role does the character play in the story?
- What does the character say and do?
- What do other characters or the narrator say about the character?
- What does the character say about him-/herself?
- Give details about the character, e.g. character traits, ambitions, aims, problems, inner *conflicts, etc.

**Step 2**  **Analysing the character**
- From your notes, draw conclusions about the character.
- Explain what the character's behaviour, thoughts and actions reveal about him/her. Why does the character act/react in this way?
- Always note down examples from the text (with line references) to give evidence for what you have concluded. ▶ SF 14: Quoting from texts, p. 361

### Writing stage

**Step 1**  **Introduction**
The introduction should include names, general information, the role the character plays in the story, etc.

**Step 2**  **Main part (body)**
The main part should include details about the character, e.g. character traits, ambitions, aims, problems, inner conflicts, etc.

**Step 3**  **Conclusion**
The conclusion should summarize why the character acts/reacts the way he/she does.

**Giving a characterization**
- Do not describe what the character does, but explain why he/she says or does something.
- Use the present tense.
- Support your findings using quotes from the text. ▶ SF 14: Quoting from texts, p. 361

**Giving a characterization**

- X appears to be ... is portrayed as ...
- This behaviour shows/indicates ...
- Evidence for this can be found in *lines ...
- The way he/she talks implies that ...
- His/Her ... shows ...
- This proves that ... is someone who can be considered courageous/optimistic/trustworthy/unreliable/disloyal/...

## SF 32  Writing an (online) article

An article is a text about current events or about a specific topic of general interest published in print (in a newspaper or magazine) or online (e.g. in an online paper or magazine or a blog). There are three types of articles: *news reports ▶ SF 33: Writing a report, p. 389, feature articles and *leading articles (also called editorials). ▶ SF 28: Argumentative writing, p. 382

- **News articles/reports** should be objective and unbiased and answer the five *wh*-questions (Who? What? When? Where? Why? And, if possible, How did it happen? What are the consequences?). Sources or people are often quoted.
- **Feature articles** put special emphasis on background information and try to give more (emotional) depth to topical events, people or issues. They are often written in a more narrative style and can also be human-interest stories.
- **Leading articles or editorials** (comparable to comments) express the writer's opinion on a particular topic.

### Planning stage

**Step 1**  **Identifying your readership and the kind of article you need to write**
- Who is your target audience (e.g. schoolmates in a school magazine, young people in an online blog, people from your area in your regional newspaper)?
- What style/*register is appropriate for your target audience?
- What type of article should you write (e.g. are you reporting on an event, should you write a lively *feature story, or are you asked and allowed to express your opinion in an editorial)?
- Is there a word limit?

**Step 2**  **Researching your topic**
- Make sure you can answer all the *wh*-questions.
- Try to find examples, good quotes and anecdotes about the event or people you want to write about that will help you make your point more clearly.
- You could also look for extras such as illustrations, statistics or photos and add them if possible and appropriate.

### Writing stage

**Step 1**  **Headline**
- A good headline should be short, but not too general. It does not have to be a full sentence.
- Often a question is more provocative because the reader then wants to know the answer.
- You can also add a subheading with additional information.

**Step 2**   **Introduction and main part (body)**
- It can be helpful to arrange your ideas in an outline.
- The first sentence or paragraph ('the lead') of a news article gives an overview of the event or story. In the introduction, you need to keep the reader's attention by presenting the most important or most exciting facts so that he/she wants to know and read more.
- After the introductory paragraph, the body of the news article usually gives the most important information first, followed by more minor facts and details. This structure is called the inverted pyramid.
- For each new idea or argument (but not for each sentence) start a new paragraph. Present your ideas/arguments in a coherent order.

**Step 3**   **Conclusion**
A good article stays in the reader's mind and makes them think.
- The last paragraph should therefore contain something that the reader will remember.
- If you asked a question at the beginning, you could come back to it.
- If you want to appeal to your readership, you could end your leading article with a call to action, a *rhetorical question or a quote.

**Tip**

**Byline**
Don't forget to include a *byline with the author's name at the beginning or end of the article.

## SF 33   Writing a report

Reports offer factual information about a recent event. The information is given in chronological order and the language used is objective and *formal.
The following instructions will guide you through the steps of writing a report.

**Planning stage**

**Step 1**   **Gathering information**
- Gather as much information about the event as possible.
- Try to answer the five *wh*-questions:
  - Who [was involved]?
  - What [happened]?
  - When [did it happen]?
  - Where [did it happen]?
  - Why [did it happen]?
  and sometimes also:
  - How [did it happen]?
  - What is the consequence?
- If your report is based on a fictitious event (e.g. from a novel or play), you might need to add missing details such as last names, place names or dates.

**Step 2**   **Ordering the information**
Put the information in chronological order. If necessary, add further details.

### Writing stage

- Start off with a summarizing sentence.
- Divide your report into paragraphs.
- Use the past tense.
- Use linking words to connect your ideas.
- Make your report sound formal and matter-of-fact by using objective language and the passive voice where possible.
- Do not state personal thoughts, feelings or opinions. Focus on the facts.
- Include quotes or witness statements as evidence. ▸ SF 14: Quoting from texts, p. 361
- If possible, add a picture/photo with a caption so that the reader can visualize what happened and who was involved.

---

**Language help**

**Writing a report**

- On ..., an incident was reported to the police.
- It is believed/assumed that ...
- ... confirmed/claimed/revealed that ...
- People are concerned about ... / that ...

---

## SF 34  Writing a summary or an outline

When you work with a written or spoken text, you are often asked to write a summary or an outline of the text. While a summary presents (all) the main information from the text in a condensed form, an outline includes only specific information or certain aspects, usually from a complex text. For example, you might be given one of these two tasks on a newspaper article about climate change:

- **Summarize** the article.
  OR
- **Outline** the effects of climate change on biodiversity in Northern Europe as described in the article.

To write a summary or to outline information, you need a good overview of the original text, its content and message. Then you have to decide what to include and what to leave out. The following steps can guide you.

### Planning stage

**Step 1**   **Skimming or scanning**

Read the task carefully so that you know what is expected of you. Then read or listen to the complete text.
- For a **summary:** Take notes or mark the most important words and phrases or sections of the text. Find out which text type you are dealing with, e.g. a *non-fictional text or a fictional text.
  ▸ SF 17–20, p. 367ff.
- For an **outline:** Scan the text (or listen out) for the aspect(s) you are asked to include. Mark this information in the text or take notes.

If you have to write a summary, read or listen to the text again and continue with these steps:

**Step 2**   **Answering the five *wh*-questions**

- Try to answer the five *wh*-questions (Who? What? When? Where? Why? And, if possible, how did it happen? What are the consequences?).

**Step 3    Distinguishing essential and non-essential information**
- Decide which passages of the text contain essential information that needs to be part of your summary and which passages can be left out.
- Do not include examples, numbers, comparisons, quotes, *imagery, *direct speech, etc. in a summary.

## Writing stage

**Step 1    Putting the key points in your own words**
- Write an introductory phrase, mentioning the title, author, source of the text as well as the topic and (for a summary) the main message.
- Do not copy from the original text. Remember to use your own words.
- Do not state your own opinion on the matter.
- Use the present tense.
- Use linking words to connect your ideas.

**Step 2    Checking your summary or outline**
- Does your summary contain the most important facts and ideas from the original text?
- Does your outline focus on the aspects in the text as specified in the task?
- Have you left out examples, unnecessary details, etc.?

**Tips**

### Writing a summary or an outline
- Your summary should be (much) shorter than the original text. Sometimes a maximum number of words is given in the task.
- You do not have to follow exactly the same order as in the original text. Rearrange your points so that your summary is logical.
- As an outline only focuses on certain aspects of the text, it is usually shorter than a summary.

**Language help**

### Summing up
- The story/article is about …
- The story takes place in … (**Not:** The story ~~plays in~~ …)
- The film deals with …
- In the podcast the reader gets to know …
- The topic of the *essay is …
- The article shows …
- The author writes/says/states/argues that …

## SF 35   Writing a formal letter or email

When applying for a place at university, asking for information from a company or organization, etc., your *letter or email should follow certain formal rules.

## Writing a formal letter

Hoehenweg 53
14197 Berlin
Germany
Tel +491234567890
Lukas.Meister@xxxx.com

Joanne Sutton
14 Springfield Place
Chelmsford
CM2 7ZA
United Kingdom

Ref. No.: 315/14

3 February 2024

**Application for an internship**

Dear Mrs Sutton

I am writing to apply for an internship at the National Gallery. I will be finishing school in July 2024, with A-levels in English, Art, History and Maths. As I have always had a particular interest in art and history, I would like to get a deeper insight into work in this field before I start my university course in art history at the University of Cologne in October 2024. As your website specifies that short-term internships are possible, I would be delighted to be given a chance to work at the National Gallery.

I enclose a copy of my CV, which shows that I have some experience of running educational classes and of working as a tour guide at a local museum in Berlin. I have also had the opportunity to take part in several art classes. As I speak English and German, I would also be able to deal with international visitors.

I would welcome the opportunity of enhancing my experience. As I am reliable, willing to learn and enthusiastic, I would certainly be a helpful addition to the National Gallery.

Thank you for considering my application. I look forward to hearing from you soon.

Yours sincerely

*Lukas Meister*
Lukas Meister

Write your contact information – your address (without your name), your phone number and your email address – in the top right corner of your letter. Do not use letters that aren't used in English like *ä, ö, ü* or *ß* and use English language placenames if they exist, e.g. Co*logne* for *Köln, Germany for Deutschland.*

Write the address of the person or company you are writing to on the left. If you have a reference number, write it below the recipient's address.

Write the date on the right.

State the subject of the letter.

Start your letter with *Dear Mr/Mrs/Ms …* (Remember to use dots after Mr./Mrs./Ms. in American English). *Dear* is used for both German 'Liebe(r)' and 'Sehr geehrte(r)'. If you do not know the recipient's name, write *Dear Sir or Madam* or *Dear Sir/Madam*. In British English, there is usually no comma after the greeting; in American English a colon after the greeting is used in formal letters.

Always start with a capital letter (e.g. *With great interest, I read …*).

State the reason you are writing in the opening paragraph.

Add more detailed information in the following paragraphs (reasons for applying, qualifications, why you are the right person for the position, etc.).

Use long forms (*I am / We are / I would*) rather than short forms (*I'm/We're/I'd*) and abbreviations.

If you are asking for information or a favour, thank the recipient in advance.

Finish your letter with *Yours sincerely* (AE: *Sincerely, Sincerely yours* or *Yours truly*). If you do not know the recipient's name, write *Yours faithfully.*
Type your name at the end of the letter, leaving space for a handwritten signature.

### Writing a formal email

- You do not need to include the recipient's address or the date in the main part of your email, as they appear automatically in the header.
- Open and close your mail the same way you would when writing a formal letter.
- Do not use emoticons, smileys, etc.
- Type your name and contact details (the email signature) at the bottom.

## SF 36 Writing an application: cover letter and CV

If you want to apply for a holiday job or a position in a company (e.g. an internship), you should send a cover letter and a CV (curriculum vitae).

### The cover letter

The cover letter for an application follows the rules of a formal letter. ▶ SF 35, p. 391 Since you are presenting yourself, it is important to avoid mistakes and to use formal language. State in what ways you are suited for the position you are applying for. Show that you have collected information about the company you are applying to and that you have a real interest in the position advertised. Mention what documents you are enclosing. At the end of the letter, express hope for a reply or an invitation to an interview.

### The CV (American English: **résumé** [ˈrezəmeɪ])

Your CV gives information about you, about your education, qualifications, etc. to the person you are applying to. A CV should be clear and effective – remember the KISS rule ('Keep it short and simple'). Use a clear and easy-to-read font, highlight particularly relevant information and do not forget to check your CV for spelling mistakes.

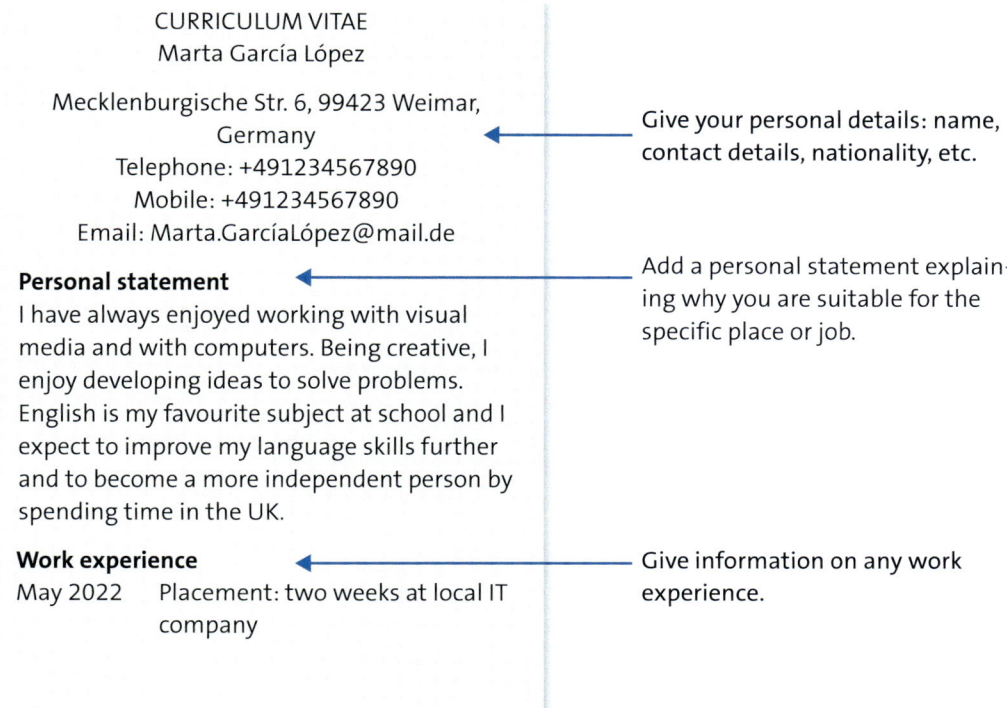

CURRICULUM VITAE
Marta García López

Mecklenburgische Str. 6, 99423 Weimar, Germany
Telephone: +491234567890
Mobile: +491234567890
Email: Marta.GarcíaLópez@mail.de

◀— Give your personal details: name, contact details, nationality, etc.

**Personal statement** ◀—
I have always enjoyed working with visual media and with computers. Being creative, I enjoy developing ideas to solve problems. English is my favourite subject at school and I expect to improve my language skills further and to become a more independent person by spending time in the UK.

Add a personal statement explaining why you are suitable for the specific place or job.

**Work experience** ◀—
May 2022    Placement: two weeks at local IT company

Give information on any work experience.

| | | |
|---|---|---|
| **Education** | | Show the stages of your education so far (schools, exams, etc.). |
| 2018–date | Secondary/High School: Alfred-Krupp-Schule, Wernigerode | |
| 2014–2018 | Primary/Elementary School Gartenstrasse, Essen | |
| **Qualifications/skills** | | List your qualifications and present your key skills, especially those the employer is looking for. |
| IT skills | Excellent knowledge of MS Word, PowerPoint, Excel, web design, Photoshop | |
| Language skills | German native speaker; good written and spoken English, basic French | |
| Technology | Winner of the gold medal 2021 for 'school inventors' in the 'Junior Ingenieur Akademie' (school engineering course) | |
| **Hobbies and interests** | | Write something about your hobbies or interests. |
| Member of school drama club, member of school computer club, member of after-school basketball club. I enjoy listening to and playing music and making films. | | |
| **References** | | Add that references are available on request. |
| Available on request | | |

## SF 37 Writing a letter to the editor

Newspapers often have a special section for *letters to the editor ('Leserbriefe'). Those on particularly interesting and controversial topics are printed there.

In a letter to the editor, a reader reacts to a *newspaper article and expresses his/her own opinion about it. The reader may agree with the author's opinion or hold a different opinion. He/she can therefore criticize, praise, comment on, add to or correct aspects with which he/she agrees or disagrees. Letters to the editor have a similar structure to other persuasive forms of writing, like written comments. The intention of the writer of a letter to the editor is that it should be published in the newspaper.

> **Info**
>
> **Editor**
> The editor is a person in charge of a newspaper (department) who decides what should be published. Editors also write articles, but usually articles are written by authors and edited by editors.

### Writing stage

A letter to the editor follows most of the conventions of a formal letter or email. ▶ SF 35: Writing a formal letter or email, p. 391

Note the following, however:
- Nowadays, letters to the editor are very often sent by email. Watch out for contact information on the magazine's or newspaper's website.
- Your letter should be brief and to the point.
- Start like this: *Sir or Madam* (leave out *Dear*).
- Refer to the article (give title, date and main topic).
- Omit the closing remarks *(Yours faithfully/sincerely)*.
- End with your name and (postal or email) address.

The main part of a letter to the editor is structured like a comment. ▶ SF 28: Argumentative writing, p. 382 However, in a letter to the editor, you limit yourself to the arguments that support your point of view.

**Language help**

#### Writing a letter to the editor
- I refer to your article '…' about … published on … 2024.
- I am writing to you after reading the article '…' about …
- I am writing to you in response to the article '…' about …
- I support / agree with / disagree with the author's opinion on …
- I disagree with this idea / the idea of …
- I approve of the author's belief in …
- I do not think that the author understands …
- In my opinion, it is essential to consider/include the perspective of …

## SF 38  Creative writing

Most creative writing tasks ask you to write ('create') a text based on an existing piece of writing ('material-based writing'). You may have to rephrase part of a story (possibly from a different perspective) or create something new, such as a letter, that is only mentioned in the original text.

### Type 1 Continuation of a story
When dealing with fictional texts, a common creative task might be to write an ending to a story.

**Planning stage**

**Step 1  Reread the original text**
Look at the *setting, events, dates, characters and their relationships in the original text and watch out for hints as to how the story might continue. Make notes.

**Step 2  Check your ideas against the original text**
Brainstorm ideas for a continuation and compare them to the original extract to make sure they do not contradict the reality depicted in the story.

**Step 3  Analyse the narrative perspective of the original text**
Identify the *narrative perspective of the original text (e.g. *first-person narrator) and consider what limitations that specific perspective might have or not have.

**Writing stage**

Create a new text that corresponds to the original. Try to imitate the style and language used in the original.

### Type 2 Change of perspective

A change of perspective means that you take over the view of one of the characters in the story from whose perspective the story is not told. You retell and evaluate ('re-create') the events from this person's point of view, e.g. in a diary entry, a letter or an *interior monologue.

In the case of a non-fictional text (e.g. a *speech or newspaper article), you usually have to evaluate a situation through the eyes of a fictitious character. You might, for example, be asked to read a text on a climate conference and then write an article from the perspective of a reporter who attended the conference.

**Example: Writing a diary entry**

You may be asked to write a diary entry from the perspective of a literary character.

**Planning stage**

- Look at the original text and ask yourself what this character thinks, feels, hopes, expects and/or fears in various situations and also what your character knows and does not know.
- Think about a *theme or question that is important to this character. The diary entry should focus on the character's experiences as described in the text.
- Think about what might have led to your character's current situation and/or what you expect to happen next.

**Writing stage**

- The style of a diary entry is usually informal and it is arranged in chronological order.
- Make it clear at what time, where, in what situation and why you are writing.
- A diary entry usually contains opinions and chit-chat as well as facts. It must not only refer to events but also comment on and evaluate them.
- The diary entry should be written to match the character's personality and language. Age, social status and other features usually determine how someone speaks or writes.

---

**Tips**

**The difference between a diary entry and an interior monologue**
- An evaluation in a diary entry looks back on events and is made in retrospect.
- An interior monologue represents the thoughts and feelings going through a character's mind. It should therefore be conceived as an immediate reaction to the events in the text extract.
- Interior monologues are normally narrated in the present tense.

---

### Type 3 Writing a film script (screenplay)

You may be asked to write the text for a film, including instructions for the actors and directions for filming. A film script has a standard format that is functional rather than attractive to read.

**Step 1   Slug line**

At the start of each *scene there is a line of text (the so-called slug line) that indicates:

- whether the scene takes place inside or outside (INT. = interior / EXT. = exterior, outside)
- the exact location
- the time of day
- the type of camera shot.

**Step 2   Screen directions and dialogue**

The slug line is followed by:

- the screen directions (describing the *action, location and objects in the scene as well as the characters)
- the dialogue, i.e. the words the characters speak.

As a rule, the present tense is used for the screen directions, similar to a picture description. The dialogue is usually written in a centre column.

Example:

> INT. ARYANE'S FLAT – MIDNIGHT – CLOSE-UP
> The two large profiles fill the screen. Aryane kisses the boy firmly, but not passionately. Then her phone rings ...
>
> ARYANE (softly)
> Are you feeling better?
>
> GREG (seen from the back, barely audible)
> Hmmm ... a little.

You may also be asked to turn a *short story or a key scene from a novel into a film script. In this case, you need to consider which aspects of the original text can be represented in the film and how and which details can be omitted without changing the message of the text.

**Tips**

**Creative writing**

- In a material-based creative writing task, you have to work on and with the original text. Do not move too far away from it, or your own text may become illogical or contradict the events of the original story.
- Think of your task as 'reading between the lines' rather than inventing completely new scenes, etc.
- Pay attention to the text type you are using. If you write a diary entry, you should focus on thoughts and feelings. If you write a letter, you must address the addressee and sign it. ▶ SF 35: Writing a formal letter or email, p. 391 If you write dialogues, you should use typical elements of spoken language.

# Listening and viewing skills

## SF 39    Essentials: listening and viewing

The ability to understand spoken English is key to speaking it. Some of the challenges of listening and viewing are listed below.

- In real-life situations, e.g. in conversations, you can usually listen to or look at what you hear or see only once. This is fundamentally different from reading where you can reread the words as many times as you like or feel necessary, e.g. when you get distracted or interrupted.
- When listening or watching, you need to decode both verbal and non-verbal messages, such as *intonation, tone of voice, *pitch, tempo, volume, facial expression and posture. These help you to identify the *speaker's attitude or intentions.
- People speak differently than they write. Many have accents and/or speak too fast, loudly, softly or even very informally. There may also be background noise that makes listening difficult.

There are different listening and viewing skills to be applied depending on the situation or task.
- **Listening/Viewing for gist** enables you to get a general idea of the content or main topic.
- **Listening/Viewing for detail** is necessary if you need to collect information about certain aspects of a spoken text. In exams, you may have to listen/view for specific information.
- **Listening/Viewing and making deductions** is drawing conclusions about the meaning or the speaker's intentions based on the information you hear or see.

A listening or viewing task may be based on a short audio (e.g. an interview, a *speech) or video (e.g. an interview, a documentary, a film clip). Listening tasks often focus on 'Anforderungsbereich I', i.e. text comprehension, and use closed test formats such as multiple choice. Viewing tasks, but also some listening tasks, go beyond simple comprehension and require you to analyse the video or audio more fully. Therefore, make sure you are familiar with the aspects to be tested. ▶ SF 2–3, p. 347.

### Tips

**Listening and viewing strategies**

**Pre-listening/Pre-viewing**
- Read the instructions carefully and make sure you know what to focus on.
- Examine the background information.
- Make predictions about the audio/video and the answers to the questions.

**While-listening/While-viewing**
- Read all the answers, even if you are sure that you have found the correct one. The differences between the right and the wrong answers are often subtle or tricky. Keep in mind that in exams, only one answer must be given.
- If you take notes, only jot down keywords or short phrases.
- If the task is to write a text, note down phrases from the audio/video to use as quotes.
- For viewing tasks, it may be helpful to work with a film diary (viewing log) in which you record the action or individual important scenes as well as your reaction to them.

## SF 40  Listening/Viewing for gist and detail

**Listening or viewing for gist** is when you try to understand what is happening, even if you do not (need to) understand every phrase or sentence. Instead, you try to pick up keywords, intonation and other clues that help you to work out the general meaning.

**Listening or viewing for detail** is when you listen/watch out for specific aspects or pieces of information to complete a task.

### Listening/Viewing for gist

Step 1  **Pre-listening/Pre-Viewing**
Read the task(s) carefully. If possible, collect information on the following:
- the *text type (e.g. podcast, interview, *feature film) and its addressee(s)
- the situation and *setting
- the number of speakers and their role, e.g. will there be conflicting points of view?
- the topic dealt with and what *points of view or concepts you are likely to encounter.

Try to predict what the listening/viewing will be about and what the speaker(s) might say.

Step 2  **While-listening/While-viewing**
- Identify the topic / main idea / main point of the text. Ask yourself: What do the speakers talk/think about ...?
- Do not try to understand every detail that is said or shown.
- Listen out for 'signpost expressions' that show somebody's train of thought, e.g. *the biggest issue is ..., the most important argument is ..., on the one hand ...*
- Remember to take notes on key points.

### Listening/Viewing for detail

Step 1  **Pre-listening/Pre-viewing**
- Examine what you know about the audio/video (its speaker(s), addressee(s), situation, setting and/or topic).
- Try to anticipate what might be said/shown in the audio/video.
- Collect keywords that are relevant to your task, e.g. names, dates or numbers.
- Prepare so that you can take notes quickly.

Step 2  **While-listening/While-viewing**
- Listen/Watch out for the aspects you collected.
- Take notes, using abbreviations and symbols.

**Tip**

**Using the breaks between listening/viewing times**
- After the first (or second) listening/viewing, look at your notes and work on the task(s).
- After the second (and/or third) listening/viewing, complete your task(s) and check your answers.

## SF 41  Analysing films, series and videos

Watching a film, series or video can make you laugh or cry, feel angry or scared. Such reactions are not only caused by the story itself but also by the way the film or series tells it. Just as written texts can provoke a reaction in their readers through the choice of words and *stylistic devices, films or series can achieve similar responses in their viewers through, for example, the camera work, lighting, sound and editing.

**Step 1**  **Pre-viewing**
- Find out what film, series or video you are going to watch and get an idea of what to expect by looking at any available information, e.g. film posters, reviews, covers, magazine information.
- Identify the genre: Is it a documentary, a feature film such as a thriller, a science-fiction/sci-fi movie, a *comedy or a drama? Is it a crime series, a non-fiction series, a sitcom or a *soap opera? Is it a news clip, a music video or a *commercial?

**Step 2**  **While-viewing**
Make notes on the story (setting, location, *plot) and the cast (*actors).

**Step 3**  **Analysing cinematic devices and their effect**
Watch the film, video or episode once more and have a closer look at the cinematic devices used (e.g. camera work, lighting, sound) and the effect they achieve. You will find details and useful terms below.

## Camera range ('Einstellungsgröße')

**long shot** ('Totale', 'Gesamtaufnahme')
a view of a situation from a distance
**establishing shot** ('Eröffnungsszene')
a long shot at the beginning of a *scene (or a sequence), often an **aerial shot** ('Luftaufnahme')
Long shots give an overall impression of the setting.

**medium shot** ('Halbnahe', 'Halbnahaufnahme')
a shot which shows one or two people from the waist up
This allows the viewer to get an idea of the interaction between the *characters.

**close-up** ('Nahaufnahme', 'Großaufnahme')
a full screen shot of one person's face or one object
This allows the viewer to see clearly the emotions a character is experiencing or to consider the role of the object that is shown.

## Camera angle ('Kameraperspektive)

**low-angle shot** ('Froschperspektive')
a shot which looks up at the subject (a person, a building, etc.) from below eye level
The character appears to be bigger than others in the scene, thus seeming powerful, dominant or dangerous.

**high-angle shot** ('Vogelperspektive')
a shot which looks down on the subject (a person, a building, etc.) from above eye level
The character appears to be smaller than others in the scene, thus seeming vulnerable, inferior or frightened.

**eye-level shot** ('Normalsicht')
a shot which is taken with the camera approximately at human eye level
This has a 'neutral' effect and gives the viewer the feeling of actually being in the scene.

**over-the-shoulder shot** ('Über-die-Schulter')
a shot of one character over the shoulder of another
In this shot, the viewer sees a character's point of view. It is useful for showing reactions during conversations.

## Camera movement ('Kamerabewegung')

**pan shot** ('Schwenk')
a shot where the camera moves horizontally (pans) – left to right or right to left – from a static position

**tilt shot** ('vertikaler Schwenk')
a shot where the camera moves up or down (tilts) from a static position

**tracking shot** ('Kamerafahrt', 'Mitschwenk')
a shot where the camera moves along tracks beside, behind or in front of a moving person or object

**zoom** ('Zoom')
a shot from a stationary camera in which the lens achieves the effect of moving towards the subject (zoom-in, 'Ranfahrt') or away from the subject (zoom-out, 'Wegfahrt')

## Editing ('Filmschnitt')
Film editing is the technique, practice and art of assembling shots into a coherent sequence.

**cut** ('Schnitt')
the point at which one shot changes (cuts) directly to another

**cross-cutting** ('Kreuzschnitt', 'Parallelmontage')
cutting separate actions together to illustrate moments that take place simultaneously

**jump cut** ('harter Schnitt', 'diskontinuierlicher Schnitt')
an abrupt and unexpected cut from one shot to another where, for example, an element of time or space has been left out

**fade-in/fade-out** ('Aufblende'/'Abblende', 'Ausblende')
the gradual appearance or disappearance of a shot – usually at the beginning or end of a scene

**(cross-)fading** ('Überblendung')
fading in (one sound or picture source) as another is being faded out

## Lighting ('Beleuchtung[sstil]', 'Lichtgestaltung')

**high-key lighting** ('High-Key-Beleuchtung[sstil]')
a style of lighting that emphasizes bright and soft lighting with few shadows to create a friendly atmosphere

**low-key lighting** ('Low-Key-Beleuchtung[sstil]')
a style of lighting where a scene is dominated by shadow and light is used without producing great contrast

**high-contrast lighting** ('kontrastreiche Beleuchtung', 'starkes Kontrastlicht')
a style of lighting that results in dark shadows and bright highlights to create eye-catching shots

## Sound ('Ton')

**soundtrack** ('Ton[spur]', 'Filmmusik')
all the sounds, speech and music recorded for a film

**on-screen sound** ('On-Ton')
sounds, speech or music whose source can be seen in the shot

**off-screen sound** ('Off-Ton')
sounds, speech or music whose source is not visible in the shot and only the viewers can hear it

**voice-over** ['– –] ('Begleitkommentar', 'Offkommentar')
a spoken commentary while other sounds including voices of the characters continue, often used to convey a character's thoughts or memories

**Tip**

### Viewing log
A viewing log can help you structure your notes. Here is one example. You may choose other categories (e.g. *images, *dialogue, costumes, mood, *characterization, plot) to serve your own purposes.

| Scene (What? Where? Who?) | Camera work + its effect | Lighting + its effect | Sound + its effect | Your reaction |
| --- | --- | --- | --- | --- |
| … | … | … | … | … |

## Film analysis / Describing cinematic devices

### Camera work – static shots

- The director uses a long shot of the scene so the viewer can see the group and the setting …
- There is a medium shot of the two characters so the viewer can see …
- The viewer sees the character in close-up / There is a close-up of the character …
- The establishing shot of the film shows …
- This scene is shot from X's point of view.
- The director uses a high-angle shot of … in order to …
- The camera takes a steady position. As a consequence, the action appears slower.

### Camera work – moving shots

- The camera pans from left to right / tilts up/down …
- We first see X as the camera tilts from … to …
- There is a tracking shot in this scene as the camera follows …
- The camera zooms in on … in order to show …
- The camera zooms out to reveal …

### Editing

- The director uses a lot of cuts in this scene …
- There are short shots and a quick succession of cuts to increase the pace of the action and make it more exciting.
- Cross-cutting is used to show X approaching the house, while Y is still asleep.
- *Flashbacks (showing past events) and flash-forwards (showing future events) are used.
- The scene gradually fades in to show …
- The director uses a fade-in in order to …
- The use of cross-fading between these two scenes makes the connection stronger / produces a/an … effect.

### Sound and lighting

- The music intensifies/fades as … / creates/builds tension/suspense/joy/…
- In this scene, the music and lyrics support the plot / underline the feeling of …
- The soundtrack is eerie and moves towards a *climax.
- The soundtrack helps to … / underlines/emphasizes …
- The soundtrack/lighting/editing establishes/reinforces the mood of the scene.

# Speaking skills

## SF 42  Essentials: speaking

Speaking is a special skill that is determined by the following factors.

- Speaking occurs 'in real time'. This means you have to react quickly in conversations, discussions or even presentations, especially in the case of mistakes or misunderstandings, but also to make your point.
- Speaking takes place in a particular environment, situation or context, i.e. under varying conditions. You react differently to different partners, you deliver a *speech to a certain target audience, you are emotionally involved in a heated argument, etc.
- Speaking tends to be *informal and conversational in *tone and *style, but may also be *formal, e.g. public speeches or academic presentations. ▶ SF 43–44, p. 405f.
- Speaking also involves non-verbal forms of communication and good speakers use them effectively to get their point across.
- Every communicative situation consists of different stages, also called speech acts (e.g. starting it, adding to it, interrupting, contradicting, etc.). Being aware of these stages enables you to keep a conversation going and make it more successful.

**Step 1  Preparing for a speaking task**
- Analyse the situation:
  - Are you talking to your teacher, classmates, a friend, an interviewer, etc.?
  - Are you taking part in a conversation, discussion, an argument, an interview, etc.?

This will help you to adapt your message to your own needs, those of your communication partner(s) or to your target audience.
- Analyse the task:
  - Is it a *monologue or a *dialogue – with one person or more?
  - Do you have to contribute to a discussion, present an idea, describe a photo or a *cartoon, give an oral presentation, etc.?
- Check you have relevant information/arguments/facts about the topic.
- Collect useful words and phrases for the topic and communicative situation in question.
- Record yourself to help identify and refine problem areas.

**Step 2  Speaking**
Successful speaking involves various expressive and receptive skills, often performed spontaneously or simultaneously. To be effective, it requires paying attention to:
- fluency
- vocabulary (including specialist vocabulary for your topic)
- rules of pronunciation
- rules of grammar
- non-verbal communication, e.g. body language, gestures and facial expression
- in some cases: intercultural communication – to avoid (cultural) misunderstandings.
  ▶ SF 12: Communicating across cultures, p. 359

As you speak, react to mistakes or misunderstandings by trying to correct them or by rephrasing what you want to say.

**Step 3    Receiving feedback and acting on it**
Sometimes you will receive feedback from your communication partner(s) or audience on the content of your speech or on your performance. This may be questions, applause, expressions of boredom, etc. Use this feedback to improve your speaking skills.

**Tips**

**Improving your speaking skills**
- Study communicative strategies, e.g. how to respond to questions, how to introduce new ideas, how to be persuasive, how to disagree, etc.
- Learn and practise words, phrases and parts of sentences so that you can use them automatically and without thinking when you speak
- Observe other people speaking to learn from their examples.

## SF 43    Giving a presentation

Informing an audience about a topic is an important skill to master and one that is useful at school and in later life. To give a successful presentation, these steps can be a helpful guide.

**Preparing a presentation**

**Step 1    The general framework for your talk**
Find out about:
- the topic of your talk
- the time limit for your presentation
- your audience and their background knowledge of the topic
- the equipment available (smartboard, blackboard, flip chart, digital/video projector, laptop).

**Step 2    Researching your subject** ▶ SF 13: Doing research, p. 360
- Collect information from different, reliable sources to ensure you cover all the relevant aspects.
- Decide which information is relevant for your presentation.
- Take notes, preferably in English.
- If you are working in a team, decide who is going to work on which aspect.

**Step 3    Structuring your presentation**
- Work out an outline for your presentation.
- Make notes to guide you through your presentation and help you to speak freely.
For team presentations:
- Decide who is going to present which parts.
- Check that the different parts create a coherent presentation.
- Make sure that everybody takes part in the presentation.

**Step 4    Making your presentation interesting, effective and easy to understand**
- Get off to a good start: refer to interesting facts or tell an anecdote to introduce the topic of your presentation.
- Remember the KISS-rule: **K**eep **i**t **s**hort and **s**imple!

- Keep your audience's attention by giving interesting or funny details or examples.
- Explain any difficult or specialist terms so the audience can follow your presentation.
- Avoid extremely long sentences and too many figures or new words. Remember that your audience can only listen to your presentation once.
- If appropriate, prepare charts, visuals, diagrams, etc. to present facts and figures visually.

**Step 5**  **Using presentation tools**
- Prepare a handout or poster or use presentation software to accompany your presentation.
- Design such material in a way that helps your audience to follow your presentation.
- Proofread your material.

**Step 6**  **Practising your presentation**
- Check the pronunciation of difficult words in a print or an online dictionary.
  ▶ SF 8: Working with dictionaries, p. 355
- Practise your presentation in front of friends or record it. If you are doing a team presentation, practise as a team. Incorporate useful feedback to improve your presentation.
- Rehearse with any technology you plan to use. Make sure it is working.
- Do not exceed your time limit.

## Doing the presentation

**Step 1**  **Introducing your presentation**
- Wait until the audience is quiet.
- Then greet them and give an overview of your presentation.
- Say that you will take any questions at the end of the presentation.

**Step 2**  **Giving your presentation**
- Speak clearly, loudly and not too fast. Make suitable pauses.
- Speak freely and do not read out complete sentences.
▶ More language
- Use 'signposting language' (e.g., 'I will begin by ...', 'more importantly ...' and 'to conclude ...') so your listeners can follow what you are saying.
- Refer to your handout, poster or slides without reading from them word for word.
- Maintain eye-contact with your audience.
- Write any new or difficult words on the board and explain them to help your audience.

**Step 3**  **Rounding off your presentation**
- Summarize the most important aspects.
- Thank your audience for their attention.
- Ask them if they have any questions.

**Tips**

### Making and using effective presentation tools
**Handout**
- Decide if you should distribute it before the presentation so your audience can follow your talk or afterwards as a reminder of the main points.
- Give it a clear structure. A handout should only contain the most relevant points of your presentation. Usually it should not be more than one page.
- Present the most important information, key quotations, diagrams and/or charts on it.
- Use bullet points, short sentences or keywords and try to avoid any redundancies.
- Indicate the sources you used.

**Poster**
- Give it a clear structure to guide the reader through the various sections.
- Make it visually attractive and informative.
- Present complex information visually, e.g. with diagrams.
- Keep a good balance between visuals and written information.
- Make sure that the writing can be read from the back of the room.
- Use bullet points, short sentences or keywords and avoid redundancies.
- Indicate the sources you used.

**Presentation software**
- Choose the right font and size.
- Use good-quality images.
- Avoid too many special effects.
- Limit the number of slides.
- Limit each slide to one idea and keep text to a minimum (6–8 lines per slide).
- Do not read from your slides and do not 'speak to them'.

**Speaking notes**
- Do not learn a full script by heart or read from it.
- Write keywords or notes on index cards.
- Number the cards and use them during your presentation.

**Language help**

**Giving a presentation**
**Introduction**
- Hello everybody. My/Our talk today is going to be on ...
- Today I'm going to talk about ...
- The topic/subject of my presentation is ...
- Today I'll be talking about / discussing ...
- First, I will give you a general idea of ... Then I'll go on to ... After that I'll tell you more about ... And, finally, I'll...
- At the end of my talk, I will explain why ... and give you some examples.
- I'll be happy to take any questions at the end of my presentation.

**Starting a new section**
- Now, let's turn to ...
- I'd now like to talk about ... / to discuss ...
- The next/second ...
- The next issue/topic/area I'd like to focus on is ...

**Conclusion**
- So, as I have pointed out, ...
- It's important to keep in mind that ...
- That was my presentation on ...
- Thank you for listening. I hope you enjoyed my/our presentation.
- Do you have any questions? / Are there any questions?

## SF 44 Preparing and giving a speech

When you give a speech, you want to get and keep your audience's attention as well as convince them of your point of view on a topic. To do so, plan your speech carefully and deliver it effectively.

### Preparing a speech

**Step 1** **Establishing the general framework for your speech**
- Determine the topic of your speech.
- Check the time available.
- Be clear on the purpose of your speech, e.g. to inspire people / lead to a specific action / …
- Find out about your audience and their background knowledge / attitudes.

**Step 2** **Brainstorming and/or researching your topic**
- Collect any ideas, stories or arguments that fit your topic.
- Form your own opinion on it.
- Make notes.

**Step 3** **Structuring your speech**
- Select the ideas that are the most relevant to the topic and message you wish to get across to your audience.
- Take notes and structure them into introduction / main part / conclusion.
- Put the ideas for the main part of your speech in a coherent order.

**Step 4** **Preparing the presentation of your speech**
- Decide whether you want to prepare a speech script. If so, print out your speech in a format that is easy to read (fonts and margins not too small).
- Write keywords or notes on index cards if you plan to speak freely. Number the cards and use them during your speech.
- Mark passages and words that you want to emphasize.

**Step 5** **Practising your speech**
- Read it out loud to check the pronunciation of difficult words.
- Make your speech sound as if you are speaking freely even if you are using a script.
- Practise it in front of friends or record it.
- Incorporate useful feedback and insights from your practice round to improve your speech.
- Make sure you do not exceed the time limit.

### Giving the speech

Remember: Giving a speech is not like reading something out (even if you have written it down).
- Wait until the audience are quiet, then greet them and state your topic.
- Develop your ideas step by step.
- Speak as freely as possible and keep your listeners' attention.
- Speak clearly, loudly and not too fast. Pause in suitable places.
- Try to maintain eye-contact with your listeners. Use facial expressions and gestures to emphasize important points.
- Thank your audience for their attention.

### Writing a speech script

If you are not a very experienced speaker, it can be helpful to write down your complete speech. Writing a speech script is also a task you might be asked to do in an exam. A speech script is a type of argumentative text that should have an introduction, a main part and a conclusion. ▶ SF 28: Argumentative writing, p. 382

**Step 1**   **Writing out your speech**
- Choose the correct *register for your specific audience, e.g. scientific, informal.
- Use clear and short sentences. Make logical connections clear by using linking words.
- Be persuasive: use *stylistic devices to convince your audience, e.g. *contrasts, *rhetorical questions, *enumerations, *alliterations, *direct address.

**Step 2**   **Writing the introduction and conclusion**
- Write a conclusion: sum up the main points, give a final effective example supporting your message, further food for thought or an appeal for action.
- When you have prepared most of your speech, think of a good introduction, e.g. a true story, a quotation, a rhetorical question, interesting statistics or a joke.

## SF 45   Taking part in an interview

At school or when applying for a job, you may be asked to take part in interviews, either asking or answering questions. It is essential to prepare for an interview and to follow some general guidelines.

### Preparing for an interview
- On the basis of your role card or the task given, prepare questions to ask (as the interviewer) or think of possible answers to questions you might be asked (as the interviewee).
- For job interviews, you need to be prepared to explain why you are suitable for the position. Research the company you are applying to and prepare some relevant questions. It might be useful to rehearse a job interview with a friend or parent.

### Mastering the interview
- Smile when saying hello or thanking your interviewer/interviewee at the end.
- Introduce yourselves and the situation.
- Speak loud enough and clearly.
- Be aware of your non-verbal communication. Maintain eye-contact with the interviewer/interviewee.
- Use a *neutral or formal register.

As an **interviewer:**
- Start off by using your prepared questions but be flexible.
- If an interesting aspect comes up, ask new questions.
- If you feel that your question was not answered fully, ask again in other words.

As an **interviewee:**
- Take time to think about your answers so your reply does not show you in a bad light.
- Do not simply answer questions with *yes* or *no,* but use your answers to show your qualifications or to express your thoughts.
- If you have not understood a question fully, ask the interviewer to clarify it.
- Always be polite.

### Language help

#### Interviewing
**Interviewer**
- Nice to meet you. / Thank you for coming.
- To start off, would you like to say something about ...? / First, let me ask you ...
- My next question would be ...
- If you think so, then why didn't you ...?

- Let's get back to my original question ...
- You just said ..., how does that relate to ...?
- Thank you very much for taking part in this interview.

**Interviewee**
- Nice to meet you too. / Thank you for inviting me today. / I am fine, thank you.
- I am not sure I have understood your question correctly. / Sorry, could you rephrase that?
- I'm glad you asked that question because ... / ... is very important to me, as ...
- A good example of the aspect you mentioned is ...
- Let me explain that in some more detail.
- Thank you for the chance to speak to you.

## SF 46 Having a discussion

In a (classroom) discussion you exchange ideas and opinions with others. Discussions may be spontaneous or more formal, e.g. in panel discussions or debates. ▶ SF 47: Having a debate, p. 412 If possible, you should prepare so that you have your arguments and useful words and phrases ready.

### Preparing a discussion

**Step 1   Researching the topic and making notes**
- Form an opinion on the topic and note down arguments.
- In a role-play, you may have to take a position which is not really your own, so make sure that your arguments are in line with *your role*.
- Think of counterarguments and of ways to refute them.
- Arrange your notes so that you have the relevant facts ready during the discussion.

**Step 2   Preparing an initial statement**
- A prepared opening statement on the topic will ease your way into the discussion.
- If you are assigned a specific role, be prepared to introduce yourself.

**Step 3   Choosing a chairperson**
It is advisable to choose a chair(person) to lead the discussion. He/she:
- moderates the discussion without taking sides
- steers the flow of the discussion
- is responsible for getting the discussion going and keeping it going.
- must be well informed about the various aspects of the discussion topic.

### Holding the discussion

**Step 1   Stating your point of view on the topic**
For example, give your prepared statement.

**Step 2   Listening to what others say and referring back to their statements**
- Say which of the arguments do not convince you and why.
- You might counter an argument by asking a provocative question.
- Remember to bring in the facts you collected to support your view.

**Step 3   Reaching an agreement**
At the end of the discussion, even if you do not fully agree with each other, you need to reach some kind of agreement which you both accept.

**Step 4** **Summarizing**

At the end of the discussion, summarize your point of view or your main arguments. If a chair-person has moderated the discussion, he/she may summarize the main line of the discussion and round it off.

### Taking part in a discussion

**Stating/Expressing your opinion**

- In my opinion/view, ...
- As far as I'm concerned, ...
- The way I see it, ...
- If you ask me, ...
- It seems to me that ...
- I (personally) think/feel/reckon/believe ...
- First of all, / To start with, I'd like to point out that ...
- There can be no doubt that ...
- I'm (absolutely) convinced that ...

**Involving a partner**

- What do you think about ...?
- Is there anything you'd like to add?
- Would you agree with that?

**Agreeing**

- I quite agree.
- I couldn't agree with you more.
- Quite!/Exactly!/Precisely!/Certainly!/Definitely!
- You're quite right.
- I agree entirely/completely.
- That's just/exactly how I see it / how I feel about it.
- You've got a good point there.

**Disagreeing politely / Contradicting**

- I'm afraid I don't quite/really agree there.
- Well, that's one way of looking at it, but ...
- I'm not convinced that ...
- Well, I have my doubts about that.
- This is true to a certain extent, but ...

**Disagreeing strongly**

- I doubt that very much.
- That doesn't convince me at all.
- I don't agree with you at all.
- I disagree entirely.
- It's not as simple as that.

**Asking for clarification**

- Excuse me, I didn't quite catch your point about ...
- I'm sorry, but I don't understand/know what you mean by ...
- Sorry, could you say that again, please?
- Could you give an example / explain that, please?

**Interrupting / Signalling that you would like to say something**
- May I interrupt? / May I interrupt you for a moment, please?
- Sorry to interrupt you but …
- Excuse me, I would like to add to that.
- That illustrates perfectly what …
- Can I just say/explain that …?
- I would just like to jump in here, to clarify that …

**Adding a point**
- Another thing is …
- We must also consider …
- I would like to add to that …
- Have you ever considered / thought about …?

**Buying time / Gaining time to think**
- Well, I would say …
- It's difficult to say exactly, but …
- If I understood the question correctly, …
- Well, that's an interesting point.
- I see what you mean.
- Why don't we see what X has to say about that?

**Summarizing your point of view**
- I have shown that …
- It has become clear that …
- Let me just state again that it is vital to …
- If we don't …, then … / In spite of everything we have heard from the other side, …

**Summarizing the course and results of the discussion**
- So, to sum up …
- In brief, …
- We have seen/heard that …
- Some are in favour of …, others against it, but in general you can say that …
- The general trend seems to be …
- On the one hand, … On the other hand, …
- All in all, this discussion has shown …

## SF 47 Having a debate

A debate is a formal discussion of a 'motion' (proposal) that ends in a vote. Similar to a discussion, the aim of a debate is to present arguments as convincingly as possible. Participants therefore need well-prepared arguments as well as rhetorical skills. There is often a set of rules that the participants have to agree on before the debate.

The starting point for the debate, the 'motion' (i.e. a controversial topic), is normally phrased as a statement starting 'This house …'.
- 'This house proposes that … (students should be allowed to use phones during lessons).'
- 'This house believes that … (minimum wages are a threat to the German economy).'
- 'This house would … (abolish the death penalty worldwide).'

**Step 1**   **Preparing the debate**
- Divide the class into two groups: one <u>for</u> the motion (the proposition or 'prop' team) and one <u>against</u> the motion (the opposition or 'opp' team).
- Choose a chair(person), judges (so-called adjudicators [əˈdʒuːdɪkeɪtəz]) and a timekeeper. Then specify a time limit for each speaker (often 3–6 minutes per speaker).
- In your team (either proposition or opposition), research the topic and collect and note down arguments for your side. Your personal opinion on the motion is not relevant here – you must argue for your team. List and rank your team's arguments in order of importance.
- Write your arguments on index cards so that you have them ready during the debate.
- Think of arguments for the opposing view and ways to refute them.
- Choose speakers for your side.
- Remaining group members are the audience, called the 'floor'.

**Step 2**   **Holding the debate**
A debate follows a clear structure:
- **1st proposal** from the team in favour of the motion
  The first speaker proposes the motion (= argues in favour of the motion) and gives some main arguments.
- **1st opposition** from the team opposing the motion
  The first speaker of this team opposes the motion (= argues against the motion).
- **2nd proposal** from the team in favour of the motion
  The second speaker of the affirmative team presents further arguments in favour of the motion. He/she also responds to the aspects mentioned by the first speaker of the opposing team, outlining where the positions conflict.
- **2nd opposition** from the team opposing the motion
  The second speaker of the opposing team presents further arguments against the motion and/or restates the position of his/her team. The main task here is to defeat the arguments presented by the team in favour of the motion.

[A short recess may be taken here to prepare for the following 'rebuttals'.]
- **1st rebuttal** from the team opposing the motion
  The team against the motion defends their arguments and tries to rebut the arguments of the affirmative team.
- **2nd rebuttal** from the team in favour of the motion
  The affirmative team supports their point of view and tries to rebut the arguments of the opposing team.
- **3rd rebuttal** from the team opposing the motion
  The opposing team gives their closing statements.
- **4th rebuttal** from the team in favour of the motion
  The affirmative team gives their closing statements.

**Info**

**Rules for the debate**
- The chair(person) controls the debate and makes sure that the rules are followed and that time limits are respected. He or she introduces the topic, the judges and speakers and calls on them to deliver their speeches.
- The judges will watch the entire debate and decide at the end which team won.

- Speakers may not interrupt each other at any point. They must wait their turn. However, in competitive debates, a member of the team opposing that of the current speaker may briefly interrupt, offering a POI (point of information) in the form of a short question or a statement (10 seconds or less).
- The time limits as given by the chair must be respected.
- Speakers must remain polite and respectful of the other team.
- Statements must be backed up by examples or proof, by referring to research, experience, etc.

**Step 3    Concluding the debate**

- The 'floor' (i.e. the audience) may ask questions and/or present their ideas on the topic.
- The 'house' (i.e. everyone present) may take a vote on the motion by a show of hands, not based on what they personally agree or disagree with, but on who made the better case by presenting the better arguments and speaking more convincingly.
- Members of the two debating teams may get some feedback from the audience.
- The judges mark each team on their style, content and strategy, comment on their performance and finally decide who is the winner of the debate.

**Language help**

### Debating

**1st proposal**
- This house firmly believes that ...
- Not only is ... but also ...

**1st opposition**
- We strongly advise against following the proposed motion because ...
- The most obvious reason for this is that ...

**2nd proposal**
- The opposing team has tried to create the impression that ...
- However, we can prove that ...
- It is therefore evident that ...

**2nd opposition**
- Again, it needs to be stated that by following the arguments, ...
- ... would lead to / cause ...

# Mediating skills

## SF 48   Essentials: mediating

### What is mediating?

Mediating basically means transferring written or spoken information in one language to another language. The main objective is 'to get the message across'. You may also use mediating skills in real-life situations where – as a mediator – you help speakers of English and your own language to understand each other or to understand a text in the other language.

### How to do a mediation task

In a mediation task, you should not translate word for word. You should select and pass on only the information that is relevant to another person, the addressee. Usually, the original text is in your native language and the text you need to produce (your mediation text) is in the second language, i.e. English. Pay attention to the following steps when working on a mediation task.

**Step 1**   **Analysing the communicative situation**
- Read the task carefully.
- Who is the addressee?
- Will you be writing or speaking? (Speaking allows you to use gestures and other non-verbal means of communication.)
- What *text type are you expected to produce? A (personal or formal) *letter, a (personal or formal) email, a *newspaper article, a school magazine, an internet article, e.g. a blog entry? ▶ SF 28-38, p. 382ff.

**Step 2**   **Selecting the relevant information**
- Select the aspects of the text that are relevant to the given task or situation.
- Answer all of the addressee's questions, but do not give any unnecessary details.
- Decide what ideas, names or technical terms you need to explain.
- Decide which (cultural) aspects or concepts that might not be familiar to the addressee you need to explain. Watch out for possible (cultural) misunderstandings.

**Tips**

### Mediating

- Do not summarize the whole text and do not translate every sentence.
- Use an appropriate *style and *register for the given situation and the text type you are expected to produce.
- Paraphrase words you do not know as well as technical terms. ▶ SF 50: Paraphrasing, p. 417
- Avoid German-sounding sentence patterns and 'false friends' such as 'spenden'/*spend*.

**Mediating from German into English**

Usually in a mediation task, you are expected to inform your (English-speaking) reader(s) about ideas which you have found in a German text.

### Preparing a German-English mediation

- Read the task carefully.
- Check what text type you are expected to produce.
- Make sure you understand the content of the original German text perfectly.
- Bear in mind what specific information the English-speaking addressee needs. Highlight keywords and sentences in the German text.
- Take notes on the relevant information you need, then structure it and phrase it in English. Use a dictionary if necessary. ▶ SF 8: Working with dictionaries, p. 355

### Doing a German-English mediation

- Make sure you use the correct text type.
- Sum up the information relevant for the addressee.
- Name the source.
- Include all the necessary explanations.
- Watch out for aspects that are specific to one culture (here: German) and explain them in more detail.
- Paraphrase any words you do not know in English. ▶ SF 50: Paraphrasing, p. 417
- Structure your text as clearly as possible.
- Remember: the mediated English text will usually be shorter than the original German text because you select only the information that is relevant.

---

**Tips**

**Mediating information from German into English**

- If the original text is German and the text you need to write is English, you can take notes on the text in either German or English.
- As you are working with a German text, you may find it easier to take notes in German. On the other hand, if your notes are in English, it will be easier for you later to write your own text in English from your notes.
- Find out on your own which method works better for you and use it in all your exams.

---

**Tips**

**Mediating from spoken source texts**

When mediating orally presented texts, such as during a real-life discussion or a listening text like a radio programme or podcast, some of the strategies above might not apply, for instance, cross checking a text or highlighting passages. However, there are other useful tips.

- In live situations, you can actively ask participants for information or clarification if needed and even rephrase what you mediated earlier.
- When listening to a recording, you can replay important passages multiple times.
- Even if you do not have access to a written copy, you can take notes while listening.

## SF 50 Paraphrasing

If you paraphrase a text or *speech, you rephrase it in different words, without changing the meaning. Paraphrasing is useful

- for summaries or outlines, i.e. to avoid copying from the original text and to show that you have really understood it
- when you do not know the exact English word or expression, e.g. when mediating into English, when writing a text or in conversation.

There are different paraphrasing techniques.

### Using antonyms ['æntənɪmz]

*Antonyms denote the opposite of the original word.

Examples:
- 'Reichtum' → *the opposite of poverty*
- 'stumpf' → *the opposite of sharp*

### Using comparisons

Comparisons help you illustrate what you mean by creating *images.

Examples:
- 'Handschuh' → *like a shoe for your hand*
- 'Wendeltreppe' → *a set of stairs shaped like a spiral*

### Definition or explanation (often using relative clauses)

With definitions or explanations, relative clauses help you add details to general terms such as *person, thing, machine, activity.*

Examples:
- 'Freiwillige/r' → a person who offers to do something but doesn't ask for money in return
- 'Wahl-O-Mat' → an internet website that is designed to help people decide which party to vote for in an election
- 'Apotheke' → a place where you can get something for headaches or other illnesses

---

**Language help**

**Paraphrasing**
- It's the opposite of ...
- It's the same as ...
- It's like ...
- It's similar to ...
- It's somebody / a person who ...
- It's something / a machine / a tool that you use to ...
- It's an animal / a plant / a building / a custom that ...
- It's a place that/where ...

# Glossary

An asterisk (*) or an arrow (▶) before a term indicates that it can be found as a separate entry in the Glossary.

| | |
|---|---|
| **accumulation** [əˌkjuːmjəˈleɪʃn] *Akkumulation, gehäufte Aneinanderreihung* | using a lot of similar words or phrases within a few lines in order to emphasize a description or impression<br>**Example:** *Motorcycles, busses, cars, coaches, bicycles, lorries, vans* were passing by – there was no way to cross the road. |
| **acronym** *Akronym, Kurzwort* | a term formed from the first letters of several words<br>**Example:** *NASA* is an acronym for **N**ational **A**eronautics and **S**pace **A**dministration. |
| **act** *Akt* | a major division in a *drama<br>Each act is usually subdivided into *scenes. |
| **action** *Handlung* | in *fictional texts, everything that happens in the story<br>▶ external action, internal action |
| **actor/actress** *Schauspieler/-in* | a person who performs in a theatre, in a film, on TV or on the radio, especially as a profession<br>The actors express themselves in the form of *dialogues, *monologues or *soliloquies. |
| **advertisement** (*infml* also: **advert/ad**) [ədˈvɜːtɪsmənt] *Werbung, Anzeige, Annonce* | a text which attempts to persuade people to do something (e.g. buy a particular product or contribute money to a cause)<br>An advertisement normally consists of pictures and text (called *copy*) and is designed to catch the attention of the reader through its *layout. |
| **alliteration** [əˌlɪtəˈreɪʃn] *Alliteration, Stabreim* | the repetition of a consonant at the beginning of neighbouring words, or of stressed syllables within such words to produce a rhythmic effect<br>**Example:** A**r**ound the **r**ugged **r**ock the **r**agged **r**ascal **r**an.<br>▶ assonance |
| **allusion** [əˈluːʒn] *Anspielung, indirekte Bezugnahme* | an indirect reference to something or somebody the reader or listener is supposed to recognize and respond to<br>An allusion may be to a work of literature, a historical event, a well-known person, etc. |
| **alternate rhyme** *Kreuzreim, alternierender Reim* | an **a b a b** *rhyme scheme where every other *line rhymes with each other |
| **analogy** [əˈnælədʒi] *Analogie, Ähnlichkeit, Vergleich* | the comparison of two things which are similar in several aspects<br>By comparing an object, situation or person to something familiar, the explanation becomes easier to understand.<br>**Example:**<br>What's in a name? That which we call a rose. /<br>By any other word would smell as sweet. /<br>So Romeo would, were he not Romeo called.<br>(William Shakespeare, *Romeo and Juliet*) |

**anaphora** [əˈnæfərə]
*Anapher*
the repetition of the same words or group of words in neighbouring sentences, *lines, *stanzas, etc. usually at the beginning of the clause
**Example:**
**In every** cry of every man,
**In every** infant's cry of fear,
**In every** voice, **in every** ban
(William Blake, 'London', 1794)

**antagonist** *Antago-*
*nist/-in, Gegner/-in,*
*Widersacher/-in*
in *fictional text, the person who opposes the *protagonist

**anticipation**
*Vorwegnahme*
the technique of hinting at later events in a *fictional text so that the reader or audience is prepared for them or can anticipate them

**antithesis** [ænˈtɪθəsɪs]
*Antithese, genaues*
*Gegenteil, Gegensatz*
an idea that is the opposite of an idea (*thesis) already put forward by a writer
Often the writer will put forward the antithesis in order to stress his or her own thesis.

**antonym** *Gegenbegriff,*
*Antonym*
a word meaning the opposite of another word
**Example:** *Sweet* is the antonym of *sour* or *savoury*.
<> synonym

**argumentative text**
*argumentativer Text*
a text that presents arguments about one or both sides of an issue
The main purpose of an argumentative text is to get a certain perspective of an issue across, i.e. the writer tries to convince the reader of his or her opinion on a topic with the help of arguments.
Typical examples are *columns, *editorials, *letters to the editor, *speeches, and *essays.
▶ text type

**article** *Artikel, Aufsatz*
a story or report in a newspaper or magazine

**assonance** *Assonanz,*
*vokalischer Gleichklang*
the repetition of the same or similar vowel sounds within stressed syllables of neighbouring words
**Example:**
the p**o**ppies bl**o**w /
Between the cr**o**sses, r**o**w on r**o**w.
(John McCrae, 'In Flanders Fields', 1915)
▶ alliteration

**atmosphere**
[ˈætməsfɪə] *Atmo-*
*sphäre, Stimmung*
the feeling or mood created by a *narrator in his/her story
The *setting, the use of language (i.e. adjectives, adverbs, choice of words, length of sentences, etc.) and *characterization all contribute to the atmosphere.

**author** *Autor/-in,*
*Verfasser/-in*
a person who writes books, *articles, *essays, etc.

**autobiography**
[ˌɔːtəbaɪˈɒɡrəfi]
*Autobiografie*
a book written by a person about his/her own life

**biography** [baɪˈɒɡrəfi] *Biografie* — a book written by a person about the life of another person

**blog** *Blog* — a regularly updated website containing blog posts or blog entries that publish information or discussions on current issues or topics

**blurb** *Umschlagtext, Klappentext* — the short promotional text on the back cover of a book or a Blu-ray case

**byline** *Zeile mit dem Namen des Verfassers oder der Verfasserin* — a line at the beginning or end of a piece of writing in a newspaper or magazine that gives the writer's name

**caricature** [ˈkærɪkətʃʊə] *Karikatur* — a crude representation of a *character which is meant to be laughed at

**cartoon** *Cartoon, Karikatur* — an amusing drawing in a newspaper or magazine that deals with human nature or a current political or social issue
Complex issues are reduced to memorable pictures. Cartoons often include *captions or speech bubbles. Techniques employed by cartoonists include *caricature, *exaggeration, *wordplay and the use of *symbols.

**character** *Charakter, Figur, handelnde Person* — a person in a *fictional text
Characters can be presented through their actions, speech and thoughts as well as through description. Characters can be classified according to their importance as main characters or minor characters and according to their type as *round characters or *flat characters.
▶ antagonist, characterization, protagonist

**characterization** [ˌkærəktəraɪˈzeɪʃn] *Charakterisierung, Kennzeichnung* — the way in which the *author of a *fictional text presents his or her *characters to the reader or, in the case of a *drama, to the audience
We usually distinguish between two ways of presenting a character: *direct/*explicit characterization (*'telling') – somebody tells the reader what sort of person a character is. When the reader has to draw conclusions about a character on the basis of their actions and words, we speak of *indirect/*implicit characterization (*'showing'). This kind of characterization is predominant in *plays.

**chunk** *Wortkombination* — words that are commonly placed together, e.g. *collocations or fixed phrases
**Examples:** give a presentation, a lame excuse, by the way, a long way off, out of my mind

**classified ads / small ads** (pl) *Kleinanzeigen* — newspaper or magazine advertisements dealing with job offers, buying, selling or renting something, etc.

**cliché** [ˈkliːʃeɪ] *Klischee, Gemeinplatz, abgedroschene Phrase* — an expression which has been overused and no longer has any effect

**cliffhanger** *offenes Ende* — an exciting situation that makes you want to know what will happen next

**climax** *Höhepunkt, Klimax* — the part of the *plot where the *suspense reaches its highest point
▶ anti-climax

| | |
|---|---|
| **cluster** *Cluster* | spontaneous association of a group of words based around a concept |
| **collocation** *Zusammen-stellung, Anordnung* | words that are commonly placed together<br>**Example**: strongly suggest, go crazy, economic growth, big decision |
| **colloquial** [kəˈləʊkwiəl] *umgangssprachlich* | *informal words and phrases, used in conversation rather than in writing |
| **column** *Kolumne; kurzer, regelmäßig erschei-nender Zeitungsartikel* | an *article that appears regularly in a newspaper or magazine<br>Columns can be *humorous or serious and they can deal with any subject, e.g. lifestyle, gossip, personal problems, finances or politics. Any opinion expressed in a column is the opinion of the writer, or 'columnist', and not of the newspaper or magazine it appears in. Thus a column is often an *argumentative text. |
| **comedy** *Komödie, Lustspiel* | a type of *drama which deals with a light topic or a serious topic in an amusing way<br>A comedy always has a happy ending. |
| **comic** *Comic* | a form of literary text; stories are conveyed with the help of texts and visual elements, often sequential |
| **coming-of-age story / story of initiation** *Entwicklungsroman, Initiationsgeschichte* | a *short story or *novel in which the process of growing up is portrayed<br>Usually the *protagonist is a child or an adolescent undergoing an experi-ence which changes his/her outlook on life and marks an important stage in his/her development towards adulthood. |
| **comment** *Kommentar, Stellungnahme* | an *argumentative text in which the writer tries to convince the reader of his/her opinion on a topic |
| **commercial** (n) [kəˈmɜːʃl] *Werbespot, Werbung* | an *advertisement on television, on the radio or on a website |
| **compound** *Kompositum* | Combination of two words to make a new word<br>**Example:** afterlife, daydream, lifestyle, cheesecake |
| **concrete poetry / shape poetry** *konkrete Poesie* | *poems in which the printed words form a shape or picture<br>The shape usually reflects the *theme or contents of the poem. |
| **conflict** *Konflikt, Kontroverse, Streit* | a struggle or opposition between different forces which produces tension |
| **connotation** *Konnota-tion, Nebenbedeutung, Beiklang* | the additional meaning and association(s) a word has beyond its literal or dictionary meaning |
| **contrast** *Kontrast, Gegensatz* | the bringing together of opposing views, words or *characters to emphasize their difference and usually to highlight one of the opposing elements<br>▶ juxtaposition |
| **couplet** *Reimpaar, Verspaar* | two successive *lines which *rhyme |
| **denotation** [ˌdiːnəʊˈteɪʃn] *Denotation, (Haupt-)Bedeutung, Begriffs-umfang* | the literal and limited meaning of a word, regardless of the ideas and emotions it might connote |

| | |
|---|---|
| **denouement** [ˌdeɪˈnuːmõ] *Auflösung, Lösung des Knotens, Ausgang* | the *resolution of the *conflict in a story that is achieved at the end of a play, book, etc. |
| **descriptive text** *deskriptiver Text, beschreibender Text* | a text that presents the physical characteristics of living things or objects ▶ text type |
| **dialogue** [ˈdaɪəlɒg] *Dialog, Gespräch* | a conversation in a book, play or film that involves at least two *actors |
| **diction** *Diktion, Ausdruck, Wortwahl* | the words a writer chooses for his/her text<br>In many argumentative texts, for example, the writer will use words that have a positive *connotation to support his/her arguments, or words with negative connotations to attack those he or she opposes. The choice of words often reveals the writer's attitudes. A writer can also use *emotive language to influence the reader's reaction. |
| **direct address** *direkte Anrede* | a way of addressing the audience directly in order to establish contact with them |
| **direct/explicit characterization** *direkte/explizite Charakterisierung* | a way of presenting a *character directly<br>The *author may provide a description of a character through the words of the *narrator (especially an *omniscient narrator), or another character in the text may comment on the character, or the character may describe him- or herself. |
| **drama / dramatic text** *Schauspiel, Drama / dramatischer Text* | a text written to be performed by *actors in a theatre or in a film<br>A drama is usually divided into several *acts. *Tragedies and *comedies are types of drama. |
| **dramatic irony** *dramatische Ironie, dramaturgische Ironie* | a situation in a *play when the audience has more knowledge of events or individuals than the other *characters and *actions can take on different meanings for the audience than for the other characters of the play |
| **dramatist/playwright** *Bühnendichter/-in, Dramatiker/-in* | the *author of a *play |
| **editorial/leader** *Leitartikel* | an *article that expresses the opinion of the newspaper's editor or another member of the editorial staff about an item of news or a political or social issue of topical interest ▶ argumentative text |
| **ellipsis** *Auslassung, Ellipse* | the shortening of sentences by dropping a word or several words which can be understood from the context<br>**Example:** *Coming? (= Are you coming?)* |
| **emotive language** *gefühlsbetonte Sprache* | words and expressions with particular *connotations that appeal to the reader's or listener's emotions |
| **emphasis** [ˈemfəsɪs] *Betonung, Nachdruck, Emphase* | special importance that is given to a word or phrase |

**enjambement / run-on line** [ɪnˈdʒæmbmənt] *Enjambement*
incomplete syntax at the end of the *line where the meaning runs over to the next line without any punctuation at the end

**enumeration** [ˌɪˌnjuːməˈreɪʃn] *Aufzählung*
the listing of words, phrases or ideas
In *instructive or *argumentative texts, the list of enumerated elements can be given numbers or dashes ('Gedankenstriche') so the reader can see each new element clearly.

**epilogue** *Epilog, Nachwort*
speech, etc. at the end of a *play, book or film/movie that comments on or acts as a conclusion to what has happened
▶ prologue

**essay** *Essay, Aufsatz*
a text form in which a writer expresses his/her personal views on some topic
Essays can vary widely in length, subject matter and *tone. Some are serious, others are light-hearted and entertaining.

**euphemism** [ˈjuːfəmɪzm] *Euphemismus*
a *stylistic device used to hide the true nature of something unpleasant by expressing it in a more pleasant, less direct way
**Example:** He passed away. (= He died.)

**exaggeration** [ɪgˌzædʒəˈreɪʃn] *Übertreibung*
a strong overstatement
Exaggeration may be used to create either a serious or comic effect.
**Example:** There were thousands of guests at Tom's party.
<> understatement

**explicit characterization** *explizite/direkte Charakterisierung*
▶ direct characterization

**exposition** *Exposition, vorbereitender Teil eines Dramas*
the first part of the *plot, in which the *characters and *setting are introduced
The exposition is also the beginning of the *action.

**expository text/writing** *expositorischer Text*
a *text type in which the writer analyses and explains some relatively complex matter in an objective and precise way

**external action** *äußere Handlung*
what the *characters do in the 'real', physical world
▶ internal action

**fable** *Fabel*
a short *narrative text in which animals represent human types or act like human beings
Fables are usually didactic since they intend to teach a moral lesson, make a satirical comment or illustrate some general truth.

**falling action** *fallende Handlung*
a structural element of a *fictional text, marked by a reduction in the *suspense of the *plot, normally following the *turning point or *climax

**feature film** *Spielfilm*
a full-length film that has a story and *characters, who are played by *actors
A feature film is based on a film script, which the director then turns into a film. Important elements in a film are the *dialogue, the use of camera techniques and the acting.

| | |
|---|---|
| **feature story** *Zeitungsreportage* | a piece of *non-fiction news writing that deals with a topic by concentrating on a particular person or on particular people<br>A feature story often takes an individual case as its starting point to discuss the different aspects of the topic on a personal level and leaves the reader to draw more general conclusions from this individual case. The writer of a feature story makes use of direct quotes from the people involved in the story thus relying on first-hand reporting. |
| **fictional text / fiction** *fiktionaler Text / Prosaliteratur, Dichtung* | a text or type of literature that does not deal with facts of the real world but creates its own world or reality<br>A piece of fiction can take different forms. The main types are *narrative prose like *short stories or *novels and *drama. |
| **figurative language** [ˈfɪɡərətɪv] *bildhafte Sprache, Bildsprache* | ► imagery |
| **first-person narrator** *Ich-Erzähler/-in* | a *character in the story who refers to him- or herself as 'I'<br>The *first-person narrator tells the *action from his or her perspective and therefore only has a *limited point of view. |
| **flashback** *Rückblende* | a part of a film, *play, etc. that goes back into the past to describe or show a *scene that happened earlier in time than the main story but is essential for the *plot |
| **flat character** *typisierte Figur („flacher Charakter")* | a *character who only has a limited number of traits and may even just represent a single quality<br>Flat characters are usually minor characters in a *fictional work.<br>► round character |
| **foot** *Versfuß* | a unit of *rhythm in a *line of a *poem consisting of an unstressed syllable followed by a stressed syllable |
| **foreshadowing** [fɔːˈʃædəʊɪŋ] *Vorwegnahme* | ► anticipation |
| **formal style** *formaler (Sprach-)Stil* | a *style that consists of difficult vocabulary, often of Latin origin, and complex sentence structure<br>Formal style is usually only used for serious purposes, e.g. *essays or academic publications, or in official situations and would not be appropriate in normal everyday conversation. |
| **frame story / frame narrative** *Rahmenhandlung* | a *novel or *short story which contains one or more quite independent stories within it (also called 'a story-in-a-story')<br>The main story provides the frame for the other stories. Often the main story consists of a *character in one *setting telling another story in another setting. |
| **free verse** *freier Vers, freie Verse* | a literary device that makes little use of *rhyme |
| **genre** [ˈʒɒ̃rə, ˈʒɒnrə] *Gattung, Genre* | a type or style of literature, e.g. science fiction |

**graphic novel** *illustrierter Roman* — a piece of *fiction in which a story is told with the help of textual and visual elements; a complex version of the text form *comic

**humour** (BE), **humor** (AE) [ˈhjuːmə] *Humor* — a quality in something that makes you laugh, e.g. at the strangeness of a *character, an *action or comment, etc. because it is unexpected or unsuitable in a particular situation

**hyperbole** [haɪˈpɜːbəli] *Übertreibung, Hyperbel* — a deliberate *exaggeration
The purpose of hyperbole is to emphasize something or to produce a humorous effect.
**Example:** I'm so hungry I could eat a horse.

**iambic pentameter** [aɪˌæmbɪk penˈtæmɪtə] *fünfhebiger Jambus* — the most common *metre in English, which consists of a *line of five feet (each *foot consists of an unstressed syllable followed by a stressed syllable)
**Example:** This **ró** / yal **thróne** / of **kíngs** / this **scépt** / red isle.
(William Shakespeare, *Richard II*)

**image/imagery** *Bild/ Bildsprache* — the use of language beyond its normal dictionary definition and meaning
All non-literal (i.e. *figurative) use of language falls into the category of imagery, e.g. *metaphors, *similes and *symbols.

**implicit/indirect characterization** *implizite/indirekte Charakterisierung* — a way of presenting a *character indirectly
The reader or audience learns of the character through *dialogue and *action, rather than through description.
▶ explicit characterization

**informal style** *informeller (Sprach-)Stil, umgangssprachlicher (Sprach-)Stil* — a *style characterized by fairly simple, often incomplete sentences, short forms (e.g. *can't, you'll*), phrasal verbs and *colloquial words
Informal style is used between friends or in a relaxed or informal situation. It may include the use of *slang and/or *taboo words.

**instructive text / instruction** *instruktiver Text / (Gebrauchs-)Anweisung* — a text that tells the reader what to do in order to achieve a certain goal
Typical examples of instructive texts are travel guides, how-to books or user's manuals. Typical features are the use of imperatives, the use of the passive voice, graphics and illustrations and printing techniques like **bold** or *italic* print, dashes, etc. ▶ text type

**interior monologue** [ɪnˌtɪəriə ˈmɒnəlɒg] *innerer Monolog* — a particular kind of *scenic presentation in which the *author depicts the thoughts and feelings passing through a *character's mind
Often an interior monologue does not follow a chronological order because when people think, their thoughts jump from one subject to another. The more common way of portraying thought is through *'reported thought', in which the thoughts are presented as reported speech, introduced by reporting verbs like *think*. ▶ soliloquy

**internal action** *innere Handlung* — what takes place in a *character's mind, i.e. the character's thoughts, feelings, memories, associations, etc.
▶ external action

**intonation** *Betonung* — (effect created by) the tone of a person's voice as they speak

**ironic / irony** [aɪˈrɒnɪk / ˈaɪrəni] *ironisch / Ironie* — saying the opposite of what you actually mean
**Example:** Oh, what a nice present! (when you actually mean 'It is rather ugly').

| | |
|---|---|
| **juxtaposition**<br>[ˌdʒʌkstəpəˈzɪʃn]<br>*Gegenüberstellung,*<br>*Nebeneinanderstellung* | a very strong *contrast of opposing ideas, arguments, views, mostly intro-<br>duced by words like for example *but, however, nevertheless* |
| **layout**  *Layout, Aufbau,*<br>*Anordnung, Gestaltung* | the way elements are arranged on a printed page<br>The layout includes elements such as the type and size of letters, the use of<br>**bold** or *italic* typeface, <u>underlining</u>, headings and sub-headings, bullets (i.e.<br>dots or other symbols used at the beginning of a text passage), the size and<br>number of *columns, the length of paragraphs, the colour and the placement<br>of illustrations. The layout determines whether a text attracts the attention<br>of the reader and is pleasant to read and it helps writers to structure their<br>texts and to emphasize certain words, phrases or passages. The layout is<br>particularly important when considering *newspaper articles, *advertise-<br>ments and brochures. |
| **leader / leading article**<br>*Leitartikel* | ▶ editorial |
| **letter**  *Brief* | a handwritten, typed or printed message that is put in an envelope and sent<br>to somebody<br>A letter can be personal or business-oriented, depending on the relationship<br>between the sender and receiver, the occasion and the purpose of the letter.<br>Letters are a very flexible text form and comprise thank-you notes, emails,<br>covering letters (*AE* cover letters), letters of complaint, *letters to the editor,<br>etc. The beginnings and endings of letters follow certain conventions. |
| **letter to the editor**<br>*Leserbrief, Leserinnen-*<br>*brief* | a *letter in which a reader expresses his/her opinion concerning an *article<br>in a newspaper or magazine or a problem which is of public interest<br>A letter to the editor may criticize or support an *article, or state a personal<br>opinion concerning a topic of current interest.<br>▶ argumentative text |
| **limited point of view**<br>*eingeschränkte*<br>*Erzählperspektive* | a method of storytelling in which the *narrator sees only what's in front of<br>him/her but does not know everything that occurs, therefore imposing<br>his/her understanding and interpretation on the *action<br>A *third-person narrator can have a limited point of view: the narrator looks<br>at the events and *characters from the perspective of one of the characters<br>or from the outside (as an observer narrator) and so does not have access to<br>the thoughts and feelings of all the characters. |
| **line**  *Zeile, Vers* | the row of words of a song or poem<br>A *sonnet, for example, always has 14 lines. |
| **literary text**  *literarischer*<br>*Text* | a piece of writing that is valued as a work of art, e.g. a *novel, *play or *poem<br>(in contrast to *non-fiction texts)<br>A literary text is often structured and held together by a specific *theme or a<br>so-called *motif, which may be a recurring image or a specific phrase or<br>sentence. |

**metaphor** ['metəfə] *Metapher* — a comparison between two things which are basically quite unlike one another without using the words *as* or *like*
The things are meant to create a picture (image) in your mind that sheds more light on a topic.
**Example:** There's daggers in men's smiles. (William Shakespeare, *Macbeth*)
▶ simile

**method card** — an individual compilation of strategies to help you with skills, language learning or exam preparation

**metre** (BE), **meter** (AE) ['miːtə] *Metrum, Versmaß* — the regular *rhythm of words in a *poem
The most common metre in English is the *iambic pentameter.

**mode of presentation** *Erzählweise* — the way a writer narrates events
There are two modes of presentation and usually a combination of both is used in a *narrative text: *scenic presentation and *panoramic presentation.

**monologue** ['mɒnəlɒg] *Monolog, Selbstgespräch* — a lengthy speech by just one character in the company of others
▶ dialogue

**motif** *Motiv, Leitmotiv, Leitgedanke* — a dominant idea in a *fictional text that is often part of the main *theme
If the motif is an *image or *metaphor and is repeated often, it may be called a 'leitmotif'.

**narrative perspective** *Erzählperspektive* — *narrator, *point of view from which a story is told
▶ narrator

**narrative prose** *Erzähl-/ Prosatext* — a *fictional story told by a *narrator and written in a continuous flow of sentences, not as a *poem or *drama
Typical examples of narrative prose are *novels and *short stories.

**narrator** BE: [nəˈreɪtə], AE: ['næreɪtər] *Erzähler/-in* — the person who tells the story in *narrative prose
There are two main types of narrator: the *first-person narrator and the *third-person narrator. The third person-narrator can have a *limited point of view or an *unlimited point of view. The third-person narrator with an *unlimited point of view is also known as an *omniscient narrator. A narrator can be *reliable or *unreliable. The narrator is not the same as the *author of a story.

**neutral style** *neutraler (Sprach)Stil* — the style generally used by educated people
Neutral style falls between *formal and *informal style. It is used in *feature stories, *news stories, etc.

**news item** *Nachricht* — a single report of news about one topic

**news(paper) article / news report / news story** *Zeitungsartikel, Zeitungsbericht* — a piece of writing about a particular subject that appears in print (in a newspaper or magazine) or digitally (e.g. on a website)
News articles can be of any length. In theory, they are meant to be objective and unbiased presentations of the facts, providing answers to the five *wh*-questions, i.e. the questions *who?, what?, when?, where?* and *why?* and often quoting sources or people as support. In practice, however, totally impartial reporting is impossible.

| | |
|---|---|
| **non-fiction / non-fictional text** *Sachliteratur, Sachbücher, Sachtexte / nichtfiktionaler Text, Sachtext* | texts that refer to the real world and are classified as *descriptive, *instructive, *argumentative or *expository texts according to their purpose<br>Examples of non-fictional texts are *news stories, *advertisements, *speeches, *letters, *essays. |
| **novel** *Roman* | a long and complex type of *fictional *narrative prose often divided into chapters<br>The *plot and structure of a novel are normally more complicated than those of shorter fictional works (like *short stories); consequently there may be a greater variety and a more detailed development of *characters and *setting. |
| **omniscient narrator** [ɒmˈnɪsiənt] *allwissende/r Erzähler/-in* | a *third-person narrator with an *unlimited point of view<br>Omniscient narrators can move freely in place and time and can enter the minds of the *characters as they wish. |
| **onomatopoeia** [ˌɒnəˌmætəˈpiːə] *Lautmalerei* | the use of a word which imitates the sounds it refers to, e.g. *buzz* or *hum*<br>In a group of words or a phrase, onomatopoeia may evoke a particular feeling, mood, sound or movement.<br>**Example:** Only the st**utt**ering rifes' rapid **ratt**le.<br>From: Wilfred Owen, 'Anthem for doomed youth'<br>The repetition of 't's and 'r's sounds like the shooting of rifles, which the words describe. |
| **open ending** *offenes Ende, offener Schluss* | the ending when a *conflict in a *fictional text is not resolved and the reader is left wondering what might happen next |
| **panoramic presentation** *panoramische Darstellung, raffender Bericht* | summarizing in just a few sentences what happens over a longer period of time (e.g. an hour, a week, months) in a story<br>► scenic presentation |
| **paradox** *Paradox(on), Widerspruch in sich* | a statement that seems impossible because it contains two opposing ideas that are both true<br>**Example:** In this rich country, there is a lot of poverty. |
| **parallelism / parallel structures** [ˈpærəlelɪzəm] *Parallelismus, Übereinstimmung, Parallelität, Ähnlichkeit / Parallelstrukturen* | the deliberate repetition of similar or identical words, phrases, sentence constructions, etc. in the same or neighbouring sentences<br>Parallelism draws the attention of the reader to certain ideas that the writer may consider important. It may be used to show that the elements are of similar importance, or it may be used in a climactic sequence, with the most important element listed at the end.<br>**Example:** Which alters[1] when it alteration finds, Or bends with the remover[2] to remove.<br>From: William Shakespeare, 'Sonnet 116'<br>[1] **alter** change<br>[2] **remover** person who goes away |
| **parody** *Parodie, komisch-satirische Nachahmung* | a *fictional text that copies or imitates someone or something in an amusing way |
| **pars pro toto** *Pars pro Toto* | a part or aspect of something representing the whole<br>**Example:** under my roof (= in my house) |

**personification**
[pəˌsɒnɪfɪˈkeɪʃn]
*Personifizierung*

the technique of representing animals or objects as if they were human beings or possessed human qualities
**Example:** the wailing wind

**persuasive text**
[pəˈsweɪsɪv] *appellativer Sachtext*

a text in which the writer attempts to appeal to a reader's or listener's emotions
Unlike *argumentative texts, persuasive texts do not use solid arguments. The most obvious example of a persuasive text is an *advertisement, but many *speeches are persuasive rather than argumentative texts.
► text type

**pitch** (1) *Tonhöhe, Stimmlage, Lautstärke*

how high or low a sound is, especially a musical note

(2) *Pitch*

a speech or set of arguments used by sb. trying to sell sth. or persuade sb. to do sth.

**play** *Schauspiel*

► drama

**playwright** *Dramatiker/-in, Bühnendichter/-in*

the *author of a *play
► dramatist

**plot** *Handlung(sgerüst)*

the structure of events in a *fictional text
The plot develops in a number of stages: *exposition, *rising action, the *climax, *turning point, *falling action and the *denouement or an *open ending. A plot will have some element of *suspense and *tension.

**poem/poetry** *Gedicht/ Lyrik*

a piece of creative writing structured by *lines, *stanzas and *rhythm
A poem can express personal thoughts and feelings (lyrical poem) or it can tell a story (narrative poem). Traditional poets make use of *rhyme whereas modern poets often use *free verse. The *speaker is the voice in which a poem is spoken, especially when the personal pronoun 'I' is used. This speaker is not always identical with the voice of the poet.

**point of view** *Erzählperspektive*

the perspective from which a story is told
The concepts of *narrator and point of view are closely related. There can be a *limited point of view, i.e. the *action, etc. are approached from one angle (possibly the point of view of a *character, including a *first-person narrator), or there can be an *unlimited point of view, i.e. the narrator can examine the action, etc. from the point of view of different characters – in this case the narrator is *omniscient.

**prologue** [ˈprəʊlɒɡ] *Prolog, Vorwort*

an introductory speech, etc. at the beginning of a *play, book or film

**props** (pl) *Requisiten*

all kinds of objects used by *actors on stage or in a film

**prose** *Prosa*

a form of written language that is formed by sentences in a continuous flow and is broken up only by paragraphs

**protagonist** *Protagonist/-in, zentrale Gestalt*

the principal *character in a *fictional text, sometimes also called the hero
His/Her opponent is called the *antagonist.

**pun** *Wortspiel*

► wordplay

| | |
|---|---|
| **quatrain** [ˈkwɒtreɪn] *Vierzeiler* | four *lines with a shared *rhyme scheme |
| **quick write** | a short written response to an open-ended question or a prompt to reflect your understanding of a topic |
| **refrain** [rɪˈfreɪn] *Refrain* | phrases or *lines repeated at intervals throughout a *poem |
| **register** *Sprachstil, der für bestimmte Situationen charakteristisch ist; Register* | the level of language used in a text, e.g. *formal, *informal, *neutral, *slang |
| **reliable narrator** *glaubwürdige/r Erzähler/-in* | a trustworthy storyteller<br>The reader may take everything the *narrator tells at face value.<br><> unreliable narrator |
| **repetition** *Wiederholung* | the deliberate use of a word or phrase more than once in a sentence or a text to create a sense of pattern or form, or to emphasize certain elements for the reader or listener |
| **reported speech** *indirekte Rede* | the reporting of what sb. has said, written or thought<br>**Example:** Direct speech: *Selma asked: 'Is Sam going to the party?'*<br>Indirect speech: *Selma asked if Sam was going to the party.* |
| **reported thought** *erlebte Rede* | in fiction: the rendering by the narrator of a character's thoughts using the third-person and the past tense / conditional, but no reporting verb<br>(> *reported speech)<br>**Example:** Direct speech: *Selma asked: 'Is Sam going to the party?'*<br>Reported thought: *Was Sam going to the party?* |
| **resolution** *Auflösung* | the moment at the end of a *drama, *novel, etc., where all the *conflicts are solved |
| **rhetorical device** *rhetorisches (Stil-)mittel* | ► stylistic device |
| **rhetorical question** [rɪˈtɒrɪkl] *rhetorische Frage (auf die keine Antwort erwartet wird)* | a question to which the answer seems obvious and is therefore not necessary<br>A rhetorical question pushes the reader or listener to a certain conclusion. For this reason, it is popular in political *speeches, etc. when a person is trying to influence others. |
| **rhyme** *Reim* | the similarity of sounds between certain words in *poems, usually at the end of *lines<br>► rhyme scheme |
| **rhyme scheme** *Reimschema* | the way a poet arranges the *rhymes in a *poem<br>Small letters are used to show that words share a rhyme. If the words 'day', 'make', 'say' and 'lake' appear at the end of four successive *lines, the rhyme scheme is written as **a b a b.**<br>► alternate rhyme, rhyming couplet |
| **rhyming couplet** *Paarreim, Reimpaar* | a *rhyme scheme that is written a a b b |

| | |
|---|---|
| **rhythm** *Rhythmus* | the arrangement of stressed and unstressed syllables in a *line of a *poem<br>► metre |
| **rising action** *(an-)*<br>*steigende Handlung* | the second part of the *plot where the *conflict or the *theme of the story in a *fictional text is developed and *suspense created |
| **round character**<br>*runde Figur* | a character in a *fictional text who has several character traits and behaves in a lifelike way<br>Usually a round character develops in the course of the story. The main characters are usually round characters.<br>► flat character |
| **run-on line**<br>*Enjambement* | ► enjambement |
| **scene** *Szene* | a smaller unit of *action in which there is no change of place or break in time<br>In a *drama a scene is a subdivision of an *act. |
| **scenic presentation**<br>*szenische Darstellung* | showing an event or describing a scene in detail as it occurs, using *dialogue, *interior monologue and depicting thoughts and emotions<br>► panoramic presentation |
| **script** *Drehbuch* | the written text of a *play or film |
| **scriptwriter** *Dreh-<br>buchautor/-in* | a person who creates *scripts for films and television |
| **setting** *Schauplatz,<br>Handlungsort* | the time and place (and often the *atmosphere as well) in a *fictional text |
| **shape poetry** *konkrete<br>Poesie* | ► concrete poetry |
| **short story** [ˌ-ˈ-]<br>*Kurzgeschichte* | a piece of *fictional *narrative prose, but considerably shorter and less complex than a *novel<br>A short story centres around one or two *characters at a decisive moment in their lives. It is limited in its *theme, *setting and *plot by its length. |
| **showing** *szenische<br>Darstellung* | ► scenic presentation |
| **simile** [ˈsɪməli]<br>*Vergleich, Gleichnis,<br>Simile* | a comparison between two things that are not really like each other. Similes use the word *like* or *as*.<br>**Example:** My love is like a red, red rose. (Robert Burns, 1794) |
| **sitcom** (= situation<br>comedy) *Sitcom, Situa-<br>tionskomödie (beson-<br>ders als Fernsehserie)* | a comic *TV/radio series which usually centres around a *character or group of characters<br>The characters are often stereotypes as they do not evolve over the series. A sitcom may be filmed in front of a live audience or have canned laughter added to make the audience aware of or to reinforce the funny lines. |
| **slang** *nachlässige, oft<br>fehlerhafte, saloppe<br>Ausdrucksweise; Slang* | very *informal language, mainly used in *dialogue between people of the same age or from a similar background, etc. |

| | |
|---|---|
| **soap (opera)** „Seifen-oper", (rührselige) Hörspiel- oder Fernsehspielserie | a regular TV or radio programme about the everyday lives of a group of people<br>The storyline of a soap (opera), unlike that of a normal *TV/radio series, develops from programme to programme and may often end with a *cliffhanger to encourage the audience to tune in to the next episode. |
| **soliloquy** [səˈlɪləkwi] Monolog, Selbstgespräch | a *speech delivered by one of the *characters in a *drama, in which he or she reveals his or her thoughts, feelings or motives to the audience<br>▶ monologue |
| **solution** (Auf-)Lösung | the successful ending of a problem, a *conflict or a difficult situation |
| **sonnet** [ˈsɒnɪt] Sonett | a special form of a *poem that consists of 14 *lines<br>There are various types of sonnets with different structures and forms. Shakespeare's sonnets comprise three *quatrains (i.e. four lines with a shared *rhyme scheme) and a *couplet (i.e. two successive lines which rhyme). |
| **speaker** lyrisches Ich | the *fictional person, in theory not identical with the poet, who speaks the text of a *poem |
| **speech** Rede, Ansprache | a spoken *non-fictional text delivered to an audience<br>The speaker normally wants to convince his/her audience to adopt his/her view on a certain topic.<br>▶ argumentative text |
| **spidergram** Wortigel | a simple diagram for organizing words that belong together because they are of the same type (phrasal verbs, prefixes and suffixes) or they express a key concept |
| **stage directions** (pl) Bühnenanweisungen | the *dramatist's description of what the stage should look like and how the *actors should perform the *drama<br>Stage directions may give information about any of the following: the *setting, the objects on stage (the *props), the *characters' appearances, clothes and manner of speaking, as well as their entrances and exits. |
| **stanza** Strophe, Vers | a group of *lines (*verses) that form a unit in a *poem because they relate to a similar thought or topic |
| **storyboard** Szenenbuch | a series of illustrations or images visualizing a scene from a movie or a *play<br>Storyboards often include additional information on the *setting, the *props, technical aspects like the camera movements or the lighting, the *characters and the *dialogue. |
| **story of initiation** [ɪˌnɪʃiˈeɪʃn] Entwicklungsroman, Initiationsgeschichtes | ▶ coming-of-age story |
| **style** Stil | the particular way in which a *fictional or *non-fictional text is written<br>Style includes elements such as *register and *tone. |

**stylistic device** *Stilmittel* — a method and technique used to produce a particular effect in a text and on the reader
The most common stylistic devices are: *accumulation, *alliteration, *allusion, *anaphora, *assonance, *contrast, *exaggeration, *irony, *juxtaposition, *metaphor, *personification, *rhetorical question, *simile, *symbol, *understatement, *wordplay.

**surprise ending** *überraschendes Ende, nicht vorhersehbarer Schluss* — an ending in which the reader's expectations regarding the course of the story are not fulfilled, but an unexpected *resolution to the *conflict is presented

**suspense** *Spannung* — a feeling of worry or excitement that is created when the reader does not know the outcome of the *conflict or *action

**suspension of disbelief** *willentliche Aussetzung der Ungläubigkeit* — expecting the reader to accept this world or story as existing or true

**symbol / symbolic** *Symbol / symbolisch* — a thing, word or phrase signifying something concrete that stands not only for itself but also for a certain abstract idea
As in the case of a *metaphor or a *simile the meaning of a symbol goes beyond the literal meaning.
**Example:** A red rose is often a symbol of love.

**synonym** *Synonym* — a word that means the same as another word
**Example:** Fast and quick are the synonyms of speedy.
<> antonym

**taboo word** *Tabuwort* — a word that is generally considered obscene, vulgar or shocking and is used only if the writer is trying to make a particular point or shock the readers

**telling** *berichtende Darstellung* — ▶ panoramic presentation

**tension** *(An-)Spannung* — the feeling evoked in the reader when a story/*drama is full of *suspense, i.e. the reader is curious about what will happen

**text type** *Textsorte, Textart* — the classification of a text according to the *writer's intentions
There are different text types: *argumentative texts, *descriptive texts, *expository texts, *instructive texts, *narrative texts, *persuasive texts.

**theme** *Thema, Gegenstand, Stoff* — the main idea or *motif (e.g. a recurring image or a specific phrase or sentence) that structures and holds together a *literary text

**thesis** [ˈθiːsɪs] *These, Behauptung, Postulat* — an idea or a view that an *author of an *argumentative text presents and discusses in a *formal way
▶ antithesis

**third-person narrator** *auktoriale/r Erzähler/-in* — a *narrator who refers to all the *characters as *he, she, they* or by their names
A third-person narrator is not a character in the story. This type of narrator can have a *limited point of view (just like a camera) or an *unlimited point of view. In the latter case, the narrator knows everything and is called *omniscient.

| | |
|---|---|
| **tone** *Ton, Stimmung* | the way in which a writer treats his/her topic, thereby reflecting his/her emotional attitude towards that topic and also towards the reader<br>The tone can be *formal, intimate, solemn, playful, serious, *ironic, *humorous, angry, etc. |
| **tragedy / tragic** *Tragödie, Trauerspiel / tragisch* | a type of *drama in which the main *character (the *protagonist) goes through a series of misfortunes towards his or her downfall<br>Usually this downfall is partly brought about by the protagonist's own faults and weaknesses. |
| **turning point** *Wendepunkt* | a sudden or surprising change of the *action in the *plot |
| **tv/radio series** [ˈsɪəriːz] *Fernseh-/Radioserie* | a regular programme on TV or radio about the lives and problems of a *character or, more usually, a group of characters<br>Each programme is self-contained, i.e. it deals with a particular issue or storyline which is concluded at the end of the programme. The lives of the characters evolve slowly over the course of a series. |
| **understatement** *Untertreibung* | a statement in which the true importance of an idea, event or fact is minimized, so that something is deliberately presented as being much less important, valuable, etc. than it really is<br>Understatement is often used for *ironic effect. The opposite is *exaggeration/overstatement. |
| **unlimited point of view** *uneingeschränkte Erzählperspektive* | a method of storytelling in which the *narrator can move freely in place and time and enter the minds of the *characters at will |
| **unreliable narrator** *unglaubwürdige/r Erzähler/-in* | an untrustworthy storyteller<br>The reader must find out just how much of what the *narrator says can be accepted. *First-person narrators are usually unreliable as they give only one perspective on the *action and the *characters.<br><> reliable narrator |
| **verse** *Vers* | a single *line of a *poem |
| **volta** *Volta, Wendung* | the *turning point in a *sonnet, which can be identified by words like *but, yet* or and *yet*<br>The volta might be a *line of the sonnet. |
| **word family** *Wortfamilie* | a group of words with a common base to which other words are added<br>**Example:** The words *signal, signature, assign, resign,* etc. belong to the word family of *sign.* |
| **wordplay / play on words / pun** *Wortspiel* | the use of a word which may be understood in two different ways or which may be put into a different context to change the meaning<br>**Example:** My family bought a boat because it was for sail. |

# The US System of Government

## System of Checks and Balances

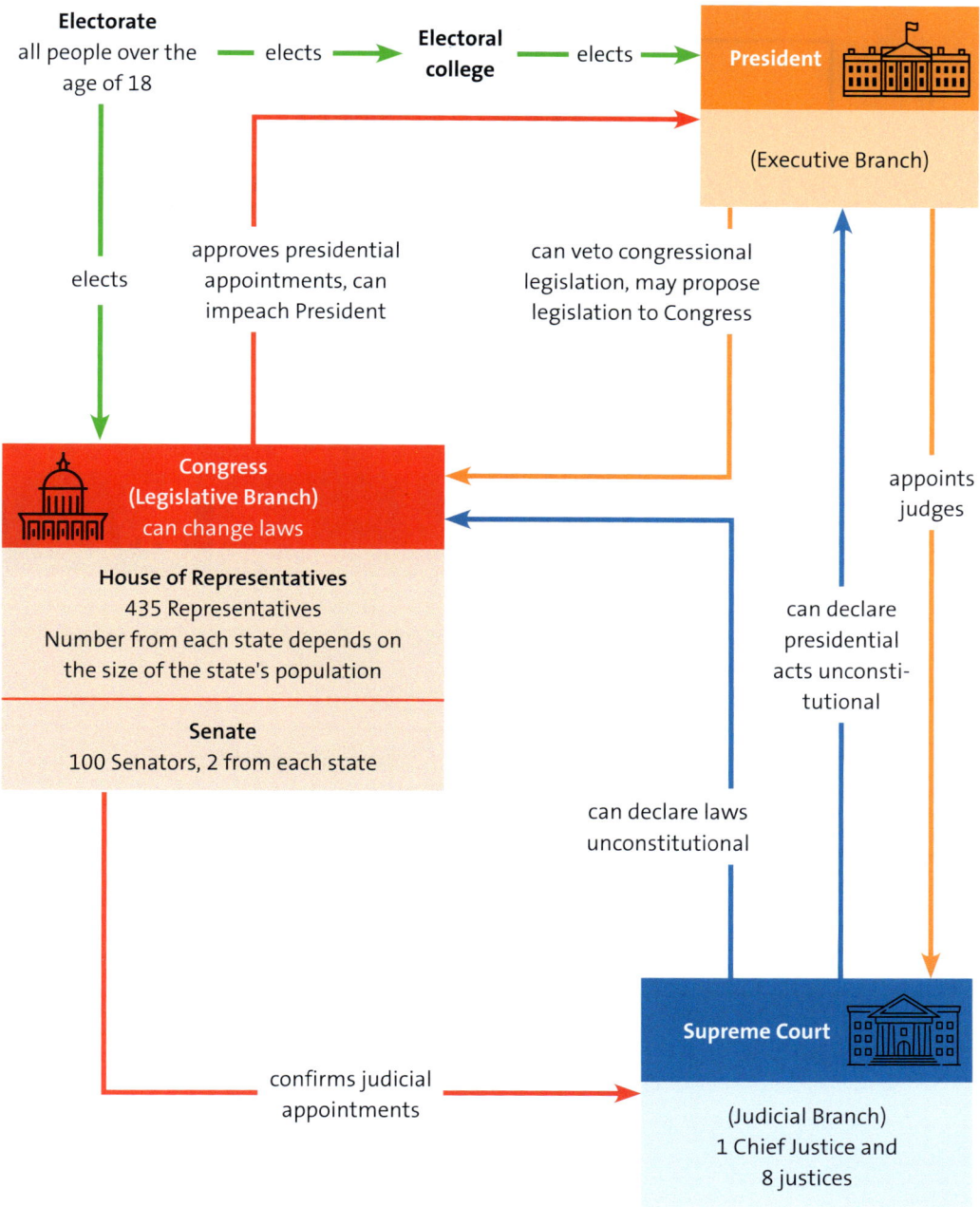

**Electorate**
all people over the
age of 18

elects → **Electoral college** → elects → **President**

(Executive Branch)

elects

approves presidential
appointments, can
impeach President

can veto congressional
legislation, may propose
legislation to Congress

**Congress
(Legislative Branch)**
can change laws

**House of Representatives**
435 Representatives
Number from each state depends on
the size of the state's population

**Senate**
100 Senators, 2 from each state

appoints
judges

can declare
presidential
acts unconsti-
tutional

can declare laws
unconstitutional

confirms judicial
appointments

**Supreme Court**

(Judicial Branch)
1 Chief Justice and
8 justices

## The British System of Government

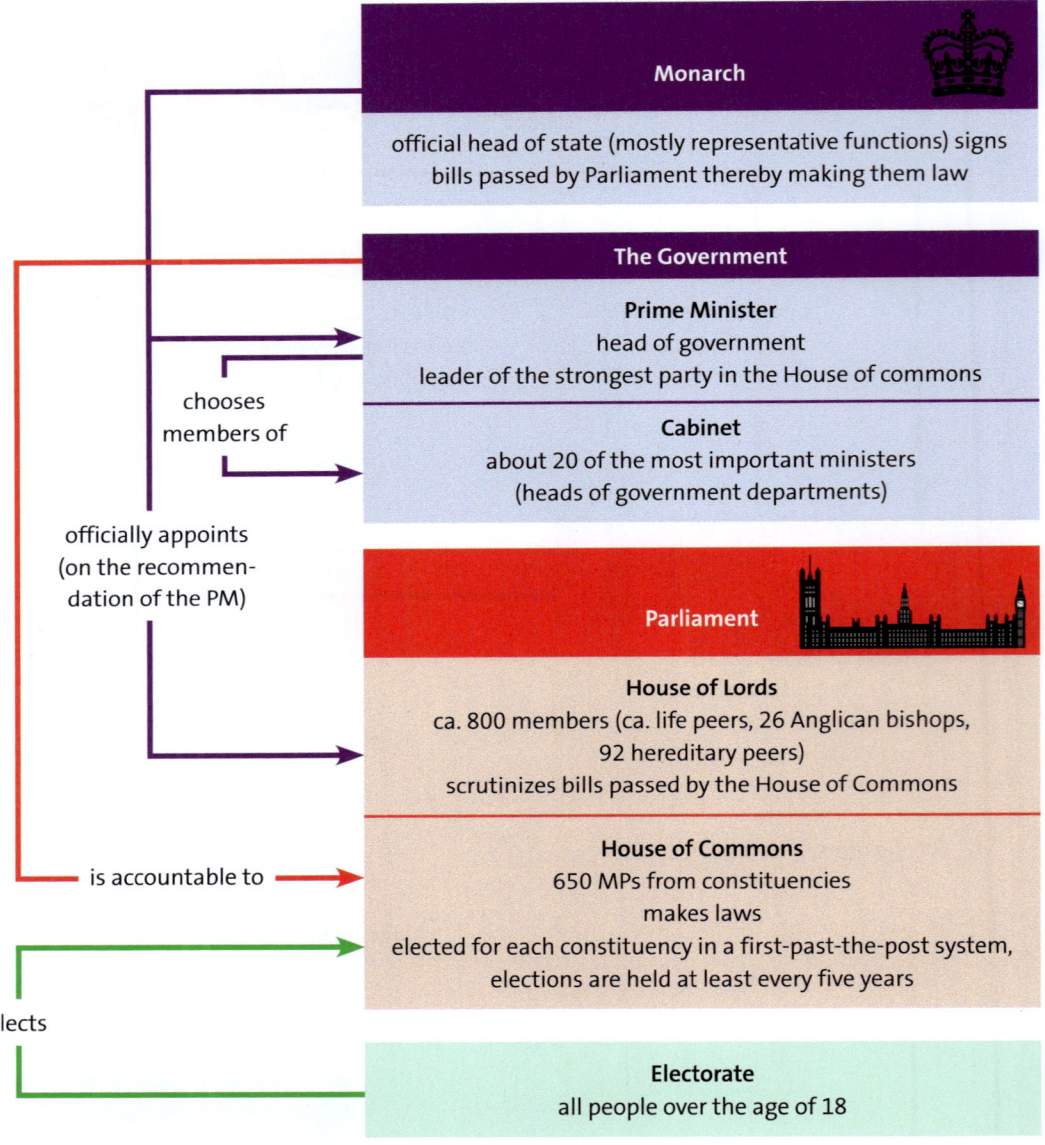

**Monarch**

official head of state (mostly representative functions) signs
bills passed by Parliament thereby making them law

**The Government**

**Prime Minister**
head of government
leader of the strongest party in the House of commons

**Cabinet**
about 20 of the most important ministers
(heads of government departments)

**Parliament**

**House of Lords**
ca. 800 members (ca. life peers, 26 Anglican bishops,
92 hereditary peers)
scrutinizes bills passed by the House of Commons

**House of Commons**
650 MPs from constituencies
makes laws
elected for each constituency in a first-past-the-post system,
elections are held at least every five years

**Electorate**
all people over the age of 18

chooses
members of

officially appoints
(on the recommen-
dation of the PM)

is accountable to

elects

## The German System of Government

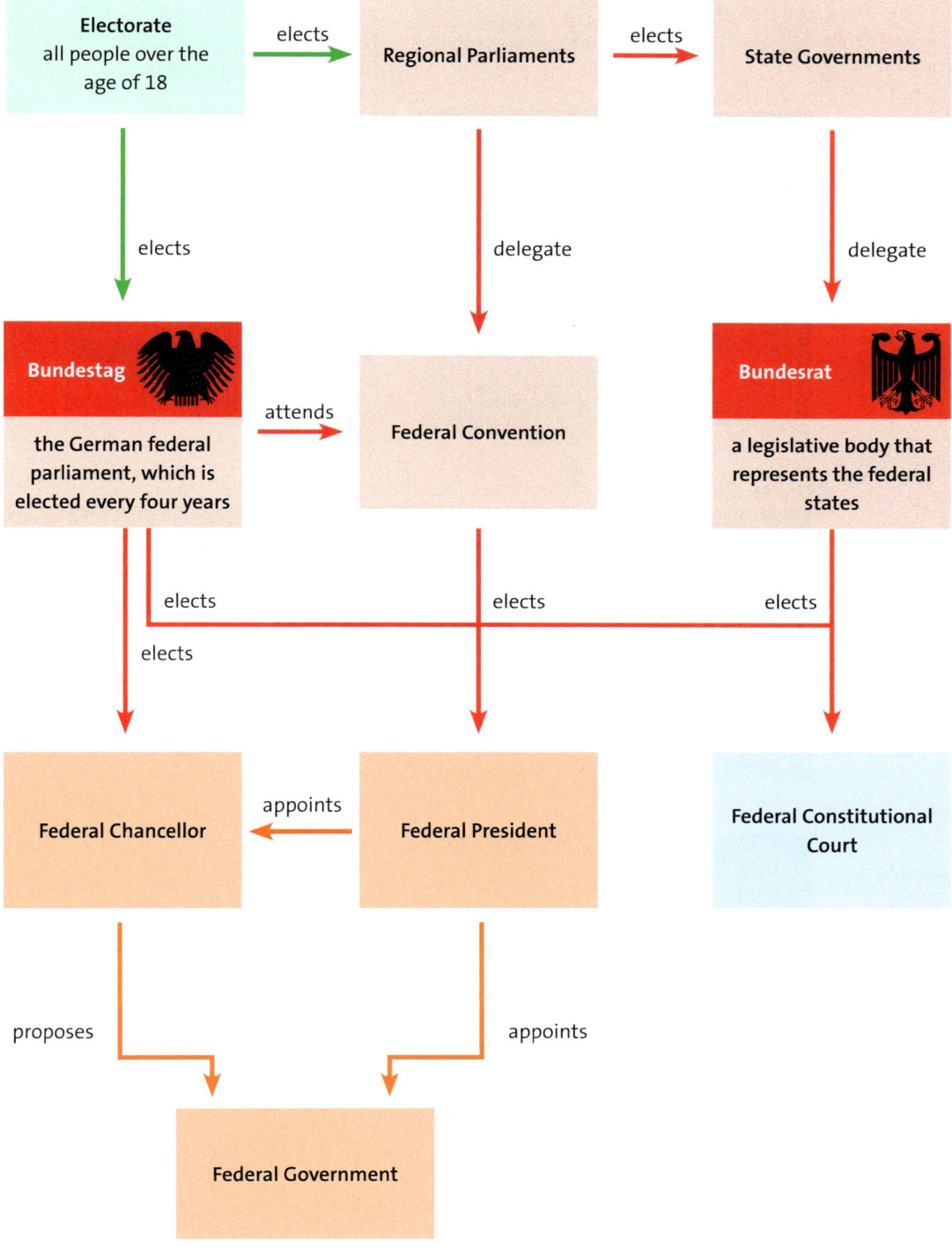

# The US System of Education

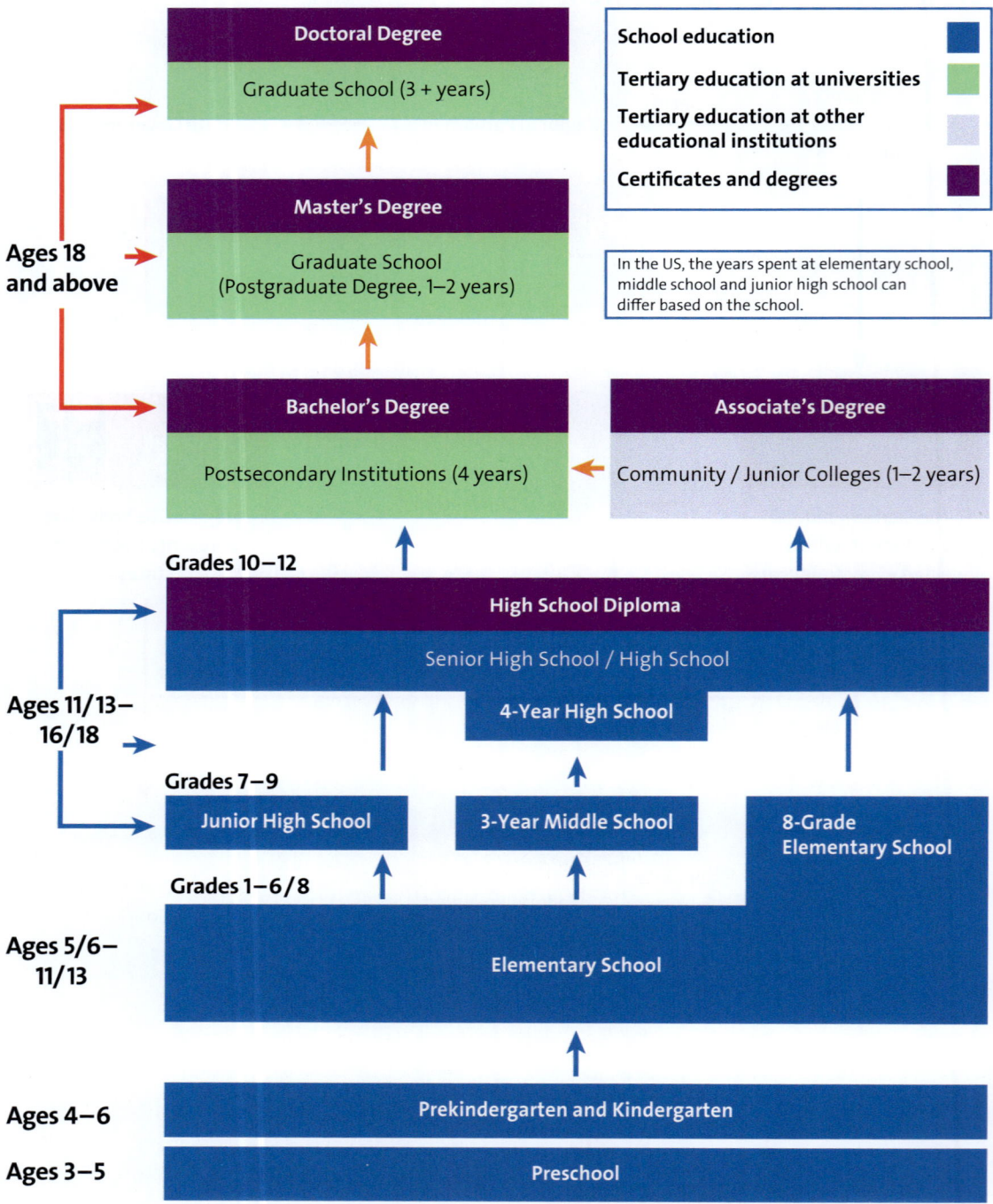

**Legend:**
- School education (blue)
- Tertiary education at universities (green)
- Tertiary education at other educational institutions (light grey)
- Certificates and degrees (dark purple)

In the US, the years spent at elementary school, middle school and junior high school can differ based on the school.

**Ages 18 and above**
- Doctoral Degree — Graduate School (3 + years)
- Master's Degree — Graduate School (Postgraduate Degree, 1–2 years)
- Bachelor's Degree — Postsecondary Institutions (4 years)
- Associate's Degree — Community / Junior Colleges (1–2 years)

**Grades 10–12**

**Ages 11/13– 16/18**
- High School Diploma — Senior High School / High School
- 4-Year High School

**Grades 7–9**
- Junior High School
- 3-Year Middle School
- 8-Grade Elementary School

**Grades 1–6/8**

**Ages 5/6– 11/13**
- Elementary School

**Ages 4–6**
- Prekindergarten and Kindergarten

**Ages 3–5**
- Preschool

*Source:* gpseducation.oecd.org

## The UK System of Education

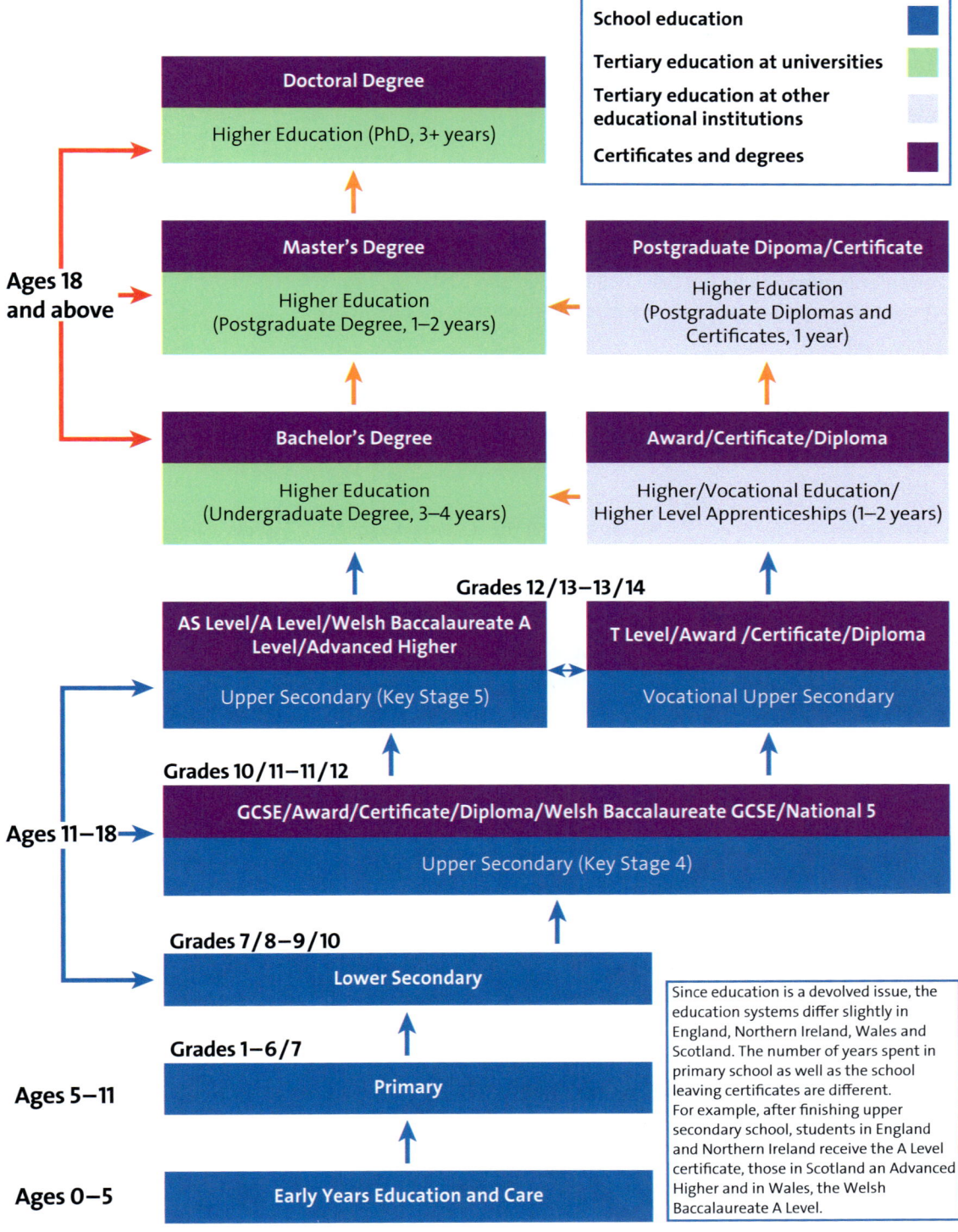

**Legend:**
- School education
- Tertiary education at universities
- Tertiary education at other educational institutions
- Certificates and degrees

**Doctoral Degree**
Higher Education (PhD, 3+ years)

**Master's Degree**
Higher Education (Postgraduate Degree, 1–2 years)

**Postgraduate Dipoma/Certificate**
Higher Education (Postgraduate Diplomas and Certificates, 1 year)

**Bachelor's Degree**
Higher Education (Undergraduate Degree, 3–4 years)

**Award/Certificate/Diploma**
Higher/Vocational Education/ Higher Level Apprenticeships (1–2 years)

**Ages 18 and above**

**Grades 12/13–13/14**

**AS Level/A Level/Welsh Baccalaureate A Level/Advanced Higher**
Upper Secondary (Key Stage 5)

**T Level/Award /Certificate/Diploma**
Vocational Upper Secondary

**Grades 10/11–11/12**

**GCSE/Award/Certificate/Diploma/Welsh Baccalaureate GCSE/National 5**
Upper Secondary (Key Stage 4)

**Ages 11–18**

**Grades 7/8–9/10**

**Lower Secondary**

**Grades 1–6/7**

**Ages 5–11**

**Primary**

**Ages 0–5**

**Early Years Education and Care**

Since education is a devolved issue, the education systems differ slightly in England, Northern Ireland, Wales and Scotland. The number of years spent in primary school as well as the school leaving certificates are different. For example, after finishing upper secondary school, students in England and Northern Ireland receive the A Level certificate, those in Scotland an Advanced Higher and in Wales, the Welsh Baccalaureate A Level.

*Source:* gpseducation.oecd.org

# Verbs for tasks

*Context Starter* uses the same special vocabulary ('Operatoren') for tasks that is used in standard tests, including the 'Abitur'. Be sure you understand what's required of you when you come across one of the verbs below.

**'Anforderungsbereich I'** COMPREHENSION
refers to text comprehension and definition.

**'Anforderungsbereich II'** ANALYSIS
focuses on text analysis and comparison and stylistic devices.

**'Anforderungsbereich III'** BEYOND THE TEXT
concentrates on discussion, comment, evaluation and text production.

| The instructions say | Example | What you are expected to do |
| --- | --- | --- |
| **analyse** *(BE)*, **analyze** *(AE)* ['ænəlaɪz] *analysieren* ANALYSIS | **Analyse** the narrative perspective in the given excerpt. | Describe and explain in detail. |
| **assess** [ə'ses] *auswerten, beurteilen, bewerten, einschätzen* BEYOND THE TEXT | **Assess** whether the statement applies to the short story as well. | Express a well-founded opinion on the nature or quality of sb./sth. |
| **comment on** ['kɒment] *kommentieren, Stellung nehmen, darlegen* BEYOND THE TEXT | **Comment** on the future of multiculturalism in the USA. | State your opinion clearly and support your view with evidence, reasons or arguments. |
| **compare** *vergleichen, kontrastieren, gegenüberstellen* ANALYSIS | **Compare** X's and Y's views on education. | Show similarities and differences. |
| **describe** *beschreiben* COMPREHENSION | **Describe** the living conditions of the family. | Give a detailed account of what sb./sth. is like. |
| **discuss** *diskutieren, erörtern* BEYOND THE TEXT | **Discuss** advantages and disadvantages of introducing fullbody scanners at airports. | Give arguments or reasons for and against, especially to come to a well-founded conclusion. |
| **evaluate** [ɪ'væljueɪt] *kommentieren, Stellung nehmen, darlegen* BEYOND THE TEXT | **Evaluate** the chances of the protagonist's plan to succeed in life. | Express a well-founded opinion on the nature or quality of sb./sth. |

| The instructions say | Example | What you are expected to do |
|---|---|---|
| **examine** [ɪgˈzæmɪn] *untersuchen* ANALYSIS | **Examine** the author's use of language. | Describe and explain in detail. |
| **explain** *erklären* ANALYSIS | **Explain** the protagonist's obsession with money. | Make sth. clear taking into account culture-related differences if necessary. |
| **interpret** [ɪnˈtɜːprɪt] *interpretieren, deuten, auswerten* BEYOND THE TEXT | **Interpret** the message the author wants to convey. | Explain the meaning or purpose of sth. |
| **illustrate** *veranschaulichen* ANALYSIS BEYOND THE TEXT | **Illustrate** the narrator's admiration for the main character. **Illustrate** the way in which school life in the USA differs from that in Germany. | Use examples to explain or make sth. clear. |
| **outline** *präsentieren, vorstellen, nennen* COMPREHENSION | **Outline** the author's views on lowering the voting age. | Give the main features, structure or general principles of sth. |
| **point out** *darstellen* ANALYSIS | **Point out** the author's main ideas on … | Present the main aspects of sth. briefly and clearly. |
| **summarize** (*also*: **sum up** / **write a summary**) *zusammenfassen* COMPREHENSION | **Summarize** the main points of the German newspaper article. | Give a concise account of the main points or ideas of a text, issue or topic. |
| **state** *darlegen* COMPREHENSION ANALYSIS BEYOND THE TEXT | **State** the author's main arguments … **State** the writer's opinion on green energy. **State** your reasons for applying for an internship. | Present the main aspects of sth. briefly and clearly. |
| **write/give a characterization of** [ˌkærəktəraɪˈzeɪʃn] ANALYSIS *charakterisieren, detailliert beschreiben und erklären* | **Write** a characterization of the heroine. **Give** a characterization of the hero in the excerpt. | Provide a thorough analysis of a character. |

**Cover**

stock.adobe.com/Boris Stroujko, Architekt Millennium Bridge: Norman Foster, Architekt St. Paul's Cathedral: Sir Christopher Wren

**Illustrationen**

2021: S. 150/u. m., S. 305, S. 309, S. 373/m. l., S. 373/u. r.; Cornelsen/Roland Beier: S. 400, S. 401; mauritius images/alamy stock photo/De Luan: S. 112/m. l.; mauritius images/alamy stock photo/Lanmas: S. 120/o. l.; mauritius images/alamy stock photo/Pictorial Press Ltd: S. 107; PEFC Deutschland e.V.: S. 2; Shutterstock.com/Benjavisa Ruangvaree Art: S. 188/o. l.; Shutterstock.com/Chipmunk131: S. 21/o. r.; Shutterstock.com/cosmaa: S. 66; Shutterstock.com/Katrine Glazkova: S. 21/u. r.; Shutterstock.com/LinGraphics: S. 192/m. l.; Shutterstock.com/MPFphotography: S. 373/m.; Shutterstock.com/okili77: S. 50; Shutterstock.com/Viktoria Kurpas: S. 257/u. r..

**Fotos**

S. 1: Cornelsen/Inhouse/Anne Weingarten; S. 17/o. r.: Shutterstock.com/Lee Yiu Tung; S. 17/u. m.: Shutterstock.com/Varavin88; S. 18/m. l.: Shutterstock.com/Dean Drobot; S. 18/o. l.: Shutterstock.com/Susan Law Cain; S. 19: Shutterstock.com/Everett Collection; S. 20/m. l.: Shutterstock.com/delcarmat; S. 20/u. m.: Shutterstock.com/pathdoc; S. 22/o. l.: Shutterstock.com/hxdbzxy; S. 22/u. l.: Shutterstock.com/Peshkova; S. 23/m.: Shutterstock.com/melitas; S. 23/m. r.: Shutterstock.com/OllgaZhog; S. 23/u. r.: Shutterstock.com/Drazen Zigic; S. 24: Shutterstock.com/BAZA Production; S. 25/m.: CartoonStock/Warren Miller; S. 25/m. l.: CartoonStock/Tim Cordell; S. 26: Shutterstock.com/michaeljung; S. 27: Shutterstock.com/SeventyFour; S. 29: Shutterstock.com/Monkey Business Images; S. 33: Shutterstock.com/creativepriyanka; S. 34: Barker, Meg-John and Scheele, Jules. Queer: A Graphic History. London: Icon Books, p. 87; S. 35: Shutterstock.com/Rittis; S. 36/m. l.: Shutterstock.com/melitas; S. 36/u. l.: Shutterstock.com/eamesBot; S. 38/o. l.: Shutterstock.com/VGstockstudio; S. 38/u. l.: Shutterstock.com/svitlini; S. 39: Shutterstock.com/Djomas; S. 41/u. r.: CartoonStock/Karsten Schley; S. 43: Shutterstock.com/Yeti studio; S. 44: Shutterstock.com/Narin Nonthamand; S. 45/m. r.: Shutterstock.com/Jacob Lund; S. 46/o. r.: Shutterstock.com/Marusya Chaika; S. 46/u. l.: Shutterstock.com/sharpner; S. 47: Galerie Bilderwelt/Bridgeman Images; S. 48/o. r.: Shutterstock.com/Photos BrianScantlebury; S. 51: Shutterstock.com/danceyourlife; S. 54/u. l.: CartoonStock/Chris Madden; S. 56/o. l.: Shutterstock.com/D. Pimborough; S. 57: stock.adobe.com/Kaspars; S. 58/m. l.: dpa Picture-Alliance/robertharding; S. 58/o. l.: CartoonStock/Mick Stevens; S. 60: dpa Picture-Alliance/ASSOCIATED PRESS/Pool Daily Telegraph/AP; S. 61/m.: mauritius images/alamy stock photo/Vuk Valcic; S. 61/u. r.: Shutterstock.com/David Smart; S. 63/o. r.: Shutterstock.com/Loredana Sangiuliano; S. 64: Shutterstock.com/PeskyMonkey; S. 65: Shutterstock.com/Lysified; S. 67/u. r.: mauritius images/alamy stock photo/Keith Skingle; S. 68: Shutterstock.com/Sarah2; S. 70: Shutterstock.com/Amir Ridhwan; S. 71/o. r.: Shutterstock.com/Yau Ming Low; S. 72: Shutterstock.com/ivosar; S. 73: Shutterstock.com/Cagkan Sayin; S. 79/o. r.: Shutterstock.com/Simon Collins; S. 80/u. l.: mauritius images/Oliver Gutfleisch; S. 81: Shutterstock.com/Barandash Karandashich; S. 82/m.: Shutterstock.com/13_Phunkod; S. 82/o. r.: Shutterstock.com/William Perugini; S. 83/m. r.: Shutterstock.com/Valeriy Karpeev; S. 83/o. r.: Shutterstock.com/Brian A Jackson; S. 83/o. r.: Shutterstock.com/Mangostar; S. 84: mauritius images/World Book Inc.; S. 87/u. r.: Shutterstock.com/Leo Fernandes; S. 89: Shutterstock.com/Chinnapong; S. 93: Shutterstock.com/SibRapid; S. 94: Shutterstock.com/ESB Professional; S. 99: Shutterstock.com/DariaRen; S. 104/o. l.: Shutterstock.com/Gorodenkoff; S. 104/u. l.: Shutterstock.com/guruXOX; S. 105: Shutterstock.com/tommaso lizzul; S. 108: Shutterstock.com/LIPING; S. 109: Shutterstock.com/igor kisselev; S. 110/m. l.: Shutterstock.com/Billion Photos; S. 111: Shutterstock.com/Vasin Lee; S. 113/o. r.: Shutterstock.com/eyes on him; S. 113/u. r.: Shutterstock.com/Jacob Lund; S. 114/m. r.: Shutterstock.com/fitzcrittle; S. 114/m. r.: stock.adobe.com/Bumble Dee; S. 114/o. r.: Shutterstock.com/Diego Cervo; S. 115/m.: Shutterstock.com/photoiva; S. 115/o. l.: Imago Stock & People GmbH/Addictive Stock; S. 115/o. r.: Shutterstock.com/PEPPERSMINT; S. 116: CartoonStock/Chris Wildt; S. 117: Shutterstock.com/Itana; S. 118/o. r.: mauritius images/Science Faction; S. 121: stock.adobe.com/dennizn; S. 123: Shutterstock.com/Christopher David

Howells; S. 126: Bridgeman Images/Photo © Christie's Images; S. 128: stock.adobe.com/Dave Newman; S. 129/m. r.: Shutterstock.com/Dean Drobot; S. 129/m. r.: Shutterstock.com/SIAATH; S. 130/o. l.: Imago Stock & People GmbH/Westend61; S. 130/u. m.: Shutterstock.com/Oskari Porkka; S. 131: stock.adobe.com/kirkikis; S. 132: Shutterstock.com/Valery Sidelnykov; S. 137/m. r.: Shutterstock.com/sirtravelalot; S. 137/u. r.: Shutterstock.com/Stuart Monk; S. 138/m. l.: stock.adobe.com/2016 Dallas Golden/Dallas; S. 138/o. l.: mauritius images/TopFoto; S. 139: Imago Stock & People GmbH/ZUMA Wire/xSgt. xCharlottexCarulli/Dodx; S. 140/m. r.: stock.adobe.com/Delphotostock; S. 141/o. r.: stock.adobe.com/zabanski; S. 144: Shutterstock.com/Maridav; S. 145: Bridgeman Images/Peter Newark American Pictures; S. 146/m. l.: Imago Stock & People GmbH/Levine-Roberts; S. 148/u. l.: Shutterstock.com/PEPPERSMINT; S. 150/u. l.: Shutterstock.com/Boydz1980; S. 151/u. l.: Shutterstock.com/canadastock; S. 152/m. r.: stock.adobe.com/JIRMoronta; S. 152/o. r.: Depositphotos/Matej Kastelic; S. 153/m. l.: Shutterstock.com/sklyareek; S. 153/m. r.: akg-images/Freese/drama-berlin.de; S. 153/o. m.: mauritius images/World Book Inc.; S. 153/o. r.: stock.adobe.com/Dirima; S. 154/m. l.: mauritius images/Axiom RF; S. 154/o. l.: akg-images/Liszt Collection; S. 154/u. l.: Shutterstock.com/IfH; S. 155/m. r.: Depositphotos/Jan Wehnert; S. 155/m. r.: mauritius images/SagaPhoto; S. 155/o. r.: Shutterstock.com/Kiselev Andrey Valerevich; S. 155/u. m.: Imago Stock & People GmbH/Heritage Images; S. 155/u. m.: mauritius images/Jim West/Alamy Stock Photos; S. 155/u. r.: mauritius images/alamy stock photo/Watchtheworld; S. 156: CartoonStock/Amy Hwang; S. 157/m.: Shutterstock.com/Mehaniq; S. 157/m. l.: Shutterstock.com/Kamira; S. 157/o. m.: Shutterstock.com/Pixel-Shot; S. 157/u. l.: Shutterstock.com/Gilmanshin; S. 158/m. r.: mauritius images/alamy stock photo/ako; S. 158/o. r.: Shutterstock.com/Supamotionstock.com; S. 159: mauritius images/alamy stock photo/360b; S. 161/m. r.: stock.adobe.com/@Franck Camhi/snaptitude; S. 161/o. m.: stock.adobe.com/fidelio; S. 162/m. l.: stock.adobe.com/Volodymyr; S. 163/m.: stock.adobe.com/Karin Jähne; S. 163/u. l.: mauritius images/alamy stock photo/IanDagnall Computing; S. 164: mauritius images/alamy stock photo/Richard Sheppard; S. 165: stock.adobe.com/Stefan Gräf; S. 168/m. l.: mauritius images/alamy stock photo/Martin Lee; S. 168/u. l.: mauritius images/alamy stock photo/Martin Lee; S. 169: Imago Stock & People GmbH/Bruno Press; S. 171: Imago Stock & People GmbH/Mary Evans; S. 172: Shutterstock.com/Monkik; S. 174/m. r.: mauritius images/SuperStock; S. 174/o. r.: Shutterstock.com/Nithid; S. 176/o. l.: mauritius images/Science Source; S. 179/o.r.: Shutterstock.com/Moremar; S. 179/u. r.: Shutterstock.com/Vladiczech; S. 180/u. l.: stock.adobe.com/saiko3p; S. 181: Shutterstock.com/ricochet64; S. 183: stock.adobe.com/lkpro; S. 184/o. l.: Shutterstock.com/Uuganbayar; S. 184/u. m.: mauritius images/alamy stock photo/Wavebreak Media ltd; S. 185/m. r.: Shutterstock.com/Juice Dash; S. 185/u. l.: Shutterstock.com/Colorlife; S. 186/o. l.: stock.adobe.com/shadowvincent; S. 187: stock.adobe.com/lkpro; S. 188/u. l.: Imago Stock & People GmbH/ZUMA Wire/xVukxValcicx; S. 190: Shutterstock.com/r.classen; S. 191/u. r.: CartoonStock/Stan Eales; S. 192/o. l.: Shutterstock.com/Drazen Zigic; S. 193: Shutterstock.com/StanislauV; S. 194: Shutterstock.com/Somchai_Stock; S. 198: Imago Sportfotodienst GmbH/USA TODAY Network; S. 201: Shutterstock.com/WellofMike; S. 202/o. l.: Shutterstock.com/helloRuby; S. 204/o. r.: mauritius images/alamy stock photo/Ireland/Stephen Barnes; S. 204/u. l.: Philip Devlin; S. 204/u. m.: stock.adobe.com/Maxim Grebeshkov; S. 206: stock.adobe.com/Peter Hermes Furian; S. 208/m. l.: mauritius images/alamy stock photo/UPI; S. 208/u. l.: mauritius images/alamy stock photo/Christian Bertrand; S. 209: Logan Werlinger, Columbia World Projects; S. 210/u. l.: mauritius images/age fotostock; S. 211: Imago Stock & People GmbH/robertharding/CarloxMorucchio; S. 212: Imago Stock & People GmbH/Cavan Images; S. 213/m. r.: Depositphotos/Momcilo Jovanov; S. 214: dpa Picture-Alliance/WHA/World History Archive; S. 215: dpa Picture-Alliance/empics/PA Wire/Brian Lawless; S. 217: mauritius images/Loop Images/Extramural Activity; S. 219/m. r.: stock.adobe.com/zwiebackesser; S. 220: mauritius images/alamy stock photo/Dermot Blackburn; S. 222: Shutterstock.com/Stephen Barnes; S. 224/u. l.: mauritius images/alamy stock photo/Irish Eye; S. 225: mauritius images/alamy stock photo/jackie ellis; S. 226/m. r.: stock.adobe.com/Fela Sanu; S. 226/o. r.: Shutterstock.com/bolarzeal; S. 227/o. l.: Shutterstock.com/Kehinde Olufemi Akinbo; S. 227/o. m.: Depositphotos/Olekcii Mach; S. 227/o. m.: Shutterstock.com/i_am_zews; S. 228/m. l.: Shutterstock.com/

# Acknowledgements

Tayvay; S. 228/u. l.: mauritius images/alamy stock photo/Peregrine; S. 228/u. m.: mauritius images/alamy stock photo/Anka Agency International; S. 230/o. l.: Shutterstock.com/Rawpixel.com; S. 230/u. r.: Shutterstock.com/Hurca; S. 232/u. l.: Shutterstock.com/grebeshkovmaxim; S. 234: stock.adobe.com/lesniewski; S. 235/o. r.: mauritius images/World Book Inc.; S. 237: Imago Stock & People GmbH/Photoshot/Nic Hutchings/agefotostock; S. 238: mauritius images/alamy stock photo/Tim Graham; S. 239/u. m.: Shutterstock.com/Dancing_Man; S. 242: Shutterstock.com/Fourth Exposure; S. 243: MASQUERADE (EGUNGUN)/Dir. Olive Nwosu/interfilm Berlin Management GmbH; S. 244/o. l.: Shutterstock.com/ChristianChan; S. 248: Shutterstock.com/Kryuchka Yaroslav; S. 250: mauritius images/alamy stock photo/Mark Thomas; S. 252/u. l.: Shutterstock.com/solarseven; S. 255/o. m.: Shutterstock.com/sun ok; S. 255/u. r.: mauritius images/Norbert Michalke; S. 256/m. r.: mauritius images/alamy stock photo/Hector Christiaen; S. 259/m.: Shutterstock.com/Naumova Marina; S. 259/m. r.: Shutterstock.com/Visual Generation; S. 259/u. m.: Shutterstock.com/Ksenia Zvezdina; S. 260/m. r.: Shutterstock.com/Andy.LIU; S. 260/m. r.: Shutterstock.com/Nesie Bird; S. 262: Shutterstock.com/Lightspring; S. 263: mauritius images/Science Photo Library; S. 264: Shutterstock.com/BAZA Production; S. 265: Shutterstock/aerogondo2; S. 266/o. l.: Shutterstock.com/Anatomy Image; S. 266/u. l.: mauritius images/alamy stock photo/Donald Cooper; S. 267: mauritius images/alamy stock photo/Donald Cooper; S. 268/m.: Shutterstock.com/aurielaki; S. 268/m.: Shutterstock.com/popicon; S. 268/m. r.: Shutterstock.com/Irina Usmanova; S. 268/m. r.: Shutterstock.com/LvNL; S. 268/o. l., m.: Shutterstock.com/Faber14; S. 268/o. r.: Shutterstock.com/gn8; S. 269/u. l.: Written – directed – animated by Kaleb Lechowski (C) Kaleb Lechowski; Hartmut Zeller – Sound, David Masterson – Voice acting; S. 269/u. m.: Written – directed – animated by Kaleb Lechowski (C) Kaleb Lechowski; Hartmut Zeller – Sound, David Masterson – Voice acting; S. 270/m. l.: dpa Picture-Alliance/Jörg Carstensen; S. 273: Shutterstock.com/Alexander Remy Levine; S. 274: Brown, Don. Drowned City: Hurricane Katrina and New Orleans. Brown – Houghton Mifflin, 2017; S. 275/u. m.: Shutterstock.com/VectorMine; S. 277: Shutterstock.com/Andrii Yalanskyi; S. 278: Shutterstock.com/Dmitry Demidovich; S. 280: Shutterstock.com/graficriver_icons_logo; S. 282/m. l.: Shutterstock.com/delcarmat; S. 282/m., m. l.: Shutterstock.com/Phumsky; S. 282/m., m. l.: Shutterstock.com/Robcartorres; S. 282/o. m.: Shutterstock.com/Sabelskaya; S. 283/m.: Shutterstock.com/Oleksandra Klestova; S. 283/o. l.: Shutterstock.com/r2dpr; S. 283/o. m.: Shutterstock.com/FuusenTango; S. 283/o. m., m., m. l.: Shutterstock.com/Phumsky; S. 283/o. m., m., m. l.: Shutterstock.com/Robcartorres; S. 285: Shutterstock.com/iku4; S. 286/o. l.: akg-images/© Omikron/SCIENCE SOURCE; S. 287/m. r.: Shutterstock.com/Meilun; S. 289: mauritius images/age fotostock/Classic Vision; S. 290: interfoto e.k./National Trust Photo Library; S. 291/u. m.: Shutterstock.com/Plastic Ghost; S. 292/m. l.: Shutterstock.com/Ruslan M.; S. 292/o. r.: Shutterstock.com/smilewithjul; S. 296: Shutterstock.com/Andrekart Photography; S. 298/o. l.: Shutterstock.com/inimalGraphic; S. 298/u. m.: Bridgeman Images/Taylor, John; S. 298/u. r.: Mathew McFarren; S. 300: Shutterstock.com/Artur Szczybylo; S. 301/u. r.: Shutterstock.com/Tharun 15; S. 302: © Deutsche Welle 2019; S. 303: Shutterstock.com/delcarmat; S. 306: CartoonStock/Lindsay Foyle; S. 314: CartoonStock/Brian Fray; S. 322/m.: Shutterstock.com/4zevar; S. 322/m.: Shutterstock.com/graphixmania; S. 322/m.: Shutterstock.com/Overearth; S. 322/m. l.: Shutterstock.com/Alena Nv; S. 322/m. l.: Shutterstock.com/CharacterFamily70; S. 322/u. l.: Shutterstock.com/Possawat Sepa; S. 322/u. m.: Shutterstock.com/Animashka; S. 322/u. m.: Shutterstock.com/elenabsl; S. 359: Shutterstock.com/Andrey_Kuzmin; S. 373/m. l.: Shutterstock.com/FallyDesign; S. 373/o. l.: Shutterstock.com/VectorsMarket; S. 373/o. m.: Shutterstock.com/Ico Maker; S. 373/u. l.: Shutterstock.com/Dychek Marina; S. 375: Shutterstock.com/Travel-Fr; S. 376: Shutterstock.com/Everett Collection; S. 379: Oseman, Alice. Heartstopper. Hodder Children's Books, 2018, p. 14; S. 407: Shutterstock.com/karen roach; S. 407/m. r.: Shutterstock.com/karen roach; S. 435: Shutterstock.com/Martial Red; S. 435: Shutterstock.com/matsabe; S. 435: stock.adobe.com/Vector Tradition; S. 435/m. l.: Shutterstock.com/matsabe; S. 435/o. r.: Shutterstock.com/Martial Red; S. 435/u. r.: stock.adobe.com/Vector Tradition; S. 436: Shutterstock.com/newelle; S. 436: Shutterstock.com/Robert Voight; S. 436/m. r.: Shutterstock.com/newelle; S. 436/o. r.: Shutterstock.com/

Robert Voight; S. 437/m. l.: © VG Bild-Kunst, Bonn 2024; Ludwig Gies: Der Bundesadler, 1953 (Grafik); S. 437/m. r.: Shutterstock.com/Radoslaw Maciejewski.

**Texte**

S. 14: 1971 Ono Music/Lenono Music/Budde Music Publishing GmbH/Text: John Lennon. John; S. 18: gemeinfrei; S. 21/m. l.: Rooney, Sally. Normal People. London, Faber & Faber Ltd., 2018, pp. 12–15 *; S. 23: Bristow, Vicky. "We are in this together." Lockdown in 2020. Poetry and prose from around the world on living in isolation and surviving the coronavirus, edited by Robin Barrat, 2020, pp. 12–13.; S. 31: Einramhof-Florian, Helene. „Fit Für Die Jungen Generationen Am Arbeitsplatz." Springer eBooks, 2022, https://doi.org/10.1007/978-3-658-39149-2 *; S. 37: Keegan, Marina. "Even Artichokes Have Doubts." The Opposite of Loneliness. Essays and Stories, Simon & Schuster UK Ltd., 2014, p. 187, pp. 198–200 *; S. 40: Rooney, Sally. Normal people. London, Faber & Faber Ltd., 2019, pp. 107–109. *; S. 42: Slater, Dashka. The 57 Bus. London, Wren & Rook, 2018, pp. 122–129. *; S. 46: gemeinfrei; S. 48: Walsh, James and Guardian readers. "Let's not make a fuss: 10 things that sum up Britishness", theguardian.com, 09.06.2014, https:// www.theguardian.com/uk-news/guardianwitness-blog/2014/jun/09/scottish-independence-10-things-that-sum-up-britishness, Copyright Guardian News & Media Ltd 2021 (accessed 30.06.2021); S. 49: Walsh, James and Guardian readers. "Let's not make a fuss: 10 things that sum up Britishness", theguardian.com, 09.06.2014, https:// www.theguardian.com/uk-news/guardianwitness-blog/2014/jun/09/scottish-independence-10-things-that-sum-up-britishness, Copyright Guardian News & Media Ltd 2021; S. 49: Walsh, James, and Guardian Readers. "Let's Not Make a Fuss: 10 Things That Sum up Britishness." The Guardian, 21 July 2021, www.theguardian.com/uk-news/guardianwitness-blog/2014/jun/09/scottish-independence-10-things-that-sum-up-britishness. Copyright Guardian News & Media Ltd 2021; S. 52: Mattinson, Deborah. "Brexit has made this country as anxious as I have ever known it", 15.06.2019, https:// www.theguardian.com/politics/2019/jun/15/brexit-made-country-angry-as-i-have-ever-known-it, Copyright Guardian News & Media Ltd 2021; S. 54: Wincott, Daniel. "The possible break-up of the United Kingdom." UK in a Changing Europe, 19 Dec. 2020, ukandeu.ac.uk/long-read/the-possible-break-up-of-the-united-kingdom/ *; S. 56: "The Guardian view on the trailblazer devolution deals: a step in the right direction", theguardian.com, 16.03.2023, https:// www.theguardian.com/commentisfree/2023/mar/16/the-guardian-view-on-the-trailblazer-devolution-deals-a-step-in-the-right-direction, Copyright Guardian News & Media Ltd 2023; S. 59: Kellner, Peter. "The Surprising Potential of King Charles's Reign." Carnegie Europe, 14 Sept. 2022, carnegieeurope.eu/2022/09/14/surprising-potential-of-king-charles-s-reign-pub-87909. *; S. 62: gemeinfrei; S. 67: Hawkins, Paul. The Bloody British – a well-meaning guide to an awkward nation. E-book, published by Paul Hawkins, 2019. *; S. 69: Coe, Jonathan. Middle England. Viking, 2018, pp. 326–327. *; S. 71: Roß, Jan. „Genug geheult". ZEIT ONLINE, 29.01.2020, https:// www.zeit.de/2020/06/brexit-grossbritannien-europaeische-union-liberalitaet (accessed 19 June 2021); S. 74: Lowe, By Keith. "Five Times Immigration Changed the UK." BBC News, 20 Jan. 2020, www.bbc.com/news/uk-politics-51134644.; S. 80: Universal/MCA Music Publishing GmbH, Berlin/Text: Aniruddha Das/John Ashok Pandit/Steven Chandra Savale/Sanjay Tailor/Saidullah Zaman.; S. 86: Ellerbeck, Stefan. "Half of US Teens Use the Internet 'Almost Constantly'. But Where Are They Spending Their Time Online?" World Economic Forum, 31 Aug. 2022, www.weforum.org/agenda/2022/08/social-media-internet-online-teenagers-screens-us. *; S. 87: Duffy, Carol Anne. Rapture, London: Picador, p. 2; S. 92: McBride, Kelly. "New NPR Ethics Policy […]". NPR.org, 29.07.2021 *; S. 96: Magoon, Nicole, et al. "Six Shifts Changing the Future of Media." Bain, 11 Aug. 2021, www.bain.com/insights/six-shifts-changing-the-future-of-media. *; S. 100: Sankaran, Vishwam. "Scientists Warn of Threat to Internet From Altrained AIs." The Independent, 20 June 2023, www.independent.co.uk/tech/ai-training-data-internet-junkb2360570. html; S. 103: Elton, Ben. Dead Famous. Bantam Press, p. 183. *; S. 110: Urner, Maren. Interview by Dirk Reelfs and Eltje Kunze. „Negative Nachrichtflut führt dazu, dass sich Menschen nicht mehr beteiligen." SMK-Blog, 30 Jun. 2021, www.bildung.sachsen.de/blog/index.php/2021/06/30/negative-nachrichtflut-fuehrt-dazu-dass-sich-menschen-nicht-mehr-beteiligen/. Accessed 13 Oct. 2021. *; S. 112: gemeinfrei; S. 118: Obama, Barack. A Promised Land. Viking/Penguin

Random House, 2020, pp. 14–16. *; S. 120: gemeinfrei; S. 122: gemeinfrei; S. 124: gemeinfrei; S. 133: Childress, Alice. Like One of the Family. Boston, Beacon Press, 1986. *; S. 134: Ehrenhalt, Alan. "Could We Please Stop Pontificating About the American Dream?" Governing, Apr. 2021, www.governing.com/assessments/could-we-please-stop-pontificating-about-the-american-dream.html. *; S. 138: Biden, Joseph R. jr. Inaugural speech, January 20, 2021. https:// www.whitehouse.gov/briefing-room/speeches-remarks/2021/01/20/inaugural-address-by-president-joseph-r-biden-jr/; S. 140: Emma Lazarus; S. 141: Spröer, Susanne. „German-American Day: So Deutsch Sind Die USA." dw.com, 28 Oct. 2020, www.dw.com/de/german-american-day-so-viel-deutsches-steckt-in-den-usa/a-45478424. *; S. 143: Tan, Amy. The Joy Luck Club. Vintage/Penguin Random House, 1989, pp. 307–309. *; S. 146: Quiñonez, Ernesto. Bodega Dreams. 1st edition, Vintage, 2000, pp. 6–7. *; S. 147: Kristof, Nicholas D., and Sheryl WuDunn. Tightrope: Americans Reaching for Hope. Vintage Books, 2020, pp. 54–68.; S. 148: Kristof, Nicholas D., and Sheryl WuDunn. Tightrope: Americans Reaching for Hope. Vintage Books, 2020, pp. 54–68. *; S. 157: Lerner, Max. "America as a Civilization: Life and Thought in the United States Today". New York, Simon & Schuster, 1957, pp. 779–781. *; S. 161: Carey, Lamont. "I can't read". Reach Into My Darkness: I Hate This Place. LaCarey Entertainment, 2013; S. 162: gemeinfrei; S. 168: „Wonderwalls: Und vor den Werken wird getanzt", ZEIT ONLINE, Eva Sager, 16.01.2023, https:// www.zeit.de/2023/03/wonderwalls-ausstellung-duesseldorf-pop-street-art?utm_referrer=https%3A%2F%2Fwww.ecosia.org%2F; S. 176: Friedman, Thomas L.. The world is flat. New York, Picador, 2007, p. 9. *; S. 179: "What is the WTO?" WTO, www.wto.org/english/thewto_e/whatis_e/whatis_e.htm. Accessed 22 June 2021. *; S. 179: "Who we are." WTO, www.wto.org/english/thewto_e/whatis_e/who_we_are_e.htm. Accessed 22 June 2021. *; S. 180: "What we do." WTO, www.wto.org/english/thewto_e/whatis_e/what_we_do_e.htm. Accessed 22 June 2021. *; S. 182: Vanham, Peter. "Here's what a Korean boy band can teach us about globalization 4.0." World Economic Forum, 18 Dec. 2018, www.weforum.org/agenda/2018/12/here-s-what-a-korean-boy-band-can-teach-us-about-globalization/. Accessed 19 May 2021. *; S. 186: Hamid, Mohsin. The Reluctant Fundamentalist. Berlin: Cornelsen Verlag, 2012, pp. 50–53. *; S. 196: Andreas Hoenig, David Hutzler und Robin Wille. „Lieferkettengesetz: Das kommt auf deutsche Unternehmen zu". dpa-Basisdienst vom 23.12.2022. Quelle: dpa *; S. 199: Kagan, Robert. "A Superpower, Like It or Not." Foreign Affairs, March/April 2021, www.foreignaffairs.com/articles/united-states/2021-02-16/superpower-it-or-not, Accessed 19 Aug 2021. *; S. 202: Brandt, Hendrik. „Kommentar: Wir sollten ein neues Verhältnis zu den USA finden". NDR.de, 06.11.2020, https:// www.ndr.de/nachrichten/info/sendungen/kommentare/Kommentar-Wir-sollten-ein-neues-Verhaeltnis-zu-USA-finden,usa924.html *; S. 204: gemeinfrei; S. 208: Buczkowska, Teresa, In: Marie-Claire Logue, ed. Being Irish. 101 Views on Irish Identity Today, The Liffey Press Ltd., 2021, pp. 20–22 *; S. 208: Leo Varadkar, In: Marie-Claire Logue, ed. Being Irish. 101 Views on Irish Identity Today, The Liffey Press Ltd., 2021, pp. 293–295 *; S. 208: McMullan, Ryan, In: Marie-Claire Logue, ed. Being Irish. 101 Views on Irish Identity Today, The Liffey Press Ltd., 2021, pp. 206–207 *; S. 210: Ruggeri, Amanda. "Ireland's light-hearted approach to life." BBC Travel, https:// www.bbc.com/travel/article/20180403-irelands-light-hearted-approach-to-life, 03.04.2018. *; S. 213: McGreevy, Ronan. "A History of Ireland for Outsiders: From Henry VIII to the Troubles." The Irish Times, 6 Mar. 2019, www.irishtimes.com/news/ireland/irish-news/a-history-of-ireland-for-outsiders-from-henry-viii-to-the-troubles-1.3816898; S. 218: https:// www.finegael.ie/speech-of-the-tanaiste-leo-varadkar-at-the-opening-of-the-2021-fine-gael-ard; S. 219: Watson, Dawn. "Queen Of The Sticklebacks." Paul McVeigh and Lisa Frank, eds. Belfast Stories, Doire Press, 2019, pp. 139–144.; S. 224: „Wird Irland wiedervereinigt?", Duncan Morrow, Miriam Dahliner, SZ vom 27.12.2022, https:// www.sueddeutsche.de/politik/nordirland-religion-konflikt-1.5718056?reduced=true; S. 226: Reporter, Guardian Staff. "My Nigeria: Five Writers and Artists Reflect on the Place They Call Home." The Guardian, 19 Oct. 2022, www.theguardian.com/global-development/2021/oct/29/my-nigeria-five-writers-and-artists-reflect-on-the-place-they-call-home.; S. 227: Reporter, Guardian Staff. "My Nigeria: Five Writers and Artists Reflect on the Place They Call Home." The Guardian, 19 Oct. 2022, www.theguardian.com/global-development/2021/oct/29/my-nigeria-five-writers-and-artists-reflect-on-the-place-they-call-home.; S. 230: Faloyin, Dipo. Africa Is Not a Country: Notes on a Bright Continent. W. W. Norton, 2023, pp. 4–6; S. 232: Cheeseman, Fola Aina and Nic. "Don't Call Nigeria a Failed State: It Is More Resilient and Inclusive Than Ever, Despite Rising Insecurity." Foreign Affairs, 19 Apr. 2023, www.foreignaffairs.com/articles/africa/2021-05-05/dont-call-nigeria-failed-state. *; S. 235: Amt, Auswärtiges. „Rede von Außenministerin Annalena Baerbock anlässlich der Übergabe der Benin-Bronzen." Auswärtiges Amt, www.auswaertiges-amt.de/de/newsroom/baerbock-uebergabe-benin-bronzen-an-nigeria/2570312. *; S. 239: Mohammed, Kenneth. "A Wealth of Sorrow: Why Nigeria's Abundant Oil Reserves Are Really a Curse." The Guardian, 19 Oct. 2022, www.theguardian.com/global-development/2021/nov/09/a-wealth-of-sorrow-why-nigerias-abundant-oil-reserves-are-really-a-curse. Copyright Guardian News & Media Ltd 2023; S. 244: Odafen, Aiwanose. Tomorrow I Become a Woman. Scribner, London 2022, pp. 19–24 *; S. 247: Salaudeen, Aisha. "These Nigerian Kids Are Creating Epic Sci-fi Short Films Using Their Phones, and Hollywood Is Paying Attention." CNN, 1 Jan. 2021, edition.cnn.com/2021/01/01/africa/critics-company-young-filmmakers-nigeria-spc-intl/index.html. *; S. 252: Asimov, Isaac. "Foreword." Encyclopaedia of Science Fiction, edited by Robert Holdstock, London, Octopus Books, 1978.; S. 254: Hawking, Stephen: Brief Answers to the Big Questions. London, John Murray, 2018, S. 208, pp. 210–211. *; S. 256: Feynman, Richard. The Quotable Feynman. Princeton, Princeton UP, 2015, p. 127. *; S. 256: Wright, Lawrence. The End of October. New York, Alfred A. Knopf, 2020, pp. 3–8; S. 261: Arlidge, John. "Why Jennifer Doudna's DNA discovery is revolutionising the way we tackle disease". The Sunday Times, 03.01.2021, www.thetimes.co.uk/article/why-jennifer-doudnas-dna-discovery-is-revolutionising-the-way-we-tackle-disease-v3jjsh588 (accessed 29.06.2021); S. 266: Prebble, Lucy. The Effect. London, Methuen Drama, 2012, pp. 55–58. *; S. 269: "R'ha". Written – directed – animated by Kaleb Lechowski (C) Kaleb Lechowski; Hartmut Zeller – Sound, David Masterson – Voice acting; S. 269: Westin, O. Micro Science Fiction. Berlin, mikrotext, 2019, p. 136, p. 140.; S. 270: "R'ha". Written – directed – animated by Kaleb Lechowski (C) Kaleb Lechowski; Hartmut Zeller – Sound, David Masterson – Voice acting *; S. 271: Ward, Jesmyn. Salvage the Bones. London, Bloomsbury Publishing, 2011, pp. 240–243. *; S. 276: Doudna, Jennifer A., and Emmanuelle Charpentier. "The new frontier of genome engineering with CRISPR-Cas9." Science, vol. 346, 2014, p. 1077, science.sciencemag.org/content/346/6213/1258096. Accessed 10 June 2021. *; S. 279: Weston, Phoebe. "Top scientists warn of 'ghastly future of mass extinction' and climate disruption". theguardian.com, 13 Jan 2021, https:// www.theguardian.com/environment/2021/jan/13/top-scientists-warn-of-ghastly-future-of-mass-extinction-and-climate-disruption-aoe (accessed 16.12.2021); S. 286: gemeinfrei; S. 287: gemeinfrei; S. 288: gemeinfrei; S. 291: gemeinfrei; S. 292: gemeinfrei; S. 293: gemeinfrei; S. 297: Anderson, Lily. The Only Thing Worse Than Me Is You. New York, St. Martin's Griffin, 2016, p. 85.; S. 297: gemeinfrei; S. 299: Tempest, Kae. "My Shakespeare". In: Context – Allgemeine Ausgabe 2022 – Oberstufe – Shakespeare – Not of an Age, But for All Time – Topics in Context – Themenheft. Cornelsen Verlag, 2022, pp. 25–26; S. 301: Nurtsch, Dr. Ceyda. „Shakespeare: aktuell und unerschöpflich." Deutsche Welle 28.04.2019, https:// www.dw.com/de/shakespeare-aktuell-und-unersch%C3%B6pflich/a-48524490. *; S. 313: Childress, Alice. Like One of the Family. Boston, Beacon Press, 1986. *; S. 313: gemeinfrei; S. 317: "What we do." WTO, www.wto.org/english/thewto_e/whatis_e/what_we_do_e.htm. Accessed 22 June 2021. *; S. 318: Kagan, Robert. "A Superpower, Like It or Not." Foreign Affairs, March/April 2021, www.foreignaffairs.com/articles/united-states/2021-02-16/superpower-it-or-not, Accessed 19 Aug 2021. *; S. 324: George, McKelle. Speak Easy, Speak Love. New York, Greenwillow Books, 2017, pp. 149–150. *; S. 326: Levy, Andrea, "Loose change", Underwords, Maia Press, 2005, pp. 67–76 *; S. 330: Dave Eggers *; S. 334: Jain, Sunita, "Fly the friendly skies", R. M. Nischik, ed., Short Short Stories Universal, Reclam; S. 337: Chimamanda Ngozi Adichie, Purple Hibiscus, Algonquin Books 2003, pp. 71–76 *; S. 342: Sandra Navidi, „Vorwort", Die DNA der USA: Wie tickt Amerika? Finanz Buch Verlag, 2022, S. 8 *; S. 343: Lieske, Tanya, „Die Zeit war grausam, brutal und sehr spannend", www.deutschlandfunk.de, 19.04.2014 *; S. 355: „Ruf." Schulwörterbuch English G 21. 3rd ed. 2020. *; S. 356/o. m.: "grim." Oxford Advanced

Learner's Dictionary. 10th ed., 2020 *; S. 356/u. m.: "Grim." Oxford Leaner's Dictionaries, www.oxfordlearn-ersdictionaries.com/definition/english/grim?q=grim. *

*: aus didaktischen Gründen gekürzt